I0100671

THE LEGAL STATUS OF THE NEGRO

By

CHARLES S. MANGUM, Jr.

THE LAWBOOK EXCHANGE, LTD.
Clark, New Jersey

ISBN 978-1-58477-081-7 (hardcover)
ISBN 978-1-61619-401-7 (paperback)

Lawbook Exchange edition 2000, 2013

The quality of this reprint is equivalent to the quality of the original work.

THE LAWBOOK EXCHANGE, LTD.
33 Terminal Avenue
Clark, New Jersey 07066-1321

Please see our website for a selection of our other publications and fine facsimile reprints of classic works of legal history:
www.lawbookexchange.com

Library of Congress Cataloging-in-Publication Data

Mangum, Charles S., (Charles Staples), 1902-
The legal status of the Negro / by Charles S. Mangum, Jr.
p. cm.
Originally published: Chapel Hill : Univ. of North Carolina Press, 1940.
Includes bibliographical references and index.
ISBN 1-58477-081-3 (cloth : alk. paper)
1. Afro-Americans—Legal status, laws, etc. 2. Afro-Americans Civil rights. 3. United States—Race relations. I. Title.

KF4757 .M33 2000
346.7301'3—dc21

99-088240

Printed in the United States of America on acid-free paper

THE LEGAL STATUS OF THE NEGRO

By

CHARLES S. MANGUM, Jr.

CHAPEL HILL

THE UNIVERSITY OF NORTH CAROLINA PRESS

1940

PRINTED IN THE UNITED STATES OF AMERICA BY EDWARDS & BROUGHTON COMPANY, RALEIGH, N. C.; BOUND BY L. H. JENKINS, INC., RICHMOND, VA.

TO MY FATHER

WHOSE INTEREST IN THE NEGRO

WAS ALWAYS GREAT

PREFACE

In this study the author has attempted a review of the statutes and cases concerning the relations of the white and colored races since the Civil War. This is not a philosophic treatise on the problems of race relations and the courts, but a statement of the law as it has been interpreted by courts all over the nation. The development of the law in this respect has been an interesting commentary on the life of the American people. The laws of the different sections of the nation seem to reflect the social customs and mores of the people themselves. In this study sectionalism and the impact of historical events cannot be overlooked. On the whole, however, the author has been struck with the way the problem has become national instead of sectional in scope. Of course this is due in large measure to the Negro migration in the second and third decades of the present century. While most of the unfairness and discrimination is still in the South, many cases of this sort have been noted in other sections of the country as well.

The problems are manifold and are not to be easily solved. A slow and thoughtful approach seems to be demanded by the circumstances which surround the relations of the Negroes with the dominant race. The white man must recognize that the Negro has fundamental rights and must try to understand that he wishes to obtain them. All the petty discriminations which he is called upon to endure make it just that much more difficult to work out a system of coöperation in interracial relations. This spirit of coöperation must be the mainspring of any successful effort to improve the conditions which exist today. The difficulties are many and varied, but it cannot be said that they are insuperable.

On the whole, it is believed that interracial relations are improving. The average man is realizing more and more that in our system of jurisprudence there are certain inequalities which must be eradicated. None of these is more important than the inequalities which are based on race. We are still much too prone to use race as a criterion in many situations where logic tells us no real distinction exists. However, it must be remembered that race prejudice is inculcated into the hearts of the great majority of white Americans, and hence it is rather difficult for them to take an altogether dispassionate view. It is easy to say that one is going to be fair to a Negro accused of crime, but it is rather difficult to give him full justice because of this ingrained prejudice. The judge on the bench and the jury in the box may not be conscious that there is unfairness, and yet this prejudice may creep into the trial unawares. It is the duty of the court, in so far as it is humanly possible, to see that justice may sometimes be not only blind, but color-blind.

The primary purpose of those who desire the welfare of the Negro race should be the improvement of interracial attitudes. An effort should be made to foster interracial coöperation and to show that fair treatment in the courts will not only bring us nearer the democratic ideal but will mean added prosperity to the nation. It is hoped that this treatise will shed light on problems of this kind and help to bring them nearer to a solution. The Negro's friends must work toward this goal.

The coöperation of the law and sociology faculties of the University of North Carolina has been of inestimable help in the preparation of this treatise, especially that of Dr. Guy B. Johnson and the late Dr. Atwell C. McIntosh. Others who gave constructive advice are Professor Charles T. McCormick, of Northwestern University; Professor William R. Vance, of Yale University; Professor James H. Chadbourn, of the University of Pennsylvania; and Dr. Guion G. Johnson, of Chapel Hill. The library staff of the University of North Carolina also rendered sterling assistance.

CHARLES S. MANGUM, JR.

Chapel Hill, N. C.
December, 1939

CONTENTS

THE
LEGAL STATUS
OF
THE NEGRO

I

WHO IS A NEGRO?

The average person in the United States would have little difficulty in identifying a member of a particular racial group provided he has had long and familiar association with that group. However, he might be totally unable to distinguish between a Japanese and a Chinese, for example, if he had had no opportunity to observe their different physical and cultural traits. The characteristics attributed to a particular race are based at least to a certain extent upon the proportionate numbers of that race in a given locality, upon social distance, and upon the amount of economic contact and competition.

The attempt to answer the question of who is a Negro brings up such sociological problems as are implied in the variance, for instance, between the definition of the term as given by the average man from Alabama and the average man from Maine, Minnesota, or Oregon. An examination of the legal definitions available in numerous statutes and court decisions also reveals dissimilarities, and these definitions themselves seem to reflect the methods which the various states have developed in meeting the problems of race relations.

There is no definite or uniform holding upon the question of who is a Negro,[1] and, in the states where the question has been raised, the courts have been far from unanimous as to the proportion of African blood necessary to classify an individual as a Negro. Some states have defined the term by a general statute, while others have defined it only with respect to particular subjects treated by their laws, such as marriage or education. In a few states, the definition of the term varies according to the subject under consideration. Thus an individual of mixed blood may be classified as a white person as far as the law with respect to marriage is concerned and as a Negro with respect to the public school system. In states where no statutory definition has been attempted, the courts are faced

[1] Note (1931) 35 L. Notes 68.

with the difficulty of deciding the query as best they may from the general connotation of the words of the specific statute under consideration or from the accepted meaning of the term as used generally in the community. In some instances where there is no statute covering a particular subject like education, the definition in an act covering another field of law may be used as a pointer to show the general meaning of the term in that jurisdiction. However, this course is not always followed.

Before the Civil War it seems to have been a general rule in the slave states that a Negro was presumed to be a slave.[2] In fact the South Carolina Court held in one early case that the word "Negro" had the fixed meaning of "a slave." [3] For the presumption to apply, however, the person must have appeared to be a Negro,[4] and, if it was doubtful to which race he belonged, there was then no basis for a presumption one way or the other.[5]

In the years following the war it became increasingly clear that the exigencies of the situation in the South demanded that there be some attempt at a legal definition of the word "Negro" or "colored person." Even at this early date there had been a good deal of racial intermixture. The laws of the southern states still made race a criterion in certain legal relationships, and hence it was necessary that there should be some definition of the term in order for one to ascertain what individuals came within its meaning. In some instances statutes were enacted defining the word "Negro" in some particular relationship, in others the courts were permitted to adopt their own definitions as the problems arose. There had even been such attempts at legal definition of the term before the war. The general defini-

[2] Mandeville v. Cookenderfer, 16 Fed. Cas. No. 9009 (C. C. D. C. 1827); Drayton v. United States, 7 Fed. Cas. No. 4074 (C. C. D. C. 1849); Miller v. McQuerry, 17 Fed. Cas. No. 9583 (C. C. D. Ohio 1853); Field v. Walker, 17 Ala. 80 (1849); Becton v. Ferguson, 22 Ala. 599 (1853); Daniel v. Guy, 19 Ark. 121 (1857); Macon & W. Ry. v. Holt, 8 Ga. 157 (1850); Adelle v. Beaureguard, 1 Mart. (o.s.) 183 (La. 1810); Gentry v. McMinnis, 33 Ky. 382 (1835); Fox v. Lambson, 8 N. J. Law 275 (1826); State v. Miller, 29 N. C. 275 (1847); Bennett v. State, 31 Tenn. 410 (1852).

[3] *Ex parte* Leland, 1 Nott & McCord 460 (S. C. 1819).

[4] Daniel v. Guy, 19 Ark. 121 (1857).

[5] See *ibid.* In this case the person was given the benefit of the doubt. The court decided that in such circumstances it could not justly take upon itself the burden of deciding contrary to the person's interest, since it was not certain that he was a Negro.

tive statute is in most instances a comparatively modern development.

In the North and West there had been many legal disabilities for Negroes prior to the adoption of the postwar amendments to the Federal Constitution. A few cases arose in which racial identity was an important issue. In Michigan, for example, it was held that persons in whose veins the white blood so far predominated that they were less than one-fourth Negro were white within the then effective state constitutional provision restricting the voting franchise to white male citizens.[6] Moreover, the Ohio Court adopted[7] the preponderance theory in interpreting laws involving the right of persons of mixed blood to vote, to have educational privileges, and to testify in court. In respect to voting this continued to be the rule until the year 1867[8] before the Fifteenth Amendment was ratified. In a case which arose in 1859, however, it was said that the words "white" and "colored" as used in the Ohio separate school law of 1853 were employed in their popular and ordinary sense. Hence it was held that children who were three-eighths Negro and five-eighths white and distinctly colored in appearance were to be regarded as colored children and therefore not eligible to be admitted to the white schools.[9]

In 1852 the Maine Court held that a person having only one-sixteenth or perhaps one-eighth African blood was not a Negro within the meaning of a statute, since repealed, prohibiting intermarriage between whites and Negroes.[10] There was also an ante-bellum statute in Massachusetts which proscribed the marriage of white persons with Negroes or mulattoes. This act was held not to prohibit the marriage of a white person and a person who was the child of a union between a mulatto and one who was wholly white.[11]

In construing an ante-bellum Connecticut statute exempting the property of "persons of color" from taxation, the court of that state ruled that a quadroon was within the mean-

---

[6] People v. Dean, 14 Mich. 406 (1866).

[7] Gray v. State, 4 Ohio Rep. 353 (1831); Thacker v. Hawk, 11 Ohio Rep. 376 (1842); Lane v. Baker, 12 Ohio Rep. 237 (1843).

[8] Anderson v. Millikin, 9 Ohio St. 568 (1859); Monroe v. Collins, 17 Ohio St. 665 (1867).

[9] Van Camp v. Bd. of Education, 9 Ohio St. 406 (1859).

[10] Bailey v. Fiske, 34 Me. 77 (1852).

[11] Inhabitants of Medway v. Inhabitants of Natick, 7 Mass. 88 (1810).

ing of the act.[12] The Indiana statute of pre-civil-war days concerning the competency of witnesses prohibited persons who had one-eighth or more Negro blood from testifying against white persons.[13]

Race distinctions have now practically disappeared from the written codes of the states north of the Mason and Dixon Line and east of the Mississippi River. The only real exception is the state of Indiana. Among the statutory provisions of that state which make a distinction because of race is one which prohibits interracial marriages between whites and persons of one-eighth Negro blood.[14]

West of the Mississippi the situation is different, for most of the states in this northwest section of the country have laws which prohibit marriage between whites and Negroes. Some of these indicate the proportion of African blood which will make a person a Negro within the statute. The Arizona[15] and Montana[16] acts would seem to interdict the marriage of white persons with all persons of Negro blood, however remote the strain. In Nebraska[17] and North Dakota[18] marriages of whites with persons of one-eighth or more Negro blood are proscribed, while in Oregon[19] the proportion is one-fourth or more. The other miscegenation statutes in this region mention no definite proportion, although several of them prohibit marriages between whites and "mulattoes." [20]

One might expect a certain uniformity in the southern and border states with respect to the statutory and judicial definitions of the term "Negro" or "colored person." However, such uniformity does not exist. Furthermore, there seems to be nothing geographical about this dissimilarity. For example, Louisiana, in the Deep South, has been far less definite in its attitude toward mixed bloods than has Virginia, in the Upper South. However, this may be at least partially explained by

[12] Johnson v. Town of Norwich, 29 Conn. 407 (1860).

[13] Graham v. Crockett, 18 Ind. 119 (1862).

[14] Ind. Stat. Ann. (Burns, 1933) §44-104.

[15] Ariz. Rev. Code Ann. (Struckmeyer, 1928) §2166 as amended by Ariz. Laws 1931, c. 17.

[16] Mont. Rev. Codes (1921) §5700.

[17] Neb. Comp. Stat. (1929) §42-103.

[18] N. D. Comp. Laws Ann. (1913) §9583.

[19] Ore. Code Ann. (1930) §14-840.

[20] See chapter on Intermarriage *infra*, notes 53, 54, 56, 61, 73.

the following review of the Louisiana decisions and the peculiar social conditions existing in that state.

The decisions of the Louisiana Court on this important phase of the Negro problem appear to be somewhat inconsistent. In an early case[21] it was said that the term "colored" had been applied to all persons who were not of the white race, including both Indians and Negroes. In 1910 the court held that anyone who has an appreciable amount of Negro blood is a member of the colored race within the meaning of the Jim Crow law.[22] In the very same year, however, the court decided[23] that an octoroon was not a member of the Negro or black race as that term was used in the 1908 act[24] punishing concubinage among members of the white and Negro races. In this case the court delivered an elaborate opinion in which it defined some of the numerous terms which are employed in describing the mixed bloods in the state. It declared that the term "Negro" does not necessarily include persons in whose veins there is only an admixture of Negro blood, and that it clearly would not be applicable to a person in whom the admixture is so slight that even a scientific expert could not be positive of its presence. The term "colored" was said to apply to those having African blood, and this was said to be the general acceptation of the term except on the Pacific coast where persons of Mongolian descent were also included when the term was used. The term "griffe" was said to have a definite meaning in Louisiana and was defined as applying to the issue of a Negro and a mulatto. It was said that the term "mulatto" indicated an individual who is too dusky to be white and too light-colored to be a griffe. The court also declared that a quadroon is of a lighter color than a mulatto.

The decision of the court in this case seems to have been influenced by the fact that the legislature, at the time when the statute was enacted, had refused to adopt a clause which defined the term "Negro" as including those persons who had one thirty-second or more Negro blood. The decision was

[21] Adelle v. Beauregard, 1 Mart. (o.s.) 183 (La. 1810).

[22] Lee v. New Orleans G. N. Ry., 125 La. 236, 51 So. 182 (1910).

[23] State v. Treadaway, 126 La. 300, 52 So. 500 (1910). The Lee case, *supra*, note 22, was cited and distinguished because the statute involved in that decision employed the word "'colored" instead of the word "Negro."

[24] La. Acts 1908, No. 87.

evidently unsatisfactory to the people of Louisiana, for, soon after, the legislature passed the present concubinage statute[25] which is a duplicate of the 1908 act except that the word "colored" is substituted for the word "Negro." This latter act has never been interpreted in respect to questions of racial identity, and hence it is not known just how far the court would follow its previous definition of the word "colored." There was much racial intermixture in ante-bellum Louisiana,[26] and this fact might possibly lead the court to take a liberal view. The only indication of the present judges' attitude is contained in an opinion handed down in a recent case.[27] In this instance a white man was seeking to annul a marriage contracted with a woman whose great-great-grandmother was alleged to have been a free woman of color. A thorough analysis of the opinion seems to indicate that the court would have declared the marriage void had the evidence been clear and more convincing.

In Virginia the terms "Negro" and "colored person" have been said to be synonymous,[28] and at present a general statute[29] defines the latter term as including all persons in whom there is ascertainable any quantum whatever of Negro blood. The statute excepts individuals having one-fourth or more Indian blood and less than one-sixteenth Negro blood. These persons are to be considered tribal Indians so long as they remain on Indian reservations. If they move, however, then they would be classified as colored. The statute formerly provided that only those who had one-fourth or more Negro blood were to be considered colored.[30] This was changed in 1910[31] to read one-sixteenth or more and then to its present form in 1930.[32] In

[25] La. Acts 1910, No. 206 (La. Crim. Code [Dart, 1932] arts. 1128-30).

[26] Daggett, *Legal Aspect of Amalgamation in Louisiana* (1933) 11 Tex. L. Rev. 162. See also Saxon, Fabulous New Orleans (1928) c. 19, pp. 177-86; Asbury, The French Quarter (1936) c. 12, pp. 350-95.

[27] Sunseri v. Cassagne, 185 So. 1 (La. 1938).

[28] Jones v. Commonwealth, 80 Va. 538 (1885).

[29] Va. Code Ann. (Michie, 1930) §67.

[30] *See* McPherson v. Commonwealth, 28 Gratt. 939 (Va. 1877); Jones v. Commonwealth, 80 Va. 538 (1885); Scott v. Raub, 88 Va. 721, 14 S. E. 178 (1891); Eubank v. Boughton, 98 Va. 499, 36 S. E. 529 (1900); Moon v. Children's Home Society, 112 Va. 737, 72 S. E. 707 (1911).

[31] Va. Acts 1910, c. 367. *See* Spencer v. Looney, 116 Va. 767, 82 S. E. 745 (1914).

[32] Va. Acts 1930, c. 85.

the latter year the legislature enacted a race registration act[33] which requires every person in the state to supply information concerning the racial composition of his ancestors in so far as it is known. The statute provides that if there is any Negro blood in the veins of the registrant he must give the generation, if known, of the intermixture. The portion of this act concerning intermarriage outlaws all unions of whites and persons of Negro blood, while another provision states that an intentionally false registration constitutes a felony.

Georgia has a history very similar to that of Virginia. Until 1927 a general statute classified as colored only those persons who had one-eighth or more Negro blood in their veins.[34] In that year, however, the law was changed to read that all persons with any ascertainable trace of Negro blood must be classified as persons of color.[35] At the same time the legislature enacted a race registration act[36] which required all persons to fill out blanks with information concerning their racial antecedents. If there proves to be any admixture of Negro blood in the veins of any registrant, then he is to be considered a person of color. Another provision of this statute which is worth specific mention here is the clause which punishes false representations with respect to the race of the registrant. Even before 1927 the law in respect to intermarriage was in accord with the later view.[37]

Alabama's record is much the same. At the present time the state has a general statute classifying all persons with any Negro blood as colored.[38] The present marriage law similarly

---

[33] VA. CODE ANN. (Michie, 1930) §5099a.

[34] GA. CODE ANN. (Michie, 1926) §2177. *See* White v. Clements, 39 Ga. 232 (1869).

[35] Ga. Laws 1927, p. 272 (GA. CODE ANN. [Michie, Supp. 1928] §2177).

[36] GA. CODE ANN. (Michie, Supp. 1928) §§2177(1)-2177(20).

[37] GA. CODE ANN. (Michie, 1926) §2941.

[38] ALA. CODE ANN. (Michie, 1928) §2. The law in Alabama was formerly more liberal. In one ante-bellum case it was decided that the offspring of a white mother by a mulatto father was not a "mulatto" within the meaning of a statute prescribing the death penalty for rape when committed by a slave, free Negro, or mulatto. Thurman v. State, 18 Ala. 276 (1850). In another ante-bellum case there was an indictment for murder which alleged that the victim was a Negro, but the proof showed that the deceased was a mulatto. The court threw the case out because this constituted a fatal variance between the pleading and the proof. Felix v. State, 18 Ala. 720 (1851). In a later case, however, it was held that an indictment charging a white person with cohabitation with a Negro was suffi-

provides that all unions between whites and persons descended from Negroes are void.[39] Before this act was changed in 1927,[40] it only prohibited marriages of whites with persons of Negro blood to the third generation inclusive.[41] This change was effected in order to make the criminal statute conform to the state constitutional provision[42] which forbade marriages of whites and persons of Negro blood no matter how remote the strain. Before the change was made, a marriage of a white person with one of Negro blood beyond the third generation was void but the act could not be punished criminally.[43] It was also held that an octoroon was within the criminal statute prior to the amendment.[44] Hence a person who was in the fourth generation from a pure-blooded Negro ancestor was within the act, such ancestor being counted as the first generation.

Texas presents an interesting parallel to the situation in Alabama before that state's criminal miscegenation statute was amended. The Texas school law provides that the terms "colored race" and "colored children" employed in the act shall include all persons of mixed blood who are descended from Negro ancestry,[45] and the separate coach law evidently refers to this when it states that the term "Negro" as used therein includes persons of African descent as defined by the state statutes.[46] The Texas statute forbidding intermarriage between members of the two races is to the effect that any union between a Caucasian and a descendant of an African is null and void.[47] However, the penal statute punishing miscegenation

---

ciently supported by proof of cohabitation with a mulatto. Linton v. State, 88 Ala. 216, 7 So. 261 (1889). [39] ALA. CODE ANN. (Michie, 1928) §5001.

[40] Ala. Acts 1927, p. 219. [41] ALA. CODE (1923) §5001. [42] ALA. CONST. §102.

[43] Weaver v. State, 22 Ala. App. 469, 116 So. 893 (1928).

[44] See *ibid.* It was said that an octoroon could be prosecuted whether the proportion of one-eighth Negro blood was reached regularly or irregularly.

[45] TEX. ANN. REV. CIV. STAT. (Vernon, 1925) art. 2900. In one early case the Texas Court declared that the term "colored man" was considered broader than the term "Negro" and included persons which the latter term did not. Pauska v. Daus, 31 Tex. 67 (1868). Moreover, there is another early Texas decision which shows that the state was once more liberal in this respect than it is today. In this instance it was held that an indictment charging a white man with marrying a Negro woman could not be supported by proof that the woman was a person of mixed blood. Frasher v. State, 3 Tex. App. 263 (1877).

[46] TEX. ANN. REV. CIV. STAT. (Vernon, 1925) art. 6417; TEX. ANN. PEN. CODE (Vernon, 1925) art. 1659.

[47] TEX. ANN. REV. CIV. STAT. (Vernon, 1925) art. 4607.

defines the term "Negro" as including only those persons who are of Negro blood to the third generation inclusive.[48] Hence we have the same situation that was presented in Alabama,[49] and the courts of Texas would probably reach a similar conclusion.

Another state which has a strict definition of the term "Negro" is Oklahoma. In that jurisdiction the state constitution[50] defines "Negro" or "colored" as meaning any person of African descent, and the intermarriage,[51] separate school,[52] and separate coach[53] laws are to the same effect.

The Tennessee law on this subject presents a rather anomalous situation. Two statutes define the term "Negro" or "a person of color" as including every person who has any Negro blood in his veins.[54] However, the constitutional provision[55] and statute[56] which forbid interracial marriages only prohibit the union of whites and persons who have Negro blood to the third generation inclusive. This is confusing to say the least, but it may be that the general interpretive statutes would govern in all instances where miscegenation was not an issue.

The Arkansas definitions are very strict. The concubinage statute[57] prohibiting cohabitation between the white and Negro races defines the term "Negro" as including any person who has any Negro blood whatever in his veins, and the separate coach law[58] expressly applies to "persons in whom there is a visible and distinct admixture of African blood." In addition to these statutory definitions, the court has construed the term as employed in the school law and has made it apply to any person having a trace of Negro blood, whether visible or not.[59]

North Carolina has dissimilar definitions in respect to intermarriage and the public schools. The marriage law prohibits the union of whites with persons of Negro descent to the third

---

[48] TEX. ANN. PEN. CODE (Vernon, 1925) art. 493.

[49] *See* Weaver v. State, note 43 *supra*.

[50] Art. XXIII, §11.

[51] OKLA. COMP. STAT. (1921) §7499. *See* Blake v. Sessions, 94 Okla. 59, 220 Pac. 876 (1923).

[52] OKLA. CONST. Art. XIII, §3; OKLA. COMP. STAT. (1921) §10,568.

[53] *Id.* at §4954.

[54] TENN. CODE (Will. Shan. & Harsh, 1932) §§25, 8396.

[55] TENN. CONST. Art. XI, §14.

[56] TENN. CODE (Will. Shan. & Harsh, 1932) §8409.

[57] ARK. DIG. STAT. (Crawford & Moses, 1921) §2603.

[58] *Id.* at §996.

[59] State *ex rel.* Black v. Bd. of Directors, 154 Ark. 176, 242 S. W. 545 (1922).

generation inclusive.[60] Like the former Alabama statute of the same type, this act has been construed to include persons who are in the fourth generation from a pure-blooded Negro ancestor, and this ancestor is to be counted as the first generation.[61] The North Carolina Court had come to the same conclusion with respect to the meaning of the words "generation inclusive" when construing a pre-civil-war statute which provided that a person of mixed blood would only cease to be a free Negro when it could be shown that his Negro ancestor was beyond the fourth generation inclusive.[62] According to this decision, a person of mixed blood must have had less than one-sixteenth Negro blood to be classified as a free white person.

The definition of a colored person used in the North Carolina marriage law was at one time held to be determinative of the issue as to what children of mixed blood, if any, should be permitted to attend the white schools.[63] However, the law in this respect was changed in 1903.[64] The school law now provides that no child with Negro blood in his veins shall attend a white school.[65] This statute was held constitutional by the State Supreme Court.[66] The definition contained in the constitutional provision concerning intermarriage was said to have application to that subject alone and not to the problems arising out of the separate school system maintained by the state.

In Florida there are two statutes which define the word "Negro" in such a manner that only those who have one-eighth or more Negro blood would be within the term.[67] In the last compilation one of these statutes is placed immediately following the statute prohibiting intermarriage between members of the two races[68] and therefore, by all indications, would apply to it. This, however, is confusing, as the state constitution prohibits interracial marriages to the "fourth generation inclu-

---

[60] N. C. Const. Art. XIV, §8; N. C. Code. Ann. (Michie, 1931) §§2495, 4340. *See* State v. Melton, 44 N. C. 49 (1852); Ferrall v. Ferrall, 153 N. C. 174, 69 S. E. 60 (1910). The statute formerly read "fourth generation inclusive." *See* State v. Watters, 25 N. C. 455 (1843).

[61] Hare v. Bd. of Education, 113 N. C. 10, 18 S. E. 55 (1893).

[62] State v. Chavers, 50 N. C. 11 (1857). *See also* State v. Dempsey, 31 N. C. 384 (1849); State v. Jacobs, 51 N. C. 284 (1859).

[63] See note 61 *supra*.

[64] N. C. Pub. Laws 1903, c. 435, §22.

[65] N. C. Code Ann. (Michie, 1931) §5384.

[66] Johnson v. Bd. of Education, 166 N. C. 468, 82 S. E. 832 (1914).

[67] Fla. Comp. Gen. Laws Ann. (Skillman, 1927) §§1, 5858.

[68] *Id.* at §5857.

sive," [69] and, according to principles which have already been discussed in connection with the Alabama and North Carolina cases, this would mean that such marriages would be proscribed if either party had one-sixteenth or more Negro blood. It may be, however, that the construction given elsewhere to the word "generation" as used in the constitutional provision may not have been thought of by the Florida lawmakers. They may have believed that the constitution and the statute dovetailed completely, and such may be the case should the state court decide that a different interpretation must be given to the words "generation inclusive." In addition to the above-mentioned statutes, the Florida act penalizing cohabitation of members of the two races includes persons having one-eighth or more Negro blood in defining the term "mulatto." [70]

In Maryland the only indication of the answer to the query is contained in the statute prohibiting intermarriage. This act prohibits unions between whites and persons of Negro descent to the third generation inclusive.[71] The Missouri statute[72] prohibiting the intermarriage of whites and Negroes makes one-eighth or more Negro blood the criterion, and the same is true of the Mississippi[73] and South Carolina[74] laws on this subject. However, the courts of the two last-mentioned states have rendered opposite decisions as to whether these definitions would apply in cases arising under the separate school laws. The South Carolina Court held that the definition contained in the marriage law would govern in this situation and that

[69] Art. XVI, §24. [70] FLA. COMP. GEN. LAWS ANN. (Skillman, 1927) §7565.

[71] MD. ANN. CODE (Bagby, 1924) art. 27, §365.

[72] MO. REV. STAT. (1929) §4263. *See* Marre v. Marre, 184 Mo. App. 198, 168 S. W. 636 (1914). [73] MISS. CONST. §263; MISS. CODE ANN. (1930) §2361.

[74] S. C. CONST. Art. III, §33. In an ante-bellum case the South Carolina Court declared that the term "mulatto" was not invariably applicable to every person who has an admixture of white and Negro blood. Persons who had a taint of African blood were not necessarily to be classified as Negroes or persons of color. The court said that a mere predominance of white blood did not of necessity make a person white legally. It was declared that a quadroon was practically certain to be regarded as a mulatto, but that the same was not always true of an octoroon. The question in all close cases was one for the jury to determine after a thorough consideration of all the evidence. The court remarked that about the only definite rule that could be laid down was that the individual was termed a mulatto or a person of color whenever the admixture of Negro blood was distinct. State v. Davis, 2 Bailey's Law 558 (S. C. 1831). See also State v. Cantey, 2 Hill's Law 614 (S. C. 1835); White v. Tax Collector, 3 Rich. Law 136 (S. C. 1846).

therefore a child with less than one-eighth Negro blood could not rightfully be forced to attend a Negro school.[75] In Mississippi the court refused to make this definition controlling in a similar case. It was decided that the word "colored" used in the separate school law of that state included all persons having an appreciable amount of Negro blood.[76]

In Kentucky there is no statutory definition of the word "Negro." In one early case the state court said that the former Virginia law providing that all persons having one-fourth or more Negro blood were to be classified as colored persons had been carried over into the Kentucky law at the time the state was carved out of territory belonging to Virginia.[77] This, however, is not the law of Kentucky today. In one instance it was held that a child having one-sixteenth Negro blood could not attend a white school. The court stated that any child having an appreciable amount of Negro blood is colored.[78] Nevertheless, it has been decided that a person who looks white, has straight hair, is of a copper color, and has other characteristics of the white man is not a mulatto within the Kentucky statute prohibiting the marriage of whites and Negroes or mulattoes.[79] Thus we cannot definitely say that there is any hard and fast rule concerning the matter in this jurisdiction.

The only indication of the meaning of the term in the District of Columbia is in a case involving the interpretation of the separate school law. Here the District Court of Appeals ruled that a child was colored within the meaning of the act when it had one-eighth or one-sixteenth Negro blood, and that this was true notwithstanding the fact that the child had none of the physical characteristics of a full-blooded Negro.[80]

In a recent case in New York a lower court decided that an octoroon was within the meaning of a restrictive covenant prohibiting the ownership of certain real estate by Negroes or persons of Negro blood.[81] However, it cannot be said that the word "Negro" would always include octoroons in this juris-

---

[75] Tucker v. Blease, 97 S. C. 303, 81 S. E. 668 (1914).

[76] Moreau v. Grandich, 114 Miss. 560, 75 So. 434 (1917).

[77] Gentry v. McMinnis, 33 Ky. 382 (1835).

[78] Mullins v. Belcher, 142 Ky. 673, 143 S. W. 1151 (1911).

[79] Theophanis v. Theophanis, 244 Ky. 689, 57 S. W. (2d) 957 (1932).

[80] Wall v. Oyster, 36 App. D. C. 50, 31 L. R. A. (N.S.) 180 (1910).

[81] Ridgway v. Cockburn, 163 Misc. 511, 296 N. Y. Supp. 936 (1937).

diction, for it must be remembered that the words "of Negro blood" were employed in this covenant.

A rather novel case concerning a restrictive covenant of this kind arose in Virginia. Here the court held that a corporation composed entirely of Negro members is not a colored person within such a covenant.[82] The corporation was considered as an entity distinct from its members.

In all this discussion of the statutes and judicial decisions governing the question of racial identity one fact stands out. There has been an increasing desire on the part of the law-makers of the South and West to discourage and stamp out miscegenation. This tendency is reflected in the recent efforts to tighten the marriage bar by means of much stricter definitions of the term "Negro" than was the case in the days of slavery and the period immediately following the Civil War. The registration statutes of Georgia and Virginia are indicative of this tendency, and it is not unlikely that other states will adopt the same policy. Those who sincerely desire that there be no amalgamation believe that these registration statutes would eventually serve the purpose of clearing up the law of racial identity. However, one should not lose sight of the fact that no matter how carefully such laws are devised or how diligently they are administered, they cannot completely stop extra-legal mixing or the passing of persons with a modicum of Negro blood into the white race by the simple means of moving into a more tolerant region.

When an issue involving racial identity comes before a court, the question arises as to just what evidence is admissible to show the race of any particular individual or that individual's ancestor within the prohibited degree of kinship, if such a degree is provided for by the constitutional provision or statute under consideration. For example, it might be necessary to show that a person of Negro blood who had married a white person had the proscribed fraction of such blood.

It is certainly true that the person who is suspected of being a Negro within the meaning of the term as defined in the particular jurisdiction concerned may be brought before the court in order to allow the jury the opportunity for an inspection.[83]

---

[82] Peoples Pleasure Park Co. v. Rohleder, 109 Va. 439, 61 S. E. 794 (1908).

[83] Linton v. State, 88 Ala. 216, 7 So. 261 (1889); Jones v. State, 156 Ala. 175,

The same is also true of the person's direct or collateral kindred.[84] This profert of the person is not necessarily final, however, for in one early case the Kentucky Court ruled that where a girl who was so exhibited was apparently white, evidence of reputation of Negro maternity was admissible to rebut the same.[85] Where for any reason the racial identity of a child is in question, that child may be exhibited to the jury.[86] Furthermore, photographs of any one of the kinsmen of the person involved whose relationship is sufficiently close are admissible,[87] and the same is true of a crayon portrait if it can be shown to be an accurate likeness of the person depicted.[88] Evidence that such persons have kinky hair or some other peculiar characteristic of the Negro is also competent.[89] In fact in one early Arkansas case it was deemed proper to require a man suspected of being colored to remove his shoes and exhibit his bare feet.[90] In this instance testimony had been introduced that the formation of the Negro's foot is peculiar.

It has been held that experts in ethnology may testify to the presence and amount of Negro blood in the veins of any given person.[91] Even though they may not be experts,[92] persons who have an intimate knowledge of the individual concerned or

---

47 So. 100 (1908); Garvin v. State, 52 Miss. 207 (1876); State v. Davis, 2 Bailey's Law 558 (S. C. 1831).

[84] Weaver v. State, 22 Ala. App. 469, 116 So. 893 (1928). *But see* Graham v. State, 23 Ala. App. 331, 125 So. 200 (1929), where a very light-colored great-aunt of a child in a bastardy proceeding was said to have been erroneously exhibited to the jury. [85] Chancellor v. Milly, 39 Ky. 23, 33 Am. Dec. 521 (1839).

[86] People v. Rabbit, 64 Cal. App. 264, 221 Pac. 391 (1923); Miller v. State, 103 Neb. 591, 173 N. W. 577 (1919); Warlick v. White, 76 N. C. 175 (1877).

[87] Weaver v. State, 22 Ala. App. 469, 116 So. 893 (1928); Spencer v. Looney, 116 Va. 767, 82 S. E. 745 (1914).

[88] Shultz v. Cousins, 242 Fed. 794 (C. C. A. 6th, 1917).

[89] Weaver v. State, 22 Ala. App. 469, 116 So. 893 (1928); State v. Chavers, 50 N. C. 11 (1857). [90] Daniel v. Guy, 23 Ark. 50 (1861).

[91] Daniel v. Guy, 19 Ark. 121 (1857); White v. Clements, 39 Ga. 232 (1869); Nave's Adm'r v. Williams, 22 Ind. 368 (1864). In Spencer v. Looney, 116 Va. 767, 82 S. E. 745 (1914), the witness was found not to possess proper qualifications. In State v. Jacobs, 51 N. C. 284 (1859), the testimony of one who was an owner and manager of slaves and who declared that he had given much attention to the effects of the admixture of the white and Negro races was ruled to be competent. He was of the opinion that he could distinguish between persons of pure white stock and those who were the descendants of Negroes or Indians and determine the amount of non-Caucasian blood.

[92] Hopkins v. Bowers, 111 N. C. 175, 16 S. E. 1 (1892); Hare v. Bd. of Education, 113 N. C. 10, 18 S. E. 55 (1893).

his family may give their opinion of his racial antecedents,[93] the matter being one of common observation.[94] In one miscegenation case from Alabama the admission of a witness' statement that the woman looked white was held not to be erroneous, since he followed this statement with a positive declaration that she was white.[95] In a similar case from Texas the court declared that a conviction could not be had on the opinion of one witness that the woman looked white in the absence of other proof of race.[96] General reputation in the community concerning the race of a particular individual is admissible,[97] and so is proof that he generally associated with persons of one race or the other.[98]

In an ante-bellum South Carolina case, evidence that a person had commonly exercised the privileges of a white man was deemed admissible to prove that he was of the Caucasian or white race.[99] In a later North Carolina case the same principle was applied where there was testimony that the ancestor of the person in question had voted at a time when only white men had that privilege.[100] Evidence that individuals had attended the white schools in their home state[101] or in the state from which they had emigrated[102] was also held to be admissible to prove race. Admissible also is testimony that a person sits in the white section of public conveyances and patronizes the white hotels and theatres.[103]

---

[93] Weaver v. State, 22 Ala. App. 469, 116 So. 893 (1928); White v. Clements, 39 Ga. 232 (1869); Cole v. District School Bd., 32 Okla. 692, 123 Pac. 426 (1912).

[94] Hopkins v. Bowers, 111 N. C. 175, 16 S. E. 1 (1892).

[95] Jones v. State, 156 Ala. 175, 47 So. 100 (1908).

[96] Moore v. State, 7 Tex. App. 608 (1880).

[97] Nave's Adm'r v. Williams, 22 Ind. 368 (1864); Cole v. District School Bd., 32 Okla. 692, 123 Pac. 426 (1912); State v. Cantey, 2 Hill's Law 614 (S. C. 1835). In one North Carolina case a question of this nature was deemed a prerequisite to a further question propounded to a witness as to the racial identity of a certain person's mother. Medlin v. Bd. of Education, 167 N. C. 239, 83 S. E. 483 (1914).

[98] Weaver v. State, 22 Ala. App. 469, 116 So. 893 (1928); Sunseri v. Cassagne, 185 So. 1 (La. 1938); Hopkins v. Bowers, 111 N. C. 175, 16 S. E. 1 (1892); State v. Davis, 2 Bailey's Law 558 (S. C. 1831). In the ante-bellum Davis case it was said that the person's social position might also be considered.

[99] State v. Cantey, 2 Hill's Law 614 (S. C. 1835).

[100] Gilliland v. Bd. of Education, 141 N. C. 482, 54 S. E. 413 (1906).

[101] Cross v. Bd. of Trustees, 121 Ky. 469, 89 S. W. 506 (1905); Sunseri v. Cassagne, 185 So. 1 (La. 1938).

[102] Cole v. District School Bd., 32 Okla. 692, 123 Pac. 426 (1912).

[103] Sunseri v. Cassagne, 185 So. 1 (La. 1938).

Evidence that a person was treated by a Negro couple as their child has been deemed competent,[104] and the same is true of testimony that nine months before the birth of her child, (the father of the children in question) the grandmother of the said children was living with a half-breed Negro.[105] Such evidence, if true, would place the children within the meaning of the term "Negro" as defined by the North Carolina statute which was under consideration in this instance.

Declarations made by the deceased relatives of the person whose race is at issue concerning the racial antecedents of the family have been held to be admissible.[106] These declarations were held to be competent evidence under the exception to the hearsay rule which permits the introduction of declarations concerning pedigree as particularly reliable testimony. In Louisiana a parish recorder's certificates of birth and marriage are admissible.[107]

Another interesting question of evidence arose in a North Carolina case where a person who claimed that his children were white made an attempt to compel the authorities of the white school to accept them as pupils. The school authorities had refused to admit the children because they believed them to be colored, and the father brought a mandamus action to compel them to do so. An attempt was made by the defendants to introduce a declaration made by the father to the effect that he had married a Negro woman. Their contention was that this declaration should be admissible as an admission by a party to the suit, within another well recognized exception to the hearsay rule. The lower court held the declaration admissible only as impeaching testimony and would not permit its use as substantive evidence, and a majority of the judges of the appellate tribunal

---

[104] Locklayer v. Locklayer, 139 Ala. 354, 35 So. 1008 (1904).

[105] Hare v. Bd. of Education, 113 N. C. 10, 18 S. E. 55 (1893).

[106] Locklayer v. Locklayer, 139 Ala. 354, 35 So. 1008 (1904); Gilliland v. Bd. of Education, 141 N. C. 482, 54 S. E. 413 (1906). Declarations made by persons who were not relatives are inadmissible. Reed v. State, 18 Ala. App. 353, 92 So. 511 (1922). In North Carolina a declaration by a grandmother that the parent was the offspring of herself by a white man was held to be inadmissible because she failed to name the man and because of the rule which disallows such testimony when the declaration was made by a person who had a motive to pervert the truth. State v. Watters, 25 N. C. 455 (1843).

[107] Sunseri v. Cassagne, 185 So. 1 (La. 1938).

were of the same opinion.[108] The father was said to have no sufficient interest in the suit to constitute him a "party" within the rule as to admissions, the children being the real parties in interest. The dissenting judge contended that the father was the real party in interest and that the declaration should have been admissible as substantive evidence.

An interesting case concerning the meaning of the term "Creole" arose in Alabama. During a trial for miscegenation the prosecution introduced a declaration made by a light-colored mulatto in making an application for a marriage license to the effect that the woman he wished to marry was a Creole. This declaration was held to be allowable as an admission.[109] The court declared that the term "Creole" was subject to various interpretations, one indicating the French-speaking inhabitants of Louisiana and neighboring states, while another designated the same sort of people with a slight admixture of Negro blood. The interpretation to be given the term as used in this particular instance was left to the jury.

---

[108] Medlin v. Bd. of Education, 167 N. C. 239, 83 S. E. 483 (1914).

[109] Parker v. State, 118 Ala. 655, 23 So. 664 (1898).

II

LIBEL AND SLANDER

There can be no doubt that the term "Negro" or "colored person," when applied to a person who is wholly of Caucasian blood, carries with it a certain degree of opprobrium. Such language constitutes a grievous insult in the South where the resentment is particularly strong as a result of historic factors and anti-Negro social attitudes which are taken judicial notice of by the southern courts.[1] The prejudice is ingrained and cannot easily be conquered even by those who believe that no real racial inferiority exists. It is so strong with the southern whites of all classes that even the most degraded would be insulted if it were intimated that there was Negro blood in their veins. In the North and West the prejudice is not so severe, and yet even in these sections of the country the imputation of Negro blood is deeply resented in most instances.

Is defamation of this kind actionable? The answer to this question is complicated by certain technical differences between libel and slander which developed with the common law.[2] It is sufficient to say that sometimes the written word may be actionable per se, that is, without proof of special damage, where the spoken word is not. Every court which has considered the question has held that writing that a white man is a Negro is libelous per se.[3] In the case of spoken words, however, the courts

---

[1] Shultz v. Cousins, 242 Fed. 794 (C.C.A. 6th, 1917); Wolfe v. Ga. Ry. & Electric Co., 2 Ga. App. 499, 58 S. E. 899 (1907); State v. Bessa, 115 La. 259, 38 So. 985 (1905); Succession of David v. Richard, 1 La. App. 237 (1924).

[2] *See* Williams v. Riddle, 145 Ky. 459, 140 S. W. 661 (1911).

[3] Upton v. Times-Democrat Pub. Co., 104 La. 141, 28 So. 970 (1900); Collins v. Oklahoma State Hospital, 76 Okla. 229, 184 Pac. 946 (1916); Hargrove v. Okla. Press Pub. Co., 130 Okla. 76, 265 Pac. 635 (1928); Flood v. News and Courier Co., 71 S. C. 112, 50 S. E. 637 (1905); Shultz v. Cousins, 242 Fed. 794 (C.C.A. 6th, Tenn., 1917). It is believed that Alabama, Georgia, Illinois, and Kentucky would concur because of expressions in the opinions of their courts. Jones v. Polk & Co., 190 Ala. 243, 67 So. 577 (1915); Atlanta Journal Co. v. Farmer, 48 Ga. App. 273, 172 S. E. 647 (1934); Wright v. F. W. Woolworth Co., 281 Ill. App. 495 (1935); Williams v. Riddle, 145 Ky. 459, 140 S. W. 661 (1911).

have disagreed. Thus the Arkansas,[4] Georgia,[5] Louisiana,[6] Mississippi,[7] South Carolina,[8] and Virginia[9] courts have employed language in their opinions which can only be interpreted as recognizing the doctrine that such an utterance is actionable per se, while a federal court in the District of Columbia[10] and state courts of Illinois,[11] Kentucky,[12] North Carolina,[13] and Ohio[14] have either held directly opposite views or else used phraseology subject to that interpretation. A thorough reading of a recent Kansas opinion[15] leads one to believe that the latter rule would prevail in that jurisdiction. Some of the states which have taken the former view have had special reasons for doing so. The Arkansas and Mississippi decisions are based upon statutes which can be interpreted as enlarging upon the common law rule. The prewar South Carolina decisions were evidently influenced by the consideration that the truth of the charge that the injured party was colored would entail the loss of many of his civil rights, the Negro then having very few privileges.[16] The Louisiana decisions may be accounted for by calling attention to the fact that it is the Roman civil law, and

[4] Morris v. State, 109 Ark. 530, 160 S. W. 387 (1913).

[5] Wolfe v. Ga. Ry. & Elec. Co., 2 Ga. App. 449, 58 S. E. 899 (1907). *See also* Bagwell v. Rice & Hutchins Co., 38 Ga. App. 87, 143 S. E. 125 (1928).

[6] Dobard v. Nunez, 6 La. Ann. 294 (1851); Spotorno v. Fourichon, 40 La. Ann. 423, 4 So. 71 (1888); May v. Shreveport Traction Co., 127 La. 420, 53 So. 671 (1910); Berot v. Porte, 144 La. 805, 81 So. 323 (1919). This is true in spite of the failure to hold an alleged defamer liable in Toye v. McMahon, 21 La. Ann. 308 (1869), where the proof did not show conclusively that the defendant uttered the language complained of or that he spoke with the intention of publicly insulting the plaintiff at a meeting of hackmen and for the purpose of causing the latter to be expelled from the Hackmens' Association. It did not appear that he had ever been a member but only that his application for membership was rejected.

[7] Scott v. Peebles, 2 Sm. & M. 546 (Miss. 1844).

[8] Eden v. Legare, 1 Bay 171 (S. C. 1791); King v. Wood, 1 Nott & McCord 184 (S. C. 1818).

[9] Spencer v. Looney, 116 Va. 767, 82 S. E. 745 (1914).

[10] Johnson v. Brown, 13 Fed. Cas. No. 7375 (C. C. D. C. 1832).

[11] Wright v. F. W. Woolworth Co., 281 Ill. App. 495 (1935).

[12] Williams v. Riddle, 145 Ky. 459, 140 S. W. 661 (1911).

[13] McDowell v. Bowles, 53 N. C. 184 (1860); Deese v. Collins, 191 N. C. 749, 133 S. E. 92 (1926).

[14] Barret v. Jarvis, cited in note to Goodenow v. Tappan, 1 Ohio Rep. 60, 83 (1823).

[15] Jones v. Gill, 145 Kan. 482, 66 P. (2d) 1033 (1937).

[16] *See* Eden v. Legare, 1 Bay 171 (S. C. 1791).

not the common law, that forms the basis of the jurisprudence of that state.[17] The Georgia Court evidently followed this Louisiana view, while the Virginia decision was supported by the citation of a South Carolina libel case. All this would lead one to believe that a holding that such language is slanderous per se is not in accordance with the accepted principles of the common law. However, it may be difficult to convince the southern white man that there is any logical distinction between libel and slander in this respect, as a person can be hurt just as much, and possibly more, by malicious gossip of this sort as he can by a malevolent statement contained in a newspaper or other publication. In a case from Kansas,[18] a state which does not even have a statute prohibiting intermarriage, it was alleged that the adoptive parents of a little girl were hounded out of a neighborhood by gossip that she was colored.

In a case from Nebraska one person said that another was a "half-breed Mexican." The court held that this was not actionable per se.[19] While in most sections of the country this appellation would not be considered as carrying anywhere near the same degree of opprobrium that the terms "Negro" and "colored" do, yet in some states, particularly in those of the Southwest, it is thought by some white men to constitute a grievous affront. In Nebraska it would probably be deemed less insulting to call a man a Mexican than to call him a Negro. Therefore we cannot positively say that the Nebraska Court would adopt the same attitude where the latter appellation was applied to a person of pure white descent. However, this case would undoubtedly be persuasive authority for the proposition that language of this kind would not be actionable per se.

In the above-mentioned District of Columbia case the plaintiff argued that the language imputing that he was of Negro descent was actionable per se because he had married a white woman in a jurisdiction where the laws made an interracial marriage a criminal offense and therefore would be subject to punishment if the charge turned out to be true. The alleged defamatory statement contained no reference to the marriage and there was no allegation that the words were spoken in reference there-

---

[17] *See* Spotorno v. Fourichon, 40 La. Ann. 423, 4 So. 71 (1888).

[18] Jones v. Gill, 145 Kan. 482, 66 P. (2d) 1033 (1937).

[19] Davis v. Meyer, 115 Neb. 251, 212 N. W. 435, 50 A. L. R. 1410 (1927).

to. The court ruled that this was fatal to the plaintiff's contention.[20]

The Kentucky Court has declared that the special damages which it is necessary to prove where the language is not actionable per se must be of a pecuniary nature. Therefore the court ruled that loss of caste with the white people with whom one is in the habit of associating was not a sufficient element of damage to warrant a recovery.[21] However, the courts of late have been taking more and more cognizance of injuries to the individual's feelings as an element of damages, and hence it would occasion no great surprise if some court took an opposite view.

The Virginia Court seems to have been the only tribunal to consider the following interesting question. In a case where the defendant had called the plaintiff and his son Negroes, the court seems to have approved the doctrine that the defendant would not be permitted to set up the truth of the charge as a defense unless it could be shown that the plaintiff had one-sixteenth or more Negro blood, for that was the criterion of an individual's race which was established in Virginia at that time.[22] Consequently, one might argue that, if a plaintiff had less Negro blood than the amount prescribed by the definitive statutes or decisions in any given jurisdiction, he would be considered a white man and could recover damages from anyone who called him a Negro without qualifying the remark.

A man who has been defamed in this manner must bring the action himself. Neither parents in Georgia[23] nor an Oklahoma wife[24] were permitted to recover damages in cases of this kind. In the case of the parents the argument was made that the imputation of Negro blood in the offspring carried with it a stigma on the parents themselves. Although the contention seems a rather sensible and reasonable one, the court would not follow this theory. In one instance the Virginia Court held that a parent is not legally responsible for the act of his young child in calling a little white girl a "Negro doll." [25]

In order for an action of this kind to succeed it is necessary

[20] Johnson v. Brown, 13 Fed. Cas. No. 7375 (C. C. D. C. 1832).
[21] Williams v. Riddle, 145 Ky. 459, 140 S. W. 661 (1911).
[22] Spencer v. Looney, 116 Va. 767, 82 S. E. 745 (1914).
[23] Atlanta Journal Co. v. Farmer, 48 Ga. App. 273, 172 S. E. 647 (1934).
[24] Hargrove v. Okla. Press Pub. Co., 130 Okla. 76, 265 Pac. 635 (1928).
[25] Mopsikov v. Cook, 122 Va. 579, 95 S. E. 426 (1918).

for the plaintiff to show that the defamatory language was employed with respect to himself and no other[26] and that the words distinctly charged that he was a Negro or mulatto and were not subject to the interpretation that the defendant had merely said that he resembled a Negro.[27] It is permissible to use innuendoes in stating such a case.[28]

Defamatory language of this kind may be qualifiedly privileged because it was rendered in some public or private investigation, and, if such is the case, malice must be shown in order to enable the maligned party to recover damages. Language recognizing this principle has been employed by the courts of Louisiana,[29] Oklahoma,[30] and Virginia.[31] In a pre-civil-war case the Louisiana Court seems to have held that malice must be shown irrespective of whether or not the statement was privileged.[32] However, this is not in accord with the modern view. In one Louisiana case the plaintiff was allowed to recover at least nominal damages where there was no ill will and the libelous publication was due to a mistake and retraction was made.[33] In a case from Alabama, however, the court refused to allow a recovery and affirmed a judgment for the defendant where the publication was in a city directory and was due to an innocent mistake.[34] The Louisiana view is legally the better one, as a man may be injured just as much by a defamatory statement which is innocently and mistakenly published as by one which is inspired by malice. The Alabama decision was probably influenced by special circumstances and by the fact that no bad motive was shown. The outcome can be accounted for only on the theory that the act of the defendant in printing the city directory was qualifiedly privileged.

The postwar constitutional amendments have had very little effect upon the social attitude of the southern white man toward the Negro. Two courts have stated that there is no reason why the rule of law which permits an action to be brought for language referring to a white man as a Negro should be altered

[26] See note 23 *supra*. [27] Atkinson v. Hartley, 1 McCord 203 (S. C. 1821).
[28] See note 23 *supra*. [29] Berot v. Porte, 144 La. 805, 81 So. 323 (1919).
[30] Collins v. Oklahoma State Hospital, 76 Okla. 229, 184 Pac. 946 (1919).
[31] Spencer v. Looney, 116 Va. 767, 82 S. E. 745 (1914).
[32] Boullemet v. Philips, 2 Rob. 365 (La. 1842).
[33] Upton v. Times-Democrat Pub. Co., 104 La. 141, 28 So. 970 (1900).
[34] Jones v. Polk & Co., 190 Ala. 243, 67 So. 577 (1915).

because of these changes in the fundamental law of the land.[35]

A novel case was brought before the Oklahoma Court in 1919. A white patient in the State Hospital for the Insane brought a libel suit against the institution because of the action of the authorities in charge in placing the complainant in a colored ward. The patient claimed that this constituted actionable libel. The court was of the opinion that the state libel statute, upon which the action was predicated, did not cover the case. There was neither spoken nor written language designating that the plaintiff was a Negro, and hence the tribunal refused to allow a recovery.[36]

In a New York case it was proved that the defendant had said that the white female plaintiff was only fit to associate with Negroes and that, before moving from her former abode in the South, she had performed labor for Negroes alone. The court held that the words were not slanderous per se and denied a recovery.[37] In the South, however, it is conceivable that much damage might result from the use of this sort of language. Testimony which brought out facts of this kind might well be considered as a sufficient proof of special damage. Where domestic servants are involved such a statement might even be held slanderous per se, since it would tend to injure the plaintiff in her chosen way of making a living. White families would not wish to employ a woman of their own race who had worked in the homes of wealthy colored persons for any length of time. In fact, such a situation is practically unheard of in the South. There is one case which might possibly be cited in support of the proposition that language of this kind is actionable, although it was decided in the eastern state of Rhode Island. In this instance a false item was published in a newspaper which represented the plaintiff, an unmarried white woman, as being in the company of a Negro man. It went on to say that she had been assaulted by her escort's colored wife because of jealousy. The true facts were that she was struck by a jealous Negro woman who had mistaken her for another person. This

[35] Flood v. News and Courier Co., 71 S. C. 112, 50 S. E. 637 (1905); Spencer v. Looney, 116 Va. 767, 82 S. E. 745 (1914).

[36] Collins v. Oklahoma State Hospital, 76 Okla. 229, 184 Pac. 946 (1919).

[37] MacIntyre v. Fruchter, 148 N. Y. Supp. 786 (Sup. Ct. 1914). See in connection with this case Kenworthy v. Brown, 45 Misc. 292, 92 N. Y. Supp. 34 (Sup. Ct. 1904).

language was found to be actionable. The appellate court ruled that a jury verdict exceeding two thousand dollars was not excessive and seemed to emphasize the fact that the plaintiff, a respectable white woman of good family, was accused of associating with colored persons in this very intimate way.[38]

In several cases it has been declared actionable to accuse a white woman of having had sexual intercourse with a Negro man.[39] A Georgia statute[40] makes a charge of this kind slanderous per se. In one instance the Michigan Court used language which might possibly be given the interpretation that such an accusation would give rise to greater damages than an imputation of incontinency with a white man.[41] This interpretation, however, would be rather exceptional in view of the fact that Michigan has no law prohibiting interracial marriages. Therefore it is doubted that the court wished its remarks to be so understood.

In a Georgia case a newspaper published an article stating that a certain group of Negroes had endorsed a certain white person's candidacy for the office of sheriff. The white man claimed that this article had caused his defeat at the polls and started a libel suit. The appellate court ruled that the article was not libelous per se.[42]

In a recent case an Oklahoma newspaper published an article stating that a Negro attorney had referred to certain accused colored persons whom he was defending on gambling charges as "niggers." The article went on to state that the club in which the Negroes were alleged to have been found gambling had been twice raided in recent months, that the attorney had for some time been proclaiming the innocence of the manager of the club, and that it was a virtuous, charitable institution. The article attributed to the attorney words which are commonly used by the more illiterate southern Negro. The attorney claimed that the article was libelous per se in that it tended to

---

[38] Luft v. Lingane, 17 R. I. 420, 22 Atl. 942 (1891).

[39] Strader v. Snyder, 67 Ill. 404 (1873); Hemming v. Elliott, 66 Md. 197, 7 Atl. 110 (1886); Hargrove v. Okla. Press Pub. Co., 130 Okla. 76, 265 Pac. 635 (1928); Smith v. Hamilton, 10 Rich. Law 44 (S. C. 1856).

[40] GA. CODE ANN. (Michie, 1926) §4434.

[41] Smitley v. Pinch, 148 Mich. 670, 112 N. W. 686 (1907).

[42] Watkins v. Augusta Chronicle Pub. Co., 49 Ga. App. 43, 174 S. E. 199 (1934).

deprive him of the confidence of his clientele and hence to injure him professionally. The court, however, refused to allow a recovery.[43] It declared that a publication which subjects a person to jest or banter, so as to affect his feelings, is not, standing alone, actionable libel. It is stated that the term "nigger" is commonly used by members of both races and is merely an abbreviated or substituted form for the word "Negro." Hence it was stated that the term had no special derogatory connotation when used to indicate a person of the colored race. It is to be noted, however, that many Negroes resent the term "nigger" when it is used in an uncivil or rude fashion.

In a Kentucky case a newspaper published an article charging the officials of a tobacco company with placing white girls under Negro foremen. The statement was untrue and the corporation initiated a libel suit. The plaintiff claimed that the article had injured its reputation and that it had caused a local labor union to place the company on its black list. The appellate court decided that the corporation had a cause of action and therefore allowed a recovery.[44]

A recent Florida case illustrates the gravity with which a southern court is likely to look upon any imputation of intimate relationships between the races. In this instance the defendant used language charging a prominent white man with attending a colored dance hall and dancing with Negro wenches. The court ruled that this language was actionable per se.[45]

From what has been said above it may be stated that southern courts take judicial cognizance of the attitude of the white man toward the Negro. Hence these courts will consider as defamatory certain statements which would not be actionable if this attitude did not exist.

---

[43] Franklin v. World Pub. Co., 183 Okla. 507, 83 P. (2d) 401 (1938).

[44] Axton Fisher Tobacco Co. v. Evening Post Co., 169 Ky. 64, 183 S. W. 269 (1916).

[45] Sharp v. Bussey, 187 So. 779 (Fla. 1939).

III

CIVIL RIGHTS

Before the Civil War slaves and even free Negroes had very few rights or privileges. This situation remained even after the Thirteenth Amendment to the Federal Constitution was adopted immediately following the war. The amendment merely prohibited slavery or involuntary servitude, except as a punishment for crime, and authorized Congress to enforce its terms by appropriate legislation. The inequality of treatment accorded to the Negroes was nation-wide, though there were of course greater inequalities in the South than in the North and West. In some sections of the country where there were almost no Negroes, such as northern New England and Wisconsin, they were given the voting franchise and other privileges which were denied to them in states where they were more numerous. In 1856 the federal citizenship of the Negro had been tested and found wanting in the famous *Dred Scott* decision.[1] In this case the Supreme Court merely took the same position taken by various state courts.[2] The *Dred Scott* decision was of course one of the contributing causes of the War Between the States, and hence it was only natural that during the war and immediately thereafter opinions were expressed in the North that the decision was no longer effective and was not to be followed in the present or the future.[3]

After the war the southern legislatures had put into effect the "Black Codes." These laws were very harsh and were undoubtedly stricter than the circumstances called for, although the whites certainly had considerable reason for enacting them into law. The Negroes were ignorant and were not accustomed to or capable of supporting or taking care of themselves financially or otherwise. They were easily swayed by "carpet-

---

[1] Dred Scott v. Sandford, 19 How. 393 (U. S. 1856).

[2] Pendleton v. State, 6 Ark. 509 (1846); Crandall v. State, 10 Conn. 339 (1834); Bryan v. Walton, 20 Ga. 480 (1856); *In re* Opinion of Justices, 44 Me. 505 (1858); Mitchell v. Wells, 37 Miss. 235 (1859); State v. Claiborne, 19 Tenn. 331 (1838). *But see* Walsh v. Lallande, 25 La. Ann. 188 (1873).

[3] *See* Smith v. Moody, 26 Ind. 299 (1866).

baggers" and "skalawags" who made them rash promises which were not even meant to be kept, such as "forty acres and a mule." These Black Codes gave the Negro population very little freedom. The colored man was free in name only in many cases. The apprentice, vagrancy, and other provisions of these statutes forced the Negro into situations where he would be under the uncontrolled supervision of his former master or other white men who were ready and willing to exploit his labor. This group of statutes angered the northern people who had no understanding of the true situation in the South, which was one of the chief reasons why the radical element in Congress, led by Thaddeus Stevens and Charles Sumner, were able to get control of the legislative branch of the government. They believed that the Negroes in the South should be allowed to exercise many if not all of the privileges which the southern white man had thought were his alone.

In 1866 Congress passed a Civil Rights Act[4] which gave the Negro citizenship and also included within its terms certain other rights and privileges. Among these were the right to make and enforce contracts, the right to hold and convey personal or real property, to sue and be parties in the courts of the nation and to be given equal benefit of the laws, to give evidence in these same courts, and to be subject to the same punishments and penalties as white persons, any law to the contrary notwithstanding. The issue concerning the validity of this statute never reached the Federal Supreme Court, for the Fourteenth Amendment superseded it before the question could be brought to a test in that tribunal. There was at least some doubt as to the validity of the Civil Rights Act. Most of the decisions in the lower federal courts and the state tribunals seemed to admit that the statute was valid,[5] but there is at least one case in which the court held that the enactment was unauthorized.[6] The question is a purely academic one today, as the Fourteenth Amendment was adopted in 1868. The amendment

---

[4] 14 Stat. 27 (1866).

[5] United States v. Rhodes, 27 Fed. Cas. No. 16,151 (C. C. D. Ky. 1866); *In re* Turner, 24 Fed. Cas. No. 14,247 (C. C. D. Md. 1867). *See also* Ellis v. State, 42 Ala. 525 (1868); State v. Gibson, 36 Ind. 389 (1871); Hart v. Hoss & Elder, 26 La. Ann. 90 (1874); State v. Hairston, 63 N. C. 451 (1869); Lonas v. State, 3 Heisk. 287 (Tenn. 1871); Frasher v. State, 3 Tex. App. 263 (1877).

[6] Bowlin v. Commonwealth, 65 Ky. 5 (1867).

guaranteed federal and state citizenship to all persons born or naturalized in the United States who are subject to the jurisdiction thereof, and of course this included the former slaves.[7] Those who were not born in this country would probably be considered as naturalized or at least capable of naturalization. The amendment also guaranteed the privileges and immunities of federal[8] citizenship, the equal protection of the laws, and the right not to be deprived of life, liberty, or property without due process of law. The purpose of these provisions was of course that "no State" should discriminate against the Negro with respect to the making and administration of laws.[9] The Civil Rights legislation was reënacted in 1870,[10] and some of the provisions of this enactment were not essentially different from the language used in the act of 1866.

These statutes not being effective, it was deemed advisable to adopt a statute with sharper teeth. Therefore in 1875 Congress passed a statute[11] which provided that all persons within the United States, regardless of race, color, or previous condition of servitude, and subject only to restrictions established by law and applying to all citizens alike, should be entitled to the full and equal accommodations and facilities of inns, public conveyances on land and water, theatres, and other places of public amusement. The act punished a violation of its provisions with fine or imprisonment and a heavy penalty to be recovered by the person aggrieved. The federal courts were given exclusive jurisdiction of offenses arising under this statute. Again the lower federal courts divided concerning the validity of this act. Two southern judges cast doubt upon its validity in their charges to grand juries,[12] and a federal court in Kentucky ruled that the statute was unconstitutional.[13] Other tribunals upheld the validity of the enactment. This was done in a case from Pennsylvania which involved the refusal of a

[7] Slaughter House Cases, 16 Wall. 36 (U. S. 1872).

[8] These privileges and immunities of federal citizenship are differentiated from those of state citizenship. *See* Minor v. Hapersett, 21 Wall. 162 (U. S. 1874).

[9] That such was the primary purpose, see Slaughter House Cases, 16 Wall. 36 (U. S. 1872).

[10] 16 STAT. 144 (1870).

[11] 18 STAT. 335 (1875).

[12] Charge to Grand Jury, 30 Fed. Cas. No. 18,258 (C. C. W. D. N. C. 1875); *id.* at No. 18,260 (C. C. W. D. Tenn. 1875).

[13] Smoot v. Ky. Cent. Ry., 13 Fed. 337 (C. C. D. Ky. 1882).

Pennsylvania clerk to accommodate a Negro except on conditions that the latter declined to accept.[14] The same result was reached in a decision against a Texas carrier for refusing to accommodate a Negro woman in the ladies' car.[15] The question was not definitely settled until 1883, when the Supreme Court held in the *Civil Rights Cases* that the Fourteenth Amendment did not authorize direct legislation of this kind against individuals.[16] The court declared that the amendment authorized only corrective legislation which seeks to penalize states or their officials for not respecting the rights guaranteed by the constitutional change, such as the right not to be deprived by the state of life, liberty, or property without due process of law. By this time the whites had regained control of the governmental machinery in the southern states, and no further attempt was made in Congress to enact federal legislation of this type. It was apparently decided that the South was to be given an opportunity to manage its local problems with respect to the Negro as best it might. It was evidently thought that the constitutional amendments would act as a check and keep the white people of the southern states from grossly disregarding the rights of the Negro in this respect.

Before the enactment of the 1875 Federal Civil Rights Act, the Reconstruction legislatures in several of the southern states, dominated by "carpetbaggers," "skalawags," and Negroes, enacted statutes[17] which were similar in tone to that legislation. Only a few cases dealing with these statutes reached the appellate courts. In Louisiana[18] and Mississippi[19] theatre proprietors were held responsible under the acts of those states for refusing to accommodate Negroes solely on account of race or color. In Louisiana the proprietor of a combination coffeehouse and saloon was held accountable.[20] Only one of these statutes,

[14] United States v. Newcomer, 27 Fed. Cas. No. 15,868 (E. D. Pa. 1876). *See also* Lewis v. Hitchcock, 10 Fed. 4 (S. D. N. Y. 1882).

[15] United States v. Dodge, 25 Fed. Cas. No. 14,976 (W. D. Tex. 1877).

[16] Civil Rights Cases, 109 U. S. 3, 3 Sup. Ct. 18 (1883).

[17] *See* Ark. Acts 1873, pp. 15-19; Fla. Laws 1873, c. 1947; La. Acts 1869, p. 57, La. Acts 1870, p. 57, La. Acts 1873, pp. 156-157; Miss. Laws 1873, c. 63; 14 S. C. Stat. 1868-70, p. 179.

[18] Joseph v. Bidwell, 28 La. Ann. 382 (1876).

[19] Donnell v. State, 48 Miss. 661 (1873).

[20] Sauvinet v. Walker, 27 La. Ann. 14 (1875).

the one in Louisiana,[21] is still on the books, and from reliable sources it has been learned that this act has simply become a dead letter and nothing is done about it. Negroes certainly do not receive accommodations, equal or otherwise, in hotels, restaurants, theatres, or other similar places of public resort which are frequented by the white people of Louisiana. Any effort by Negroes to assert the privileges which this act seems to grant would undoubtedly be met by repeal. In fact such an attempt would probably lead to a great deal of friction between the races and would hurt the Negro cause.

The Reconstruction constitutions of the states which had seceded from the Union contained provisions which seemed to be on the same order as the Thirteenth and Fourteenth amendments to the Federal Constitution. At least the wording is somewhat similar and certain fundamental rights are guaranteed by both. There are clauses which are in very much the same vein as the due process clause, and some provisions do not differ a great deal from the language employed by the framers of the Fourteenth Amendment in guaranteeing the rights of citizenship and the equal protection of the laws. Northern as well as southern states enacted statutes which were similarly worded. A Connecticut statute[22] of this general type is still on the books. The framers of the Louisiana Constitution went a bit further than this and put in a provision[23] which is worded like the above Civil Rights Acts, but this clause was left out when the whites, having regained control, adopted a new constitution in 1879. There is just a possibility that the repeal of this clause would be construed to carry with it the abrogation of the above statute which had been enacted with this provision in view.[24]

In Georgia the court held that these state constitutional provisions guaranteed the Negro equal rights and hence would invalidate a prewar statute which provided that anyone who had one-eighth or more Negro blood was ineligible to hold office.[25]

The legislation of Delaware and Tennessee during the

---

[21] La. Gen. Stat. Ann. (Dart, 1932) §§1070-73. The act of 1873 was repealed by La. Acts 1902, p. 27, but the 1869 act is still on the books.

[22] Conn. Gen. Stat. (1930) §6065.

[23] La. Const. (1868) art. 13.

[24] *See* Joseph v. Bidwell, 28 La. Ann. 382 (1876).

[25] White v. Clements, 39 Ga. 232 (1869).

twenty-year period following the war was in a tone very different from that of the Civil Rights Acts. Delaware enacted a statute which authorized the proprietor of any inn, hotel, tavern, restaurant, or other place of public entertainment or refreshment, theatre, or other place of amusement to decline to serve or accommodate persons who were offensive to the major portion of his clientele.[26] The object of this act was obviously to keep the Negroes from entering such places and demanding service. Tennessee enacted a statute in 1875[27] which was very similar to the Delaware act. This statute seems to authorize the proprietor of any hotel or public house, the owner or lessee of any theatre, or the management of any public carrier except railways to refuse accommodations to any person whom he does not wish to make provision for or entertain. The railway exception specifically mentions all commercial railways, including street and interurban lines. The constitutionality of these statutes has never been tested. If they were brought to such a test, it is possible that they would be held invalid as inferentially authorizing the places of public accommodation mentioned in the acts to make discriminatory regulations based on color alone. This could then be regarded as an instance of the discriminatory state action which is barred by the Fourteenth Amendment. Since the validity of these statutes has never been questioned in the courts, they still remain effective in their respective jurisdictions except as the law is changed by a Tennessee act of 1885.[28] This act provides that all well-behaved persons shall be admitted to theatres, shows, parks, places for the observation of scenery, or any other public place of amusement without regard to the particular route or means of transportation used to go to and from such places, but states that nothing contained in the statute is to be construed to deprive the proprietors of such places of their "existing rights" to provide separate accommodations for whites and Negroes. A violation of the act is punished criminally and provision is made for enforcement by injunction if necessary. The number of Negroes who attend white theatres in Tennessee at present is probably very small, and these are segregated in such places as balconies.

[26] DEL. CODE (1915) §§3575-76.

[27] TENN. CODE (Will. Shan. & Harsh, 1932) §5262.

[28] *Id.* at §§5257-61.

What is the situation in southern states where there are no statutes which touch upon this problem? In North Carolina language very similar to that used in the Delaware statute was employed by the court in considering the duty of an innkeeper to receive customers.[29] This opinion seems to recognize that the South is committed to the policy of a separation of the races in places of public accommodation and amusement which is as rigid and complete as the law will permit under the circumstances. According to the language employed in this instance, we would suppose that the court recognized the right of an innkeeper or proprietor of any restaurant or other like place of public resort to refuse to allow Negroes within their establishments. In the North there are indications that a different rule of law would obtain. In one case the New York intermediate appellate court has held that the existence of a Civil Rights Act in that state would not prevent anyone who has been refused accommodations by an innkeeper from being successful in an action at common law.[30] There is nothing in the opinion to signify to what race the plaintiff belonged. The Michigan Court also made remarks which seem to recognize the existence of such a common law right. These remarks were made in a comparatively early case involving the refusal of the proprietor of a restaurant to give a Negro customer equal accommodations.[31] Their force is weakened, however, by the fact that the court also cited the Michigan Civil Rights Act which was on the statute books even at this early date. Hence we see that there may be different views in the North and South with respect to the rules of the common law on a controversial matter like this one.

In respect to the actual practice of innkeepers and proprietors of restaurants, theatres, and other places of public resort in handling the problem here presented, we have diverse practices in different sections of the nation. The only general

[29] State v. Steele, 106 N. C. 766, 782, 11 S. E. 478, 484 (1890). The court declared that the guests of a hotel "cannot be lawfully prevented from going in or be put out . . . unless they be persons of bad or suspicious character, or of vulgar habits, or so objectionable to the patrons of the house, on account of the race to which they belong, that it would injure the business to admit them to all portions of the house."

[30] Cornell v. Huber, 102 App. Div. 293, 92 N. Y. Supp. 434 (2d Dep't 1905).

[31] Ferguson v. Gies, 82 Mich. 358, 46 N. W. 718 (1890).

rule which can be stated with any degree of certainty is that the more Negroes there are in a community, the more they will be discriminated against. In the South it is an almost unheard of occurrence for a Negro or mulatto to request accommodations in a place of this kind which is frequented only by whites. Some theatres permit Negroes in balconies set aside for their special use. The Negroes have their own hotels and restaurants, their own theatres and pleasure resorts. The exceptions to this practice are so few that they only serve to prove the rule. In most southern communities any Negro who made an attempt to enter a white hotel or theatre would be thrown out unceremoniously and without delay. He would be labeled as an undesirable colored person and would probably lose his means of livelihood, for he is largely dependent on the good will of white employers for his economic subsistence. In some portions of the South more serious results might follow, such as a beating.

In the states of the North and Middle West, where the prejudice against the Negro has been growing in recent years, it seems that the colored man cannot obtain accommodations in the best of the urban hotels. This is particularly true of the hotels in the resorts and larger cities which cater to the tourist trade. The proprietors of these establishments always have some reason other than race or color for refusing to admit colored persons who apply for accommodations. They are always "overcrowded" or have some other trumped up excuse. The same is true of the restaurants and similar establishments which cater to the socially elite among the whites. These places also refuse to serve lower-class foreigners and other unwanted persons. All sorts of methods are employed to keep the Negroes from entering this type of establishment, for the Civil Rights Acts would seem to cover most of these places. The proprietor of a restaurant may order his employes to delay serving Negroes until they are tired of waiting. There are also instances where the proprietor will instruct his servants to put too much salt on the Negro customers' food so that they will not return in the future. There are other subterfuges just as effective as these. Theatres and other places of amusement sometimes refuse the Negro accommodations. Other places of public accommodation also have this problem to a more or less varying degree. In urban centers where Negroes are present in large numbers the prejudice is likely to be greater than in urban or rural districts where there are relatively few colored persons. The desire for jobs has made the Negroes who migrated from the South settle in the great industrial cities of the North and Middle West. Here they have become more or less segregated in communities like New York's Harlem. In these communities the Negroes have their own hotels, restaurants, motion picture theatres, dance halls, barbershops. Some white persons attend the night clubs and cabarets, but they are either faddists or persons who have no objection to associating with the Negro on a basis of social equality.

In an effort to prevent discrimination of the kind above described, most of the states in the North and Middle West have adopted Civil Rights Acts which are very much like the congressional act of 1875. A few states in the Far West have also enacted laws of this type.

Strange though it may seem, there are no such statutes in Maine, New Hampshire, or Vermont. It is true that both Maine[32] and New Hampshire[33] have legislation which prohibits a place of public accommodation from issuing any notice or advertisement that is calculated to suggest discrimination against any religious sect, nationality, or class, enumerating business establishments which are within the terms of the statute. It is not believed, however, that the word "class" would be construed as relating to discrimination against the Negro on account of race or color. This is rendered more plausible by the fact that a recent codification in Pennsylvania contained statutes of both types.[34]

Eighteen states of the above sections of the nation have Civil Rights Acts which are clearly meant to apply to racial discrimination. These states are California,[35] Colorado,[36] Con-

---

[32] ME. REV. STAT. (1930) c. 134, §§7-10.

[33] N. H. PUB. LAWS (1926), c. 171, §§3, 4, 6.

[34] PA. STAT. ANN. (Purdon, 1930) tit. 18, §§1211, 1214-18.

[35] CAL. CIV. CODE (Deering, 1931) §§51-52. See also *id.* at §§53-54, a statute which may be construed to cover racial as well as other kinds of discrimination. This act enumerates opera houses, theatres, melodeons, museums, circuses, caravans, racecourses, fairs, and other places of amusement.

[36] COLO. STAT. ANN. (Mills, 1930) §§754 (a)-(e). See also *id.* at §§5858 (a)-(e).

necticut,[37] Illinois,[38] Indiana,[39] Iowa,[40] Kansas,[41] Massachusetts,[42] Michigan,[43] Minnesota,[44] Nebraska,[45] New Jersey,[46] New York,[47] Ohio,[48] Pennsylvania,[49] Rhode Island,[50] Washington,[51] and Wisconsin.[52] The statutes are more or less specific concerning places which are meant to be regulated. Some of them contain long lists of places of public resort, while others mention only a few or none at all. The statutes differ in the type or types of remedy to be employed in seeking redress. Thus seven states provide for a criminal prosecution only,[53] one makes provision for a civil action alone,[54] seven allow both a criminal action and either a suit for a penalty or a civil action for damages,[55] while the remaining three permit both types of redress but state that success in an action of either kind shall bar all other proceedings.[56]

It has been held, however, that a civil action may be maintained in a jurisdiction where the only remedy specifically pro-

---

[37] CONN. GEN. STAT. (Supp. 1933) §1160b.

[38] ILL. REV. STAT. (Cahill, 1933) c. 38, §§104-107, as amended by Ill. Laws 1935, p. 708. See also *id.* at §§550-555.

[39] IND. STAT. ANN. (Burns, 1933) §§10-901, 10-902.

[40] IOWA CODE (1931) §§13,251-52.

[41] KAN. REV. STAT. (1923) §21-2424.

[42] MASS. ANN. LAWS (1933) c. 272, §98, as amended in 1934. See also Mass. Acts & Resolves 1933, c. 117.

[43] MICH. COMP. LAWS (Supp. 1933) §17, 115-146 to 147.

[44] MINN. STAT. (Mason, 1927) §7321.

[45] NEB. COMP. STAT. (1929) §§23-101 to 102.

[46] N. J. COMP. STAT. (Supp. 1924) Civil Rights, Pt. 39, §§1-2, as amended by N. J. Laws 1935, c. 247.

[47] N. Y. CONSOL. LAWS (Cahill, 1930) c. 7, §§40-41; *id.* at c. 41, §514.

[48] OHIO CODE (Throckmorton, 1929) §§12,940-41; BALDWIN'S CODE SERV., Mar., 1934, §6064-25; BALDWIN'S CODE SERV., Jan., 1938, §12,940.

[49] Pa. Laws 1935, No. 132.

[50] R. I. Pub. Laws 1925-26, c. 658.

[51] WASH. REV. STAT. ANN. (Remington, 1932) §2686.

[52] WIS. STAT. (1931) §340.75.

[53] Connecticut, Iowa, Michigan, Nebraska, Pennsylvania, Rhode Island, and Washington.

[54] California. See also the above-discussed Louisiana act, *supra* note 21, which allows recovery for exemplary as well as compensatory damages.

[55] Illinois, Kansas, Massachusetts (advertising statute only criminal), Minnesota, New Jersey (action of debt in the name of the state, the aggrieved party being entitled to attorney's fees up to fifty dollars and costs), New York, and Ohio.

[56] Colorado, Indiana, and Wisconsin.

vided for is a criminal action.[57] In a Massachusetts case[58] it is said that preponderance of evidence is enough to make the defendant responsible in a civil suit under the statute of that state, and this would probably be the rule elsewhere as well. In this jurisdiction the statute provided for both a suit for a penalty and a criminal prosecution. The complainant was held to be bound by a release, the terms of which had been agreed upon by the defendant and himself. He had agreed that if the defendant would plead guilty to an indictment under the statute and pay the fine assessed against him, he would be content to accept the result in full satisfaction of any claim which he might have because of the defendant's discrimination against him. It has been decided in an Illinois case[59] that the proceeding to recover the penalty provided for by the statute of that state, although civil in form, is really an action to recover a penalty for a criminal offense. The punishment provided by these statutes varies a great deal. It may be said, however, that the later enactments usually make provision for harsher punishment.

In one case from Illinois a court of equity refused to take jurisdiction over a case in which it was alleged that a Negro was not permitted to use a public bathing pool and pavilion. The court declared that the penalty provided for by the Civil Rights Act was an adequate remedy at law and that therefore a court of equity had no jurisdiction.[60] This case was decided in accordance with the familiar principle of equity jurisprudence that a court of equity will give no relief where there is an adequate remedy at law. The Illinois act was amended in 1935 to permit the abatement of a nuisance in such a case.

There can be no doubt that these statutes are constitutional. They have been held valid in many instances as a warranted exercise of the state's police power over places of public ac-

---

[57] Ferguson v. Gies, 82 Mich. 358, 46 N. W. 718 (1890); Bolden v. Grand Rapids Operating Co., 239 Mich. 318, 214 N. W. 241 (1927); Anderson v. Pantages Theatre Co., 114 Wash. 24, 194 Pac. 813 (1921); Randall v. Cowlitz Amusements, Inc., 194 Wash. 82, 76 P. (2d) 1017 (1938).

[58] Bryant v. Rich's Grill, 216 Mass. 344, 103 N. E. 925 (1914). *See also* Deveaux v. Clemens, 17 Ohio C. C. 33, 9 Ohio C. D. 647 (1898).

[59] Thorne v. Alcazar Amusement Co., 210 Ill. App. 173 (1918).

[60] White v. Pasfield, 212 Ill. App. 73 (1918).

commodation.[61] However, the question arises as to just what businesses can be so regulated. Are there any enterprises holding themselves out to the public which cannot be brought within the scope of these statutes by specific mention in the acts themselves? This question has been recently brought to the fore by an amendment to the Ohio statute which made the act of that state apply to retail stores for the sale of merchandise,[62] a change that came about as the direct result of a decision that such an establishment which sold women's wearing apparel was not within the act as it had read prior to the amendment.[63] One commentator seems to be of the opinion that this extension of the statute cannot be justified because a retail store is not so clothed with a public interest that it can be regulated in such a manner.[64] However, it is doubtful if the courts would hold that such regulation of retail stores was not a legitimate use of the police power, especially in view of the fact that the regulation of other establishments of a semiprivate nature, such as barbershops, skating rinks, and theatres, has been approved.

Can a place of public resort or amusement which is mentioned in or included within the meaning of these statutes provide equal but separate accommodations for Negroes? Segregation of this type has been declared illegal in controversies involving the application of these acts to theatres[65] and restaurants,[66] and hence it is supposed that it would also be taboo in all establishments which could be brought within the scope of the particular statute involved. Since this is true, there would

[61] Darius v. Apostolos, 68 Colo. 323, 330, 190 Pac. 510, 511 (1920); Pickett v. Kuchan, 323 Ill. 138, 153 N. E. 667 (1926); Bolden v. Grand Rapids Operating Co., 239 Mich. 318, 214 N. W. 241 (1927); Donnell v. State, 48 Miss. 661 (1873); People v. King, 110 N. Y. 418, 18 N. E. 245 (1888); Commonwealth v. George, 61 Pa. Super. Ct. 412 (1915). *See also* Western Turf Ass'n v. Greenberg, 204 U. S. 359, 27 Sup. Ct. 384 (1907).

[62] See BALDWIN'S OHIO CODE SERV., Jan., 1938, §12,940.

[63] Noble v. Sissle, 53 Ohio App. 405, 5 N. E. (2d) 410 (1936).

[64] See Note (1938) 12 U. OF CIN. L. REV. 60.

[65] Jones v. Kehrlein, 49 Cal. App. 646, 194 Pac. 55 (1920); Baylies v. Curry, 30 Ill. App. 105 (1889); Joyner v. Moore-Wiggins Co., 152 App. Div. 266, 136 N. Y. Supp. 578 (4th Dep't 1912). *But see* Commonwealth v. George, 61 Pa. Super. Ct. 412 (1915), where the court seems to have taken an opposite view. However, this would probably not be the case under the modern act. See Note (1935) 84 U. OF PA. L. REV. 75.

[66] Ferguson v. Gies, 83 Mich. 358, 46 N. W. 718 (1890).

seem to be even stronger reasons which would prevent the proprietor of such a place of public accommodation from offering to its Negro customers facilities which are inferior to those which are furnished for its white patrons. In fact this sort of unequal treatment has been held to be discriminatory in cases[67] arising under these acts. It has been decided that proof showing that the agents of a theatre company had refused to sell a Negro plaintiff a ticket to the desired section of the house will entitle the latter to recover.[68] This is, of course, subject to the defense that all seats in the desired section of the house are occupied or sold at the time the plaintiff made his request for accommodations.[69] It is also violative of the statute to require a Negro to move to a section to which members of his race are assigned.[70] In one rather interesting case from New York a Jew and a Negro entered a restaurant together and asked to be served. They were refused accommodations because of a house rule that white and colored persons should not sit together. The court refused to allow a recovery, thereby putting its stamp of approval on the house rule.[71] The regulation was said to be a proper exercise of the proprietor's authority over his own establishment. This decision is somewhat out of line with the other authorities which have been considered in respect to this problem, as the spirit of the law would certainly include such a situation. An Ohio case presents another effort to keep the races apart in public places. In this instance the management of a dance hall attempted a different type of segregation. A house rule was put into effect which set aside certain hours when the hall was to be used by white patrons only and other hours when it could be used exclusively by colored persons. The State Appellate Court refused to approve this device and held

[67] Crosswaith v. Bergin, 95 Colo. 241, 35 P. (2d) 848 (1934); Fruchey v. Eagleson, 15 Ind. App. 88, 43 N. E. 146 (1896); Puritan Lunch Co. v. Forman, 29 Ohio C. A. 289, 34 Ohio C. D. 526 (1918).

[68] Pickett v. Kuchan, 323 Ill. 138, 153 N. E. 667 (1926); Bolden v. Grand Rapids Operating Co., 239 Mich. 318, 214 N. W. 241 (1927).

[69] Hull v. Eighty-sixth St. Amusement Co., 144 N. Y. Supp. 318 (1st Dep't 1913).

[70] Joyner v. Moore-Wiggins Co., 152 App. Div. 266, 136 N. Y. Supp. 578 (4th Dep't 1912); Guy v. Tri-State Amusement Co., 7 Ohio App. 509 (1917); Randall v. Cowlitz Amusements, Inc., 194 Wash. 82, 76 P. (2d) 1017 (1938).

[71] Cohn v. Goldgraben, 103 Misc. 500, 170 N. Y. Supp. 407 (1st Dep't 1918).

that the Civil Rights Act had been violated.[72]

Does a Negro who invokes the protection of these statutes have to be acting in good faith in requesting accommodations? Is it necessary for him to show that he entered the establishment with a bona fide desire for service? The answers to these questions seem to be in the negative, for an Ohio court has allowed a recovery even though the complainant entered a restaurant with the express purpose of causing a violation of the statute.[73] Furthermore, where the reason given by a proprietor for his refusal to serve a Negro can be shown to be frivolous or trumped up for the particular occasion, the real reason being racial antipathy, the former will not be permitted to use this excuse as a shield.[74] The *bona fides* of a claim of this kind is ordinarily a question for the jury. In one New York case it was indubitably shown by an examination of the testimony that a restaurant's tardiness in service was caused by the fact that it took some time to fill the plaintiff's order. In this instance a judgment in the plaintiff's favor was reversed as being contrary to the weight of the evidence.[75]

It has been deemed proper for proprietors of places of public resort to make and enforce house rules applicable to all persons alike irrespective of race, such as regulations against the admittance of unclean, untidy, intoxicated, or diseased persons.[76] Furthermore, discriminations which are not based on racial, or in some instances religious, grounds are not usually within the purview of these anti-race-discrimination statutes.[77] In one case from California, however, the Court of Appeals applied the statute of that state in an instance where a person of foreign extraction was discriminated against at a hotel.[78] On the other hand, in a New York case where an African-born

---

[72] Youngstown P. & F. S. Ry. v. Tokus, 4 Ohio App. 276 (1915).

[73] Young v. Pratt, 11 Ohio App. 346 (1919).

[74] Wilson v. Rozetti, 88 Misc. 37, 150 N. Y. Supp. 145 (1st Dep't 1914).

[75] Beckett v. Pfaeffle, 157 N. Y. Supp. 247 (1st Dep't 1916).

[76] Larson v. R. B. Wrigley Co., 183 Minn. 28, 235 N. W. 393 (1931); Noble v. Higgins, 95 Misc. 328, 158 N. Y. Supp. 867 (Sup. Ct. 1916).

[77] Matthews v. Hotz, 173 N. Y. Supp. 234 (1st Dep't 1918); Grannan v. Westchester Racing Ass'n, 153 N. Y. 449, 465, 47 N. E. 896 (1897); Finnesey v. Seattle Baseball Club, 122 Wash. 276, 210 Pac. 679 (1922).

[78] Piluso v. Spencer, 36 Cal. App. 416, 172 Pac. 412 (1918). *See also* Prowd v. Gore, 57 Cal. App. 458, 207 Pac. 490 (1922).

Negro was refused service at a saloon, it was held that allegation and proof of citizenship was essential to a recovery under the act of that state.[79] Lack of proof of this essential fact also prevented a proprietor of a Nebraska barbershop from being held responsible.[80] In California, however, citizenship seems to be immaterial.[81]

In one case from Iowa there was an indictment against the proprietor of a barbershop for refusing to shave a customer. One would suppose that he was a Negro, though the opinion is silent as to his racial identity. This indictment was held to be insufficient for the reason that it failed to allege that there was no good reason for the refusal and because it did not aver that immediately after the refusal the defendant proceeded to shave other customers.[82] In this instance the court seems to require unneeded allegations, as the facts which it says are essential to proper pleading seem to be matters of proof rather than matters of pleading.

There seems to be a doctrine in Michigan[83] and New York[84] which exempts the proprietor of restaurants or other places within the statute from responsibility for the action of his servants in refusing to accommodate Negroes or in discriminating against them, provided he has given express orders to make no difference in the service because of race or color. However, this is contrary to the usual rules of agency law, as the servant would certainly seem to be clothed with apparent authority in this type of case. In fact the doctrine seems to have been definitely rejected in Colorado[85] and Wisconsin.[86] The Michigan and New York decisions would appear to permit a proprietor

[79] Fuller v. McDermott, 87 N. Y. Supp. 536 (1904).

[80] Messenger v. State, 25 Neb. 674, 41 N. W. 638 (1889).

[81] Prowd v. Gore, 57 Cal. App. 458, 207 Pac. 490 (1922).

[82] State v. Hall, 72 Iowa 525, 34 N. W. 315 (1887).

[83] Goldsberry v. Kamochos, 255 Mich. 647, 239 N. W. 513 (1931).

[84] Hubert v. Jose, 148 App. Div. 718, 132 N. Y. Supp. 811 (2d Dep't 1912); Hart v. Hartford Lunch Co., 81 Misc. 237, 142 N. Y. Supp. 515 (Sup. Ct. 1913). Evidence of this fact was deemed admissible but not conclusive in Thomas v. Williams, 48 Misc. 615, 95 N. Y. Supp. 592 (1905). A statement made by the defendant's waitress who had disappeared to the effect that his orders were that Negroes should not be served was ruled to be hearsay and therefore inadmissible in Robinson v. Zappas, 227 App. Div. 208, 237 N. Y. Supp. 235 (4th Dep't 1929).

[85] Crosswaith v. Thomason, 95 Colo. 240, 35 P. (2d) 849 (1934).

[86] Bryan v. Adler, 97 Wis. 124, 72 N. W. 268 (1897).

to avoid liability by a blanket order to his waiters or other employes to the effect that they are not to refuse to serve Negroes. The servants are usually financially irresponsible and the complainant is therefore left without an effective remedy. This tends to defeat the purpose and efficacy of the statute.

Of course an employer should not be held responsible for the acts of his servants which are not within the scope of the employment. In one Ohio case relief against the lessee of a theatre was denied because the colored plaintiff had failed to allege that the agent was acting within the scope of the duties which had been assigned to him.[87]

All of these statutes with the exception of the one in Washington, the act of that state being general in form,[88] refer to specific places of a public character. They all have a general clause which specifies the types of places to which they are applicable. These general clauses mention one or more of the following types of establishments: places of public accommodation;[89] places of public amusement;[90] places of public resort;[91] public places where refreshments are served on the premises;[92] public places conducted for hire, gain, or reward;[93] places of entertainment;[94] and public places of assemblage.[95] Generally speaking, the courts have not been very liberal in their construction of these provisions. When an establishment is neither specifically mentioned in the statute[96] nor within the common-

[87] Anderson v. Rawlings, 18 Ohio C. C. 381, 10 Ohio C. D. 112 (1899).

[88] Statute changed to general form from common form in 1909. Laws of Washington 1909, c. 249, §434.

[89] California, Colorado, Connecticut, Illinois, Indiana, Massachusetts (advertising statute), Michigan, Minnesota, New Jersey, New York, Ohio, Pennsylvania, Rhode Island, Washington, Wisconsin.

[90] California, Colorado, Connecticut, Illinois, Indiana, Iowa, Kansas, Massachusetts, Michigan, Minnesota, Nebraska, New Jersey, New York, Ohio, Pennsylvania, Rhode Island, Washington, Wisconsin.

[91] Connecticut, Illinois (advertising statute only), Massachusetts (advertising statute only), New Jersey, New York, Pennsylvania, Washington.

[92] Connecticut, Iowa, Minnesota, New Jersey, New York, Pennsylvania. Service "on the premises" is not mentioned in the Iowa and Minnesota acts, but this may be inferred.

[93] Massachusetts.

[94] Kansas and Minnesota. See also Virginia act providing for segregation in theatres. VA. CODE ANN. (Michie, 1930), §§1796 (a)-(b).

[95] Washington. See also Virginia act cited in *ibid.*, which also mentions public halls.

[96] *See* Gibbs v. Arras Bros., 222 N. Y. 332, 118 N. E. 857 (1918); Campbell v. Eichert, 155 Misc. 164, 278 N. Y. Supp. 946 (Sup. Ct. 1935).

law notion of a place of public accommodation,[97] it is not likely that the Civil Rights Act will be held to cover such a place. The necessity of a license cannot be made a test,[98] although the Iowa Court has employed language in one opinion[99] which seems to make the license requirement a criterion. The Rhode Island statute specifically applies to licensed places only, while the Massachusetts act includes unlicensed establishments as well as those which are licensed.[100]

In New York a case arose which involved the refusal of a bootblack to serve a Negro. The question was whether this kind of establishment would be a place of public accommodation within the statute. The New York Court of Appeals, when faced with the difficulties which arose from the use of such general provisions as those described above, applied the doctrine of *ejusdem generis.*[101] This is a rule of statutory construction which stipulates that where general words follow an enumeration of terms having a specific or particular meaning, such general words are not to be given a broad construction, but are to be construed as applying only to those persons, places, or things of the same general kind or class as those specifically mentioned in the statute. Applying this doctrine, the court decided that a bootblacking stand was not within the statute. In a case from Colorado which also involved a bootblacking stand the court refused to apply this doctrine.[102] The tribunal was evidently of the opinion that the doctrine would have no application because the types of business establishments specifi-

---

[97] *See* Faulkner v. Sollazi, 79 Conn. 541, 65 Atl. 947 (1907); Burks v. Bosso, 180 N. Y. 341, 73 N. E. 58 (1905), *rev'g* 81 App. Div. 530, 81 N. Y. Supp. 384 (4th Dep't 1903).

[98] Faulkner v. Sollazi, 79 Conn. 541, 65 Atl. 947 (1907); Gibbs v. Arras Bros., 222 N. Y. 332, 118 N. E. 857 (1918).

[99] Bowlin v. Lyon, 67 Iowa 536, 25 N. W. 766 (1885).

[100] The Massachusetts act was amended to include places licensed and unlicensed, thus obliterating the effect of the decision in Commonwealth v. Sylvester, 95 Mass. 247 (1866), in which it had been held that a Negro who had been refused the privileges accorded to other persons in a billiard parlor must allege that the place was licensed in order that an action might be maintained, and the plaintiff was denied relief because he failed to do so.

[101] Burks v. Bosso, 180 N. Y. 341, 73 N. E. 58 (1905). *But see* Babb v. Elsinger, 147 N. Y. Supp. 98 (1st Dep't 1914), in which the court applied the rule and pointed out that no calling had been more subject to legislative control than that of the saloonkeeper, thus distinguishing this case from Burks v. Bosso.

[102] Darius v. Apostolos, 68 Colo. 323, 190 Pac. 510 (1919).

cally mentioned in the Colorado statute bear no common analogy to one another, except that they are all for pecuniary profit. This is the reason assigned for the refusal to follow the New York decision. The doctrine was applied in a Minnesota case involving racial discrimination in a saloon.[103] An Ohio court once refused to apply the doctrine because it was thought that its adoption would lead to a result which the legislature never intended,[104] but just recently it was resorted to in the above-mentioned case in which the Ohio statute was held not to be applicable to a retail store where women's wearing apparel is sold.[105]

It may be that the fact that the later statutes mention so many diversified establishments is one of the chief reasons why the courts have developed these rules of interpretation, the idea being that the legislatures would never have omitted the unmentioned public places without a specific intent to do so. Of course the above Colorado decision militates against this proposition, since the statute of that state is at least fairly detailed. However, there are a good many cases which lend support to this view. Thus a beauty parlor has been held not to be within the very detailed modern New York statute,[106] while both a skating rink[107] and a cabaret which was known as a concert hall[108] were held to be within the less specific older Empire State act.[109] The Wisconsin statute, which is not very detailed, has been held to apply to a skating rink.[110] Ohio, with a statute of this same type, has applied it to both a public dancing pavilion established by a street railway company[111] and a bowling alley at a pleasure resort.[112] There are other instances where courts have construed such general language as not including estab-

---

[103] Rhone v. Loomis, 74 Minn. 200, 77 N. W. 31 (1898).

[104] Youngstown P. & F. S. Ry. v. Tokus, 4 Ohio App. 276 (1915).

[105] Noble v. Sissle, 53 Ohio App. 405, 5 N. E. (2d) 410 (1936). See note 63 *supra*. *See also* Fowler v. Benner, 13 Ohio N. P. (N.S.) 313 (1912).

[106] Campbell v. Eichert, 155 Misc. 164, 278 N. Y. Supp. 946 (Sup. Ct. 1935).

[107] People v. King, 42 Hun 186 (N. Y. 1886), *aff'd* 110 N. Y. 418, 18 N. E. 245 (1888).

[108] Cremore v. Huber, 18 App. Div. 231, 45 N. Y. Supp. 947 (2d Dep't 1897).

[109] See N. Y. CONSOL. LAWS (Cahill, 1930) c. 41, §514.

[110] Jones v. Broadway Rink Co., 136 Wis. 595, 118 N. W. 170 (1908).

[111] Youngstown P. & F. S. Ry. v. Tokus, 4 Ohio App. 276 (1915).

[112] Johnson v. Humphrey Pop-Corn Co., 24 Ohio C. C. 135 (1902), 4 Ohio C. C. (N.S.) 49, 14 Ohio C. D. 135 (1902), *aff'd* 70 Ohio St. 478, 72 N. E. 1160 (1904).

lishments which could be said to be just as much of a public character as some of those mentioned above, as witness the refusal to apply the statutes in cases involving a Connecticut barbershop[113] and an Ohio saloon.[114] While there is no set rule of interpretation in respect to these general clauses, it can be stated, and without the danger of being too brash, that there is a tendency toward a stricter interpretation of these laws. It is possible that this tendency may be the result of an increase of racial antagonism in many of the states of the North and Middle West which are in the group having Civil Rights Acts. As the Negroes have migrated in large numbers to these states, there has undoubtedly been an increase in this antagonism among the whites. This leads to a desire on the part of the better class of white persons to avoid social contact as far as possible. Hence the Negroes are not wanted in such places as the better hotels, restaurants, and theatres.

From what has been said in one case from New York, it would probably not be an exaggeration to say that these general clauses have a rather limited effect in that state. In this instance the Court of Appeals was considering whether the Civil Rights Act would apply to saloons. The court declared that if the statute did apply to establishments other than those specifically mentioned, they were those "devoted to the general advantage, comfort or benefit, and essential or directly auxiliary to the prosperity, health, development or happiness of the citizen." [115] This is rather broad language, but it could hardly be interpreted to include saloons. Hence it was held that the statute did not apply.

In some of the more recent statutes these general provisions are disconnected from the enumeration of those establishments which are specifically mentioned. The general provisions are placed in the first part of the statute along with the description of the offense, followed by a separate sentence which states that a place of public accommodation, amusement, or resort within the meaning of the act "shall be deemed to include" various enumerated establishments. There are statutes of this type in

[113] Faulkner v. Sollazi, 79 Conn. 541, 65 Atl. 947 (1907).
[114] Kellar v. Koerber, 61 Ohio St. 388, 55 N. E. 1002 (1899).
[115] Gibbs v. Arras Bros., 222 N. Y. 332, 118 N. E. 857 (1918).

several jurisdictions.[116] The general type of Civil Rights Act may be termed conjunctive. This kind of a statute specifically enumerates certain establishments and then adds a conjunctive clause reading "or any other place of public accommodation or amusement" or employing similar language. It is possible that the general provisions of statutes of the disconnected type might be given a stricter interpretation than those in the statutes which are conjunctive in form. In respect to statutes of the former type it might be a little easier for the courts to reach the conclusion that the legislature meant to make the act apply to the enumerated public places and no others. Generally we may say that the tendency in recent years has been toward a stricter interpretation of statutes of both types.

Thirteen of these state statutes have provisions punishing anyone who incites or aids in the commission of an act of discrimination.[117] In one Ohio case it was said that the criminal or civil liability of an aiding or inciting principal is not barred by the conviction of the agent or employe, when he has instructed the latter to commit the act of discrimination complained of.[118]

Four states have provisions in their Civil Rights Acts prohibiting the issuance, publication, circulation, display, posting, or mailing of any communication, notice, or advertisement, written or printed, to the effect that any of the accommodations, privileges, facilities, or advantages of the public places named therein will be withheld from any person because of his race or color.[119] Three of these statutes make the production of any such advertisement presumptive evidence of guilt, but also provide that the enactment shall not be construed as prohibiting the mailing of a private communication sent in response to a specific written inquiry.[120] The codes of three other states contain similar separate statutes punishing the advertising of

[116] Connecticut, New Jersey, New York, and Pennsylvania. See also separate advertising acts of Colorado, Illinois, and Massachusetts, *infra* note 121.

[117] California, Colorado, Illinois, Indiana, Iowa, Massachusetts, Minnesota, Nebraska, New Jersey, New York, Ohio, Pennsylvania, and Wisconsin.

[118] Davis v. Euclid Ave. Garden Theatre Co., 17 Ohio C. C. (N.S.) 495, 32 Ohio C. D. 250 (1911).

[119] Michigan, New Jersey, New York, and Pennsylvania.

[120] New Jersey, New York, and Pennsylvania.

racial discrimination by places of public resort.[121] These statutes also contain an enumeration of the establishments to which they apply. In all three jurisdictions this list includes certain public places which are not mentioned in the more usual type of civil rights legislation, while in two of these states[122] the advertising statutes fail to mention establishments which the common form of statute specifically enumerates. In respect to the three states which have statutes of both types, it might be thought that the two acts would be construed together, so as to permit the punishment of those who practice racial discrimination in establishments mentioned in the separate advertising statutes but not in those of the ordinary type. However, this proposition has been negatived in a Colorado case.[123]

From what has been said above it is deemed proper to discuss in detail the establishments to which these Civil Rights Acts are applicable. The places of public resort will be classified. Those places which are specifically enumerated will be mentioned, as will various establishments which have been construed to be within or without the terms of the general provisions which have been discussed above. These establishments can be divided into three general classes as follows: places where lodging, food, or other refreshments are provided; places where some kind of amusement or other similar form of entertainment, athletic, aesthetic, or appealing to the spirit, is offered; and places where services not included in either of the other two classes are rendered.

The statutes differ a great deal with respect to the variety of establishments specifically mentioned. The general provisions have received divers interpretations as to the places of public resort covered thereby. One can never be sure that any particular establishment not mentioned in the act is within the general provisions of the statute in a given jurisdiction unless the question has been squarely presented on a previous occasion. Therefore, it seems best to confine this discussion to an analysis of the statutes themselves and the reported cases interpreting them. The Washington act, being entirely general in form,

[121] Colorado, Illinois, and Massachusetts. COLO. STAT. ANN. (Mills, 1930) §§5858a-5858e; ILL. REV. STAT. (Cahill, 1933) c. 38, §§550-555; Mass. Acts & Resolves 1933, c. 117.

[122] Illinois and Massachusetts.

[123] Darius v. Apostolos, 68 Colo. 323, 190 Pac. 510 (1919).

would no doubt seem to include many establishments to which it has not yet been construed to apply, and the same would be true to a varying extent with respect to a great many if not all of the general provisions in the other states. But to delve into this maze of probable interpretation would lead one too far afield. Conjectures and surmises will not be indulged in except where they are deemed advisable or necessary to clearness. Southern statutes and decisions concerning segregation in such places of public resort will be alluded to wherever necessary. Of the eighteen states which have civil rights legislation only seventeen will be considered in this detailed review of the statutory provisions, Washington being left out for the above-mentioned reason. The application of these acts to educational institutions and various types of public carriers is considered elsewhere.[124]

PLACES WHERE LODGING AND/OR REFRESHMENTS ARE FURNISHED

Inns, Hotels, etc.—All save one[125] of these states make specific reference to inns, eight[126] referring to hotels, and five[127] mentioning taverns and roadhouses. In addition to these there is a Utah statute penalizing any innkeeper who refuses without just cause to accommodate any guest.[128] This act makes no mention of discrimination on account of race or color, but might well be considered as covering this as well as other forms of unfairness. The separate Colorado and Illinois advertising acts, mentioned above, refer to inns, hotels, and taverns, while the similar Massachusetts statute mentions inns alone. This Massachusetts act as well as other statutes of the usual type which refer only to inns would probably be construed to cover all places of like nature whatever they may be called, as the term "inn" is generally considered as being synonymous[129] with "hotel" and

---

[124] See chapter on Education, notes 260-267; chapter on Carriers, note 99.

[125] Minnesota.

[126] California, Connecticut, Illinois, Kansas, Minnesota, New Jersey, New York, and Pennsylvania.

[127] Connecticut, Illinois, New Jersey, New York, and Pennsylvania.

[128] UTAH REV. STAT. ANN. (1933) §103-29-2.

[129] Foster v. State, 84 Ala. 451, 4 So. 833 (1888); *In re* Brewster, 39 Misc. 689, 80 N. Y. Supp. 666 (Essex Co. Ct. 1903).

"tavern." In one case arising under the Indiana Civil Rights Act a hotel is described as "a house for entertaining travelers, an inn or public house of the better class." [130]

There are places called taverns and roadhouses which are not lodginghouses but are more like night clubs or cabarets. Whether such an establishment would be held to be included within the meaning of the word "taverns" or "roadhouses" is an open question. These terms are used along with the words "hotels" and "inns" in such a way as to suggest that they are referring to lodginghouses rather than to such places of entertainment or amusement. In four[131] of the five states where the statutes of the usual type mention both taverns and roadhouses, places of the night club variety which are called by these names might be held to be within other provisions of these statutes enumerating establishments where food and/or beverages are sold at retail on the premises.

The statutes of the usual type in three states[132] and the three separate advertising acts just mentioned attempt a further description of the kind of lodging house which is intended to be within the meaning of such terms as "inn" or "hotel." For example, the language employed in the Pennsylvania act would make it apply to "inns, taverns, roadhouses, hotels, whether conducted for the entertainment of transient guests or for the accommodation of those seeking health, recreation, or rest," and similar language is used in the other statutes in this group. This language was evidently placed in the statutes in order to clarify them with respect to the type of hotel the legislatures meant to be included. The provision may have been placed in the New York statute as a result of a decision[133] in that state that a so-called family hotel which was in the nature of an apartment house was not within the meaning of the statute in effect at that time—an act which was not so detailed as the modern one. This case involved the refusal of the proprietor of such an establishment to accommodate a person of Jewish extraction. While the change in the wording of the statute prob-

[130] Fruchey v. Eagleson, 15 Ind. App. 88, 43 N. E. 146 (1896).

[131] Connecticut, New Jersey, New York, and Pennsylvania.

[132] New Jersey, New York, and Pennsylvania.

[133] Alsberg v. Lucerne Hotel Co., 46 Misc. 617, 92 N. Y. Supp. 851 (Sup. Ct. 1905).

ably would not affect the law as announced in this case, it was evidently thought that a more concise definition of the term "hotel" was called for.

A California court has decided that the term "hotel" as employed in that state's Civil Rights Act includes public resort hotels as well as those for temporary lodging and refreshment.[134] Thus the court reached the same result by judicial interpretation as that obtained by the elaborate statutory provisions noted above. The tribunal was evidently influenced in its decision by the fact that the legislature had amended the statute in such a manner as to embrace hotels as well as inns, thus making a rather unusual distinction.

An interesting case came before the Indiana Court of Appeals in 1896. In this instance a Negro who had come to a city with the University of Indiana football team was refused equal accommodations in the local hotel. The proprietor had contracted with the manager of the opposing team to furnish the necessary facilities. The court held that the proprietor was responsible under the Civil Rights Act.[135] Situations of this kind are continually arising in the South when northern athletic teams go into that section to compete with southern teams. Negro members of the northern team are not allowed to stay in the white hotels and there are no Civil Rights Acts under which the Negro can assert such a right.

In Nebraska the Civil Rights Act has been held to be applicable in an instance where a Negro messenger boy for the Republican State Central Committee was denied the privilege of using the hotel elevator.[136] Politics may well have had a great deal to do with the bringing of this action.

In the South hotel accommodations are provided for the two races in separate establishments. The Negroes have their own hotels, inns, and lodginghouses. Of course there are Negro servants in the white hotels, and this gives rise to certain unavoidable contacts between members of the two races. The hotels have sought to prevent these contacts by providing separate accommodations wherever necessary. In carrying out

[134] Piluso v. Spencer, 36 Cal. App. 416, 172 Pac. 412 (1918).

[135] Fruchey v. Eagleson, 15 Ind. App. 88, 43 N. E. 146 (1896).

[136] Hoover v. Haynes, 65 Neb. 557, 91 N. W. 392 (1902) (case reversed on question of damages), rehearing denied in 93 N. W. 732 (1903).

this policy they have provided separate toilet facilities for Negro employes. In Alabama a statute forbids the use by members of either race of toilet facilities in hotels and restaurants which were furnished for the accommodation of persons of the other.[137] The statute requires separate toilets for Negro servants in establishments for whites.

Before leaving the subject of hotels, it is thought that a very interesting Massachusetts statute should be discussed. This act made it unlawful for women under twenty-one years of age to enter any hotel or restaurant conducted by Chinese and penalized the proprietors of these establishments for allowing such young girls to come there. The ostensible purpose of the enactment was to stamp out prostitution which had become a lucrative business with several of the Chinese proprietors. The Chinese claimed that the statute was invalid because it violated the equal protection clause of the Fourteenth Amendment to the Federal Constitution. It was argued that the statute made a reasonable classification and therefore was valid under the familiar doctrine of constitutional law allowing such classifications. The court refused to be swayed by this argument and held that the act violated the Fourteenth Amendment.[138] It was said to be an unwarranted exercise of the police power. The court declared that the statute made an unreasonable classification because it permitted the entry of girls into any hotel managed by other persons no matter what the moral status of the place might be, but made unlawful the entry of girls into any such place managed by Chinese no matter how high the moral tone of the establishment might be. The tribunal came to the conclusion that there was no rational basis for the proposition that all hotels run by Chinese are immoral or corrupt merely because of their management by members of that race.

Restaurants, Cafes, etc.—All the statutes of the usual type with the exception of two, those of Kansas and Massachusetts, mention restaurants, and such establishments are also included by the separate advertising act in the Bay State as well as those in Colorado and Illinois. The Kansas Court has decided that a

[137] ALA. CODE ANN. (Michie, 1928) §4465.

[138] *In re* Opinion of Justices, 207 Mass. 601, 94 N. E. 558 (1911).

restaurant or lunch room is not within the act of that state.[139] The tribunal argued that the general words "place of entertainment" were used in strict association with the words "or amusement" and hence denoted the same kind of establishment. On the other hand, Massachusetts has held that a combination restaurant and barroom is within the meaning of its statute.[140] The Illinois act specifically mentions cafes and that of Iowa, lunch counters and chophouses. The New York and Pennsylvania statutes include buffets. The same states which mention restaurants also employ the term "eating houses" with the exception of Minnesota and Nebraska. In addition to these specific provisions there is the above-mentioned general language in six states,[141] which seeks to render the statutes applicable to all public places where refreshments are sold on the premises.

Negroes have been refused accommodation or equal treatment at restaurants in numerous instances. In some of these cases relief was granted,[142] while in others it was denied[143] for various reasons, such as lack of proof, inadmissibility of the plaintiff's evidence, and the application of the above-mentioned Michigan and New York agency doctrine. In one case from Illinois a trial judge instructed the jury that a restaurant proprietor was responsible under the Civil Rights Act if he failed to serve the Negro plaintiff. The statute created a liability only if he denied a Negro service on account of race or color or incited such a denial. The court declared that the instruction was erroneous, since the word "fail" is much broader than the word "deny." [144]

[139] State v. Brown, 112 Kan. 814, 212 Pac. 663 (1923).

[140] Bryant v. Rich's Grill, 216 Mass. 344, 103 N. E. 925 (1914).

[141] Connecticut, Iowa, Minnesota, New Jersey, New York, and Pennsylvania. "On the premises" inferred in Iowa and Minnesota.

[142] Crosswaith v. Bergin, 95 Colo. 241, 35 P. (2d) 848 (1934); Ferguson v. Gies, 82 Mich., 358, 46 N. W. 718 (1890); Wilson v. Razetti, 88 Misc. 37, 150 N. Y. Supp. 145 (Sup. Ct. 1914); Puritan Lunch Co. v. Forman, 29 Ohio C. A. 289, 35 Ohio C. D. 526 (1918); Young v. Pratt, 11 Ohio App. 346 (1919); Bryan v. Adler, 97 Wis. 124, 72 N. W. 368 (1897).

[143] Goldsberry v. Kamochos, 255 Mich. 647, 239 N. W. 513 (1931); Hubert v. Jose, 148 App. Div. 718, 132 N. Y. Supp. 811 (2d Dep't 1912); Hart v. Hartford Lunch Co., 81 Misc. 237, 142 N. Y. Supp. 515 (Sup. Ct. 1913); Beckett v. Pfaeffle, 157 N. Y. Supp. 247 (1st Dep't 1916); Robinson v. Zappas, 227 App. Div. 208, 237 N. Y. Supp. 235 (4th Dep't 1929).

[144] Grace v. Moseley, 112 Ill. App. 100 (1904).

An interesting case came up in a New York federal court under provisions of the now defunct Federal Civil Rights Act of 1875. This case was decided the year before the statute was declared unconstitutional by the Supreme Court. The plaintiff alleged that he had been denied the privileges of an inn; to wit, a restaurant. The statute mentioned inns but not restaurants. The court approved this method of pleading and held the defendant liable to the penalties provided in the statute.[145] It was declared that the word "restaurant" had no fixed legal meaning. A place known by that name might or might not be an inn, and hence it was quite possible for an establishment called a restaurant to be within the meaning of the statute.

In an Iowa case a Negro was refused service in a booth at a pure food show. A coffee merchant had rented the booth for the purpose of advertising his product. Here he dispensed cups of coffee gratis to prospective buyers of his wares. This booth was held not to be within the Iowa statute.[146]

Boardinghouses are mentioned only in the Kansas statute, and it is believed that very few if any of the other acts would be held applicable to these establishments. A contract for board is usually considered a matter of private concern. In one Iowa case where the statute of that state was construed to be applicable to an establishment where meals were served to all who desired accommodations, the court has inferred that the statute would not apply to an establishment where meals were served to particular individuals in pursuance of a previous arrangement.[147] The court was evidently of the opinion that the issue of the application of the statute to any particular establishment should be determined by considering the actual manner of conducting the business rather than considering only the signs and advertisements which are put forward by the management.

Two states specifically mention drugstores,[148] while five include soda fountains.[149] A soda fountain located in a drugstore

[145] Lewis v. Hitchcock, 10 Fed. 4 (S. D. N. Y. 1882).

[146] Brown v. J. H. Bell Co., 146 Iowa 89, 123 N. W. 231 (1909).

[147] Humburd v. Crawford, 128 Iowa 743, 105 N. W. 330 (1905) (a very strong dictum).

[148] New York and Pennsylvania.

[149] California, Illinois, New Jersey, New York, and Pennsylvania. *See* Hutson v. Owl Drug Co., 79 Cal. App. 390, 249 Pac. 524 (1926), in which the evidence

was held not to be a place of public accommodation within the general language of the Washington act,[150] but an opposite decision was recently rendered in Ohio.[151] Furthermore, before the Illinois statute was amended to include specifically soda fountains, an establishment which only sold refreshing drinks by the glass was held not to be within the act.[152] Three states mention confectionaries[153] and five, ice cream parlors.[154] A place of this general type has been held to be outside the scope of the Indiana statute,[155] but a court in the neighboring state of Ohio has ruled that such an establishment is within the meaning of the statute in effect in that jurisdiction.[156] Besides mentioning all or some of these places specifically, the New Jersey, New York, and Pennsylvania acts refer to establishments where fruit preparations and other beverages are sold for consumption on the premises.

Four states now specifically mention saloons,[157] but two of them, Minnesota and New York, have amended[158] their statutes to include these establishments as the direct result of a decision by the highest court of both states that saloons were not within the meaning of the general provisions of the acts.[159] The decision of the New York Court of Appeals was rendered despite the fact that the lower courts in that state had in several instances applied the statute in cases involving saloons or similar establishments.[160] In one Iowa case the court used language

---

was held to be sufficient to uphold a Negro's claim of discrimination at a soda fountain.

150 Goff v. Savage, 122 Wash. 194, 210 Pac. 374 (1922). As above stated, the Washington act is in general terms only.

151 Eckerd Drug Store v. Gordie, 14 Ohio Law Abs. 513 (1933). A peculiar thing about this case is that the jury decided that the establishment was within the statute and the court approved.

152 Cecil v. Green, 161 Ill. 265, 43 N. E. 1105 (1896), *aff'g* 60 Ill. App. 61 (1895).

153 New Jersey, New York, and Pennsylvania.

154 California, Illinois, New Jersey, New York, and Pennsylvania.

155 Chochos v. Burden, 74 Ind. App. 242, 128 N. E. 696 (1920).

156 Fowler v. Benner, 13 Ohio N. P. (N.S.) 313 (1912).

157 Minnesota, New York, Pennsylvania, and Wisconsin. Before the 1935 amendment the Illinois act mentioned saloons.

158 Minn. Laws 1899, c. 41; N. Y. Laws 1918, c. 196, as pointed out in Springer v. McDermott, 173 N. Y. Supp. 413 (1st Dep't 1919).

159 Rhone v. Loomis, 74 Minn. 200, 77 N. W. 31 (1898); Gibbs v. Arras Bros., 222 N. Y. 332, 118 N. E. 857 (1918).

160 Babb v. Elsinger, 147 N. Y. Supp. 98 (1st Dep't 1914); Tobias v. Riehm,

which might have been interpreted to mean that saloons and soda fountains were within the statute of that state.[161] This having been brought to its attention, the tribunal filed a supplementary opinion declaring that the language used was merely a citation of cases from other states to the effect that the statutes of those jurisdictions covered these establishments.[162] The court said that this was not even entitled to be considered as a dictum and therefore would not bind the tribunal if such a case should arise in the future. The New York and Pennsylvania statutes also mention barrooms and other stores, parks, or enclosures where spirituous or malt liquors are sold. In fact it is said in one Pennsylvania case that the renewal of a liquor license would be refused if it should appear that the dealer had discriminated against anyone because of his race or color.[163] The Massachusetts act has also been held to apply in an instance where a barkeeper refused to serve a Negro.[164] The Ohio act has recently been amended to include the new liquor stores[165] which were established after the repeal of the prohibition amendment to the Federal Constitution. Prior to this change in the statute, however, the Ohio Supreme Court had refused to apply it in a case involving discrimination in a saloon.[166] The court declared that it would not infer that the legislature had meant the statute to apply to saloons, since the proprietor would then be placed in an embarrassing position where he could not safely decline to serve a Negro or a member or any other minority race, whether that person be intoxicated or sober. In the above-mentioned Minnesota decision[167] the court said that the most likely reason for the legislature's omission of saloons from the original Civil Rights Act of that state was the fear that the racial antipathies of the

---

162 N. Y. Supp. 976 (1st Dep't 1917); Matthews v. Hotz, 173 N. Y. Supp. 234 (1st Dep't 1918). Relief was denied in Fuller v. McDermott, 87 N. Y. Supp. 536 (1904), only because the Negro plaintiff was not a citizen or did not prove himself to be such.

[161] Brown v. J. H. Bell Co., 146 Iowa 89, 123 N. W. 231 (1909).

[162] Supplementary opinion filed in Brown v. J. H. Bell Co., 146 Iowa 89, 123 N. W. 231 (1909), on petition for a rehearing. Reported in 124 N. W. 901 (1910).

[163] Russ' Application, 20 Pa. Co. Ct. 510 (1898).

[164] Bryant v. Rich's Grill, 216 Mass. 344, 103 N. E. 925 (1914).

[165] Ohio Code Serv. (Baldwin, Mar., 1934) §6064-25.

[166] Kellar v. Koerber, 61 Ohio St. 388, 55 N. E. 1002 (1899).

[167] Rhone v. Loomis, 74 Minn. 200, 77 N. W. 31 (1898).

people would be fanned into flame in these establishments and that this would cause race riots. There was much to be said in favor of this argument, as among those who are under the influence of spirituous liquors there is a known propensity to become violent.

In the South, of course, the situation is wholly different. Here a policy of segregation is the order of the day. The Negroes have their own establishments where liquors may be obtained, legally or illegally. In former days there were places of this kind which served the members of both races, but in separate apartments with a common entrance. In Louisiana an effort was made to put a stop to this practice. In 1908 the legislature enacted a statute which provided that bars for white and colored patrons must be conducted in separate buildings.[168] In a case which came before the appellate court during the following year, the proprietor of a saloon had partitioned his establishment into two rooms, one for white patrons and the other for colored, with an opening behind the bar for the sake of convenience. He was thereby enabled to serve both races at the same time with a minimum of effort and expense. The court, however, declared that this arrangement failed to meet the specifications of the statute, for the requirement of separate and distinct buildings was positively mandatory. Therefore the proprietor was said to be subject to punishment under the statute. However, it was the opinion of the tribunal that a tax collector could not compel him to pay the price of two licenses.[169] In the absence of specific legislation of this type, the Alabama[170] and Florida[171] courts have held that it is not unlawful to segregate the members of the two races in such establishments. No particular method of segregation is called for by these decisions, and it seems that only one license is required.

Places of Amusement

Theatres.—At the outset it may be said that theatres are mentioned in all save two of the seventeen states which have

[168] La. Acts 1908, p. 236.

[169] State *ex rel.* Tax Collector v. Falkenheiner, 123 La. 617, 49 So. 214 (1909). A case similar to this one is Town of Vidalia v. Falkenheiner, 123 La. 625, 49 So. 217 (1909).

[170] Hochstadler v. State, 73 Ala. 24 (1882).

[171] Galloway v. Strauss, 67 Fla. 426, 65 So. 588 (1914).

statutes that enumerate particular establishments as coming within the purview of the acts. The two exceptions are Kansas and Wisconsin. The courts of these two states would probably hold that theatres are within the general provisions of the acts. In fact the Kansas Supreme Court has used language in one opinion[172] which would lead one to believe that theatres are within the scope of the statute of that state. Furthermore, the entirely general Washington statute has been held to apply in the case of a theatre.[173] Negroes have brought numerous prosecutions and suits against theatre proprietors, and they have been successful in many instances.[174] In one New York case relief was refused because the seats which the complainant desired were not available.[175] In another case from the same jurisdiction the court excluded certain evidence to the effect that a theatre proprietor had given his employes instructions to make no discriminations. The court was of the opinion that this evidence was erroneously excluded, as it would clearly tend to avoid the liability of the principal in accordance with the peculiar New York agency doctrine already mentioned.[176]

It has been seen from the above general discussion that theatre proprietors cannot lawfully segregate the races in states which have Civil Rights Acts. However, in jurisdictions where there is no such legislation, the management may adopt regulations of its own calling for race separation in such establishments.[177] A Missouri court has recently held that persons operating a municipal auditorium under a license from the city authorities may adopt their own regulations with respect to

[172] State v. Brown, 112 Kan. 814, 212 Pac. 663 (1923).

[173] Anderson v. Pantages Theatre Co., 114 Wash. 24, 194 Pac. 813 (1921); Randall v. Cowlitz Amusements, Inc., 194 Wash. 82, 76 P. (2d) 1017 (1938).

[174] Jones v. Kehrlein, 49 Cal. App. 646, 194 Pac. 55 (1920); Prowd v. Gore, 57 Cal. App. 458, 207 Pac. 490 (1922); Baylies v. Curry, 128 Ill. 287, 21 N. E. 595 (1889), *aff'g* 30 Ill. App. 105 (1889); Thorne v. Alcazar Amusement Co., 210 Ill. App. 173 (1918); Pickett v. Kuchan, 323 Ill. 138, 153 N. E. 667 (1926); Bolden v. Grand Rapids Operating Co., 239 Mich. 318, 214 N. W. 241 (1927); Miller v. Stampul, 83 N. J. Law 278, 84 Atl. 201 (1912); Joyner v. Moore-Wiggins Co., 152 App. Div. 266, 136 N. Y. Supp. 578 (4th Dep't 1912); Davis v. Euclid Ave. Garden Theater Co., 17 Ohio C. C. (N.S.) 495, 32 Ohio C. D. 250 (1911); Commonwealth v. George, 61 Pa. Super. Ct. 412 (1915).

[175] Hull v. Eighty-sixth Street Amusement Co., 144 N. Y. Supp. 318 (1st Dep't 1913).

[176] Thomas v. Williams, 48 Misc. 615, 95 N. Y. Supp. 592 (1905).

[177] Younger v. Judah, 111 Mo. 303, 19 S. W. 1109 (1892); De La Ysla v. Publix Theatre Corp., 82 Utah 598, 26 P. (2d) 818 (1933) (Filipinos).

admission and the seating of persons of different races who purchase tickets for the entertainment.[178] In this instance it could not be shown that there had been any discrimination against Negroes in granting admission to performances under the direct auspices of the city or in granting permits to use the auditorium for entertainments. In fact the building was shown to have been used by both colored and white organizations which desired a place of this kind for theatrical or other similar functions.

A Virginia statute requires segregation in every theatre, motion-picture show, opera house, public hall, or other place of public entertainment which accepts both white and colored patrons.[179] This act punishes as a misdemeanor any violation of its provisions by either the proprietor or a patron of either race. The Louisiana Civil Rights Act and the Delaware and Tennessee Reconstruction legislation concerning theatres have been discussed above.[180] In the other southern states no statutes have been found covering segregation in theatres. In South Carolina, however, there is an act which stipulates that all circuses and other tent shows must provide separate entrances for their white and colored customers.[181]

Theatres cannot be considered in the same category as public conveyances and other public utilities. In the absence of statute the proprietors of these establishments do not have to admit those persons whom they do not wish to accommodate.[182] At common law a ticket to a performance in a theatre is nothing more than a revocable license. Occasionally a Negro or a member of some other race obtains a ticket to a performance where members of his race are not wanted. If this occurs in a jurisdiction where there is no Civil Rights legislation, to what extent is the proprietor liable to the ticket holder in case he refuses to admit him? Several courts have decided that he may be held responsible in an action on the contract but not in an action sounding in tort.[183] This limits the Negro's right of

---

[178] Harris v. City of St. Louis, 111 S. W. (2d) 995 (Mo. App. 1938).

[179] VA. CODE ANN. (Michie, 1930) §§1796 (a)-(b).

[180] See notes 21, 26, and 27 *supra*.

[181] S. C. CODE (1932) §1271.

[182] People *ex rel.* Burnham v. Flynn, 189 N. Y. 180, 82 N. E. 169 (1907).

[183] Burton v. Scherpf, 83 Mass. 133 (1861); Taylor v. Cohn, 47 Ore. 538, 84 Pac. 388 (1906); De La Ysla v. Publix Theatre Corp., 82 Utah 598, 26 P. (2d) 818 (1933). What is said in Drew v. Peer, 93 Pa. St. 234 (1880), to the effect that

recovery in such cases to a paltry sum and is probably the chief reason for the infrequency of litigation of this kind. Why should one start legal proceedings over the price of a theatre ticket? Hence only test cases have reached the appellate courts. There have been instances where Negroes have refused to depart amiably upon request after the theatre management had decided to revoke their tickets. In one such case it was held that the management would be justified in using enough force to oust the obstinate party.[184] In another instance, however, it was said that the theatre would be responsible in a tort action if it could be shown that the employes used excessive force.[185]

Suppose some Negro should somehow obtain possession of a transferable ticket to a performance in a southern theatre which had no separate accommodations and did not admit members of his race. Suppose he threw caution to the winds and presented himself at the theatre. When he was refused admittance, as he surely would be, is there any reason for believing that he would be allowed to maintain a suit against the proprietors? According to what has previously been said with respect to the southern common-law rule concerning hotels and restaurants, it is not very likely that a theatre proprietor would be forced to accept the Negro. The colored assignee of the ticket would not be placed in a better position than his assignor. Hence the theatre management could revoke its agreement and be subject to suit only for the purchase price. An opposite view would be utterly at odds with southern tradition. The insignificance of the damages recoverable in such an action and the danger of stirring up race hatred in the community seem to have been sufficient deterrents to proceedings of this kind, as no such case has been found in the published reports from this section of the country. Furthermore, a theatre in any section of the country could avoid trouble of this sort by using

---

the purchaser's right is not a mere license and is more in the nature of a lease is declared to be obiter dictum in Horney v. Nixon, 213 Pa. St. 20, 61 Atl. 1088 (1905), the court in that case holding that a ticket was a revocable license. The dictum in Drew v. Peer is followed in the case of Ferguson v. Chase, 28 Wash. Law Rep. 797 (Nov. 22, 1900), which has been severely criticized. See Note (1901) 14 Harv. L. Rev. 455.

[184] Burton v. Scherpf, 83 Mass. 133 (1861).

[185] Drew v. Peer, 93 Pa. St. 234 (1880).

non-transferable tickets, as was done in New York to prevent ticket scalping.[186]

Motion-picture theatres are specifically mentioned in the Civil Rights Acts of five states,[187] and the Ohio statute has been held to include such establishments within its terms.[188] Furthermore, it is probable that the statutes of the other states which mention theatres in general would be construed to apply to this particular kind of theatre. A Connecticut statute enacted in 1925 provided that no motion-picture house should show any film which ridiculed or cast reflections upon the Negro as a race.[189] There is a very similar Illinois act which applies not only to motion pictures, but also to plays, dramas, sketches, and lithographs.[190] Moreover, there is a general Connecticut statute which penalizes any person who, by his advertisements, ridicules an individual or holds him up to contempt because of his race or color.[191]

Music Halls.—Five[192] of the statutes of the usual type and the three separate advertising acts[193] mention music halls. The Illinois act, while it does not mention music halls specifically, includes concerts in its enumeration. Before the New York act was amended to apply specifically to such a variety of establishments, a place which was known as a concert hall but which was evidently somewhat in the nature of a cabaret was held to be within the general provisions of the statute.[194] The term "theatres" used in most of these statutes would undoubtedly be construed to cover a majority of the establishments which are known as music halls. Roof gardens are also specifically mentioned in the New Jersey, New York, and Pennsylvania statutes. The term "roof garden" is applied to various kinds of establishments. A place which goes by that name is usually located at the top of some metropolitan hotel or other building.

[186] Collister v. Hayman, 183 N. Y. 250, 76 N. E. 20 (1905).

[187] Connecticut, Michigan, New Jersey, New York, and Pennsylvania.

[188] Guy v. Tri-State Amusement Co., 7 Ohio App. 509 (1917).

[189] Conn. Laws 1925, c. 177.

[190] ILL. REV. STAT. (Cahill, 1933) c. 38, §457.

[191] CONN. GEN. STAT. (1930) §6066.

[192] Connecticut, New Jersey, New York, Pennsylvania, and Rhode Island.

[193] Separate advertising acts of Colorado, Illinois, and Massachusetts, *supra* note 121.

[194] Cremore v. Huber, 18 App. Div. 231, 45 N. Y. Supp. 947 (2d Dep't 1897).

It may be an establishment where one sits and listens to orchestral or vocal music, it may be in the nature of a cabaret, it may be merely a place for dancing, or it may be a combination of all three of these types. It might be assumed that the statutes were meant to cover roof gardens of all kinds, since no clarification of the term is attempted. However, more will be said with respect to places of the cabaret and dancing type.

Dance Halls, etc.—Not a single one of the statutes specifically mentions dance halls. Nevertheless, a public dance hall was held to be within the scope of the Ohio act in a case involving discrimination against Jews.[195] A place which was in the nature of a cabaret was declared to be within the older New York statute,[196] but it may be that this decision would not be followed today in view of what has been said above concerning the more specific modern acts of New York and other states. Relief seems to have been denied to a prospective customer in a California cabaret only because the court upheld the defendant's claim that all seating space not already occupied had been reserved.[197]

As noted above, the New Jersey, New York, and Pennsylvania acts mention roof gardens. While it is probable that roof gardens of the cabaret and dancing type would be held to be within the meaning of these statutes, it is possible that a distinction might be drawn between places of this sort and establishments of the music hall type. This possible distinction is brought out in the New York case discussed in the following paragraph.

Dance halls or pavilions which were established and conducted by interurban or street railway companies in conjunction with amusement parks owned by them have been held to be included as public places within the meaning of the Ohio[198] and New York[199] statutes. However, the language of the New York Court of Appeals clearly indicates that the chief reason for deciding that such a place was within the statute was the fact that the dance hall belonged to and was managed by a public

[195] Anderson v. State, 30 Ohio C. D. 510 (1918).

[196] Cremore v. Huber, 18 App. Div. 231, 45 N. Y. Supp. 947 (2d Dept. 1897).

[197] Gilmore v. Paris Inn, 10 Cal. App. (2d) 353, 51 P. (2d) 1103 (1935).

[198] Youngstown P. & F. S. Ry. v. Tokus, 4 Ohio App. 276 (1915).

[199] Johnson v. Auburn & S. E. R. R., 222 N. Y. 443, 119 N. E. 72 (1918), *rev'g* 169 App. Div. 864, 156 N. Y. Supp. 93 (4th Dep't 1915).

conveyancing corporation, a public utility of a type which is surely within the act. Hence there is at least some room to doubt that a dance hall which was not so owned and operated would be held to be covered by the statute. In fact such an interpretation is indicated by the opinion of the New York Appellate Division in which a distinction is drawn between dance halls where persons dance with each other and those where exhibitions of dancing are featured.[200] The latter type of establishment could be classified under the head of theatres and would therefore be within all acts which applied thereto.

Bathhouses and Bathing Accommodations.—Bathhouses are specifically mentioned in the usual type of statute in six states[201] and also in the three separate advertising acts.[202] The Illinois statute mentions bathrooms and this would almost certainly be construed to mean bathhouses. The New Jersey act also refers to public seashore accommodations and boardwalks. The New York statute has been held to apply to a public bathing establishment at the beach.[203]

In a Colorado case a complaint was made by Negro school children against rules adopted by the authorities of the school which they attended. The regulations provided for separate social functions and swimming classes for white and colored pupils. There is a state constitutional provision in Colorado prohibiting any special distinction or classification of pupils on account of race or color,[204] which was held to invalidate this attempt at segregation on the part of the school authorities.[205] A New Jersey court has rendered a similar decision in respect to school swimming facilities[206] without the aid of such a constitutional provision.

An Oklahoma act of 1935[207] invested the State Conservation Commission with authority to make rules and regulations providing for the segregation of the white and colored races in

[200] Johnson v. Auburn & S. E. R. R., 169 App. Div. 864, 156 N. Y. Supp. 93 (4th Dep't 1915).

[201] California, Iowa, New Jersey, New York, Pennsylvania, and Rhode Island.

[202] Separate advertising acts of Colorado, Illinois, and Massachusetts, *supra* note 121.

[203] Norman v. City Island Beach Co., 126 Misc. 335, 213 N. Y. Supp. 379 (Sup. Ct. 1926).

[204] COLO. CONST. Art. IX, §8.

[205] Jones v. Newlon, 81 Colo. 25, 253 Pac. 386 (1927).

[206] Patterson v. Trenton Bd. of Education, 11 N. J. Misc. 179, 164 Atl. 892 (1933).

[207] Okla. Sess. Laws 1935, c. 70, §12.

respect to the exercise of fishing, boating, and bathing privileges in waters under its control. In 1937,[208] however, this authority was transferred to the State Planning and Resources Board.

Skating Rinks, etc.—Skating rinks have been deemed worthy of mention by the legislatures of seven states.[209] Such an establishment has also been held to be within the Wisconsin act.[210] The Iowa Court, while it decided that an unlicensed rink was not within the statute of that state, employed language which would seem to indicate that there would have been a different result had the proprietor been licensed.[211] Furthermore, relief appears to have been denied in an Ohio case involving a place of this kind only because there was no evidence to show that the doorkeeper, who had refused to admit the Negro plaintiff, was entrusted with anything more than authority to take up tickets.[212] A skating rink was also held to be within an earlier New York act in which such places were not mentioned specifically.[213] Bicycle rinks were evidently deemed of sufficient importance to be referred to in the Illinois statute.

Bowling Alleys.—The detailed New Jersey, New York, and Pennsylvania acts mention bowling alleys, and the Ohio Court has held that they are within the statute of that state.[214]

Billiard and Pool Parlors.—The New Jersey, New York, and Pennsylvania statutes also refer to billiard and pool parlors. Moreover, it appears that the only reason for the refusal of the Massachusetts Court to hold that such an establishment was within the scope of an earlier act in that state was that the plaintiff did not allege that the place was licensed.[215]

In contrast to this is a Georgia statute which provides that no license shall be issued to a person of either race to operate

---

[208] Okla. Sess. Laws 1937, p. 79.

[209] California, Illinois, Massachusetts, New Jersey, New York, Pennsylvania, and Rhode Island.

[210] Jones v. Broadway Rink Co., 136 Wis. 595, 118 N. W. 170 (1908).

[211] Bowlin v. Lyon, 67 Iowa 536, 25 N. W. 766 (1885).

[212] Lyon v. Akron Skating Rink Co., 18 Ohio C. C. (N.S.) 202, 32 Ohio C. D. 690 (1908).

[213] People v. King, 110 N. Y. 418, 18 N. E. 245 (1888), *aff'g* 42 Hun 186 (N. Y. 1886).

[214] Johnson v. Humphrey Pop-Corn Co., 24 Ohio C. C. 135 (1902), *aff'd* 70 Ohio St. 478, 72 N. E. 1160 (1904).

[215] Commonwealth v. Sylvester, 95 Mass. 247 (1866).

a billiard room to be patronized by members of the other.[216]

Recreation Parks.—The statutes of Connecticut, New Jersey, New York, and Pennsylvania mention recreation parks. In addition to this, New York also has a special statute which forbids discrimination against any person or group of persons in the prices charged for admission to any building, park, inclosure, or other places which are open to the public at stated periods.[217] This act might very well be construed to outlaw racial discrimination in such places.

In the southern states the situation is entirely different. Here a policy of segregation is the order of the day. It has been held that certain municipalities are empowered to acquire property on which to establish park or other recreational facilities for the separate enjoyment of members of the colored race, similar playgrounds for the whites having been already provided.[218] Furthermore, the Georgia Court has approved a private grant of park land to a municipality which was conditioned upon its use by white people only.[219] In one North Carolina case an attempt was made to invalidate a private grant thus conditioned on the ground that the municipality had provided no similar facilities for Negroes. However, there was nothing in the record of this litigation to show that such was the case. The court held that this lack of evidence precluded an attack upon the validity of the conveyance on the ground that the acceptance of the gratuitous deed would constitute discrimination of an unconstitutional variety.[220] In this case the court made the remark that "in any event the matter must be left to the sound discretion of the governing authorities, to be exercised according to the needs and requirements of either race, and without discrimination between them." From this language it may well be argued that the Negroes could bring a mandamus action to force the city authorities to provide park or playground facilities for the colored population. The city

---

[216] GA. CODE ANN. (Michie, 1926) §1762 (22).

[217] N. Y. CONSOL. LAWS (Cahill, 1930) c. 41, §515.

[218] Wrightsman v. Gideon, 296 Mo. 214, 247 S. W. 135 (1922); Page v. Commonwealth, 157 Va. 325, 160 S. E. 33 (1931); Mayes v. Mann, 164 Va. 584, 180 S. E. 425 (1935). See Missouri statute authorizing city school boards to establish separate playgrounds. Mo. REV. STAT. (1929) §9333.

[219] City of Barnesville v. Stafford, 161 Ga. 588, 131 S. E. 487 (1925). *But see* Berry v. City of Durham, 186 N. C. 421, 119 S. E. 748 (1923).

[220] *Ibid.*

fathers might decide to have separate parks or they might deem it advisable to provide separate facilities in the same park, a device which has received the approval of the Kentucky Court.[221] The latter might prove to be a necessity in view of the municipality's straitened financial condition. It is probable that the authorities would be forced to adopt one of these alternatives or else admit Negroes to the parks on a basis of equality with the whites.

Racecourses.—Racecourses[222] are mentioned in the Civil Rights Acts of New York and Pennsylvania. Even before the New York statute was amended so as to mention them specifically, the intermediate appellate court held that racecourses were within the scope of the act as it then read.[223] While it is true that this case was reversed by the Court of Appeals,[224] the reason assigned therefor was that the only kind of discrimination covered by the act was that based upon race, color, or religion. The complainant had not brought his case within any one of these categories, and therefore the desired relief could not be obtained under this statute. However, this reversal does not interfere with the point here made that racecourses were within the act. The state of Arkansas recently required racecourses to segregate their white and Negro customers.[225]

Miscellaneous Places of Amusement.—The New Jersey, New York, and Pennsylvania statutes mention fairs,[226] gymnasiums, and shooting galleries. From what has been intimated in a Washington case[227] in respect to the character of a baseball park, it is probable that such a place would be held to be within the Civil Rights Act of that state. The refusal of the management to allow the plaintiff on the premises in this particular

---

[221] Warley v. Board of Park Commr's, 233 Ky. 688, 26 S. W. (2d) 554 (1930).

[222] Racecourses are mentioned in California anti-discrimination statute, CAL. CIV. CODE (Deering, 1931) §§53-54. See note 35 *supra*. This act has been applied in a case involving discrimination at a racecourse against a person who was not of African descent. *See* Greenberg v. Western Turf Ass'n, 140 Cal. 357, 73 Pac. 1050 (1903), 148 Cal. 126, 82 Pac. 684 (1905).

[223] Grannan v. Westchester Racing Ass'n, 16 App. Div. 8, 44 N. Y. Supp. 790 (2d Dep't 1897).

[224] Grannan v. Westchester Racing Ass'n, 153 N. Y. 449, 47 N. E. 896 (1897).

[225] Ark. Laws 1937, No. 230.

[226] Fairs are mentioned in California anti-discrimination statute, CAL. CIV. CODE (Deering, 1931) §§53-54. See note 35 *supra*.

[227] Finnesey v. Seattle Baseball Club, 122 Wash. 276, 210 Pac. 679 (1922).

instance was based upon his reputation as a gambler and not upon his race or color. Hence the statute was said not to be applicable. A Texas statute[228] prohibits whites and Negroes from engaging in boxing matches against one another.

Miscellaneous Public Places

Cemeteries.—There are statutes[229] in New Jersey and New York outlawing racial discrimination by cemeteries. However, a cemetery which was incorporated was held not to be a "place of public accommodation or amusement" within the Illinois Civil Rights Act.[230] The court reached this conclusion in spite of a clause in the act itself which prohibited racial discrimination in the prices to be charged for lots or graves in any cemetery or other place for burying the dead. The court evidently based its decision upon the fact that this particular portion of the statute was set off from the rest of its provisions and was therefore an independent clause. It would have been very easy for the legislature to enumerate cemeteries along with the other places of public accommodation mentioned in the principal clause in the statute if it had wished to do so. In fact the failure to do this evidently militated against the opposing view. The provision was interpreted as being a unit distinct in itself. Whether such was the intention of the legislature is a matter of judicial interpretation, and the view of the court is perhaps strengthened by the fact that the principal clause enumerates funeral hearses and fails to mention cemeteries. While the court was probably right in its interpretation of this detached provision, the decision makes it of little practical value as a deterrent to racial discrimination. The cemeteries could simply refuse to sell any lots at all to Negroes. However, it is supposed that there must have been some cemeteries which had adopted the practice of charging colored persons an exorbitant price. Otherwise the statute would never have been so worded.

Barber Shops and Beauty Parlors.—Barber shops are

---

[228] Tex. Gen. Laws 1933, c. 241, §11.

[229] N. J. Comp. Stat. (1911) p. 1810, §213; N. Y. Consol. Laws (Cahill, 1930) c. 41, §514.

[230] People *ex rel.* Gaskill v. Forest Home Cemetery Co., 258 Ill. 36, 101 N. E. 219 (1913). See chapter on Property Rights, notes 104-106, for other cases involving cemeteries.

specifically mentioned in the statutes of twelve states[231] and in the separate advertising acts of Colorado, Illinois, and Massachusetts. The Connecticut Court, however, has held that a barber shop is not within the statute of that state.[232] In this instance the tribunal declared that the legislature had never meant that the act should cover this type of establishment. Because of the complainants' failure to plead certain essential facts, relief was refused in two afore-mentioned cases[233] which involved racial discrimination in barber shops situated in states whose statutes, at that time as well as at present, contained specific references thereto. The Pennsylvania statute would hardly be held to cover barber shops, as the enumeration of establishments is the same as that in the New York act with the exception that it makes no mention of barber shops.

A New York court has held that a beauty parlor which is not affiliated with a barber shop is not within the scope of the statute of that state, although barber shops are mentioned in the act.[234] However, the court reserved its opinion as to whether the act would apply to an establishment where the barber shop and beauty parlor were operated together under the same management.

Formerly a great many of the barber shops in the South were operated by Negroes. Although the white barbers have largely encroached upon this means of earning a livelihood, there are still a number of Negro establishments where only white patrons are served. The Negroes have lost their one-time monopoly on this trade because of a lack of enough capital to buy necessary equipment and a want of proper sanitation in their places of business. Ignorance of the proper methods of conducting a modern business establishment has also had its effect, as the white barbers, because of more efficient management, offered service at a lower operating cost. Of course the Negro barbers

---

[231] California, Colorado, Illinois, Indiana, Iowa, Massachusetts, Michigan, Minnesota, Nebraska, New York, Ohio, and Wisconsin.

[232] Faulkner v. Sollazi, 79 Conn. 541, 65 Atl. 947 (1907).

[233] State v. Hall, 72 Iowa 525, 34 N. W. 315 (1887); Messenger v. State, 25 Neb. 674, 41 N. W. 638 (1889). See notes 80 and 82 *supra*. In respect to the problem here presented it is immaterial whether the facts which were not pleaded were provable or not.

[234] Campbell v. Eichert, 155 Misc. 164, 278 N. Y. Supp. 946 (Sup. Ct. 1935).

still serve the members of their own race, but this is not nearly so lucrative as the employment which is given by the wealthier white customers.

Sometimes opposition to Negro barbers develops in a southern community. For example, the city of Atlanta passed an ordinance to the effect that no Negro barber should be allowed to serve white children under fourteen years of age. The Negroes decided to contest the validity of this enactment, and the Georgia Court declared the ordinance unconstitutional as a violation of the due process and equal protection clauses of the Fourteenth Amendment.[235] Furthermore, in pursuance of its equity powers, the court granted an injunction against the enforcement of the ordinance. There was no adequate remedy at law because repeated prosecutions were threatened which would seriously interfere with and perhaps destroy the Negro barbers' lawful business.

Bootblacking Stands.—The Colorado Court has held that a bootblacking stand is a place of public accommodation within the scope of the statute of that state.[236] In reaching this conclusion the Colorado Court refused to follow the reasoning in an earlier New York decision to the effect that bootblacking stands which were not located in barber shops were outside the scope of the Empire State act.[237] The question arises as to whether the New York decision would have been the same if the bootblacking stand had been located in a barber shop, as is the case in many instances. The opinion of the Court of Appeals gives no indication as to what the answer to this query would be.

In the South the majority of the bootblacks are Negroes. The whites have not encroached upon this occupation as they have in the case of the tonsorial art.

Libraries.—Libraries are specifically mentioned in the acts of three states.[238] Furthermore, the West Virginia Court has held that Negroes could not be excluded from a public library which had been established under a statute allowing the Board

[235] Chaires v. City of Atlanta, 164 Ga. 755, 139 S. E. 559 (1927).

[236] Darius v. Apostolos, 68 Colo. 323, 190 Pac. 510 (1919). For additional discussion of this case, see note 102 *supra*.

[237] Burks v. Bosso, 180 N. Y. 341, 73 N. E. 58 (1905).

[238] New Jersey, New York, and Pennsylvania.

of Education to levy a tax for that purpose.[239] The refuted contention in this case was that the library was an integral part of the state public school system and that therefore the Negroes could not lawfully be admitted under the West Virginia separate school law. However, since there is no Civil Rights Act in this jurisdiction, the library management would surely be permitted to establish separate accommodations in the same building for white and colored persons. There is a certain amount of southern segregative legislation concerning the separation of the races in public libraries.[240]

Hospitals, Clinics, etc.—The New Jersey, New York, and Pennsylvania acts mention hospitals, clinics, and dispensaries. Drugstores are also referred to in New York and Pennsylvania.

Miscellaneous.—Garages are mentioned in the New Jersey, New York, and Pennsylvania statutes. The Illinois act refers to elevators and rest rooms and that of Massachusetts to public meetings. The statutes of New Jersey, New York, and Pennsylvania also contain provisions which expressly state that the acts will not apply to an establishment which is in its nature distinctly private, and there is little doubt that the statutes of the other states would be given a similar interpretation.

Business Regulations

Business is usually a matter of strictly private concern in the United States, and hence a great deal of the discrimination against persons of the colored race which occurs in our daily

---

[239] Brown v. Bd. of Education, 106 W. Va. 476, 146 S. E. 389 (1929), (1930) 33 L. Notes 215.

[240] North Carolina directs the state librarian to fit up and maintain a separate place in the state library for the accommodation of colored patrons. N. C. Code Ann. (Michie, 1931) §6585. Oklahoma commands the maintenance of separate accommodations for persons of the colored race in public libraries located in cities having a Negro population of one thousand or more. Okla. Comp. Stat. (1921) §9528. In Texas separate branches for Negroes to be administered by a Negro custodian are required in all county free libraries. Tex. Ann. Rev. Civ. Stat. (Vernon, 1925) art. 1688. In Missouri the city boards of education are authorized to establish and maintain separate libraries for white and colored persons in connection with the proper management of the municipal school districts. Mo. Rev. Stat. (1929) §9333. In Kentucky a statute authorizes the establishment of separate library facilities for Negroes in certain cities. The statute provides that no tax shall be levied on the property of the race which is not permitted to have free access to the library established under other provisions of the act. See Ky. Stat. Ann. (Carroll, Supp. 1933) §§2741d-6,

lives cannot be prevented. The restraints of the Fourteenth Amendment to the Federal Constitution are limited to state action and therefore cannot be employed to outlaw business practices which are unfair to the Negro as a race. Of course any statutory regulation of business establishments which expressly discriminated against colored persons or individuals of any other race would be unconstitutional, as would also any racial discrimination by state, county, or municipal boards or officials acting under the authority granted to them by statute or ordinance.

A case of the latter variety was brought up to the Federal Supreme Court from California. A San Francisco ordinance had set up a board of control which was given authority to issue permits to persons who desired to conduct a laundry business. It was established that the board had used its authority in such a manner as to discriminate against the Chinese. The evidence showed that the board had refused permits to Chinese while granting the requests of white persons who were similarly situated in wooden buildings without proper safeguards against fire. While this ordinance was not discriminatory on its face, the Supreme Court declared the enactment unconstitutional because it clothed the board with arbitrary power to grant or withhold a permit at its own caprice.[241] There were no checks on this autocratic power and no standards were furnished which would guide the board in the administration of the authority conferred by the ordinance. The court based its decision on the additional ground that the discriminatory use of the authority granted to the board under this ordinance was state action and therefore constituted a denial of the equal protection of the laws, which is guaranteed by the Fourteenth Amendment. This latter doctrine could be employed to nullify any attempt at race discrimination on the part of state, county, or municipal boards or officials acting under authority granted by statute or ordinance.

In a recent Illinois case an attempt was made to restrain the

---

2741d-8. This statute is very similar to those Kentucky school laws the constitutionality of which was so much in doubt. See chapter on Education, notes 338 and 340.

[241] Yick Wo v. Hopkins, 118 U. S. 356, 6 Sup. Ct. 1064 (1885), rev'g *In re* Yick Wo, 68 Cal. 294, 9 Pac. 139 (1885). *See* Bullock v. Wooding, 123 N. J. Law 176, 8 A. (2d) 273 (1939) (bathing beach ordinance).

enforcement of an ordinance which outlawed solicitation of passengers for hire in a certain park district. The complainant claimed that the authorities had enforced the ordinance against colored taxicab drivers while allowing the whites to continue to solicit business. This, if true, would clearly constitute unconstitutional discrimination against the Negroes. The complaint, however, was held defective in that it failed to allege either that the white taxicab drivers did or that the colored plaintiffs did not solicit passengers for hire.[242]

When the Negroes first began to migrate from the South to the northeastern and middle western states, it was believed by many persons that they would not be able to stand the rigors of the colder climate and that they would die or be invalided in great numbers. For this reason certain life insurance companies adopted the practice of charging higher premiums in their sales of policies to Negroes than were exacted from the whites. This practice was considered discriminatory by numbers of northern and western people. The pressure of this mass opinion upon the lawmakers became so great that a number of legislative bodies made an effort to put a stop to the practice. Six states, Connecticut,[243] Massachusetts,[244], Michigan,[245] New Jersey,[246] New York,[247] and Ohio,[248] enacted statutes outlawing this and other forms of racial discrimination which might arise in the course of the life insurance business. The New York act forbids the refusal of a Negro's application because of his race alone. The New Jersey and Ohio statutes provide that nothing contained in the acts shall be construed as forcing any company or agent to issue a policy to "any person."

These last provisions, if construed strictly, could be interpreted to mean that no company or agent can be forced to insure a colored person even if he seems to be just as good a risk as some white person whom the company has accepted. However, a more liberal and far better interpretation would be

---

[242] Chicago Park District v. Lattipee, 364 Ill. 182, 4 N. E. (2d) 86 (1936).

[243] CONN. GEN. STAT. (1930) §§4183-85.

[244] MASS. ANN. LAWS (1933) c. 175, §122.

[245] MICH. COMP. LAWS (1929) §12,457.

[246] N. J. COMP. STAT. (1911), p. 2865, §83.

[247] N. Y. CONSOL. LAWS (Cahill, 1930) c. 30, §90 as amended by N. Y. Laws 1935, c. 736.

[248] OHIO CODE (Throckmorton, 1929) §§9401-02, 12954-55.

that the insurance company could reject a Negro applicant only if the refusal is based on a reason other than race or color. The latter interpretation would be far more effective, since the stricter construction would permit the insurance companies to refuse Negro applicants with impunity, a result which would injure the Negro greatly. However, it may be said that there is no great danger of a general refusal of all life insurance companies in these states to do business with colored persons. The increase in business resulting from the issuance of policies to the now considerable Negro population would probably far offset any fear of the Negro death rate. In fact the rigorous northern climate has not proved to be such a big bugaboo as had been expected. The Connecticut, Massachusetts, and Ohio acts require the refusal of a Negro's application to be accompanied by an examining official's certificate stating that the application had been rejected for reasons other than the applicant's race or color. In Ohio this clause would seem to establish that the suggested liberal interpretation of the above doubtful provision is the correct one. Even with this clause added, however, the statute may not be an effective deterrent to discrimination against Negroes, for it may prove rather difficult to show that the insurer's refusal to issue a policy is based on the applicant's race or color. The New Jersey act applies only to contracts which are made with persons who are residents of the state at the time of the application. The statutes of all six states have provisions stating that all contracts or policy clauses which are contrary to the acts are void. Four[249] penalize the officers and agents as well as the corporation for racial discrimination of this kind, while the New York act subjects only the corporation to punishment.

New York has a somewhat similar statute which forbids racial discrimination by mutual life insurance associations.[250] However, it contains a provision which states that such an association formed by the members of a secret or fraternal order cannot be forced to accept persons into the organization. North Carolina has found it necessary to enact a statute to prevent racial discrimination with respect to the payment of benefits out of

[249] Connecticut, Massachusetts, Michigan, and Ohio.

[250] N. Y. CONSOL. LAWS (Cahill, 1930) c. 41, §1191 (4).

the Firemen's Relief Fund which was raised by taxing the fire insurance companies.[251]

Virginia denies the privilege of chartering fraternal beneficiary associations which admit both whites and Negroes to membership or which have both white and Negro officers and punishes anyone who violates or seeks to violate the act.[252] This statute also prohibits any such association from carrying on business within the state. A somewhat similar North Carolina act forbids mutual associations or fraternal orders of this kind to do business in that state.[253]

In one Arkansas case[254] it was held that a mutual life insurance company may separate its membership into white and colored divisions by contract. The agreement in this instance was worded in such a way as to entitle a Negro policyholder to only those assessments which had been obtained from Negro members. The court held that this was true even though the few assessments from Negroes which were collectable would fail to raise even one-twentieth of the amount stated on the face of the policy. Furthermore, it was shown that the amount recoverable in this action would have been materially increased had assessments upon the white members been permitted.

The Wisconsin Civil Rights Act contains a clause which makes it unlawful to decline to furnish any type of automobile insurance or to charge higher rates therefor because of the race or color of the applicant. This provision was in all likelihood placed in the statute in order to break up a practice of charging higher rates to Negroes. The practice probably developed as a result of the then more or less general impression that Negroes were careless and irresponsible.

The Professions

In respect to the professions there is a dearth of statutory and case material. However, there are a few acts and decisions

[251] N. C. Code Ann. (Michie, 1931) §6073.

[252] Va. Code Ann. (Michie, 1930) §4302a.

[253] N. C. Code Ann. (Michie, 1931) §6494. However, it is interesting to note that burial associations with white and colored divisions are authorized by a recent statute. N. C. Pub. Laws 1937, c. 239, §2.

[254] Young v. Farmers Mutual Life Ins. Co., 175 Ark. 1045, 1 S. W. (2d) 74 (1928).

which are worthy of note. Statutes in Colorado.[255] and Florida[256] provide that no person shall be denied a license to practice law because of race, while a North Carolina act[257] states that no applicant for a license to practice dentistry shall be denied the privilege for a like reason. The latter state formerly had a statute which made it mandatory upon the management of any public or private hospital, sanatorium, or institution which admitted colored patients to employ colored nurses to wait upon the inmates of their own race,[258] but this act was repealed in 1925.[259] There is a somewhat similar statute now in effect in Alabama which makes it unlawful for a white female nurse to serve or be required to serve in wards or rooms in hospitals, public or private, in which Negro men are patients.[260] A Mississippi statute commands that all colored patients in state eleemosynary institutions shall be attended by colored nurses.[261]

In an early case the Maryland Court decided that a statute limiting the privilege of admission to the state bar to white male citizens was not unconstitutional.[262] The court argued that admission to the bar is a matter for state control and that it cannot be termed a privilege or immunity of federal citizenship within the purview of the Fourteenth Amendment to the Federal Constitution. The court was evidently influenced in its decision by the similar reasoning of the Federal Supreme Court in a case concerning a refusal to grant a law license to a woman.[263] The Maryland Court seems to have overlooked the provision in the Fourteenth Amendment forbidding any action by the states which would deny the equal protection of the laws. Should the question ever reach the Supreme Court, it is practically certain that a statute of this kind would be declared unconstitutional. This conclusion is based on two decisions of the Supreme Court itself which, when taken together, support the contention that such a statute would be invalid. In one of these cases the high tribunal held that the right to vote is not a privilege

[255] COLO. STAT. ANN. (Mills, 1930) §284.

[256] FLA. COMP. GEN. LAWS ANN. (Skillman, 1927) §4196.

[257] N. C. CODE ANN. (Michie, 1931) §6632.

[258] N. C. CONSOL. STAT. (1919) §6740. [259] N. C. Pub. Laws 1925, c. 23.

[260] ALA. CODE ANN. (Michie, 1928) §§5011-12.

[261] MISS. CODE ANN. (1930) §4619. [262] *In re* Taylor, 48 Md. 28 (1877).

[263] Bradwell v. State, 16 Wall. 130 (U. S. 1872).

or immunity of citizenship within the meaning of the amendment,[264] while in the other it decided that a Texas statute which denied the Negro the privilege of voting in the Democratic primary was unconstitutional because the colored man is thereby denied the equal protection of the laws.[265] The present Maryland law concerning the admission of applicants to the bar makes no such racial distinction,[266] and it is believed that there is little chance that another case of this sort will arise in this or any other state. Applicants of the Negro race who can pass the bar examinations are now becoming members of the legal profession in the South as well as elsewhere, and the same may be said with respect to the medical, dental, and other professions.

Sometimes there is opposition, even in the northern states, to admitting Negroes to membership in semisocial organizations such as the state bar and medical societies. These controversies, however, rarely reach the courts. In fact only one reported case has been found in which a situation of this kind was considered. In this instance a Negro applied for membership in the New York Pedic Society, an organization established by a special act of the state legislature which had as its objective the improvement and elevation of the practice of chiropody within that jurisdiction. The by-laws of the society provided that an applicant for membership must receive a majority vote of the members of the organization in order to obtain favorable action on his petition. At the first meeting at which the matter was considered the Negro chiropodist received a majority of the votes cast, but this result was not reached without the opposition of some of the members. In fact, even after the vote was taken, the chairman refused to declare the petitioner elected to membership. Moreover, at a later meeting the minority who had opposed the Negro's admission attempted to change the by-laws in such a manner that five dissenting votes would constitute a rejection. The Negro applied for a writ of mandamus

[264] Minor v. Hapersett, 21 Wall. 162 (U. S. 1874).

[265] Nixon v. Herndon, 273 U. S. 536, 47 Sup. Ct. 446 (1927). The principle as here involved is not affected by the fact that this statute concerned primary and not general elections, for a similar act pertaining to general elections could be declared invalid on this same ground as well as under the Fifteenth Amendment, if the principle here announced is followed to its logical limits.

[266] See Md. Laws 1904, p. 240; 1914, p. 1108.

directing the society to admit him. The appellate court granted the relief desired by the applicant.[267] The court declared that the approval of a majority of the members of the organization had entitled the petitioner to membership and that the subsequent attempt to change the by-laws was ineffective because it had failed to satisfy a provision contained therein which expressly provided that they were not to be altered or amended except with the approval of three-fourths of the active members attending the annual meeting.

Controversies of this kind may become more numerous and increasingly important as professional organizations take over various public functions. In many states the admission of applicants to one or more of the professions has been placed in the hands of state societies of this type. The same can be said with respect to the ousting of undesirables.

Fraternal Associations

It was only natural that the social life of the freedmen should be patterned after that of their former masters. It was necessary for the emancipated Negro to adjust himself to the social and economic life which went on about him. Hence many customs and institutions of the whites were adopted by Negroes when they were forming what became the colored society of today, no matter whether it be in Harlem or the Deep South. Among the institutions which were copied from the white society are the various types of fraternal associations and organizations. Sometimes the Negroes would adopt the name, colors, signs, symbols, paraphernalia, and ritual of similar white fraternal orders. To this usurpation of their insignia the white organizations seriously objected in several instances. Hence we have a number of attempts by the white orders to enjoin the use of their insignia by associations whose membership consisted of persons of the colored race.

The question involved in this type of case is whether there has been an unlawful usurpation. The courts of Georgia,[268] New

[267] Hillery v. Pedic Soc. of State of New York, 189 App. Div. 766, 179 N. Y. Supp. 62 (1st Dep't 1919).

[268] Creswill v. Grand Lodge, Knights of Pythias, 133 Ga. 837, 67 S. E. 188 (1910); Faisan v. Adair, 144 Ga. 797, 87 S. E. 1080 (1916), 148 Ga. 403, 96 S. E. 371 (1918).

Jersey,[269] Tennessee,[270] and Texas[271] seem to have recognized the existence of the right to the exclusive use of name and insignia in cases involving usurpations by Negro organizations of similar name. In New York the Court of Appeals restrained a Negro order from using a name similar to that of a white fraternal organization but refused to enjoin the use of the fraternal colors and the peculiar names of its officers.[272]

Even if such a right is recognized, the injured order must not wait too long to object to its violation. In fact in two of the above-mentioned instances the Federal Supreme Court reversed the decisions of the state courts on the ground that the white fraternal order had been guilty of laches in not objecting promptly.[273] In both cases the court seems to have been of the opinion that there had been a fatal delay and that the decisions of the state courts that there had been no laches had no basis whatsoever in the testimony. It was decided that the clear weight of the evidence supported the Negro organizations' claim that there had been laches. The white orders had waited for years before objecting to the Negro organizations and had done other acts inconsistent with their theory. Therefore it was said that the state courts had decided erroneously. In both instances the appellate jurisdiction of the Federal Supreme Court was evidently based on the fact that the defendants were incorporated in the District of Columbia under a federal statute. Thus it was decided that a question concerning a federal right was involved. The court declared that it had a right to consider the point as to whether the federal right had been denied in substance and effect by interposing a non-federal ground of decision having no fair support.

There has been much sentiment among some of the Negroes of the northern states for a more militant campaign in favor

[269] Supreme Lodge, Loyal Order of Moose v. Independent, Benevolent & Protective Order of Moose, 98 N. J. Eq. 598, 131 Atl. 219 (1925).

[270] Benevolent Order of Elks v. Improved Benevolent Order of Elks, 122 Tenn. 141, 118 S. W. 389 (1909).

[271] Burrell v. Michaux, 273 S. W. 874 (Tex. Civ. App. 1925) *aff'd* 286 S. W. 176 (Tex. Com. App. 1926).

[272] Benevolent & Protective Order of Elks v. Improved Benevolent & Protective Order of Elks, 205 N. Y. 459, 98 N. E. 756 (1912).

[273] Creswell v. Grand Lodge, Knights of Pythias, 225 U. S. 246, 32 Sup. Ct. 822 (1912); Ancient Egyptian Arabic Order v. Michaux, 279 U. S. 737, 49 Sup. Ct. 485 (1929).

of equal rights in places of public accommodation and amusement. One of the results of this movement has been the enactment of the Illinois and Pennsylvania Civil Rights Acts of 1935. There have been efforts to put sharper teeth in the acts of other states as well. That this is no new movement is shown when one considers a Pennsylvania case which was decided as far back as 1893. In this instance there was a devise by a Negro testator to trustees for the promotion, aid, and protection of the colored citizens of the United States in the enjoyment of their civil rights. The trustees were directed to form a corporation for this purpose and were given authority to employ all legal and moral means to prevent discrimination against the Negro and to render financial aid to persons or organizations with that purpose in view. In case the trust could not be substantially executed, the property was to be conveyed to those persons who would have inherited it had the devisor died intestate. This instrument was held to have established a valid charitable trust.[274] There is no reason why this and other charitable trusts in favor of the Negro[275] should not be given the approval of the courts.

In this connection it is proper to notice a recent New Jersey statute.[276] This act makes it a misdemeanor for anyone to publish, circulate, or disseminate propaganda designed to promote race or religious hatred.

---

[274] Lewis' Estate, 152 Pa. St. 477, 25 Atl. 878 (1893).

[275] *See* Jackson v. Phillips, 96 Mass. 539 (1867); Godfrey v. Hutchins, 28 R. I. 517, 68 Atl. 317 (1907). Cf. American Colonization Society v. Soulsby, 129 Md. 605, 99 Atl. 944 (1917). In the Jackson case the cy-pres doctrine was applied.

[276] N. J. Laws 1935, c. 151.

IV

EDUCATION

The problems arising from the legal aspects of Negro education are many and varied. In the first place one must face the fact that the Negro has migrated into the northern, middle western, and even the western states in great numbers and has become a considerable portion of the population in quite a few of them. This has produced friction between the races in these jurisdictions and has made the school problem national instead of sectional in scope. There has been a considerable group of persons in these states which has opposed the instruction of the children of the white and colored races in the same school. Most of the states east of the Mississippi River and north of the Mason and Dixon Line have enacted legislation which sought to prevent any effort at a policy which might be construed as an attempt to discriminate against or discredit the Negro in any manner whatsoever, and this is true of a number of the western states as well. These laws tell their own story of the necessity for some attempt at curbing race prejudice in the public schools.

In the South where segregation is mandatory, the problems which arise are chiefly those dealing with equality or inequality of educational facilities. The question of equal housing and teaching force, and the problem growing out of the inequality of the legislative appropriations for the white and colored schools seem to have received little or no attention in the southern courts. However, there has been much judicial expression on the constitutional guarantee of equality in general, and this has also been the case with taxation in a few particular jurisdictions. Some states have very elaborate statutory provisions, while others barely mention the separation, with all sorts of variations between these two extremes.

Furthermore, the policy of racial segregation in the public schools is not confined to the South, for a number of jurisdictions in other sections of the country have adopted a somewhat similar scheme. Particularly is this true of the states of the

Southwest which have been populated to a great extent by immigrants from Texas and the states of the Old South. In Alabama,[1] Arkansas,[2] Delaware,[3] Florida,[4] Georgia,[5] Kentucky,[6] Louisiana,[7] Mississippi,[8] Missouri,[9] North Carolina,[10] Oklahoma,[11] South Carolina,[12] Tennessee,[13] Texas,[14] Virginia,[15] West Virginia,[16] and the District of Columbia[17] all public schools must be separate and pupils of the white and Negro races are not permitted to attend the same school.

In Arizona the legislature has authorized two distinct methods of segregation of the Negro pupils in the grammar grades or primary schools,[18] and it has been decided that either method may be followed and that one does not exclude the other.[19] The state court has also decided that the segregation is mandatory.[20] Boards of school trustees may also segregate the Negroes in any high school provided there be twenty-five or more of the race within the district; but this is only permitted after a majority of the voters have signified their assent at an election called upon the petition of 15 per cent of the school electors.[21]

---

[1] ALA. CONST. §256; ALA. SCHOOL CODE (1927) §§124, 207.

[2] ARK. DIG. STAT. (Crawford & Moses, 1921) §8915; ARK. DIG. STAT. (Castle, Supp. 1931) §8747s3.

[3] DEL. CONST. Art. X, §2; DEL. REV. CODE (1915) §2296; Del. Laws 1921, c. 160, art. 3, §§23, 34. See also Del. Laws 1929, c. 222.

[4] FLA. CONST. Art. XII, §12.

[5] GA. CONST. Art. VIII, §1, ss. 4, ¶1; GA. CODE ANN. (Michie, 1926) §§1551 (8), 1551 (89), 1551 (118).

[6] KY. CONST. §187; KY. STAT. ANN. (Carroll, Supp. 1934) §4399-43. This statute superseded the following repealed acts: KY. STAT. ANN. (Carroll, 1930) §2978a-31 (cities of first class), §3235a-34 (cities of second class), §3470 (cities of third class), §3587a-18 (cities of fourth class). These statutes were repealed by Ky. Laws 1934, c. 65.

[7] LA. CONST. Art. XII, §1.

[8] MISS. CONST. §207; MISS. CODE ANN. (1930) §6586.

[9] MO. CONST. Art. XI, §3; MO. REV. STAT. (1929) §9216.

[10] N. C. CONST. Art. IX, §2; N. C. CODE ANN. (Michie, 1931) §5384.

[11] OKLA. CONST. Art. I, §5, Art. XIII, §3; OKLA. COMP. STAT. (1921) §§10,567, 10,574.

[12] S. C. CONST. Art. XI, §7; S. C. CODE (1932) §5406.

[13] TENN. CONST. Art. XI, §12; TENN. CODE (Will. Shan. & Harsh, 1932) §2377, (Supp. 1932) §2393-9 (high schools).

[14] TEX. CONST. Art. VII, §7; TEX. ANN. REV. CIV. STAT. (Vernon, 1925) arts. 2719, 2900.

[15] VA. CONST. §140; VA. CODE ANN. (Michie, 1930) §680.

[16] W. VA. CONST. Art. XII, §8; W. VA. CODE (1931) c. 18, art. 5, §14 (as amended in Michie, Supp. 1933).

[17] D. C. CODE (Supp. 1933) tit. 7, §§249, 252.

[18] ARIZ. REV. CODE ANN. (Struckmeyer, 1928) §1011 (2), 1025.

[19] Burnside v. Douglas School Dist., 33 Ariz. 1, 261 Pac. 629 (1927).

[20] Harrison v. Riddle, 44 Ariz. 331, 36 P. (2d) 984 (1934).

[21] ARIZ. REV. CODE ANN. (Struckmeyer, 1928) §1085.

In Kansas the several boards of education in cities of the first class are given authority by statute to establish and maintain separate primary schools for Negro children, and this permission is extended to include the high schools in Kansas City.[22] This power to separate the races in such cities has been given the approval of the state court,[23] and so has a regulation adopted by the Kansas City board to the effect that all white pupils should attend a high school in the morning and all colored pupils, in the afternoon.[24] However, authority is not given to establish separate high schools in cities of the first class except in Kansas City, and the ninth grade is a high school grade, whether in junior or senior high school, to which a colored child is entitled to be accepted as a pupil.[25] Wichita, although a city of the first class, was held to be governed in this respect by a special act, one clause of which provided that no discrimination should be made because of race or color, a provision which was held to negative any authority the municipality might have to establish separate schools under the general law.[26] Of course second-class cities cannot derive power from the above statute to establish separate schools.[27]

In Maryland the law declares it to be the duty of the county board of education to establish one or more separate schools for Negroes in the county provided that the colored population of any such district shall, in the board's judgment, warrant such an establishment of colored educational facilities.[28] The control of these units is given to a district board of school trustees appointed by the county board.[29]

---

[22] KAN. REV. STAT. (1923) §72-1724.

[23] Reynolds v. Topeka Bd. of Education, 66 Kan. 672, 72 Pac. 274 (1903); Williams v. Parsons Bd. of Education, 79 Kan. 202, 99 Pac. 216 (1908); Wright v. Topeka Bd. of Education, 129 Kan. 852, 284 Pac. 363 (1929); Foster v. Topeka Bd. of Education, 131 Kan. 160, 289 Pac. 959 (1930).

[24] Richardson v. Bd. of Education, 72 Kan. 629, 84 Pac. 538 (1906).

[25] Thurman-Watts v. Bd. of Education of Coffeyville, 115 Kan. 328, 222 Pac. 123 (1924).

[26] Rowles v. Wichita, 76 Kan. 361, 91 Pac. 88 (1907).

[27] Ottawa Bd. of Education v. Tinnon, 26 Kan. 1 (1881); Knox v. Bd. of Education, 45 Kan. 152, 25 Pac. 616 (1891); Cartwright v. Bd. of Education, 73 Kan. 32, 84 Pac. 382 (1906); Woolridge v. Bd. of Education, 98 Kan. 397, 157 Pac. 1184 (1916).

[28] MD. CODE ANN. (1924) art. 77, §200, as amended by Md. Laws 1937, c. 552.

[29] MD. CODE ANN. (1924) art. 77, §201.

Indiana,[30] New Mexico,[31] New York,[32] and Wyoming[33] allow the establishment of separate schools for Negroes if the authorities believe that such separation is necessary or proper. The law of Wyoming provides that this shall be done only when there are fifteen or more colored children in the particular district desiring such segregation. The Indiana act provides that any colored student is entitled to enter the regular public schools if a separate school is not provided, or even if such a school is provided, if the particular pupil in question is entitled to enter a grade which is of higher rank than any grade provided by the separate school. This latter clause would contain within its spirit at least any grade which was not taught in such school. The Indiana act has also been held to include high schools.[34] New Mexico authorizes separate schools for Negroes wherever the local governing bodies approve and the consent of the State Board of Education is obtained, but the facilities offered in these schools must be equal to those in the white schools.[35] In New York the trustees of any union school district or any district organized under a special act may establish separate schools provided that the facilities are equal and that the inhabitants of such district shall so determine at any annual meeting or a meeting called for that particular purpose.[36] The act also provides that teachers employed in the Negro schools must be legally qualified.[37] This act is not rendered invalid by the state constitutional provision guaranteeing a system of free common schools where all children may be educated,[38] by the state Civil Rights Act,[39] or by the since invalidated federal civil

---

[30] IND. STAT. ANN. (Burns, 1933) §28-5104.

[31] N. M. STAT. ANN. (Courtright, 1929) c. 120, §1201.

[32] N. Y. CONSOL. LAWS (Cahill, 1930) c. 41, §921.

[33] WYO. REV. STAT. ANN. (Courtright, 1931) c. 99, §332.

[34] Greathouse v. Bd. of School Comm'rs of Indianapolis, 198 Ind. 95, 151 N. E. 411 (1926).

[35] N. M. STAT. ANN. (Courtright, 1929) c. 120, §1201.

[36] N. Y. CONSOL. LAWS (Cahill, 1930) c. 41, §921.

[37] *Id.* at §922.

[38] People *ex rel.* Cisco v. School Bd. of Queens, 161 N. Y. 598, 56 N. E. 81 (1900), *aff'g* 44 App. Div. 469, 61 N. Y. Supp. 330 (Sup. Ct. 1899). N. Y. constitutional provision construed, Art. IX, §1. *See also* Chrisman v. Mayor of Brookhaven, 70 Miss. 477, 12 So. 458 (1892), where a very similar provision was held not to prevent the establishment of a separate school for whites outside of the state-supported system.

[39] People *ex rel.* King v. Gallagher, 93 N. Y. 438 (1883), *aff'g* 11 Abb. New Cas. 187 (1882).

rights legislation.[40] The separation is authorized in spite of another statutory provision declaring that no person shall be refused admission into the public schools on account of race or color.[41] At one time the Oklahoma law was optional also.[42]

Separation of the races was once possible in Massachusetts,[43] but the legislature abolished the practice before the Civil War.[44] An early Nevada act stipulated that Negroes, Mongolians, and Indians were not permitted to attend the public schools in that state.[45] It provided for their education in separate units if the authorities so desired, these schools to be supported out of the public school fund. This act was ruled unconstitutional in so far as it excluded Negroes from the public schools, but the court also let it be known that this proposition did not interfere with the right of the school trustees to establish separate schools.[46] However, separate schools are no longer authorized in Nevada. An ante-bellum Pennsylvania statute permitted the school directors to establish separate schools for colored children if such a school could be located in a place where it would provide accommodations for twenty or more colored pupils.[47] This act was held not to permit the Wilkes-Barre city authorities to unite two districts, each of which had less than the required number of colored children, and build a combined school for Negroes.[48] Opposition soon developed against the dual system, and the statute was repealed in 1881.[49] Separate schools were also legalized in Ohio for quite a while,[50] but the statute authorizing their establishment

[40] Dallas v. Fosdick, 40 How. Prac. 249 (N. Y. 1869).

[41] N. Y. Consol. Laws (Cahill, 1930) c. 41, §920.

[42] *See* Marion v. Territory, 1 Okla. 210, 32 Pac. 116 (1893).

[43] Roberts v. City of Boston, 59 Mass. 198 (1849).

[44] Mass. Acts & Resolves 1854-55, pp. 674-75.

[45] Nev. Laws 1864-65, p. 426.

[46] State *ex rel.* Stoutmeyer v. Duffy, 7 Nev. 342 (1872).

[47] Pa. Laws 1854, No. 610, §24.

[48] Commonwealth v. Williamson, 30 Leg. Int. 406 (1873).

[49] Pa. Laws 1881, p. 76.

[50] *See* State *ex rel.* School Directors v. City of Cincinnati, 19 Ohio Rep. 178 (1850); Van Camp v. Bd. of Education, 9 Ohio St. 406 (1859); State *ex rel.* Garnes v. McCann, 21 Ohio St. 198 (1871); United States v. Buntin, 10 Fed. 730 (C. C. S. D. Ohio 1882). *See also* Chalmers v. Stewart, 11 Ohio Rep. 386 (1842), where a subscriber to the common school fund was said to be released from his obligation if colored children should be admitted to the school. In Stewart v. Southard, 17 Ohio Rep. 402 (1848), decided before the Negro had any right to equal educational advantages, it was said that school directors

was repealed in 1887.[51] California for a short time after the Civil War provided separate colored schools,[52] but the authorization was soon removed.[53] Other states which once had separate schools for colored children and which now have abandoned the policy are Illinois,[54] Iowa,[55] Montana,[56] and New Jersey.[57]

The authorization to establish separate schools need not be state-wide, as one city alone may be granted such power.[58] Where this has been done, however, other cities and towns in the jurisdiction are not permitted to establish a similar system.[59]

The Negro race is not the only one for which separate schools are provided. In the eighties a child of Chinese parentage was refused admittance to a school in California, and it was held that the teacher could not justify his action on the ground that the board of education had authorized it.[60] As a result of this decision the state legislature immediately gave the authorities the right to establish separate schools for Mongolian children.[61] Fifteen years before this action the legislature had enacted a statute authorizing separate schools for Negro and Indian children.[62] Thus we see that the Mongolians had in a very short time replaced the Negroes as the unpopular race in California. The separate school for Mongolian children continued on into the twentieth century[63] and is still authorized at the present

could not be held responsible for an error in allowing colored children to enter a school. The white plaintiff had removed his children from the school in protest. It could not be shown that the directors had acted with corrupt motives. The court declared that the action of the directors was probably an error.

[51] Ohio Laws 1887, p. 34.

[52] Cal. Laws 1869-70, pp. 838-839; Ward v. Flood, 48 Cal. 36 (1874).

[53] Cal. Laws 1880, p. 47; Wysinger v. Crookshank, 82 Cal. 588, 23 Pac. 54 (1890).

[54] BOND, THE EDUCATION OF THE NEGRO IN THE AMERICAN SOCIAL ORDER (1934) 382; STEPHENSON, RACE DISTINCTIONS IN AMERICAN LAW (1910) 189.

[55] Iowa Laws 1858, c. 52, §30, ss. 4.

[56] Mont. Ter. Laws 1872, p. 627.

[57] STEPHENSON, RACE DISTINCTIONS IN AMERICAN LAW (1910) 189.

[58] See KAN. REV. STAT. (1923) §72-1724; Dallas v. Fosdick, 40 How. Prac. 249 (N. Y. 1869).

[59] Thurman-Watts v. Bd. of Education of Coffeyville, 115 Kan. 328, 222 Pac. 123 (1924).

[60] Tape v. Hurley, 66 Cal. 473, 6 Pac. 129 (1885).

[61] Cal. Laws 1885, p. 100; Wysinger v. Crookshank, 82 Cal. 588, 23 Pac. 54 (1890).

[62] Cal. Laws 1869-70, p. 839. Afterwards CAL. POL. CODE (Haymond & Burch, 1874) §1669.

[63] See STEPHENSON, RACE DISTINCTIONS IN AMERICAN LAW (1910) 159-163; Baldwin, *The Japanese Question* (1907) 7 COL. L. REV. 85; Mahon, *The Japa-*

time.[64] This same act includes authority to establish separate schools for Indian children. Furthermore, the school boards are empowered to receive financial aid from the federal government under contracts therewith to help educate the Indians.[65] However, where there is no separate school provided for Indian children by the local school authorities and the only school which the Indian child in question could attend is one under federal control, the child is entitled to enter the regular school of the district and may enforce this right by means of a writ of mandamus.[66]

North Carolina authorizes[67] separate educational facilities for the "Cherokee Indians of Robeson County" and the "Indians of Person County," formerly known as "Croatans" and "Cubans," the groups which are traditionally supposed to be descended from Sir Walter Raleigh's Lost Colony which disappeared from Roanoke Island. The act specifically denies the privileges of such schools to all persons of Negro blood to the fourth generation inclusive. The state court has given its approval to this statute, at the same time deciding that one whose ancestor within the prohibited degree had been a slave was presumed to be a Negro until proved otherwise and was therefore not entitled to admission to the Indian school.[68]

In North Dakota the legislature recently declared that it did not "believe it would be expedient to have the Indian children mingle with the white children in our educational institutions by reason of the vastly different temperament and mode of living and other differences and difficulties of the two races." [69] South Dakota has enacted legislation forcing Indian parents or those *in loco parentis* to send all their eligible children to

---

nese Question (1914) 48 Am. L. Rev. 698. *See also* Cal. Pol. Code (Deering, 1923) §1662.

[64] Cal. Gen. Laws (Deering, 1931) Vol. III, Act 7519, §3.3, 3.4.

[65] *Id.* at §3.10.

[66] Piper v. Big Pine School Dist., 193 Cal. 664, 226 Pac. 926 (1924).

[67] N. C. Code Ann. (*Michie, 1931*) §*5445*. See also §*6258 ss.* 1. These schools are not only for those Croatans who resided in the district when the law was enacted in 1885 but also for those who had since then become residents in good faith from adjacent territory. Goins v. Trustees, 169 N. C. 736, 86 S. E. 629 (1915). Two Indian normal schools are also established in this state. N. C. Code Ann. (Michie, 1931) §§5775b, 5843-49.

[68] McMillan v. School Committee, 107 N. C. 609, 12 S. E. 330 (1890).

[69] N. D. Laws 1933, p. 438.

schools operated by the federal government where food and clothing are furnished,[70] and has also passed a statute giving financial aid to school districts containing Indian lands.[71] In Alaska separate schools for Indian children may be maintained.[72] During the Civil War the Rhode Island Court held that members of Indian tribes were not entitled to send their children to the public schools, the state having provided a school especially for them.[73] A local act requiring certain Indian children to attend school in Jackson and Swain counties in North Carolina was declared not to be invalid because of racial discrimination.[74] Statutory authority to establish separate Indian schools is also given in Mississippi.[75]

In Mississippi trouble arose over the assigning of certain Chinese pupils to colored schools. This action of the school authorities was upheld by the state court, the reasoning being that all persons who are not "white" are "colored" and that a Chinaman is not white.[76] The Federal Supreme Court upheld this view, declaring that a state is not required to establish separate schools for all races just because it has done so in the case of a particular race.[77] The courts have also given their approval of the practice invoked by certain schools in Texas of teaching the Mexican children in separate schools in the elementary grades because they have their own peculiarities and customs and are not familiar with the English language.[78] These

[70] S. D. Laws 1931, c. 138, §§290-293. [71] S. D. Laws 1933, c. 12.

[72] Sing v. Sitka School Bd., 7 Alaska 616 (1927). Indians who were semi-civilized were not admitted to public schools in 1908. Davis v. Sitka School Bd., 3 Alaska 481 (1908). But the act establishing the University of Alaska contains a provision outlawing discrimination because of color. Alaska Laws 1935, c. 49, §24.

[73] Ammons v. Charlestown School Dist., 7 R. I. 596 (1863).

[74] State v. Wolf, 145 N. C. 440, 59 S. E. 40 (1907).

[75] Miss. Code Ann. (1930) §§6789-90.

[76] Rice v. Gong Lum, 139 Miss. 760, 104 So. 105 (1925); Bond v. Tij Fung, 148 Miss. 462, 114 So. 332 (1927).

[77] Gong Lum v. Rice, 275 U. S. 78, 48 Sup. Ct. 91 (1927). The case has received much attention in the law journals: (1928) 8 B. U. L. Rev. 132, (1928) 16 Calif. L. Rev. 346, (1928) 32 L. Notes 147, (1929) 2 Miss. L. J. 258, (1928) 2 St. John's L. Rev. 215, (1928) 13 St. Louis L. Rev. 156, (1928) 37 Yale L. J. 518. Two widely divergent views on the policy of race segregation are presented in the notes from the California and St. John's Law Reviews on one side and the note from Law Notes on the other.

[78] School Dist. v. Salvatierra, 33 S. W. (2d) 790 (Tex. Civ. App. 1930), *app. dismissed*, 284 U. S. 580, 52 Sup. Ct. 28 (1931).

statutes and decisions definitely show that there will be a movement or tendency to segregate any racial group which has customs differing widely from those of the dominant racial group in any given community, as witness the segregation of the people called Moors in the Delaware schools.[79]

In South Carolina at one time schools were established for mulattoes which were independent of both the white and Negro schools, thus creating a third class of separate educational units in certain portions of that state.[80] This was a convenient way of handling the problem growing out of the fact that the state constitution[81] permitted the intermarriage of persons wholly white and those with less than one-eighth Negro blood, thus inferentially classifying the latter group as white persons. This was done under the authority of a statute giving the school trustees authority to suspend or dismiss a pupil when the best interests of the school made such action necessary.

The general rule, however, is that separate schools for any race cannot be established without express constitutional or statutory authority.[82] Although Illinois is one of the states which has consistently upheld this view, the Court of Appeals of that state in one instance set its approval upon the action of certain school authorities in an urban district in sending all the white pupils in the district to other schools.[83] The board claimed that these pupils had a right to go elsewhere if they were permitted to do so by the governing body. The prosecution had produced some evidence that this action was forcing an overcrowded situation in the schools to which these white pupils

---

[79] Del. Laws 1921, c. 160, art. 3, §34. See also Del. Laws 1935, c. 189 (Moors or Indians).

[80] Tucker v. Blease, 97 S. C. 303, 81 S. E. 668 (1914).

[81] Art. III, §33.

[82] Wysinger v. Crookshank, 82 Cal. 588, 23 Pac. 54 (1890); People *ex rel.* Longress v. Bd. of Education of Quincy, 101 Ill. 308 (1882); People *ex rel.* Peair v. Bd. of Education of Upper Alton, 127 Ill. 613, 21 N. E. 187 (1889); People *ex rel.* Bibb v. Mayor of Alton, 193 Ill. 309, 61 N. E. 1077 (1901); Clark v. Bd. of Directors, 24 Iowa 266 (1868); Smith v. Directors of the Ind. School Dist. of Keokuk, 40 Iowa 518 (1875); Dove v. Independent School Dist. of Keokuk, 41 Iowa 689 (1875); Knox v. Bd. of Education, 45 Kan. 152, 25 Pac. 616 (1891); Bd. of Education v. State, 45 Ohio St. 555, 16 N. E. 373 (1888); Dayton Bd. of Education v. State *ex rel.* Reese, 114 Ohio St. 188, 151 N. E. 39 (1926); Crawford v. Dist. School Bd., 68 Ore. 388, 137 Pac. 217 (1913) (Indians); Kaine v. Commonwealth, 101 Pa. St. 490 (1882).

[83] People v. McFall, 26 Ill. App. 319 (1886).

had been transferred, and had thereby compelled at least some of the Negro children in these outside districts to attend the school in the said district which was attended only by Negroes and taught exclusively by Negro instructors. The court gave as its reasons for upholding the authorities the fact that all of the colored pupils in the outside schools were not forced out by this action and that there must be some discretion vested in the board of education to move the children around as it might see fit. It declared that the evidence produced proved neither that there was discrimination against the Negro nor that the object of the shifting of pupils was the establishment of a separate school for Negroes. In this instance it seems that the court was trying to escape the effect of the doctrine forbidding discrimination or segregation and hit upon this evidential scheme of carrying out its purpose, knowing full well that local public opinion was behind it in so deciding. There are many instances of this extralegal segregation in northern communities to which the Negroes have migrated in large numbers.[84]

In an earlier Illinois case, decided before the establishment of the doctrine by the courts of that state, it was held that a taxpayer had a right to interfere in order to prevent public funds from being used to maintain a separate school for three or four colored children, the number being too few for practical separation.[85]

Separate school laws have been held not to violate the provisions of the Fourteenth Amendment.[86] In states where separation is constitutionally provided for, laws which are silent on the subject of just what schools they are meant to include are not rendered invalid because of the possibility of discrimination

[84] BOND, THE EDUCATION OF THE NEGRO IN THE AMERICAN SOCIAL ORDER (1934) c. 18.

[85] Chase v. Stephenson, 71 Ill. 383 (1874). The doctrine is discussed but not decided upon in this case.

[86] Gong Lum v. Rice, 275 U. S. 78, 48 Sup. Ct. 91 (1927); United States v. Buntin, 10 Fed. 730 (C. C. S. D. Ohio 1882); Wong Him v. Callahan, 119 Fed. 381 (C. C. N. D. Cal. 1902); Dameron v. Bayless, 14 Ariz. 180, 126 Pac. 273 (1912); Cory v. Carter, 48 Ind. 327 (1874); People *ex rel.* King v. Gallagher, 93 N. Y. 438 (1883); State *ex rel.* Garnes v. McCann, 21 Ohio St. 198 (1871); Greenwood v. Rickman, 145 Tenn. 361, 235 S. W. 425 (1921); Martin v. Bd. of Education, 42 W. Va. 514, 26 S. E. 348 (1896). The validity of such laws had been upheld before the adoption of the amendment. Lewis v. Henley, 2 Ind. 332 (1850); State *ex rel.* School Directors v. City of Cincinnati, 19 Ohio Rep. 178 (1850).

against the Negro by those persons responsible for the fair administration of such laws.[87] Neither will an act be declared unconstitutional because one of its provisions mentions the white race and not the colored in such a way as to invalidate the provision if considered alone, when non-discriminatory as regards the entire act.[88] The same is true with respect to the remaining portions of an act where one of its clauses contains language which is patently discriminatory, provided, of course, that the statute or its purpose is not materially altered or affected by the deletion of the invalid portion.[89] However, where specific provisions for the establishment of schools baldly state that they are for whites and such is the only interpretation that is possible, they are considered void and of no effect.[90] Moreover, a statute which by implication excludes Negro children from any share in the common school fund has been held to be in conflict with the Fourteenth Amendment and therefore invalid.[91] Of course the amendment had put an end to all statutory provisions expressly limiting the use of the school funds to white children alone.[92]

Whether the separation is required by constitution or statute or is optional, equal facilities must be provided for each race.[93] In fact impartial treatment is expressly guaranteed in a number of the states.[94] Whenever this requirement has not been

[87] Prowse v. Bd. of Education, 134 Ky 365, 120 S. W. 307 (1909); Lowery v. School Trustees, 140 N. C. 33, 52 S. E. 267 (1905); Smith v. School Trustees, 141 N. C. 143, 53 S. E. 524 (1906); Whitford v. Bd. of Commissioners, 159 N. C. 160, 74 S. E. 1014 (1912); Powell v. Hargrove, 136 S. C. 345, 134 S. E. 380 (1926). The same is true with regard to an order or notice for a bond issue for school purposes. Fall v. Read, 194 Ky. 135, 238 S. W. 177 (1922); Story v. Bd. of Comm'rs, 184 N. C. 336, 114 S. E. 493 (1922).

[88] Bonitz v. Bd. of Trustees of Ahoskie School, 154 N. C. 375, 70 S. E. 735 (1911).

[89] Lowery v. School Trustees, 140 N. C. 33, 52 S. E. 267 (1905).

[90] McFarland v. Goins, 96 Miss. 67, 50 So. 493 (1909); Williams v. Bradford, 158 N. C. 36, 73 S. E. 154 (1911).

[91] Dawson v. Lee, 83 Ky. 49 (1885).

[92] *See* State Bd. of Education v. Bd. of Public Education, 186 Ga. 783, 199 S. E. 641 (1938).

[93] Bertonneau v. Bd. of School Directors, 3 Fed. Cas. No. 1361 (C. C. D. La. 1878); United States v. Buntin, 10 Fed. 730 (C. C. S. D. Ohio 1882); Daviess County Bd. of Education v. Johnson, 179 Ky. 34, 200 S. W. 313 (1918); People *ex rel.* King v. Gallagher, 11 Abb. N. C. 187 (N. Y. 1882), *aff'd* 93 N. Y. 438 (1883).

[94] Ariz. Rev. Code Ann. (Struckmeyer, 1928) §1085 (high schools); Del. Const. Art. X, §2; Fla. Const. Art. XII, §12; Ga. Code Ann. (Michie, 1926) §1551 (89); Ind. Stat. Ann. (Burns, 1933) §28-5104; Ky. Const. §187 (im-

mentioned in either constitution or statute, the Arkansas Court has said that it is implied.[95] In the same case it is said that the maintenance of equal facilities for both races may be enforced by a writ of mandamus directed against the school authorities with the object of compelling them to provide therefor. Discrimination against the Negro must be clearly shown in order to upset any action by the school officials who are entrusted with the duty of carrying out the law in this respect.[96] The same is true when a complainant wishes to show an official distribution of the school fund which is unfair to the Negro. In such a situation it must be shown that the method of providing funds for the Negro schools is insufficient or discriminatory.[97] Such an unfair distribution must be averred[98] and proved[99] in order to establish a case of discrimination. One court has said it is unlawful to apportion the school funds with respect to the scholastic population and then limit the school terms for each race accordingly.[100] The requirement of equal facilities, however, does not mean that the accommodations provided for each race must be identical.[101] Thus the fact that one school has swimming facilities and another has not does not constitute

---

partial distribution of school fund and some of statutes above cited, *supra* note 6, guaranteed same benefits to both races); Mo. Rev. Stat. (1929) §§9217, 9346; N. M. Stat. Ann. (Courtright, 1929) c. 120, §1201; N. Y. Consol. Laws (Cahill, 1930) c. 41, §921; N. C. Const. Art. IX, §2, N. C. Code Ann. (Michie, 1931) §5384; Okla. Const. Art. XIII, §3, Okla. Comp. Stat. (1921) §10567; Tex. Const. Art. VII, §7, Tex. Ann. Rev. Civ. Stat. (Vernon, 1925) art. 2900; Va. Code (Michie, 1930) §680.

[95] Maddox v. Neal, 45 Ark. 121 (1885).

[96] *See* State *ex rel.* Mitchell v. Gray, 93 Ind. 303 (1883); State *ex rel.* Cheeks v. Wirt, 203 Ind. 121, 177 N. E. 441 (1931), (1932) 7 Ind. L. J. 395. In both cases evidence of unfairness was not deemed sufficient.

[97] Jones v. Bd. of Education, 90 Okla. 233, 217 Pac. 400 (1923). In this case the facts seemed to indicate that there was discrimination in providing accommodations, but relief was refused because funds already set aside for the use of the white schools could not be diverted into other channels, such as the schools for Negroes. See in this connection School Dist. v. Bd. of Comm'rs, 135 Okla. 1, 275 Pac. 292 (1928); Bd. of Comm'rs v. School Dist., 135 Okla. 248, 275 Pac. 302 (1928). It will not be presumed that an apportionment is discriminatory. Fall v. Read, 194 Ky. 135, 238 S. W. 177 (1922).

[98] Reid v. Mayor of Eatonton, 80 Ga. 755, 6 S. E. 602 (1888).

[99] Galloway v. Bd. of Education, 184 N. C. 245, 114 S. E. 165 (1922).

[100] Maddox v. Neal, 45 Ark. 121 (1885).

[101] Bertonneau v. Bd. of School Directors, 3 Fed. Cas. No. 1361 (C. C. D. La. 1878); Daviess County Bd. of Education v. Johnson, 179 Ky. 34, 200 S. W. 313 (1918); State *ex rel.* Gaines v. Canada, 342 Mo. 121, 113 S. W. (2d) 783 (1937); People *ex rel.* King v. Gallagher, 93 N. Y. 438 (1883).

discrimination where other physical educational opportunities are offered in the latter.[102] However, it has been said in one Kentucky case that the term "educational facilities" embraces all the expenses of education and not simply a furnished school building.[103]

The need for Negro schools which are more on a par with those for white children is strikingly presented in a recent case from Maryland. In this instance a community located near the city of Baltimore had no high school for its colored population. The number of Negro children of high school age was very small, and the practice in years past had been to send the ones who were qualified to the colored high schools in the city. The expense was borne by the local community. The city schools, however, would not permit such transfer pupils, whether white or colored, to enter their classes unless they passed a special examination which was given for the twofold purpose of testing their capabilities and of keeping down the number of transfers.

A Negro girl who had finished the course offered in the local colored elementary school took this examination and failed to make a passing grade. She then repeated the seventh grade in the local elementary school on the advice of the authorities. Again she took the examination and again she failed. The *State Manual of Standards* provides that any pupil possessing an elementary school certificate signifying completion of the course offered therein is entitled to enter a school of higher grade. The Negro thereupon brought a mandamus action to force her acceptance into the local white school of higher grade. The court declared that the procedure outlined in the *Manual* was not mandatory and that the custom of giving the examination had superseded it in this instance. Since the examination was given to whites and Negroes alike, it was decided that discrimination against persons of the colored race could not be sufficiently proved to warrant interference by the courts.[104] While this case is no doubt decided in accordance with sound principles of law, no one could possibly read the opinion without getting

---

[102] State *ex rel.* Cheeks v. Wirt, 203 Ind. 121, 177 N. E. 441 (1931).

[103] Woodford County Bd. of Education v. Bd. of Education, 264 Ky. 245, 94 S. W. (2d) 687 (1936), interpreting KY. STAT. ANN. (Carroll, Supp. 1934) §§4399-3, 4399-49, applying to fifth- and sixth-class cities.

[104] Williams v. Zimmerman, 172 Md. 563, 192 Atl. 353 (1937).

the impression that Maryland does not supply its Negro children with equal educational advantages. A Negro child who has successfully completed a seventh grade twice ought to be fully prepared to pass any reasonable examination for entrance into the eighth grade in any school in the state. Hence this is a clear indication of the inferiority of facilities in this particular Negro elementary school if not in others as well. The court also said that the Negro girl had chosen the wrong remedy.

The courts cannot enjoin the establishment of separate schools in an optional state because there is apprehension that there will be discrimination on the part of those who are entrusted with the duty of carrying out the law. Some act which is unfair to the Negro or at least the intention of committing some such act is necessary for the interference of a court of equity in such matters.[105] The courts are very hesitant about interfering in matters involving the administration of the schools, such as the competency of teachers and the overcrowding of particular units.[106] However, in the event that a clear case of discrimination can be shown, whether it be in an optional or compulsory jurisdiction, the courts must step in and invalidate unfair administrative action.[107] If the separate school law is optional, the school authorities cannot be forced to establish schools for colored pupils if the scheme is impracticable.[108] But when the law is compulsory an equality in facilities or at least a just administration of the law may be enforced by mandamus, that being the proper remedy rather than action by the same method to force the white schools to admit Negro pupils.[109]

The fact that a statute provides for an official known as a "visitor" for the schools of one race and not the schools of the other does not necessarily render the act invalid for that reason.[110] The effect of this statute was not to give the schools

---

[105] Greathouse v. Bd. of School Comm'rs, 198 Ind. 95, 151 N. E. 411 (1926).

[106] *See* State *ex rel.* Mitchell v. Gray, 93 Ind. 303 (1883).

[107] Williams v. Bd. of Education, 45 W. Va. 199, 31 S. E. 985 (1898).

[108] State *ex rel.* Oliver v. Grubb, 85 Ind. 213 (1882).

[109] Black v. Lenderman, 156 Ark. 476, 246 S. W. 876 (1923); Cory v. Carter, 48 Ind. 327 (1874) (Indiana separate school law compulsory before 1877, see Ind. Laws 1877, c. 81); Martin v. Bd. of Education, 42 W. Va. 514, 26 S. E. 348 (1896). *See also* State *ex rel.* Dellande v. School Bd., 33 La. Ann. 1469 (1881); Williams v. Zimmerman, 172 Md. 563, 192 Atl. 353 (1937).

[110] KY. STAT. ANN. (Carroll, 1930) No. 4434a-16, construed by Daviess County

for one race the benefit of another official in addition to a trustee, but to provide an officer who, with the exception of being a member of a certain division board, merely took the place of a trustee. Neither is an act unconstitutional which provides for only one board of education for the schools of both races.[111]

The schools must be made accessible to all colored children,[112] but the fact that they must go a greater distance in order to reach their school than the white children who are similarly situated is immaterial[113] if the mileage is not unreasonable.[114] That the colored children must cross railway tracks in order to reach their school, a danger which they would not be forced to run were they admitted elsewhere, cannot be urged as racial discrimination, since the danger of crossing railway tracks is no more to be feared than the danger of the ordinary street crossing under modern conditions.[115] However, where the railroad tracks were so situated as to imperil the lives of colored children on going to and from school, a different result was reached.[116] Indiana has recently noticed this problem and has enacted a statute[117] providing that if any colored child in a city of the first class which has separate schools is, for the reason that such schools have been established, forced to travel a distance one-half mile greater than the distance between his home and the nearest white school, he shall be provided with suitable transportation facilities at the public expense. Missouri has provided transportation facilities for those colored children who, because of the fact that there are only a few in the district, are denied a local separate school.[118] The statute provides for their transfer to another colored school in some adjoining district. There is also a provision in the Missouri statute concerning colored consolidated high schools which states that they must be conveniently located at a spot where

Bd. of Education v. Johnson, 179 Ky. 34, 200 S. W. 313 (1918). Statute repealed by Ky. Laws 1934, c. 65.

[111] Prowse v. Bd. of Education, 134 Ky. 365, 120 S. W. 307 (1909).

[112] United States v. Buntin, 10 Fed. 730 (C. C. S. D. Ohio 1882).

[113] Dameron v. Bayless, 14 Ariz. 180, 126 Pac. 273 (1912).

[114] Roberts v. City of Boston, 59 Mass. 198 (1849); People *ex. rel.* Dietz v. Easton, 13 Abb. Pr. (N.S.) 159 (N. Y. 1872); State v. Bd. of Education, 7 Ohio Dec. Reprints 129 (1876).

[115] Dameron v. Bayless, 14 Ariz. 180, 126 Pac. 273 (1912).

[116] Williams v. Parsons' Board of Education, 79 Kan. 202, 99 Pac. 216 (1908).

[117] Ind. Acts 1935, c. 296.

[118] Mo. Rev. Stat. (1929) §9217.

they will serve the most pupils from the standpoint of transportation.[119] The school authorities in Kentucky may provide transportation facilities for colored pupils attending consolidated schools out of the general funds,[120] and where a Negro parent has paid the cost of transportation because of failure of the authorities to provide therefor, he may recover only the amount paid after a demand upon the said authorities.[121] A recent South Carolina enactment requires school bus drivers to be of the same race as the children they transport.[122]

An enumeration of children according to color is provided for by the statutes of at least six states,[123] and Virginia,[124] along with Georgia,[125] which incidentally is one of the above six, has enacted race registration acts which undoubtedly would have the same effect. Proceedings may be instituted in Missouri and probably elsewhere to correct a mistaken enumeration,[126] or one which has been fraudulently made,[127] in order to force the authorities to take cognizance of the fact that the number of properly qualified Negro children in the district has become sufficient for the establishment of a separate colored school. The Missouri statute formerly required fifteen,[128] a figure which has now been reduced to eight.[129] There is a similar provision in West Virginia which requires ten Negro pupils, except where circumstances render it practicable to establish

---

[119] *Id.* at §9347.

[120] Bd. of Education v. Fultz, 241 Ky. 265, 43 S. W. (2d) 707 (1931), interpreting KY. STAT. ANN. (Carroll, 1930) §4426a-11. Statute repealed by Ky. Laws 1934, c. 65. Probably superseded in this respect by KY. STAT. ANN. (Carroll, Supp. 1934) §4399-20.

[121] Warren v. Bd. of Education, 258 Ky. 212, 79 S. W. (2d) 681 (1935).

[122] S. C. Acts 1935, No. 185.

[123] GA. CODE ANN. (Michie, 1926) §1551 (77); MISS. CODE ANN. (1930) §6746; MO. REV. STAT. (1929) §9212; OKLA. COMP. STAT. (1921) §10,577; TEX. ANN. REV. CIV. STAT. (Vernon, 1925) arts. 2817, 2819; W. VA. CODE (1931) c. 18, art. 5, §14 (as amended in Michie, Supp. 1933). Kentucky once had such a statute, KY. STAT. ANN. (Carroll, 1930) §4523, but this act was repealed by Ky. Laws 1934, p. 197.

[124] VA. CODE ANN. (Michie, 1930) §5099a.

[125] GA. CODE ANN. (Michie, Supp. 1928) §§2177 (1)-2177(20).

[126] State *ex rel.* Logan v. Shouse, 257 S. W. 827 (Mo. App. 1924).

[127] State *ex rel.* Morehead v. Cartwright, 122 Mo. App. 257, 99 S. W. 48 (1907).

[128] *See* Lehew v. Brummel, 103 Mo. 546, 15 S. W. 765 (1890); State *ex rel.* Morehead v. Cartwright, 122 Mo. App. 257, 99 S. W. 48 (1907); State *ex rel.* Logan v. Shouse, 257 S. W. 827 (Mo. App. 1924).

[129] MO. REV. STAT. (1929) §9217.

a separate school for a smaller number.[130] In Oklahoma ten is the minimum number deemed feasible by the legislature for the establishment of a separate school for either whites or Negroes,[131] and the Arkansas Court has reached a similar result in its interpretation of the law of that state.[132] Missouri,[133] Oklahoma,[134] and West Virginia[135] have provided by statute for those persons who are deprived of educational facilities because there are too few of their race in the district to permit the establishment of a separate school for them. The acts give them the right to attend the schools in an adjacent district at the expense of their own unit. The same principle has been upheld in a recent Arizona decision.[136] A local act authorizing such a transfer of pupils of one race was ruled discriminatory by the North Carolina Court,[137] but this probably would not be followed today. Such a decision would undoubtedly cause difficulties in many instances where such practices are necessary.

A threatened transfer of this kind was about to take place in a district in Arkansas where whites were in the minority and hence were the ones who were going to be transferred. A sufficient number of other white children came into and made their homes in the district to increase the school population of their race to a point where the school authorities of the district were in duty bound to maintain a separate unit for them. The children who were about to be moved were allowed to stay in their own district in spite of the pendency of the action to transfer them elsewhere.[138]

The Mississippi law provides for a discontinuance of any separate school where the average daily attendance over the period of a month is less than five pupils,[139] and it is reasonable to suppose that the children who have been attending such

---

[130] W. Va. Code (1931) c. 18, art. 5, §14 (as amended in Michie, Supp. 1933).

[131] Okla. Comp. Stat. (1921) §10,575.

[132] Wesley v. Baker, 153 Ark. 529, 241 S. W. 14 (1922).

[133] Mo. Rev. Stat. (1929) §9217. *See* Lehew v. Brummel, 103 Mo. 546, 15 S. W. 765 (1890); State *ex. rel.* Herman v. St. Louis County Ct., 311 Mo. 167, 277 S. W. 934 (1925).

[134] Okla. Comp. Stat. (1921) §10,576.

[135] W. Va. Code (1931) c. 18, art. 5, §14 (as amended in Michie, Supp. 1933). See also W. Va. Acts 1935, c. 50.

[136] Harrison v. Riddle, 44 Ariz. 331, 36 P. (2d) 984 (1934).

[137] Hooker v. Town of Greenville, 130 N. C. 472, 42 S. E. 141 (1902).

[138] Wesley v. Baker, 153 Ark. 529, 241 S. W. 14 (1922).

[139] Miss. Code Ann. (1930) §6586.

school will be transferred elsewhere if possible. A recent Indiana statute, enacted for the purpose of discontinuing public schools where the average daily attendance during the preceding year has been twelve or less, contains a proviso that it shall not be construed as authorizing the suspension of any separate school for Negroes where such was the only colored school in that particular school unit.[140] The Missouri law has been construed to allow the discontinuance of a colored school and the discharge of the teacher, although under contract for the full term, if the average attendance is less than eight pupils per month.[141]

In 1899 the Federal Supreme Court approved a decision by the Georgia Court upholding the action of a county board of education in abandoning a certain Negro high school while it contributed to the support of a high school for whites and also left in operation a similar high school for white girls.[142] The court was evidently of the opinion that it was far better for the interests of the community as a whole that the board should contribute all its available funds allocated to colored education to the support and maintenance of a colored common school. In this school were enrolled four hundred colored children while there were only fifty or sixty Negroes who were sufficiently advanced to enable them to enter high school. The fund was evidently not large enough to adequately support both types of colored schools and there was no evidence of bad faith. It was decided that the board had not acted unlawfully in refusing to divide the fund. However, according to principles announced in the recently decided *Gaines* case,[143] it is almost certain that the court would reverse its position if a case with similar facts should be presented today.

If territory is taken from one school district and added to a consolidated district and the school population of one race in the remaining portion of the former is thereby rendered insuf-

---

[140] Ind. Acts 1935, c. 77.

[141] Dehart v. School District, 214 Mo. App. 651, 263 S. W. 242 (1924).

[142] Cumming v. Bd. of Education, 175 U. S. 528, 20 Sup. Ct. 197 (1899), *aff'g* 103 Ga. 641, 29 S. E. 488 (1898). *See also* Blodgett v. Bd. of Education, 105 Ga. 463, 30 S. E. 561 (1898).

[143] State of Missouri *ex rel.* Gaines v. Canada, 305 U. S. 337, 59 Sup. Ct. 232 (1938). See *infra* note 256. For an adverse criticism of Cumming case see Note (1933) 82 U. OF PA. L. REV. 157, 162.

ficient for the maintenance of a school for that race, this portion must be added to some other district or such action will be illegal.[144]

In Delaware the county school commissioners have been given authority to alter, divide, unite, or consolidate the colored school districts whenever such action is deemed best for the pupils,[145] and Missouri has specifically provided for county consolidated high schools for Negroes to be conveniently located so as to serve the largest possible number of pupils.[146] The latter state also authorizes several school districts to maintain a joint elementary colored school.[147] The Mississippi law concerning the consolidation of schools has been held to be valid, as there is nothing in the statute which gives the several boards of education authority to establish consolidated schools for whites and not for Negroes.[148] The administration of this law may not be attacked by Negroes for unfairness where it does not affirmatively appear that there are enough colored pupils in the territory to justify the maintenance of such a school[149] or that equal facilities are not provided.[150] All the consolidation laws in the South would probably receive this same construction.

An effort on the part of school authorities to unite two districts for the purpose of obtaining enough colored children to satisfy the minimum requirements for the establishment of a separate school for Negroes under the old and now defunct Pennsylvania separate school law failed to win approval. The court declared that the statute permitting such procedure did not contemplate a situation where this was done on account of race.[151] Under the old compulsory separate school law in Indiana it was decided that the authorities might consolidate several districts into one provided that there was an insufficient number of Negro pupils in one or more of these districts to establish a separate school therefor.[152] The court also said that

[144] Myers v. Bd. of Superintendents, 156 Miss. 251, 125 So. 718 (1930) (race not stated).

[145] DEL. REV. CODE (1915) §2280.

[146] MO. REV. STAT. (1929) §§9346-49.

[147] *Id.* at §9217.

[148] Trustees v. Bd. of Supervisors, 115 Miss. 117, 75 So. 833 (1917); Barrett v. Cedar Hill Consol. School Dist., 123 Miss. 370, 85 So. 125 (1920).

[149] Trustees v. Bd. of Supervisors, 115 Miss. 117, 75 So. 833 (1917).

[150] Barrett v. Cedar Hill Consol. School Dist., 123 Miss. 370, 85 So. 125 (1920). No petition for such a colored school was ever presented in this instance.

[151] Commonwealth *ex. rel.* Brown v. Williamson, 30 Phila. Leg. Int. 406 (1873).

[152] Cory v. Carter, 48 Ind. 327 (1874).

if such a plan proved impracticable, educational facilities must be furnished to each individual who by the operation of the said law is deprived thereof, using such children's proportional part of the school fund to finance tutoring or any other method employed. However this may have been, the present optional Indiana law provides that when any Negro pupil in a district which has a separate school has reached a grade not taught in that school he shall be entitled to the advantages of the white school in the unit where such grade is provided.[153]

The Mississippi statute demands not only separate schools but also separate districts which shall be arranged in such a manner as to provide school facilities for the greatest possible number of pupils of both races,[154] and such was also the construction placed upon a now repealed Kentucky statute. In so interpreting the act the highest Kentucky tribunal held that the county board of education had authority to establish a colored common school within the boundaries of a white graded school district,[155] the establishment of school districts for both races being a function of the board.[156] In these two jurisdictions the districts have not been required to be coexistent.[157] In

[153] IND. STAT. ANN. (Burns, 1933) §28-5104.

[154] MISS. CODE ANN. (1930) §6586.

[155] Grady v. Larue County Bd. of Education, 149 Ky. 49, 147 S. W. 928 (1912), construing KY. STAT. ANN. (Carroll, 1930) §4426a-2. Statute repealed by Ky. Laws 1934, c. 65.

[156] Prowse v. Bd. of Education, 134 Ky. 365, 120 S. W. 307 (1909).

[157] Grady v. Larue County Bd. of Education, 149 Ky. 49, 147 S. W. 928 (1912); Shadrack v. Bd. of Trustees, 188 Ky. 345, 222 S. W. 78 (1920); Bryant v. Barnes, 106 So. 113 (Miss. 1925). The Shadrack case was decided under the act of 1920 pertaining to the maintenance of separate schools in cities of the fourth class giving such cities the privilege of establishing a separate system of education under the control of white and colored boards separately maintained, although not forcing it upon them in case they do not desire it. KY. STAT. ANN. (Carroll, 1930) §3587a-18. This statute had taken the place of the repealed §3588a under which it had been decided that a city of this class might change the management of its graded schools from a city system to a district system, separating the city schools into three white and three colored districts. Miller v. Feather, 176 Ky. 268, 195 S. W. 449 (1917). This change had not been permitted before the enactment of the last-mentioned statute according to the law as announced in Taylor v. Russell, 117 Ky. 539, 78 S. W. 411 (1904). Before the repeal of §§3588 and 3588a, cities of the fourth class had the option of maintaining separate schools in one district under one board of education or in separate districts under separate boards. Moss v. City of Mayfield, 186 Ky. 330, 216 S. W. 842 (1919). The trustees in charge of a white graded school district have also been held to have no obligation to provide schools for colored children, such being the duty of the county authorities.

North Carolina, the authorities have the option of establishing one district with one school committee governing its affairs or separate districts and school committees for each race.[158] The county board is authorized to consult the conveniences and necessities of both races in fixing the boundaries of the districts. In Arkansas the court was of the opinion that it was the duty of the authorities to so lay off the district that all pupils, whether white or colored, may have the privilege of attending school.[159] The state legislatures may commit the duty of establishing separate schools to any proper local body, such as the governing bodies of school districts, towns, or counties.[160]

In Oklahoma the districts are organized to include the schools of both races, the one with the majority of pupils being designated as the district school with its privilege of having the members of the district board named from the personnel of its own race, while the school of the minority race is termed the "separate" school.[161] This statute also contains a proviso giving the county superintendent of public instruction authority to designate which school or schools in each district shall be the separate school and which the district school and what class of pupils, white or colored, shall attend each. Under this proviso, which is certainly a "joker" if there ever was one, the county superintendent has the lawful authority to designate the white school as the district school,[162] even if the Negro children in the district outnumber the whites.[163] In other words, the court interpreted the statute to mean that the school having the fewest

---

Raley v. Bd. of Education, 224 Ky. 50, 5 S. W. (2d) 484 (1928); State Bd. of Education v. Brown, 232 Ky. 434, 23 S. W. (2d) 948 (1929). In the Raley case it was also said that since the repeal of §4468a-1 of the KY. STAT. ANN. (Carroll, 1922) by Ky. Acts 1922, c. 8, there was no existing law which would authorize the establishment of new white or colored graded schools in Kentucky, but those which had been established prior to the repeal were said to have a continuing existence.

[158] N. C. CODE ANN. (Michie, 1931) §5480. *See also* Storey v. Bd. of Comm'rs, 184 N. C. 336, 114 S. E. 493 (1922).

[159] County Court v. Robinson, 27 Ark. 116 (1871).

[160] Bd. of Education v. Bd. of County Comm'rs, 14 Okla. 322, 78 Pac. 455 (1904). See also dictum in Cotteral v. Barker, 34 Okla. 533, 126 Pac. 211 (1912), to the effect that the duty may be delegated to the district board.

[161] OKLA. COMP. STAT. (1921) §10,569.

[162] Jelsma v. Butler, 80 Okla. 46, 194 Pac. 436 (1920).

[163] Jumper v. Lyles 77 Okla. 57, 185 Pac. 1084 (1919); State *ex rel.* Gumm v. Albritton, 98 Okla. 158, 224 Pac. 511 (1923).

number of pupils would be the separate school unless the county superintendent ruled otherwise.[164] The constitutionality of this statute has been tested and upheld,[165] but of course if such juggling of schools resulted in an inequality of Negro school facilities when compared with the white, the action should be declared invalid.[166] Moreover, it has been held that this cannot be done where the circumstances show it to be a gross abuse of the discretion given the superintendent and that the result will be a great injustice to the Negro majority.[167]

The West Virginia statute expressly requires separate buildings for the schools of each race,[168] and the same would probably be inferred from the acts of all the other states having separate school facilities.[169] The policy behind the separation clearly demands that such must be the case. In Kentucky it has been decided that the local authorities have discretionary power to exchange the white and colored school buildings for the sake of the convenience of all concerned, the size and facilities of the two edifices being equal.[170] However, the Oklahoma Court refused to approve the action of a board of county commissioners in making such an exchange for the reason that the officers of the school district and not the commissioners have authority to direct which race shall use the various buildings.[171] It is easily inferable from the opinion that the exchange was unfair to the Negroes.

Sometimes the character of a neighborhood changes so that a school building which has been used for one race is no longer thought to be suitable for the children of that race. In such cases the local authorities are permitted a good deal of dis-

---

[164] Jumper v. Lyles, 77 Okla. 57, 185 Pac. 1084 (1919).

[165] State *ex rel.* Gumm v. Albritton, 98 Okla. 158, 224 Pac. 511 (1923); Muskogee School Dist. v. Hunnicutt, 51 Fed. (2d) 528 (E. D. Okla. 1931), *aff'd* 283 U. S. 810, 51 Sup. Ct. 653 (1931).

[166] State *ex rel.* Gumm v. Albritton, 98 Okla. 158, 224 Pac. 511 (1923) (dictum). Even if there were an inequality of facilities, a court of equity could not interfere because there is an adequate remedy at law in the form of a mandamus proceeding to compel an additional tax levy to support the Negro school. Muskogee School Dist. v. Hunnicutt, 51 Fed. (2d) 528 (E. D. Okla. 1931). [167] Moore v. Porterfield, 113 Okla. 234, 241 Pac. 346 (1925).

[168] W. VA. CODE (1931) c. 18, art. 5, §14, as amended by Michie, Supp. 1933.

[169] *See* County Ct. v. Robinson, 27 Ark. 116 (1871).

[170] Roberts v. Louisville School Bd., 16 Ky. Law Rep. 181, 26 S. W. 814 (1894).

[171] School Dist. v. Overholser, 17 Okla. 147, 87 Pac. 665 (1906).

cretion in the use of the building. In one case from North Carolina a schoolhouse which had formerly been used by whites was designated for the use of Negroes because of such a change in the racial aspects of the neighborhood. Certain white residents objected and sought an injunction, but the court held that the local authorities were justified in what they had done.[172] In a Kansas case it was said that the fact that the white school building was a more imposing edifice than the one allotted to Negroes does not necessarily render the facilities unfair.[173] The court said that an identity of accommodations is not required. However, the housing facilities should not be so unequal as to be discriminatory. It has been held that a court may issue an injunction to prevent school district authorities from disposing of a colored schoolhouse for the purpose of raising funds for the white school, no other suitable accommodations having been provided for the Negroes.[174]

The fact that a school building has been bought with money out of funds which had been allocated to Negro education does not impress on the acquired realty a perpetual trust for the benefit of Negro children, to prevent a fair exchange.[175] However this may be, Texas found it necessary to enact a statute providing that a schoolhouse constructed in part by the voluntary contributions of parents or guardians of either race, white or colored, for the benefit of children of that race, shall not be used by the other without the consent of the trustees of the district involved.[176] This act would seem not to protect the Negro sufficiently, as the white school authorities may sometimes be antagonistic to his interests. The elaborate Oklahoma statute makes special provision for the erection of a schoolhouse for the pupils of either race who lack facilities of this kind and also the placing of such schoolhouse at a point convenient to those who will use it.[177] The act also provides for the sale of

[172] Messer v. Smathers, 213 N. C. 183, 195 S. E. 376 (1938).

[173] Reynolds v. Topeka Bd. of Education, 66 Kan. 672, 72 Pac. 274 (1903).

[174] Bd. of Education of Kingfisher v. Bd. of Comm'rs, 14 Okla. 322, 78 Pac. 455 (1904).

[175] Roberts v. Louisville School Bd., 16 Ky. Law Rep. 181, 26 S. W. 814 (1894).

[176] TEX. ANN. REV. CIV. STAT. (Vernon, 1925) art. 2755.

[177] OKLA. COMP. STAT. (1921) §§10,577, 10,578, 10,585. These provisions do not apply to independent school districts, which are defined in §10,404 as being constituted in every city of the first class and each incorporated town maintaining a fully accredited four-year high school.

any building which has not been used for separate school purposes for the preceding two years.[178] In the District of Columbia the statute states that the authorities must provide proper housing and teaching facilities.[179]

The West Virginia Court has held that where school officials disobey the mandate of the law by limiting the Negro school term to a much shorter period than the white, a teacher in the Negro school is permitted to recover her proper salary for the full term allowed the white school.[180] In this instance the court took a practical view of the case, evidently realizing that full relief could not be given by mandamus. West Virginia now guarantees Negro teachers salaries equal to those paid the whites.[181] The Delaware Constitution provides that there shall be no discrimination in the payment of teachers' salaries on account of race.[182] Oklahoma provides that the teachers in her separate schools shall be paid by warrants upon the separate school fund in the hands of the treasurer.[183] In an old case from Missouri it was held that the state statutes did not create a separate fund and that therefore warrants for Negro teachers' salaries were properly drawn upon the district fund, which was responsible for the payment of both white and Negro teachers.[184] In an early Ohio case, decided before separate schools were abolished in that state, a writ of mandamus was ruled to be the proper remedy to enforce the payment of teachers' salaries by the city authorities out of a city's school funds.[185] A salary schedule was provided by a Delaware act of 1927,[186] and this enactment guaranteed that there would be no discrimination on account of race or color. A Maryland act set up an elaborate schedule for the salaries of colored teachers.[187] As the

[178] OKLA. COMP. STAT. (1921) §§10,586, 10,587, *et seq.*

[179] D. C. CODE (Supp. 1933) tit. 7, §§249, 252.

[180] Williams v. Bd. of Education, 45 W. Va. 199, 31 S. E. 985 (1898).

[181] W. VA. CODE (1931) c. 18, art. 7, §2.

[182] Art. X, §2.

[183] OKLA. COMP. STAT. (1921) §10,583. In connection with these warrants for teachers' salaries and other expenses of separate schools, see School Dist. v. Cap. Nat. Bank, 7 Okla. 45, 54 Pac. 309 (1898); American State Bank of Boynton v. Bd. of Comm'rs, 143 Okla. 1, 286 Pac. 902 (1930). As to what funds are available for teachers' salaries, see Sams v. Bd. of Comm'rs, 72 Okla. 84, 178 Pac. 668 (1919).

[184] State *ex rel.* Humphries v. Thompson, 64 Mo. 26 (1876).

[185] State *ex rel.* School Directors v. City of Cincinnati, 19 Ohio Rep. 178 (1850).

[186] Del. Laws 1927, c. 156.

[187] MD. ANN. CODE (Bagby, 1924) art. 77, §§202-203.

salaries provided in this schedule are not on a par with those paid to white teachers, a test case was recently brought to determine whether or not the statute was constitutional. The authorities sought legal advice and were told that the statute was invalid.[188] It is probable that the settlement obtained in this case will result in more equal treatment being meted out to the Negro teachers of Maryland.

Mississippi provides for separate teachers' examinations.[189] The duty of employing teachers for the separate schools in Oklahoma devolves upon the county superintendent,[190] while in Missouri the same is left to the school board of directors.[191] In Maryland,[192] North Carolina,[193] and West Virginia[194] statutes make provision for a supervisor or director of Negro schools. In Maryland this officer must be a white man, and for this reason the validity of the act of that state might well be questioned. The North Carolina act provides for both clerical and professional assistants. West Virginia also has a body known as the advisory counsel for Negro schools,[195] while Alabama has an advisory board for Negro institutions appointed by the state board of education.[196]

Florida makes it a criminal offense for teachers of one race to instruct pupils of the other in the public schools,[197] while the West Virginia law commands that all teachers in Negro schools must be Negroes also.[198] Georgia refuses to allow any payment from the public school fund to a teacher who is guilty of receiving or teaching white and colored pupils in the same school.[199] Oklahoma punishes a similar wilful act as a misdemeanor, fining the teacher and canceling his or her certificate

---

[188] See 6 INT. JURID. ASS'N MONTHLY BULL. 100 (Feb. 1938). *See also* Mills v. Lowndes, 26 F. Supp. 792 (D. C. D. Md. 1939).

[189] MISS. CODE ANN. (1930) §6589.

[190] OKLA. COMP. STAT. (1921) §§10,579, 10,581. Independent districts, *supra* note 177, excepted.

[191] MO. REV. STAT. (1929) §9217.

[192] MD. ANN. CODE (Bagby, 1924) art. 77, §35 (4).

[193] N. C. CODE ANN. (Michie, 1931) §5405.

[194] W. VA. CODE (1931) c. 18, art. 3, §9.

[195] *Id.* at art. 2, §2, as amended in Michie, Supp. 1933, with duties outlined in c. 18, art. 2, §§16, 17, which were added in 1933 Supp.

[196] ALA. SCHOOL CODE (1927) §50.

[197] FLA. COMP. GEN. LAWS (Skillman, 1927) §8112.

[198] W. VA. CODE, (1931) c. 18, art. 5, §14, as amended in Michie, Supp. 1933.

[199] GA. CODE ANN. (Michie, 1926) §1551 (118).

without the privilege of renewal for one year.[200] California makes it unlawful for a teacher to reflect upon citizens because of their race or color.[201]

Four states, Florida,[202] Kentucky,[203] Oklahoma,[204] and Tennessee,[205] have enacted statutes punishing any individual or corporation which allows the mingling of the students of the white and colored races in the same school, college, or other institution of learning, whether public or private, and penalizing all teachers or instructors who shall permit such intermingling. The first two named also punish the persons of either race who attend such a school, while the Oklahoma act is worded in such a manner as to punish only those of the white race who thus violate its provisions. The Tennessee act is silent on this matter.

The Kentucky act was patently aimed at an institution called Berea College, a corporation engaged in just such a project as it was the purpose of the statute to prohibit, the education of whites and Negroes in the same institution. Almost immediately after its passage arrangements were made to have a test case brought involving the validity of the statute. The State Court of Appeals decided that the statute was a reasonable exercise of the state's police power except in so far as it prohibited the teaching of the races within twenty-five miles of one another. The latter provision was said to be unreasonable. The statute was declared not be violative of the equal protection clause of the Fourteenth Amendment to the Federal Constitution or the due process clause of the same.[206] The privilege of teaching Negroes and whites in the same school was declared not to be a property right. The court evidently had before it another ground for deciding the case against the college. This ground was the reserved power of the state to alter or amend the charters of the corporations it has chartered.

The case was taken up to a higher tribunal, but the Federal

---

[200] OKLA. COMP. STAT. (1921) §10,570.

[201] CAL. GEN. LAWS (Deering, 1931) Act 7519, §3.50.

[202] FLA. COMP. GEN. LAWS (Skillman, 1927) §8107.

[203] KY. STAT. ANN. (Carroll, 1930) §§4526a(1-4). Superseded by Carroll, Supp. 1934 §4363-8.

[204] OKLA. COMP. STAT. (1921) §§10,571-73.

[205] TENN. CODE (Will. Shan. & Harsh, 1932) §§11,395-97.

[206] Berea College v. Commonwealth, 123 Ky. 209, 94 S. W. 623 (1906).

Supreme Court refused to consider the constitutionality of the act. It declared that where there are two grounds for a state court's decision, one federal and the other non-federal, the highest tribunal will refuse to give an opinion on the federal question. Here it was held that the decision of the state court could be upheld on the point regarding the reserved power of the state over corporations, and therefore the validity of the statute was not a proper issue upon which the appellant could demand a decision.[207] Since the appellant was a corporation, the Supreme Court also ruled that it was unnecessary to consider the validity of the statute as affecting individuals who might wish to establish and operate such a school. This case was loaded with political dynamite, and it probably would not be far amiss to say that the court was glad it could find a way to sidetrack the main issue of the validity of the statute. This is the last pronouncement upon either this statute or the similar acts in the other states mentioned. The power to amend or alter the charters of corporations is carried in this instance to the extent of allowing the legislature to enact laws concerning them which might be unconstitutional if applied to individuals. The Kentucky Court, however, refused to approve a statute which sought to deprive corporations of the right to establish a Negro industrial school by making the establishment of such schools depend upon the concert of a majority of the voters in the precinct.[208]

Separate higher educational facilities are maintained in all of the southern and border states, even where the prohibition against mixed schools is statutory and not constitutional. Alabama provides for a Negro normal school[209] and an agricultural and mechanical institute,[210] makes an appropriation to the Tuskegee Normal and Industrial Institute,[211] and gives the state board of education authority to appoint an advisory council for Negro institutions.[212] In an early case the state court decided that a legislative diversion of a portion of the colored

[207] Berea College v. Kentucky, 211 U. S. 45, 29 Sup. Ct. 33 (1908). Case discussed thoroughly by Stephenson in article (1909) 43 Am. L. Rev. 695. At least one commentator has argued that the statute is invalid. Note (1933) 82 U. of Pa. L. Rev. 157.

[208] Col. Trust Co. v. Lincoln Institute, 138 Ky. 804, 129 S. W. 113 (1910).

[209] Ala. School Code (1927) §§474 *et seq.*

[210] *Id.* at §§494–499. [211] *Id.* at §601. [212] *Id.* at §50.

school fund for the purpose of establishing a colored university was unauthorized.[213]

Arkansas has established an Agricultural, Mechanical, and Normal School for Negroes which is run in conjunction with the State University.[214] This institution was held to be a necessary expense of the state government.[215] Hence the act providing for it was not subject to the objection that the proposition had not received a two-thirds vote as required by the state constitution for all such expenses which were not necessary.

Delaware has a State College for Colored Students.[216] High school as well as college courses are made available in this institution.[217] The state also provides separate teachers' institutes.[218] Florida has established an Agricultural, Mechanical, and Normal College for Negroes.[219] Georgia[220] has a State Teachers and Agricultural College for Negroes at Forsyth, a School of Agriculture and Mechanic Arts, and the Georgia State Industrial College for Colored Youth at Savannah. Kentucky supplies higher educational facilities at the Kentucky State Industrial College and the West Kentucky Industrial College.[221] In Louisiana persons of color are provided for at Southern University[222] and the Louisiana Negro Normal and Industrial School.[223] Maryland has provided certain industrial schools for colored persons[224] and the State Normal School for Negro teachers.[225] Some facilities are also provided at Princess Anne Academy.

---

[213] Elsberry v. Seay, 83 Ala. 614, 3 So. 804 (1888).

[214] ARK. DIG. STAT. (Castle, Supp. 1927) §§9604 (a-i); (Supp. 1931) §9604a.

[215] Hudson v. Higgins, 175 Ark. 585, 299 S. W. 1000 (1927).

[216] DEL. REV. CODE (1915) §§2349-57.

[217] Del. Laws 1921, c. 160, art. 1, §8, ¶21.

[218] DEL. REV. CODE (1915) §§535, 2302.

[219] FLA. COMP. GEN. LAWS ANN. (Skillman, 1927) §§814, 815. In §804 is a provision which limits the enrollment of Florida State College for Women to persons of the white race.

[220] GA. CODE ANN. (Michie, 1926) §§1397, 1562 (9-12); (Supp. 1932) §257 (59).

[221] KY. STAT. ANN. (Carroll, Supp. 1934) §§4527 (59)-(80). There were formerly separate institutes for teachers, KY. STAT. ANN. (Carroll, 1930) §4525, and a Trade & Training School for the Negroes of Normal District No. 2, KY. STAT. ANN. (Carroll, 1930) §§4526e-(1)-(16), but these statutes were repealed by Ky. Laws 1934, c. 65.

[222] LA. GEN. STAT. ANN. (Dart, 1932) §§2453-64. This statute provides for an Industrial and Normal School and also a Model Industrial and Agricultural School to be located at the university.

[223] *Id.* at §§2465-69.

[224] MD. ANN. CODE (Bagby, 1924) art. 77, §§211-214.

[225] *Id.* at §256.

Mississippi has established the Alcorn Agricultural and Mechanical College for Negroes.[226] The municipal separate school districts have also been authorized to establish junior colleges and agricultural high schools.[227] This would seem to give the colored school districts this privilege as well as the white districts. Moreover, the state has authorized its county school boards to establish two agricultural high schools, one for each race.[228] In Missouri there are Lincoln University for Negroes[229] and separate institutes for colored teachers.[230] North Carolina supplies the North Carolina College for Negroes,[231] the Negro Agricultural and Technical College,[232] and colored normal schools.[233]

In Oklahoma there is the Colored Agricultural and Normal University.[234] This institution provides such higher educational facilities as are deemed advisable by the authorities in charge. These facilities include the agricultural, mechanical, and industrial arts. The state also provides Negro teachers' institutes.[235] South Carolina has established the Colored Normal, Industrial, Agricultural, and Mechanical College at Orangeburg.[236] Tennessee maintains at Nashville an Agricultural and Industrial Normal College for Negroes.[237] In Texas there is the Negro Teachers and Industrial College at Prairie View.[238] Virginia maintains a State College for Negroes.[239] Certain lands have also been allocated to Hampton Institute,[240] a colored institution of college grade which is located in the state. The colored population of West Virginia is provided for at West Virginia State College[241] and Bluefield Colored Institute.[242]

It is safe to say that none of the above state-supported

[226] MISS. CODE ANN. (1930) §§7195-96 [227] *Id.* at §6685. [228] *Id.* at §6674.

[229] MO. REV. STAT. (1929) §§9616-24. Section 9624 provides that near-by Negro children who are unable to attend school elsewhere because of the lack of proper facilities may be given instruction at Lincoln University. Section 9618 authorizes an increase in facilities up to the standards set by the University of Missouri.

[230] *Id.* at §9477. [231] N. C. CODE ANN. (Michie, 1931) §§5912 (g)-(h).

[232] *Id.* at §§5826-32. [233] *Id.* at §§5775, 5775a, 5850.

[234] OKLA. COMP. STAT. (1921) §§10,803-20. [235] *Id.* at §10,535.

[236] S. C. CODE (1932) §§5800-5806.

[237] TENN. CODE (Will. Shan. & Harsh, 1932) §§2398, 2403, 2404.

[238] TEX. ANN. REV. CIV. STAT. (Vernon, 1925) arts. 2638-43.

[239] VA. CODE ANN. (Michie, 1930) §947-969.

[240] *Id.* at §853. [241] W. VA. CODE (1931) c. 18, art. 13, §1.

[242] *Id.* at art. 14, §1, as amended in Michie's 1933 Supp.

colleges is on a par with the corresponding institutions provided for the whites. Various courses which are given in the white institutions are not provided in the colored colleges. This is particularly true with respect to graduate and professional training. The equipment is not up to standard and the teaching force is oftentimes inadequate. Thus there is very little graduate work done in these Negro colleges. As the Negro is becoming better educated, there is a crying need for the members of the race who wish to enter the professions or do graduate work in their chosen fields. The separate school system of the South prevents them from attending the white universities, and the studies which they wish to pursue are not offered at the Negro institutions. Hence some plan will have to be devised in the near future which will give the progressive Negro an equal opportunity in this respect.

In the last few years most of the states in the northern tier of the territory which has the separate school system have enacted the so-called scholarship laws. These statutes provide funds to enable advanced Negro students to obtain the desired courses in out-of-state institutions. A recipient of one of these scholarships could go to some other institution where such work is offered and take any course which is given in the white higher educational institutions of the state but not at the colored colleges. The states which adopted this type of legislation were Kentucky,[243] Maryland,[244] Missouri,[245] Oklahoma,[246] Tennessee,[247] Virginia,[248] and West Virginia.[249] The Oklahoma and Tennessee acts specifically refer to transportation costs as an item to be considered in the computation of the amount of money needed. The Virginia act is worded a little differently from those of the other states. It gives the collegiate heads the authority to refuse to allow anyone, irrespective of race, the privilege of attending the state educational institution under their control, provided that the person desiring admission is objectionable for any reason whatsoever. The purpose of this peculiar wording seems to have been the avoidance of consti-

[243] Ky. Laws 1936, c. 43. [244] Md. Laws 1933, c. 234; 1935, c. 577; 1937, c. 506.

[245] Mo. Rev. Stat. (1929) §9622; Mo. Laws 1933, p. 87; 1935, pp. 113-114.

[246] Okla. Sess. Laws 1935, c. 34, art. I.

[247] Tenn. Pub. Acts 1937, c. 256. [248] Va. Acts 1936, c. 352.

[249] W. Va. Code (1931) c. 18, art. 13, §2, as amended in Michie's 1933 Supp.

tutional difficulties under the Fourteenth Amendment. The statute's validity has been impugned on the ground that it establishes no proper standard by which prospective students at the state-supported educational institutions may be judged.[250] The act would seem to allow administrative officials of the State University and colleges of the state to determine at their own pleasure whether any person, be he white or colored, should be afforded the opportunity of attending these institutions. The statute could be attacked on this theory as well as others.

The first Maryland act[251] of this kind provided for the fair distribution, according to the ratio of whites to Negroes in the state, of the funds received under the terms of a federal statute known as the Morrill Act and concerning land-grant educational institutions. Under the terms of this state statute the part of the funds rightfully belonging to the Negroes would be apportioned to them. This money would be used at the discretion of the Board of Regents of the State University as the state appropriation or any part thereof for the Princess Anne Academy or to establish scholarships at Morgan, a colored institution located in the state, for worthy colored students who are unable to obtain access to advanced studies because they are not available at Princess Anne. A later act[252] set up a commission on higher education for Negroes with authority to carry out the purposes of the former statute and established scholarships to the amount of two hundred dollars.

Under this setup was tried the first of the cases which were begun with a view to testing the constitutionality of statutes of this type. A Negro named Murray, after being refused admittance to the University of Maryland law school, applied for a writ of mandamus to force the university to enroll him. The defendants contended that the scholarship law would satisfy the constitutional guarantee of equal protection of the laws. The State Court of Appeals ruled that the amount of the scholarship obtainable under the statute would not cover the increased tuition, living, and traveling expenses which he would be forced to bear at an out-of-state institution.[253] The

[250] Note (1936) 45 YALE L. J. 1296.

[251] Md. Laws 1933, c. 234.

[252] *Id.* 1935, at c. 577.

[253] Pearson v. Murray, 169 Md. 478, 182 Atl. 590 (1936). See Notes: (1936)

court also pointed out that the colored plaintiff could only obtain the specialized course in the law of Maryland, the state in which he desired to practice, at the state-supported law school. This institution was the only one where such a specialized course was taught. The court did not decide whether an adequate system of scholarships would satisfy the constitutional guarantee of equality.

The Maryland legislature's answer to this decision was the 1937 scholarship law which made more adequate provision for Negroes who desire professional and graduate training and appointed a body to look into the advisability of adding Morgan College to the colored educational system of the state.[254]

Then came the celebrated *Gaines* case from Missouri. This controversy, like the Maryland case, involved an attempt by a Negro to gain entrance into the law school at the State University. The state court held that the scholarship law satisfied the constitutional guarantee of equal protection by providing an equality of educational opportunity for Negroes.[255] The tribunal distinguished the Maryland case on two grounds: First, it was argued that the laws of Missouri authorize Lincoln University to establish a law school whenever it is deemed necessary or practical to do so, whereas the laws of Maryland make no such provision. Second, it was argued that Missouri had provided adequate funds to meet the expense of the scholarship program, while Maryland had not. The court attempted to answer the afore-mentioned specialized law course argument by pointing out that the University of Missouri, like the state-supported universities in neighboring states, gave a law course which was designed to prepare its graduates for the practice of the profession in any state in the union where the common law forms the groundwork of the system of jurisprudence. This argument seems to have convinced the Missouri judges. The efficacy of the reasoning appears to be somewhat doubtful, how-

20 MINN. L. REV. 673, (1936) 21 ST. LOUIS L. REV. 260, (1936) 45 YALE L. J. 1296.

[254] Md. Laws 1937, c. 506.

[255] State *ex rel.* Gaines v. Canada, 342 Mo. 121, 113 S. W. (2d) 783 (1937). However, the court did rule that so much of the 1935 appropriations act as limited the amount of the scholarships to the difference between the tuition in Missouri and in the adjacent states was unconstitutional in that it violated a state constitutional provision that no bill shall contain more than one subject and that shall be expressed in its title.

ever, in view of the fact that state university law schools generally emphasize the statute and case law of their own particular jurisdiction.

The case was taken to the Federal Supreme Court, and that tribunal reversed[256] the decision of the state court. The court declared that Missouri must supply an equal opportunity for white and Negro residents of the state to obtain courses which are offered at any one of its state-supported educational institutions. Under the scholarship law the white resident is afforded an opportunity to have a legal or other professional education within the state, while the same educational advantages are denied to Negroes. The important fact is that the state has provided these facilities for one race and not the other, and the fact that there never has been a demand for such courses at the Negro institution is immaterial. This lack of facilities cannot lawfully be met by the establishment of scholarships at out-of-state institutions where colored persons are permitted to enter on an equal footing. What would be an unconstitutional discrimination in respect to educational opportunities cannot be justified by a resort to facilities of this kind in other states. "That resort may mitigate the inconvenience of the discrimination but cannot serve to validate it." The court also declared that the mere statutory declaration that facilities of a professional and graduate grade would be established whenever practicable or necessary in the opinion of the Board of Curators of Lincoln University would not require the board to establish such facilities for Negroes if they thought best not to do so. The board was provided with the scholarship alternative. The fact that this scholarship plan was only a temporary one pending the establishment of a law department at Lincoln University did not excuse the discrimination. For these reasons the plaintiff's failure to request that facilities for a legal education be provided at Lincoln University was not of importance in this case.

How will non-resident Negroes who wish to attend southern

[256] State of Missouri *ex rel.* Gaines v. Canada, 305 U. S. 337, 59 Sup. Ct. 232 (1938). Justices Butler and McReynolds dissented. See Notes: (1939) 6 U. of Chi. L. Rev. 301, (1939) 17 N. C. L. Rev. 280, (1939) 27 Geo. L. J. 331, (1939) 87 U. of Pa. L. Rev. 478. *See also* State *ex rel.* Gaines v. Canada, 131 S. W. (2d) 217 (Mo. 1939).

state-supported institutions of higher learning be affected by the decision in the *Gaines* case? Will the principles announced therein be extended to include persons of color who come into the state for the express purpose of attending these institutions? The Fourteenth Amendment prohibits a state from denying equal protection of the laws to any person "within its jurisdiction." One commentator has argued that non-resident Negroes who come into the state for the purpose of attending these institutions would be protected from arbitrary discrimination on the basis of race alone.[257] It may be, however, that the Supreme Court will come to a different conclusion when the question is presented. An actual domicile in the state might be required.

There is little or no effort at northern institutions of higher learning or technical schools to segregate persons of the colored race. It is true, however, that New Jersey has established a Manual Training and Industrial School for Colored Youths at Bordentown.[258] This school is certainly an anomaly and can be explained only upon the hypothesis that the people feel that such an institution is needed because of the peculiar problems of the Negro in our world of today. This does not mean, however, that all other schools of this type in the state are closed to Negroes, for racial discrimination of this sort is prohibited by other legislation. This is of course assuming that such a school is under the supervision of the state regents, as provided by the civil rights legislation.

The statutory provisions governing the University of Nevada contain a clause stating that there shall be no discrimination in the admission of students on account of race or color.[259] The Kansas Civil Rights Act threatens to punish the trustees or regents of any state university, college, or other school of public instruction for making any distinction on account of race or color or previous condition of servitude.[260] This statute, however, does not prevent the limited separate school law which is in force in the state from operating to its fullest extent, as has been seen above in discussing the New

[257] Note (1939) 17 N. C. L. Rev. 280, 284.

[258] N. J. Comp. Stat. (1911) pp. 4791-92, §§201-204, pp. 4814-16, §§262-267.

[259] Nev. Comp. Laws (Hillyer, 1929) §7734.

[260] Kans. Rev. Stat. (1923) §21-2424. See also §76-307.

York law.[261] The New Jersey,[262] New York,[263] and Pennsylvania[264] Civil Rights Acts include, in their enumeration of places of public accommodation to which such acts apply, kindergartens, primary and secondary schools, high schools, academies, colleges, universities, and all other educational institutions under the supervision of the state regents or other similar authority. These statutes expressly state that they are not to be applied to private institutions. A New York court, however, has held that where a business school has been incorporated by the regents, and has received a provisional charter from them, it is not a private school within the exception.[265] The court declared that the burden of proof was upon the school to show that it was a private institution. A recent amendment to the New York statute extended it to any educational institution "supported in whole or in part by public funds or by contributions solicited from the general public." [266] The Michigan Civil Rights Act mentions "all public educational institutions of the State." [267]

Private schools and colleges, even though they are located in northern states, cannot be forced to admit Negro students, for the Fourteenth Amendment applies only to institutions of a public character.[268] The private nature of a Maryland school was said not to have been changed because the institution had made a contract with a municipality which provided that each member of the city council could appoint one pupil each year.[269] In this instance one of the councilmen had chosen a Negro as his appointee. However, where the particular Negro involved has been previously admitted to the private school or college, it seems quite probable that the courts would recognize a contract right to continue his attendance, a breach of which would

[261] See note 39 *supra*.

[262] N. J. Comp. Stat. (Supp. 1924) Civil Rights, §1.

[263] N. Y. Consol. Laws (Cahill, 1930) c. 7, §40. See also c. 41, §514.

[264] Pa. Laws 1935, Act 132.

[265] McKaine v. Drake Business School, 107 Misc. 241, 176 N. Y. Supp. 33 (Sup. Ct. 1919).

[266] See N. Y. Laws 1935, c. 737.

[267] Mich. Comp. Laws (Supp. 1933) §17,115(146).

[268] State *ex rel.* Clark v. Maryland Institute, 87 Md. 643, 41 Atl. 126 (1898); Booker v. Grand Rapids Medical College, 156 Mich. 95, 120 N. W. 589 (1909).

[269] State *ex rel.* Clark v. Maryland Institute, 87 Md. 643, 41 Atl. 126 (1898).

entitle the student to recover damages but not to specific performance.[270]

Trusts which have as their express purpose the educational improvement of the colored race are valid. In one case from Rhode Island an instrument of this kind which left the property to organizations to be named by designated trustees was held to create a valid charitable trust.[271] A Kentucky statute[272] formerly authorized various state and county officials to administer all gifts or devises which express an intention to aid in the education of the colored children of the state. This act, however, was repealed in 1934 when a new school law was enacted.[273]

Segregation of the races in the public schools is expressly prohibited in Colorado, Idaho, Michigan, and Minnesota, either by statute or constitutional provision.[274] One of these, Minnesota, provides that any school district so classifying pupils according to race or color shall lose its apportionment of the public school funds for the period over which such segregation shall continue. An attempt in a Colorado school to segregate the Negro pupils as far as swimming facilities and scholastic social functions were concerned was held discriminatory and unauthorized,[275] and the same was held in New Jersey with respect to an attempt to prohibit a Negro pupil from taking singing lessons except with those of his own race.[276] As a contrast to these decisions, however, the Ohio court has ruled that a colored girl student at the State University can be denied

---

[270] See dictum in Booker v. Grand Rapids Medical College, 156 Mich. 95, 120 N. W. 589 (1909).

[271] Godfrey v. Hutchins, 28 R. I. 517, 68 Atl. 317 (1907). In this connection see Kinnaird v. Miller's Executor, 25 Gratt. 107 (Va. 1874), where a testator left property in trust for the purpose of establishing a manual labor school for "children." The court declared that this bequest should be construed to be for the benefit of white children alone in view of the fact that in 1859, the date when the will was drawn, such a grant for Negro children would have been illegal. The court argued that the gift was not invalid as being violative of the Fourteenth Amendment, as that constitutional provision is not applicable to private bequests.

[272] KY. STAT. ANN. (Carroll, 1930) §4522.

[273] Ky. Laws 1934, c. 65.

[274] COLO. CONST. ART. IX, §8; IDAHO CONST. ART. IX, §6; MICH. COMP. LAWS (1929) §§7156 (L), 7368; MINN. STAT. (Mason, 1927) §2999.

[275] Jones v. Newlon, 81 Colo. 25, 253 Pac. 386 (1927), (1927) 31 L. NOTES 150.

[276] Patterson v. Bd. of Education, 11 N. J. Misc. 179, 164 Atl. 892 (1933).

the privilege of rooming, dining, and sharing common toilet and bathroom facilities with white students, these being purely social privileges.[277]

Ten states, Connecticut,[278] Illinois,[279] Massachusetts,[280] Michigan,[281] Minnesota,[282] New Jersey,[283] New York,[284] Pennsylvania,[285] Rhode Island,[286] and Washington,[287] either by statute or constitutional provision, provide that there shall be no racial discrimination in the public schools—or else the state laws are subject to this interpretation. In all of these states except New York, which has a separate school law, segregation of the Negroes in separate rooms or buildings is not permitted, the decisions of the courts to this effect having been discussed above. This is also the law even in a number of states where there

---

[277] State *ex rel.* Weaver v. Bd. of Trustees of Ohio State University, 126 Ohio St. 290, 185 N. E. 196 (1933).

[278] CONN. GEN. STAT. (1930) §833.

[279] ILL. REV. STAT. (Cahill, 1933) c. 122, §§385, 386. *See* People *ex rel.* Peair v. Bd. of Education of Upper Alton, 127 Ill. 613, 21 N. E. 187 (1889); People *ex rel.* Bibb v. Mayor of Alton, 179 Ill. 615, 54 N. E. 421 (1899), 193 Ill. 309, 61 N. E. 1077 (1901), 209 Ill. 461, 70 N. E. 640 (1904). In the first hearing of the Bibb case it was held to be error to confine the proof of discrimination to the plaintiff's children alone, evidence showing similar acts of discrimination against other Negro children having been excluded in the lower court. It was also erroneous to refuse to permit the president of the school board to testify concerning his instructions regarding the admission of Negro children. Evidence as to what the school officials said while carrying out these orders was also ruled competent.

[280] MASS. ANN. LAWS (1933) c. 76, §5.

[281] MICH. COMP. LAWS (1929) §§7156(1), 7368. *See* People v. Bd. of Education, 18 Mich. 400 (1869).

[282] MINN. STAT. (Mason, 1927) §2998.

[283] N. J. COMP. STAT. (1911) p. 4767, §125. See exclusion cases, State *ex. rel.* Pierce v. Union Dist. School Trustees, 46 N. J. Law 76 (1884), *aff'd* 47 N. J. Law 348 (1885); Raison v. Bd. of Education, 103 N. J. Law 547, 137 Atl. 847 (1927). In State *ex rel.* Jefferson v. Bd. of Education, 64 N. J. Law 59, 45 Atl. 775 (1899), the relator, wishing to transfer his child to a school nearer his residence, was told that he would have to follow the procedure outlined in the school law in order to obtain his rights. The complainant in the Raison case had not followed this procedure, but the court ruled he did not have to do this because this case was one of exclusion while the Jefferson case was one of transfer, and that therefore the cases differed.

[284] N. Y. CONSOL. LAWS (Cahill, 1930) c. 41, §920.

[285] PA. STAT. ANN. (Purdon, 1930) tit. 24, §1377. Where evidence concerning discrimination is conflicting, the question is left to the jury. Taylor v. Entriken, 214 Pa. St. 303, 63 Atl. 606 (1906); Mayo v. Morton School Dist., 72 Pa. Super. Ct. 247 (1919).

[286] R. I. Gen. Laws (1923) §1041.

[287] WASH. CONST. Art. IX, §1.

are no statutes forbidding discrimination.[288] Minnesota and New Jersey punish a member of a board of education who is responsible for any such act of discrimination,[289] while the Illinois act makes it criminal for any school official or other person to exclude or aid in excluding any child because of its color or to engage in acts of intimidation with that object in view.[290]

As a penalty for not carrying out the provisions of the Missouri separate school law, the statute visits the school district whose board of directors is responsible therefor with a deprivation of all public school funds for so long as such board shall refuse to comply therewith.[291]

Separate kindergartens are provided for in Delaware, although the establishment of public institutions of this kind is left to the discretion of the local authorities.[292] In Missouri the legislature has authorized the city boards of education to establish and maintain separate playground and library facilities for whites and Negroes.[293] It is also worthy of note here that the West Virginia Court, in considering a case involving the exclusion of a Negro from a public library, refused to identify the institution with the public school system because the local board of education was given control of it by statute.[294] The refuted contention was that the library was an integral part of the public schools and hence subject to the separate school law which demanded that there should be no such close association as that desired by the Negroes, who wanted the same privileges as the whites.

As the Negro blood is mixed with the white throughout the nation, be it accomplished by legal or illegal unions, it becomes increasingly important to have some criterion set up as the dividing line between white and colored persons. This is nowhere better illustrated than in the public schools where questions concerning the race of certain pupils frequently arise in states where separate schools are conducted. In an early Indiana case

---

[288] Clark v. Bd. of Directors, 24 Iowa 266 (1868); Bd. of Education v. State, 45 Ohio St. 555, 16 N. E. 373 (1888).

[289] MINN. STAT. (Mason, 1927) §2998; N. J. COMP. STAT. (1911) p. 4767, §125.

[290] ILL. REV. STAT. (Cahill, 1933) c. 122, §§385, 386.

[291] MO. REV. STAT. (1929) §9217.

[292] DEL. REV. CODE (1915) §2296.

[293] MO. REV. STAT. (1929) §9333.

[294] Brown v. Bd. of Education, 106 W. Va. 476, 146 S. E. 389 (1929), (1930) 33 L. NOTES 215.

it was decided that a prospective pupil who applied for a writ of mandamus to gain entrance into a school must have affirmatively alleged that he was neither a Negro or a mulatto.[295] During the ante-bellum period in Ohio it was held that anyone with a preponderance of white blood was entitled to the benefit of the common school fund,[296] but later in the same period the court of that state ruled that certain children who were five-eighths white but distinctly colored in appearance could be refused admission to a white school.[297] Moreover, the District of Columbia Court of Appeals has ruled that a child having one-sixteenth or more Negro blood, but without physical characteristics of the Negro race, is nevertheless considered as a colored person within the meaning of the separate school law.[298] The laws of Oklahoma,[299] Texas,[300] and North Carolina[301] employ language particularly applicable to schools, which excludes from the white schools all children who have the least modicum of Negro blood, however remote the strain may be. In the latter state the courts had formerly held that a person who had one-eighth or more Negro blood was not entitled to admission into the white schools.[302] The court used the criterion of the third generation inclusive which is used to establish the validity or invalidity of a marriage between a white person and a person of Negro descent.

However, this criterion was expressly denied in Mississippi, for the court of that state declared that all persons having an appreciable amount of Negro blood were colored within the meaning of the school law.[303] The latter rule also obtains in Kentucky, where the white school authorities were held to be justified in refusing to admit a child who had one-sixteenth Negro blood.[304] A very similar rule appears to be in effect in Arkansas, for the court of that state has declared that anyone

[295] Draper v. Cambridge, 20 Ind. 268 (1863).

[296] Lane v. Baker, 12 Ohio Rep. 237 (1843).

[297] Van Camp v. Bd. of Education, 9 Ohio St. 406 (1859).

[298] Wall v. Oyster, 36 App. D. C. 50, 31 L. R. A. (N.S.) 180 (1910).

[299] OKLA. CONST. Art. XIII, §3; OKLA. COMP. STAT. (1921) §10,568.

[300] TEX. ANN. REV. CIV. STAT. (Vernon, 1925) Art. 2900.

[301] N. C. CODE ANN. (Michie, 1931) §5384. *See* Johnson v. Bd. of Education, 166 N. C. 468, 82 S. E. 832 (1914).

[302] Hare v. Bd. of Education, 113 N. C. 10, 18 S. E. 55 (1893).

[303] Moreau v. Grandich, 114 Miss. 560, 75 So. 434 (1917).

[304] Mullins v. Belcher, 142 Ky. 673, 134 S. W. 1151 (1911).

with a trace of Negro blood in his veins is a Negro.[305] In South Carolina, however, it was ruled that the marriage criterion governed and that a person with less than one-eighth Negro blood could not be placed in a Negro school.[306] The difficulty was avoided in this instance because the court permitted the authorities to establish schools for such persons distinct from both Negro and white schools.

There are also a number of southern states which have defined the words "Negro" or "colored person" by statute. Thus Florida[307] has defined such terms as including all those persons who have one-eighth or more Negro blood, while Alabama,[308] Georgia,[309] Tennessee,[310] and Virginia[311] have enacted statutes which include within the term "Negro" or "colored person" all persons who have any Negro blood whatever. These statutes apply generally and not to the school problem alone. The Virginia act formerly included only those persons who had at least one-fourth Negro blood,[312] while before 1927 the Georgia statute[313] included those persons having one-eighth or more Negro blood.

When a pupil has in the past attended a school for one race which was later closed to him, he may be presumed to be of that race, and hence he is not required to state his race in his effort to obtain a writ of mandamus to force his admittance into the school.[314]

In a Virginia case at the turn of the century a person who evidently had some Negro blood applied to local school authorities for permission to send his children to the white school. The authorities ruled that the children had at least one-fourth Negro blood and refused the request. The parent then sought a writ of mandamus. The lower court ruled that the children were legally white and issued the writ. The case was taken to a higher tribunal and the appellate court held that a writ of mandamus

---

305 State *ex rel.* Black v. Bd. of Directors, 154 Ark. 176, 242 S. W. 545 (1922).

306 Tucker v. Blease, 97 S. C. 303, 81 S. E. 668 (1914).

307 FLA. COMP. GEN. LAWS ANN. (Skillman, 1927) §5858.

308 ALA. CODE ANN. (Michie, 1928) §2.

309 GA. CODE ANN. (Michie, Supp. 1928) §§2177, 2177(13).

310 TENN. CODE (Will. Shan. & Harsh, 1932) §25.

311 VA. CODE ANN. (Michie, 1930) §67.

312 Eubank v. Boughton, 98 Va. 499, 36 S. E. 529 (1900). Later changed to one-sixteenth. See Note (1912) 17 VA. L. REG. 692.

313 GA. CODE ANN. (Michie, 1926) §2177.

314 Cross v. Bd. of Trustees, 121 Ky. 469, 89 S. W. 506 (1905).

9

will not be granted in a case of this kind where the power of the local authorities is discretionary.[315] An additional ground for the decision was that the petitioner had not taken advantage of the provision of the school law for an appeal to the county superintendent. In a substantially similar case, however, the Mississippi Court held that the applicant was entitled to a judicial determination of his race.[316] This was decided in spite of the fact that the Mississippi school law provided for an appeal to the superintendent of education. The Mississippi view is the better one, for otherwise the plaintiff would have no recourse if the school authorities decided against him. Probably the correct view is that taken by the Arkansas Court in a similar controversy. In this instance the court ruled that the finding of the school authorities, when supported by substantial proof, will not be disturbed by the courts unless it can be shown that the authorities have acted arbitrarily and have disregarded the weight of the testimony.[317]

Evidence of general reputation in the community is admissible at such a hearing.[318] However, a question asked of a witness, the wording of the inquiry being "who was said to be her mother," was ruled out as hearsay evidence.[319] In this instance the witness was not first asked the general reputation as to the race of the ancestor involved, and this was said to be fatal. Persons who have long known the applicant and his family are also permitted to give an opinion as to his race,[320] and testimony tending to show that the person in question was received and treated by his neighbors and the community at large as a white person is also competent.[321] Testimony that the applicant's grandmother was living with a Negro nine months before the birth of her child, the applicant's parent, is also considered admissible.[322] Evidence tending to show the nature and extent of the family's associations with whites or

[315] Eubank v. Boughton, 98 Va. 499, 36 S. E. 529 (1900).

[316] Moreau v. Grandich, 114 Miss. 560, 75 So. 434 (1917).

[317] State *ex rel.* Black v. Bd. of Directors, 154 Ark. 176, 242 S. W. 545 (1922).

[318] Gilliland v. Bd. of Education, 141 N. C. 482, 54 S. E. 413 (1906); Cole v. District School Bd., 32 Okla. 692, 123 Pac. 426 (1912).

[319] Medlin v. County Bd. of Education, 167 N. C. 239, 83 S. E. 483 (1914).

[320] Cole v. District School Bd., 32 Okla. 692, 123 Pac. 426 (1912).

[321] Gilliland v. Bd. of Education, 141 N. C. 482, 54 S. E. 413 (1906).

[322] Hare v. Bd. of Education, 113 N. C. 10, 18 S. E. 55 (1893).

Negroes is competent.[323] However, a declaration made by the applicant's father that he had married a Negro was ruled out as being hearsay evidence. An attempt was made to get this testimony in as an admission by a party to the suit in accordance with the familiar exception to the hearsay rule. The court ruled that it was only admissible as impeaching evidence because the children's father had no sufficient interest in the suit to make the declaration admissible under the exception.[324] Evidence that the applicant's ancestor had voted at a time when Negroes were not permitted to exercise the franchise was held competent to show that he was white,[325] as was also testimony that the applicant had attended the white school in another state where separate schools for the white and Negro races were maintained.[326]

California has found it necessary to ban all textbooks or other means of instruction containing any matter reflecting upon citizens because of their race or color.[327] Kentucky has enacted a statute providing that when free textbooks have first been distributed to children of one race, they may not at a later date be distributed to the other.[328] There was also at one time a Delaware statute authorizing the distribution of free textbooks in all the colored schools of the state with the exception of those located in the city of Wilmington.[329] The Delaware Constitution now provides that there shall be no discrimination in furnishing free textbooks.[330]

Race prejudice sometimes develops at vocational training schools in the northern states. A situation of this sort evidently prevailed at some of the schools of beauty culture in Minnesota, for the legislature of that state enacted a statute outlawing discrimination at these schools on account of race or color.[331]

---

[323] Cole v. District School Bd., 32 Okla. 692, 123 Pac. 426 (1912).

[324] Medlin v. County Bd. of Education, 167 N. C. 239, 83 S. E. 483 (1914). There is a strong dissent by Walker, J., to the effect that the father was the real party in interest and that therefore this bit of testimony should have been admitted as substantive evidence.

[325] Gilliland v. Bd. of Education, 141 N. C. 482, 54 S. E. 413 (1906).

[326] Cole v. District School Bd., 32 Okla. 692, 123 Pac. 426 (1912).

[327] Cal. Gen. Laws (Deering, 1931) Act 7519, §3.51.

[328] Ky. Stat. Ann. (Carroll, 1930) §4421c-11.

[329] *See* Bd. of Education v. Griffin, 9 Houston 334, 32 Atl. 775 (Del. 1892).

[330] Art. X, §2.

[331] Minn. Laws 1927, c. 245, §10.

Negroes may not be taxed to support white schools only, and a statute which is subject to any such interpretation is in conflict with the equal protection clause of the Fourteenth Amendment.[332] A white person, however, may not set up this objection, for the law is not prejudicial to him.[333]

The North Carolina Constitution contains a provision guaranteeing that there shall be no discrimination to the prejudice of either race in the public schools.[334] Statutes were enacted which directed that the funds to be raised by taxation on the property of white persons were to be devoted to the support of the white schools, while the funds raised by taxation on the property of Negroes were to go to the support of the Negro schools. In several cases[335] the state court ruled that this method of taxation was in violation of the above constitutional provision. Moreover, the Oklahoma Court has declared that such an arrangement is in conflict with provisions of the Fourteenth Amendment, being unfair to the Negro.[336]

In connection with this problem a rather peculiar and puzzling situation developed in Kentucky. A statute which denied to the Negroes any participation in the proceeds of the annual school tax on the property of white persons was held by the state court in 1885 to be in conflict with the Fourteenth Amendment.[337] A statute very similar to the afore-mentioned North Carolina acts was also declared invalid by a federal district court.[338] The effect of an arrangement like this is to give the Negro school facilities far inferior to the white. Furthermore, it was later held in a federal court that a statute levying taxes

---

[332] Marshall v. Donovan, 73 Ky. 681 (1874); McFarland v. Goins, 96 Miss. 67, 50 So. 493 (1909).

[333] Marshall v. Donovan, 73 Ky. 681 (1874); Norman v. Boaz, 85 Ky. 557, 4 S. W. 316 (1887). This same principle is recognized in several cases where school laws have been subject to claims of discrimination against the Negro in other ways. Reid v. Mayor of Eatonton, 80 Ga. 755, 6 S. E. 602 (1888); Eakins v. Eakins, 20 S. W. 285 (Ky. 1892); Daviess County Bd. of Education v. Johnson, 179 Ky. 34, 200 S. W. 313 (1918); Powell v. Hargrove, 136 S. C. 345, 134 S. E. 380 (1926).

[334] Art. IX, §2.

[335] Puitt v. Commissioners, 94 N. C. 709 (1886); Riggsbee v. Town of Durham, 94 N. C. 800 (1886); Duke v. Brown, 96 N. C. 127, 1 S. E. 873 (1887); Markham v. Manning, 96 N. C. 132, 2 S. E. 40 (1887).

[336] Porter v. Comm'rs of Kingfisher County, 6 Okla. 550, 51 Pac. 741 (1898).

[337] Dawson v. Lee, 83 Ky. 49 (1885). *See also* State Bd. of Education v. Bd. of Public Education, 186 Ga. 783, 199 S. E. 641 (1938).

[338] Claybrook v. City of Owensboro, 16 Fed. 297 (D. Ky. 1883).

on the property of white persons alone and applying the proceeds of such tax for the benefit of the white schools exclusively was also invalid.[339] Right in the teeth of these decisions, however, the legislature continued to enact statutes which seem to be invalid when considered in their light.[340] Moreover, the state court appeared to recognize the validity of these acts in several instances without considering their constitutionality.[341] One of these statutes which had application to cities of the fourth class[342] was finally ruled invalid in so far as it prevented the Negro schools from receiving their just share of the tax upon corporate property, for the act appeared to allow the white schools the proportion of the fund derived from such tax which the white stockholders bore to the colored.[343] The court came to the conclusion that the proper way to apportion the fund was according to the number of white and colored children in the territory.

In a comparatively old case, moreover, it was decided that white taxpayers could not object that colored persons were not allowed to vote at an election authorized by a local act providing for submission to white voters only. The election had been

---

[339] Davenport v. Cloverport, 72 Fed. 689 (D. Ky. 1896).

[340] See KY. STAT. (Carroll, 1903) §4487; KY. STAT. ANN. (Carroll, 1915) §3588a.

[341] *See* Bd. of Education v. Trustees of Colored School Dist., 18 Ky. Law Rep. 103, 35 S. W. 549 (1896); Munfordville Mercantile Co. v. Bd. of Trustees, 155 Ky. 382, 159 S. W. 954 (1913); Thornton v. White, 162 Ky. 796, 173 S. W. 167 (1915).

[342] KY. STAT. ANN. (Carroll, 1915) §3588a.

[343] Trustees of Colored Schools v. Trustees of White Schools, 180 Ky. 574, 203 S. W. 520 (1918); Moss v. City of Mayfield, 186 Ky. 330, 216 S. W. 842 (1919); Mueller v. Phillips, 186 Ky. 657, 217 S. W. 1010 (1920). A rehearing was refused in the Trustees case, the court ruling that the case had been properly brought against the white trustees and was not required to be brought against the city as contended for by the defendant, 181 Ky. 303, 204 S. W. 86 (1918), but the plaintiff's claim was finally defeated, the court deciding that there was no trust relationship and that hence the claim was barred by the five-year statute of limitations. 181 Ky. 810, 205 S. W. 904 (1918). In the Mueller case the claim was denied because such funds are not permitted to be used for any purpose except that for which they were collected, the tax having been assessed for the benefit of the white schools. The corporations which had paid the tax were not involved in this suit and their rights were not adjustable in this action. They might object if they saw fit to do so. The method of distribution of tax funds here invoked seems to have been continued in Kentucky even after the repeal of §3588a in 1920. Commonwealth v. Sebree Deposit Bank, 202 Ky. 589, 260 S. W. 388 (1924); Louisville, H. & St. L. Ry. v. Powell, 213 Ky. 563, 281 S. W. 532 (1926).

called to decide whether a tax should be levied for the support of the schools. The court declared that it would presume that the legislature had intended that the white property owners only should be taxed, since otherwise there would be taxation without representation.[344] The state court, however, has thrown some doubt upon the validity of this method of taxation as applied to individuals as exemplified by one of the above statutes by remarking that it is "a very questionable right." [345] The principle, however, seems to have been recognized at least as late as 1921. In that case the court declared[346] that although the legislature has in some instances adopted this method with respect to local school taxes, it is not required to do so, and therefore white persons may be taxed to support the Negro schools as was done by the instant statute. The above general statutes have now been repealed,[347] and there are no longer any school statutes of this type in the state which are subject to the claim of invalidity on this ground.

Negro voters have been held to be entitled to vote at an election to decide whether a special tax should be levied under the Kentucky statute permitting a consolidation[348] or at an election of members of the county board of education.[349] It has also been declared by the court that all legal voters, regardless of color, have a right to vote upon any proposition concerning the county common schools.[350] In a case arising under one of the above-repealed statutes,[351] however, it was held not to be improper to deny Negroes the right to vote at an election to

---

[344] Eakins v. Eakins, 20 S. W. 285 (Ky. 1892).

[345] Trustees of Colored Schools v. Trustees of White Schools, 180 Ky. 574, 203 S. W. 520 (1918). In this connection see Note (1933) 82 U. OF PA. L. REV. 157, 162.

[346] City of Pineville v. Moore, 190 Ky. 357, 227 S. W. 477 (1921).

[347] KY. STAT. (Carroll, 1903) §4487 was repealed by Ky. Laws 1916, c. 24, p. 162, and was then superseded by KY. STAT. ANN. (Carroll, 1922) §4468a-1; KY. STAT. ANN. (Carroll, 1915) §3588a was repealed in 1920 by what was KY. STAT. ANN. (Carroll, 1930) §3587a-1 *et seq.* The latter was in turn superseded by KY. STAT. ANN. (Carroll, Supp. 1934) §§4399-17 *et seq.*

[348] County Bd. of Education v. Bunger, 240 Ky. 155, 41 S. W. (2d) 931 (1931), construing KY. STAT. ANN. (Carroll, 1930) §4426-2.

[349] Wright v. Lyddan, 191 Ky. 58, 229 S. W. 74 (1921), construing the act of 1920 which in a modified form was the now repealed KY. STAT. ANN. (Carroll, 1930) §4399a-1c. *See also* Bd. of Education v. Bunger, 240 Ky. 155, 41 S. W. (2d) 931 (1931).

[350] *Ibid.*

[351] KY. STAT. (Carroll, 1903) §4487.

decide whether there should be an issuance of bonds to establish a white school.[352]

In the only Kentucky case in the state court which seems to have considered the constitutionality of the method of taxation employed in the above-repealed statutes, it was held that a city has authority to issue bonds for the additional support of the white school with the consent of those taxed.[353] The levy was on the property of the whites only and the submission of the question at the election had been to the white voters alone. The tax was supplementary to the regular state school funds which had been divided equitably between the white and colored schools. It is extremely doubtful that this distinction would receive the approval of the Federal Supreme Court, as it would allow the white property owners, who own most of the more valuable property in the South, to escape taxation for Negro schools except for the amount contributed to the state school fund. That this fund was insufficient to maintain the schools on the high plane which the whites desired for their own school is shown by their willingness to vote the supplement. Furthermore, such property as was owned by the Negroes would almost certainly be of such comparatively insignificant value that a tax thereon would not support a colored school with anywhere near equal facilities. Would this be equality of educational opportunity? A statute which denied poor children the advantages which it gave to the offspring of wealthier parents would probably be declared invalid in spite of the fact that the additional facilities were paid for by a tax upon the wealthy. Yet this or a similar situation would be the result in a great many instances under the law as announced in this decision of the Kentucky Court. This is carrying the principle of separation entirely too far. Furthermore, an earlier Kentucky act employing practically the same or a very similar method of taxation was declared invalid as being in conflict with the Fourteenth Amendment in one of the above-mentioned federal decisions,[354] and at least some of the above North Carolina cases are somewhat

[352] Munfordville Mercantile Co. v. Bd. of Trustees, 155 Ky. 382, 159 S. W. 954 (1913).

[353] Crosby v. City of Mayfield, 133 Ky. 215, 117 S. W. 316 (1909). This case is adversely criticized in a Note (1933) 82 U. of Pa. L. Rev. 157, 162.

[354] Davenport v. Cloverport, 72 Fed. 689 (D. Ky. 1896). See note 339 *supra*.

similar. Therefore it cannot be doubted that the validity of this method of taxation for school purposes, even where it is supplementary, is at least uncertain, the Federal Supreme Court never having had the question presented to it.

It has been suggested that the North Carolina and Kentucky decisions differ because of the difference in the wording of the constitutions of the two states,[355] the fundamental document of the former state providing that there shall be no discrimination with respect to the separate schools in favor of or to the prejudice of either race,[356] while that of the latter states that there shall be no discrimination on account of race or color in the distribution of the school fund.[357] The term "school fund" might possibly be given the meaning of the state school fund mentioned above. However, this contention fails to take into consideration the above argument that the statute is in conflict with the Fourteenth Amendment, and it is not too bold to doubt its constitutionality on this ground, considering all that has been said above.

Since it has been decided in Kentucky that such a method of taxation, when supplementary to the state school fund, is valid, the provision of the state constitution[358] requiring a two-thirds vote of a municipality for the approval of a tax which exceeded its income and revenue has been declared to be satisfied if two-thirds of the white voters cast their ballots in favor of a proposition concerning the white schools alone.[359] A similar result was reached some years later with respect to a proposition to incur an indebtedness for a Negro school building in the same town.[360] Two-thirds of the Negro voters had approved the project and the indebtedness was held down so as not to exceed 2 per cent of the value of the property of colored persons plus the proportional amount of the corporate property computed as pointed out above. Another clause in the state constitution[361] limited such indebtedness to 2 per cent of the taxable property in the taxing district.

Under a Kentucky act which provided for the collection and apportionment of the property tax on railway and bridge com-

[355] STEPHENSON, RACE DISTINCTIONS IN AMERICAN LAW (1910) 198.
[356] N. C. CONST. Art. IX, §2. [357] KY. CONST. §187. [358] §157.
[359] Crosby v. City of Mayfield, 133 Ky. 215, 117 S. W. 316 (1909).
[360] Moss v. City of Mayfield, 186 Ky. 330, 216 S. W. 842 (1919). [361] §158.

panies,[362] a statute which has since been repealed,[363] the white school districts were given authority to tax such companies and divide the proceeds between the white and colored schools according to the number of children of each race in the territory.[364] The statute formerly applied only to railway corporations,[365] but bridge companies were included when it was re-enacted in 1906.[366] It was held before the change that it would apply to railways alone.[367] However, it was held[368] that it superseded the above-mentioned statute concerning cities of the fourth class as to the tax on railways in the method of distribution, the 1906 act coming after the passage of this statute. Where the colored district's boundaries extended beyond the limits of the white district, the apportionment was made on the basis of the number of white and colored children in the white district.[369] It was also held that the terms "common school districts" and "graded school districts" used in the act were synonymous, and therefore the words "colored common school district" were said to include a colored common school whether graded or ungraded.[370] In the year of its repeal this statute was declared discriminatory and hence unconstitutional to the extent that it required a railway company to pay the white graded school rate on the proportion of its property the tax on which is devoted to the support of the colored schools, since the state constitution provided that taxes must be uniform and that all corporate property must be assessed at the same tax rate paid by individuals.[371]

Mississippi is the only state where anything on the same order as the above-criticized Kentucky legislation has been upheld. The court of that state in a comparatively early case declared that an act authorizing the issuance of bonds for the

---

[362] Ky. Stat. Ann. (Carroll, 1922) §4101. [363] Ky. Acts 1926, c. 82.

[364] *See* Harrodsburg Ed. District v. School Trustees, 105 Ky. 675, 49 S. W. 538 (1899); Hickman College v. Trustees, 111 Ky. 944, 65 S. W. 20 (1901); Commonwealth *ex rel.* Trustees v. Ferguson, 128 S. W. 95 (Ky. 1910).

[365] Ky. Stat. (Carroll, 1903) §4101. [366] Ky. Acts 1906, c. 22, p. 142.

[367] Bd. of Education v. Trustees of Colored School Dist., 18 Ky. Law Rep. 103, 35 S. W. 549 (1896).

[368] Thornton v. White, 162 Ky. 796, 173 S. W. 167 (1915).

[369] Bd. of Trustees v. Morris, 24 Ky. Law Rep. 1420, 71 S. W. 654 (1903).

[370] Bd. of Trustees v. West, 163 Ky. 568, 174 S. W. 10 (1915).

[371] Louisville, H. & St. L. Ry. v. Powell, 213 Ky. 563, 281 S. W. 532 (1926), discussing Ky. Const. §§171, 174.

support of a school exclusively for whites, entirely outside the system of free public schools and to be supported by a tax on the whites alone, did not violate a state constitutional provision requiring taxation to be uniform.[372] The opinion also stated that the contention that the act violated the Federal Constitution was without force. This case could be used to support the above-criticized Kentucky doctrine concerning the authorization of supplementary taxation for the benefit of one race only, but its force as a precedent is very much weakened by the fact that the court did not see fit to make its statement that the act did not violate the Federal Constitution more specific and support it with reasoning. The court seemed to take the validity of the act for granted on this particular point.

As a contrast to these attempts to divide the burden according to race, an early Indiana statute provided that a certain school tax should be levied without regard to the race of the owner of the property taxed.[373]

In one instance in Missouri bonds were voted for the purpose of purchasing school sites and of erecting and furnishing schoolhouses, one for white children and one for colored. The bond issue for separate schools was held not to violate a state constitutional provision prohibiting a submission of more than a single proposition to popular vote.[374]

In Oklahoma the county excise board is required to levy a tax sufficient to maintain the separate schools according to the estimate made by the county commissioners or, in independent school districts, the board of education.[375] This shall include the cost of maintaining, superintending, supervising, and administering the separate schools, the purchase of building sites, and the erection of buildings. When the tax is collected, it is directed to be paid over to the several boards of education in the various districts to be expended upon the orders of such boards for the purpose for which it was levied. Under this statute the board of education in an independent dis-

---

[372] Chrisman v. City of Brookhaven, 70 Miss. 477, 12 So. 458 (1892). *But see* McFarland v. Goins, 96 Miss. 67, 50 So. 493 (1909).

[373] *See* Cory v. Carter, 48 Ind. 327 (1874).

[374] State *ex rel.* Carrollton School Dist. v. Gordon, 231 Mo. 547, 133 S. W. 44 (1910).

[375] OKLA. COMP. STAT. (1921) §10,574. See also amendment to this statute. Okla. Laws 1937, p. 176.

trict has been held to be the agent of the county in respect to a creation of an indebtedness for the maintenance of separate schools, such being a liability of the county.[376] If the maximum tax permitted to be levied by the county commissioners for the maintenance of separate schools is not sufficient to maintain such schools without discrimination, the burden of supplementing such funds is upon the school district which may levy taxes within state constitutional limitations.[377] It has been decided that the state aid funds in Oklahoma, including the proceeds of the gross production tax as well as ad valorem taxes, shall be apportioned according to the scholastic enumeration of white and colored pupils in the district, and the portion which rightfully belonged to the minority school, in this case the one for Negroes, must be used for the benefit of such school.[378]

The Delaware Code of 1915 provided that all the provisions of the act concerning the making of the assessment lists for the white schools must also apply to the colored schools with exceptions where certain sums to be raised were required to be less for the colored districts.[379]

The North Carolina Court once declared that the colored school children must have the same per capita share of school funds as the white children.[380] But this declaration was not necessary to the decision of the case and was soon afterwards repudiated in another case in which it was decided that all that was required was that there be no racial discrimination in the distribution of the school fund, equality of facilities being provided for the Negro schools.[381] In this instance the court said

[376] American State Bank of Boynton v. Bd. of Comm'rs, 143 Okla. 1, 286 Pac. 902 (1930).

[377] Olson v. Logan County Bank, 29 Okla. 391, 118 Pac. 572 (1911), construing Art. X, §9, of OKLA. CONST. See also in this connection Lusk v. White, 68 Okla. 316, 173 Pac. 1128 (1916); Bd. of Education v. Excise Bd., 86 Okla. 24, 206 Pac. 517 (1922).

[378] Bd. of Comm'rs v. School District, 137 Okla. 193, 279 Pac. 326 (1929). *See also* Bd. of Education of Sapulpa v. Bd. of Comm'rs, 127 Okla. 132, 260 Pac. 22 (1927); School District v. Creek County Comm'rs, 135 Okla. 1, 275 Pac. 292 (1928).

[379] §2293 referring to §2292.

[380] Hooker v. Town of Greenville, 130 N. C. 472, 42 S. E. 141 (1902) (dictum).

[381] Lowery v. School Trustees, 140 N. C. 33, 52 S. E. 267 (1905). See in accord with this decision: Smith v. School Trustees, 141 N. C. 143, 53 S. E. 524 (1906); Bonitz v. Bd. of Trustees of Ahoskie School, 154 N. C. 375, 70 S. E. 735 (1911).

that "the school term shall be of the same length during the school year, and that a sufficient number of teachers, competent to teach the children in each building or section, shall be employed at such prices as the board may deem proper." It has also been decided that a clause in a statute providing that the trustees shall dispose of the school fund to be realized under the act in such a way as to them would seem just confers no arbitrary discretion upon them, for it was implied that the funds would be distributed according to the above principles.[382]

The Mississippi Constitution of 1890 contains a provision that no public money shall be appropriated for any public institution in the state which makes any distinction among the citizens of the state,[383] but this provision was held not to preclude the establishment and financing of separate schools for whites and Negroes.[384]

To show how the system of overlapping districts which has been employed in Kentucky and Mississippi may be used to discriminate against the Negro, a case which presents this unfairness to at least a certain extent will now be discussed. An exclusively colored community in Mississippi established a school district and levied a one-cent tax on the property in the district to pay the expenses thereof. A neighboring white community established a consolidated school district embracing the territory of the community and other surrounding terrain, including the property of the colored school district, and levied a tax at the same rate to support the consolidated school. The Negroes, who owned the property in the colored district, claimed that they were being taxed for a school from which they received no benefit, and resisted the latter tax on the ground that such an arrangement was discriminatory and therefore unlawful. The court decided that every acre of land in the state was taxable for both white and colored schools no matter who owned the property, for the Mississippi scheme required the members of both races to support schools for both. Hence it refused to invalidate the tax. It was remarked that it would be impractical to have districts for white and colored which were coterminous. The court answered the contention

[382] Smith v. School Trustees, 141 N. C. 143, 53 S. E. 524 (1906).
[383] Art. I, §21.
[384] Chrisman v. City of Brookhaven, 70 Miss. 477, 12 So. 458 (1892).

that Negroes received no benefit from the tax by saying that the whole community was certainly improved by education in general, an argument that is obviously subject to criticism. The court also said that the ownership of the property in the colored district might well change, thus shifting the burden of the tax for that district upon the shoulders of white purchasers. The colored plaintiffs failed in their attempt to enjoin the collection of the tax to support the white school.[385] This decision would seem to grate on the sense of justice of a fair-minded citizen. In answer to the court's last argument it might be remarked that it would be entirely possible for such a shift of property ownership to take place under the taxation scheme here approved, as the Negroes might well be forced to sell because of inability to pay taxes.

It would seem that where there are no white children in a community and the group is so situated geographically that it may be set apart by itself, that particular neighborhood might be left out of the districting for the white schools. This would certainly seem fairer to the Negro, and a statutory amendment to this effect should not be too difficult to frame. However, this amendment should not be drafted in such a way as to apply to towns and cities where the races live in segregated sections close to one another as they do in almost every town of any size in the South, as the law might then permit the dominant white race to evade all taxation for the support of the Negro school by an unfair gerrymander. Therefore the proposed amendment should be so worded as to apply only to communities such as the one in the above case, a district which could well be separated from the rest of the school system without doing irreparable injury to the finances of any other district.

The central theme running through the above discussion of the statutes and decisions on this important subject is the guarantee of equal educational opportunity for the children of all races. The fact that such a guarantee of equal facilities exists does not mean that it is carried out in the southern states. In fact it is the exception and not the rule for the Negro schools in that part of the nation to be anywhere near as efficient as those

---

[385] Bryant v. Barnes, 106 So. 113 (Miss. 1925).

for the whites. The inequalities are manifest to anyone who has even a cursory knowledge of the present status of education in the South. To begin with, the per capita expenditure for the education of Negro children in 1930 was far less than the amount spent for the maintenance of the white schools.[386] The Negro schools are not provided with proper housing facilities in a great many localities where the white children have imposing structures in which they are given advantages denied the pupils of the colored race.[387] In the rural districts the lack of proper buildings is perhaps emphasized to a greater degree than in the towns and cities.[388] Whether in urban or rural districts, the teaching force in the Negro schools is usually inferior in training to that employed in the schools of the dominant race. There is a scarcity of properly trained Negro teachers,[389] the educational facilities for Negroes who desire to enter the teaching profession being comparatively poor.[390] On the whole the Negro teachers are far less competent. Of course there are numerous exceptions to this rule, but in general the white teachers have had superior advantages and are much better prepared for their profession. The teacher load is heavier in the Negro schools,[391] and the salaries are lower for Negroes than they are for whites.[392] It has been suggested that the meager salaries paid Negro teachers may be justified to a certain extent by the lower level of living expense prevailing among the Negroes,[393] and this is no doubt true to a certain extent. However, one author answers this by saying that the Negro teacher is thereby forced to accept the lower standard of living which his race has been compelled to adopt on account of racial prejudice.[394] Low

[386] SCHRIEKE, ALIEN AMERICANS (1936) 159. See also NEGRO YEAR BOOK for 1931-32, 204.

[387] See table of investment in public school property for whites and Negroes in *ibid.* For inadequacy of physical equipment in Negro schools, see NEGRO EDUCATION, Bul. 38, 1916, Bureau of Education, Interior Dep't, pp. 32-33.

[388] See SCHRIEKE, *op. cit. supra* note 386, at 158-161.

[389] BOND, THE EDUCATION OF THE NEGRO IN THE AMERICAN SOCIAL ORDER (1934) 267-270, 277-283.

[390] See NEGRO EDUCATION, Bul. 38, 1916, Bureau of Education, Interior Dep't, c. 5, on Preparation of Teachers (Vol. I, pp. 71-80).

[391] See table of comparative number of pupils per teacher for white and Negro schools in NEGRO YEAR BOOK for 1931-32, 205.

[392] See tables of teachers' salaries in NEGRO YEAR BOOK for 1931-32, 206, or *ibid.*, for 1937-38, 171; BOND, *op. cit. supra* note 389, at 152-163, 270-272.

[393] See *id.*, at 271.

[394] *Id.*, at 273.

standards prevail in many colored schools,[395] and in some instances the school terms for Negroes are shorter than those for the whites.[396] A lack of teaching equipment may also be noticed in the colored schools.[397]

One difficulty which has caused hardship in the past, the task of providing transportation for rural Negroes whose homes are remote from the school, has been obviated to a great extent in some localities through the use of school busses which gather up the children in the morning and carry them home after the day's work is over. Without this service, a great many of the poorer Negro farmers were unable to send their children to school. Their homes were not within walking distance of the schoolhouse. This difficulty obtains today wherever transportation is not provided. In some instances transportation facilities have been provided for white schools in the towns for the benefit of white children in the surrounding countryside. In such cases the rural Negro may be forgotten and forced to attend a poorly equipped colored school or perhaps be left without any adequate educational facilities whatever. It has been said that new services like transportation and other special advantages such as laboratories and gymnasiums have tended to increase the inequality of the schools for the two races, for the states and counties spend large amounts of money on these services for the white children while allowing the Negro schools to stagnate in inadequate buildings with poor facilities.[398]

In the past and to a lesser extent in the present the control of the public schools in the southern states has been or still is in the hands of the local educational authorities.[399] The county and city boards levy the local taxes on which the life of the school system depends and distribute the appropriations which are derived from state funds. They allocate the funds at their disposal to the various units in their jurisdiction. State equalization funds may not be effective in preventing discrimination against Negro schools. They are usually administered by the local authorities who collect from the fund on a per

395 SCHRIEKE, *op. cit. supra* note 386, at 160-161.

396 See table in NEGRO YEAR BOOK for 1931-32, 205; BOND, *op. cit. supra* note 389, at 291-292.

397 SCHRIEKE, *op. cit. supra* note 386, at 161.

398 BOND, *op. cit. supra* note 389, at 165-167.

399 SCHRIEKE, *op. cit. supra* note 386, at 166-169.

capita basis. In counties where there are great numbers of Negro children the authorities may obtain large amounts of money from the fund on the basis of numbers of children of both races and then spend the greater portion of the money for the benefit of the white schools.[400]

There are many ways in which local authorities may discriminate against the Negro schools. The colored teachers may be paid lower salaries than the white even though both have the same grade certificate. The equipment and library facilities of the colored schools may be neglected in favor of those for the whites. Of course absolute equality of facilities is practically impossible to achieve and would be undesirable in many instances even if it were feasible. There must be some attention given to local situations and problems. Thus where the cause of the Negro would best be served by an agricultural or other type of technical school, this kind of educational institution should be established. There must always be a certain amount of local control of school finances and, since this is inevitable, there will be a tendency on the part of school boards which are made up of white men to give the schools for the children of their own race the lion's share. The increasing amount of state supervision and control of school finances which has been noted in some states in recent years may do much toward remedying this inequality.[401]

The average school official in the South is far more interested in the welfare of the white schools than he is in the colored. Thus a truant officer may force white parents to send their children to school while Negro parents in the same community are negligently permitted to disregard the compulsory attendance laws. Better attendance in the urban colored schools might be expected, since the rural children are forced to travel greater distances in order to reach their schoolhouses. However, one writer has come to the conclusion that this is true only with respect to the younger children, the older ones having a better opportunity to secure remunerative employment in the cities.[402]

It is surprising to note the prejudice with which a great many southern whites view the whole subject of Negro educa-

---

[400] BOND, *op. cit. supra* note 389, at 232-252; SCHRIEKE, *op. cit. supra* note 386, at 168-169. [401] *Id.* at 169-171. [402] BOND, *op. cit. supra* note 389, at 221.

tion. Their sincere opinion that the Negro should not be given educational opportunities comparable to those which are provided for the white children is at least partly due to the strong belief that better facilities in the colored schools would not yield a proper return in human values. This belief is a heritage from slavery. Of course there is also the attitude that the educated Negro will lose the humility which has characterized his relations with the southern white man ever since Reconstruction. The white laboring man is no doubt influenced in his opposition to better educational facilities for Negroes by the fear that Negroes will enter skilled trades and thereby create a new and very effective rivalry in a field in which the whites have not had as much competition as they have where the task requires less training and education. However, certain far-sighted leaders and some others realize that the Negro must be given better schools. They believe that improved colored school facilities will benefit not only the Negroes but also the whites. They feel that the colored man is entitled to a good high school education in subjects which may be selected with a view to the peculiar social situation in the South. The Negro must be trained for the jobs which are available under present conditions. Cultural training in the arts and sciences must for the present be subordinated to an education which is more suitable to his needs. In this way the greatest number will be benefited. The curriculum for the colored schools needs a great deal of study with a view toward revision.

Philanthropic organizations such as the General Education Board, set up and supported by the Rockefeller money, and the Rosenwald, Jeanes, and Phelps-Stokes funds have done much toward helping Negro schools and educating the southern whites into a more tolerant attitude concerning the educational needs of the colored man.[403] These organizations and others like them have built schoolhouses and made educational advantages available to many Negroes who would otherwise have been left without proper facilities. They poured money into higher educational institutions and industrial schools for Negroes like Fisk University, and Hampton and Tuskegee institutes. It is

[403] LEAVELL, PHILANTHROPY IN NEGRO EDUCATION (1930); BOND, *op. cit.*, *supra* note 389 at c. 7; SCHRIEKE, *op. cit. supra* note 386 at c. 6; HOLMES, THE EVOLUTION OF THE NEGRO COLLEGE (1934) c. 13.

10

necessary for those who direct this philanthropy to coöperate with the southern whites who are interested in Negro education and to avoid antagonistic attitudes toward the dual educational system which prevails in the South. They have gone a long way toward securing this coöperation in some sections. It has been suggested that southern men who understand the nature and difficulties of the problem should be chosen to carry on the work.[404] In this way the foundations may greatly assist in stimulating the interest of the white authorities in the advantages to be gained from a thorough and well-organized system of Negro schools.

The state-supported institutions of higher learning for Negroes are far inferior to their sister institutions for whites. Most of the inequalities which have been noted herein with respect to the public schools for whites and Negroes are also present in the Negro normal and technical schools which are established with the idea of giving the colored man an opportunity to obtain advanced work. There is hardly one among them that could compare with any good white college in the same area. Equipment in these schools is poorer than that in white universities and technical schools of college grade supported by the state, and there is little if any opportunity for doing graduate work. Little research can be undertaken because of the lack of proper equipment and library facilities. These state-supported schools, however, have assumed an increasing portion of the task of supplying higher educational advantages for Negroes.[405] One school in each of the seventeen states which maintain a compulsory separation of the races in the schools is a federal land-grant college.[406] These land-grant schools, as well as similar institutions for whites, came into existence with the above-mentioned federal legislation known as the first and second Morrill Acts. These statutes made provision for agricultural and mechanical colleges throughout the nation, which are now supported partly by funds derived from the sale of public lands, distributed as provided for in the second Morrill Act, and partly by state appropria-

---

[404] See Schrieke, *op. cit. supra* note 386, at 163-164.

[405] Holmes, *op. cit. supra* note 403, at 150.

[406] See list of Land-Grant Colleges for Negroes in Holmes, *op. cit. supra* note 403, at 153; same in Negro Year Book for 1931-32, 232.

tions. The first Morrill Act,[407] adopted in 1862, made no provision for a fair division of the funds obtained under the statute between the white and Negro institutions in states having the dual system. The result of this omission was that most of the money was expended for the white colleges. However, an attempt was made in at least four states, Kentucky, Mississippi, South Carolina, and Virginia, to give the Negro a square deal in the division of the fund.[408] Because of the failure of most of the states to be fair to the Negro in this respect the second Morrill Act,[409] enacted in 1890, provided that no state with the dual system could come under the terms of the statute unless it agreed to a just and equitable division of the fund between the technical schools for each race. All of these states had accepted this condition within a few years.

There is very little opportunity for a southern Negro who has limited financial resources to do graduate work or obtain professional training. In 1932 the only southern schools of medicine, dentistry, and pharmacy open to Negroes were located at Howard University in Washington and Meharry College at Nashville, Tennessee, neither of which is a state institution.[410] There were law schools at Howard and at two Baptist institutions, Simmons University in Louisville and Virginia Union University in Richmond.[411] Any Negro who desires professional training is therefore forced to attend one of these schools or to go to a northern institution where the graduate courses are open to all persons regardless of color. We have seen that some of the upper tier of southern states attempted to overcome this inequality of facilities by adopting a system of state scholarships which entitled the recipients to financial aid at institutions, in or out of the jurisdiction, where the desired course of study is offered. Now that the legality of this method of providing facilities for the higher education of the Negro has been tested and found wanting, the gauntlet has been thrown down to the southern states. It would seem that they must either establish adequate graduate and professional schools for Negroes or else allow men of the colored race to attend the state universities. It is believed that an attempt will be made to estab-

---

[407] 12 STAT. 503 (1862).
[408] HOLMES, *op. cit. supra* note 403, at 150-151.
[409] 26 STAT. 417 (1890).
[410] See NEGRO YEAR BOOK for 1931-32, 236.
[411] *Ibid.*

lish the separate schools, for the southern whites are as yet in no mood to adopt the other method. The separate graduate and professional schools which are established will probably not be on a par with the state-supported schools which at present do not enroll members of the colored race. Hence the same problem of adequacy which has arisen in connection with the public schools will have to be fought out along this front also.

The above-mentioned Maryland and Missouri cases are but the forerunners of a great wave of controversies concerning the higher education of the Negro in the South. In fact there have been other attempts to enter the white universities. In 1933 a Negro made an effort to force the authorities at the University of North Carolina to accept him as a student in its pharmacy school. The trial judge was of the opinion that the plaintiff had chosen the wrong remedy and dismissed the case on this ground.[412] The university authorities also questioned the plaintiff's right to enter the school on the ground that he had failed to satisfy entrance requirements. The colored organization behind this attempt decided to drop the case without an appeal. Proceedings of a somewhat similar nature were also started in Tennessee.[413] A great deal of this type of litigation may be expected in the near future.

It has been learned from reliable sources that no race conflicts or other disagreeable consequences have arisen because of the presence of the Negro at the University of Maryland law school. However, the colored man should not be unduly optimistic about pinning his faith on the legalistic method altogether. The overwhelming majority of southern whites are opposed to admitting Negroes to the white institutions of higher learning, and the apparently easy social adjustments which have resulted at the Maryland school might not follow such a bold stroke in the more prejudiced Lower South.

One commentator[414] has expressed skepticism as to whether the separate facilities for professional training which will be furnished the Negro "will as a practical matter equal the opportunities for acquiring a professional education on a liberal out-of-state scholarship plan." Hence the Negroes in those

---

[412] See Raleigh News and Observer, Mar. 29, 1933, p. 9.

[413] See NEGRO YEAR BOOK for 1937-38, 142.

[414] Note (1939) 6 U. OF CHI. L. REV. 301, 305.

states which had the scholarship plan may very well have temporarily lost rather than gained as a result of the decision in the *Gaines* case. However, it is probable that the ultimate result of the decision will be beneficial, for the southern legislatures will have to pay at least some attention to the problem.

The foregoing discussion seems to indicate that the legal guarantee of equal educational facilities for colored persons is not carried out in practice. The Negro schools are certainly inferior and very little is done to remedy the situation. As a final remark on the subject, however, it may be said that a school law which obviously would not supply equal facilities for both races should be declared unconstitutional. In one Oklahoma case it was shown that a state school law would not provide an equal educational system for Negroes except in certain districts where there were quite a number of children of that race. The state court held that the entire act was discriminatory and declared it invalid.[415]

[415] Porter v. Comm'rs of Kingfisher County, 6 Okla. 550, 51 Pac. 741 (1898).

V

PROPERTY RIGHTS

Southern white people are averse to living in close proximity to Negroes unless the latter are their servants. This is one of those facts which cannot be disregarded in studying the problems of race relations. The result of this feeling has been a very decided segregation. Practically every community of any size in the South has its "nigger town." Sometimes there may be a Negro family living in a white neighborhood, but this is rather rare. The white people either squeeze the Negroes out or else move out themselves. The only thing that will ordinarily make southern whites live in a Negro-sprinkled city block is economic necessity. In the big cities and commercial centers there are areas where the whites are getting out because of the encroachment of business establishments. The ones who leave may sell to Negroes, thus hastening the exodus. A problem is created with respect to the relations of these Negroes with the whites who are left behind.

The same problem has been harassing the inhabitants of northern and middle western cities ever since the Negro immigration of the early years of the present century to the great industrial centers in these areas. There are many segregated Negro communities in the northern states, like New York's Harlem. The better class of whites are probably even less sympathetic toward the Negro and his problems than their southern brothers. Class hatred has increased in the North in the past few years, and the Negro is, by reason of his economic position, on the side of labor in its never-ending struggle with capital.

With all this aversion to living near Negroes prevailing among the whites, some lawful way to keep Negroes out of white neighborhoods was sought. White landlords, not caring about the feelings of the majority of property owners in the block, would rent their property to what were considered by them to be desirable Negro tenants. The neighbors were helpless to prevent the Negroes from moving in. Relief was sought through legal means. Segregation ordinances were passed in a number of southern cities. When these failed to accomplish their purpose because of constitutional difficulties, restrictive covenants in deeds were adopted as the best way to accomplish the desired results. Although this method was not approved by all the courts in the land, many jurisdictions have sanctioned the device. A typical covenant of this kind provides that the property shall not be owned or occupied by persons of the Negro race.

Thus the law concerning the ownership and occupancy of real property has been brought into contact with problems of racial discrimination and segregation. In considering these matters, the courts have in many instances diverged from their usual policy of upholding the doctrines of the separatists. In abandoning their customary attitude toward problems of like nature, the courts have probably been influenced by the fact that white property owners would otherwise be deprived of the privilege of selling or renting houses in a restricted area to Negroes. The white landlords are not desirous of giving up any rights over the property which they own.[1] Under a segregation ordinance or restrictive covenant, if valid, the white landlord might find it very difficult to sell or rent his property to desirable whites and could not legally transfer it to Negroes.[2] This would be especially true where the premises are in a dilipated condition and the property unfit for anyone except low-caste Negroes who are unable to better their lot.[3] It has been said, however, that this possibility of loss would in most instances be more than offset by the protection which the landowners would receive. There is danger of an influx of Negroes into a white community brought about by the machinations of unscrupulous real-estate dealers who are seeking to reduce property values to a point where they may buy in cheap.[4]

[1] Note, *Segregation Ordinances* (1915) 1 VA. L. REG. (N.S.) 330.

[2] See *ibid.* In the note it is argued that such a situation would not last long in the South, since a city block which was occupied by both races would soon be deserted by all the whites, especially under an ordinance of the type illustrated in Hopkins v. City of Richmond, 117 Va. 692, 86 S. E. 139 (1915), which prohibited one race from living in a block where the other race was in the majority. However, the commentator does not take into consideration the fact that some people must stay where they are because of economic necessity.

[3] *See* Brice v. City of Dallas, 300 S. W. 970 (Tex. Civ. App. 1927).

[4] See note 1 *supra.*

Much of the opposition to segregation ordinances was therefore due to this attitude of the white property owner. Some doubt existed in the judicial mind as to the efficacy of an attack on an ordinance by white persons both because of the absence of damages to the landlord or vendor by reason of the theoretical equality of whites and Negroes as prospective renters or purchasers[5] and because of the lack of a sufficient interest to maintain a suit.[6] However, such contentions have been negatived by expressions in an opinion of the Supreme Court itself.[7]

The first instance of a race segregation ordinance came before a California federal court in 1890. The city of San Francisco passed an ordinance which required all Chinese inhabitants to move from that portion of the city theretofore occupied by them to another part of the city. The court ruled that this ordinance was void because it violated the Fourteenth Amendment and the treaty with China.[8]

About 1910 certain southern cities began enacting segregation ordinances, the avowed purposes of which were to discourage friction between the white and Negro races and to keep them from intermingling socially and to some extent commercially.[9] The city of Baltimore was among the first to employ the device. The validity of this ordinance was tested and was found wanting.[10] There was no saving clause preserving and protecting the vested rights of present property owners. The court disapproved of the ordinance because a great deal of confusion and uncertainty would be caused thereby. However, the court based its decision mainly upon the municipality's lack of authority to enact the ordinance, a position which was

[5] Minor, *Constitutionality of Segregation Ordinances* (1912) 18 VA. L. REG. 561.

[6] Land Development Co. v. New Orleans, 13 F. (2d) 898 (E. D. La. 1926). The case is adversely commented upon in (1926) 36 YALE L. J. 273.

[7] Buchanan v. Warley, 245 U. S. 60, 38 Sup. Ct. 16 (1917).

[8] *In re* Lee Sing, 43 Fed. 359 (C. C. N. D. Cal. 1890).

[9] Hunting, *The Constitutionality of Race Distinctions and the Baltimore Negro Segregation Ordinance* (1911) 11 COL. L. REV. 24.

[10] State v. Gurry, 121 Md. 534, 88 Atl. 228, 546 (1913). *Cf.* Carey v. City of Atlanta, 143 Ga. 192, 84 S. E. 456 (1915), in which the conveyance to the Negro which was complained of took place between the enactment of the original ordinance and the passage of the amendment protecting vested interests. Hence the interesting question of the relation back of the amendment presented itself.

assented to by the North Carolina Court a year later.[11] The court of that state declared that such an ordinance was not authorized by the general welfare clause of a city's charter in view of the fact that the general policy of the state was to discourage the emigration of Negro labor. This argument is unconvincing when one considers the other forms of segregation which are practiced and made lawful in the state.[12] The Virginia Court took a more legally acceptable view in respect to this point, deciding that such an ordinance was authorized by the welfare clause.[13]

There were two distinct types of these ordinances. There were those which arbitrarily set apart certain districts for each race. The above San Francisco ordinance is somewhat on that order. Then there is also the type which merely requires residential districts to be allotted to each race according to principles which apply without discrimination to either race. Ordinances of this latter type were thought to be far less subject to constitutional objections.[14] In fact such ordinances which protected vested rights of present property owners were declared to be valid in several state courts.[15] One of these, the Virginia Court, declared that such an ordinance does not deny the equal protection of the laws guaranteed by the Fourteenth Amendment because it operates alike on all persons and property under the same circumstances and conditions.[16] In coming to

[11] State v. Darnell, 166 N. C. 300, 81 S. E. 338 (1914).

[12] See note 1 *supra*.

[13] Town of Ashland v. Coleman, 19 VA. L. REG. 427 (1913); Hopkins v. City of Richmond, 117 Va. 692, 86 S. E. 139 (1915).

[14] See note 5 *supra*.

[15] Hopkins v. City of Richmond, 117 Va. 692, 86 S. E. 139 (1915); Harris v. City of Louisville, 165 Ky. 559, 117 S. W. 472 (1915); Harden v. City of Atlanta, 147 Ga. 248, 93 S. E. 401 (1917). The Kentucky Court declared that the ordinance was a legitimate exercise of the police power because it would tend to prevent miscegenation and promote peaceful interracial relations. The Georgia Court distinguished the Harden case from its former decision in Carey v. City of Atlanta, 143 Ga. 192, 84 S. E. 456 (1915), by stating that in the prior decision the ordinance had left vested rights unprotected, but a critical survey of that case shows that the opinion of the court was based upon the ordinance's invalidity, independent of the question as to whether or not vested rights were guaranteed, and hence there is little doubt that the Harden case represents an about face on the part of the court. Some uncertainty remains as to this, however, because of the afore-mentioned peculiar circumstances of the Carey case, *supra* note 10.

[16] Hopkins v. City of Richmond, 117 Va. 692, 86 S. E. 139 (1915).

this conclusion the court is probably correct,[17] for the act in question seems only to combine principles announced separately by the Supreme Court in upholding the Jim Crow laws[18] and a New Orleans ordinance segregating prostitutes.[19] In fact, the action of the New Orleans Commission Council in enacting an ordinance segregating white and Negro prostitutes in separate districts was held to be invalid only because the act provided that the girls might not select their places of abode when not engaged in their uncommendable trade.[20] An ordinance which failed to take reasonable consideration of population densities and numbers might well be declared void because it denied equal protection.[21]

An then the question of the constitutionality of these ordinances reached the Supreme Court in an appeal from the *Harris* case from Kentucky.[22] The action had been brought against a white owner for a violation of the Louisville ordinance in disposing of his property to a Negro. The court decided that the ordinance passed the legitimate bounds of the police power in that it interfered with the right of the property owner to dispose of his real estate to anyone he might select and that it was unconstitutional because it violated the due process clause of the Fourteenth Amendment.[23] The court refused to be swayed by the argument that such an ordinance tends to prevent miscegenation and to promote peaceful relations between the races.

No sooner had this decision been handed down than southern municipal authorities sought a way out of the difficulty created thereby. Many schemes were devised for the purpose of getting around the decision. One of these attempts took the form of an ordinance forbidding the occupancy of a dwelling on a city block by members of one race where the block is inhabited only by the other race, vested rights being of course protected. The Maryland Court decided that this ordinance

[17] See note 9 *supra.*

[18] Plessy v. Ferguson, 163 U. S. 537, 16 Sup. Ct. 1138 (1896).

[19] L'Hote v. City of New Orleans, 177 U. S. 587, 20 Sup. Ct. 788 (1900).

[20] City of New Orleans v. Miller, 142 La. 163, 76 So. 596 (1917).

[21] See note 1 *supra.*

[22] Harris v. City of Louisville, 165 Ky. 559, 177 S. W. 472 (1915).

[23] Buchanan v. Warley, 245 U. S. 60, 38 Sup. Ct. 16 (1917). Two convictions under similar ordinances which had been upheld by state courts were reversed in deference to this decision. Irvine v. City of Clifton Forge, 124 Va. 781, 97 S. E. 310 (1918); Glover v. City of Atlanta, 148 Ga. 285, 96 S. E. 562 (1918).

was not different in principle from one which makes it unlawful for members of one race to occupy quarters on a block where the other race is in the majority and declared the enactment invalid.[24] Another attempt was made in New Orleans, where the city fathers passed an ordinance prohibiting both races from establishing residences in certain districts without the written consent of a majority of the race who occupied most of the property in the particular district involved. The state court distinguished the case from the above decision of the Supreme Court by reason of the "consent" provision and declared that the act was merely a zoning ordinance within the police power of the state. It therefore refused to hold that the ordinance was violative of the Fourteenth Amendment.[25] The Supreme Court, however, declined to accept any such specious reasoning and reversed the case.[26] An attempt was made in a Virginia city to base a segregation ordinance on the miscegenation statutes. The enactment prohibited the use as a residence of any building on a block occupied mainly by those with whom intermarriage is forbidden. The court ruled that the attempt to distinguish the case from other instances where the ordinance had been condemned was only an effort to evade the law.[27] The main purpose behind the miscegenation statutes is to keep the races from having too much to do with one another, and hence the attempted distinction is not a real one.

Another effort was made in Texas to make an ordinance ef-

---

[24] Jackson v. State, 132 Md. 311, 103 Atl. 910 (1918).

[25] Tyler v. Harmon, 158 La. 439, 104 So. 200 (1925), 160 La. 943, 107 So. 704 (1926).

[26] Harmon v. Tyler, 273 U. S. 668, 47 Sup. Ct. 471 (1927). See also Note on state court decision in (1926) 36 YALE L. J. 274. After the reversal, the state court held that a vendor was not entitled to specific performance of an agreement to purchase land where the vendee decided to buy upon the misrepresentation that the property, which was only suitable for Negroes to live in, was in a Negro neighborhood as determined by the above ordinance. The vendor contended that since the Supreme Court had ruled the ordinance invalid he was entitled to a decree in his favor. The court held that subsequent events such as the reversal could not affect the fact that the misrepresentation had actually been made with intent to deceive and that the obligations of the parties must be determined as of the date when the contract was entered into. Leopold Weil Bldg. & Improvement Co. v. Heiman, 167 La. 67, 118 So. 694 (1928). This case is of doubtful soundness and is certainly opposed to the doctrine that an unconstitutional law is void *ab initio*.

[27] City of Richmond v. Deans, 37 F. (2d) 712 (C. C. A. 4th, 1930) *aff'd* 281 U. S. 704, 50 Sup. Ct. 407 (1930).

fective. Certain citizens of the city of Dallas, both white and colored, entered into a voluntary agreement to district the city in such a manner as to segregate the two races. The city then enacted an ordinance punishing criminally a breach of the agreement. In a suit to enjoin the enforcement of this ordinance, the court asserted that since a direct segregation ordinance is invalid, an enactment punishing the breach of an agreement to do the same thing is also of no effect. Hence any action under the ordinance might be enjoined.[28] It was said on another hearing of this same case that it is the privilege of a party to the contract, subject only to civil liability for its breach, to terminate the agreement at any time he sees fit to do so, an attempt to deprive him of the privilege being without due process of law.[29] The court also held that the state statute[30] authorizing such city ordinances was invalid. In another case arising under this same ordinance certain signers of the above agreement who would be damaged if the particular property in question was rented to Negroes sought to intervene in an action to enjoin prosecutions thereunder. The action had been brought by property owners whose premises were fit only for Negro tenants and had always been occupied by them. The trial court had sustained the intervenors' plea in abatement on the ground that they were necessary parties to the suit, but this was held to be error.[31] The court declared that the original plaintiffs had the right to have the validity of the ordinance tested without regard to the effect the decision would have on adjoining property owners. The case was then taken to the Texas Commission of Appeals, and that court said that those persons who would profit by the upholding of the ordinance were not necessary parties except as regards the cancellation of the agreement on which the ordinance was based or in so far as the validity of the agreement itself was attacked.[32]

[28] Liberty Annex Corp. v. City of Dallas, 289 S. W. 1067 (Tex. Civ. App. 1927), *aff'd* on ground that the agreement did not cover the particular property in question. 295 S. W. 591 (Tex. Com. App. 1927).

[29] City of Dallas v. Liberty Annex Corp., 19 S. W. (2d) 845 (Tex. Civ. App. 1929). The case is commented upon in (1930) 8 TEX. L. REV. 298.

[30] Tex. Gen. & Sp. Laws Reg. Sess. 1927, c. 103. Louisiana and Virginia had similar statutes. See La. Acts 1912, p. 139; VA. CODE ANN. (Michie, 1930) §§3043-53.

[31] Brice v. City of Dallas, 300 S. W. 970 (Tex. Civ. App. 1927).

[32] City of Dallas v. Brice, 12 S. W. (2d) 541 (Tex. Com. App. 1929).

The latest attempt to evade the above decisions of the Supreme Court was an effort by the governor of Oklahoma to give effect to an Oklahoma City ordinance of this type through the use of his emergency military power. He authorized the enactment of this ordinance by a proclamation in which he declared a state of martial law to exist. There had been threatened inroads of Negroes into certain sections of the city occupied by whites which had created a rather tense interracial situation. The state court held that the ordinance was unconstitutional and enjoined its enforcement.[33] Continued occupancy by Negroes in the prohibited areas would subject them to prosecution for a separate offense for every day that they remained, and hence the requested injunction was granted. The failure of the federal courts to invalidate this ordinance in a recent case was due to poor pleading and the fact that jurisdictional requirements were not met, the plaintiff evidently being confused as to the proper procedure to be followed in such an instance.[34]

All these efforts by southern cities to segregate the Negro by municipal ordinance having failed, there is nothing in the form of state action which can be employed to prevent Negroes from entering and living in white neighborhoods. To make sure of this, a Kansas statute provides that nothing contained in a certain zoning act of 1921 shall be construed as authorizing the governing bodies of cities which are within the act to discriminate against anyone because of his race or color.[35] A federal statute also guarantees to the Negro the same rights with respect to real estate as those possessed by whites.[36] However, a Negro may contract away his rights in the same way that whites do. In one case from Alabama a Negro property owner had entered into a contract to permit no colored picnicking or bathing parties on his land. The court held that this agreement was enforceable by injunction.[37]

There have been other efforts to deprive the Negro of property rights which have been attempted by state constituted authorities. Such was the Kentucky Homestead Act of 1866

---

[33] Allen v. Oklahoma City, 175 Okla. 421, 52 Pac. (2d) 1054 (1935). See Note (1936) 35 MICH. L. REV. 137.

[34] Jones v. Oklahoma City, 78 F. (2d) 860 (C. C. A. 10th, 1935).

[35] KAN. REV. STAT. (1923) §13-1107.

[36] 8 U. S. C. A. §42 (1926).

[37] Moseby v. Roche, 233 Ala. 280, 171 So. 351 (1936).

which was held to be invalid in so far as Negroes were excluded from its benefits.[38] Furthermore, an attempt was made in a North Carolina case to prevent a city from accepting a dedication of certain lands by a private citizen. The grant stipulated that the lands were to be used as a public park for the benefit of the white race. The persons who were attempting to defeat the grant argued that a municipality must either permit members of the white and Negro races to intermingle in its parks and public playgrounds or else furnish separate recreational facilities to each race according to its needs and requirements. Therefore it was contended that the city could not accept the grant, since the terms of the conveyance made its use by Negroes impossible. However, the exception by which these persons questioned the efficacy of the acceptance failed to state facts showing that the city authorities would actually be discriminating against its Negro population by approving the grant. They did not prove that there would be an inequality in facilities, and hence the court refused to hear them further.[39] What would have happened if these facts had been shown, we cannot say. However, a private grant of land to a municipality to be used exclusively for the benefit of its white citizens has been given the approval of a southern court.[40] Private grants of realty to be used for the establishment and maintenance of white[41] or Negro[42] schools also seem to have been approved.

It was a very common practice in the years immediately following the Civil War for the former slave states to enact legislation providing that children of slave marriages should be entitled to inherit the property of their parents as legitimate heirs. The Tennessee statute was construed by the court of that state

[38] Eubank v. Eubank, 7 Ky. Law Rep. 295 (1885); Custard v. Poston, 8 Ky. Law Rep. 260, 1 S. W. 434 (1886).

[39] Berry v. City of Durham, 186 N. C. 421, 119 S. E. 748 (1923).

[40] City of Barnesville v. Stafford, 161 Ga. 588, 131 S. E. 487 (1925). The provision in the instrument was construed as a condition subsequent.

[41] Tucker v. Smith, 199 N. C. 502, 154 S. E. 826 (1930), construed only as marking out purpose of grant and not as a condition subsequent.

[42] Bd. of Education v. St. Patrick's R. C. Church, 15 Del. Chan. 286, 136 Atl. 833 (1927). In this case it was ruled that the maintenance of a Negro school for nineteen years was a sufficient compliance with the covenant that the property should be used for Negroes and that the action of the authorities in using the property for white children for quite a while thereafter was not unlawful.

as not extending the right of inheritance to collateral kindred. In other words the act only applied to lineal descendants. A case was taken to the Federal Supreme Court to decide whether the statute, as so construed, was valid. It was contended that the act violated the equal protection clause of the Fourteenth Amendment because the laws of descent for white and colored persons were thereby made dissimilar. The court refused to adopt this theory and ruled that the classification was a reasonable one in view of the peculiar circumstances which had obtained in the southern states after the war.[43]

When the whites saw all their attempts at segregating the Negro population by state or municipal action going awry, they sought some lawful means of accomplishing their purpose of keeping the colored man out of white residential sections. One of the most effective methods of keeping unwanted racial elements, Negro or Mongolian, out of white districts is by placing in deeds conditions and restrictive covenants which prohibit ownership and/or occupancy by these unacceptable ones. Agreements among landowners are also employed extensively for this purpose, and there should be no great difference in the principles of law applicable, whichever method may be used.[44] There is a tacit understanding in the South that no Negroes shall be permitted to own property or reside in white districts, and in one instance the Alabama Court took cognizance of such a custom.[45] However, the whites desire a more certain way of accomplishing their purpose. The question as to whether the above-mentioned covenants and conditions are valid is at present one of real property law rather than a constitutional problem, as it has been decided by the Supreme Court that the Four-

[43] Jones v. Jones, 234 U. S. 615, 34 Sup. Ct. 935 (1914). A construction of this Tennessee statute which permitted children of slave marriages to inherit property under certain circumstances and which discriminated in favor of those whose parents resided in Tennessee and against those whose parents lived elsewhere is not subject to criticism as denying equal protection of the laws. Napier v. Church, 132 Tenn. 111, 177 S. W. 56 (1915). It has been held that such a statute, which is quite usual in the southern states, applies only to the offspring of sexual relationships excusable by reason of the customs of slavery and not to the offspring of immoral unions of a type not so condoned. Christopher v. Mungen, 61 Fla. 513, 55 So. 273 (1911).

[44] Bruce, *Racial Zoning by Private Contract* (1928) 13 VA. L. REG. (N.S.) 526.

[45] Wyatt v. Adair, 215 Ala. 363, 110 So. 801 (1926).

teenth Amendment does not apply, because a deed is the action of an individual and not of the state.[46]

The difficulty as far as real property law is concerned is in deciding just how far the modern courts are going to follow the policies laid down in England in the Middle Ages[47] encouraging freedom from restrictions on alienation of estates.[48] It has been said that the Supreme Court, in one of its more important decisions,[49] refused to set up a policy of its own in opposition to the policy of the individual states.[50] The problem is one which each jurisdiction must decide for itself. The authorities are in a somewhat confused state,[51] and the result in any jurisdiction where the question is a new one largely depends upon how the particular community and the appellate judges feel about the question at issue. Of course, the state's former attitude toward restrictions on alienation in general would no doubt influence the court in its consideration of the problem, but even this might not be allowed to interfere where there was an ingrained prejudice one way or the other. This is illustrated by the fact that the southern states have uniformly upheld such covenants whenever the question has been presented.[52] Other portions of the country have not been so consistent in this respect. There are a lot of things which enter into a decision of this kind. One commentator has recently re-

---

[46] Corrigan v. Buckley, 271 U. S. 323, 46 Sup. Ct. 521 (1926), *aff'g* 55 App. D. C. 30, 299 Fed. 899 (1924). The Supreme Court thus supported decisions rendered by several state tribunals. Los Angeles Inv. Co. v. Gary, 181 Cal. 680, 186 Pac. 596 (1919); Queensborough Land Co. v. Cazeaux, 136 La. 724, 67 So. 641 (1915); Parmalee v. Morris, 218 Mich. 625, 188 N. W. 330 (1922); Porter v. Barrett, 233 Mich. 373, 206 N. W. 532 (1925). *See also* United Coöperative Realty Co. v. Hawkins, 269 Ky. 563, 108 S. W. (2d) 507 (1937). A contrary decision had been rendered by a California federal court at an earlier date in respect to a covenant not to rent property to Chinese. Gandolfo v. Hartman, 49 Fed. 181 (C. C. S. D. Cal. 1892).

[47] Quia Emptores, 18 Edw. I, c. 1.

[48] See Bruce, *Racial Zoning by Private Contract* (1928) 13 VA. LAW REG. (N.S.) 526.

[49] Corrigan v. Buckley, 271 U. S. 323, 46 Sup. Ct. 521 (1926).

[50] Bruce, *Racial Zoning by Private Contract in the Light of the Constitution and the Rule Against Restraints on Alienation* (1927) 21 ILL. L. REV. 704.

[51] Note (1919) 4 MINN. L. REV. 68.

[52] Allmond v. Jenkins, 165 Ga. 334, 140 S. E. 879 (1927); Queensborough Land Co. v. Cazeaux, 136 La. 724, 67 So. 641 (1915); Koehler v. Rowland, 275 Mo. 573, 205 S. W. 217 (1918). *See also* Eason v. Buffaloe, 198 N. C. 520, 152 S. E. 496 (1930).

marked that there should be more dependence upon sociological data, population, and other statistical information in deciding whether or not and to what extent these restrictions should be declared valid and enforceable.[53]

Total restraints on alienation which are unlimited as to time are held to be void all over the country, but there is a difference of opinion on the question as to whether a covenant for an unlimited time but applying only to a limited class of persons is in the same category.[54] The permanency of the restrictive agreement never seems to have been the deciding point in any case involving a covenant against Negro ownership or occupancy,[55] though it has been an important element in such a decision.[56]

In California the whole problem is complicated by the presence of the Japanese and Chinese, and the covenants generally include them as well as the Negro.[57] Some of the covenants that have come before the courts in this state contain restrictions upon everyone except Caucasians, while others mention one or more of the unwanted races. Various conditions and covenants in deeds providing that the property conveyed thereby shall not be sold, released, and the like, to persons belonging to the above racial groups have been held invalid as restraining alienation.[58] These restrictions vary as to time, but there is nothing to indicate that the courts were influenced to any great extent by the length of the period that the covenant would be effective. In coming to the conclusion that such covenants were void the courts were swayed by the fact that there is a California statute interdicting restraints on alienation

---

[53] Martin, *Segregation of Residences of Negroes* (1934) 32 MICH. L. REV. 721.

[54] Bruce, *Racial Zoning by Private Contract* (1928) 13 VA. L. REG. (N.S.) 526.

[55] See note 53 *supra.*

[56] Foster v. Stewart, 134 Cal. App. 482, 25 P. (2d) 497 (1933); Porter v. Barrett, 233 Mich. 373, 206 N. W. 532 (1925); Williams v. Commercial Land Co., 34 Ohio Law Rep. 558 (1931).

[57] In fact all the Pacific coast states have alien land laws. *See* State v. Kosai, 133 Wash. 442, 234 Pac. 5 (1925).

[58] Title Guarantee & Trust Co. v. Garrott, 42 Cal. App. 152, 183 Pac. 470 (1919), (1919) 4 MINN. L. REV. 68; Los Angeles Inv. Co. v. Gary, 181 Cal. 680, 186 Pac. 596 (1919); Janss Inv. Co. v. Walden, 196 Cal. 753, 239 Pac. 34 (1925), (1926) 20 ILL. L. REV. 723; DuRoss v. Trainor, 122 Cal. App. 732, 10 P. (2d) 763 (1932).

generally.[59] However, covenants restricting the occupancy[60] of property by these racial groups have been held to be valid and enforceable whether they are contained in deeds[61] or in agreements by property owners[62] which have been brought to the actual or constructive notice of prospective purchasers. The two covenants, the one restraining alienation and the other prohibiting occupancy, may be so interwoven as to be inseparable, and, if this is true, the whole provision is invalidated.[63] However, they are not so enlaced in many instances and are usually separable.[64] There is no time limit in respect to these occupancy covenants, as a permanent one was upheld in the *Walden* case.[65] Some of these provisions contain an exception with respect to domestic servants living in the homes of white persons.[66] At times they may be construed as conditions subsequent,[67] an estate being defeated upon the violation thereof. As a result of these decisions a person who is not of Caucasian blood could own but not occupy property to which one of these occupancy covenants applied.

Michigan agrees with California concerning the invalidity of covenants restraining alienation to Negroes[68] and the validity

---

[59] CAL. CIV. CODE (Deering, 1931) §711.

[60] Commentator in (1926) 20 ILL. L. REV. 723 believes that there is no real difference between covenants restraining alienation and those preventing occupancy by these racial groups.

[61] Los Angeles Inv. Co. v. Gary, 181 Cal. 680, 186 Pac. 596 (1919); Janss Inv. Co. v. Walden, 196 Cal. 753, 239 Pac. 34 (1925); Letteau v. Ellis, 122 Cal. App. 584, 10 P. (2d) 496 (1932).

[62] Wayt v. Patee, 205 Cal. 46, 269 Pac. 660 (1928); Littlejohns v. Henderson, 111 Cal. App. 115, 295 Pac. 95 (1931). *See also* Schulte v. Starks, 238 Mich. 102, 213 N. W. 102 (1927).

[63] Foster v. Stewart, 134 Cal. App. 482, 25 P. (2d) 497 (1933).

[64] Los Angeles Inv. Co. v. Gary, 181 Cal. 680, 186 Pac. 596 (1919); Janss Inv. Co. v. Walden, 196 Cal. 753, 239 Pac. 34 (1925); Letteau v. Ellis, 122 Cal. App. 584, 10 P. (2d) 496 (1932); DuRoss v. Trainor, 122 Cal. App. 732, 10 P. (2d) 763 (1932).

[65] Janss Inv. Co. v. Walden, 196 Cal. 753, 239 Pac. 34 (1925). One learned commentator believes that there should be a time limit even as to occupancy covenants. Bruce, *Racial Zoning by Private Contract* (1928) 13 VA. L. REG. (N.S.) 526. This view may possibly find support in Foster v. Stewart, 134 Cal. App. 482, 25 P. (2d) 497 (1933).

[66] *Ibid. See also* Burke v. Kleiman, 277 Ill. App. 519 (1934); Ridgway v. Cockburn, 163 Misc. 511, 296 N. Y. Supp. 936 (Sup. Ct. 1937).

[67] Los Angeles Inv. Co. v. Gary, 181 Cal. 680, 186 Pac. 596 (1919).

[68] Porter v. Barrett, 233 Mich. 373, 206 N. W. 532 (1925); Schulte v. Starks, 238 Mich. 102, 213 N. W. 102 (1927).

of occupancy covenants.[69] Ohio[70] and West Virginia[71] have also refused to sustain covenants restraining alienation. On the other hand, the Illinois intermediate appellate court seems to have given its approval to both kinds of covenants.[72] Both types also seem to have been upheld in a recent New York case.[73] There appears to have been no reported case concerning the validity of such restrictions in any other northern or middle western state.

In the South and in some of the western states the approval of the courts has been given. Covenants preventing alienation to Negroes for varying periods of time have been held valid in the District of Columbia[74] and in the states of Colorado,[75] Georgia,[76] Louisiana,[77] and Missouri,[78] and indications are that they would be upheld in Kansas[79] and North Carolina.[80] The Maryland Court has recently upheld an agreement prohibiting Negro occupancy or use.[81]

---

[69] Parmalee v. Morris, 218 Mich. 625, 188 N. W. 330 (1922); Schulte v. Starks, 238 Mich. 102, 213 N. W. 102 (1927). The court in the Parmalee case said its reason for upholding the covenant was that it could make no true distinction between these covenants and other restrictions upon occupancy which had been declared valid in Michigan. It is suggested in a Note in (1926) 35 YALE L. J. 755 that the court would be denying due process of law to the other groups excluded by these other covenants against occupancy if it failed to uphold these covenants against the Negro.

[70] Williams v. Commercial Land Co., 34 Ohio Law Rep. 558 (1931).

[71] White v. White, 108 W. Va. 128, 150 S. E. 531 (1929).

[72] Burke v. Kleiman, 277 Ill. App. 519 (1934); Lee v. Hansberry, 291 Ill. App. 517, 10 N. E. (2d) 406 (1937).

[73] Ridgway v. Cockburn, 163 Misc. 511, 296 N. Y. Supp. 936 (Sup. Ct. 1937).

[74] Corrigan v. Buckley, 55 App. D. C. 30, 299 Fed. 899 (1924) (21 years); Torrey v. Wolfes, 56 App. D. C. 4, 6 F. (2d) 702 (1925) (permanent); Russell v. Wallace, 58 App. D. C. 357, 30 F. (2d) 981 (1929) (no time limit); Cornish v. O'Donoghue, 58 App. D. C. 359, 30 F. (2d) 983 (1929) (permanent); Edwards v. West Woodridge Theatre Co., 60 App. D. C. 362, 55 F. (2d) 524 (1931) (no time limit).

[75] Chandler v. Ziegler, 88 Colo. 1, 291 Pac. 822 (1930) (permanent).

[76] Allmond v. Jenkins, 165 Ga. 334, 140 S. E. 879 (1927) (no time limit).

[77] Queensborough Land Co. v. Cazeaux, 136 La. 724, 67 So. 641 (1915) (25 years).

[78] Koehler v. Rowland, 275 Mo. 573, 205 S. W. 217 (1918) (25 years); Porter v. Johnson, 232 Mo. App. 1150, 115 S. W. (2d) 529 (1938) (15 years).

[79] Clark v. Vaughan, 131 Kans. 438, 292 Pac. 783 (1930) (15 years).

[80] Eason v. Buffaloe, 198 N. C. 520, 152 S. E. 496 (1930) (no time limit); St. Louis Union Trust Co. v. Foster, 211 N. C. 331, 190 S. E. 522 (1937) (21 years).

[81] Meade v. Dennistone, 173 Md. 295, 196 Atl. 330 (1938).

The rule against perpetuities should not be allowed to interfere with the enforcement of these covenants, especially in jurisdictions where it is considered as the rule against the remoteness of vesting. Where it is so held, as it is in the great majority of states, this rule of property law would not be permitted to defeat one of these covenants or agreements on the ground that it would tie up property so that it could not be aliened freely.[82]

These provisions against Negroes may sometimes be construed as conditions allowing re-entry rather than just restrictive covenants,[83] but in one instance a vendor who had violated the terms of the deed by which the land had been conveyed to him was given an opportunity to cancel his sale to a Negro before the rescission of the original deed could be demanded.[84] Most of these covenants run with the land,[85] but it is possible that one might be construed to be merely personal where the instrument does not expressly provide that such shall be the case.[86]

A court of equity will enforce such covenants[87] and kindred provisions prohibiting Negro occupancy[88] by injunction. This will be done even though the instrument containing the covenant includes a clause providing for a two-thousand-dollar penalty in case of a breach, the penalty being deemed inadequate relief under the familiar doctrine that a court of equity will not take jurisdiction in a case where there is an adequate remedy at law.[89] It is true that a changed situation may develop when

[82] Koehler v. Rowland, 275 Mo. 573, 205 S. W. 217 (1918); Martin, *Segregation of Residences of Negroes* (1934) 32 MICH. L. REV. 721.

[83] Koehler v. Rowland, 275 Mo. 573, 205 S. W. 217 (1918).

[84] Queensborough Land Co. v. Cazeaux, 136 La. 724, 67 So. 641 (1915).

[85] See note 84 *supra*.

[86] *See* Wayt v. Patee, 205 Cal. 46, 269 Pac. 660 (1928).

[87] Lee v. Hansberry, 291 Ill. App. 517, 10 N. E. (2d) 406 (1937); Queensborough Land Co. v. Cazeaux, 136 La. 724, 67 So. 641 (1915); Edwards v. West Woodridge Theatre Co. 60 App. D. C. 362, 55 F. (2d) 524 (1931).

[88] Wayt v. Patee, 205 Cal. 46, 269 Pac. 660 (1928); Meade v. Dennistone, 173 Md. 295, 196 Atl. 330 (1938); Schulte v. Starkes, 238 Mich. 102, 213 N. W. 102 (1927). In the Schulte case it was said that evidence that Negro occupancy would diminish the value of neighboring property was admissible to give equity jurisdiction.

[89] Torrey v. Wolfes, 56 App. D. C. 4, 6 F. (2d) 702 (1925). Such a penalty clause is not unique. *See* Cornish v. O'Donoghue, 58 App. D. C. 359, 30 F. (2d) 983 (1929).

there has been such an influx of colored persons into the neighborhood surrounding the restricted property as to make the enforcement of these covenants or agreements inequitable and unsuitable under existing social conditions, thereby rendering the restrictions nugatory as to purpose. In such cases the courts refuse to enforce the covenants.[90] However, it is not every minor incursion of this kind that will have this effect.[91] The courts may refuse to allow such a change in neighborhood to influence their decisions because the evidence shows that the covenantors anticipated Negro occupation of surrounding territory at the time the agreement was made.[92] In one recent case from the District of Columbia a white owner of property wished to remove a restriction of this kind as a cloud upon his title because Negroes had occupied all houses on an adjoining block and were quite numerous in the vicinity. Opposition developed among the white property owners in the restricted area, and the court agreed with them that the desired relief should not be granted. The majority opinion stated that the plaintiff had not alleged sufficient facts and that the presence of Negroes in the neighborhood did not necessarily render the property unfit for white occupants.[93]

It is sometimes important to ascertain just what persons are included within the prohibitions of these covenants. Mulattoes who obviously have Negro blood in their veins would almost certainly be within the restrictions, and they might even be construed as covering those persons who have only a modicum of Negro blood. A state's former attitude in respect to problems of racial identity, discussed in another chapter, would no doubt be controlling here. There seem to be only three cases dealing with this phase of the problem. A New York court has held that a man who was three-fourths Negro and his octoroon wife were within the terms of a covenant which prohibited the

[90] Bruce, *Racial Zoning by Private Contract in the Light of the Constitution and the Rule Against Restraints on Alienation* (1927) 21 Ill. L. Rev. 704. *See* Letteau v. Ellis, 122 Cal. App. 584, 10 P. (2d) 496 (1932); Clark v. Vaughan, 131 Kan. 438, 292 Pac. 783 (1930); Pickel v. McCawley, 329 Mo. 166, 44 S. W. (2d) 857 (1931).

[91] Burke v. Kleiman, 277 Ill. App. 519 (1934); Meade v. Dennistone, 173 Md. 295, 196 Atl. 330 (1938); Koehler v. Rowland, 275 Mo. 573, 205 S. W. 217 (1918).

[92] Porter v. Johnson, 232 Mo. App. 1150, 115 S. W. (2d) 529 (1938).

[93] Grady v. Garland, 67 App. D. C. 73, 89 F. (2d) 817 (1937).

ownership or occupancy of a certain lot by Negroes or persons of Negro blood.[94] In a West Virginia case it was decided that the word "Ethiopian" was used in a deed as denoting Negroes, although the term does not so signify when it is employed in its strictest sense.[95] In the other case the Virginia Court held that a corporation composed of Negro stockholders did not come within the meaning of a covenant of the usual type, the corporation being considered a separate entity.[96] The wisdom of this decision is doubtful. There is the possibility that some wealthy Negro who desired a residence in some exclusive white neighborhood might incorporate his family and thus avoid the restrictions which had been written into the deeds with the object of keeping out members of his race. The successful culmination of such an attempt would require only a slight extension of the doctrine approved in this case. The decision extends the idea of the separate corporate person to a situation where the reason behind the conception fails. It should be possible for private property owners, whether they be white or colored, to make such contracts with one another or with the management of a new subdivision. The corporate fiction should not be permitted to defeat the aim of those who desire a congenial community.

A good many questions may arise as to when these covenants against Negro ownership or occupancy shall go into effect, the formalities which are necessary to complete their effectiveness, and the persons who will be permitted to enter into and enforce them. An agreement among property owners that no Negroes shall be allowed in the restricted area may be so worded as to require the signatures of all or a certain proportion of the said owners as a condition precedent to its effectiveness,[97] and the courts will allow a reasonable period of time in which these signatures may be obtained.[98] In one case from California

[94] Ridgway v. Cockburn, 163 Misc. 511, 296 N. Y. Supp. 936 (Sup. Ct. 1937).

[95] White v. White, 108 W. Va. 128, 150 S. E. 531 (1929).

[96] Peoples Pleasure Park Co. v. Rohleder, 109 Va. 439, 61 S. E. 794, 63 S. E. 981 (1908).

[97] Foster v. Stewart, 134 Cal. App. 482, 25 P. (2d) 497 (1933); Pickel v. McCawley, 329 Mo. 166, 44 S. W. (2d) 857 (1931); Thornhill v. Herdt, 130 S. W. (2d) 175 (Mo. App. 1939); Veal v. Hopps, 183 Okla. 116, 80 P. (2d) 275 (1938).

[98] Russell v. Wallace, 58 App. D. C. 357, 30 F. (2d) 981 (1929). The circum-

only two of the twenty-three signers had acknowledged the instrument and neither of these two owned the particular piece of property in question. A Negro vendee acquired this lot without knowing of the agreement. The court said that the agreement, being improperly acknowledged, could not be considered as giving the Negro constructive notice. Therefore the recorded instrument was declared to be ineffective in relation to the Negro.[99] In a North Carolina case there was a general development scheme to restrict a certain tract to white ownership and occupancy. The promoter had already conveyed a few lots, and the deeds contained such restrictions. These purchasers were said to have a right to object if the rest of the property covered by a general scheme was not so conveyed. In order to prove that such a general plan existed a recorded map dividing the tract into lots was introduced. However, this map was said to be not alone sufficient to show the existence of the plan. The particular lots in controversy were held not to be under a general scheme and therefore not subject to the demand that they be transferred with restrictions.[100]

In a Missouri case there was an agreement to sign a contract by which Negroes could be kept out of a certain land tract. One of the participants in the agreement perfected a conveyance to a Negro who had notice of the pact. The contract had never been executed, but other participants in the agreement to sign demanded redress for its breach. The court refused to grant either equitable or legal relief.[101] The remedy by cancellation of the offensive conveyance was refused because neither the Negro nor the defendant's wife had signed the agreement to execute the contract. It was said that specific performance of the agreement to sign would be ineffectual, since the alienation of the lot to the Negro had already been consummated and nothing could be done to upset it. The court refused to grant damages for the breach of the agreement to sign because of the plaintiff's failure to plead damages or a consideration adequately. Had there been more specific pleading, however, the

stances must be taken into consideration in order for the court to determine what a reasonable time is.

[99] Du Ross v. Trainor, 122 Cal. App. 732, 10 P. (2d) 763 (1932).

[100] Eason v. Buffaloe, 198 N. C. 520, 152 S. E. 496 (1930). *See also* St. Louis Union Trust Co. v. Foster, 211 N. C. 331, 190 S. E. 522 (1937).

[101] Mueninghaus v. James, 324 Mo. 767, 24 S. W. (2d) 1017 (1930).

plaintiff would probably have been allowed to recover damages.

It has been decided that no one may enforce a restrictive covenant of this kind unless he is in privity with the original covenantee.[102] However, a person who has an interest in the property, such as a residuary devisee or a life tenant who has control and beneficial use, may enter into an agreement with a view toward protecting the neighborhood against Negro intrusion.[103]

The desire of white persons to remain apart from the Negro is also seen in the separate cemeteries of the South. A white family would be much averse to burying their loved ones in a cemetery where the races were mixed. However, there are many burying grounds in the South where the Negro graves are situated in a lot adjoining the white tombs. Sometimes there is a wall between, sometimes just a path. It has been held that private cemetery corporations, no matter in what section of the country they are located, may limit burial in their grounds to members of the white race.[104] However, this would not interfere with the vested rights of those Negroes who have either reserved a lot at the time of the transfer of the property to the corporation[105] or have acquired their lots before the regulation excluding Negroes was put into effect.[106] Two northern states, New Jersey and New York, prohibit racial discrimination in cemeteries.[107] The Illinois Civil Rights Act provides that there shall be no racial discrimination in the prices which may be charged for a cemetery lot,[108] but it has been held that this statute would not prevent a private corporation from put-

[102] Toothaker v. Pleasant, 315 Mo. 1239, 288 S. W. 38 (1926).

[103] Russell v. Wallace, 58 App. D. C. 357, 30 F. (2d) 981 (1929).

[104] Forest Lawn Memorial Park Ass'n v. DeJarnette, 79 Cal. App. 601, 250 Pac. 581 (1926); People *ex rel.* Gaskill v. Forest Home Cemetery Co., 258 Ill. 36, 101 N. E. 219 (1913). There is a suggestion in the Illinois case that the decision might have been different if the corporation had been a quasi-public one with the right of eminent domain.

[105] Richmond Cemetery Co. v. Walker, 29 Ky. Law Rep. 1252, 97 S. W. 34 (1906). The person to be interred was almost white.

[106] People *ex rel.* Gaskill v. Forest Home Cemetery Co., 258 Ill. 36, 101 N. E. 219 (1913); Mount Moriah Cemetery Ass'n v. Commonwealth, 81 Pa. St. 235, 22 Am. Rep. 743 (1876).

[107] N. J. Comp. Stat. (1911) p. 1810, §213; N. Y. Consol. Laws (Cahill, 1930) c. 41, §514.

[108] Ill. Rev. Stat. (Cahill, 1933) c. 38, §104.

ting into effect a regulation excluding Negroes altogether.[109]

There have been instances where fraudulent representations have been relied upon with the result that white persons have been disappointed in their wish to live apart from Negroes. In such cases the white person should be allowed to obtain some redress from the persons responsible for the deception. In one case from Colorado a vendor, wishing to facilitate the sale of a certain lot in a subdivision, falsely represented to a buyer that all the other lots in the neighborhood had been conveyed with restrictions against Negro ownership and occupancy. It was held that the buyer was entitled to damages.[110] In a Missouri case a white plaintiff successfully brought a suit to set aside a conveyance to an agent of a realty company who falsely represented that he desired the property for himself, but who in reality was merely acting as a dummy for a Negro who paid all the purchase price and to whom the plaintiff had already refused to sell because he did not wish to convey to a Negro.[111]

In the absence of fraud, the Washington Court refused to rescind a contract to convey real estate which the vendor declined to execute because the purchaser was a Negro, a fact which was unknown to the vendor at the time of the sale.[112] The court declared that there was no evidence that the purchaser deliberately concealed the fact that he was a Negro nor that he knew that this fact, if known, would have prevented the sale. The court does not state that proof of these facts would have made a difference in its opinion, and hence it is rather difficult, if not impossible, to understand the exact scope of the decision. It is possible, however, that the purchaser's knowledge of the vendor's racial antipathy might have made a difference in the court's decision. Another case similar to this one arose in Michigan. In this instance a vendor sold property to a female purchaser, the deed containing the common provision saying that the latter could not sell or assign her interest without the former's consent. The vendor gave his approval to a proposed transfer on condition that the property should not be sold to

[109] People *ex rel.* Gaskill v. Forest Home Cemetery Co., 258 Ill. 36, 101 N. E. 219 (1913). [110] Chandler v. Ziegler, 88 Colo. 1, 291 Pac. 822 (1930).

[111] Keltner v. Harris, 196 S. W. 1 (Mo. 1917).

[112] Cole v. Hunter Tract Improvement Co., 61 Wash. 365, 112 Pac. 368 (1910).

Jews or Negroes. A contract was made with a person who, though he appeared to be white, had Negro blood. In the absence of convincing evidence that this person knew the exact terms of the condition or had made false statements concerning his race, the court refused to grant the vendor's request that the sale be rescinded.[113]

It has been decided that a landowner may erect small and cheap tenement houses close to the line of an adjacent owner and lease them to orderly Negro tenants,[114] and may also advertise unrestricted property as being for sale to members of the Negro race.[115] Moreover, he may do these things even though one of his purposes is to annoy neighboring real-estate owners who do not care for the propinquity of Negroes.[116] In New York it has been held that a landlord cannot be prevented from renting an apartment to Negroes even though his ulterior motive is to force certain white tenants to vacate the property.[117] However, the Alabama Court has decided that there is a custom which is an implied element of every contract of this kind that Negroes shall not be permitted in an apartment building which had been and was still being used by whites.[118] In this case a landlord rented to Negroes an apartment in a building in which there were common toilet facilities. The court declared that a white tenant might consider this action as a constructive eviction and could recover damages for this and the mental anguish caused thereby. In Louisiana an attempt was made to handle

[113] Henze v. Saunders, 215 Mich. 646, 184 N. W. 443 (1921).

[114] Falloon v. Schilling, 29 Kans. 292, 44 Am. Rep. 642 (1883).

[115] Holbrook v. Morrison, 214 Mass. 209, 100 N. E. 1111 (1913).

[116] Falloon v. Schilling, 29 Kans. 292 (1883); Holbrook v. Morrison, 214 Mass. 209, 100 N. E. 1111 (1913). There is suggestion in the Holbrook case that equity might have intervened if the sole purpose of the advertising had been to plague the neighboring property owners.

[117] Schoolhause v. Browning, 116 Misc. 338, 190 N. Y. Supp. 353 (Sup. Ct. 1921).

[118] Wyatt v. Adair, 215 Ala. 363, 110 So. 801 (1926). This case is fully commented upon in (1926) 12 Corn. L. Q. 400, in which the commentator grants the correctness of the decision in the far South and intimates that a similar doctrine should apply in the North because of the bad motive for the action. In stating that the question is a new one in New York, he evidently overlooked Schoolhause v. Browning, 116 Misc. 338, 190 N. Y. Supp. 353 (Sup. Ct. 1921). His argument that the action of the judiciary in implying the covenant might be considered as state action which is prohibited by the Fourteenth Amendment can be answered by stating that the only thing the court did was to imply individual action.

this matter by statute. An act was adopted which provides that no person or corporation shall rent an apartment in an apartment house or other like structure to a person who is not of the same race as the other occupants.[119] The statute makes exceptions for domestic servants and states that buildings with partitions or separate entrances for white and colored tenants are also under the prohibition of the law. A violation of the act is made a misdemeanor punishable by fine and imprisonment. Hence we see that there may be sectional differences in the manner in which the states handle situations of this kind.

An interesting case came before a Missouri Court of Appeals in 1914. A landlord had leased property in a white neighborhood to a Negro tenant. The whites in the district were opposed to the entrance of Negroes into their part of the city. It was shown that the landlord had the premises ready for occupancy at the time when the lessee's right of entry accrued. Under these circumstances it was held that the landlord was not responsible for the action of third parties in preventing the Negro from entering the residence in an unfriendly neighborhood.[120]

The federal statute[121] punishing any conspiracy to deprive a person of the rights guaranteed by the Constitution and laws of the United States has been twice employed to protect the property rights of Negroes. A conspiracy to drive a Negro from the homestead which he had established in conformity with federal laws was held to be indictable under this act,[122] as was also a plot to prevent Negroes from leasing and cultivating land in a community where there was much race hatred.[123]

Negro individuals and organizations are permitted to use their property in the same manner as whites, and the fact that such a use is offensive to the white neighbors should not be allowed to influence the courts unduly. The nuisance doctrine will not be held to apply except where similar acts, if indulged

[119] LA. CODE CRIM. PROC. ANN. (Dart, 1932) arts. 1315-17.

[120] Brown v. Hall, 186 Mo. App. 150, 171 S. W. 586 (1914). The interference in this instance was by municipal police who were trying to prevent bad feeling between the races from being engendered, the white people being antagonistic toward the Negroes.

[121] 18 U. S. C. A. §51 (1926), REV. STAT. §5508 (1875).

[122] United States v. Waddell, 112 U. S. 76, 5 Sup. Ct. 35 (1884). It is not stated that the person injured was a Negro, but from the circumstances that are mentioned one can reason that he was of that race.

[123] United States v. Morris, 125 Fed. 322 (E. D. Ark. 1903).

in by white persons, would constitute an illegal interference with some neighboring property owner's comfort or convenience. The courts will not enjoin the erection of small tenement houses for Negroes close to the line of an adjacent owner[124] or the construction of a garage, the upper story of which overhangs the plaintiff's second floor, to be occupied by Negro servants.[125] Neither can a Negro college be interfered with because it permits a portion of its property to be divided into building lots and sold for the purpose of establishing a residential colony for colored persons.[126] Negro religious bodies may use their property in any legitimate manner, and people in the neighborhood are not permitted to object to the mode of worship unless it amounts to a breach of the peace or is for some other reason illegal.[127] The same principles apply to a Negro hospital, although its maintenance must be enjoined if it is being conducted in an indecent, obnoxious, and unsanitary manner.[128] In one Georgia case it was held that a Negro cemetery cannot be regarded as a nuisance per se.[129]

In an interesting case from Texas it was held that a Negro property owner may recover compensatory and punitive damages from a white man for malicious interference with a contractor who was building a house on the plaintiff's lot.[130] The owner was building the structure as an investment and had told the defendant that he would not rent it to anyone who was objectionable to the latter. In spite of this reassurance the defendant acted unlawfully.

One other point deserves consideration. In Colorado a corporate lessee of a dance hall sublet it with a provision in the sublease that the hall should not be used in a "disreputable" manner. The occupant made a contract with a Negro organization for the use of the hall on Christmas and New Year's evenings. After its use by the Negroes on the first of these occasions, the

[124] Falloon v. Schilling, 29 Kans. 292 (1883).

[125] Woods v. Kiersky, 14 S. W. (2d) 825 (Tex. Com. App. 1929).

[126] Diggs v. Morgan College, 133 Md. 264, 105 Atl. 157 (1918).

[127] Boyd v. Board of Council of Frankfort, 117 Ky. 199, 77 S. W. 669 (1903); Spencer Chapel M. E. Church v. Brogan, 104 Okla. 123, 231 Pac. 1074 (1924). See in connection with this point City of Louisiana v. Bottoms, 300 S. W. 316 (Mo. App. 1927).

[128] Giles v. Rawlings, 148 Ga. 575, 97 S. E. 521 (1918).

[129] Hall v. Moffett, 177 Ga. 300, 170 S. E. 192 (1933).

[130] Day v. Hunnicutt, 160 S. W. 134 (Tex. Civ. App. 1913).

corporation took over the property and refused to allow the organization to proceed with the party scheduled for New Year's. The corporation claimed that the sublessee had breached the above provision of the agreement by renting the hall to Negroes, and sued for the installments of rent which the sublessee had refused to pay after the doors were closed. The court held that a Negro dancing club was not "disreputable" per se and that the corporation's interference constituted an eviction which prevented a recovery.[131]

A recent case from Louisiana presents an interesting contrast to the case just discussed. A New Orleans public-service company had control of a ball park which was located in a white neighborhood. It leased the park to an amusement company which desired to stage athletic contests therein, the contract containing a provision that the latter would not use the park in an objectionable or offensive manner. The lessee allowed Negro baseball teams to play a game in the park, and a fight ensued which caused a great deal of unfavorable comment on the part of the white residents. The lessor corporation realized that such use of its park would create ill will against it. Therefore it notified the lessee that the latter must cease using the park for Negro games, citing the above provision of the lease. The lessee acted on the advice of its attorney. It cancelled all other Negro games which had been booked for the park and then sued the lessor for damages alleged to have been caused by the latter's supposed breach of contract in refusing to allow such games. The state court held that such a use would come within the above provision because it was offensive to the white persons in the neighborhood, and relief was refused for this reason.[132] The court stated that the Fourteenth Amendment did not apply to the case because the action was that of an individual and not of the state.

The decisions in these two cases seem to be opposed to one another in principle. The only substantial difference is in the word employed to describe the type of person or thing that is not wanted. A person or event may be "objectionable" without being "disreputable." However, the cases are enough alike

---

[131] Central Business College v. Rutherford, 47 Colo. 277, 107 Pac. 279 (1910).

[132] Modern Amusements v. New Orleans Public Service, 183 La. 898, 165 So. 137 (1936).

to present an interesting comparison. The dissimilarity of the results in the two cases may be better understood when one remembers that they were decided by courts in widely separated sections of the country. A Colorado judge could hardly be expected to take the same attitude toward race relationships that would prevail among the Louisiana jurists. However, the fact that such a case arose in Colorado is proof enough that at least some race prejudice exists in that state.

VI

INVOLUNTARY SERVITUDE

Before 1860 approximately half of the United States was slave territory. Then came the Civil War and the adoption of the Thirteenth Amendment to the Federal Constitution, which abolished slavery and prohibited involuntary servitude except as a punishment for crime. The typical southern state constitution of the postwar period and the fundamental documents of a goodly number of other states contain similar provisions in their Bill of Rights or elsewhere in their texts.

This created a very serious situation in the southern states. Several millions of freedmen were thereby turned loose on the community with little or no provision for their welfare. There were very few remunerative jobs to be had, and the Negroes wandered about and lived as best they could. Of course some remained with their former masters and helped them make an attempt to build up something out of the desolation which engulfed most of the plantation owners. An attempt was made to exercise some measure of authority over the ignorant and vagrant Negroes. The legislatures enacted the so-called Black Codes, and these statutes contained provisions which were very harsh indeed. Chief among the provisions were apprentice laws which practically returned the Negro to the old master and slave relationship under another name. There were vagrancy laws and other types of statutes designed to give the white man authority over the freedmen.

This was the way that the whites chose to handle the difficult problem confronting them. It was thought in the North, and not without reason, that this was merely an attempt to perpetuate slavery in a different guise. The northern people had a somewhat sketchy idea of the conditions in the South which had prompted this legislation. They were not familiar with the abysmal ignorance of the overwhelming majority of the Negroes. They did not understand the necessity for at least some measure of legal control over the freedmen. They did not realize that the Negroes, while basking in the sun of their newly found freedom, were being deceived by the fabulous promises of "forty acres and a mule" made by "skalawags" and "carpetbaggers." A defense of the Black Codes is not attempted here, as some of the provisions were extremely rigorous and certainly had a tendency to re-establish the old master and slave relationship under a new name. However, the southern legislators had a very serious situation before them and were merely trying to make something out of the chaotic conditions which followed the war and the emancipation of the slaves. These Black Codes had a great deal to do with the rise of the radical elements in Congress and hence were to some extent responsible for the dark blot of Reconstruction.

The provisions of the Maryland statute failed to give the same protection to Negro apprentices that was given to whites. Hence the act was declared to be in conflict with the Congressional Civil Rights Act of 1866 and therefore of no effect.[1] Although the validity of this piece of federal legislation was never tested in the Supreme Court,[2] the principle involved in this Maryland case was carried over into the equal protection clause of the Fourteenth Amendment.

The second section of the Thirteenth Amendment gave Congress authority to enforce its purposes by appropriate legislation. In accordance with the power thus given to it, Congress enacted statutes proscribing peonage and various other tortuous methods which might be employed to circumvent the purposes and spirit of the amendment.[3] Although the original purpose of this legislation was to stamp out the system of Indian peonage which had existed in New Mexico,[4] its aim was to abolish involuntary servitude wherever found, no matter what racial element was the victim.[5] There is no doubt about the validity of these statutes.[6]

The term "peonage" has been defined by the courts. One court has defined it as being a condition of compulsory service

---

[1] *In re* Turner, 24 Fed. Cas. No. 14,247 (C. C. D. Md. 1867).

[2] See chapter on Civil Rights, p. 27.

[3] REV. STAT. §§1990, 1991, 5526, 5527 (1875). Section 1990 is now 8 U. S. C. A. §56 (1926). In this connection see also COMP. STAT. (1901) pp. 1266-67.

[4] *See* Jaremillo v. Romero, 1 N. M. 190 (1857).

[5] *In re* Lewis, 114 Fed. 963 (C. C. N. D. Fla. 1902).

[6] United States v. McClellan, 127 Fed. 971 (S. D. Ga. 1904); Clyatt v. United States, 197 U. S. 207, 25 Sup. Ct. 429 (1905).

based on the indebtedness of the victim, which indebtedness is the cord by which he is bound to the person to whom he owes the obligation.[7] There are various ways in which the crime may be committed. In one case from Florida it was shown that a master, desiring to have a Negro servant returned to him to work out a debt, caused the delinquent one to be arrested on a warrant procured by himself. After the incarceration he obtained the Negro's release on the latter's promise to return to his employ and pay the debt. It was shown that the master had charged the Negro with a crime with the express purpose of extorting his promise to return. The court held that this constituted peonage.[8] In a South Carolina case a federal court held that one is guilty of peonage who by reason of his superior economic and social position induces a party to labor for the purpose of paying debts by threats of prosecution under criminal statutes, if by reason of such threats the will of the party is overcome.[9] Again, it has been said that one is guilty of peonage if he falsely pretends to another that the latter is accused of a criminal offense and offers to prevent his conviction if he will pay the prosecutor a sum of money in satisfaction, thus inducing him to sign a labor contract to reimburse the one who is supposed to have paid such sum for him and to submit to a deprivation of liberty in the meantime.[10] Such is also the case where someone having authority over a criminal farms him out to the person who has been his surety, as permitted by state law, beyond the time provided for in his sentence.[11] A state of peonage has also been held to exist under an Alabama statute providing additional punishment for breaking a contract to work for a surety who has paid one's fine.[12] Any magistrate who connives at chicanery of this kind may be successfully indicted on a peonage charge[13] and may also be prosecuted under a federal statute[14] punishing a conspiracy to deprive a person of his constitutional rights.

[7] *In re* Peonage Charge, 138 Fed. 686 (C. C. N. D. Fla. 1905). *See also* Clyatt v. United States, 197 U. S. 207, 25 Sup. Ct. 429 (1905); United States v. Clement, 171 Fed. 974 (D. S. C. 1909).

[8] *In re* Peonage Charge, 138 Fed. 686 (C. C. N. D. Fla. 1905).

[9] United States v. Clement, 171 Fed. 974 (D. S. C. 1909).

[10] Peonage Cases, 123 Fed. 671 (M. D. Ala. 1903). [11] *Ibid.*

[12] United States v. Reynolds, 235 U. S. 133, 35 Sup. Ct. 86 (1914).

[13] Peonage Cases, 123 Fed. 671 (M. D. Ala. 1903).

[14] 18 U. S. C. A. §51 (1926), Rev. Stat. §5508 (1875).

In order to obtain a conviction of the crime of peonage it is only necessary to show that the culprit acted wilfully and knowingly and proof that he acted corruptly is not required.[15] A federal court in Georgia has held that a person may be prosecuted under these statutes in spite of the fact that the same act might be punishable under state law as kidnapping or false imprisonment.[16] Where the fear of prosecution is self-engendered and is not the result of action on the part of the master or employer, it has been held that there is no basis for a charge of peonage.[17]

The statutes contain provisions making it a crime to return to a state of peonage persons who have escaped from that predicament. In one case the indictment charged that the defendant had knowingly returned certain Negroes to a condition of peonage. As the proof failed to show that the victims had ever in the past been in such a state, the court ruled that there was a fatal variance between the pleading and the proof and that this required a reversal of a conviction.[18] In the absence of any attempt at coercion or undue influence, an agreement by a debtor to labor for one suggested by his creditor instead of the creditor himself cannot be termed involuntary servitude.[19]

A different situation is presented by a state statute which provides for the punishment of any laborer, renter, or share cropper who shall leave without the consent of his employer or landlord before the expiration of his contract and make another agreement with a third party without giving the latter notice of the prior contract. The Mississippi Court held that this act was unconstitutional.[20] The same has been said to be true with respect to a state statute making it a misdemeanor to wilfully violate a contract of hire conditioned upon the continued cultivation of land and upon the faith of which money or goods have been advanced, no offer of restitution being made.[21] The

[15] United States v. Clement, 171 Fed. 974 (D. S. C. 1909).

[16] United States v. McClellan, 127 Fed. 971 (S. D. Ga. 1904).

[17] United States v. Clement, 171 Fed. 974 (D. S. C. 1909).

[18] Clyatt v. United States, 197 U. S. 207, 25 Sup. Ct. 429 (1905).

[19] Potts v. Riddle, 5 Ga. App. 378, 63 S. E. 253 (1908).

[20] State v. Armstead, 103 Miss. 790, 60 So. 778 (1912).

[21] State v. Oliva, 144 La. 51, 80 So. 195 (1918), overruling all that is said to the contrary in State v. Murray, 116 La. 655, 40 So. 930 (1906), a decision which is in line with a former erroneous decision of the South Carolina Court in State v. Williams, 32 S. C. 123, 10 S. E. 876 (1890), later corrected in *ex parte* Hollman,

court also said that it was immaterial that the service had been begun voluntarily. In another instance there was an Alabama statute penalizing the breaking of a contract to labor or cultivate lands when such breach is accompanied by the laborer's failure to give his next prospective employer notice of his failure to fulfill the terms of his prior contract. This act was also held to violate the Thirteenth Amendment and to countenance a status indictable under the peonage statutes.[22]

When it appeared that statutes of the above type would not stand the constitutional test, the southern legislators sought other means of forcing the Negro tenant farmers to carry out their contracts. The lot of the southern Negro tenant farmer is notoriously hard, and yet the legislators were not totally without justification in their attempt to find some way of making the Negroes live up to their agreements. There were large numbers of the colored population who had very little sense of responsibility. Landlords had a great deal of trouble in holding their Negro tenants, and most of the latter were financially unable to pay damages for a breach of contract.

The legislators evidently still believed that the best method of accomplishing their purpose was the threat of a jail sentence. They set about the task of finding some method which would not violate constitutional guarantees. Quite a few of the states of the Lower South enacted statutes making it a criminal offense to enter into such a contract with an intent to defraud, adding a clause which made the refusal of the tenant or laborer to perform the contract presumptive or prima-facie evidence of such an intention. Statutes of this type were held valid by the state courts of Alabama[23] and Georgia.[24] The Alabama case was appealed to the Federal Supreme Court, and after quite

---

79 S. C. 9, 60 S. E. 19 (1908) and *ex parte* Drayton, 153 Fed. 986 (D. S. C. 1907), both of which also held the statute to be invalid as not bearing equally on the laborers in violation of the Fourteenth Amendment, although the courts gave different reasons therefor. The Hollman case decided that the statute was invalid because it punished the laborer and not the landlord for a breach of contract, whereas the federal court based its holding on the fact that the act made an unreasonable classification, applying only to agricultural laborers.

[22] Peonage Cases, 123 Fed. 671 (M. D. Ala. 1903).

[23] Bailey v. State, 158 Ala. 18, 48 So. 498 (1908).

[24] Townsend v. State, 124 Ga. 69, 52 S. E. 293 (1905). Prima-facie provision is left out of court's discussion of Georgia statute but an examination shows it to have been included.

a battle that tribunal ruled that the statute was unconstitutional.[25] Although a state may enact legislation providing that proof of one fact shall be prima-facie evidence of another, there must be a rational relation between the two. The court said that there was no such rational relation in this instance and held that this set up constituted peonage and hence violated the Thirteenth Amendment. The tribunal was evidently influenced by the fact that there is a rule of evidence in Alabama that an accused person cannot testify with respect to uncommunicated motives or intentions. Immediately an attempt was made to uphold similar statutes in other states which had no such rule of evidence. It was argued that the cases were distinguishable on this ground, and some jurists agreed that this was a differentiating feature.[26] However, the language of the Supreme Court in the Alabama case is not subject to this interpretation and clearly denies the validity of the statute on the above constitutional grounds. The evidential rule is mentioned only as an additional factor which entered into the court's decision.

These acts usually appeared in two sections, the first being devoted to a description of the fraudulent crime, the second to the presumption arising from the refusal to perform the contract. A question arose concerning separability of the two sections of these statutes. It has been held that the first section is valid in spite of the unconstitutionality of the second.[27] The courts employed the familiar doctrine that statutory provisions which are not invalid in themselves will not be declared void because other portions of the same act are unconstitutional, unless the sections of the act are so tied in with one another that the purpose of the entire statute would fail of accomplishment if the invalid section should fall. Sometimes it has been deemed unnecessary to use the second section of the acts because there was an abundance of evidence on which to base the charge of fraud without employing the presumption. In an instance where this is the case a writ of habeas corpus, brought by one who claims

[25] Bailey v. Alabama, 219 U. S. 219, 31 Sup. Ct. 145 (1911).

[26] Wilson v. State, 138 Ga. 489, 75 S. E. 619 (1912). *See also* Phillips v. Bell, 84 Fla. 225, 94 So. 699 (1922).

[27] Latson v. Wells, 136 Ga. 681, 71 S. E. 1052 (1911); Phillips v. Bell, 84 Fla. 225, 94 So. 699 (1922).

that the act under which he has been convicted is unconstitutional, may be properly denied.[28] In another case the Georgia Court refused to issue a writ of habeas corpus where the defendant in the criminal prosecution had pleaded guilty to a charge of violating the statute's first section.[29] Hence it seems that statutes of this type which do not contain the presumption are not objectionable on constitutional grounds, and the courts have so held.[30]

It has been held that separate school[31] or coach[32] laws do not create a "badge of slavery" and hence are not violative of the Thirteenth Amendment. Furthermore, it was decided in the *Civil Rights Cases*[33] that the amendment gave Congress no authority to enact civil rights legislation guaranteeing equal accommodations for all persons, irrespective of race, in inns, public conveyances, and other places of public accommodation and amusement.

In one instance certain portions of the Reconstruction legislation protecting individuals from an infringement of their constitutional rights[34] were invoked where an effort was being made to force Negroes to break labor contracts. Certain citizens of the state of Arkansas conspired and engineered an oppressive plot to prevent these Negroes from making and carrying out such contracts. The Supreme Court held that no right guaranteed by the Thirteenth Amendment or other constitutional provision was involved in this case and that therefore the federal courts had no jurisdiction of the offense charged.[35] The court declared that such a conspiracy was entirely within the province of the state tribunals. However, one of these same statutes has been held to cover a case where farm labor by Negroes has been induced by fraudulent representa-

[28] *Ibid.* [29] Latson v. Wells, 136 Ga. 681, 71 S. E. 1052 (1911).

[30] Bailey v. Alabama, 211 U. S. 452, 29 Sup. Ct. 141 (1908); Thomas v. State, 13 Ala. App. 431, 69 So. 908 (1915). The seeming contrariety of Goode v. Nelson, 73 Fla. 29, 74 So. 17 (1917), to this view may be explained by a look at the statute, unavailable to us at present, which may contain a second section similar to those which were declared void above, a fact which does not appear in the case itself. [31] Ward v. Flood, 48 Cal. 36 (1874).

[32] Plessey v. Ferguson, 163 U. S. 537, 16 Sup. Ct. 1138 (1896).

[33] Civil Rights Cases, 109 U. S. 3, 3 Sup. Ct. 18 (1883); Charge to Grand Jury, 30 Fed. Cas. No. 18, 260 (C. C. W. D. Tenn. 1875).

[34] REV. STAT. §§1978, 1979, 5508, 5510 (1875).

[35] Hodges v. United States, 203 U. S. 1, 27 Sup. Ct. 6 (1906).

tions that wages would be paid and later continued by force, brutality, and threats of violence.[36] There is a thin line of distinction between the two cases. One case involved a forcible interference with the right of persons to work for whomsoever they pleased, while in the other the victims were forced to work for the conspirators. Both involved the right of the individual to a free opportunity to work for wages.

There is a common-law rule that one can recover damages from anyone who entices away one's servant. Moreover, an Arkansas enticement statute, applying to the luring of renters as well as laborers, has been held not to be in conflict with the Thirteenth Amendment or the peonage statutes.[37] However, in one South Carolina case it was said that a judge's instruction to the jury in an enticement suit was subject to the interpretation that one could be held responsible for enticing away the employe of another even though the employe had breached his contract of his own volition and the defendant had not attempted to hire him until after he had done so. The appellate court held that such an interpretation of the common-law rule against enticements would countenance involuntary servitude.[38] The employe would practically be forced by economic necessity to continue his employment because, under the above instruction, everyone with whom he sought work after giving up his job would be faced with an enticement suit and hence would not hire him.

There is a rule of law that personal service contracts are not specifically enforceable. This means that an individual cannot be forced to perform such an agreement and is subject only to damages for its breach. In one pre-civil-war case from the free state of Indiana a Negro woman had made such an agreement and then refused to carry it out. The court declared that a holding that such a contract was specifically enforceable would amount to a coercion of the woman into a state of involuntary servitude and that this was unlawful under the fundamental law of Indiana at that time.[39]

---

[36] Smith v. United States, 157 Fed. 721 (C. C. A. 8th, 1907), *cert. denied* 208 U. S. 618, 28 Sup. Ct. 569 (1908).

[37] Johns v. Patterson, 138 Ark. 420, 211 S. W. 387 (1919).

[38] Shaw v. Fisher, 113 S. C. 287, 102 S. E. 325 (1920).

[39] *In re* Mary Clark, 1 Blackford 122, 12 Am. Dec. 213 (Ind. 1821).

Vagrancy statutes are not invalid unless they fail to take account of the ability of a person to provide for himself and family without labor or gainful occupation or the scarcity of jobs.[40] The type of statute[41] or municipal ordinance[42] which requires a specified period of labor on the public roads for every able-bodied man in the community has been held not to compel involuntary servitude within the meaning of anti-slavery constitutional provisions.

A discussion of this problem would be incomplete without at least some reference to the effect of the Thirteenth Amendment on contracts for the purchase and sale of slaves. Today this problem is merely academic, but we think it worth a passing glance. Did the amendment annul all such contracts? Typical of the legislation enacted in the South as a remedy for the situation created by the freeing of the slaves is the Georgia constitutional provision reading that no debt could be enforced the consideration of which was a slave or the hire thereof. The validity of this provision was soon questioned, and the Federal Supreme Court held that it was void because it violated the obligation-of-contracts clause of the Federal Constitution.[43] Under quite similar circumstances the Louisiana Court at an earlier date had held that the amendment necessarily annulled the state laws under which slave contracts were enforceable.[44] The constitutional provision reads that the states shall enact no laws impairing the obligations of contracts and hence the prohibition does not apply to legislation by the federal govern-

[40] *Ex parte* Hudgins, 86 W. Va. 526, 103 S. E. 327 (1920). See also *In re* Thompson, 117 Mo. 83, 22 S. W. 863 (1893), where the court held invalid a state statute which authorized any person convicted of vagrancy by a jury to be hired out to the highest bidder. The court was of the opinion that an offender could be convicted under the terms of a later vagrancy statute providing a lesser punishment. No sufficient reason for this holding appears, the only possible views seeming to be that the second statute repealed the first, a point which is raised but decided to be unnecessary to a decision because of the declared unconstitutionality of the statute, or that the punishments provided in both statutes may be used in the alternative.

[41] Butler v. Perry 240 U. S. 328, 36 Sup. Ct. 258 (1916).

[42] *In re* Dassler, 35 Kan. 678, 12 Pac. 130 (1886); State *ex rel.* Curtis v. City of Topeka, 36 Kan. 76, 12 Pac. 310 (1886).

[43] White v. Hart, 13 Wall. 646 (U. S. 1871). See in this connection Osborn v. Nicholson, 13 Wall. 654 (U. S. 1871); Calhoun v. Calhoun, 2 S. C. 283 (1870).

[44] Wainwright v. Bridges, 19 La. Ann. 234 (1867); Armstrong v. Lecomte, 21 La. Ann. 527 (1869).

ment. It was argued in this instance that the laws had been annulled by federal action and therefore there was no violation of the obligation-of-contracts clause. The cases were not appealed, and hence it is not known whether or not the Supreme Court would have adopted the above theory.

Situations exist today in the South as well as in other sections of the nation where Negroes are held in circumstances which approach involuntary servitude. It is for those who have the welfare of the race at heart to ferret out these cases of peonage or near-peonage and stir up feeling against the wrongdoers. In so doing, however, care should be taken not to increase race prejudice.

VII

LABOR AND RELATED PROBLEMS

The feeling that the Negro is inferior is not confined to the upper stratum of society in either the North and West or the South, although the racial prejudice among the lower classes is far more pronounced in the latter section. This is particularly true of the laboring classes who come in contact with the colored man in their daily struggle for economic subsistence and are brought face to face with his competition at every turn. The fact that Negro labor is cheap and hence tends to lower wages does not lessen the already existent racial antipathy. It has been said that the Negro is looked down upon in the South because it is only human for white laborers to despise anyone who is lower in the social scale than themselves. This explains much of the feeling among the white laborers that the Negro should not be elevated even to their low social plane. This antipathy has to a greater or less extent pervaded most sections of the North and Middle West to which the Negroes have migrated in any great numbers. Of course this dislike is far less intense in these sections of the country than in the South, but nevertheless it is a factor to be reckoned with. Friction has arisen in many industrial centers, but up to the present time there has been comparatively little litigation or regulation by either state or municipal authorities. The settlement of labor disputes and the problems of segregation in industrial plants have generally been left for private industry to handle. However, the courts have of late had to step in more frequently, and even a few of the legislative bodies have found that the problems of Negro labor must receive at least some attention.

The first instance in which a controversy of this kind arose involved an attempt to use the Reconstruction statutes[1] protecting constitutional rights. There had been a conspiracy in Arkansas to prevent certain Negroes from making or carrying out labor contracts. It was alleged that this had been done be-

[1] 8 U. S. C. A. §§42, 43; 18 U. S. C. A. §§51, 52 (1926). These statutes were Rev. Stat. §§1978, 1979, 5508, 5510 (1875).

cause of the color of the victims. The Federal Supreme Court held[2] that under these statutes it had no jurisdiction of an individual offense of this kind, since only state action or the action of state or municipal officials is considered indictable under these acts. The acts complained of had been carried out by persons who were not in any way connected with state or municipal governments.

In another early case there had been a conspiracy among the officers and citizens of an Oklahoma town to keep Negroes from entering its environs. A white man brought a Negro laborer into the town, and the former was beaten by a group of citizens. In Oklahoma there was no statutory liability in this kind of case. Hence it was held that the municipality could not be held responsible in this instance.[3]

Several eastern and middle western states have deemed it advisable to enact regulations seeking to prevent discrimination against Negro laborers. Thus Illinois,[4] New York,[5] Ohio,[6] and Pennsylvania[7] have enacted statutes which make racial discrimination unlawful with respect to public employment. New York has extended this to the public utilities.[8] The same is true of a recent Delaware act providing relief for the unemployed.[9]

There is a notion in certain portions of the South that the Negro laborer is not as competent as the average white laborer in respect to the skilled trades. In an early case from Texas, however, the court would not allow the race of certain Negro railway employes to be used to show their competency or incompetency for their appointed tasks.[10] In a Georgia case it was said to be improper to make a reference in the courtroom to the race or color of certain Negro inspectors of defective goods in a manufacturing plant.[11]

The problem of industrial segregation in the South is usually left in the hands of private business. In a few instances, however, the southern legislatures have found it advisable to inter-

---

[2] Hodges v. United States, 203 U. S. 1, 27 Sup. Ct. 623 (1906).
[3] Wallace v. Town of Norman, 9 Okla. 339, 60 Pac. 108 (1900).
[4] Ill. Rev. Stat. (Cahill, 1933) c. 38, §§107 (1)-(8).
[5] N. Y. Consol. Laws (Cahill, 1930) c. 41, §514.
[6] Ohio Laws 1935, pp. 151-152. [7] Pa. Laws 1935, Act 382.
[8] N. Y. Consol. Laws (Cahill, Supp. 1933) c. 7, §42.
[9] Del. Laws 1933, c. 1, §7.
[10] Missouri Pac. Ry. v. Christman, 65 Tex. 369 (1886).
[11] Atlanta Coca-Cola Bottling Co. v. Shipp, 170 Ga. 817, 154 S. E. 243 (1930).

fere. Thus a North Carolina statute[12] provides that there must be separate toilets for whites and Negroes in all manufacturing plants located in towns and cities of one thousand or more inhabitants. A Texas statute[13] requires separate bathing and locker facilities in the coal mines of that state. Moreover, the South Carolina legislature has found it desirable to segregate the races in cotton textile factories.[14] This act denies the two races the use of the same means of entrance and exit at the same time, the same pay ticket windows, stairways, lavatories, toilets, or drinking utensils. Several necessary exceptions are made for the sake of convenience and comfort.

That industrial segregation is considered of prime importance by the white laborers of the South is illustrated by a Kentucky libel case. In this instance a newspaper article charged that a tobacco company had placed a Negro foreman over certain white female employes. Testimony was introduced to the effect that the article had caused the company to be placed on the unfair list by the local labor union. The article was held libelous per se and a recovery allowed.[15]

In a recent Georgia case a Negro communist was convicted of an attempt to incite an insurrection under the terms of a state statute punishing such a venture.[16] He had distributed communistic literature among the people of his own race, and certain documents of that nature were found on his person when arrested and in the room where he had lodged. A perusal of this literature demonstrated that it would certainly tend to stir up the Negroes, however justly or unjustly, against the employers of labor and the landlords. Some of it favored a separate Negro commonwealth to be carved from the boundaries of the state. It called for Negro coöperation with the white communists in the North as well as in the South, and declared that the Negro must fight not only against inequality but also against the whole system by which that inequality is enforced.

---

[12] N. C. CODE ANN. (Michie, 1931) §§6559-64.

[13] TEX. ANN. REV. CIV. STAT. (Vernon, 1925) art. 5920, TEX. ANN. PEN. CODE (Vernon, 1925) art. 1612.

[14] S. C. CODE (1932) §1272.

[15] Axton Fisher Tobacco Co. v. Evening Post Co., 169 Ky. 64, 183 S. W. 269 (1916).

[16] GA. CODE ANN. (Michie, 1926) PEN. CODE §§56-57. For history of statute see Michie's Annotations and Gibson v. State, 38 Ga. 571 (1869).

The court held that the evidence supported the conviction, but in doing so construed the statute as applying to all attempts to incite an insurrection instead of limiting it to attempts to incite immediate insurrection as it had been construed by the trial court.[17] The defendant then attempted to defeat the indictment on the ground that the statute was unconstitutional in that it failed to set forth a sufficient standard of guilt. He claimed that the description of the crime was much too vague and uncertain and that the act violated the guarantee in the Fourteenth Amendment that a person may not be deprived of life, liberty, or property without due process of law. The state court decided that the defendant had not sufficiently raised the question in the lower court and that he was not allowed to do so for the first time in the appellate tribunal.[18] The Negro then appealed to the Federal Supreme Court and there also met with a rebuff. The defendant argued that there is an exception to the above rule concerning the necessity of raising a question in the lower court and claimed that the exception would apply in this case. The exception which he claimed was relevant is that the rule does not apply where the appellate court places upon a statute a construction different from that which the trial court has given it. While admitting that such an exception existed, the Supreme Court declared that it did not apply in this particular instance because the highest court in the state in a previous case[19] had placed the same construction upon the statute as it had done in the instant case, thereby precluding any possibility of ignorance of the proper construction of the statute except that caused by the negligence of the appellant's attorney, who is presumed to know of this decision by the highest court in his home state.[20] Hence, it was unnecessary to rule upon the validity of the statute. This, however, was not the end of the litigation, for the Negro then applied for a writ of habeas corpus, claiming that the

[17] Herndon v. State, 178 Ga. 832, 174 S. E. 597 (1934).

[18] Herndon v. State, 179 Ga. 597, 176 S. E. 620 (1934).

[19] Carr v. State, 176 Ga. 55, 166 S. E. 827 (1932), 176 Ga. 747, 169 S. E. 201 (1933).

[20] Herndon v. Georgia, 295 U. S. 441, 55 Sup. Ct. 794 (1935). Justices Brandeis, Cardozo, and Stone dissented. A petition for a rehearing was denied. 296 U. S. 661, 56 Sup. Ct. 82 (1935). See Notes: (1935) 30 Ill. L. Rev. 530, (1936) 20 Minn. L. Rev. 216.

act was unconstitutional. The lower state court was inclined to agree with him as to the invalidity of the statute, but the State Supreme Court refused to hold that the act violated the Fourteenth Amendment.[21]

Again the case was taken to the highest tribunal in the land. The construction given the statute in the state court had been that the accused would be guilty if he intended that violence should occur at any time within which he might reasonably expect his influence to continue to be directly operative in causing the desired action by those persons whom he sought to persuade. As so construed, the Supreme Court held that the act was so vague and indeterminate as to the standard of guilt that it violated the fundamental notions of due process of law.[22] The act was said to unduly disregard the freedom of speech and of assembly.

There is a statute in Virginia which makes it a felony to incite groups of either race to acts of violence against the other.[23] This act would no doubt be valid, as the elements of the crime are sufficiently described.

Even where Negroes are not permitted to join a labor union, they may be protected under its agreements with the employer. Thus a Negro brakeman on a passenger train was allowed to sue as a third party beneficiary under a wage agreement between a railway company and its white employes organized as a union.[24] The agreement applied to both white and Negro laborers. The union had a very substantial interest in the welfare of the Negro brakeman. The company had attempted to defend itself by showing that no Negro was or could be a member of the union. It was also declared that the company should not be permitted to pay a Negro porter's wages and require him to perform the duties of a brakeman, all the while dubbing him a porter.

Negro employes may be used to break up a strike among the white workers, thereby creating racial conflict and leading to acts of intimidation and violence. It has been said in one case

---

[21] Lowry v. Herndon, 182 Ga. 582, 186 S. E. 429 (1936).

[22] Herndon v. Lowry, 301 U. S. 242, 57 Sup. Ct. 732 (1937). Justices Butler, McReynolds, Southerland, and Vandervanter dissented. See Note (1937) 50 Harv. L. Rev. 1313.

[23] Va. Code Ann. (Michie, 1930) §4392.

[24] Yazoo & Miss. V. R. R. v. Sideboard, 161 Miss. 4, 133 So. 669 (1931).

of this kind from Tennessee that such acts of intimidation may be enjoined even when it can be shown that the same type of threats would not necessarily have prevented other white workers from continuing on the job.[25] Here two sets of affidavits made by the Negroes were introduced in evidence. The white laborers insisted that the first set of sworn statements, which were unfavorable to them, should be rejected because they were influenced by an increase in wages given the Negroes in order to insure a continuation of labor on their part. The company countered this by insisting that the later set of affidavits, which were inconsistent with the first, were influenced by the aforementioned acts of intimidation. The federal appellate court declared that the action of the trial judge in finding that the facts were as stated in the first set of affidavits could not be disturbed unless contrary to the weight of all the evidence, and such was not found to be the case in this instance.

Courts in Maryland[26] and New York[27] have decided that the ordinary rules of law governing labor disputes and picketing do not apply where Negro leaders have persuaded their followers to boycott certain mercantile establishments in urban districts where most of the patronage is colored. In both instances the controversy was entirely a racial one and the boycott had been started with a view to forcing these business establishments to employ Negroes in clerical and other positions which were filled by whites. The Negro pickets had used tactics which would be permitted under the ordinary rules applying to labor disputes in industrial plants. In both jurisdictions the Negro pickets were enjoined from interfering in this manner with the legitimate business of the aforesaid establishments. The Maryland Court declared that the Negroes might organize with the boycott in view, hold public meetings, employ propaganda, personally solicit coöperation among the colored customers, and attempt to convince the merchants of the unfairness of their discriminatory policy. Anything beyond this was said to be illegal. The New York tribunal denied that there was any right of picketing, peaceful or otherwise, in this type of con-

[25] King v. Weiss & Lesh Mfg. Co., 226 Fed. 257 (C. C. A. 6th, 1926).

[26] Green v. Samuelson, 168 Md. 421, 178 Atl. 109 (1935).

[27] Beck Shoe Corporation v. Johnson, 153 Misc. 363, 274 N. Y. Supp. 946 (Sup. Ct. 1934). See Notes: (1935) 48 HARV. L. REV. 691, (1935) 83 U. OF PA. L. REV. 381.

troversy. It suggested that the Negroes themselves might be the chief sufferers if picketing was permitted in this kind of case. The principle contended for would also allow white persons to boycott and picket business establishments for the purpose of forcing the proprietors to hire white persons only. Thus a boomerang would be created which might conceivably do the Negro irreparable harm, for the white man is usually in a far more strategic position and can better accomplish his ends in this respect.

A parallel case from the District of Columbia reached the Federal Supreme Court. The situation was further complicated because of the Norris-La Guardia Act[28] restricting the right of all federal courts to issue injunctions in controversies arising out of labor disputes. It was conceded that no injunction would issue if the statute were applicable. The act defines "labor dispute" as including "any controversy concerning terms or conditions of employment, or concerning the association or representation of persons in negotiating, fixing, maintaining, changing, or seeking to arrange terms or conditions of employment, regardless of whether or not the disputants stand in the proximate relation of employer and employee." In this instance no employer-employe relationship existed and the Negro organization conducting the boycott was not engaged in a competing business. The factual situation was practically the same as in the cases mentioned above. The organization was merely picketing the establishment and arranging for the dissemination of information concerning the refusal of the proprietor to employ Negro clerks. The Supreme Court held that the Norris-La Guardia Act was applicable in this racial controversy and declared that a federal court could not lawfully issue an injunction in such a case.[29] In this instance the court took a step which may be extended to other situations where the employer-employe relationship does not exist. The case seems to go a long way in restricting the right of the federal courts to issue injunctions.

A somewhat similar case came before a Pennsylvania court.

[28] 29 U. S. C. A. §§101-115 (Supp. 1937). Section 113c defines the term "labor disputes."

[29] New Negro Alliance v. Sanitary Grocery Co., 303 U. S. 552, 58 Sup. Ct. 703 (1938), *rev'g* 67 App. D. C. 359, 92 F. (2d) 510 (1937). Justices Butler and McReynolds dissented.

In this instance the threat of a boycott was used to force the proprietor of a theatre to discharge two satisfactory white employes and replace them with Negroes. One of the discharged employes sought an injunction to prevent a continuation of the Negro organization's policy. An attempt was made to distinguish the above case from the District of Columbia on the ground that in that case the Negro organization was only attempting to influence the employer with respect to future employes, whereas in the present controversy the organization was trying to make the employer discharge satisfactory white men to make room for Negroes. The court appears to have accepted this distinction.[80] The injunction was granted preventing the organization from using unfair tactics, but the court recognized a right to a reasonable amount of picketing in racial controversies of this kind. The court refused to apply the state labor relations act, saying that it was not meant to cover such disputes.

This phase of the Negro problem has as yet scarcely been touched by the courts. However, one may take the liberty of prophesying that this is one of the fields from which much litigation will arise in the not-too-far-distant future.

---

[80] Stevens v. West Philadelphia Youth Civic League, 34 Pa. D. & C. 612 (1939).

VIII

JIM CROW LAWS AND REGULATIONS

The courts and legislative bodies of the nation have paid a great deal of attention to the aspect of the Negro problem which has arisen out of the unavoidable contacts between persons of the white and colored races in all types of public conveyances. Even where a policy of segregation is adopted, as is the case in the southern states, such contacts are inevitable. The same racial antipathy is found here that is encountered in other semisocial relationships, and consequently it is considered necessary to the continued tranquillity of the southern states for these carriers to separate the races as far as possible. The southern and border states have sought to handle the matter by means of Jim Crow laws and regulations which make it unlawful for any carrier to which such rules apply to transport white and colored passengers in the same vehicle or the same portion thereof.[1] That the problem is not wholly southern is evidenced by the Civil Rights Acts which have been enacted in a majority of the eastern and middle western states with the intention of preventing all exclusion and discrimination by public carriers on account of race or color.

The Jim Crow laws of the South are filled with exceptions. When a consideration arising out of long experience with the problem is shown to overbalance the advantages to be obtained from a strict and unbending continuance of the policy behind these laws, the legislatures usually recognize this and place exceptions in the statutes to take care of these situations. Thus provisions have been inserted which exempt various types of cars or trains and certain classes of individuals from the operation of the acts.

Oklahoma and all the former slaveholding states, with the exception of Delaware, Missouri, and West Virginia, have made provision by statute for an enforced separation of the white

[1] Stephenson, *Race Distinctions in American Law* (1909) 43 AM. L. REV. 694, 734.

and Negro races on railways operated in the jurisdiction,[2] and even Delaware has an act which may be termed an optional Jim Crow statute.[3] These acts will apply to all railways of the type generally accepted as falling within that term. They would probably be construed in most instances to include interurban lines even though the statute does not specifically mention them, as is the case in several instances. Most of the statutes contain provisions punishing the carrier for a failure to carry out the terms of the law, making such a dereliction of duty a misdemeanor.[4] There are also provisions in the majority of these acts punishing conductors and other train officials for refusing to execute the mandates of the law in this respect.[5] Most of the states also punish passengers for wilfully refusing to obey the

---

[2] Ala. Code Ann. (Michie, 1928) §§9968-69; Ark. Dig. Stat. (Crawford & Moses, 1921) §§986-97; Fla. Comp. Gen. Laws Ann. (Skillman, 1927) §§6617-19, 7751-52; Georgia Code Ann. (Michie, 1926) §§2716-22; Ky. Stat. Ann. (Carroll, 1930) §§795-801; La. Gen. Stat. Ann. (Dart, 1932) §§8130-32; Md. Ann. Code (Bagby, 1924) art. 27, §§332-38; Miss. Code Ann. (1930) §§1115, 6132; N. C. Code Ann. (Michie, 1931) §§3494-97; Okla. Comp. Stat. (1921) §§4952-61; S. C. Code (1932) §§8396-8400, 1702-03; Tenn. Code (Will. Shan. & Harsh, 1932) §§5518-20; Tex. Ann. Rev. Civ. Stat. (Vernon, 1925) art. 6417, Tex. Ann. Pen. Code (Vernon, 1925) arts. 1659-60; Va. Code Ann. (Michie, 1930) §§3962-69.

[3] Del. Code (1915) §3577. Act states that any carrier of passengers may assign a particular place to such of their customers as would be offensive to the major portion of the travelling public, but guarantees equal accommodations if the price charged is the same.

[4] Ark. Dig. Stat. (Crawford & Moses, 1921) §994; Fla. Comp. Gen. Laws Ann. (Skilman, 1927) §§6619, 7751; Ky. Stat. Ann. (Carroll, 1930) §797; Md. Ann. Code (Bagby, 1924) art. 27, §434; Miss. Code Ann. (1930) §1115; Okla. Comp. Stat. (1921) §4956 (penalty recoverable in state's name); S. C. Code (1932) §8400 (penalty recoverable for state's benefit), *see* Sturkie v. So. Ry. 71 S. C. 208, 50 S. E. 782 (1905); Tenn. Code (Will. Shan. & Harsh, 1932) §5520; Tex. Ann. Rev. Civ. Stat. (Vernon, 1925) art. 6417 (penalty recoverable in state's name); Va. Code Ann. (Michie, 1930) §3964. Georgia and North Carolina appear to allow recovery of a penalty by the wronged individual. Ga. Code Ann. (Michie, 1926) §2716 (civil action); N. C. Code Ann. (Michie, 1931) §3497. Louisiana and Florida punish the corporation's officers and directors. La. Gen. Stat. Ann. (Dart, 1932) §8132; Fla. Comp. Gen. Laws Ann. (Skillman, 1927) §7751. Alabama has no such provision.

[5] Ark. Dig. Stat. (Crawford & Moses, 1921) §992; Fla. Comp. Gen. Laws Ann. (Skillman, 1927) §7751; Ga. Code Ann. (Michie, 1926) §2721, Pen. Code §537; Ky. Stat. Ann. (Carroll, 1930) §800; La. Gen. Stat. Ann. (Dart, 1932) §8131; Md. Ann. Code (Bagby, 1924) art. 27, §436; Miss. Code Ann. (1930) §1115; Okla. Comp. Stat. (1921) §4961; S. C. Code (1932) §1702; Tenn. Code Ann. (Will. Shan. & Harsh, 1932) §5520; Tex. Ann. Pen. Code (Vernon, 1925) art. 1659; Va. Code Ann. (Michie, 1930) §3966.

law.[6] The conductors in charge of trains operated in these states are in practically every instance given police power to enforce the regulations.[7] They may insist that the law must be obeyed and, if necessary, may put it into effect by force.

Under these acts it has been held that a person subjects himself to criminal indictment by entering a coach or compartment set aside for members of the race to which he does not belong.[8] The same was held where a person was guilty of "remaining" in the wrong coach after being requested by the conductor to get out, although his original purpose in entering the coach had been merely to pass through to another car.[9]

A failure to carry out the requirements of the statute may be used as the basis for a civil suit against the railway company for physical injuries suffered in consequence,[10] but only if such failure be the proximate cause of the injury inflicted.[11] A white passenger may sue the railway company on the theory that he has been humiliated at being forced to ride in close proximity to a Negro who has been allowed to remain in the white coach.[12] It might also be supposed that a Negro passenger would be permitted to maintain a successful suit for damages on this same ground where a white man was wrongfully in the Negro

---

[6] ALA. CODE ANN. (Michie, 1928) § 5365; ARK. DIG. STAT. (Crawford & Moses, 1921) §992; FLA. COMP. GEN. LAWS ANN. (Skillman, 1927) §7752; GA. CODE ANN. (Michie, 1926) §2719; LA. GEN. STAT. ANN. (Dart, 1932) §8131; MD. ANN. CODE (Bagby, 1924) art. 27, §435; OKLA. COMP. STAT. (1921), §4957; S. C. CODE (1932) §1703; TEX. ANN. PEN. CODE. (Vernon, 1925) art. 1659; VA. CODE ANN. (Michie, 1930) §3983.

[7] ALA. CODE ANN. (Michie, 1928) §9969; ARK. DIG. STAT. (Crawford & Moses, 1921) §993; FLA. COMP. GEN. LAWS ANN. (Skillman, 1927) §6617; GA. CODE ANN. (Michie, 1926) §2718; KY. STAT. ANN. (Carroll, 1930) §799; LA. GEN. STAT. ANN. (Dart, 1932) §8131; MD. ANN. CODE (Bagby, 1924) art. 27, §435; MISS. CODE ANN. (1930) §6132; OKLA. COMP. STAT. (1921) §4957; S. C. CODE (1932) §1703; TENN. CODE (Will. Shan. & Harsh, 1932) §5519; TEX. ANN. REV. CIV. STAT. (Vernon, 1925) art. 6417, TEX. ANN. PEN. CODE (Vernon, 1925) art. 1659; VA. CODE ANN. (Michie, 1930) §3965. North Carolina has no such provision.

[8] *In re* Escalade, 150 La. 638, 91 So. 135 (1921). *See also* State v. Omes, 149 La. 676, 90 So. 20 (1921), where an information was ruled defective for failure to make essential allegations.

[9] Brown v. State, 110 Ga. 771, 36 S. E. 68 (1900), construing GA. CODE ANN. (Michie, 1926) §2719.

[10] Louisville & E. Ry. v. Vincent, 29 Ky. Law Rep. 1049, 96 S. W. 898 (1906).

[11] Hines, Director-General of Rys. v. Meador, 145 Ark. 356, 224 S. W. 742 (1920); Royston v. Ill. Cent. R. R., 67 Miss. 376, 7 So. 320 (1889).

[12] Payne v. Stevens, 125 Miss. 582, 88 So. 165 (1921).

coach. In some instances Negroes could hardly be said to be humiliated at being compelled to ride with white persons, but it is not inconceivable that such a case of mortification might arise. A dirty, disreputable white man might be seated beside or near a respectable Negro man or woman. If such a case did arise, it would be only natural to suppose that the court, for the sake of consistency, would allow a recovery. Where the facts were not so strong, however, the Negro's attorney might have a rather difficult task in convincing the average white jury that there had been any humiliation.

In one Alabama case it was held that a train official was not justified in attempting to move a white passenger from a Negro coach while the train was running at a dangerous rate of speed.[13]

Sometimes a person of one race will enter a coach set aside for the other without the knowledge or fault of the responsible employes of the railway company. In a case of this kind where a passenger has either wilfully or negligently violated the law, notice to these responsible officials is essential to a recovery. Unless such notice can be shown, passengers who claim to have been injured because of the alleged infraction of the separate coach law cannot maintain a successful suit.[14] Notice to lesser employes or employes who are not at the time responsible for the management of the train is insufficient.[15] The duty of the lesser employe under such circumstances is to report the matter to his superiors.[16]

To allow a recovery for physical injury, circumstances must be such as to give the proper officials warning that there is danger from trespassers who have boarded the train.[17] Some-

[13] Carleton v. Central of Ga. Ry., 155 Ala. 326, 46 So. 495 (1908), 163 Ala. 62, 51 So. 27 (1909).

[14] Hillman v. Ga. R. R. & Bk. Co., 126 Ga. 814, 56 S. E. 68 (1906); Bailey v. Louisville & N. Ry., 19 Ky. Law. Rep. 1617, 44 S. W. 105 (1898); Louisville & N. R. R. v. Renfro's Adm'r, 142 Ky. 590, 135 S. W. 266 (1911); Hale v. Chesapeake & O. Ry., 142 Ky. 835, 135 S. W. 398 (1911).

[15] Walker v. Int. & G. M. Ry., 54 Tex. Civ. App. Rep. 406, 117 S. W. 1020 (1909); Baker v. Ill. Cent. Ry., 215 S. W. 556 (Tex. Com. App. 1919), *rev'g* Baker v. Tex. & P. Ry., 184 S. W. 664 (Tex. Civ. App. 1915).

[16] Louisville & N. R. R. v. Renfro's Adm'r, 142 Ky. 590, 135 S. W. 266 (1911); Walker v. Int. & G. M. Ry., 54 Tex. Civ. App. Rep. 406, 117 S. W. 1020 (1909).

[17] Savannah, F. & W. Ry. v. Boyle, 115 Ga. 836, 42 S. E. 242 (1902); Segal v. St. Louis, S. W. Ry., 35 Tex. Civ. App. Rep. 517, 80 S. W. 233 (1904).

times an injury will occur because of racial feeling engendered by the presence of members of either race in a coach which has been assigned to persons of the other. Where a situation of this kind is brought about because of a knowing or negligent failure on the part of train officials to carry out the provisions of the separate coach law, the railway company may be held liable for an injury which was inflicted by fellow passengers as a result of such neglect.[18] In one case from Tennessee a railway company had failed to provide proper accommodations for colored passengers. The railway was held responsible for an injury to a Negro who was manhandled by white persons intent upon putting him out of a coach for ladies which had been set aside for the use of white passengers only.[19] Furthermore, the Mississippi Court held a railway liable where its conductor assaulted a Negro who was attempting to pass through the white coach into the one which was reserved for colored persons.[20] In one Kentucky case a railway company was deemed responsible for an injury caused when its officials, though warned by a previous racial clash in one of its coaches, had permitted Negroes to remain unguarded on the platform of the same coach, in a position to renew the conflict whenever opportunity offered.[21] In another case from the same jurisdiction, however, it was decided that a white passenger could not recover damages where he had voluntarily passed into the colored coach to avoid crowded conditions in the coach set apart for the members of his own race.[22]

A passenger who is in the wrong coach may maintain an action where the fact that he is so seated is not connected in any way with the act that caused the injury complained of, such act being no dereliction of duty under the separate coach law or regulation but a failure to observe or comply with some other rule of law.[23] An illustration will serve to clarify the rule

[18] So. Ry. v. Lee, 167 Ala. 268, 52 So. 648 (1910); Richmond & D. Ry. v. Jefferson, 89 Ga. 554, 16 S. E. 69 (1892); Quinn v. Louisville & N. R. R., 98 Ky. 231, 32 S. W. 742 (1895); Wood v. Louisville & N. R. R., 101 Ky. 703, 42 S. W. 349 (1897).

[19] Murphy v. Western & A. R. R., 23 Fed. 637 (C. C. E. D. Tenn. 1885).

[20] Louisville, N. O. & T. Ry. v. Crayton, 69 Miss. 152, 12 So. 271 (1891).

[21] Louisville & N. R. R. v. McEwan, 21 Ky. Law Rep. 487, 51 S. W. 619 (1899).

[22] Chesapeake & O. Ry. v. Austin, 137 Ky. 611, 126 S. W. 144 (1910).

[23] Fla. Cent. & P. Ry. v. Sullivan, 120 Fed. 799 (C. C. A. 5th, 1903).

of law here presented. A train in which a white passenger has seated himself in the coach for Negroes is demolished in a collision caused by the negligence of a railway company's employes. Can it be said that the passenger's presence in the colored coach was a sufficient contributing cause to bar a recovery for injuries sustained in the accident? There can be only a negative answer to such a query.

There is a suggestion in a rather old Tennessee case that a recovery for personal injuries would not be allowed if the Negro's only purpose in entering the white coach, which she claimed was better equipped than the other coach in which the races were mixed, was to harass the company.[24] There was evidence that the Negro plaintiff had acted with the ulterior motive of bringing an action because of the railway company's alleged failure to provide equal accommodations for the two races.

The states of Kentucky,[25] Texas,[26] and North Carolina[27] have decisions to the effect that a railway company is not liable to an indictment or statutory penalty where it has furnished the required separate accommodations, but one of its officials has allowed the passengers, white and colored, to become unlawfully mixed in the same coach. In the first two states mentioned the official at fault is said to be the only party who is criminally liable in this situation. According to this view a railway's agents might be extremely negligent and yet not render the carrier criminally responsible.[28] The advisability of such a holding is doubtful to say the least. There are expressions in the Kentucky cases which would deny the application of this doctrine to civil cases. In one Oklahoma case this point formed the basis of a refusal to allow a recovery in a civil suit.[29] However, some

[24] Chesapeake, O. & S. R. R. v. Wells, 85 Tenn. 613, 4 S. W. 5 (1887).

[25] Louisville & N. R. R. v. Commonwealth, 99 Ky. 663, 37 S. W. 79 (1896); Commonwealth v. Ill. C. Ry., 141 Ky. 502, 133 S. W. 1158 (1911).

[26] State v. G., H. & S. A. Ry., 184 S. W. 227 (Tex. Civ. App. 1916).

[27] Merritt v. Atlantic C. L. R. R., 152 N. C. 281, 67 S. E. 579 (1910).

[28] This is brought out by the dissent in the Merritt case, *supra* note 27. Moreover, the majority opinion leaves a particularly bad situation in North Carolina because there is no provision in that state for the punishment of officers who fail to do their duty in this respect.

[29] Stratford v. Midland Valley R. R., 36 Okla. 127, 128 Pac. 98 (1912). The Negro was an interstate passenger and hence the state law should not have been applied at all.

doubt has been thrown upon the correctness of this decision by a later ruling,[30] although the court in the second case attempted to distinguish the two decisions by stating that in the former instance the plaintiff was where he had no right to be, whereas in the latter the opposite was true. This argument can hardly be wholly accepted. If the plaintiff was where he had no right to be, he could have been thrown out of court on that theory, and there would then have been no necessity to enter into a discussion of the respective liabilities of the railway and its official under the statute. The strict application of this doctrine, particularly in civil cases, would go far toward defeating the purpose behind the statute. Therefore, it is believed that this limit on the liability of the carrier for the acts of its employes should not be approved. The doctrine has never been applied to civil cases except in the one instance from Oklahoma.

In most states which have Jim Crow legislation, an honest mistake by a conductor or other official in seating a person in the coach which has been assigned to members of the other race, thereby causing humiliation, however unjustifiably, to white passengers, does not excuse the railway company from civil liability.[31] However, there is authority which seems opposed to such a holding.[32] The Louisiana Court has held that the discretion given train officials in this respect must be exercised at their own peril and that of the railway company as well.[33]

Humiliation at being made to ride in a coach with Negroes may be considered as an element of damages in such instances of honest mistake as well as in cases where there is no possible excuse.[34] In these cases it is also permissible to show that the

[30] Chicago, R. I. & P. Ry. v. Sharp, 87 Okla. 98, 209 Pac. 646 (1922).

[31] So. Ry. in Ky. v. Thurman, 121 Ky. 716, 28 Ky. Law Rep. 699, 979, 90 S. W. 240 (1906); Louisville & N. Ry. v. Ritchel, 148 Ky. 701, 147 S. W. 411 (1912); Lee v. New Orleans G. N. R. R., 125 La. 236, 51 So. 182 (1910) (recovery denied because plaintiffs failed to prove themselves white); Missouri, K. & T. Ry. v. Ball, 25 Tex. Civ. App. Rep. 500, 61 S. W. 327 (1901).

[32] Norfolk & W. Ry. v. Stone, 111 Va. 730, 69 S. E. 927 (1911).

[33] *Ex parte* Plessy, 45 La. Ann. 80, 11 So. 948 (1893).

[34] Chicago, R. I. & P. Ry. v. Allison, 120 Ark. 54, 178 S. W. 401 (1915); Louisville & N. Ry. v. Ritchel, 148 Ky. 701, 147 S. W. 411 (1912); Texas & P. Ry. v. Johnson, 2 Willson, Tex. Civ. App. Rep., 154, Par. 186 (1884); Missouri, K. & T. Ry. v. Ball, 25 Tex. Civ. App. Rep. 500, 61 S. W. 327 (1901); Norfolk & W. Ry. v. Stone, 111 Va. 730, 69 S. E. 927 (1911). *But see* Little Rock Ry. & Electric Co. v. Putsche, 84 Ark. 623, 104 S. W. 554 (1907) (Str. Ry.).

injured party is a person of culture and refinement.[35] In a proper case the court may award punitive damages,[36] namely those damages which are allowed to the plaintiff not to compensate him for the injury sustained, but to punish the malicious, wicked, or wanton conduct on the part of a defendant or his or its agents. This may even be true when no compensatory damages, that is, damages measured by the injury suffered, are awarded.[37] It has been held that a passenger must at least use ordinary care to minimize the damages resulting from a breach of the statute.[38] The Kentucky Court held in one instance that if, after being ousted from the white coach by a brakeman who had mistaken her for a mulatto, a female white passenger is allowed to return immediately, she may recover only for her trouble in going from the white coach and back, unless it could be shown that the brakeman's conduct was insulting.[39] Texas denies a recovery unless the plaintiff suffers some special damage of a kind not sustained by other passengers who have had no such close contact as the plaintiff with the person who is in the wrong coach.[40]

Sometimes it is thought advisable to adopt a special statute with respect to particular situations. Thus North Carolina recently enacted a statute authorizing the utilities commissioner to make special Jim Crow regulations for trains of not more than one car unit.[41] Separate toilet facilities are specifically mentioned in the act. There is a somewhat similar act in South Carolina.[42]

There are a great many exceptions which have been inserted in the Jim Crow statutes. In some instances exceptions have been conjured up by the courts when the exigencies of a situation so demand. Ten states expressly except nurses or attendants in charge of persons of the opposite race who are unable to take

---

[35] Louisville & N. Ry. v. Ritchel, 148 Ky. 701, 147 S. W. 411 (1912).

[36] Norfolk & W. Ry. v. Stone, 111 Va. 730, 69 S. E. 927 (1911).

[37] Louisville & N. Ry. v. Ritchel, 148 Ky. 701, 147 S. W. 411 (1912).

[38] Chesapeake & O. Ry. v. Austin, 137 Ky. 611, 126 S. W. 144 (1910).

[39] So. Ry. in Ky. v. Thurman, 121 Ky. 716, 28 Ky. Law Rep. 699, 979, 90 S. W. 240 (1906).

[40] Norwood v. Galveston Ry., 12 Tex. Civ. App. Rep. 560, 34 S. W. 180 (1896); Weller v. Mo., K. & T. Ry., 187 S. W. 374 (Tex. Civ. App. 1916).

[41] N. C. Pub. Laws 1935, c. 270.

[42] S. C. Acts 1935, No. 142.

care of themselves;[43] six except railway employes;[44] while eight except police officers in charge of prisoners.[45] This proves that the legislatures realize that in some instances convenience should be given primary consideration. The separation policy will not be allowed to override expediency. In the case of the latter exception, the North Carolina Court held that a railway's regulation requiring a white officer with a Negro prisoner to ride in the colored coach was a reasonable one.[46] The statute gave no specific directions as to what should be done in this situation, but only provided that the railway company was not bound to supply separate accommodations where such circumstances existed. It has been declared in Kentucky that this exception is in favor of the officer alone, and hence a Negro prisoner in the custody of a white officer cannot object if he is made to travel in a colored coach.[47] In those states where the statute fails to make this exception it has been held that the carrier or its officials may make reasonable rules in case such a situation arises, the policy of separation outlined in the statute not being intended to cover these peculiar circumstances.[48] The carrier may make a regulation that the white officer must ride with his prisoner in the colored coach.[49] Even

[43] FLA. COMP. GEN. LAWS ANN. (Skillman, 1927) §6617; GA. CODE ANN. (Michie, 1926) §2722; KY. STAT. ANN. (Carroll, 1930) §801; LA. GEN. STAT. ANN. (Dart, 1932) §8132; MD. ANN. CODE (Bagby, 1924) art. 27, §438; N. C. CODE ANN. (Michie, 1931) §3494; S. C. CODE (1932) §8399; TENN. CODE (Will. Shan. & Harsh, 1932) §5518; TEX. ANN. REV. CIV. STAT. (Vernon, 1925) art. 6417, TEX. ANN. PEN. CODE (Vernon, 1925) art. 1660; VA. CODE ANN. (Michie, 1930) §3968.

[44] ARK. DIG. STAT. (Crawford & Moses, 1921) §988; KY. STAT. ANN. (Carroll, 1930) §801; MD. ANN. CODE (Bagby, 1924) art. 27, §438; OKLA. COMP. STAT. (1921) §4958; TEX. ANN. REV. CIV. STAT. (Vernon, 1925) art. 6417, TEX. ANN. PEN. CODE (Vernon, 1925) art. 1660; VA. CODE ANN. (Michie, 1930) §3968.

[45] ARK. DIG. STAT. (Crawford & Moses, 1921) §988; KY. STAT. ANN. (Carroll, 1930) §801; LA. GEN. STAT. (Dart, 1932) §8132; MD. ANN. CODE (Bagby, 1924) art. 27, §438; N. C. CODE ANN. (Michie, 1931) §3494; OKLA. COMP. STAT. (1921) §4958; S. C. CODE (1932) §8399; VA. CODE ANN. (Michie, 1930) §3968 (provides also for those in charge of lunatics).

[46] Huff v. Norfolk So. R. R., 171 N. C. 203, 88 S. E. 344 (1916).

[47] Louisville & N. R. R. v. Catron, 102 Ky. 323, 43 S. W. 443 (1897).

[48] Spenny v. Mobile & O. R. R., 192 Ala. 483, 68 So. 870 (1915), disapproving reasoning but upholding decision reached in 12 Ala. App. 375, 67 So. 740 (1914); Illinois C. R. R. v. Cox, 132 Miss. 471, 96 So. 685 (1923), construing Tenn. statute; Gulf, C. & S. F. Ry. v. Sharman, 158 S. W. 1045 (Tex. Civ. App. 1913).

[49] Illinois C. R. R. v. Cox, 132 Miss. 471, 96 So. 685 (1923). See also other cases cited in note 48 *supra*.

where the officer fails to comply with the regulation, he may recover if the conduct of the train official in attempting to carry out his orders is inexcusable or unnecessarily insulting.[50] In Texas it was decided that the separate coach law does not prevent a white peace officer from entering a Negro coach in the performance of his duty when notified that there was a disturbance therein.[51] The court in this instance said that the fact that the coach had become quiet in the meantime was immaterial.

Certain types of trains and coaches have been exempted from the operation of these Jim Crow laws in many states. Four jurisdictions exempt express trains;[52] two exempt narrow gauge and branch lines;[53] one exempts relief trains;[54] one exempts excursion trains;[55] one permits special trains for the members of either race where regular schedules are not interferred with;[56] and eight exempt freight trains,[57] some expressly mentioning cabooses.

With respect to the latter exception, it was held to be error for an Oklahoma judge to instruct a jury that if a railway required or permitted members of both races to occupy a caboose on a freight train, such would constitute a violation of the separate coach law.[58] In a case from Kentucky the only train run on a certain branch line was one having a caboose as the only suitable place for passengers. The railway company sold

---

[50] Illinois C. R. R. v. Cox, 136 Miss. 123, 100 So. 520 (1924).

[51] Mo., K. & T. Ry. v. Brown, 158 S. W. 259 (Tex. Civ. App. 1913).

[52] Md. Ann. Code (Bagby, 1924) art. 27, §438; N. C. Code Ann. (Michie, 1931) §3494; S. C. Code (1932) §8399; Va. Code Ann. (Michie, 1930) §3968.

[53] N. C. Code Ann. (Michie, 1931) §3495 (consent of Utilities Commission necessary); S. C. Code (1932) §8399.

[54] N. C. Code Ann. (Michie, 1931) §3494.

[55] Tex. Ann. Rev. Civ. Stat. (Vernon, 1925) art. 6417, Tex. Ann. Pen. Code (Vernon, 1925) art. 1660.

[56] Okla. Comp. Stat. (1921) §4960.

[57] Ark. Dig. Stat. (Crawford & Moses, 1921) §997; Ky. Stat. Ann. (Carroll, 1930) §801; Md. Ann. Code (Bagby, 1924) art. 27, §438; Okla. Comp. Stat. (1921) §4958; S. C. Code (1932) §8399 (applies to freights with one passenger coach attached for local travel); Tenn. Code (Will. Shan. & Harsh, 1932) §5518 (if passenger coach is carried, the races must be separated); Tex. Ann. Rev. Civ. Stat. (Vernon, 1925) art. 6417, Tex. Ann. Pen. Code (Vernon, 1925) art. 1660; Va. Code Ann. (Michie, 1930) §3968. In North Carolina the Utilities Commission may allow certain lines that run mixed trains to disregard the statute because of the small number of Negro passengers. N. C. Code Ann. (Michie, 1931) §3495.

[58] St. Louis, I. M. & S. Ry. v. Freeland, 39 Okla. 60, 134 Pac. 47 (1913).

tickets to persons of both races, making no effort at segregation. An indictment was brought against the company for its failure to supply separate accommodations. The prosecution contended that this train was bound to be considered a passenger train because the company was required by law to run at least one train daily. The court decided that these facts formed no basis for a criminal action under the provisions of the separate coach law.[59] The train was a freight, and the prosecution brought the action under the wrong statute. A successful action might have been brought under the statute requiring one passenger train daily. In another case from the same jurisdiction, a railway company ran a passenger train over a certain route. On Sundays a freight was run over the same route. A criminal action was brought against the railway company for its alleged failure to supply equal accommodations for Negroes on a train which was run on a certain Sunday. The indictment alleged that a colored passenger was compelled to travel in a baggage car which had no fire, seats, or other conveniences. The court declared that the train in this instance was a freight, and therefore the statute did not require the railway to carry a separate coach or to have separate accommodations on such a train carrying a combination car used as a caboose.[60] The court also said that the indictment was insufficient because it did not include an allegation that the baggage car had been set apart for the use of colored persons. Hence we see that poor pleading at least contributed a little toward the failure of these two Kentucky indictments. In a later criminal case, however, the Kentucky Court held that a train composed of an engine and one coach divided into two compartments, one being used for freight and baggage and the other for passengers, is not a freight train with an attached caboose within the meaning of the exception.[61] The court said that it was necessary that a train be primarily a freight in order to be within the meaning of the exception. A caboose was defined as a car with or without compartments fitted up for the accommodation of the conductor, brakemen, and chance passengers.

Three states exempt pullman cars from the operation of the

[59] So. Ry. in Ky. v. Commonwealth, 129 Ky. 87, 110 S. W. 372 (1908).
[60] Louisville & N. R. R. v. Commonwealth, 117 Ky. 345, 78 S. W. 167 (1904).
[61] Mammoth C. R. R. v. Commonwealth, 176 Ky. 747, 749, 197 S. W. 406 (1917).

Jim Crow law,[62] thereby relieving the railways of the duty to segregate passengers and to provide equal accommodations for the two races. These provisions may possibly be challenged because they would allow the railways to disregard the cardinal principle of public utility law which demands that there shall be no unreasonable discrimination among passengers. If such exceptions were approved, the carrier would be permitted to make unfair distinctions based on the passengers' race or color, and it might be argued that this would constitute a denial of equal protection of the laws as prohibited by the Fourteenth Amendment. A Virginia statute authorizes railway officials to reject any passenger who wishes accommodations in any pullman, chair, palace, dining, or compartment car if they deem it advisable to do so.[63] This statute is probably unconstitutional because it would give railway employes a blanket authority to accept or reject any passenger without setting up any standard of conduct which would subject the passenger to summary refusal or eviction. Under this act a conductor might refuse to carry a Negro on account of his race or color, and this would amount to rank discrimination.

Three other states have clauses which provide that railways may haul pullman or chair cars for the exclusive use of the members of either race.[64] Diners are also mentioned in two of these jurisdictions.[65] The constitutionality of the Oklahoma proviso has been discussed by the Supreme Court. The lower federal court had held that the proviso made a reasonable classification and that hence it did not violate the equal protection guarantee of the Constitution. It declared that there was little demand for such luxuries among the Negroes in Oklahoma, in fact not enough to warrant the railways' supplying such accommodations. The Supreme Court declined to adopt this reasoning, however, and stated that the proviso was invalid.[66] Thus it is safe to say that this type of clause is uncon-

[62] MD. ANN. CODE (Bagby, 1924) art. 27, §438 (applies also to parlor cars); N. C. CODE ANN. (Michie, 1931) §3494; VA. CODE ANN. (Michie, 1930) §3968.

[63] *Id.* at §4007.

[64] ARK. DIG. STAT. (Crawford & Moses, 1921) §989; OKLA. COMP. STAT. (1921) §4958; TEX. ANN. REV. CIV. STAT. (1925) art. 6417, TEX. ANN. PEN. CODE (Vernon, 1925) art. 1660.

[65] Oklahoma, Texas.

[66] McCabe v. Atchison, T. & S. F. Ry., 235 U. S. 151, 35 Sup. Ct. 69 (1914), *rev'g* on this point the case in 186 Fed. 966 (C. C. A. 8th, 1911), but *aff'g* the decision for lack of proper pleading.

stitutional. Therefore, it may be said that the railways are required to furnish equal accommodations for both races, no matter what the demand for the special facilities may be.

In Georgia a special statute makes compulsory the separation of the races on pullmans.[67] The act provides that nothing in it shall be construed to compel railways to carry Negroes either in sleeping or in parlor cars. There is an exception in the case of nurses or servants traveling with their employers. Penalties are provided for the breach of this statute, and railway employes are given police power to enforce it.[68]

Jim Crow statutes may well be construed to require separate pullman accommodations for the two races. Such has been the construction placed upon the Mississippi act.[69] However, it has been said in two cases, one from Kentucky and the other from Texas, that a railway company cannot be held criminally responsible for not providing separate pullman accommodations where the pullman company's employes and not the railway's employes are in sole control of the sleeping car.[70] The courts also emphasized the fact that the only renumeration which the railways obtained from hauling pullman cars was an inducement for increased travel over their roads.

Another question arises in connection with the increased cost of maintaining separate pullman accommodations. A railway company in Mississippi, where the statute was construed to require separate facilities in pullmans, claimed that the additional expense of carrying colored pullman coaches would be practically prohibitive because of the paucity of Negro pullman passengers. The state court decided that this inconvenience to the railway did not constitute a deprivation of property without due process of law prohibited by the Fourteenth Amendment, the additional cost of furnishing separate accommodations not being confiscatory.[71] There have been some objections by railway corporations to the increased expense which the whole system of Jim Crow laws puts upon them. It is believed,

---

[67] GA. CODE ANN. (Michie, 1926) §2724.

[68] *Id.* at §§2724-25, GA. CODE ANN. (Michie, 1926) PEN. CODE §538.

[69] Alabama & V. Ry. v. Morris, 103 Miss. 511, 60 So. 11 (1912); So. Ry. v. Norton, 112 Miss. 302, 73 So. 1 (1916).

[70] Commonwealth v. Illinois C. R. R., 141 Ky. 502, 133 S. W. 1158 (1911); State v. G. H. & S. A. Ry., 184 S. W. 227 (Tex. Civ. App. 1916).

[71] So. Ry. v. Norton, 112 Miss. 302, 73 So. 1 (1916).

however, that, without statutory requirements, most of the railways in the South would segregate the Negroes, for public opinion probably would demand a separation of the races.

It was decided in a Tennessee case that the Arkansas statute does not require either separate or partitioned dining cars.[72] The court in this instance approved a railway company's regulation to the effect that its diners must serve meals at different hours for white and colored passengers. However, the railway was held responsible for the negligence of one of its employes in making a call for white persons at a time when Negroes were about to be served.

Whenever an unexpected emergency occurs, the railway is excused from a strict compliance with the provisions of the Jim Crow laws, though there are expressions in the cases which seem to require as much separation and as quick a solution of the difficulty as is possible under the circumstances.[73] This is true whether the emergency occurs because of an unusual influx of white or colored passengers[74] or a breakdown in equipment.[75] However, this defense was not successful in a case where the company had advertised an excursion and it was shown that the Negro plaintiff might have been given proper accommodations in a colored coach if the railway officials had placed some of the following trains in advance.[76] The legislatures of three states have realized that emergencies may sometimes occur and have given train conductors statutory authority to act when such a situation arises.[77] The Arkansas statute contains a provision relieving a railway from the operation of the

---

[72] Shelton v. Chicago, R. I. & P. Ry., 139 Tenn. 378, 201 S. W. 521 (1918).

[73] Bradford v. St. L., I. M. & S. Ry., 93 Ark. 244, 124 S. W. 516 (1910); Weller v. Mo., K. & T. Ry., 187 S. W. 374 (Tex. Civ. App. 1916).

[74] Bradford v. St. L., I. M. & S. Ry., 93 Ark. 244, 124 S. W. 516 (1910); St. L. & S. F. R. R. v. Petties, 99 Ark. 415, 138 S. W. 961 (1911); Anderson v. Gulf & S. I. R. R., 147 Miss. 164, 113 So. 188 (1927); Norris v. So. Ry., 84 S. C. 15, 65 S. E. 956 (1909). In one case it is said that a press of business will not excuse non-compliance, but the opinion does not state whether the increase of traffic was expected or unexpected. So. Kan. Ry. of Tex. v. State, 44 Tex. Civ. App. Rep. 218, 99 S. W. 166 (1906).

[75] Chesapeake & O. Ry. v. Commonwealth, 119 Ky. 519, 84 S. W. 566 (1905); Weller v. Mo., K. & T. Ry., 187 S. W. 374 (Tex. Civ. App. 1916).

[76] Williams v. Int. & G. N. Ry., 28 Tex. Civ. App. Rep. 503, 67 S. W. 1085 (1902).

[77] N. C. Code Ann. (Michie, 1931) §3496; S. C. Code (1932) §8398; Va. Code Ann. (Michie, 1930) §3967.

law when a coach is disabled, at least until another can be provided.[78] The defense of emergency is an affirmative one, and hence the attorney for the railway company must plead it if he expects to make use of it at the trial.[79]

All of these state statutes with only one exception, South Carolina, give express permission to use partitioned or compartment cars, one portion for whites and the other for Negroes.[80] Five of these[81] require signs designating the race which is to use the particular coach or compartment. In a Kentucky case where the gravamen of the offense charged was a violation of this requirement, it was held that it was not prejudicial to reject evidence brought forward to prove that the railway had actually supplied separate coaches, such evidence being immaterial on the issue involved.[82]

It has been decided that the Oklahoma statute requires separate entrances to the coaches, including a step box wherever necessary.[83] In this instance a Negro passenger refused to use the step box for whites, there being none provided for Negroes. The railway contended that the Negro was contributorily negligent in refusing to use the step box which was offered. The Negro secured a verdict, and the court declared that the issue of contributory negligence was properly left to the jury.

---

[78] ARK. DIG. STAT. (Crawford & Moses, 1921) §987.

[79] Illinois C. R. R. v. Redmond, 119 Miss. 765, 81 So. 115 (1919).

[80] ALA. CODE ANN. (Michie, 1928) §9968; ARK. DIG. STAT. (Crawford & Moses, 1921) §§986, 990 (railway may use only one such coach on lines more than thirty miles in length); FLA. COMP. GEN. LAWS ANN. (Skillman, 1927) §6618 (cannot do so without consent of Railroad Comm.); GA. CODE ANN. (Michie, 1926) §§2717, 2720 (may be proportioned according to usual travel of each race on road); KY. STAT. ANN. (Carroll, 1930) §795; LA. GEN. STAT. ANN. (Dart, 1932) §8130; MD. ANN. CODE (Bagby, 1924) art. 27, §432; MISS. CODE ANN. (1930) §6132; N. C. CODE ANN. (Michie, 1931) §3494; OKLA. COMP. STAT. (1921) §4955; TENN. CODE (Will. Shan. & Harsh, 1932) §5518; TEX. ANN. REV. CIV. STAT. (Vernon, 1925) art. 6417, TEX. ANN. PEN. CODE (Vernon, 1925) art. 1659; VA. CODE ANN. (Michie, 1930) §3962. The S. C. act provides that railways under forty miles in length shall furnish separate apartments, the exact meaning of which has never been judicially determined. S. C. CODE (1932) §8399. Does it mean that these short lines may use partitioned or compartment coaches?

[81] KY. STAT. ANN. (Carroll, 1930) §795; MD. ANN. CODE (Bagby, 1924) art. 27, §432; OKLA. COMP. STAT. (1921) §4955; TEX. ANN. REV. CIV. STAT. (Vernon, 1925) art. 6417, TEX. ANN. PEN. CODE (Vernon, 1925) art. 1659 (does not specifically mention compartment cars, but its application can be implied from context); VA. CODE ANN. (Michie, 1930) §3962.

[82] Chesapeake & O. Ry. v. Commonwealth, 149 Ky. 386, 149 S. W. 826 (1912).

[83] St. Louis-S. F. Ry. v. Loftus, 109 Okla. 141, 234 Pac. 607 (1925).

In a case from Kentucky a coach was partitioned, part of it being used as a smoker for whites and part as a compartment for Negroes. This coach was the only one set aside for Negroes on that train, and the result was that there was only one toilet available for colored persons of both sexes. The white coaches on the train had separate toilets, and it was claimed that this constituted unequal treatment of persons of the two races. It was held that the principle of equality was not violated by this difference in facilities.[84] The chief reason advanced by the court for its decision was that not more than 15 per cent of the travelers on this particular line were Negroes. Although, as said in the instant case, equality does not require identity,[85] still it is a judicial untruth to declare that accommodations for the two races are equal when both sexes of one race must use the same toilet while separate toilets are furnished in the coaches which are set aside for the exclusive use of members of the other race. The decision is therefore clearly contrary to the established rule that railways must provide equal accommodations for Negroes.[86] While it is true that only 10 or 15 per cent of the passenger traffic on this particular road was colored, the smallness of this demand, as has been already pointed out in the discussion of the pullman exceptions, would not justify a railway's discriminatory policy of furnishing unequal accommodations. Moreover, it has been decided in other instances that if separate toilets for the sexes and smoking facilities are provided for one race, such conveniences must also be furnished for the other.[87] In one case a Negro passenger was made to ride in a partitioned coach, half of which was set apart for Negroes and the other portion used as a smoking compartment for both

---

[84] Louisville & N. R. R. v. Commonwealth, 160 Ky. 769, 170 S. W. 162 (1914).

[85] Plessy v. Ferguson, 163 U. S. 537, 16 Sup. Ct. 1138 (1896), approving *Ex parte* Plessy, 45 La. Ann. 80, 11 So. 948 (1893); McCabe v. Atchison, T. & S. F. Ry., 235 U. S. 151, 35 Sup. Ct. 69 (1914); Logwood v. Memphis & C. R. R., 23 Fed. 318 (C. C. W. D. Tenn. 1885); Illinois C. R. R. v. Redmond, 119 Miss. 765, 81 So. 115 (1919).

[86] Brown v. Memphis & C. R. R., 5 Fed. 499 (C. C. W. D. Tenn. 1880); Houck v. So. P. R. R., 38 Fed. 226 (C. C. W. D. Tex.), 4 I. C. C. 441 (1888); Texas & P. Ry. v. Johnson, 2 Willson, Tex. Civ. App. Rep. 154, par. 186 (1884); Gray v. Cin. So. R. R., 11 Fed. 683 (C. C. S. D. Ohio, 1882); Gaines v. Seaboard A. L. Ry., 16 I. C. C 471 (1909).

[87] Illinois C. R. R. v. Redmond, 119 Miss. 765, 81 So. 115 (1919); Henderson v. Galveston, H. & S. A. Ry., 38 S. W. 1136 (Tex. Civ. App. 1896).

races. It was shown that there were superior accommodations for white persons who were on the same train. The court held that the railway had not furnished equal facilities.[88] The same result was reached where a Negro having a first-class ticket was forced to ride in a distinctly second-class coach where the two races were mixed and crowded together and smoking was permitted.[89]

A railway may be required to furnish for both races whatever accommodations are needed to supply a reasonably anticipated demand, but the carriers would not be held responsible for an unusually large number of white or Negro passengers.[90] This duty to furnish reasonable accommodations may be entirely independent of the Jim Crow statute. There is usually a statute stating that such a duty exists. This type of act makes no mention of the races, but only requires accommodations for all passengers. In a case from Kentucky a railway company was indicted under the terms of the separate coach law. The indictment alleged that the railway had violated this statute. However, it was shown that the railway had furnished separate coaches for both races. The only way in which the company had been at fault was in not providing sufficient facilities for white passengers, and they had been forced to ride, if at all, in the Negro coach. The court declared that the gravamen of the offense described in the indictment was not the failure to furnish separate coaches but a failure to supply a sufficient number of coaches for whites. It therefore held that the indictment had been brought under the wrong statute.[91]

The indictment must also be drawn under the correct section of the Jim Crow law. In another Kentucky case the indictment was brought under the section requiring railways to furnish separate coaches, while the alleged facts showed only a failure to supply equal accommodations to the passengers of both races. It was held that the indictment had been brought under the improper section of the statute.[92] The proper procedure would have been an indictment under the section providing that

[88] Heard v. Georgia R. R., 1 I. C. C. 719 (1888).

[89] Council v. Western & A. R. R., 1 I. C. C. 638 (1887).

[90] Chesapeake & O. Ry. v. Austin, 137 Ky. 611, 126 S. W. 144 (1910).

[91] Commonwealth v. Louisville & N. Ry., 27 Ky. Law Rep. 932, 87 S. W. 262 (1905).

[92] Illinois C. Ry. v. Commonwealth, 25 Ky. Law Rep. 295, 74 S. W. 1076 (1903).

railways must furnish equal accommodations. It is not necessary to go into a lot of detail in the indictments under the separate coach law. Thus an indictment which follows the wording of the statute and alleges a willful violation on a particular occasion has been held sufficient.[93]

In civil suits against railway companies to recover damages for injuries caused by violations of separate coach laws all essential allegations are necessary to a successful termination of the action. Thus, where a woman asked for damages because the railway's agents had forced her to ride in the Negro coach, the complaint was ruled defective in as much as it failed to allege that the plaintiff was white.[94]

The fact that at a particular time there are no Negroes on a train does not excuse noncompliance with the separate coach law.[95] It was the duty of a railway company to make preparations for the carriage of both races on all regular trains,[96] and a failure to carry out this duty completes the offense.[97] However, only one such offense is possible with each train. Hence, where a train was broken up one day and reassembled the next, it cannot be considered a double offense under the statute.[98]

Practically all of the eastern and middle western states and a few in the far west have Civil Rights Acts.[99] A typical statute

---

[93] Chesapeake & O. Ry. v. Commonwealth, 119 Ky. 519, 84 S. W. 566 (1905).

[94] Southern Ry. v. Thurman, 25 Ky. Law Rep. 804, 76 S. W. 499 (1903).

[95] So. Kansas Ry. of Texas v. State, 44 Tex. Civ. App. Rep. 218, 99 S. W. 166 (1906).

[96] Louisville & N. R. R. v. Commonwealth, 171 Ky. 355, 188 S. W. 394 (1916); So. Kans. Ry. of Tex. v. State, 44 Tex. Civ. App. Rep. 218, 99 S. W. 166 (1906).

[97] Louisville & N. R. R. v. Commonwealth, 171 Ky. 355, 188 S. W. 394 (1916).

[98] See *ibid.*

[99] CAL. CIV. CODE (Deering, 1931) §§51-52; COLO. STAT. ANN. (Mills, 1930) §§754a-b; CONN. GEN. STAT. (Supp. 1933) §1160b; ILL. REV. STAT. (Cahill, 1933) c. 38, §§104-5 as amended by Ill. Laws 1935, p. 708; IND. STAT. ANN. (Burns, 1933) §§10-901-2; IOWA CODE (1931) §§13,251-52; KANS. REV. STAT. (1923) §21-2424; MASS. ANN. LAWS (1933) c. 272, §98; MICH. COMP. LAWS (Supp. 1933) §17,115 ss. 146-47, re-enacting MICH. COMP. LAWS (1929) §16,809-11; MINN. STAT. (Mason, 1927) §7321; NEB. COMP. STAT. (1929) §§23-101-2; N. J. COMP. STAT. (Supp. 1924) tit. 39, §§1-2, amending N. J. COMP. STAT. (1911) p. 1442, §§1-2; N. Y. CONSOL. LAWS (Cahill, 1930) c. 7, §§40-41, c. 41, §514; OHIO CODE (Throckmorton, 1929) §§12940-41 as amended in BALDWIN'S CODE SERV., Jan. 1938; Pa. Laws 1935, Act 132; R. I. Pub. Laws 1925-26, c. 658; WASH. REV. STAT. ANN. (Remington, 1932) §2686 (statute general, does not mention carriers or other places of public accommodation specifically); WIS. STAT. (1931) c. 340, §75 (340.75). The Louisiana Civil Rights Act prohibiting carriers from making

of this kind provides that there shall be no racial discrimination by public carriers on land or water. These acts either punish such unfair conduct as a crime or else assess penalties against those who are responsible, and in some instances both remedies are provided. In an action under one of these statutes the act of the railway in refusing to transport a Negro passenger or giving him less commodious accommodations must be shown to have been motivated by racial antipathy.[100] A very similar act of Congress applying to interstate and intrastate passengers alike was enacted in 1875 as a portion of the Reconstruction legislation.[101] The purpose of the radical legislators in enacting this statute was to force the South to accept Negroes in certain places of public accommodation and amusement. The act was declared unconstitutional by the Supreme Court in the *Civil Rights Cases*.[102] The court held that the Fourteenth Amendment authorized no such direct legislation against individual action. It declared that the power to enact laws under the amendment was limited to corrective legislation punishing states or their officials for not respecting the rights guaranteed thereby, such as the right not to be deprived of life, liberty,

any regulations discriminating against persons because of their race or color has been superseded with respect to railways and buses by the Louisiana Jim Crow laws. See Louisiana Civil Rights Act. LA. GEN. STAT. ANN. (Dart, 1932) §§1070-73. In so far as the statute applied to interstate travel, it was declared unconstitutional in Hall v. DeCuir, 95 U. S. 485 (1877). In respect to the question as to the total invalidity of the statute, see note 133 *infra,* and Annotation to LA. GEN. STAT. ANN. (Dart, 1932) §1070.

Utah once had a statute making it a misdemeanor for an innkeeper or a carrier to refuse to receive anyone as a guest or passenger. UTAH COMP. STAT. (1917) §8445. The portion of the act concerning carriers is left out of the 1933 Revisal, UTAH REV. STAT. ANN. (1933) §103-29-2, probably because the codifiers deemed it unnecessary to so bolster the common law rule.

The Michigan, New Jersey, New York, and Pennsylvania Civil Rights Acts prohibit the advertising of any racial discrimination. The same is done by special statutes covering such advertising in Colorado, Illinois, and Massachusetts. COLO. STAT. ANN. (Mills, 1930) §§5858a-5858e; ILL. REV. STAT. (Cahill, 1933) c. 38, §§550-555; Mass. Acts & Resolves 1933, c. 117.

[100] Williams v. Chicago, R. I. & P. Ry., 90 Kan. 478, 135 Pac. 671 (1913); Central R. R. of N. J. v. Green, 86 Pa. St. 421 (1878).

[101] 18 STAT. 335 (1875).

[102] Civil Rights Cases, 109 U. S. 3, 3 Sup. Ct. 18 (1883). *In accord are* Smoot v. Kentucky C. Ry., 13 Fed. 337 (C. C. D. Ky. 1882); United States v. Washington, 20 Fed. 630 (C. C. W. D. Tex. 1883). *See* Butts v. Merchants' & Miners' Transportation Co., 230 U. S. 126, 33 Sup. Ct. 964 (1913), as applied to carriers within sphere of federal control.

or property without due process of law or the right to equal protection of the laws.

Before the Supreme Court's ruling was handed down, there had been a difference of opinion as to the validity of this statute. Some of the litigation involved rights on railways. One court came to the conclusion that the act would not apply in a case of local travel because it was enacted to protect the rights of national citizenship and not state citizenship.[103] The court declared that the privilege of local travel was a right of the latter variety. As an additional reason for deciding against the plaintiff the court pointed out that he had not averred that the alleged discrimination had been practiced because of race or color.

In one case from Texas a federal court seems to have granted the validity of the Civil Rights Act.[104] In the course of its opinion the court suggested that the statute would not be applicable where the carrier furnished equal but separate accommodations for both races. Hence, under this interpretation, a railway could not be indicted or penalized for making Jim Crow regulations if the accommodations for the two races were equal. From this it might be supposed that railways could segregate passengers according to race even in a state where there is a Civil Rights Act. However, when one considers the decisions under the state Civil Rights Acts concerning other places of public accomodation and amusement,[105] it is not very probable that the practice of segregation would be permitted. In fact the Pennsylvania Court intimated as much in one instance where it upheld the right to segregate under the common law.[106] This view also derives support from a decision by the Federal Supreme Court.[107] In this instance there was a grant of certain privileges to a railway company in the District of Columbia. A clause in the charter provided that "no person shall be excluded from the cars because of race or color." This clause was construed to force a mixture of the races in the

---

[103] Cully v. B. & O. Ry., 6 Fed. Cas. No. 3,466 (D. Md. 1876).

[104] United States v. Dodge, 25 Fed. Cas. No. 14,976 (W. D. Tex. 1877).

[105] See chapter on Civil Rights, notes 65 and 66.

[106] *See* West Chester & P. R. R. v. Miles, 55 Pa. St. 209 (1867).

[107] Alex. & W. Ry. v. Brown, 17 Wall. 445 (U. S. 1873).

coaches and not to permit the railway to adopt a Jim Crow policy.

In a jurisdiction where there is neither a separate coach law nor a Civil Rights Act, it has been held that railway companies, if they so desire, may make their own Jim Crow regulations.[108] Missouri and West Virginia are in this category, but there is no segregation on the railways of these two states at the present time.

The above-mentioned Delaware optional Jim Crow statute gives all types of public carriers the privilege of assigning to a particular place in their vehicles any person or group of persons whose presence is offensive to the major portion of the traveling public, provided that equal accommodations are supplied for such persons.[109] However, segregation is not practiced in Delaware today.

Ten states make statutory provision for separate waiting room accommodations for the two races in stations or depots,[110] and one of these also requires separate facilities in station restaurants where meals are served.[111] In the absence of statutory regulation, a southern court has held that a railway company may establish rules requiring separate waiting rooms.[112] Generally speaking, southern waiting rooms usually provide separate accommodations for the white and Negro races. The

---

[108] Chilton v. St. Louis & I. M. Ry., 114 Mo. 88, 21 S. W. 457 (1893). *See* West Chester & P. R. R. v. Miles, 55 Pa. St. 209 (1867), and a suggestion in Chicago & N. W. Ry. v. Williams, 55 Ill. 185 (1870), cases which were decided before these states adopted Civil Rights legislation. *See also* Britton v. Atlantic & C. A. Ry., 88 N. C. 536 (1883).

[109] DEL. REV. CODE (1915) §3577.

[110] ALA. CODE ANN. (Michie, 1928) §9964; ARK. DIG. STAT. (Crawford & Moses, 1921) §§950, 986; FLA. COMP. GEN. LAWS ANN. (Skillman, 1927) §§6625, 6712 (may extend time for compliance therewith); LA. GEN. STAT. ANN. (Dart, 1932) §§8133-35 (distinct act with penalties for its violation and having exceptions in favor of nurses and police officers in charge of prisoners); MISS. CODE ANN. (1930) §7079; N. C. CODE ANN. (Michie, 1931) §§1043, 3494; OKLA. COMP. STAT. (1921) §4953 (seems to apply to all interurban and street railways as well); S. C. CODE (1932) §8413 (separation of races not specifically mentioned but may be implied from context); TEX. ANN. REV. CIV. STAT. (Vernon, 1925) art. 6498; VA. CODE ANN. (Michie, 1930) §3716. The Mississippi, North Carolina, and Virginia laws authorize the Corporation or Utilities' Commissioners to make provision for separate waiting-room facilities for white and colored passengers.

[111] S. C. CODE (1932) §8403.

[112] Smith v. Chamberlain, 38 S. C. 529, 17 S. E. 371 (1893).

Arkansas Court has upheld the constitutionality of the waiting room statute of that state.[113]

In Arkansas an indictment under this statute must allege facts showing in what respect the facilities for one race were inferior to those provided for the other,[114] which waiting room, white or Negro, was inferior,[115] and should particularly describe the circumstances surrounding the offense.[116] Thus an indictment which follows the language of the statute and goes no further is not sufficient in that state.[117] It has also been held erroneous to join the station agent as a party in the action.[118]

In one instance a statute requiring separate waiting rooms was construed to apply only to those stations where there are depots.[119] In this case it was held that a flag station store over which the railway company exercised no control was not a station within the meaning of such a statute in spite of the fact that railway tickets were sold there.

It has been decided that separate waiting room facilities must be supplied at all proper times.[120] The accommodations for whites and Negroes must be substantially equal. In one case from Oklahoma the railway had placed its Negro waiting room in a cold spot where the heat from a stove in the station agent's office, separated from the waiting room by a lattice partition, could not properly warm the prospective Negro passengers. The court decided that this proved that the railway had not provided equal facilities for Negroes.[121] In a South Carolina case it was held that accommodations cannot be considered unequal because at some past time tobacco chewing and smoking had been tolerated in the Negro waiting room, whereas these pastimes had not been permitted in the waiting room for

[113] State v. St. Louis & S. F. R. R., 83 Ark. 254, 103 S. W. 625 (1907).

[114] Choctaw, O. & G. R. R. v. State, 75 Ark. 279, 87 S. W. 426 (1905).

[115] State v. St. Louis & S. F. R. R., 83 Ark. 254, 103 S. W. 625 (1907).

[116] St. Louis & S. F. Ry. v. State, 68 Ark. 251, 57 S. W. 796 (1900).

[117] Choctaw, O. & G. R. R. v. State, 75 Ark. 279, 87 S. W. 426 (1905). Dissenting opinion takes view that indictment is good since it follows wording of statute.

[118] St. Louis & S. F. Ry. v. State, 68 Ark. 251, 57 S. W. 796 (1900).

[119] St. Louis, I. M. & S. Ry. v. State, 61 Ark. 9, 31 S. W. 570 (1895).

[120] St. Louis, S. W. Ry. v. Green, 99 Ark. 572, 139 S. W. 307 (1911); Neal v. So. Ry., 92 S. C. 197, 75 S. E. 405 (1912).

[121] St. Louis, I. M. & S. Ry. v. Lewis, 39 Okla. 677, 136 Pac. 396 (1913).

whites.[122] There was no evidence that either of these pursuits had been indulged in on the particular occasion in question.

A railway company is not permitted to offer to persons of one race accommodations in the waiting room which has been set apart for members of the other.[123] A passenger's refusal to enter the waiting room assigned to members of the race to which he does not belong has been held not to bar a recovery[124] or to minimize the damages resulting from a failure to obey the mandate of the law.[125] In one Oklahoma case the colored waiting room was poorly heated, and a Negro refused to pass through the white waiting room in order that he might reach the fire in the station agent's office. The court declared that this refusal could not be considered as the sole proximate cause of injuries suffered because of the railway's failure to provide equal accommodations.[126] This case presents a situation which is vastly different from those mentioned above, and evidence of such a refusal should at least be admissible to minimize the damages.

In the North Negroes are allowed to intermingle with the whites at stations, and the Illinois Civil Rights Act has been held to apply in a case where a Negro was denied the privilege of riding in a depot elevator.[127] The Civil Rights Acts of Connecticut, New Jersey, New York, and Pennsylvania mention stations.

And now the constitutionality of these Jim Crow regulations will be discussed. It has been held that separate coach laws are not in conflict with the equal protection clause of the Fourteenth Amendment.[128] An equality of accommodations is guaranteed and the classification is said not to be unfair. In Missouri where there is neither a Jim Crow statute nor a Civil

---

[122] Smith v. Chamberlain, 38 S. C. 529, 17 S. E. 371 (1893).

[123] St. Louis, S. W. Ry. v. Green, 99 Ark. 572, 139 S. W. 307 (1911).

[124] *Ibid;* Neal v. So. Ry., 92 S. C. 197, 75 S. E. 405 (1912).

[125] See note 123 *supra.* [126] See note 121 *supra.*

[127] Dean v. Chicago & N. Ry., 183 Ill. App. 317 (1913).

[128] Plessy v. Ferguson, 163 U. S. 537, 16 Sup. Ct. 1138 (1896), aff'g *Ex parte* Plessy, 45 La. Ann. 80, 11 So. 948 (1893); Chesapeake & O. Ry. v. Commonwealth, 179 U. S. 388, 21 Sup. Ct. 101 (1900), *aff'g* 21 Ky. Law Rep. 228, 51 S. W. 160 (1899); McCabe v. Atchison, T. & S. F. Ry., 235 U. S. 151, 35 Sup. Ct. 69 (1914); Anderson v. Louisville & N. Ry., 62 Fed. 46 (C. C. D. Ky. 1894); Ohio V. Ry's Receiver v. Lander, 104 Ky. 431, 47 S. W. 344 (1898); Illinois C. R. R. v. Redmond, 119 Miss. 765, 81 So. 115 (1919).

Rights Act, the state court has upheld the validity of a railway's regulation directing a separation of the races on its coaches.[129] The fact that a certain railway supplies less commodious facilities to the members of one race does not render the statute invalid, as this is not the fault of the act itself.[130]

These separate coach laws, when limited to intrastate traffic, have been held to be a proper exercise of the state's police power.[131] However, where the act is written in such a manner as to include interstate as well as local traffic, a different problem is presented. In the *Anderson* case from Kentucky, a case which was decided by a federal court in the nineties, a statute which received such an interpretation was held to be void *in toto* because it interfered with interstate commerce.[132] Whether this case would be followed today we do not know. However, the famous Louisiana steamboat case gives us at least an inkling as to the attitude of the Supreme Court toward the application of such a statute to interstate passengers. The Louisiana Civil Rights Act which had been enacted during Reconstruction provided that carriers shall not make rules or regulations which discriminate against any person by reason of his race or color. A steamboat plying between points in different states adopted Jim Crow regulations. It was held that the Civil Rights Act was invalid in so far as it had any application to interstate passengers.[133] The court does not decide whether the act would

[129] Chilton v. St. Louis & I. M. Ry., 114 Mo. 88, 21 S. W. 457 (1893). *See also* West Chester & P. R. R. v. Miles, 55 Pa. St. 209 (1867) *and* Chicago & N. W. Ry. v. Williams, 55 Ill. 185 (1870), cases which occurred before the Civil Rights Acts in the respective states were enacted. In the latter case there was no such regulation shown to be in effect on the defendant's road and therefore the railway was not excused for having excluded a Negro woman from the ladies' car.

[130] McCabe v. Atchison, T. & S. F. Ry., 186 Fed. 966 (C. C. A. 8th, 1911), *reviewed,* 235 U. S. 151, 35 Sup. Ct. 69 (1914).

[131] Louisville, N. O. & T. Ry. v. Mississippi, 133 U. S. 587, 10 Sup. Ct. 348 (1890), *aff'g* 66 Miss. 662, 6 So. 203 (1889); Chesapeake & O. Ry. v. Com. of Ky., 179 U. S. 388, 21 Sup. Ct. 101 (1900), *aff'g* 21 Ky. Law Rep. 228, 51 S. W. 160 (1899); McCabe v. Atchison, T. & S. F. Ry., 186 Fed. 966 (C. C. A. 8th, 1911); Ohio V. Ry's Receiver v. Lander, 104 Ky. 431, 47 S. W. 344 (1898); Hart v. State, 100 Md. 595, 60 Atl. 457 (1905); Illinois C. Ry. v. Redmond, 119 Miss. 765, 81 So. 115 (1919).

[132] Anderson v. Louisville & N. Ry., 62 Fed. 46 (C. C. D. Ky. 1894). See also (1910) 19 YALE L. J. 445. But see what is said regarding application to interstate traffic in Smith v. State, 100 Tenn. 494, 46 S. W. 566 (1898).

[133] Hall v. DeCuir, 95 U. S. 485 (1877), *rev'g* DeCuir v. Benson, 27 La. Ann. 1 (1875).

be unconstitutional with respect to intrastate traffic, but there is enough said in the opinion to give the impression that the statute would not be held entirely void.

The Jim Crow statutes have been held in a number of instances to have no application to interstate passengers.[134] However, the Mississippi statute has been held to apply to carriers which are operating as connecting links in a chain of railways which are engaged in interstate transportation, both terminals and the whole line between them being situated within the state.[135] Another similar case came before the Supreme Court in 1920. In this instance there was a distinct operation of a train within the state of Kentucky. Such a road was authorized by the corporate charters of a foreign interurban railway company and its local subsidiary. This line was run as a link in a system which was engaged in interstate carriage. The court held that the state Jim Crow statute was applicable and that there was no interference with interstate commerce.[136] However, it has been held that a passenger going from one jurisdiction to another is not deprived of his status as an interstate traveler on the first leg of his journey because this first leg is within the boundaries of the first jurisdiction or by reason of the fact that he must change cars before reaching the second.[137]

The Jim Crow laws will not be construed as affecting the

[134] Wash. B. & A. Ry. v. Waller, 53 App. D. C. 200, 289 Fed. 598 (1922) (interurban), construing MD. STAT.; State *ex rel.* Abbott v. Hicks, 44 La. Ann. 770, 11 So. 74 (1892); Hart v. State, 100 Md. 595, 60 Atl. 457 (1905); O'Leary v. Ill. C. R. R., 110 Miss. 46, 69 So. 713 (1915); Carrey v. Spencer, 36 N. Y. Supp. 886 (Sup. Ct. 1895), construing TENN. STAT. This is true notwithstanding the following cases which would seem to make such statutes apply to interstate passengers. So. Ry. v. Norton, 112 Miss. 302, 73 So. 1 (1916); Smith v. State, 100 Tenn. 494, 46 S. W. 566 (1898); Pullman Palace Car Co. v. Cain, 15 Tex. Civ. App. Rep. 503, 40 S. W. 220 (1897). It is not necessary to negative in the complaint the proposition that the plaintiff might be an interstate passenger, such being a matter of defense. State v. Jenkins, 124 Md. 376, 92 Atl. 773 (1914) (interurban). The Alabama statute contains a provision negativing its application to interstate passengers who have made contracts for transportation into the state from a jurisdiction where a similar policy of segregation does not prevail. ALA. CODE ANN. (Michie, 1928) §9969.

[135] Alabama & V. Ry. v. Morris, 103 Miss. 511, 60 So. 11 (1912), dismissed on recommendation of appellant's counsel, 234 U. S. 766, 34 Sup. Ct. 675 (1914).

[136] South C. & C. S. Ry. v. Kentucky, 252 U. S. 399, 40 Sup. Ct. 378 (1920) *and* Cin., C. & E. Ry. v. Kentucky, 252 U. S. 408, 40 Sup. Ct. 378 (1920), *aff'g both cases in* 181 Ky. 449, 205 S. W. 603 (1918).

[137] Washington, B. & A. Ry. v. Waller, 53 App. D. C. 200, 289 Fed. 598 (1922) (interurban).

interstate passenger traffic unless they are subject to no other interpretation,[138] as it is not to be presumed that state legislators would enact laws pertaining to interstate passengers. Congress has remained discreetly silent since the days of the Civil Rights Act, and hence the problem and its control have been left in the hands of the individual carriers. The railways in various sections of the country have therefore been permitted to handle the problem in any way they saw fit. Southern carriers have thereupon adopted a Jim Crow policy. It has been said that congressional inaction is equivalent to a declaration that railways and other interstate carriers may make such regulations.[139] Congress certainly has the power to act but has not acted.[140] Interstate carriers' regulations separating the races on trains running across the state boundaries between North and South have been approved by the courts.[141] In order for such regulations to be effective, however, they must be brought to the passenger's notice, at least constructively.[142]

Suppose a railway company wished to separate the races on trains operated between points located in two northern states which had Civil Rights Acts. According to the Louisiana steamboat case, discussed above, the State Civil Rights Acts would be invalid if construed to apply to interstate traffic as well as that within the boundaries of the respective states. Hence these acts, which do not specifically mention interstate carriers, would probably not be construed to have any application at all to the passenger traffic between the two states. Accordingly, no reason is perceived which would prevent the railway from adopting a segregation policy. Of course an instance of this kind is extremely unlikely to occur. Any railway which adopted such Jim Crow regulations would soon be beset by cries of racial discrimination and prejudice. In fact there would be the distinct danger of a boycott by the Negroes and their white friends. The criticism would hurt the business of the com-

---

[138] Ohio V. Ry's Receiver v. Lander, 104 Ky. 431, 47 S. W. 344 (1898).

[139] Minor, *Constitutionality of Segregation Ordinances* (1912) 18 VA. L. REG. 561, 569. See also Baker, *The Segregation of White and Colored Passengers on Interstate Trains* (1910) 19 YALE L. J. 445.

[140] *Ibid.* The author suggests that some such action should be taken.

[141] Chiles v. Chesapeake & O. Ry., 218 U. S. 71, 30 Sup. Ct. 667 (1910) *aff'g* 125 Ky. 299, 101 S. W. 386 (1907); Washington, B. & A. Ry. v. Waller, 53 App. D. C. 200, 289 Fed. 598 (1922).

[142] *Ibid.*

pany at least enough to worry the management. It might even force an abandonment of the policy.

On the other hand, if a southern carrier refused to adopt a Jim Crow policy for its interstate passengers, it might feel the force of the public anger. It is almost certain that the wave of public opinion would compel the carrier to renounce its innovation. The prejudice is still sufficiently intense in the truly southern states to force a return to the policy of segregation. In the border states the prejudice might not be sufficiently strong to necessitate an abandonment of a nonsegregative policy. In fact Negro passengers on interstate trains are not required to move their seats when coming south into Maryland. Except in Kentucky and Maryland, where the law requires separation on intrastate trains, public opinion would probably be overwhelmingly against the practice of local separation. The railways in Kentucky have separate accommodations for interstate as well as intrastate passengers.

All except three of the above southern states having railway Jim Crow laws also require separate accommodations on street railways.[143] The three exceptions are Alabama, Kentucky, and Maryland. All of these laws with the lone exception of the Florida statute contain penal and police provisions which are the equals of the similar Jim Crow laws applying to railways.[144]

---

[143] ARK. DIG. STAT. (Crawford & Moses, 1921) §§998-1003; FLA. COMP. GEN. STAT. ANN. (Skillman, 1927) §§6620-24; GA. CODE ANN. (Michie, 1926) §§2716-22, construed to include street railways because of language used in §2718; LA. GEN. STAT. ANN. (Dart, 1932) §§8188-90; MISS. CODE ANN. (1930) §§6133-35; N. C. CODE ANN. (Michie, 1931) §§3536-38; OKLA. COMP. STAT. (1921) §§4952-58, 4960-61; S. C. CODE (1932) §§8490-97; TENN. CODE (Will. Shan. & Harsh, 1932) §§5527-32; TEX. ANN. REV. CIV. STAT. (Vernon, 1925) art. 6417, TEX. ANN. PEN. CODE (Vernon, 1925) arts. 1659-60; VA. CODE (Michie, 1930) §§3978-83.

[144] Louisiana and Mississippi provide for action to be taken against the directors and officers instead of the corporation itself. LA. GEN. STAT. ANN. (Dart, 1932) §8190; MISS. CODE ANN. (1930) §6135. The Georgia provision is of course the same, the railway act applying. The North Carolina act punishes the officers but not the company. N. C. CODE ANN. (Michie, 1931) §3536. South Carolina punishes the superintendent and the officers but not the company. S. C. CODE (1932) §8495. It is also doubtful if the police power given the conductor by the Tennessee statute extends so far as to allow him to put a passenger off a car. TENN. CODE (Will. Shan. & Harsh, 1932) §5529. The Florida statute contains no penal or police provisions at all, unless FLA. COMP. GEN. LAWS ANN. (Skillman, 1927) §§7751-52 be construed to apply to street railways as well as steam railways.

The imposition of such penalties is not beyond the power of the state legislature.[145]

According to an interpretation of the Tennessee statute, the street railway is required to do more than merely designate the portion of its cars which is set aside for each race, for it has the additional duty of keeping races separate.[146] The same statute gives the conductor authority to change the line of division for the two races in the street cars and to assign seats in accordance therewith. It also has a clause punishing the passenger's refusal to take the seat assigned to him. The court has declared that these provisions do not constitute an unlawful delegation of authority.[147]

Three states give the conductors on street railways authority to change the line of division between the races,[148] and the statutes of at least three others could easily be so interpreted.[149] Five states provide for signs designating the portion of the car which is to be used for the accommodation of each race.[150] Two others require screens or partitions.[151] The Arkansas statute states that the conductor may "require" a passenger to change his seat, and this term has been held synonymous with "compel." [152] A street railway company in Texas has been held responsible for insulting conduct to a white female passenger on the part of its conductor. He had moved the sign designating the separate divisions for the races, his act signifying that the woman was a Negro.[153] The portion of the Louisiana act re-

---

[145] State v. Pearson, 110 La. 387, 34 So. 575 (1903).

[146] Nashville Ry. & Light Co. v. State, 144 Tenn. 446, 234 S. W. 327 (1920).

[147] Morrison v. State, 116 Tenn. 534, 95 S. W. 494 (1906).

[148] ARK. DIG. STAT. (Crawford & Moses, 1921) §1000; TENN. CODE (Will. Shan. & Harsh, 1932) §5529; VA. CODE ANN. (Michie, 1930) §3980.

[149] GA. CODE ANN. (Michie, 1926) §2719, interpreted this way in Savannah Electric Co. v. Lowe, 27 Ga. App. 350, 108 S. E. 313 (1921); N. C. CODE ANN. (Michie, 1931) §3537; S. C. CODE (1932) §§8491-92.

[150] FLA. COMP. GEN. LAWS ANN. (Skillman, 1927) §6622; OKLA. COMP. STAT. (1921) §4955; S. C. CODE (1932) §8498 (construed to apply to street as well as interurban railways); TENN. CODE (Will. Shan. & Harsh, 1932) §5528; TEX. ANN. REV. CIV. STAT. (Vernon, 1925) art. 6417, TEX. ANN. PEN. CODE. (Vernon, 1925) art. 1659.

[151] LA. GEN. STAT. ANN. (Dart, 1932) §8188; MISS. CODE ANN. (1930) §6133 (adjustable). Florida makes provision for adjustable screens which may be used in place of signs. FLA. COMP. GEN. LAWS ANN. (Skillman, 1927) §6621.

[152] Little R. Ry. & Electric Co. v. Hampton, 112 Ark. 194, 165 S. W. 289 (1914).

[153] San Antonio Traction Co. v. Lambkin, 99 S. W. 574 (Tex. Civ. App. 1907); San Antonio Traction Co. v. Davis, 101 S. W. 554 (Tex. Civ. App. 1907).

quiring screens or partitions has been interpreted to denote adjustable ones.[154] However, it was declared in this same case that a conductor had no right, by moving the partition, to place a passenger in the compartment thus designated for members of the race to which he did not belong, especially when no seats were vacant in the portion of the car which was left for members of his own race. The Mississippi Court has decided that the posting of signs does not constitute a sufficient compliance with the statutory requirement of adjustable screens.[155] It was said that the signs did not come up to the stated specifications. In another case the court declared that a failure to comply with this Mississippi statutory requirement would prevent the employes from making a valid arrest in accordance with the police powers given to them by the act.[156]

There is a difference of opinion concerning the liability of the company and its employes for a mistake in the racial identity of a passenger which causes physical injury or humiliation. Two state courts in the Lower South have taken the view that the street railway is liable in such a case.[157] However, the Virginia Court has declared that there is no liability unless there has been an abuse of discretion, thus excusing honest mistakes.[158] The North Carolina statute contains a provision absolving the company and its employes for any mistake of this kind which they may make.[159] It may be that this difference of opinion is caused by the more liberal attitude which is displayed in the states of the Upper South toward the problems of race relations.

The Arkansas and Georgia courts have refused to permit a recovery for mental suffering in cases where white women were insulted by street railway employes in attempts to enforce the

---

[154] Alexander v. New O. Ry. & Light Co., 129 La. 959, 57 So. 283 (1912).

[155] So. Light & Traction Co. v. Compton, 86 Miss. 269, 38 So. 629 (1905) (statute declared unsuitable but authoritative); Waldauer v. Vicksburg Ry. & Light Co., 88 Miss. 200, 40 So. 751 (1906). With respect to signs on motor buses on streets of Mississippi city, see Mississippi Power & Light Co. v. Garner, 179 Miss. 588, 176 So. 280 (1937).

[156] Waldauer v. Vicksburg Ry. & Light Co., 88 Miss. 200, 40 So. 751 (1906).

[157] Wolfe v. Ga. Ry. & Electric Co., 124 Ga. 693, 53 S. E. 239 (1905), 2 Ga. App. 499, 58 S. E. 899 (1907); May v. Shreveport Traction Co., 127 La. 420, 53 So. 671 (1910).

[158] Va. Ry. & Power Co. v. Deaton, 147 Va. 576, 137 S. E. 500 (1927).

[159] N. C. Code Ann. (Michie, 1931) §3538.

law.[160] However, this is not the general rule,[161] and two later cases[162] from the two states mentioned probably nullify the earlier decisions.

In a Texas case a street railway company was held to be responsible where one of its employes, while ejecting a Negro from the portion of the car set apart for whites, overstepped his statutory authority by assaulting the Negro on the street after rightfully putting him off the car.[163] The act was said to be within the scope of the employment, and therefore the carrier was liable.

There are a good many exceptions distributed through the statutes relating to Jim Crow accommodations on street cars, although they are not so numerous as in those which apply to ordinary steam railways. Thus two states exempt from the operation of the statute officers in charge of prisoners;[164] three exempt company employes engaged in operating the cars;[165] while nine exempt nurses in charge of children or infirm persons.[166] Two courts have held that the latter exception is a reasonable classification and that it does not violate the equal protection guarantee of the Fourteenth Amendment.[167] Chil-

---

[160] Little Rock Ry. & Electric Co. v. Putsche, 84 Ark. 623, 104 S. W. 554 (1907); Ga. Ry. & Electric Co. v. Baker, 1 Ga. App. 832, 58 S. E. 88 (1907).

[161] Conley v. Central Ky. Traction Co., 152 Ky. 764, 154 S. W. 41 (1913) (interurban); May v. Shreveport Traction Co., 127 La. 420, 53 So. 671 (1910). See also Note on Railways, *supra* note 34.

[162] Chicago, R. I. & P. Ry. v. Allison, 120 Ark. 54, 178 S. W. 401 (1915); Wolfe v. Ga. Ry. & Electric Co., 2 Ga. App. 499, 58 S. E. 899 (1907).

[163] Dallas Consol. Street Ry. v. Gilmore, 138 S. W. 1134 (Tex. Civ. App. 1911).

[164] OKLA. COMP. STAT. (1921) §4958; VA. CODE ANN. (Michie, 1930) §3982.

[165] OKLA. COMP. STAT. (1921) §4958; TEX. ANN. REV. CIV. STAT. (Vernon, 1925) art. 6417, TEX. ANN. PEN. CODE (Vernon, 1925) art. 1660; VA. CODE ANN. (Michie, 1930) §3982.

[166] FLA. COMP. GEN. LAWS ANN. (Skillman, 1927) §6623; GA. CODE ANN. (Michie, 1926) §2722; LA. GEN. STAT. ANN. (Dart, 1932) §8190; MISS. CODE ANN. (1930) §6135; N. C. CODE ANN. (Michie, 1931) §3536; S. C. CODE (1932) §8493; TENN. CODE (Will. Shan. & Harsh, 1932) §5527; TEX. ANN. REV. CIV. STAT. (Vernon, 1925) art. 6417, TEX. ANN. PEN. CODE (Vernon, 1925) art. 1660; VA. CODE ANN. (Michie, 1930) §3982.

[167] Crooms v. Schad, 51 Fla. 168, 40 So. 477 (1906) (ordinance); Morrison v. State, 116 Tenn. 534; 95 S. W. 494 (1906). An earlier Florida decision, State v. Patterson, 50 Fla. 127, 39 So. 398 (1905), would probably not be followed if the question came before the Federal Supreme Court. The reasoning of the state court was that such an act, when interpreted to apply only to colored nurses in charge of white persons and not to white nurses in charge of colored persons, was discriminatory in favor of the Negro nurses. It is doubtful if the doctrine

dren and invalids require the constant care and attention of their nurses, and hence the exception has received the approval of the courts. The other two exceptions mentioned would probably be approved also.

The statutes of four states expressly provide that street railways are not to be prevented from operating special cars for the exclusive accommodation of either racial group if the regular cars are also operated on schedule,[168] and the acts of two others are subject to a like interpretation.[169]

All these statutes, with the exception of those in North Carolina, Tennessee, and Virginia, expressly permit the use of separate cars for each race, and the laws of these three jurisdictions would probably not be construed in such a manner as to prevent the practice if any company chose to employ it. In fact a municipal ordinance requiring racial segregation on street cars has been said to permit a company operating cars to choose either this method or the usual one of separating the races in the same car.[170]

In those southern jurisdictions where there is no Jim Crow legislation affecting street railways and also no Civil Rights Acts, the operating companies may establish and put into effect regulations which require a separation of the races on the cars. Such a regulation on a street railway in an Alabama city has been approved by the court of that state.[171] The street railways in the border states would no doubt be permitted to adopt similar regulations if they desired to do so. The Kentucky railway statute has definitely been held to have no application to

of McCabe v. Atchison, T. & S. F. Ry., 235 U. S. 151, 35 Sup. Ct. 69 (1914) cited *supra* note 66, could be carried to such absurd and unrealistic lengths, there being practically no white nurses in charge of Negroes on street cars in the southern states.

[168] ARK. DIG. STAT. (Crawford & Moses, 1921) §1003; FLA. COMP. GEN. LAWS ANN. (Skillman, 1927) §6624; OKLA. COMP. STAT. (1921) §4960; TENN. CODE (Will. Shan. & Harsh, 1932) §5532.

[169] S. C. CODE (1932) §8496; TEX. ANN. REV. CIV. STAT. (Vernon, 1925) art. 6417, TEX. ANN. PEN. CODE (Vernon, 1925) art. 1660. The South Carolina act might be construed to allow regular cars to be run for either race exclusively, and, if so construed, would be subject to the objections to the validity of such a statute which are raised in McCabe v. Atchison, T. & S. F. Ry., 235 U. S. 151, 35 Sup. Ct. 69 (1914), cited *supra* note 66. The Texas act mentions an excursion car, which probably means a special car and not a regularly scheduled one.

[170] Patterson v. Taylor, 51 Fla. 275, 40 So. 493 (1906).

[171] Bowie v. Birmingham Ry. & Elec. Co., 125 Ala. 397, 27 So. 1016 (1900).

street railways.[172] However, this would not prevent the operators of street cars and busses from segregating the races if they saw fit to do so.[173] In the other border states there is no segregation on street railways or city busses.

The Civil Rights Acts of the North and West would clearly apply to racial discrimination on street railways,[174] the statutes usually mentioning all carriers on land. It would be logical to suppose that segregation on the cars would be illegal under these laws, since such is the usual construction with respect to other places of public accommodation. In one case from California, decided during the Reconstruction period, a refusal to permit a Negro to ride on account of race or color was held to render a street railway company liable even in the absence of a Civil Rights Act.[175] This is a case of an absolute refusal to allow a Negro to ride, and hence is not authority for the proposition that such a carrier cannot segregate its passengers according to race.

A street railway in a middle western state has been held responsible for the act of its agents in transporting a Negro passenger to a park where there was a conspiracy to assault all Negroes who entered the grounds.[176] The park was owned by the carrier, and it was shown that the railway employes knew of the conspiracy and had made no effort to warn the Negro of his danger. In a Missouri case a street railway was held liable where its employes knowingly permitted a Negro to travel on and alight from a car which was going into a section of a city where a mob was attacking all colored persons.[177] This decision can only be sustained by adopting the theory that the carrier had a legal duty to provide a safe place of egress on or off the street.

The North Carolina street railway act has been extended to motor busses operated in the urban, interurban, or suburban

[172] Louisville Ry. v. Commonwealth, 130 Ky. 738, 114 S. W. 343 (1908).

[173] *See* Brumfield v. Consolidated Coach Co., 240 Ky. 1, 40 S. W. (2d) 356 (1931).

[174] *See* Bartolini v. Grays Harbor Ry. & Light Co., 88 Wash. 341, 153 Pac. 4 (1915) (discrimination against Italian).

[175] Pleasants v. North Beach & M. Ry., 34 Cal. 586 (1868).

[176] Indianapolis S. Ry. v. Dawson, 31 Ind. App. 605, 68 N. E. 909 (1903).

[177] Williams v. East St. L. & S. Ry., 207 Mo. App. 233, 232 S. W. 759 (1921).

transportation of passengers.[178] Recently a case arose under the provisions of this act. A Negro woman boarded a street bus and found a seat at the end of the vehicle which was set apart for colored passengers. She seated herself in that end of the bus in the last seat except the long seat across the rear. Afterwards a white couple got on and complications arose. The bus was so crowded that the only single seat available for the white man was the one beside the Negro woman. Since the statute prohibited him from taking this seat beside a member of the other race, he and the bus driver requested her to move to the long rear seat. She refused to do this but offered to get off if her fare was refunded. She was arrested and found guilty of a violation of the statute by the lower court. She appealed and the State Supreme Court held that the above-mentioned facts failed to show the "wilful" violation required by the statute. The tribunal declared that the defendant had acted unlawfully but not wilfully so. It was said that the term "wilful" implies that the act was done purposely and deliberately, with no thought as to whether or not the party had a right to do it.[179]

This decision seems to be a bit doubtful. What could be more wilful than the defendant's refusal to obey the instructions of the bus driver? Ignorance of the law is no excuse. It cannot be said that the defendant was not acting wilfully because she believed that she was within her rights under the statute. The decision might possibly be supported on a ground not mentioned by the opinion. It might be argued that the long seat across the rear of the bus would not be considered as a seat within the terms of the statute. If this be the proper interpretation, the defendant was within her rights and could not be accused of violating the law, wilfully or otherwise. She would then have been in the last available seat set aside for her race and the bus driver would have no authority to require her to move to the long rear seat. This case illustrates the increasing liberality with which some courts are dealing with matters of race relationships.

The adjustable screen provisions of the Mississippi Street Railway Act do not apply to busses employed instead of street

[178] N. C. Pub. Laws 1933, c. 489.

[179] State v. Harris, 213 N. C. 758, 197 S. E. 594 (1938). The word "wilful" was deleted from the statute by N. C. Pub. Laws 1939, c. 147. See *Statutory Changes in North Carolina* (1939) 17 N. C. L. Rev. 375.

15

cars.[180] The drivers, however, are given authority to segregate the races on busses of this kind.

The four states of North Carolina, Oklahoma, Texas, and Virginia specifically include interurban lines within the terms of their Jim Crow laws.[181] Maryland and South Carolina have separate statutes applying to electric railways,[182] and these can be said to include electric interurban lines. The Maryland act has reference only to lines extending twenty miles beyond the limits of any incorporated city or town. Alabama, Arkansas, Louisiana, and Tennessee expressly exempt street railways from the operation of their railway statutes,[183] and therefore it may be argued that these acts apply to all other railways of any importance including interurban lines. The Florida, Georgia, and Kentucky acts are subject to a similar interpretation as far as interurban railways are concerned,[184] and the Kentucky Court has definitely held that such lines are within the meaning of the statute of that state.[185] The Mississippi statutes contain no language from which their application to interurban roads can be inferred, but they would probably be construed to apply to such railways should the question arise.

The Kentucky Court has held that an interurban railway company did not evade responsibility under the law of that state by leasing its road to a street railway to which the Jim

---

[180] Miss. Laws 2d Ex. Sess. 1936, c. 23.

[181] N. C. CODE ANN. (Michie, 1931) §3536; OKLA. COMP. STAT. (1921) §4952; TEX. ANN. REV. CIV. STAT. (Vernon, 1925) art. 6417, TEX. ANN. PEN. CODE (Vernon, 1925) art. 1659; VA. CODE ANN. (Michie, 1930) §3978. *See* Chester v. State, 84 Tex. Cr. Rep. 269, 206 S. W. 685 (1918).

[182] MD. ANN. CODE (Bagby, 1924) art. 27, §§443-448 (act very similar to railway statute); S. C. CODE (1932) §8498. *See* State v. Jenkins, 124 Md. 376, 92 Atl. 773 (1914); Wash., B. & A. Ry. v. Waller, 53 App. D. C. 200, 289 Fed. 598 (1922).

[183] ALA. CODE ANN. (Michie, 1928) §9968; ARK. DIG. STAT. (Crawford & Moses, 1921) §987; LA. GEN. STAT. ANN. (Dart, 1932) §8130; TENN. CODE (Will. Shan. & Harsh, 1932) §5518.

[184] FLA. COMP. GEN. LAWS ANN. (Skillman, 1927) §6618 (see also §6711 giving railway commissioners authority to make Jim Crow regulations for all common carriers); GA. CODE ANN. (Michie, 1926) §§2716-18; KY. STAT. ANN. (Carroll, 1930) §795.

[185] Louisville Ry. v. Commonwealth, 130 Ky. 738, 114 S. W. 343 (1908); Conley v. Central Ky. Traction Co., 152 Ky. 764, 154 S. W. 41 (1913); South C. & C. S. Ry. v. Commonwealth, 181 Ky. 449, 205 S. W. 603 (1918); Louisville & I. R. R. v. Garr, 209 Ky. 841, 273 S. W. 540 (1925).

Crow law does not apply.[186] It is the character of the road and not the character of the management that is the crux of the matter.

Maryland, North Carolina, and Virginia have Jim Crow legislation applying specifically to steamship lines.[187] Officers in charge of prisoners and nurses in charge of children or invalids are excepted from the provisions of all these acts. The Maryland and Virginia statutes command that separate sleeping and dining accommodations be furnished,[188] while in Maryland separate toilet facilities are required.[189] The Virginia act contains a provision for separate and noncommunicating waiting rooms at wharves,[190] but there is a proviso which states that the statute will not apply to any wharf where no wharfage is charged.[191] A Florida statute authorizes the State Railroad Commission to make rules and regulations for the separation of the races on railways and other common carriers,[192] and one cannot perceive any reason why this act does not give that administrative body power to make Jim Crow regulations for water carriers under its authority. The statutes of the other southern states are all silent as to the separation of the races on steamship lines with the exception of South Carolina. That state in 1904 amended its railway Jim Crow law so as to include steam ferries.[193]

The State Civil Rights Acts usually mention conveyances by water when enumerating the places of public accommodation and amusement to which they apply. In fact a steamboat was held to be within the Louisiana act of this kind which was

---

[186] Louisville Ry. v. Commonwealth, 130 Ky. 738, 114 S. W. 343 (1908).

[187] MD. ANN. CODE (Bagby, 1924) art. 27, §§439-442; N. C. CODE ANN. (Michie, 1931) §3494-95, 3497; VA. CODE ANN. (Michie, 1930) §§4022-26.

[188] MD. ANN. CODE (Bagby, 1924) art. 27, §439; VA. CODE ANN. (Michie, 1930) §4022.

[189] MD. ANN. CODE (Bagby, 1924) art. 27, §442.

[190] VA. CODE ANN. (Michie, 1930) §4026. The Corporation Commission is authorized to require separate accommodations at wharves. *Id.* at §3716.

[191] *See* Hunter v. Commonwealth, 107 Va. 909, 60 S. E. 102 (1908). This statute was construed so as not to have reference to an instance where a life tenant contracted with a steamboat company for the use of his wharf upon payment to him of a percentage of the proceeds of the traffic over it. The proviso exempts those wharves where no wharfage is charged the public, and there was no such charge at this particular wharf.

[192] FLA. COMP. GEN. LAWS ANN. (Skillman, 1927) §6711.

[193] S. C. Acts 1904, No. 249, pp. 438-9. See S. C. CODE (1932) §8396.

enacted during the period of Reconstruction.[194] Where the act does not specifically mention water carriers the courts would probably include them by implication. In accordance with the Supreme Court's decision in the *Civil Rights Cases*,[195] the Civil Rights Act of 1875 was ruled to be unconstitutional in a case involving the expulsion of a Negro from the dining room of a steamboat.[196]

It has been decided that southern steamship companies and those engaged in interstate traffic may make reasonable regulations for the separation of the races on their boats.[197] In accordance with the principles announced in the railroad cases, the accommodations for Negroes must be on a par with the corresponding facilities for whites.[198] A federal court in New York decided in one instance that a second-class Negro passenger on a steamship may recover for a breach of contract where he was forced to accept steerage accommodations or none at all.[199] In another case a Negro family had purchased berths in anticipation of using them on a journey on a steamship. The head of the family offered to pay the difference in the price of berths and the staterooms which the Negroes had decided they would rather have. The management refused to make the exchange unless they offered to pay the full price of the staterooms in addition to what they had already paid for the berths.

---

[194] *See* DeCuir v. Benson, 27 La. Ann. 1 (1875). The case was reversed by the Supreme Court in Hall v. DeCuir, 95 U. S. 485 (1877), cited *supra* note 133, for reasons not interfering with point here involved.

[195] Civil Rights Cases, 109 U. S. 3, 3 Sup. Ct. 18 (1883). For a discussion of this case see note 102 *supra.*

[196] Cooper v. New Haven Steam-Boat Co., 18 Fed. 588 (S. D. N. Y. 1883). A similar case of an earlier date was thrown out because the plaintiff did not allege citizenship. United States v. Taylor, 3 Fed. 563 (C. C. S. D. Ill. 1880).

[197] Green v. City of Bridgeton, 10 Fed. Cas. No. 5, 754 (S. D. Ga. 1879); The Sue, 22 Fed. 843 (D. Md. 1885); McGuinn v. Forbes, 37 Fed. 639 (D. Md. 1889). See also the ante-bellum case of Day v. Owen, 5 Mich. 520 (1858), where a demurrer to a plea setting up such a regulation as a defense to an action by a Negro was held not to be well taken. The reasonableness of the rule was declared to be an issuable fact which must be decided by the jury under proper instructions from the court.

[198] Green v. City of Bridgeton, 10 Fed. Cas. No. 5,754 (S. D. Ga. 1879); The Sue, 22 Fed. 843 (D. Md. 1885). *See* also Coger v. N. W. Union Packet Co., 37 Iowa 145 (1873), where a Negro was ejected from a ship's dining room and given inferior accommodations elsewhere, a regulation to this effect being deemed unreasonable.

[199] Billinger v. Clyde S. S. Co., 158 Fed. 511 (C. C. S. D. N. Y. 1908).

The court held that the first transaction was a completed contract and that therefore the refusal to exchange was not actionable.[200] There was some evidence that staterooms were available, although this was not found to be a fact from all that is said in the opinion. Suppose that this could be shown along with the fact that no white person had even been denied the privilege of exchanging accommodations in this manner. Wouldn't this be as clear an instance of racial discrimination as anyone could find?

Nine states have special Jim Crow laws requiring a separation of the races on motor carriers.[201] The above-mentioned Florida statute[202] giving the Railroad Commission authority to prescribe rules for the separation of the races on railway or other common carriers might be construed to permit the regulation of motor carriers as well as steamship lines. Texas has recently amended its Jim Crow law in such a manner as to make it apply to motor carriers.[203] This amendment was passed by the legislature in order to eliminate the result of a decision that motor carriers, although operated by a street railway company, were not within the statute.[204] The Alabama, Mississippi, North Carolina, and Oklahoma acts require separate waiting room facilities in bus stations. The North Carolina act excepts servants and attendants, officers in charge of prisoners, and specially chartered vehicles from the operation of the law. The Oklahoma act excepts officers in charge of prisoners and employes. In Texas the exceptions would be the same as for railroads. In all of the truly southern states a policy of segregation is followed in the absence of statutory regulation.

Under the Georgia and North Carolina statutes a motor carrier would be able to limit itself to the transportation of passengers of one race only. The wording of the statutes is such that the carriers are specifically permitted to do this. It is en-

---

[200] Miller v. N. J. Steam-boat Co., 58 Hun 424, 12 N. Y. Supp. 301 (1890).

[201] ALA. CODE ANN. (Michie, Supp. 1936) §6270 (109); Ark. Acts 1937, No. 124; GA. CODE ANN. (Michie, Supp. 1932) §§1770 (60lll), 1770 (60yyyy); LA. GEN. STAT. (Dart, 1932) §§5307-09; MISS. CODE ANN. (Supp. 1933) §5595-9; N. C. CODE ANN. (Michie, 1931) §2613p; Okla. Sess. Laws 1931, c. 41; S. C. Acts 1937, No. 242; VA. CODE ANN. (Michie, 1930) §§4097z, 4097aa.

[202] FLA. COMP. GEN. LAWS ANN. (Skillman, 1927) §6711.

[203] Tex. Gen. & Sp. Acts 1935, c. 147.

[204] Patillo v. State, 120 Tex. Cr. Rep. 568, 47 S. W. (2d) 847 (1932).

tirely possible that some carrier might wish to avail itself of the privilege so recognized by the law. A provision of this kind is subject to the constitutional objections which were advanced by the Supreme Court to invalidate the pullman clause of the Oklahoma railway statute.[205] A similar municipal bus franchise was approved by the Florida Court,[206] but this decision clearly violates the principles announced by the Supreme Court in the above decision.

The North Carolina motor vehicle statute also has a provision that nothing therein contained shall be construed in such a manner as to declare busses or taxicabs to be common carriers. This proviso is an effort to avoid the basic proposition that motor carriers are public or private according to the circumstances under which they operate, and it has been remarked that "the fourteenth amendment prevents the legislature from declaring a carrier private or public unless there is a reasonable basis for so doing." [207] Furthermore more light is shed upon the matter when one examines a case decided by the North Carolina Court under the law as it was prior to the enactment of the statute. The Corporation Commission, now the Utilities Commissioner,[208] had been given authority by statute to make rules and regulations for motor bus transportation.[209] At the instance of the Interracial Commission, the appellate court decided that the Corporation Commission could be required to order public motor carriers to provide equal though separate bus and station accommodations for white and Negro passengers.[210] Another effect of this decision is that there can now be no doubt that the ordinary motorbus line in North Carolina is a common carrier.[211] Of course a private carrier would not be governed by the same principles of law.

[205] McCabe v. Atchison, T. & S. F. Ry., 235 U. S. 151, 35 Sup. Ct. 69 (1914), cited *supra* note 66. The apparent invalidity of the North Carolina provision has been discussed in *A Survey of Statutory Changes in North Carolina in 1929* (1929) 7 N. C. L. Rev. 363; Note (1930) 8 N. C. L. Rev. 455.

[206] Sanders v. City of Daytona Beach, 95 Fla. 279, 116 So. 188 (1928).

[207] Frost v. Ry. Comm. of Cal., 271 U. S. 583, 46 Sup. Ct. 605 (1926); Note (1930) 8 N. C. L. Rev. 455, 457.

[208] N. C. Pub. Laws 1933, c. 134.

[209] N. C. Pub. Laws 1927, c. 136, §7.

[210] State *ex rel.* Corporation Commission v. Interracial Commission, 198 N. C. 317, 151 S. E. 648 (1930), (1930) 8 N. C. L. Rev. 455. Another commentator in a Note (1930) 39 Yale L. J. 1207 has declared that in this case the North Carolina Court has taken an "affirmative stand for the protection of Negroes."

[211] See Note (1930) 8 N. C. L. Rev. 455.

The Alabama and Mississippi motorbus acts apply specifically to interstate as well as intrastate passengers.[212] However, there is this difference between the two statutes. While the Mississippi act applies to all interstate passengers, the Alabama act excepts all persons who are traveling from states which do not have the Jim Crow system. As we have seen above, a state Jim Crow law or Civil Rights Act which threw a burden on interstate passenger traffic would be unconstitutional. Moreover, if one follows the decision of the Kentucky federal court in the abovementioned *Anderson* case,[213] all Jim Crow laws which threw a burden on interstate traffic would be considered wholly void and hence not effective even where the travel was strictly intrastate. It is doubtful, however, whether this decision, in so far as the total invalidity of the statute is concerned, would be followed today. Furthermore, there is another point which must at least be mentioned. A state may regulate interstate commerce in a field where Congress has not seen fit to legislate if its laws are not burdensome to such traffic. Could the Alabama act be upheld on the theory that it applies only to those interstate bus passengers who are traveling to or from states which have the Jim Crow system and therefore creates no burden upon the interstate carriers? Would it be possible to differentiate between these two statutes on any such narrow distinction?

There have been a number of personal injury suits which have arisen under these motor vehicle statutes. In a recent Mississippi case a white passenger sued a bus company because the driver had wrongfully directed a Negro to sit beside him. The plaintiff made no particular objection, and it was shown by the company that there was another available seat to which he could have moved had he so desired. The court was of the opinion that the plaintiff had a duty to minimize the damages by moving to the vacant seat and therefore refused to give anything more substantial than nominal damages.[214] In a case which arose under the Georgia act a white woman alleged that she was humiliated and insulted because a Negro girl had sat down beside her on a motor bus. The complaint did not state

---

[212] In this connection see a similar provision in a recent North Carolina railway act. N. C. Pub. Laws 1935, c. 270.

[213] Anderson v. L. & N. Ry. 62 Fed. 46 (C. C. D. Ky. 1894), cited *supra* note 132.

[214] City Bus Co. v. Thomas, 172 Miss. 424, 160 So. 582 (1935).

that the bus company's employes were in any way responsible for what had occurred. Because of this omission the court held that a cause of action had not been stated.[215] The tribunal intimated that the plaintiff could have recovered in this type of case for humiliation, insult, mortification, or embarrassment where it could be shown that the carrier's agents were at fault. In Mississippi a motor carrier was held liable where it failed to furnish proper partitions between the white and colored compartments as required by statute.[216]

A case recently arose in the District of Columbia concerning the application of the Virginia statute. A colored woman refused to accede to the request of a bus driver who had asked her to exchange seats in accordance with the statutory requirements. The driver then summoned police officers, but the woman, who was an interstate passenger, continued to resist and used profane language. The officers then arrested her for disorderly conduct and she was ejected from the coach, hauled before the local court, and punished. She brought a suit against the bus company, but the court declared that the driver was not at fault and that the company was not responsible in any way.[217] It seems that the plaintiff was punished by the local court for disorderly conduct and not for a violation of the Jim Crow statute. The court appears to have made the mistake of applying the state law to an interstate passenger. However, the company probably had Jim Crow regulations for such passengers which were similar to those contained in the statute.

In a Kentucky case it was said that a motor carrier, in the absence of statutory requirements, may make its own regulations for the separation of the races on busses.[218] In this instance it was the practice of the carrier to reserve seats. The employes were held to be justified in refusing to transport a Negro in one of the seats which had been reserved when there were no other seats available. In Kentucky there seems to be a general rule that a bus driver can seat passengers with due regard for their comfort. Some drivers interpret this as an

---

[215] Hames v. Old South Lines, 52 Ga. App. 420, 183 S. E. 503 (1935).

[216] Mississippi Power & Light Co. v. Garner, 179 Miss. 588, 176 So. 280 (1937).

[217] Kinchlow v. Peoples' Rapid Transit Co., 66 App. D. C. 382, 88 F. (2d) 764 (1937).

[218] Brumfield v. Consolidated Coach Corp., 240 Ky. 1, 40 S. W. (2d) 356 (1931).

authorization to separate the races. However, all the drivers do not follow this practice. The same sort of unofficial segregation seems to be in use by some Missouri motorbus drivers. In Maryland a policy of segregation is generally followed on intrastate buses. As far as can be ascertained, the motor carriers of Delaware and West Virginia do not practice segregation.

The situation is different in a state which has a Civil Rights Act. In a Kansas case a bus driver ordered a Negro to the rear of the vehicle where white people were smoking, and the Negro was made sick by the tobacco fumes. The court held that this was an instance of racial discrimination within the meaning of the statute.[219]

Air lines are chiefly interstate carriers and hence the legal principles governing interstate passengers on other types of carriers would ordinarily apply to this comparatively new mode of transportation. There are no Jim Crow laws applying to air carriers. As for the Civil Rights Acts of the North and West, the only ones which specifically mention air carriers are the Illinois and Ohio acts and the Massachusetts statute which prohibits discriminatory advertising. Very few, if any, of the others would be held to have any application whatsoever,[220] since they mention land and water carriers specifically and contain no reference to aerial transports. However, airdromes are mentioned in the New Jersey, New York, and Pennsylvania acts. Hence the commercial air lines would practically always be permitted to make their own regulations for seating passengers in their planes.[221] They may mix or segregate the races as they wish. There are very few Negro passengers and hence the problem has not arisen.

There can be no doubt that at least some of the accommodations furnished for the colored race under the provisions of Jim Crow laws and regulations are far inferior to those which are supplied for the use of white passengers. In a good many instances the Negro cars or coaches are dirty, dingy, old, or in some other respect inferior to those provided for the whites.

---

219 White v. So. Kansas Stage Lines Co., 136 Kan. 51, 12 P. (2d) 713 (1932). See case involving northern bus line's warranty against racial discrimination on a trip from New York to Alabama on connecting carriers. Battle v. Cen. Greyhound Lines, 171 Misc. 517, 13 N. Y. Supp. (2d) 357 (1939).

220 Quindry, *Airline Passenger Discrimination* (1932) 3 J. Air L. 479.

221 See note 220 *supra*.

While there has never been a reported case where filth was made the crux of a decision that a carrier had been at fault in not furnishing equally clean and up-to-date accommodations for colored passengers, the basis for such an action exists today on some of the more important railways in the South. The probable reason why this and other unfairness has not been brought to the attention of the state appellate courts is that no one is sufficiently interested in the plight of the Negro in this respect. The matter is one for collective and not individual initiative.

IX

CHARITABLE AND PENAL INSTITUTIONS

It is an established fact that a policy of racial separation and segregation has been adopted in respect to the inmates of state-established charitable and penal institutions throughout the South. The same is also true of that region which is occupied by what are commonly known as the border states.

In some of the eastern and middle western states reliable information has been obtained that some of the institutions have separate living quarters for Negroes. In certain of these institutions separate cottages or cells are provided for the colored inmates. Even where this is true, however, the Negroes are not usually segregated in other activities, such as labor and school work, although they are sometimes given separate dining accommodations. The institutions for delinquent girls in some of these states seem to be particularly insistent that a policy of segregation be adopted or continued. In a few jurisdictions this type of institution is the only one where any attempt at separation is made. In New England and other sections of the country where there are comparatively few Negroes, segregation is not even attempted or desired.

While it is true that not all of the southern charitable and penal institutions are required by law to separate the white and Negro races, it is the policy of the governing boards to adopt the usual plan of segregation. In some instances it has been thought wise to establish separate institutions for the two races. In cases where this has not been done the statute establishing the institution usually gives the board of control the right to make all needful rules and regulations which it may see fit to establish for the proper management of the institution. Hence regulations may be put into effect segregating the races in these establishments. In some states certain facilities are provided for the whites and no corresponding service for the members of the colored race. This is clearly a violation of the spirit of the constitutional guarantee of equality. It is our wish to call attention to these inequalities in order to set in motion an effort to rectify unfair discriminations of this kind. Where at least some facilities for Negroes are provided, the question of adequacy will not be too greatly emphasized. It is rather difficult to determine the adequacy of accommodations of this type, for the South is notoriously backward in respect to facilities for the whites as well as for the Negroes. It is our purpose to point out only the most glaring of the existing inequalities. One of the chief reasons for so limiting this discussion is the difficulty experienced in obtaining full and satisfactory data concerning the true conditions in these eleemosynary and penal institutions. We shall now turn our attention to the various types of institutions with a view to portraying just what is done in the several states with respect to this problem. Full information could not be obtained from some states.

Hospitals and Asylums for Persons of Unsound Mind

In Maryland,[1] North Carolina,[2] Oklahoma,[3] Virginia,[4] and West Virginia[5] the statutes provide for a separate institution for the Negro insane. A Louisiana act of 1902[6] provided for a separate institution for Negroes, but in 1904[7] the statute was amended and all mention of the colored race omitted. Hence Negroes are now cared for at the state hospitals which admit persons of both races. The statutes of Georgia,[8] Kentucky,[9] Mississippi,[10] and Tennessee[11] require the separation of the two races in the insane asylums in those states. In Alabama the Negro insane are cared for at the Searcy Hospital, in Mobile County. In Arkansas, Florida, Missouri, South Carolina, and Texas the colored insane are admitted to mental hospitals which have accommodations for members of both races, though of course they are segregated.

In 1919 a rather novel case came before the Oklahoma Court. At this time the state had no separate institution for the Ne-

[1] Md. Ann. Code (Bagby, 1924) art. 59, §§60-65.

[2] N. C. Code Ann. (Michie, 1931) §6153.

[3] Okla. Sess. Laws 1935, c. 26, art. 3, §1.

[4] Va. Code Ann. (Michie, 1930) §§1004-05.

[5] W. Va. Code (1931) c. 27, art. 2, §§2, 3.

[6] La. Acts 1902, No. 92.

[7] La. Acts 1904, No. 143. See also La. Gen. Stat. Ann. (Dart, 1932) §3896.

[8] Ga. Code Ann. (Michie, 1926) §§1598, 1611.

[9] Ky. Stat. Ann. (Carroll, 1930) §216aa-46. The colored wards at the Central State Hospital are overcrowded.

[10] Miss. Code Ann. (1930) §§4540-42.

[11] Tenn. Code (Will. Shan. & Harsh, 1932) §4434.

groes, and the law decreed a separation of the races at all the state-supported hospitals for the insane.[12] A white person had been placed in that portion of the Oklahoma State Hospital which had been set apart for the Negro inmates, and claimed that this amounted to a libel and sued the hospital for damages under the libel statute. The court ruled that this action did not constitute a violation of the statute, since only written and other usual types of defamation were covered by its language.[13]

Institutions for Feeble-minded Persons

The information which we have been able to obtain concerning the care of the feeble-minded of the Negro race is very sketchy. Five states, Alabama,[14] Kentucky,[15] Mississippi,[16] Missouri,[17] and Tennessee,[18] require their institutions of this type to provide separate accommodations for Negroes. We have reliable information that there are no Negroes in either the Mississippi or Tennessee institutions at the present time. In Arkansas there are no special facilities for the feeble-minded of either race, but some patients are treated at the State Hospital for Nervous Diseases. Delaware and Louisiana have facilities for colored persons in their institutions for the feeble-minded. In Virginia a statute[19] was enacted providing for a colony for such persons of color to be located in a separate department at the Negro insane asylum, but the state gave the institution no material financial help. A building was erected which is now being used to care for a mixed population of idiots, imbeciles, and insane persons. In North Carolina patients of this type are cared for at the colored insane asylum at Goldsboro,[20] but more adequate facilities have been recommended.[21] In Florida, Georgia, Oklahoma, and South Carolina it appears that accommodations have been provided for the

[12] Okla. Comp. Stat. (1921) §9109.

[13] Collins v. Oklahoma State Hospital, 76 Okla. 229, 184 Pac. 946 (1919).

[14] Ala. Code Ann. (Michie, 1928) §1481.

[15] Ky. Stat. Ann. (Carroll, 1930) §216aa-46.

[16] Miss. Code Ann. (1930) §7275.

[17] Mo. Rev. Stat. (1929) §8694.

[18] Tenn. Code (Will. Shan. & Harsh, 1932) §4523.

[19] Va. Code Ann. (Michie, 1930) §§1092-93.

[20] N. C. Pub. Laws 1933, c. 342.

[21] Report of N. C. Charitable, Penal, and Correctional Institutions (1934) p. 6.

whites and not for the Negroes. Reliable information concerning the other southern and border states is sadly lacking.

EPILEPTICS

The answers to our questionnaires gave us little information about the care of those persons of both races afflicted with epilepsy. A Virginia statute,[22] the same one which dealt with the Negro insane, authorizes the establishment of a colony for colored epileptics, but no provision has been made for them up to the present time. The Missouri act[23] establishing the State School for the Feeble-minded provides for the care of epileptics of both races, although they must be housed separately. Some states care for epileptics in institutions for the feeble-minded, while others have facilities for them in the hospitals for the insane. For the care of the Negroes afflicted with this malady, North Carolina and West Virginia have at least some facilities in their insane asylums. In Arkansas, however, there are no special facilities for the epileptics of either race, and the same is also true of Georgia, Kentucky, and Mississippi. In three states, Oklahoma, Tennessee, and Texas, at least some facilities are provided for the white epileptics but none for the colored. For the other southern and border states the author has been unable to obtain accurate information.

THE BLIND AND DEAF

Separate institutions for the colored blind and deaf are established by statute in Kentucky,[24] Louisiana,[25] Oklahoma,[26] Texas,[27] Virginia,[28] and West Virginia.[29] In Arkansas[30] separate facilities are also maintained. In North Carolina[31] the Negro and

[22] VA. CODE ANN. (Michie, 1930) §1004. [23] MO. REV. STAT. (1929) §8694.

[24] KY. STAT. ANN. (Carroll, 1930) §§282, 283, 283a, 298d-3, 310, 311.

[25] LA. GEN. STAT. ANN. (Dart, 1932) §§2498-2502. Before this institution was established separation of the races was decreed in the State School for the Blind. LA. GEN. STAT. ANN. (Dart, 1932) §2476.

[26] OKLA. COMP. STAT. (1921) §§9078-82.

[27] TEX. ANN. REV. CIV. STAT. (Vernon, 1925) arts. 3221-3222. This statute has been amended. See 1934 Supp.

[28] VA. CODE ANN. (Michie, 1930) §§979-985a.

[29] W. VA. CODE (1931) c. 18, art. 18, §§1-2.

[30] There is an Arkansas statute providing that there shall be no discrimination on account of race in the admission of pupils into the deaf-mute institution. ARK. DIG. STAT. (Crawford & Moses, 1921) §9362.

[31] The statute authorizes the establishment of such an institution for Negroes

white institutions are located on opposite sides of the city of Raleigh but are under the same superintendent. Alabama formerly had a separate institution for colored dependents of this kind, but it has now been consolidated[32] with the institution for the whites, in which the races are segregated. In Georgia and South Carolina the Negroes are given separate accommodations in the same institution which provides for the care of the whites. In Maryland both races are given accommodations at the State School for the Blind, while a statute[33] authorizes the commitment of deaf Negro minors to the same institution. Reliable information has been obtained from the Tennessee welfare authorities to the effect that there are no facilities for the colored blind and deaf in that state, but the statute which established the State Institution for the Deaf provides for the segregation of the races.[34] In the other states in this group available information was so inadequate that a conclusion concerning the actual practice could not be reached.

Tuberculosis Sanatoriums

Separate institutions for the care of Negroes who are afflicted with tuberculosis are established by statute in Arkansas,[35] Maryland,[36] Oklahoma,[37] Texas,[38] and West Virginia.[39] Alabama not only commands the segregation of colored persons committed to its institutions for the care of those suffering from this dread disease[40] but also makes provision for separate accommodations for white and colored tubercular convicts.[41] In Virginia the Piedmont Sanatorium at Burkeville is maintained as a separate institution for Negroes. In Delaware, Georgia, Missouri, North Carolina, and South Carolina at least some facilities for colored tubercular patients are provided at the state sanatoriums. In Missouri an increase of the accommodations for Negroes has been recommended. At least some facili-

---

on the grounds of the school for blind white persons. N. C. Code Ann. (Michie, 1931) §§5872, 5876.

[32] Ala. School Code (1927) §577.

[33] Md. Ann. Code (Bagby, 1924) art. 30, §14.

[34] Tenn. Code (Will. Shan. & Harsh, 1932) §4560

[35] Ark. Dig. Stat. (Castle, Supp. 1927) §9619a.

[36] Md. Ann. Code (Bagby, 1924) art. 43, §250. See also Md. Laws 1937, c. 126.

[37] Okla. Comp. Stat. (1921) §8965.

[38] Tex. Gen. & Sp. Laws 1935, c. 131.

[39] W. Va. Code (1931) c. 26, art. 6, §§1-2.

[40] Ala. Code Ann. (Michie, 1928) §1276.

[41] *Id.* at §33.

ties for colored persons afflicted with the disease are provided in Kentucky and Tennessee, but these accommodations are very poor and could very well be augmented by the extension of the service to larger numbers. The Dibert Tubercular Sanatorium at New Orleans, Louisiana, does not admit Negroes, and we have been unable to obtain reliable information concerning the treatment of tubercular patients of the colored race in this and the other states in the group which are not mentioned above.

In Arkansas a controversy arose when the trustees of the institution for tubercular Negroes chose a building site in a neighborhood where there were few colored persons, and the white property owners objected to the location of the institution on the ground that such an establishment in the district would be a departure from the state's policy of racial segregation. The court refused to listen to this argument and declared that the matter was one peculiarly within the province of the legislature, and that body had authorized the trustees to select a suitable spot for the institution and had left the choice to their discretion.[42]

Orphans and Abandoned Children

Homes for the colored orphans and abandoned children of the South are usually supplied by agencies which are not connected with the state government. The churches and other religious groups do much toward supplying the needs of the Negro in this respect. While the facilities for colored orphans are not on a par with those provided for the whites, at least some accommodations for destitute colored children are supplied by religious organizations and various relief and welfare agencies, both state and federal.

Orphanages for Negro children are established by statute in Oklahoma,[43] Texas,[44] and West Virginia.[45] In Delaware the colored orphans and abandoned children are committed to the care of the St. Joseph's Society for Colored Missions.[46] In Tennessee[47] the rules and regulations concerning orphanages are

[42] Mitchell v. Deisch, 179 Ark. 788, 18 S. W. (2d) 364 (1929).
[43] Okla. Comp. Stat. (1921) §§9052-53, 9078-82.
[44] Tex. Ann. Rev. Civ. Stat. (Vernon, Supp. 1934) art. 3221.
[45] W. Va. Code (1931) c. 26, art. 2, §§1-3.
[46] Del. Rev. Code (1915) §2265.
[47] Tenn. Code (Will. Shan. & Harsh, 1932) §4581.

made specifically applicable to colored as well as to white institutions. According to a Kentucky statute,[48] a considerable appropriation has been made to carry on the work of the Home Society for Colored Children. In Indiana a statute[49] provides that any association formed for the purpose of maintaining an asylum exclusively for colored orphans shall be entitled to the allowance authorized by the state for the care of all orphan children. There is a separate home for Negro orphans in Marion County in this state, but this is a county home and not a state institution.

In Colorado a controversy arose because of the refusal of a city council to grant a building permit to a group of persons who wished to establish a home for orphans and aged people of the colored race. The group brought an action of mandamus to force the issuance of the permit. The state court decided that the city council had committed a gross abuse of discretion in refusing to grant the permit in the absence of proof that the maintenance of the institution would be a nuisance or a menace to the public health.[50]

In Virginia a very unusual case arose when the State Children's Home Society attempted to take two minor white children away from their mother, who was a widow, because she had taken as her second husband a man who had less than one-fourth Negro blood in his veins. The state law at that time did not prohibit such marriages unless the intended spouse had one-fourth or more Negro blood. Except for the social necessity of Negro association, there was nothing in the circumstances surrounding the case to show that the children, who were wholly white, were not fully provided for or that the home of these two persons who had defied custom and convention was not a fit place in which to raise them. The state court refused to take the children away from their mother and hence the action was unsuccessful.[51]

A Tennessee statute[52] requires separate accommodations for

[48] KY. STAT. ANN. (Carroll, 1930) §§331h (1-2).

[49] IND. STAT. ANN. (Burns, 1933) §22-2615.

[50] City Council v. United Negroes Protective Ass'n, 76 Colo. 86, 230 Pac. 598 (1924).

[51] Moon v. Children's Home Society, 112 Va. 737, 72 S. E. 707 (1911). A more thorough discussion of this case will be found in the chapter on Domestic Relations, note 227.

[52] TENN. CODE (Will. Shan. & Harsh, 1932) §4658.

16

whites and Negroes in an institution which the state maintains for the children of both sexes who are homeless or have been led into a life of sin and vice through bad associations with the criminal or immoral element in the population of the Commonwealth. There is a home for friendless colored children in Maryland. In several other states there are associations or agencies for the care of friendless and homeless Negro waifs.

Aged and Infirm

The Negro aged and infirm are cared for in the various county homes and through the several relief agencies, both state and federal. The new methods established by the various social security programs also play a major part in the care of such indigent colored persons. Alabama,[53] North Carolina,[54] and Virginia[55] have statutes requiring a segregation of the Negro inmates of certain types of local institutions which have been established to care for aged and infirm paupers. In Mississippi an institution known as the State Charity Hospital is required to furnish separate accommodations for the races.[56] Throughout the South segregation is the order of the day in county and district homes for paupers.

Separate institutions are not usually established for Negro paupers. However, West Virginia has a state institution known as the Home for Colored Aged and Infirm which is located at Huntington.[57] Delaware has made a biennial appropriation[58] to aid the inmates of the Layton Home for Aged Colored People.

State Penitentiaries, etc.

Throughout the truly southern states segregation of the races has been the rule in the state prisons. In various activities the Negro convicts are usually kept apart to a certain extent by the prison authorities. They are worked in separate gangs and have separate cells or other quarters. In the border states a similar policy of separate living quarters has been put into effect. In West Virginia, however, whites and Negroes are

---

[53] Ala. Code Ann. (Michie, 1928) §2806(21).
[54] N. C. Code Ann. (Michie, 1931) §1343f.
[55] Va. Code Ann. (Michie, 1930) §2812e. [56] Miss. Code Ann. (1930) §4594.
[57] W. Va. Code (1931) c. 26, art. 4, §§1-3.
[58] See Del. Laws 1919, c. 153; 1935, c. 52.

worked together in the same gang and there are mixed gatherings at prison motion pictures and sporting events.

Segregation is made mandatory by statute at the state prisons in Alabama,[59] Arkansas,[60] Florida,[61] Georgia,[62] Louisiana,[63] Mississippi,[64] North Carolina,[65] Texas,[66] and Virginia,[67] and for the female convicts in Tennessee.[68] Otherwise the segregation is a matter of policy and regulation by prison officials.

To a greater or less extent the same policy of segregation is carried out at the prison farms, convict camps, jails, and other types of prisons in the southern states. Separate housing facilities are usually provided for the white and Negro prisoners. Although this policy may not be carried out in some isolated spots, this is the exception and not the rule.

Segregation in convict camps is commanded by statute in Arkansas,[69] Florida,[70] Georgia,[71] Louisiana,[72] North Carolina,[73] and Texas;[74] and in the jails of Alabama,[75] Arkansas,[76] Florida,[77] Louisiana,[78] Mississippi,[79] and North Carolina,[80] and the county workhouses of Tennessee[81] the separation is also mandatory. Segregation is likewise decreed at the Industrial Prison Farm in Georgia.[82]

---

59 ALA. CODE ANN. (Michie, 1928) §3643.
60 ARK. DIG. STAT. (Crawford & Moses, 1921) §9681.
61 FLA. COMP. GEN. LAWS ANN. (Skillman, 1927) §8589.
62 GA. CODE ANN. (Michie, 1926) PEN. CODE §1201.
63 LA. CODE CRIM. PROC. ANN. (Dart, 1932) art. 1432. See also art. 1495.
64 MISS. CODE ANN. (1930) §5762.
65 N. C. CODE ANN. (Michie, 1931) §7740.
66 TEX. ANN. REV. CIV. STAT. (Vernon, 1925) art. 6184.
67 VA. CODE ANN. (Michie, 1930) §5048n.
68 TENN. CODE (Will. Shan. & Harsh, 1932) §12,119.
69 ARK. DIG. STAT. (Crawford & Moses, 1921) §§5395, 9681.
70 FLA. COMP. GEN. LAWS ANN. (Skillman, 1927) §8613.
71 GA. CODE ANN. (Michie, 1926) PEN. CODE §§679, 1201.
72 LA. CODE CRIM. PROC. ANN. (Dart, 1932) art. 1495.
73 N. C. CODE ANN. (Michie, 1931) §7740.
74 TEX. ANN. REV. CIV. STAT. (Vernon, 1925) art. 6184.
75 ALA. CODE ANN. (Michie, 1928) §§4806, 4877.
76 ARK. DIG. STAT. (Crawford & Moses, 1921) §9681.
77 FLA. COMP. GEN. LAWS ANN. (Skillman, 1927) §§8545-48.
78 LA. CODE CRIM. PROC. ANN. (Dart, 1932) art. 1495.
79 MISS. CODE ANN. (1930) §3334. 80 N. C. CODE ANN. (Michie, 1931) §1318.
81 TENN. CODE (Will. Shan. & Harsh, 1932) §12,022.
82 GA. CODE ANN. (Michie, 1926) PEN. CODE §1265. See also Supp. 1932, PEN. CODE §1221 (i).

Institutions for Delinquent Boys

Separate institutions for delinquent Negro boys are established by statute in Alabama,[83] Arkansas,[84] Louisiana,[85] Maryland,[86] North Carolina,[87] South Carolina,[88] Virginia,[89] and West Virginia.[90] In Louisiana, however, no such institution is in operation at present. Another statute[91] was enacted which authorized the maintenance of a separate department for colored juveniles at the state prison farm until the colored reformatory could be erected. In this state there is also the Milne Municipal Boys Home at New Orleans, an institution which accepts boys of both races. Oklahoma formerly had an institution with accommodations for delinquent colored juveniles of both sexes.[92] This institution was located at Taft, but the department for boys was moved[93] and established at Boley. Tennessee also maintains a separate reformatory for delinquent Negro boys at Pikeville. Texas formerly had such a separate institution,[94] but it has now been consolidated with the similar institution for the whites.[95] In this reformatory the races are no doubt separated. There is also the Harris County Training School for Delinquent Colored Youths located at Houston. In Florida, Kentucky, and Missouri the colored youths are admitted to the same institution as the whites but are segregated.

[83] Ala. School Code (1927) §§709-719. This statute established the Alabama Reform School for Juvenile Negro Law Breakers. The law was amended by Ala. Gen. Acts 1931, pp. 670-671. See also *ibid.* p. 364.

[84] Ark. Dig. Stat. (Castle, Supp. 1927) §§811a, 811b.

[85] La. Code Crim. Proc. Ann. (Dart, 1932) arts. 1476-84.

[86] Md. Ann. Code (Bagby, 1924) art. 27, §§605-611. Section 605 has been amended. Supp. 1929 §605. See also Md. Laws 1937, c. 70.

[87] N. C. Code Ann. (Michie, 1931) §§5912 (a)-(f).

[88] S. C. Code (1932) §§2021-23.

[89] Va. Code Ann. (Michie, 1930) §1961. See Va. Acts 1920, c. 344.

[90] W. Va. Code (1931) c. 28, art. 2, §§1-2.

[91] La. Code Crim. Proc. Ann. (Dart, 1932) art. 1424. Parish industrial schools for Negroes are authorized by La. Acts 1938, No. 222.

[92] Okla. Comp. Stat. (1921) §§9189-97.

[93] Okla. Comp. Stat. (Supp. 1926) §9189-1.

[94] Tex. Ann. Rev. Civ. Stat. (Vernon, 1925) art. 5131. While the law was in this state it was held that a complaint charging a youth with delinquency need not allege to which race he belonged. It was said that the fact that the state then provided separate places of confinement for delinquent juveniles of the two races did not make such an allegation necessary. Tippins v. State, 86 Tex. Cr. Rep. 205, 217 S. W. 380 (1919).

[95] Tex. Acts 1927, cc. 159, 214.

In Kentucky the separation is made mandatory by statute.[96] A Florida statute[97] specifies separate buildings for the inmates of each race which must not be nearer to each other than a quarter of a mile. This statute also states that the whites and Negroes shall not be associated or made to work together. In Missouri the Negro inmates of the reformatory at Algoa Farms are separated from the whites. In Georgia a statute[98] dealing with the State Training School for Boys requires segregation of the races during the hours of labor. At present, however, there is no state-supported reformatory for the boys of either race in this jurisdiction. Nevertheless, Fulton County has separate institutions of this kind which are located in two suburbs of the city of Atlanta. In Delaware the colored delinquent boys are admitted to the same institution as the whites. In Mississippi there is no special provision made for delinquent Negro boys.

Institutions for Delinquent Girls

Separate institutions for delinquent and incorrigible colored girls are authorized by statute in Delaware,[99] Georgia,[100] Maryland,[101] Missouri,[102] Oklahoma,[103] Tennessee,[104] Texas,[105] Virginia,[106] and West Virginia.[107] The Georgia institution is not in operation at present, as no appropriation has been made by the state for the furtherance of the project. There are no buildings and the act was evidently passed because someone had offered a building site for the institution. In Alabama delinquent Negro girls are provided for at the State Juvenile Reform School[108] in a separate department. In Kentucky a

---

[96] Ky. Stat. Ann. (Carroll, 1930) §2095b-20.

[97] Fla. Comp. Gen. Laws Ann. (Skillman, 1927) §8636.

[98] Ga. Code Ann. (Michie, 1926) Pen. Code §1249.

[99] Del. Laws 1921, c. 155.

[100] Ga. Laws 1937, p. 682.

[101] Md. Ann. Code (Bagby, 1924) art. 27, §§589-590, 644-653 (§648 as amended in Supp. 1929); Md. Laws 1931, c. 367.

[102] Mo. Rev. Stat. (1929) §§8375-88.

[103] Okla. Comp. Stat. (1921) §§9189-97. The girls' site was left undisturbed by the change in the law cited *supra* note 93.

[104] Tenn. Code (Will. Shan. & Harsh, 1932) §§4696-4708.

[105] Tex. Gen. & Sp. Laws 1927, c. 293.

[106] Va. Code Ann. (Michie, 1930) §1961a.

[107] W. Va. Code (1931) c. 28, art. 4, §§1-2.

[108] Ala. School Code (1927) §§709-719. See note 83 *supra*.

separate department for colored girls has also been established in order to put into actual practice the segregation required by statute.[109] In North Carolina and South Carolina recommendations have been made by the public welfare authorities that some provision should be made for the delinquent colored girls of the two states.[110] The Efland and Fairwold institutions, established and managed by the colored womens' clubs of these two states respectively, have been in operation but are inadequate efforts to supply a need which the states themselves should shoulder. In these two states, as well as in Arkansas, Florida, Louisiana, and Mississippi, white girls are provided with facilities of this sort, whereas the Negro girls are not given the opportunity for improvement and education which these institutions afford. This is one of the most flagrant violations of the spirit of the constitutional guarantee of equal treatment by the states discovered in this investigation.

In Illinois, Michigan, and Nebraska the girls' reformatory is the one institution at which we have found the policy of segregating whites and Negroes. The colored girls are provided with separate cottages or other living quarters. In several of the other northern and middle western states segregation is practiced in this as well as other institutions.

In a novel case from Nebraska a young woman was charged with bad conduct and was sent to the girls' reformatory. She was later released and brought an action of false imprisonment and malicious prosecution against those persons responsible for her confinement. Among other bits of testimony offered to prove damages she presented evidence that she had been compelled to sleep with a Negro girl during her stay at the institution.[111] There are divers persons, even in the North, who would be greatly humiliated at being forced into such an intimate relationship with a person of another race. The appellate court sefused to reverse a decision that this evidence was admissible.[111]

We have seen that at least some of the institutional services rendered the public are unequally administered from a racial standpoint. Certain services are rendered to the unfortunate of

---

[109] KY. STAT. ANN. (Carroll, 1930) §2095b-28.

[110] Report of North Carolina Charitable, Penal, and Correctional Institutions (1934) p. 6; Report of Board of Public Welfare of South Carolina (1926) p. 14.

[111] Scott v. Flowers, 60 Neb. 675, 84 N. W. 81 (1900).

one race and not the other. In some cases the services which are given to the whites are so superior that the inequality can be ascertained without much examination into the actual facts. In others the inequality will appear only after a thorough investigation has been made. There are very few separate institutions for Negroes in the South which are on a par with the corresponding establishments for the whites. It is to be hoped that the South will remedy this some time in the near future.

X

MARRIAGE AND OTHER DOMESTIC PROBLEMS

In approaching a study of the sexual aspect of interracial relations one must remember that a problem of great moment is under consideration. There are a great number of persons in the country who have antipathies toward certain groups of individuals because of their race or color. In no field of jurisprudence is this antipathy more noticeable than in the field of law surrounding the marital status and the relations of men and women to one another.

Of course it is true that these antipathies may be dissimilar in different parts of the nation. The aversion is usually far more prevalent in sections of the country where there are sizable racial minorities which threaten the ascendency of the dominant white race, however trivial the danger may appear to be. In the South such a mass antipathy has as its object the Negro; in the Far West, the Mongolian. There are also antipathies toward the Indian and the Malay, in all probability of a lesser intensity only because persons of these races are relatively few in number and are inferior in economic power and importance. There is also much feeling against the Jews in many, we might say practically all, sections of the country.

Wherever such an antipathy exists, there is of course a tendency to avoid social or semi-social contacts with the objectionable race whenever possible, especially in such an intimate relationship as marriage. This feeling has been responsible for the enactment of laws outlawing interracial marriages and other sex relations.

It was once believed by certain scientists that the progeny of an interracial marriage entered into by persons of the white and Negro races would be far inferior to both parents. However, this theory has now been exploded and it is thought today that the normal offspring of such a union would be at least the physical equal of either of its parents. Most of the reputable authorities on the subject have come to the conclusion that there is no actual racial inferiority per se. The intermixture of white blood certainly does not make the resulting issue any the less intelligent or efficient.[1] Nevertheless, the imported Negroes have not sufficiently advanced from the uncivilized state in which the race lived in Africa a few generations ago for them to have become the intellectual equal of the white man, although there are notable exceptions.

The intermixture of white blood cannot be wholly prevented, as there will always be sexual relations between members of the two races in spite of the fact that intermarriage is prohibited by the laws of a great many of the states. It has been argued by some that since the prohibitory statutes have not had the effect of retarding racial amalgamation, the wisdom of such a policy might well be questioned because it would prevent the legitimation of the children of this type of illicit union.[2] The proponents of this view fail to realize that the present temper of the southern white man would not tolerate a policy permitting mixed marriages. Any attempt to so change the law would be doomed to failure. In fact such an effort could only have the result of stirring up the racial prejudice of the white man to such fever heat that it would act as a boomerang against the Negroes. The white man in the South has made up his mind that he wants no intermarriage with the Negro, and nothing is going to change this attitude as yet, if ever. In fact, the state of Mississippi has enacted a criminal statute punishing anyone for publishing, printing, or circulating any literature in favor of or urging interracial marriage or social equality.[3]

There is still some concubinage but it has decreased in recent years. It is largely in the lower stratum of society, and is not at all prevalent even there, as the white laboring classes look down upon the Negro in practically the same way that their employers do. Of course the Negro prostitute cannot be prevented from carrying on her illicit trade as long as there are evil or immoral white men in the community. Thus amalgamation cannot be wholly curbed.

In Louisiana there has been so much infusion of Negro blood that it has been said that a marriage license would be refused

---

[1] Notes (1927) 13 VA. L. REG. (N.S.) 311, (1927) 36 YALE L. J. 858. See Shannon, *Racial Integrity of the American Negro* (1933) 144 CONTEMP. REV. 581.

[2] Notes (1927) 13 VA. L. REG. (N.S.) 311, (1927) 36 YALE L. J. 858.

[3] MISS. CODE ANN. (1930) §1103.

only in cases where the admixture is evident from the appearance or other characteristics of the party making the application.[4] Marriages of white persons to individuals with only a slight admixture of Negro blood are usually attacked only by those interested in the succession to property. The courts of the state have been very lenient in their treatment of the children of mixed ancestry. In spite of these facts, however, an attempt to change the laws of Louisiana in this respect would no doubt meet with a harsh rebuff.

The feeling against intermarriage is not wholly southern, for it extends into most of the far western states, where it is exemplified by statutes prohibiting unions between whites and Negroes. The prejudicial attitude even extends into the East and Middle West. Here intermarriage is generally lawful but is usually frowned upon by the better class of white people in the community.

All of the former slaveholding states, most of the states of the Far West[5] beyond Iowa and Minnesota, and one lone middle western jurisdiction, Indiana, prohibit marriages between whites and Negroes.[6] A large majority of these states have provisions under which offenders may be punished. Some make a

---

[4] Daggett, *Legal Aspects of Amalgamation in Louisiana* (1933) 11 Tex. L. Rev. 162.

[5] Kansas, New Mexico, and Washington excepted.

[6] Ala. Code Ann. (Michie, 1928) §5001, Ala. Const. §102; Ariz. Rev. Code Ann. (Struckmeyer, 1928) §2166 as amended by Ariz. Laws 1931, c. 17; Ark. Dig. Stat. (Crawford & Moses, 1921) §7039; Cal. Civ. Code (Deering, 1931) §60; Colo. Stat. Ann. (Mills, 1930) §4729; Del. Rev. Code (1915) §2992; Fla. Comp. Gen. Laws Ann. (Skillman, 1927) §5857, Fla. Const. Art. XVI, §24; Ga. Code Ann. (Michie, 1926) §2941 (Michie, Supp. 1928) §2177 (14); Idaho Code Ann. (1932) §31-206; Ind. Stat. Ann. (Burns, 1933) §44-104; Ky. Stat. (Carroll, 1930) §2097; La. Civ. Code Ann. (Dart, 1932) art. 94; Md. Ann. Code (Bagby, 1924) art. 27, §365; Miss. Const. §263, Miss. Code Ann. (1930) §2361; Mo. Rev. Stat. (1929) §§2974, 4263; Mont. Rev. Codes (1921) §5700; Neb. Comp. Stat. (1929) §32-103; Nev. Comp. Laws (Hillyer, 1929) §10,197; N. C. Const. Art. XIV, §8, N. C. Code Ann. (Michie, 1931) §§2495, 4340; N. D. Comp. Laws Ann. (1913) §9582; Okla. Comp. Stat. (1921) §7499; Ore. Code Ann. (1930) §14-840; S. C. Const. Art. III, §33, S. C. Code (1932) §§1438, 8571; S. D. Comp. Laws (1929) §128; Tenn. Const. Art. XI, §14, Tenn. Code (Will. Shan. & Harsh, 1932) §8409; Tex. Ann. Rev. Civ. Stat. (Vernon, 1925) art. 4607; Utah Rev. Stat. Ann. (1933) §40-1-2 ss. 5; Va. Code Ann. (Michie, 1930) §§5087, 5099a ss. 5; W. Va. Code (1931) c. 48, art. 1, §19; Wyo. Rev. Stat. Ann. (Courtright, 1931) c. 68, §118. Nine other states formerly prohibited such marriages according to a list given by Franklin Johnson, Development of State Legislation Concerning the Free Negro (1919) 9.

violation of the law a felony,[7] while in others it is only a misdemeanor.[8]

The constitutionality of statutes prohibiting and punishing interracial marriages or cohabitation is no longer in doubt. Such laws have been held not to violate the guarantees of the Fourteenth Amendment.[9] In fact it was said in one instance that the privileges and immunities of federal citizenship guaranteed by the amendment do not include the right to marry outside of one's own race.[10]

The Federal Civil Rights Act of 1866 gave the Negro the same rights possessed by white men in the making and en-

---

Iowa—omitted in 1851.

Kansas—marriage statute prohibited interracial unions in KAN. STAT. (1855) c. 108, §3—omitted two years later. Kan. Laws 1857, c. 49.

Maine—repealed in 1883. See Me. Laws 1883, p. 16 (c. 203 P. P. 1883). *Cf.* Bailey v. Fiske, 34 Me. 77 (1852).

Massachusetts—repealed in 1840 (1843). See Mass. Acts 1843, c. 5. *Cf.* Inhabitants of Medway v. Inhabitants of Natick, 7 Mass. 88 (1810).

Michigan—prior interracial marriages legalized in 1883. See MICH. COMP. LAWS (1929) §12,695. *Cf.* People v. Brown, 34 Mich. 399 (1876).

New Mexico—repealed in 1866. See N. Mex. Laws 1866, p. 90.

Ohio—repealed in 1887. See Ohio Laws 1887, p. 34.

Rhode Island—repealed in 1881. See R. I. Acts Jan. Sess. 1881, p. 108.

Washington—repealed in 1867. See Wash. Laws 1867, pp. 47-48.

[7] ALA. CODE ANN. (Michie, 1928) §5001; FLA. COMP. GEN. LAWS ANN. (Skillman, 1927) §7562; GA. CODE ANN. (Michie, 1928 Supp.) §2177 (14); IND. STAT. ANN. (Burns, 1933) §10-4222 (knowingly); MD. ANN. CODE (Bagby, 1924) art. 27, §365; MISS. CODE ANN. (1930) §2361; MO. REV. STAT. (1929) §4263; N. C. CODE ANN. (Michie, 1931) §4340; N. D. COMP. LAWS ANN. (1913) §9582; OKLA. COMP. STAT. (1921) §7500; ORE. CODE ANN. (1930) §14-841 (knowingly) (also punishes attempt); S. D. COMP. LAWS (1929) §128; TENN. CODE ANN. (Will. Shan. & Harsh, 1932) §8410; TEX. ANN. PEN. CODE (Vernon, 1925) art. 492 (knowingly); VA. CODE ANN. (Michie, 1930) §4546 as amended by Va. Acts 1932, p. 68.

[8] COLO. STAT. ANN. (Mills, 1930) §4730 (knowingly); DEL. REV. CODE (1915) §2992; NEV. COMP. LAWS (Hillyer, 1929) §10,198; S. C. CODE (1932) §1438; W. VA. CODE (1931) c. 48, art. 1, §19; WYO. REV. STAT. ANN. (Courtright, 1931) c. 68, §119 (knowingly).

[9] Pace v. Alabama, 106 U. S. 583, 1 Sup. Ct. 637 (1882), *aff'g* 69 Ala. 231 (1881); *In re* Hobbs, 12 Fed. Cas. No. 6550 (C. C. N. D. Ga. 1871); Ford v. State, 53 Ala. 150 (1875); Green v. State, 58 Ala. 190 (1877), *directly overruling a contrary decision in* Burns v. State, 48 Ala. 195 (1872); Wilson v. State, 20 Ala. App. 137, 101 So. 417 (1924); Dodson v. State, 61 Ark. 57, 31 S. W. 977 (1895); State v. Gibson, 36 Ind. 389 (1871); State v. Jackson, 80 Mo. 175 (1883); State v. Hairston, 63 N. C. 451 (1869); State v. Reinhardt, 63 N. C. 547 (1869); Lonas v. State, 3 Heisk. 287 (Tenn. 1871). See *In re* Paquet's Estate, 101 Ore. 393, 200 Pac. 911 (1921) (Indians).

[10] State v. Jackson, 80 Mo. 175 (1883).

forcing of contracts. A controversy arose as to whether the marriage status was a contract within the meaning of this statute, and it was finally decided by a majority of the courts that such was not the case.[11] It was also decided that the marital status is not a contract within the meaning of the provision in the Federal Constitution prohibiting a state from enacting laws which impair the obligation of contracts.[12] Furthermore the Georgia Court has held that a statute outlawing interracial marriages is not inconsistent with a clause in the state constitution which provided that the "social status" of citizens must never be the subject of legislation.[13]

The segregation of Negro and white prostitutes has been said to be within the power of the authorities in the city of New Orleans.[14] Furthermore, the Texas Court upheld a Fort Worth ordinance making it unlawful for whites and Negroes to have sexual intercourse with one another within the city limits.[15] In another instance the authorities in a Texas city passed an ordinance which made it unlawful for white men to visit Negro women at their residences unless it appeared that the visitor fell within certain stated exceptions, such as doctors, collectors, or deliverymen. The ordinance was held to be invalid because individuals would thereby be deprived of liberty without due process of law.[16]

The fact that statutes which inflict penalties upon a man and a woman of different races for illicit cohabitation make the punishment more severe than in an instance where such conduct is indulged in by members of the same race has been held not to render these laws invalid.[17] The punishment is directed against the offense itself and not the particular persons, white or col-

---

[11] *In re* Hobbs, 12 Fed. Cas. No. 6550 (C. C. N. D. Ga. 1871); Ellis v. State, 42 Ala. 525 (1868); Green v. State, 58 Ala. 190 (1877), *overruling* Burns v. State, 48 Ala. 195 (1872); State v. Gibson, 36 Ind. 389 (1871); State v. Hairston, 63 N. C. 451 (1869); Lonas v. State, 3 Heisk. 287 (Tenn. 1871); Frasher v. State, 3 Tex. App. 263, 30 Am. Rep. 131 (1877). This is true in spite of what is said to the contrary in Hart v. Hoss & Elder, 26 La. Ann. 90 (1874).

[12] *Ex parte* Kinney, 14 Fed. Cas. No. 7825 (C. C. E. D. Va. 1879); State v. Tutty, 41 Fed. 753 (C. C. S. D. Ga. 1890).

[13] Scott v. State, 39 Ga. 321 (1869).

[14] City of New Orleans v. Miller, 142 La. 163, 76 So. 596 (1917).

[15] Strauss v. State, 76 Tex. Cr. Rep. 132, 173 S. W. 663 (1915).

[16] *Ex parte* Cannon, 94 Tex. Cr. Rep. 257, 250 S. W. 429 (1923).

[17] Pace v. Alabama, 106 U. S. 583, 1 Sup. Ct. 637 (1882).

ored, committing it. Under the usual type of statute the crime of miscegenation requires the unlawful acts of two parties, and therefore the acquittal of one participant demands the acquittal of the other.[18] This is not necessarily true where the statute requires proof of a guilty knowledge, as one party only can be held responsible under such an act.[19] Statutes have been enacted which punish only the white person. The only state which at the present time has such an act is West Virginia.[20] While a now repealed Texas statute of this kind was given the approval of the courts in that state during the period which followed the Civil War,[21] it by no means follows that such a miscegenation act would be approved today. In the Texas cases it was argued that the statute made a reasonable classification in view of the fact that the Negroes had no proper sense of moral responsibility at that time. However, it is exceedingly doubtful if such a statute would be upheld today, since it is true that most of the southern colored people now know that a marriage of this kind is unlawful.

Several of the southern states have had a chequered career on this subject of interracial marriage. In Arkansas the marriage bar was first enacted in 1838, was left out of the 1874 Code, but reappeared in the Revisal of 1884. It was held, however, that the original act had never ceased to be the law, as a statute of this kind was not subject to repeal by implication.[22] In Louisiana intermarriage was barred by a statute which was contained in the compilations of 1810 and 1825.[23] This act continued to be the law through the year 1865[24] and on down to 1870 when it was removed from the books.[25] The statutory

[18] Reed v. State, 20 Ala. App. 496, 103 So. 97 (1925).

[19] Bell v. State, 33 Tex. Cr. Rep. 163, 25 S. W. 769 (1894).

[20] W. VA. CODE (1931) c. 48, art. 1, §19.

[21] *Ex parte* Francois, 9 Fed. Cas. No. 5047 (C. C. W. D. Tex. 1879); Frasher v. State, 3 Tex. App. 263, 30 Am. Rep. 131 (1877); Francois v. State, 9 Tex. App. 144 (1880). See also the ante-bellum case of State v. Brady, 28 Tenn. 74 (1848).

[22] Dodson v. State, 61 Ark. 57, 31 S. W. 977 (1895).

[23] Daggett, *Legal Aspect of Amalgamation in Louisiana* (1933) 11 TEX. LAW REV. 162, 170.

[24] *See* Succession of Mingo, 143 La. 298, 78 So. 565 (1918). *Cf.* Succession of Dreux, Manning's Unrep. Cas. 217 (La. 1878). In this instance the marriage was in 1857.

[25] *See* Succession of Colwell, 34 La. Ann. 265 (1882).

bar in its present form was not enacted until 1894.[26] In Mississippi the bar was set up in 1865,[27] was left out of the 1870 Code, but reappeared in the compilation of 1880.[28] In contrast to the Arkansas situation the North Carolina statute, which was originally adopted in 1830, was said to have been repealed by a general provision in the 1836 Revisal repealing all prior acts not contained therein.[29] This was evidently a mere oversight and the statute was re-enacted in 1838.[30] In South Carolina a marriage bar was set up in 1865[31] but this provision was left out of and seems to have been repealed by the Revisal of 1872.[32] Soon after the whites had regained supremacy in 1876, however, a movement was launched to replace the bar. In 1879 the legislature enacted a statute outlawing intermarriage.[33] Even in a situation where the attempted interracial union occurred at a time when such marriages were lawful, the state court held that there was a presumption that no white man or woman would enter into such a relationship with persons of color.[34] Hence the cohabitation of persons of different races was deemed nothing more than mere concubinage unless the presumption could be overcome by proof.

A majority of these state laws outlawing marriages between whites and Negroes punish ministers or local officials who knowingly perform a ceremony in violation thereof.[35] Ten states

[26] *See* Succession of Davis, 126 La. 178, 52 So. 266 (1910); Succession of Yoist, 132 La. 309, 61 So. 384 (1913); Minor v. Young, 148 La. 610, 87 So. 472 (1921), 149 La. 583, 89 So. 757 (1921).

[27] Miss. Laws 1865, c. 4, §3, p. 82.

[28] MISS. REV. CODE (1880) §1147. In 1872 the Tennessee Court was of the opinion that there was no marriage bar in Mississippi. State v. Bell, 66 Tenn. 9 (1872).

[29] State v. Hooper, 27 N. C. 201 (1844).

[30] N. C. Laws 1838-39, c. 24. *See* State v. Fore, 23 N. C. 378 (1841); State v. Hooper, 27 N. C. 201 (1844).

[31] 13 S. C. Stat. 1861-66, p. 270. See also S. C. Sess. Laws, Ex. Sess., 1866, pp. 393-4.

[32] See S. C. REV. STAT. (1872) p. 843. *See* Kennington v. Catoe, 68 S. C. 470, 47 S. E. 719 (1904). *Cf.* State v. Ross, 76 N. C. 242 (1872).

[33] S. C. Stat. 1879-82, p. 3. *See* State v. Paulk, 18 S. C. 514 (1882).

[34] Lloyd v. Rawl, 63 S. C. 219, 41 S. E. 312 (1902); Rutledge v. Tunno, 69 S. C. 400, 48 S. E. 297 (1904); Tedder v. Tedder, 108 S. C. 271, 94 S. E. 19 (1917).

[35] ALA. CODE ANN. (Michie, 1928) §5002; CAL. PEN. CODE (Deering, 1931) §359; COLO. STAT. ANN. (Mills, 1930) §4730; DEL. REV. CODE (1915) §2992; FLA. COMP. GEN. LAWS ANN. (Skillman, 1927) §§7564, 5860; GA. CODE ANN. (Michie, 1926) PEN. CODE §678, (Michie, Supp. 1928) §2177 (17); IND. STAT. ANN. (Burns, 1933) §10-4223 (implied); MD. ANN. CODE (Bagby, 1924) art. 27, §358; MONT. REV. CODES (1921) §5704; NEV. COMP. LAWS (Hillyer, 1929) §10,199; N. C. CODE ANN. (Michie, 1931) §4341; N. D. COMP. LAWS ANN. (1913)

provide for the punishment of those officials who knowingly issue a license to persons of different races,[36] three punish anyone who assists in performing such a ceremony,[37] while one lone jurisdiction punishes anyone who counsels a union of this kind.[38] The Oklahoma law contains a provision penalizing those who conceal the record.[39]

In Texas the statute provides that proof of marriage by mere reputation in the community is not sufficient to convict an accused defendant.[40] Here one must also notice the wording of a Virginia statute, hereinafter referred to, which inflicts punishment on those who go out of the state for the purpose of evading the miscegenation laws. This statute provides that mere cohabitation is evidence of the attempted marriage.[41]

The Virginia law authorizes the temporary withholding of a license to marry in case there is a reasonable doubt as to the race of either applicant, pending any investigation deemed necessary.[42] The Georgia race registration act provides that anyone who makes an intentionally false statement as to his or her race or color in applying for a marriage license is guilty of a felony.[43] The Georgia and Virginia race registration acts provide for the punishment of those who swear falsely in making out their registration certificates.[44] At least four states, two of which have no laws prohibiting interracial marriages,

§9585; Okla. Comp. Stat. (1921) §§7501-02; Ore. Code Ann. (1930) §14-842; S. C. Code (1932) §1438; Va. Code Ann. (Michie, 1930) §4547; W. Va. Code (1931) c. 48, art. 1, §19; Wyo. Rev. Stat. Ann. (Courtright, 1931) c. 68, §119. Several of these acts do not require a guilty knowledge specifically, but it is thought that such would be implied. The California act is not specifically directed at interracial marriages but would clearly include them.

[36] Ala. Code Ann. (Michie, 1928) §5002; Del. Rev. Code (1915) §2992; Fla. Comp. Gen. Laws Ann. (Skillman, 1927) §§7563, 5859; Ga. Code Ann. (Michie, 1926) Pen. Code §678 (Michie, Supp. 1928) §2177 (16); Ind. Stat. Ann. (Burns, 1933) §10-4223 (implied); N. C. Code Ann. (Michie, 1931) §4341; N. D. Comp. Laws Ann. (1913) §8584; Okla. Comp. Stat. (1921) §7502; Ore. Code Ann. (1930) §14-842; W. Va. Code (1931) c. 48, art. 1, §20. A California statute makes the issuance of the license in such a case unlawful. Cal. Civ. Code (Deering, 1931) §69.

[37] Del. Rev. Code (1915) §2992; Ind. Stat. Ann. (Burns, 1933) §10-4223; Nev. Comp. Laws (Hillyer, 1929) §10,199.

[38] Ind. Stat. Ann. (Burns, 1933) §10-4223.

[39] Okla. Comp. Stat. (1921) §7502.

[40] Tex. Ann. Pen. Code (Vernon, 1925) art. 494.

[41] Va. Code Ann. (Michie, 1930) §4540.

[42] *Id.* at §5099a ss. 4.

[43] Ga. Code Ann. (Michie, Supp. 1928) §2177 (15).

[44] *Id.* at §2177 (7); Va. Code (1930) §5099a ss. 2.

require applicants for a license to state to what race they belong.[45] Mississippi even requires bills of divorce to state the race of both parties.[46] In Georgia it was evidently deemed necessary to forbid the marrying of white couples by Negro ministers. A state statute permits colored clergymen to marry Negroes only.[47]

An interracial marriage is absolutely void in those states where it is unlawful and is not just voidable.[48] The point becomes important in considering bigamous marriages. In an early case from Michigan, a state where such marriages were then unlawful, a Negro was charged with bigamy. His attempted second marriage was with a white woman. As a defense to the indictment he set up the fact that the second marriage was an interracial one and hence could not be used as the basis of the crime charged. However, the court refused to accept this reasoning. It held that the marriage was none the less bigamous because it could have been declared void for another reason, namely, that the union was an interracial one.[49] A more serious question would no doubt arise where the first marriage was interracial in character. In this situation one commentator has suggested that it would be far better to consider the interracial marriage as being ineffective by operation of law as soon as it is celebrated.[50] The second marriage will then not be considered bigamous. According to this theory, the penalties provided by the above miscegenation statutes would be assessed for the illegal attempt to contract a marriage with a person whom the state refuses to permit one to marry. This is a far better theory than one which would treat the marriage itself as the criminal act. The state would then be inflicting penalties on the parties for consummating a union which is not in the strict sense a marriage at all, being void. These statutes prohibiting interracial marriages do not apply retrospectively, and hence

[45] Cal. Civ. Code (Deering, 1931) §69; Ga. Code (Michie, Supp. 1928) §2177 (8) Pa. Stat. Ann. (Purdon, 1930) tit. 48, §13; R. I. Acts & Resolves 1927, c. 1064.

[46] Miss. Code Ann. (1930) §1426.

[47] Ga. Code Ann. (Michie, 1926) §2179.

[48] Estate of Gregorson, 160 Cal. 21, 116 Pac. 60 (1911). See also N. C. Code Ann. (Michie, 1931) §2495; Va. Code Ann. (Michie, 1930) §5087.

[49] People v. Brown, 34 Mich. 339 (1876). *Cf.* note 6 *supra.*

[50] Peck, *Necessity for Prior Valid Marriage in Prosecution for Bigamy* (1910) 15 Va. L. Reg. 905, 909.

marriages entered into prior to their enactment would not be declared illegal.[51]

The states differ with respect to the amount of Negro blood which will prevent a person of mixed ancestry from contracting a valid marriage with a white person. Arkansas,[52] California,[53] Colorado,[54] Delaware,[55] Idaho,[56] Kentucky,[57] Mississippi,[58] South Carolina,[59] Tennessee,[60] and Wyoming[61] specifically mention mulattoes in their statutory provisions, but in most instances they are silent as to the amount of Negro blood which would cause one to be included within the term.[62] Some of the statutes of these and other states are more specific. Thus the three states of Maryland, North Carolina, and Tennessee prohibit the marriage of whites to persons of Negro blood to the third generation inclusive.[63] It has been decided in North Carolina that one whose great-grandfather was a full-blooded Negro is within the prohibition.[64] This is the same as declaring that a white person cannot legally marry an individual who has one-eighth or more Negro blood in his veins. The Florida Con-

---

[51] Minor v. Young, 148 La. 610, 87 So. 472 (1921); Scott v. Epperson, 141 Okla. 41, 284 Pac. 19 (1930).

[52] ARK. DIG. STAT. (Crawford & Moses, 1921) §7039.

[53] CAL. CIV. CODE (Deering, 1931) §60.

[54] COLO. STAT. ANN. (Mills, 1930) §4729.

[55] DEL. REV. CODE (1915) §2992. [56] IDAHO CODE ANN. (1932) §31-206.

[57] KY. STAT. ANN. (Carroll, 1930) §2097 construed to include old Virginia statute, adopted when Kentucky became a state, prohibiting only marriages between whites and those who have one-fourth or more Negro blood. McGoodwin v. Shelby, 182 Ky. 377, 206 S. W. 625 (1918); Theophanis v. Theophanis, 244 Ky. 689, 51 S. W. (2d) 957 (1932).

[58] MISS. CODE ANN. (1930) §2361, MISS. CONST. §263 (one-eighth Negro blood not permitted).

[59] S. C. CODE (1932) §§1438, 8571 (one-eighth Negro blood not permitted by S. C. CONST. Art. III, §33).

[60] TENN. CONST. Art. XI, §14, TENN. CODE (Will. Shan. & Harsh, 1932) §8409.

[61] WYO. REV. STAT. ANN. (Courtright, 1931) c. 68, §118.

[62] Miss., S. C. & Tenn. excepted—*cf.* previous notes 58, 59, 60.

[63] MD. ANN. CODE (Bagby, 1924) art. 27, §365; N. C. CONST. Art. XIV, §8, N. C. CODE ANN. (Michie, 1931) §§2495, 4340, changed from fourth generation, as shown by State v. Watters, 25 N. C. 455 (1843)—*cf.* Ferrall v. Ferrall, 153 N. C. 174, 69 S. E. 60 (1910); TENN. CONST. Art. XI, §14, TENN. CODE (Will, Shan. & Harsh, 1932) §8409 (§§25, 8396, making the term "Negro" include persons who have any trace of Negro blood in their veins, would not change this).

[64] Hare v. Board of Education, 113 N. C. 10, 18 S. E. 55 (1893). *See also* Weaver v. State, 22 Ala. App. 469, 116 So. 893 (1928).

stitution prohibits marriages to the fourth generation inclusive.[65] Reasoning from the above North Carolina decision, this would outlaw marriages of whites with persons having one-sixteenth or more Negro blood. The statutory definition of the term "Negro," placed immediately after the statute prohibiting intermarriage in the last codification of the state law, is a person of one-eighth or more Negro blood.[66] Thus an apparent conflict is seen, and this inconsistency should be called to the attention of the Florida legislature. Should a case arise under the law as it exists today, the courts would probably follow the constitutional definition. In six states the statutes are worded in such a manner as to outlaw marriages of whites with persons of one-eighth or more Negro blood.[67] This gives the same result as the prohibition against unions with persons who are of Negro blood to the third generation inclusive. In Oregon the proscribed proportion of Negro blood is one-fourth or more.[68]

In no less than seven states language is employed which may be construed as prohibiting marriages of whites with persons who have any Negro blood, however remote the strain may be.[69]

---

[65] Art. XVI, §24. [66] FLA. COMP. GEN. LAWS ANN. (Skillman, 1927) §5858.

[67] IND. STAT. ANN. (Burns, 1933) §§10-4222, 44-104; MISS. CONST. §263, MISS. CODE ANN. (1930) §2361; MO. REV. STAT. (1929) §4263—*see* Marre v. Marre, 184 Mo. App. 198, 168 S. W. 636 (1914); NEBR. COMP. STAT. (1929) §42-103; N. D. COMP. LAWS ANN. (1913) §9583; S. C. CONST. Art. III, §33. *See* Tucker v. Blease, 97 S. C. 303, 81 S. E. 668 (1914). [68] ORE. CODE ANN. (1930) §14-840.

[69] ALA. CONST. §102, ALA. CODE ANN. (Michie, 1928) §5001; ARIZ. REV. CODE ANN. (Struckmeyer, 1928) §2166; GA. CODE ANN. (Michie, 1926) §2941, (Supp. 1928) §§2177 (13)-(14); MONT. REV. CODES (1921) §5700; OKLA. COMP. STAT. (1921) §7499; TEX. ANN. REV. CIV. STAT. (Vernon, 1925) art. 4607; VA. CODE ANN. (Michie, 1930) §§67, 5099a. Before 1927 the Alabama marriage statute prohibited unions with persons who had Negro blood to the third generation inclusive. *See* Green v. State, 59 Ala. 68 (1877). In 1927 the legislature changed the act to conform with the state constitution. Ala. Acts 1927, p. 219. Before this amendment a marriage of a white person and a person who had less Negro blood than that prescribed in the statute was void but could not be punished criminally. Weaver v. State, 22 Ala. App. 469, 116 So. 893 (1928). Very much the same situation is presented by the present Texas statutes, for TEX. ANN. PEN. CODE (Vernon, 1925) arts. 492-493 punishes only those marriages where one of the parties has Negro blood to the third generation inclusive. Before 1910 the Virginia law nullified only those marriages where one of the parties had one-fourth or more Negro blood. *See* McPherson v. Commonwealth, 28 Gratt. 939 (Va. 1877); Jones v. Commonwealth, 80 Va. 538 (1885); Moon v. Children's Home Soc., 112 Va. 737, 72 S. E. 707 (1911). The statute was changed in 1910 to read one-sixteenth or more. Va. Acts 1910, c. 357. *See* Note (1912) 17 VA. LAW REG. 692. The statute was changed to its present form in 1930. Va. Acts 1930, c. 85.

Louisiana proscribes marriages of whites with "persons of color." [70] In a recent opinion the Louisiana Court intimated that it would annul the marriage of a white man with a woman whose great-great-grandmother was a Negro.[71] It has been said, however, that marriage licenses are refused in this state only in instances where the Negro blood is easily discernible.[72] The Nevada statute[73] punishing any white person who cohabits with a "black person" also mentions mulattoes, and this might possibly be construed to apply to the marriage act as well, since that section of the statute has no provision which is interpretive. In South Dakota, Utah, and West Virginia there is no indication in the statutes as to the amount of Negro blood which will render a person of mixed ancestry incapable of contracting a marriage with a white person. In these three states the term "mulatto" is not even used.

An interesting question is presented in an Arizona case. A white man sought the annulment of his marriage to a woman who he claimed was a Negro, a contention which was evidently well supported by the plaintiff's evidence. The woman contended that the state statute prohibiting interracial marriages would prevent a person of mixed Caucasian and Negro ancestry from marrying anyone and was therefore invalid as an unreasonable restriction. She offered no proof that she was of mixed blood, and therefore the court held that she was not entitled to raise the question.[74] The difficulty is made to appear of no great moment, however, when one considers the fact that each individual must be a Negro or not according to the local law, depending upon the amount of African blood one may have and still retain the legal status of a white person. An early case from Maine throws some light upon this matter. Before the repeal of the law outlawing marriages of whites and Negroes of that state, it was held that a person having one-sixteenth or perhaps one-eighth Negro blood was legally white and therefore incapable of contracting a valid marriage with a mulatto.[75] Here it is also interesting to note what was said by

[70] LA. CIV. CODE ANN. (Dart, 1932) art. 94.

[71] Sunseri v. Cassagne, 185 So. 1 (La. 1938).

[72] Daggett, *Legal Aspect of Amalgamation in Louisiana* (1933) 11 TEX. L. REV. 162.

[73] NEV. COMP. LAWS (Hillyer, 1929) §10,200.

[74] Kirby v. Kirby, 24 Ariz. 9, 206 Pac. 405 (1922).

[75] Bailey v. Fiske, 34 Me. 77 (1852).

the Louisiana Court in respect to the ante-bellum statute prohibiting interracial marriages in that state. The court declared that the statute contained no provision outlawing the marriage of a free Negro and a person of mixed blood.[76] In the South today there is little or no objection to such marriages, no matter how small the percentage of Negro blood in one of the contracting parties. If it is known that an individual has the least modicum of Negro blood, then he or she is considered a suitable mate for colored persons only.

In a case which arose long before the Civil War and prior to the repeal of the Massachusetts law prohibiting interracial marriages, the court of that state took a very liberal attitude in defining the term "mulatto" used in the statute. The court declared that only those persons who were the progeny of a pure white man or woman and a pure Negro could be considered mulattoes. Hence it was held that the issue of a mulatto and a white woman was not prohibited from making a valid marriage contract with a white person.[77] This decision was no doubt influenced by the attitude of the state toward slavery, for the abolitionist sentiment was present in Massachusetts even at this early date.

There is a clause in the Missouri miscegenation statute which provides that the jury trying a party accused of violating the law may determine the proportion of Negro blood from his or her appearance. The state court held that this provision did not conflict with the Fourteenth Amendment.[78]

No action is needed to invalidate the marriage of a white person and a Negro, the union being null and void *ab initio*, and this illegality may be set up in court by any party to whom the alleged marriage is opposed, directly or collaterally.[79] Moreover, in one instance the Mississippi constitutional provision prohibiting such marriages was held by the court of another state to be self-executing.[80]

It is only natural that problems should arise out of the

---

[76] Succession of Fortier, 51 La. Ann. 1562, 26 So. 554 (1899).

[77] Inhabitants of Medway v. Inhabitants of Natick, 7 Mass. 88 (1810).

[78] State v. Jackson, 80 Mo. 175 (1883).

[79] Succession of Minvielle v. Barjac, 15 La. Ann. 342 (1860); Carter v. Veith, 139 La. 534, 71 So. 792 (1916).

[80] Succession of Gabisso, 119 La. 704, 44 So. 438 (1907).

desire of certain persons to evade these laws by going into a state where marriages of whites and Negroes are lawful. Several states have statutes[81] which are aimed at preventing this practice as far as possible. These statutes nullify interracial marriages, even if the parties go to another jurisdiction where such unions are not made illegal, should they go with an intention of returning and with the purpose of evading the law of their home state. Other states, such as Georgia[82] and Louisiana,[83] have general marriage evasion acts which may be interpreted as invalidating all such extraterritorial interracial marriages.[84] There are decisions to this same effect by the courts of these and other states.[85] However, there is also authority to the contrary.[86]

An entirely different situation is revealed where members of the white and colored races have contracted a marriage in a jurisdiction where such a union is lawful and are domiciled there at the time the marriage was celebrated. If the parties later move into some state where such matches are illegal, the better view is that the marriage is a valid one.[87] However, courts have sometimes taken an opposing view,[88] for the full faith and credit clause of the Federal Constitution does not force a state to recognize a marriage if the union is contrary to the local idea of public morality.[89] Some few states have enacted statutes which invalidate all marriages of persons who come to the jurisdiction with the intention of returning to their home

[81] DEL. REV. CODE (1915) §2992; MISS. CODE ANN. (1930) §2361; MONT. REV. CODES (1921) §5703; TEX. ANN. PEN. CODE (Vernon, 1925) art. 492; VA. CODE ANN. (Michie, 1930) §§4540, 5089. [82] GA. CODE ANN. (Michie, 1926) §2943.

[83] LA. GEN. STAT. ANN. (Dart, 1932) §2186.

[84] State v. Tutty, 41 Fed. 753 (C. C. S. D. Ga. 1890).

[85] Dupre v. Executor of Boulard, 10 La. Ann. 411 (1855); Jackson v. Jackson, 82 Md. 17, 33 Atl. 317 (1895) (dictum); State v. Kennedy, 76 N. C. 251 (1877); Eggers v. Olson, 104 Okla. 297, 231 Pac. 483 (1924); Baker v. Carter, 180 Okla. 71, 68 P. (2d) 85 (1937); Kinney v. Commonwealth, 30 Gratt. 858 (Va. 1878) —same result reached in *Ex parte* Kinney, 14 Fed. Cas. No. 7825 (C. C. E. D. Va. 1879); Greenhow v. James' Executors, 80 Va. 636 (1885).

[86] Inhabitants of Medway v. Inhabitants of Needham, 16 Mass. 157 (1819); State v. Hand, 87 Neb. 189, 126 N. W. 1002 (1910)—see 43 L.R.A. (N.S.) 358.

[87] Succession of Caballero v. Executor, 24 La. Ann. 573 (1872); State v. Ross, 76 N. C. 242 (1872).

[88] State v. Bell, 66 Tenn. 9 (1872). Subject to a like interpretation is language used in Jackson v. Jackson, 82 Md. 17, 33 Atl. 317 (1895).

[89] *See* DeBouchel v. Candler, 296 Fed. 482 (N. D. Ga. 1924).

state, and contract a marriage proscribed by the laws of the latter.[90]

In a Florida case an interracial marriage entered into by parties domiciled in a jurisdiction where such a ceremony was lawful was held to be a valid one for purposes of inheritance.[91] In Kentucky it was said that a void interracial marriage cannot generally be used as a basis for a claim of inheritance.[92]

In Texas a man made a representation to a purchaser of his alleged wife's land that his marriage to the woman was void because he was a Negro and she a white woman. On the faith of this representation the purchaser did not require him to join in the conveyance as required by law for all conveyances by married women. The court held that the man was estopped from claiming any interest in the property of the woman whom he had declared was not his lawful wife.[93]

In an early California case the testimony established that a white man, while on his way west before the Civil War, contracted a marriage in Utah with his female Negro slave. The court declared that his intention to free her could be inferred from the fact that he had taken her as his mate. The marriage was deemed a valid one, as there was at that time no Utah law which prohibited interracial marriages.[94]

In a Missouri case a white man and a colored woman had lived together for a long while without making an effort to legalize their union by a marriage ceremony. During this period the woman had been emancipated along with other slaves. Children were born to the union, but the couple finally separated some years after the woman had gained her freedom. The progeny of this alleged common-law marriage claimed a portion of their father's estate after his death. The claim was opposed by the woman whom he had married after he had left his alleged common-law wife. The court declared that the relationship had not developed into a common-law union. There

[90] See LA. GEN. STAT. ANN. (Dart, 1932) §2187; MASS. GEN. LAWS (1921) c. 207, §11; VT. GEN. LAWS (1917) §3515. It is possible that there are other states which have laws of this nature.

[91] Whittington v. McCaskill, 65 Fla. 162, 61 So. 236 (1913).

[92] Moore v. Moore, 30 Ky. Law Rep. 383, 98 S. W. 1027 (1907).

[93] Stewart v. Profit, 146 S. W. 563 (Tex. Civ. App. 1912).

[94] Pearson v. Pearson, 51 Cal. 120 (1875).

was some evidence that the deceased had recognized the colored woman as his wife after emancipation, but this was said to have been rebutted by the fact that he afterwards left her. As to the cohabitation before the war, the court made a point of the fact that the miscegenation statute forbade interracial marriages, subjecting to punishment those who disregarded its mandates. The tribunal declared that the parties would not have been likely to subject themselves to the penalties of the law in this respect.[95]

Negro slaves were not usually married, although on some plantations ceremonies were performed. There was of course much promiscuity, but there were many slaves who lived together as man and wife. This relationship was not a very stable one, for the man and woman were sometimes torn apart at the will of a master who found it to his advantage to sell one without the other. In some instances a slave would "take up with" a man or woman on some adjoining plantation. Before the war the laws pertaining to the marriage of free Negro couples were the same as those for the whites.[96] In the case of the former, however, the law enforcement was probably very lax.

After emancipation the problem of the domestic instability of the freedmen arose. The emergency called for some novel remedy to meet the extraordinary situation. The ante-bellum promiscuity and want of a stable sex relationship among the slaves would seem immoral according to the white man's civilization and religious teachings, but most of the southern whites did not look upon it as especially evil. The Negroes were chattels and were not considered as being subject to the same moral code as the whites. Some masters even encouraged some degree of promiscuity because of the desire to have larger families of slave children, since every child who was born was an asset to the owner. There were numbers of slave children who did not know who their fathers were. Hence we see what a problem was

[95] Keen v. Keen, 184 Mo. 358, 83 S. W. 526 (1904). The Federal Supreme Court affirmed the decision on the ground that the question of a common law marriage was a purely local one and that the allegation that the judgment violated the Fourteenth Amendment was insufficient in that it failed to state the reasons for the alleged conflict with the Constitution. Keen v. Keen, 201 U. S. 319, 26 Sup. Ct. 494 (1906).

[96] Indicated by statement in Downs v. Allen, 78 Tenn. 652, 666 (1882).

presented to the southern lawmakers when the Negroes were freed and made citizens with theoretically the same rights as white men and women.

The southern legislatures met this difficulty by the enactment of statutes providing that all former slaves then cohabiting as man and wife should be considered as lawfully wedded couples. The offspring of these unions were legitimated and made capable of inheriting property. The laws were not all alike, but the essentials were very similar.[97] These statutes were not intended to apply to interracial cohabitations, but only to those unions where the parties had been prevented from marrying by the laws or customs of slavery.[98] There are exceptions to this, however, as the validating acts in Florida[99] and Louisiana[100] were extended to include prior marriages of whites and Negroes.

There are various statutory provisions which outlaw the marriages of white persons with members of races other than the

[97] Ala. Acts 1868, Ordinance No. 23, p. 175 (see also Ala. Code Ann. (Michie, 1928) §7377); Ark. Dig. Stat. (Crawford & Moses, 1921) §7040; Fla. Comp. Gen. Laws Ann. (Skillman, 1927) §§5861, 5864 (see also Supp. 1936, §5480 [10]); Ga. Code Ann. (Michie, 1926) §§2178, 2180; Ky. Stat. Ann. (Carroll, 1930) §§1399a, 1399b (1-2); La. Acts 1868, No. 210 (see also La. Gen. Stat. Ann. [Dart, 1932] §2193); Md. Code Ann. (Bagby, 1924) art. 62, §15; Miss. Laws 1865, c. 4, §3, p. 82; N. C. Code Ann. (Michie, 1931) §§2497, 1654 (13); S. C. Code (1932) §8569-70; Tenn Code (Will. Shan. & Harsh, 1932) §§8397-8401; Tex. Ann. Rev. Civ. Stat. (Vernon, 1925) art. 4609; Va. Code Ann. (Michie, 1930) §5091; W. Va. Code (1931) c. 48, art. 1, §16. Illinois found it necessary to enact a similar statute. Ill. Rev. Stat. (Cahill, 1933) c. 89, §18. The Arkansas law was in force in Indian Territory before it became the state of Oklahoma. *In re* McDade's Estate, 95 Okla. 120, 218 Pac. 532 (1923). A Missouri act of 1864 required a remarriage to validate the union of persons of color. Mo. Laws 1864, p. 68. Later the legislature passed an act legitimizing the issue of slave unions. Mo. Rev. Stat. (1929) §317. The Louisiana act is construed to validate slave marriages in Johnson's Heirs v. Raphael, 117 La. 967, 42 So. 470 (1906), but what is said in that case regarding the necessity for an actual marriage ceremony is negatived in several other later cases. Marzette v. Cronk, 141 La. 437, 75 So. 107 (1917); Succession of Blackburn, 154 La. 618, 98 So. 43 (1923); Smith v. Rambo, 131 So. 524 (La. App. 1930). However, it has been decided that cohabitation after emancipation was necessary. Wiley v. Bowman, 144 La. 181, 80 So. 243 (1918); Succession of Blackburn, 154 La. 618, 98 So. 43 (1923). A ceremony of any kind is deemed reliable evidence of a slave marriage. Succession of Tyson, 186 La. 516, 172 So. 772 (1937).

[98] Kinard v. State, 57 Miss. 132 (1879); Clements v. Crawford, 42 Tex. 601 (1875); Oldham v. McIver, 49 Tex. 556 (1878). What is said to the contrary in Honey v. Clark, 37 Tex. 686 (1873) is overruled in the later Texas cases.

[99] Fla. Comp. Gen. Laws Ann. (Skillman, 1927) §5863.

[100] See La. Gen. Stat. Ann. (Dart, 1932) §2196.

Negro. Thus some fifteen states, most of which are in the Far West, have enacted laws which expressly or impliedly forbid marriages between persons of the Caucasian and Mongolian races.[101] Ten states expressly or impliedly prohibit the marriage of whites and Malays,[102] five bar unions of whites and Indians,[103] and there are a few other prohibitions of minor importance.[104] Indians and Negroes are forbidden to marry each other in Louisiana[105] and Oklahoma.[106] North Carolina prohibits the

[101] ARIZ. REV. CODE ANN. (Struckmeyer, 1928) §2166 as amended by Ariz. Laws 1931, c. 17; CAL. CIV. CODE (Deering, 1931) §60; GA. CODE ANN. (Michie, Supp. 1928) §§2177 (13), 2177 (14); IDAHO CODE ANN. (1932) §31-206; MISS. CODE ANN. (1930) §2361 (one-eighth or more); MO. REV. STAT. (1929) §2974; MONT. REV. CODES (1921) §§5701-02; NEB. COMP. STAT. (1929) §42-103 (one-eighth or more); NEV. COMP. LAWS (Hillyer, 1929) §10,197; ORE. CODE ANN. (1930) §14-840 (one-fourth or more Chinese); S. C. CODE (1932) §§1438, 8571 (white woman permitted to marry white man only); S. D. COMP. LAWS (1929) §128; UTAH REV. STAT. ANN. (1933) §40-1-2 ss. 6; VA. CODE ANN. (Michie, 1930) §5099a; WYO. REV. STAT. ANN. (Courtright, 1931) c. 68, §118.

[102] ARIZ. REV. CODE ANN. (Struckmeyer, 1928) §2166 as amended by Ariz. Laws 1931, c. 17; Cal. Stat. 1933, cc. 104, 105; GA. CODE ANN. (Michie, Supp. 1928) §§2177 (1), 2177 (14); Md. Laws 1935, c. 60; NEV. COMP. LAWS (Hillyer, 1929) §10,197; ORE. CODE ANN. (1930) §14-840 (one-fourth or more Kanaka); S. C. CODE (1932) §§1438, 8571 (white woman permitted to marry white man only); S. D. COMP. LAWS (1929) §128; VA. CODE ANN. (Michie, 1930) §5099a; WYO. REV. STAT. ANN. (Courtright, 1931) c. 68, §118. The California act was passed as a result of the decision in Roldan v. Los Angeles County, 129 Cal. App. 267, 18 P. (2d) 706 (1933), commented upon in (1933) 22 CALIF. L. REV. 116, in which the court held that a Filipino was not a "Mongolian" within the marriage statute.

[103] ARIZ. REV. CODE ANN. (Struckmeyer, 1928) §2166 as amended by Ariz. Laws 1931, c. 17; GA. CODE ANN. (Michie, Supp. 1928) §§2177 (13), 2177 (14) (West Indian); N. C. CODE ANN. (Michie, 1931) §2495 (to third generation); ORE. CODE ANN. (1930) §14-840 (more than one-half); S. C. CODE (1932) §1438, 8571 (mestizo included). *See* State v. Melton, 44 N. C. 49 (1852); *In re* Paquet's Estate, 101 Ore. 393, 200 Pac. 911 (1921). Washington formerly had such a statute. See *In re* Wilbur's Estate, 8 Wash. 35, 35 Pac. 407 (1894). Such a marriage is valid where there is no statutory prohibition. *See* Wells v. Thompson, 13 Ala. 793 (1848). Such a marriage is without legal effect in a state which prohibits it even if the ceremony took place on an Indian Reservation, there being but one law as to marriage in the jurisdiction. *In re* Walker's Estate, 5 Ariz. 70, 46 Pac. 67 (1896); *In re* Wilbur's Estate, 8 Wash. 35, 35 Pac. 407 (1894).

[104] Arizona forbids marriages with Hindus, ARIZ. REV. CODE ANN. (Struckmeyer, 1928) §2166 as amended by Ariz. Laws 1931, c. 17. Georgia and Virginia prohibit marriages with Asiatic Indians. GA. CODE ANN. (Michie, Supp. 1928) §§2177 (13), 2177 (14); VA. CODE ANN. (Michie, 1930) §5099a.

[105] LA. GEN. STAT. ANN. (Dart, 1932) §2185.

[106] OKLA. COMP. STAT. (1921) §7499. Indians forbidden to marry persons who are descendants of any Negro. *See* Blake v. Sessions, 94 Okla. 59, 220 Pac. 876 (1923); Eggers v. Olson, 104 Okla. 297, 231 Pac. 483 (1924). Such a marriage was not prohibited in Indian Territory before annexation to Oklahoma, and a

union of Cherokee Indians of Robeson County with persons of Negro blood to the third generation inclusive.[107] In Maryland a union of a Malay and a Negro is unlawful.[108]

Sometimes situations may arise in respect to the marital relationship where a person with Negro blood either fraudulently represents himself or herself to be white or else fraudulently conceals the fact that he or she is of mixed racial origin. This is made possible because of the goodly number of mulatto men and women who appear to be white but who have a strain of Negro blood in their veins. Where the percentage of Negro blood is not sufficient to invalidate the marriage according to the local law and when it appears that the prospective white spouse had been informed before the ceremony that his or her affianced mate had Negro blood, it has been held that a suit for divorce cannot be instituted or avoided for the reason that the former had been deceived or had entered into the marriage without a proper knowledge of the facts.[109] There seems to be little doubt that most courts would hold that fraudulent concealment of the fact that a person has Negro blood would be grounds for an annulment of the marriage. The Virginia Court decided in one instance that a white man could not be convicted of seducing a woman under promise of marriage if she knew she had Negro blood and was therefore incapable of contracting a valid marriage with him according to the law of that state.[110] The question of fraud also arose in a Massachusetts breach-of-promise suit in which the defendant sought to prove that the plaintiff had wrongfully concealed the fact that she had Negro blood. The court declared that the mere fact that she was of mixed racial origin, even if this fact could be proved, would not be sufficient defense in and of itself. However, it was said that when the plaintiff was talking with the defendant of her antecedents in the South, she omitted facts which might have caused him to investigate her racial origin more carefully. For the failure of the lower court to take care of this con-

marriage of this kind before that event was therefore not affected by the statute. *See* Scott v. Epperson, 141 Okla. 41, 284 Pac. 19 (1930).

[107] N. C. CODE ANN. (Michie, 1931) §2495. [108] Md. Laws 1935, c. 60.

[109] Theophanis v. Theophanis, 244 Ky. 689, 51 S. W. (2d) 957 (1932); Ferrall v. Ferrall, 153 N. C. 174, 69 S. E. 60 (1910).

[110] Wood v. Commonwealth, 159 Va. 963, 166 S. E. 477 (1932), commented upon in (1933) 37 L. NOTES 130, 133.

tingency in its charge to the jury, a judgment in the plaintiff's favor was reversed and the case remanded.[111]

The much publicized Rhinelander case from New York involved a white husband's efforts to obtain an annulment of his marriage to a woman who he claimed had Negro blood. He alleged that she had made fraudulent statements to him prior to the marriage that she had no colored blood in her veins. At the trial she failed to take the witness stand and deny that she had made these statements. The lower court decided in her favor, and the husband appealed on the ground that this failure to take the stand in her own defense created a conclusive presumption that she had actually made the alleged statements. The appellate court declared that no such conclusive presumption would arise from her refusal to take the stand in her own behalf, although the natural result of her failure to testify would be to prejudice the jury against her cause.[112] The jury was charged that it might draw such inferences as it wished from the failure to call witnesses.

A somewhat analogous situation is seen where a man is persuaded to marry a woman by false representations that he is the father of her small infant, and the child afterwards turns out to have Negro blood. In an early North Carolina case it was shown that a marriage between two persons of the white race had been induced by the wife's false representations that a child born to her was the result of illicit relations of the couple before marriage. The offspring afterwards developed the features of a Negro, but its color at the time of the marriage was not so obvious as to be detected by a man of ordinary diligence and intelligence. Under these circumstances the state court held that a divorce should be granted.[113]

Cases have reached the courts where Negro men have made offensive or improper advances toward white women. Thus in one New York case a person of Negro blood was indicted for disorderly conduct because he had sent letters proposing marriage to a white woman with whom he had had no previous so-

---

[111] Van Houten v. Morse, 162 Mass. 414, 38 N. E. 705 (1894).

[112] Rhinelander v. Rhinelander, 219 App. Div. 189, 219 N. Y. Supp. 548 (2d Dep't, 1927), *aff'd* 245 N. Y. 510, 157 N. E. 838 (1927).

[113] Barden v. Barden, 14 N. C. 548 (1832). *But see* Scroggins v. Scroggins, 14 N. C. 535 (1832), in which certain essential elements of Barden case were either lacking or insufficiently pleaded.

cial intercourse. The court held that reception of evidence that he was a colored man did not deprive him of the equal protection of the laws guaranteed by the Fourteenth Amendment.[114] In a somewhat similar case from Kentucky, however, the court took a different view. In this instance a Negro man and his associates wrote a letter to a white girl proposing that she meet them at a certain place. The letter stated that one of them loved her and contained expressions which might have been construed as suggestive proposals of immoral relations. The appellate court declared that the communicaton would have been considered as a mere harmless joke if it had been written by white youths instead of Negroes. Therefore it was held that the defendants were not subject to punishment under a statute penalizing a conspiracy to frighten anyone.[115] Some of the language in the letter would seem to suggest indecencies, and therefore the accuracy of the decision is rather doubtful.

In one Alabama case it is said that an idea prevails in the South that a white woman, even though she may be a prostitute, will not readily yield her body to the embraces of a Negro. In this instance a Negro was being tried for the rape of a white woman who was a self-confessed prostitute. The appellate court ruled that testimony that she bore the reputation of having practised lewdness with other Negroes was admissible to negative this widespread notion.[116] While it is generally true that a white prostitute will not allow a Negro to have sexual intercourse with her, there are many instances in the South today where such immorality is permitted or even sought after by the lowest type of fallen women.

Hence the legislatures of quite a number of southern and western states have found it expedient to enact statutes expressly punishing members of different races and sexes for living in a state of concubinage or for indulging in acts of sexual intercourse with one another, whether it be fornication or adultery.[117] Illicit interracial sexual relationships are also

---

[114] People v. Robinson, 73 Misc. 343, 132 N. Y. Supp. 674 (Ct. Gen. Sess. 1911).

[115] Alexander v. Commonwealth, 215 Ky. 832, 287 S. W. 29 (1926).

[116] Story v. State, 178 Ala. 98, 59 So. 480 (1912).

[117] ALA. CODE ANN. (Michie, 1928) §5001; ARK. DIG. STAT. (Crawford & Moses, 1921) §§2601-05; FLA. COMP. GEN. LAWS ANN. (Skillman, 1927) §7565; LA. CODE CRIM. PROC. ANN. (Dart, 1932) arts. 1128-30; NEV. COMP. LAWS (Hillyer, 1929)

punishable under ordinary statutes prohibiting unlawful cohabitation generally.[118] Louisiana has even gone to the extent of enacting a statute which specifically penalizes cohabitation between a Negro and an Indian.[119] Texas punishes the continuance of a cohabitation between a white person and a Negro after a marriage either in or out of the state,[120] but the marriage is an essential element of the offense and must be averred and proved.[121] There is no other general cohabitation statute in Texas which specifically affects interracial relations, but one of the cities of the state was allowed to put an ordinance of this kind into effect.[122]

The fact that a marriage license had been secured and a ceremony actually performed would constitute no defense to an indictment under these illicit relations statutes, as the marriage is of no effect.[123] However, where the prosecution is relying on the marriage as its only proof of an illegal act, the defendant may show that the commission of the person who performed the ceremony had expired, leaving him with neither *de jure* nor *de facto* authority.[124]

The Alabama courts have held that an indictment under the statute is sufficient if it follows the statutory wording.[125] In some instances the clause prohibiting intermarriage and the clause penalizing fornication and adultery are contained in the same statute. In one Alabama case the indictment alleged that the culprits did intermarry or live in adultery or fornication with each other. The court refused to hold that the pleading was bad. It declared that the prosecution had thereby made provision for difficulties that might present themselves at the

§10,200 (applies to Mongolians, Malays, and Indians also); N. D. COMP. LAWS ANN. (1913) §9588; S. D. COMP. LAWS (1929) §128 (Mongolians and Malays included); TENN. CODE (Will, Shan., & Harsh, 1932) §§8409-10. The Nevada act may be construed to punish the white person only, a construction which would probably make it invalid. See *supra* p. 241.

[118] Kinard v. State, 57 Miss. 132 (1879); Stewart v. State, 64 Miss. 626, 2 So. 73 (1887).

[119] LA. CODE CRIM. PROC. ANN. (Dart, 1932) arts. 1131-34.

[120] TEX. ANN. PEN. CODE (Vernon, 1925) art. 492.

[121] Moore v. State, 7 Tex. App. 608 (1880).

[122] Brown v. State, 98 Tex. Cr. Rep. 416, 266 S. W. 152 (1924).

[123] Green v. State, 59 Ala. 68 (1877).

[124] Williams v. State, 23 Ala. App. 365, 125 So. 690 (1930).

[125] Wilson v. State, 20 Ala. App. 137, 101 So. 417 (1924), *cert. denied.* 211 Ala. 613, 101 So. 423 (1924).

trial as to which one of the alternatives was actually presented by the evidence.[126] During the Reconstruction period, however, the Tennessee Court held that an indictment was not good which contained a charge that the person involved was a Negro or a mulatto or a person of Negro blood to the third generation and put all the alternatives in one count. The opinion stated that it was necessary to separate them into three distinct counts.[127] Nevertheless, the Alabama Court has said that a conviction of the crime of ordinary concubinage (living together in a state of fornication or adultery without the interracial features) may be had under an indictment charging miscegenation, the lesser offense being necessarily included in the felony.[128] Where the statute requires the offense to be "knowingly" committed, it has been decided that such knowledge need not be alleged in the indictment, the word being used in reference to proof and not to pleading.[129] It has been said that the absence of an intention to violate the law is no defense, for a conviction is proper if the parties had intercourse without such intention.[130]

In respect to the Louisiana statute it has been said that it is not required that the legislature should specifically define either "concubinage" or "cohabitation" as used in the act, as the meaning of these words is perfectly plain.[131]

It has been decided that one act or even an occasional act of sexual intercourse will be insufficient to convict a culprit under the Alabama law without proof that there is an intention to continue the relationship at some future date.[132] The crux of the matter is, of course, the intention with which the act is committed,[133] for it is perfectly possible that circumstances may show an intention to continue the intercourse without a definite agreement to that effect.[134] One act is sufficient if ac-

---

[126] Williams v. State, 23 Ala. App. 365, 125 So. 690 (1930).

[127] Robeson v. State, 50 Tenn. 266 (1871).

[128] Bryant v. State, 76 Ala. 33 (1884).

[129] Robeson v. State, 50 Tenn. 266 (1871).

[130] Hoover v. State, 59 Ala. 57 (1877).

[131] State v. Daniel, 141 La. 900, 75 So. 836 (1917).

[132] Jackson v. State, 23 Ala. App. 555, 129 So. 306 (1930).

[133] Linton v. State, 88 Ala. 216, 7 So. 261 (1889); Jones v. State, 156 Ala. 175, 17 So. 100 (1908); Jackson v. State, 23 Ala. App. 555, 129 So. 306 (1930).

[134] Linston v. State, 88 Ala. 216, 7 So. 261 (1889).

companied by the intention to continue to live together,[135] as is also cohabitation for a single day.[136] In one case arising under this same statute the defendant requested that the judge instruct the jury that only one act of illicit intercourse is not sufficient to convict even when combined with an agreement that it would be repeated should an opportunity offer itself. The trial judge had refused to give this instruction and the appellate court upheld him. It declared that the requested instruction was not only an erroneous statement of the law but also contrary to the evidence, more than one act of illicit intercourse having been indulged in according to the undisputed facts.[137] Indictments under the similar Florida and Louisiana statutes have been held good where they alleged that the offense was committed on a specified day.[138]

On the other hand, the Arkansas interracial concubinage statute and the Mississippi general cohabitation act seem to require a stricter interpretation than the Alabama law. Perhaps this is explained by the fact that the former punishes illicit "cohabitation" while the latter penalizes living in "adultery or fornication," and perhaps not. However this may be, the first-mentioned states seem to require a dwelling together with at least a certain degree of permanence in order that a conviction may be secured.[139] Furthermore, it has been decided in both jurisdictions that occasional clandestine illicit relations do not come within the purview of the statutes.[140]

The Arkansas and Louisiana statutes denounce concubinage, whether it be open or secret.[141] It has been declared that the words "cohabitation" and "concubinage" do not require legis-

---

[135] Jackson v. State, 23 Ala. App. 555, 129 So. 306 (1930).

[136] Linton v. State, 88 Ala. 216, 7 So. 261 (1889). *See also* State v. Harris, 150 La. 383, 90 So. 686 (1922).

[137] Love v. State, 124 Ala. 82, 27 So. 217 (1899).

[138] Parramore v. State, 81 Fla. 621, 88 So. 472 (1921); State v. Harris, 150 La. 383, 90 So. 686 (1922).

[139] Hovis v. State, 162 Ark. 31, 257 S. W. 363 (1924); Wilson v. State, 178 Ark. 1200, 13 S. W. (2d) 24 (1929); Kinard v. State, 57 Miss. 132 (1879).

[140] Hovis v. State, 162 Ark. 31, 257 S. W. 363 (1924); Kinard v. State, 57 Miss. 132 (1879).

[141] Ark. Dig. Stat. (Crawford & Moses, 1921) §2602; La. Code Crim. Proc. Ann. (Dart, 1932) art. 1129. *See* State v. Daniel, 141 La. 900, 75 So. 836 (1917). But *cf.* Jones v. Kyle, 168 La. 728, 123 So. 306 (1929), a case involving a legacy by a white man to a colored woman.

lative definition, being terms of ordinary import.[142] The Florida law has a provision punishing all persons of different race and opposite sex who habitually occupy the same room at night,[143] and a somewhat similar statute is in effect in North Dakota.[144]

The question may arise as to what persons are included within the terms of these acts. In one Alabama case an indictment charging cohabitation with a Negro was held to be supported by proof of cohabitation with a mulatto.[145] However, the Louisiana Court has held that an octoroon is not a member of the Negro or black race within the 1908 statute of that state denouncing interracial concubinage.[146] Soon afterwards the legislature changed the word "Negro" to "colored." [147] The Arkansas act includes within its definition of the term "Negro" any person who has any Negro blood whatsoever,[148] while the Florida statute applies to persons who are one-eighth or more colored.[149]

Evidence of prior and subsequent acts of interracial cohabitation or illicit intercourse between the parties are admissible to show formation of the relationship.[150] Moreover, such illegal relationships may be inferred from circumstantial evidence, eyewitnesses not being necessary.[151] In one Alabama case a

[142] State v. Daniel, 141 La. 900, 75 So. 836 (1917).

[143] Fla. Comp. Gen. Laws Ann. (Skillman, 1927) §7566. *See* Parramore v. State, 81 Fla. 621, 88 So. 472 (1921), in which it was held that the prosecution would have to prove that habit of living together had been practised within two years of the date of the indictment.

[144] N. D. Comp. Laws Ann. (1913) §9587.

[145] Linton v. State, 88 Ala. 216, 7 So. 261 (1889).

[146] State v. Treadaway, 126 La. 300, 52 So. 500 (1910). This decision was evidently influenced by the fact that the legislature, at the time when it was considering the enactment of the statute, had voted down a proposal to define the term "Negro" so that it would include persons who have one-thirty-second or more Negro blood. According to Daggett, *The Legal Aspect of Amalgamation in Louisiana* (1933) 11 Tex. L. Rev. 162, little attempt is made to enforce this statute, and the line between the races is very hazy and lacks legal interpretation which would reduce the matter to a certain formula.

[147] La. Acts 1910, No. 206. This act was a duplicate of the 1908 act except for this one change. However, since there was no reference to the former act, both are supposed to have remained on the statute books at least until the next codification. *See* Daggett, *op. cit., supra* note 146, at 173.

[148] Ark. Dig. Stat. (Crawford & Moses, 1921) §2603.

[149] Fla. Comp. Gen. Laws Ann. (Skillman, 1927) §7565.

[150] Smith v. State, 16 Ala. App. 79, 75 So. 627 (1917); Lewis v. State, 18 Ala. App. 263, 89 So. 904 (1921); Parramore v. State, 81 Fla. 621, 88 So. 472 (1921); State v. Harris, 150 La. 383, 90 So. 686 (1922); Stewart v. State, 64 Miss. 626, 2 So. 73 (1887).

[151] Lewis v. State, 18 Ala. App. 263, 89 So. 904 (1921).

white male's statements which tended to show his feelings toward a colored woman and his actions relative to her were held to be admissible against him.[152] But it has been held that he cannot be convicted on the unsupported testimony of his alleged accomplice.[153] In fact the Arkansas statute specifically provides that there shall be no conviction of the crime on the uncorroborated testimony of the woman.[154] Testimony that a white man had been seen to care for the mulatto child of a Negress has also been held admissible against him.[155] However, evidence that a Negro defendant was foolishly fond of women was said to be irrelevant.[156] In an Alabama case a white female defendant had made a statement that she did not have to work because her Negro beau kept her up and had admitted that she was his woman. This testimony was held to be admissible against her but not against her paramour, he having been absent at the time the statement was made.[157] In a Texas case a white man who was caught in a compromising position in a room with a Negro woman made a declaration that he had had no sexual intercourse with her. This declaration was held to be admissible under the familiar rule of evidence allowing such testimony to come in as part of the *res gestae*.[158]

Circumstantial evidence will not always be considered a sufficient basis for a conviction, and especially is this the case when the supposed culprits are able to bring forward other testimony which tends to explain the compromising situation in which they were discovered.[159]

Proof that the parties are legally considered as being of different races, one white and the other Negro, is of course essential to a conviction for the crime of miscegenation.[160] The Virginia Court has held that the prosecution must produce proof of how much Negro blood a defendant or his or her paramour has, and cannot succeed in its effort to convict the ac-

[152] Smith v. State, 16 Ala. App. 79, 75 So. 627 (1917).
[153] Jackson v. State, 23 Ala. App. 555, 129 So. 306 (1930).
[154] Ark. Dig. Stat. (Crawford & Moses, 1921) §2605.
[155] Lewis v. State, 18 Ala. App. 263, 89 So. 904 (1921).
[156] Cauley v. State, 92 Ala. 71, 9 So. 456 (1890).
[157] McAlpine v. State, 117 Ala. 93, 23 So. 130 (1897).
[158] Strauss v. State, 76 Tex. Cr. Rep. 132, 173 S. W. 663 (1915).
[159] Fields v. State, 24 Ala. App. 193, 132 So. 605 (1931).
[160] Metcalf v. State, 16 Ala. App. 389, 78 So. 305 (1918); Brown v. State, 98 Tex. Cr. Rep. 416, 266 S. W. 152 (1924).

cused unless it is able to show that he or she has enough Negro blood to be classified as a person of color according to the local miscegenation act.[161] The burden of proving that a particular individual is a Negro within the statute is upon the prosecution,[162] and the state officials in charge of such cases must prove this fact beyond a reasonable doubt.[163] However, an Alabama Court has said in one instance that it is unnecessary for the prosecution to fully trace the supposed colored person's antecedents, such proof being extremely difficult if not impossible to obtain in most instances.[164]

What evidence is admissible in attempting to prove the race of anyone accused of miscegenation or of his or her accomplice? Of course the technical rules of evidence complicate this matter to a great extent, but there are certain types of testimony which have been held to be acceptable. Thus it has been declared that either the defendant or his or her paramour may be brought into court for the purpose of giving the jury an opportunity of viewing the person in question and ascertaining whether or not the said individual is a Negro.[165] The same is true with respect to the immediate direct or collateral kindred of the person involved.[166] It is permissible to introduce testimony to the effect that the person whose race is at issue is in the habit of associating with one race or the other,[167] but such associations may be explained by circumstances or other evidence which shows that there is some other reason for the rather unusual social contact.[168] In one Alabama case it was held necessary to accompany evidence of the association of the

---

[161] Jones v. Commonwealth, 80 Va. 538 (1885).

[162] Williams v. State, 26 Ala. App. 53, 152 So. 264 (1934); Flores v. State, 60 Tex. Cr. Rep. 25, 129 S. W. 1111 (1910).

[163] Keith v. Commonwealth, 165 Va. 705, 181 S. E. 283 (1935).

[164] Wilson v. State, 20 Ala. App. 137, 101 So. 417 (1924).

[165] Linton v. State, 88 Ala. 216, 7 So. 261 (1889); Jones v. State, 156 Ala. 175, 47 So. 100 (1908).

[166] Weaver v. State, 22 Ala. App. 469, 116 So. 893 (1928). A conviction in Virginia was reversed because the prosecution failed to call as a witness the mother of the person whose racial identity was in question. It was shown that the mother was accessible. Jones v. Commonwealth, 79 Va. 213 (1884).

[167] Wilson v. State, 20 Ala. App. 137, 101 So. 417 (1924); Weaver v. State, 22 Ala. App. 469, 116 So. 893 (1928); Sunseri v. Cassagne, 185 So. 1 (La., 1938); Hopkins v. Bowers, 111 N. C. 175, 16 S. E. 1 (1892).

[168] Fields v. State, 24 Ala. App. 193, 132 So. 605 (1931); Marre v. Marre, 184 Mo. App. 198, 168 S. W. 636 (1914).

defendant's mother with a Negro man with proof of the time when such familiarity occurred.[169] Testimony to the effect that the former spouse of the person in question was white or colored, as the case may be, is admissible,[170] as is also evidence that the person has been treated by a Negro couple as their offspring.[171] It may even be shown that a Negro performed the marriage ceremony which is alleged to be illegal.[172]

A witness who is not an expert may be given an opportunity to state his opinion of the race of the party about whom the inquiry is being conducted.[173] However, a statement that the party looks like a member of either race has been ruled improper,[174] and the same has been held with respect to a declaration made in court that the person in question is a Negro within the third degree, that being the exact issue before the court and hence a conclusion of law.[175] Proof that one of the party's none-too-distant ancestors had kinky hair and other racial characteristics of the Negro has also been held to have been properly introduced.[176]

In a Texas case it is said that declarations of racial identity made by a person during appearances in court in a civil case are admissible in a criminal prosecution under the miscegenation statute.[177] This bit of evidence came in as an admission, an exception to the hearsay rule. Another exception to this same rule which allows declarations in respect to pedigree to be admitted has been said to apply in cases of miscegenation, [178] but such evidence is not admissible where statements concerning race were not made by members of the family of the person in question.[179] In one North Carolina case such evidence was held to

[169] Williams v. State, 26 Ala. App. 53, 152 So. 264 (1934).

[170] Locklayer v. Locklayer, 139 Ala. 354, 35 So. 1008 (1903); Bell v. State, 33 Tex. Cr. Rep. 163, 25 S. W. 769 (1894).

[171] Locklayer v. Locklayer, 139 Ala. 354, 35 So. 1008 (1903).

[172] *Ibid.*

[173] Jones v. State, 156 Ala. 175, 47 So. 100 (1908); Wilson v. State, 20 Ala. App. 137, 101 So. 417 (1924), *cert. denied,* 211 Ala. 613, 101 So. 423 (1924); Weaver v. State, 22 Ala. App. 469, 116 So. 893 (1928); Hopkins v. Bowers, 111 N. C. 175, 16 S. E. 1 (1892).

[174] Jones v. State, 156 Ala. 175, 47 So. 100 (1908); Moore v. State, 7 Tex. App. 608 (1880).

[175] Weaver v. State, 22 Ala. App. 469, 116 So. 893 (1928).

[176] *Ibid.* (photographs would also be admitted).

[177] Bell v. State, 33 Tex. Cr. Rep. 163, 25 S. W. 769 (1894).

[178] Locklayer v. Locklayer, 139 Ala. 354, 35 So. 1008 (1903).

[179] Reed v. State, 18 Ala. App. 353, 92 So. 511 (1922).

be inadmissible where the declaration was very uncertain as to the identity of the man who had had intercourse with the grandmother by whom the statement had been made, the act being attributed by her to some white man and not to any particular white man.[180] The court declared that in this instance there was a motive to pervert the truth.

Where the evidence is plainly provocative of the notion that the dark color of the person's skin is caused by an admixture of Indian, Creole, or South European blood, it is not likely that a case of miscegenation will be made out.[181] In one Alabama case it was said that the fact that a dark-skinned individual comes from Sicily is not conclusive evidence that he or she is wholly white.[182] The meaning of the term "Creole" in any given bit of testimony is a question to be decided by the jury under proper instructions from the court.[183] The term is subject to divers interpretations, one designating the French-speaking inhabitants of Louisiana and other near-by states, another indicating a people of the same kind with a slight intermixture of Negro blood.

When an issue arises concerning the race of any particular child of any illicit interracial sexual relationship, it is permissible to bring the child into court and allow the jury to view it.[184] Such proof is considered highly reliable and about the best possible under the circumstances. However, the color of the child is sometimes deceiving. There may be instances where the Negro blood will appear after many generations, although such cases are comparatively rare.

Children of illegal interracial marriages do not generally come within the purview of statutes legitimizing the offspring

---

[180] State v. Watters, 25 N. C. 455 (1843).

[181] Ill. Land and Loan Co. v. Bonner, 75 Ill. 315 (1874); Reed v. State, 18 Ala. App. 353, 92 So. 511 (1922); Bartelle v. United States, 2 Okla. Cr. Rep. 84, 100 Pac. 45 (1909). Of course this would not be true where the marriage of a white person with the race mentioned is prohibited and made a crime.

[182] Rollins v. State, 18 Ala. App. 354, 92 So. 35 (1922).

[183] Parker v. State, 118 Ala. 655, 23 So. 664 (1897).

[184] People v. Rabbit, 64 Cal. App. 264, 221 Pac. 391 (1923); Miller v. State, 103 Nebr. 591, 173 N. W. 577 (1919); Warlick v. White, 76 N. C. 175 (1877). If there be evidence that the person in question has Indian blood, his color may be referred to that source. Ill. Land and Loan Co. v. Bonner, 75 Ill. 315 (1874).

of void marriages[185] or statutes permitting bastard children to be legitimized after birth.[186] The usual rule is that decreed by the Nebraska statute which states that the issue of all attempted illegal interracial marriages shall be deemed illegitimate.[187] However, Indiana has enacted a statute legitimizing such offspring.[188] Where there is no statute outlawing such a union between whites and Negroes, the child has been deemed capable of inheriting property.[189] In one case from South Carolina it was held that the offspring of an illicit relationship between a white man and a female Negro slave, born prior to emancipation and before interracial marriages were outlawed in that state, could inherit property from its maternal grandmother, its mother having predeceased the same.[190]

The Georgia Court has decided that a Negro concubine has just as much right as a white one to make the white father of her offspring responsible for its care and upkeep in bastardy proceedings.[191] In a Maryland case it was shown that a bastardy statute provided that a white woman should go to jail if she failed to divulge the name of her illegitimate child's father. The state court held that this act did not violate the equal protection clause of the Fourteenth Amendment.[192] The tribunal cited the argument put forward by the Federal Supreme Court in the famous miscegenation case from Alabama.[193] It is difficult to understand why the court mentioned this decision, as

---

[185] *In re* Walker's Estate, 5 Ariz. 70, 46 Pac. 67 (1896); Keen v. Keen, 184 Mo. 358, 83 S. W. 526 (1904).

[186] Greenhow v. James' Executor, 80 Va. 636, 56 Am. Rep. 603 (1885).

[187] NEBR. COMP. STAT. (1929) §42-328.

[188] IND. STAT. ANN. (Burns, 1933) §44-107.

[189] Kennington v. Catoe, 68 S. C. 470, 47 S. E. 719 (1904). The marriage took place before enactment of law which prohibited interracial unions.

[190] Lloyd v. Rawl, 63 S. C. 219, 41 S. E. 312 (1902). The child was born before the repeal in 1872 of the statute under which the case was decided, and hence the status was determined before that date. The Georgia Court in interpreting a prewar statute declared that property in the form of Negro slaves could be transmitted by descent to the illegitimate offspring of a free Negro and that it did not matter that the mother of such children was a white woman, if such actually was the case. Bryan v. Walton, 20 Ga. 480 (1856).

[191] Smith v. DuBose, 78 Ga. 413 (1887).

[192] Plunkard v. State, 67 Md. 364, 10 Atl. 225 (1887). In this case a dissenting judge was of the opinion that the statute made a direct distinction on the basis of race and color and was therefore invalid. Plunkard v. State, 10 Atl. 309 (1887).

[193] Pace v. Alabama, 106 U. S. 583, 1 Sup. Ct. 637 (1882). See note 17 *supra.*

the two cases are not at all alike and present situations which are entirely dissimilar. The court evidently based its decision upon the ground that neither the white mother of the illegitimate child nor her alleged paramour, be he white or colored, was prejudiced by the fact that the statute did not apply to Negro as well as white mothers of bastard children. The court seems to be arguing the case from the standpoint of the Negro rather than of the white men and women who are directly involved. This is shown by the fact that the court asks how Negro mothers can be said to be deprived of equal protection of the laws because the statute does not apply to them. It is believed that the court's decision was erroneous. The statute makes a direct distinction on the basis of color alone and is therefore clearly within the prohibition of the equal protection clause as interpreted by decisions on other phases of the race problem. That a white woman is not prejudiced by the fact that the law does not include Negro mothers cannot be urged as a ground of distinction. Furthermore, we cannot overlook the fact that under this act white mothers of illegitimate children were made to divulge the name of the father or go to jail, whereas the Negro mothers were not forced to do so. This statute differs from the type of miscegenation act which penalizes the white person only. Courts have indicated that this type of statute, mentioned above, made a reasonable classification within the familiar doctrine that the equal protection will thereby be satisfied.[194] The Negro had not at that time acquired a proper sense of moral responsibility and therefore the classification was considered a reasonable one. It could not be said that the above bastardy statute was constitutional under this doctrine. What is reasonable about such an act?

Maryland now has a criminal statute penalizing any white woman who shall suffer herself to be got with child by a Negro or mulatto.[195] It is doubtful if this act could be supported today, since Negro women have become far more morally conscious than they were just after emancipation. Hence the application of this statute to white women alone would be less

---

[194] *Ex parte* Francois, 9 Fed. Cas. No. 5047 (C. C. W. D. Tex. 1879); Frasher v. State, 3 Tex. App. 263, 30 Am. Rep. 131 (1877). See note 21 *supra*.

[195] MD. ANN. CODE (Bagby, 1924) art. 27, §415.

likely to be approved under a reasonable classification argument.

A rather unique situation is presented in Louisiana, chiefly due to the influences and peculiarities of the civil law which forms the basis of the jurisprudence of that state. Thus, before the Civil War, a child of an illicit relationship between members of the white and Negro races was denied the privilege of legitimation by any method whatsoever, although the formal acknowledgment of such a child was especially provided for.[196] There is a difference in the results of the two processes in Louisiana, legitimation being far more efficacious as far as acquisition of rights of inheritance is concerned. The child of such a union between persons of different races was then precluded from proving its descent from the white father, but might make proof of its colored maternal descent provided the woman was unmarried.[197] Children who were not acknowledged by the white father were incapable of receiving any property from him by inheritance or certain other methods of transfer.[198] The acknowledgment was required by law to be in writing,[199] but this provision was eliminated along with the marriage bar when the state code was revised by the Reconstructionists in 1870.[200]

In this same year, however, the state legislature enacted a statute to meet the situation created by the numbers of children of mixed blood in the jurisdiction. This statute provided that parents might legitimize their natural offspring by notarial act before two witnesses if at the conception of such child there was no other legal impediment to the marriage of the parents than that they were of different races or that one of them was a slave.[201] Another statute provided that no acknowledgment

[196] Daggett, *Legal Aspect of Amalgamation in Louisiana* (1933) 11 TEX. L. REV. 162, 178. See also Succession of Fletcher, 11 La. Ann. 59 (1856).

[197] LA. CIV. CODE (1825) arts. 226, 230, as pointed out in Lange v. Richoux, 6 La. Rep. 560 (1834). See also remark made by a dissenting judge in Taylor v. Allen, 151 La. 82, 91 So. 635, 653 (1921), to the effect that the Code of 1825 merely prohibited proof of paternal descent.

[198] Robinett v. Verdun's Vendees, 14 La. Rep. 542 (1840).

[199] LA. CIV. CODE (1825) art. 221, as interpreted in Succession of Hebert, 33 La. Ann. 1099 (1881).

[200] See Succession of Hebert, 33 La. Ann. 1099 (1881).

[201] La. Acts 1870, No. 68, §1. This statute is now LA. GEN. STAT. ANN. (Dart, 1932) §4884.

shall be made in favor of children whose parents were incapable of contracting a valid marriage at the time of the offspring's conception.[202] This statute would seem to prevent the acknowledgment of children whose conception is the result of illicit relationships between whites and Negroes before the marriage bar was removed in 1870, as interracial marriages were illegal up to that date.[203] However, the court came to the conclusion that the act did not prevent the legitimation or acknowledgment of such children,[204] and in supporting its position the court declared that the statute would only apply to the children of incestuous and adulterous associations in view of the fact that the section of the former code[205] for which this act was substituted mentioned only these two types of illegal relationships. The court also mentioned the above statute of 1870 which permitted the legitimation of children of mixed blood by notarial act, and declared that this demonstrated that the public policy of the state was in favor of a greater freedom of action in respect to the recognition of these children. The re-establishment of the marriage bar in 1894 was held not to have the effect of nullifying the law with respect to acknowledgments of illegitimate children of mixed blood born prior to that date.[206]

The method of legitimation by notarial act is not exclusive of other methods of acknowledgment.[207] It is a sufficient acknowledgment if the parent signifies his or her intention of treating the child as the natural offspring of the illicit relationship, thereby showing a desire to admit the responsibility therefor, and it is permissible to prove such an intention by the con-

---

[202] LA. CIV. CODE (1870) art. 204.

[203] *See* Succession of Mingo, 143 La. 298, 78 So. 565 (1917).

[204] Succession of Colwell, 34 La. Ann. 265 (1882). See also in this connection Succession of Hebert, 33 La. Ann. 1099 (1881); Succession of Segura, 134 La. 84, 63 So. 640 (1913). In so far as the case of Succession of Davis, 126 La. 178, 52 So. 266 (1910), is contrary to this view, it is probably erroneous.

[205] LA. CIV. CODE (1825) art. 222.

[206] Succession of Yoist, 132 La. 309, 61 So. 384 (1913); Succession of Segura, 134 La. 84, 63 So. 640 (1913); Murdock v. Potter, 155 La. 145, 99 So. 18 (1923). In so far as the decision in Succession of Davis, 126 La. 178, 52 So. 266 (1910), purports to give the marriage statute a retroactive effect, it has been specifically overruled by Murdock v. Potter. Daggett, *Legal Aspect of Amalgamation in Louisiana* (1933) 11 TEX. L. REV. 162, 181.

[207] Hart v. Hoss & Elder, 26 La. Ann. 90 (1874); Murdock v. Potter, 155 La. 145, 99 So. 18 (1923).

duct of the parties.[208] However, it has been held that a white man's casual admission of paternity with respect to the child of a Negro woman is an insufficient acknowledgment, as there should be proof that he was in the habit of so recognizing the child.[209]

In one case the parents attempted to legitimize the mulatto offspring of such an illicit relationship by a marriage celebrated in 1865. The court ruled that the marriage was void and that it therefore failed to accomplish its purpose.[210] The law at that date was, as it had been at the time the children were conceived, that interracial marriages and the legitimation of the children of mixed illicit unions were illegal. The Reconstruction legislation had not then gone into effect. In another instance a marriage celebrated after the bar against intermarriage was removed in 1870 was held to have legitimated offspring conceived before the marriage and prior to the removal of the bar.[211]

As to children of such illicit unions born after the marriage bar was reëstablished in 1894, there has been no direct decision that they can or cannot be legitimized or acknowledged.[212] It is true that there are expressions in the opinions of the Louisiana courts which might lead one to believe that such a legitimation or acknowledgment cannot now be accomplished.[213] However, it must be remembered that the above-mentioned statute of 1870 is still on the books.[214] This statute would seem to still permit

[208] Succession of Hebert, 33 La. Ann. 1099 (1881); Succession of Fortier, 51 La. Ann. 1562, 26 So. 554 (1899); Murdock v. Potter, 155 La. 145, 99 So. 18 (1923). Contrary expressions in Minor v. Young, 148 La. 610, 87 So. 472 (1921), 149 La. 583, 89 So. 757 (1921), may be disregarded.

[209] Succession of Vance, 110 La. 760, 34 So. 767 (1903).

[210] Succession of Mingo, 143 La. 298, 78 So. 565 (1917).

[211] Succession of Colwell, 34 La. Ann. 265 (1882) *See also* Hart v. Hoss & Elder, 26 La. Ann. 90 (1874).

[212] Daggett, *Legal Aspect of Amalgamation in Louisiana* (1933) 11 TEX. L. REV. 162, 182.

[213] There is a statement in Barranco v. Davis, 138 So. 192 (La. App. 1931) to the effect that the issue of such a void marriage cannot be acknowledged. A dictum in Prieto v. Succession of Prieto, 165 La. 710, 717, 115 So. 911, 913 (1928) reads: "With respect to Article 204 [La. CIV. CODE ANN. (Dart, 1932) art. 204, being the same as LA. CIV. CODE (1870) art. 204, cited *supra* note 202] it has been held that, as long as the impediment to the marriage of white and black persons was removed, a child of such parents, who were incapable of contracting marriage at the time of its conception, may be legitimated; but, under the present law, no such exception can be made."

[214] LA. GEN. STAT. ANN. (Dart, 1932) §4884.

legitimation of these unfortunate children by notarial act, and hence it cannot be said without at least some doubt that legitimation or even acknowledgment would not be permitted. The state court has been very lenient in its attitude toward these children,[215] for it is evidently thought that they should not be too heavily penalized for the misdeeds of their parents. Hence it is doubted if the courts would take the view indicated in their opinions should the question be squarely presented. It might be said, however, that the above legitimation statute of 1870 was only meant to serve the special purpose of legitimizing those children of persons who in ante-bellum days had not been permitted to marry but were later allowed to do so. If this theory could be supported, then the statute would not apply to a child conceived after the marriage bar had been restored. However, it is also worthy of note that one of the present Louisiana statutes dealing with legitimation definitely provides that nothing in that particular act shall be construed to prohibit a white man from so recognizing his colored progeny.[216]

A child of mixed parentage who has been lawfully acknowledged by its mother may inherit from her[217] and also from its brothers and sisters.[218] However, the acknowledgment is absolutely essential to the acquisition of any such right.[219] In one instance the acknowledged and legitimated natural child of a union between a Negro woman and a man of mixed blood was permitted to inherit from an aunt who was also of mixed blood.[220] The legitimated child can claim a great deal more in this respect than an acknowledged one,[221] but it is not feasible to discuss the differences between the two in a treatise of this sort. In another case certain claimants of an inheritance withheld from the court the fact that they were their deceased white father's illegitimate children by a colored woman who had been a slave in Kentucky at the time they were born. The Kentucky law at that time made them incapable of receiving property by inheritance in such a case. The Louisiana tribunal held that the

---

[215] Daggett, *Legal Aspect of Amalgamation in Louisiana* (1933) 11 TEX. L. REV. 162. [216] LA. GEN. STAT. ANN. (Dart, 1932) §4883.

[217] Murdock v. Potter, 155 La. 145, 99 So. 18 (1923).

[218] Succession of Gravier, 125 La. 733, 51 So. 704 (1910).

[219] *Ibid.* [220] Succession of Fortier, 51 La. Ann. 1562, 26 So. 554 (1899).

[221] Daggett, *Legal Aspect of Amalgamation in Louisiana* (1933) 11 TEX. L. REV. 162, 175.

claimants had committed a fraud upon the court in attempting to conceal this fact.[222]

The above principles have been applied by the Louisiana Court in an instance where a white man made an effort to legitimize his mulatto offspring by an act of adoption. The children were the result of his illicit relations with a colored woman. A statute provided that no child who is incapable of acknowledgment could be adopted.[223] His ability to accomplish a valid act of adoption under such circumstances was questioned. The court declared that the test was whether or not a marriage of the parents would have been lawful at the time of the conception. There being no such legal impediment at that time, the court held that the adoption was sufficient under the law.[224]

Texas has found it advisable to enact a statute providing that no Negro shall adopt a white child and that no white person shall adopt a Negro child.[225] South Carolina makes it a criminal offense for those responsible for the welfare of white children to surrender such a child into the control, custody, support, or maintenance of any Negro except a nurse employed in the home of a white family.[226]

A very interesting case arose in Virginia in 1911. A white widow of a good family with white children married a man who had Negro blood in his veins. The marriage of a white person and a person with less than one-fourth Negro blood was legal at the time this union was consummated. The husband had Negro blood but not enough to invalidate the marriage according to the statutory definition of the word "Negro" prevailing in the state at that time. The white welfare authorities attempted to take the children away from their mother and place them in an institution for homeless white children. These officials argued that the children were entitled to mingle with persons of their own race. They attempted to show that the children were not mixing with whites in the home of their stepfather and were confined to associations with colored people. The evidence showed that there was nothing disreputable about the home of

---

[222] Succession of Taylor, 28 La. Ann. 367 (1876).
[223] La. Civ. Code Ann. (Dart, 1932) art. 214.
[224] Hodges' Heirs v. Kell, 125 La. 87, 51 So. 77 (1910).
[225] Tex. Ann. Rev. Civ. Stat. (Vernon, 1925) art. 46.
[226] S. C. Code (1932) §1446.

the mother and her second husband and that the children were receiving an education of no mean calibre. Having found this to be the case, the court decided that it could not justifiably take the children away from their mother or deprive her of her rights over them merely because she had married a man who was socially undesirable to a large portion of the white population.[227]

One commentator has remarked that the court was here confronted with a situation where a group of persons of mixed blood were considered Negroes socially but not legally, and that the problem could only be solved by the adoption of a statutory definition which would more fully represent and concur with popular sentiment.[228] He declares that the court was pulled in two directions—in one way by its duty to follow the law as laid down in the statute, in the other by its desire to respect the actual facts and circumstances surrounding the case. According to his analysis, the court would have been glad to have seen its way clear to take the children away from the mother and send them to a home where they would be associated with persons of their own race. He makes a point of the fact that the Virginia legislature, after the marriage but before the case was decided, had changed the statutory definition of the term "colored person." [229] After this change the statute read that all persons who have one-sixteenth or more Negro blood were to be considered as persons of color, and this remained the law until the statute was again altered in 1930.[230] He argues that this would at least give the court authority to treat the husband as colored for the purpose of deciding the issue of the childrens' custody, since he was at least one-sixteenth Negro. He also contends that the court should have used the broad equity powers it undoubtedly possesses in cases involving the custody of children generally. By the use of this power he seems to think that the court could have avoided overlooking what he evidently believes to have been the best interests of these innocent victims of a situation over which they themselves had no control.

This was an exceedingly difficult case to decide equitably, since so much can be said on both sides. The legal principles are

[227] Moon v. Children's Home Society, 112 Va. 737, 72 S. E. 707 (1911).

[228] Note (1912) 17 Va. L. Reg. 692.

[229] Va. Laws 1910, c. 357.

[230] Va. Laws 1930, c. 85.

clearly on the side of the mother. However, when one considers the peculiar social situation in the South and the sore plight in which these children would find themselves in a few years, one finds oneself doubting whether the court rendered a proper and just decision. Here is presented an instance where two currents of public policy converge into one another and clash, and the court, unable to avoid the issue, must decide which of the streams it wishes to follow.

Only one other point merits consideration here. In a case from Louisiana a controversy arose as to who should inherit the property of a deceased Negro woman who was the unacknowledged child of slave parents. The father and mother had "taken up" with one another with the consent of their master and without the least semblance of a marriage ceremony. It was shown that they had not cohabited after emancipation. The father had married another woman and had had children by her. One of the male offspring of this marriage claimed the right of inheritance from his illegitimate half sister. The court held that she was a bastard and that therefore the claimant could not inherit from her according to Louisiana law.[231]

[231] Jones v. James, 12 La. App. 224, 125 So. 761 (1930).

XI

MOB DOMINATION AND VIOLENCE

The freedom of the Negro was gained by means of war, and therefore it is quite natural that violence and strife should continue to play a part in the subsequent history of interracial relations. This is especially true when one looks back over the Reconstruction period with the lack of understanding on the part of high northern officials of conditions existing in the South at the time. When looked upon in the light of history, the excesses of the Ku Klux Klan were inevitable. Although its original purpose had been to combat the intolerable situation created by the carpetbaggers and scalawags, the Klan soon degenerated and became a lawless and undisciplined body of men bent upon violence which had little if any justification. The better class of whites soon recognized this and refused to participate in the depredations carried on in the name of the order. That the manifestation of the spirit of the Klan should continue to be present in the South is regrettable in the extreme, but time is no doubt the only efficient healer of wounds engendered by passion, prejudice, and injustice. One has only to visit a southern community at a time when some Negro is on trial for the rape or murder of a white person to obtain a vivid picture of the hate and passion and desire for vengeance which is often aroused in the hearts of the southern whites.

Nowhere is the spirit of mob violence so strong as it is in the courtroom or just outside while a person who is accused of some particularly heinous crime is being tried. The air is charged with an undercurrent of tension and there is a feeling of suspense, as if some exciting incident may occur at any moment. Under circumstances of this kind it is rather difficult for the jury or even the judge to escape being influenced by the feeling which permeates the throng. In cases of this sort the defendant may not be given a fair trial. Thus the appellate courts are sometimes faced with the problem of deciding whether a Negro has had a fair trial, free from the spirit of the mob.

An important case of this type occurred in Georgia just a

few years before the World War. A Jew named Leo Frank was indicted for the crime of murdering a girl. The circumstances surrounding the crime were extremely revolting, and there was a great deal of feeling against him all over the state. The trial was conducted in an atmosphere of tension and excitement. There were decided threats of taking the defendant out of the hands of the authorities and lynching him. The accused was found guilty and sentenced, and he appealed to the State Supreme Court. One of his contentions on appeal was that the trial had been dominated by the mob. The highest court in the state found that there was not sufficient evidence of this to vitiate the proceedings in the lower tribunal, and also declared that Frank had waived his right of appearance when the verdict was rendered.[1]

He then applied to the federal courts for a writ of habeas corpus on the ground that he had been denied his constitutional rights. From the federal court's refusal to grant this writ he appealed to the United States Supreme Court. A majority of that tribunal was of the opinion that if the trial could have been shown to have been dominated by the mob, then there would have been a denial of the due process of law guaranteed by the Fourteenth Amendment. The court therein recognized the existence of a federal right of freedom from mob rule at trials of criminals in the state courts. However, the court was also of the opinion that the whole procedure of the state courts, including the action of the appellate court, must be considered in deciding whether or not Georgia had actually denied due process of law to the petitioner. In accordance with this reasoning, consideration must be given to the fact that the state appellate court in the instant case had decided against the petitioner the very issue on which he had based his case. The court came to the conclusion that the petitioner had not been denied due process of law and therefore denied the relief asked.[2] One factor which greatly influenced the Supreme Court in reaching a decision in this case was the act of the appellant's attorneys in bringing up from the state courts that evidence which was favorable to their client and no other.[3] The testimony which was unfavorable

[1] Frank v. State, 141 Ga. 243, 80 S. E. 1016 (1914).

[2] Frank v. Mangum, 237 U. S. 309, 35 Sup. Ct. 582 (1915).

[3] See Schofield, *Leo Frank's Case* (1916) 10 Ill. L. Rev. 479. In this article

was not set before the federal tribunal. In this case the federal courts may well have been justified in refusing to interfere without the allegation of additional facts or reasons why the state appellate court's findings should not have been treated with the respect due them according to the principles of comity.[4]

A few years later another case of this same type came before the Supreme Court. Five Negroes were indicted for murder in Arkansas. The crime was one of the incidents that grew out of the Elaine race riots.[5] The defendants were convicted and appealed to the State Supreme Court on the ground that they had been accorded anything but a fair trial. They claimed that the feeling against them during the trial had been very intense and that the danger of mob violence had been great indeed. The state appellate court refused to disturb the decision of the lower court. It stated that the evidence of mob domination was insufficient to overcome the presumption of a fair trial.[6] In this instance the court admitted that the facts alleged as a basis for the claim of mob domination were true, but held that they did not constitute sufficient grounds for reversal. The Negroes then applied to the federal district court for a writ of habeas corpus. A demurrer, a form of pleading which admits the facts alleged for the purpose of ruling on the sufficiency of the complainant's alleged cause of action, was filed to the petition. The district court refused to grant the desired relief, and the petitioners appealed to the Supreme Court. That tribunal declared that the demurrer had admitted the alleged facts concerning mob

---

the author declares that the *scientia* of the decision is the test of due process in this connection, and makes the statement that the want of *scientia* in the lower court may be enough to authorize and require reversal by the state appellate court and yet not sufficient to authorize and require reversal by a federal court for want of due process. He believes that the want of *scientia* must be so gross as to shock the reason and judgment of mankind by crossing the line which separates judicial discretion from arbitrary power. He also makes the statement that due process is nothing more or less than an intellectual process of reason and judgment in the exercise of judicial discretion. He states that the dissenting justices had a very reasonable position in declaring that it was for the Supreme Court to set up a standard and then decide whether the proceeding in the challenged state tribunal comes up to such standard or falls below it. The failure on the court's part to do this he terms judicial abdication.

[4] See Notes: (1915) 28 HARV. L. REV. 793, (1923) 37 HARV. L. REV. 247.

[5] A good description of the circumstances surrounding the case may be found in Note (1933) 18 ST. LOUIS L. REV. 117.

[6] Hicks v. State, 143 Ark. 158, 220 S. W. 308 (1920).

domination at the trial at least for the purpose of showing that the trial had been unfair. Evidently a majority of the justices were of the opinion that the state appellate court had not exercised its "corrective process" to the proper extent. The court declared that in such an instance the federal court should decide for itself whether the facts alleged in support of the petitioners' claim were true and whether these facts could be so far explained as to leave the state court proceedings undisturbed. After an examination of the evidence, the court came to the conclusion that the whole personnel of the trial court had been swept on to the conviction by an irresistible wave of mob psychology. It declared that "if the case is that the whole proceeding is a mask—that the counsel, judge, and jury were swept to the fatal end by an irresistible wave of public passion, and that the state courts failed to correct the wrong, neither perfection in the machinery for correction nor the possibility that the trial court and counsel saw no other way of avoiding an immediate outbreak of the mob can prevent this court from securing to the petitioners their constitutional rights." Therefore it was held that the trial had been without due process of law and that the writ of habeas corpus should have been granted.[7]

It has been remarked that in considering the problem raised by these two cases the courts are presented with a twofold issue: First, was the trial court mob dominated; and second, if an affirmative answer is given to the first question, was the domination sufficient to violate the due process clause?[8] In determining this it is important to ascertain whether the decision in the state appellate court was also mob dominated. One commentator has found the attitude of the court in the two cases to be rather confusing,[9] and the decision in the Arkansas case has been adversely criticized in some quarters.[10] The decisions may perhaps be better understood by a consideration of the possibility that they might be the result of a shifting of the members of the court or of the shifting of the social outlook of some of the justices.[11] Another commentator has said that the criminal is hereby provided with just one more avenue of escape from the

[7] Moore v. Dempsey, 261 U. S. 86, 43 Sup. Ct. 265 (1923).

[8] Note (1923) 33 YALE L. J. 82.

[9] Note (1932) 31 MICH. L. REV. 245.

[10] Note (1923) 33 YALE L. J. 82.

[11] See Note (1923) 37 HARV. L. REV. 247.

hands of justice or at least a method of delaying its application.[12] However, this argument is somewhat specious in that it fails to take into consideration the fact that courts were established with the idea of obtaining justice, and that in a great many instances there is certainly a duty to protect those who are charged with heinous crimes from the spirit of mob violence which is sometimes present when passions are aroused. Nevertheless, caution and circumspection should be exercised in the use of the writ of habeas corpus in such cases.[13]

The most likely explanation of the seemingly conflicting attitudes taken by the Supreme Court in these two cases is that in the Arkansas case the defendant in the habeas corpus proceeding demurred, thereby admitting the alleged facts to be true, while in the Frank case he did not commit this error.[14] Furthermore, Frank's lawyers did their client no good by bringing before the court only that evidence which was favorable to his theory of the case. It is probably the better view in cases of this type to allow the federal courts to examine the facts on which the claim of mob rule is based in order to determine whether or not the allegation of unfairness is true, but consideration should of course be given the action of the state appellate court to ascertain the extent to which the "corrective process" described in the Frank case has been applied.[15]

In several instances the state appellate courts have reversed decisions of inferior tribunals because of mob domination at trials. Thus the South Carolina Court gave a new trial where a hostile crowd overran the courthouse during a murder trial.[16] The mob in this instance filled the space within the bar and immediately around the judge and witnesses so that the counsel for the accused was unable to see the jury until he actually addressed them. This demonstration was calculated to overawe the jury and force them to render a verdict adverse to the accused. The court evidently came to the conclusion that the trial had not been so protected against extraneous influences as to give the unprejudiced mind the impression of the fair and impartial

---

[12] Note (1923) 7 MINN. L. REV. 513.

[13] *Ibid.;* Note (1932) 31 MICH. L. REV. 245.

[14] See Note (1923) 37 HARV. L. REV. 247.

[15] *Ibid.;* Notes: (1923) 7 MINN. L. REV. 513, (1932) 31 MICH. L. REV. 245.

[16] State v. Weldon, 91 S. C. 29, 74 S. E. 43 (1912).

trial by jury guaranteed by the state constitution. In another instance of the same kind which occurred in Georgia perhaps two hundred of the audience in the courtroom became excited and began pouring over the benches in a manner which seemed to indicate that they were preparing to lynch a defendant charged with rape. Although the disturbance was quelled by the prompt action of the judge, the appellate court reversed the conviction which had been thereafter obtained.[17] The court declared that the crucial point in such cases is not whether the jury was actually influenced by these demonstrations, but whether such threats of violence were calculated to influence the jury in reaching its verdict. In this case all the jurymen made affidavits to the effect that the demonstration had had no influence upon them in coming to a decision, but the court dismissed this attempt to uphold the verdict by asking two very pertinent questions: Can anyone swear with certainty that such circumstances have had no influence upon him? Can any one of us tell just how much our minds may be influenced by the applause or excitement of a crowd which surrounds us?

In another case of this kind it was shown that during the trial of a Georgia Negro for rape a large mob had congregated in the courthouse square and had threatened to lynch the defendant. It is probable that the mob would have accomplished its purpose if it had not been for the presence of two hundred national guardsmen. The spirit of mob violence obtained to such an extent that the defendant, even if he had been acquitted, would never have been allowed to leave the courtroom without protection. The federal courts, to which the case was taken on a writ of habeas corpus, were quite evidently of the opinion that the state had not made its "corrective process" available to the prisoner.[18]

There are other instances of threatened mob violence at trials of Negroes for crimes where the courts for various reasons have declined to interfere. Circumstances are sometimes such that the appellate courts cannot be certain that the trial was anything but fair. In one such case two convicted Kentucky Negroes claimed that they had been tried in an atmosphere laden with

[17] Collier v. State, 115 Ga. 803, 42 S. E. 226 (1902).

[18] Downer v. Dunaway, 53 F. (2d) 586 (C. C. A. 5th, 1931). See same case in 1 F. Supp. 1001 (M. D. Ga. 1932).

the spirit of mob violence. They applied to the federal courts for a writ of habeas corpus. The Circuit Court of Appeals denied the requested relief because the preponderance of the evidence clearly demonstrated that the trial had been a fair one and that it had been conducted under the immediate protection of the state militia which had been called out to protect the defendants against unlawful violence.[19]

A good example of the above-mentioned "corrective process" is found in a fairly recent North Carolina case. In this instance a Negro was convicted of the murder of a young white girl under circumstances which suggested that there might have been an attempted rape, although there was no direct evidence that such had been the case. At the trial the accused was assaulted by the father and brother of the deceased with the evident purpose of taking him from the custody of the court and lynching him. The disorder was promptly suppressed and members of a military company were brought forward and formed a cordon about the prisoner. Thereafter the trial proceeded in an orderly manner, and in his charge the judge warned the jury not to be influenced by what had occurred. The State Supreme Court declared that it was not unreasonable to conclude that under the circumstances the impressive conduct of the trial judge had had far more influence upon the jury than the improper conduct of certain members of the audience. Therefore it refused to interfere in the matter and affirmed the decision on this ground.[20] This case illustrates the idea that the "corrective process" may be exercised in the trial courts as well as those of appellate jurisdiction.

Sometimes the fear of mob violence is so great that a Negro will confess that he is guilty of the crime with which he is charged. Whether innocent or guilty, a confession wrung from him under such circumstances should not be used as the basis for a conviction. In a recent case from Oklahoma an ignorant Negro, with the terror of an assembled mob in his mind, confessed to the crime of rape of a white woman. The trial was hastily held and the defendant convicted on the basis of this confession. The appellate court took a very just attitude toward

---

[19] Bard v. Chilton, 20 F. (2d) 906 (C. C. A. 6th, 1927). *See also* Carruthers v. Reed, 102 F. (2d) 933 (C. C. A. 8th, 1939).

[20] State v. Newsome, 195 N. C. 552, 143 S. E. 187 (1928).

the Negro and declared that under the circumstances the defendant could not voluntarily do anything, much less confess himself guilty of a heinous crime. The writ of habeas corpus requested by the appellant was therefore granted for the reason that he had been denied the constitutional guarantee of due process of law.[21]

This case was merely the forerunner of the far more important decision by the Supreme Court in the Mississippi torture case. In this instance three ignorant Negroes were suspected of murdering a white man. There was no sufficient evidence on which a conviction could possibly have been obtained except certain confessions which had been wrung from the lips of the accused men by brutality and violence amounting to torture. The state appellate court had ruled that these confessions were admissible in evidence because the counsel appointed by the lower court to defend the Negroes had failed to move for the exclusion of the confessions after they were shown to have been obtained by torture.[22] The Negroes' attorney believed that his motion of exclusion, made at the time the confessions were first introduced and overruled by a court not then cognizant of the way in which they had been obtained, was a sufficient objection to their admissibility. The appellate court, however, declined to adopt this reasoning. An appeal was then taken to the Federal Supreme Court, and that tribunal was of the opinion that the use of these confessions was a clear case of denial of due process of law. The court said that a "state is free to regulate the procedure of its courts in accordance with its own conceptions of policy, unless in so doing it offends some principle of justice so rooted in the traditions and conscience of our people as to be ranked as fundamental." [23] The court evidently realized that it would be a terrible miscarriage of justice if the contention of the state as to a technical point of this kind was upheld. It was a life and death matter to these poor Negroes. It had been through no fault of theirs that the

[21] *Ex parte* Hollins, 54 Okla. Cr. Rep. 70, 14 P. (2d) 243 (1932).

[22] Brown v. State, 173 Miss. 542, 158 So. 339, 161 So. 465 (1935). For antebellum cases where state courts protected slaves who were forced to confess, see SYDNOR, SLAVERY IN MISSISSIPPI (1933) 84-85.

[23] Brown v. Mississippi, 297 U. S. 278, 56 Sup. Ct. 461 (1936). See Notes (1936) 36 COL. L. REV. 832, (1936) 24 ILL. B. J. 359, (1936) 12 IND. L. J. 66, (1936) 20 MINN. L. REV. 821. *See* Chambers v. Florida, 60 Sup. Ct. 472 (U. S. 1940).

confessions had been allowed to form the basis of the case against them. It was their attorney's misunderstanding of the rules of procedure which had caused their plight.

A Negro who has been accused of any crime which arouses race prejudice in the community in which his case is to be tried should beyond a doubt be entitled to a change of venue if he can show that there exists in the said community such feeling against him as would prevent him from receiving a fair trial.[24] There are usually statutory provisions in the state law which can be construed to give such a right. It is doubly true where the prejudice has become so great that it manifests itself in threats of mob violence and lynching.[25] Similar principles govern the granting of continuances.[26] Thus a trial may be deferred a few weeks in order to allow the prevailing sentiment in favor of violence to die down. Where this is done, however, it is wise to remove the prisoner to a safer place of confinement or else station guards for his protection.

The usual procedure is to change the venue to some adjoining county, but sometimes it is necessary to remove the case further away from the scene of the crime. An Alabama statute provides for removal to the nearest county which is free from exception, this to be done only once,[27] and the constitutionality of this provision has been upheld in one of the cases growing out of the Scottsboro incident.[28]

Georgia has a special statute which provides that a judge of the superior court may on his own initiative or on the motion of the defendant grant a change of venue when in his judgment there is danger that a person accused of crime will be taken forcibly from the custody of the law and lynched or hurt.[29] A right of appeal from an adverse ruling on the supposed culprit's motion is expressly reserved. The statute also provides that the case shall take precedence over all others in the State Supreme Court and that a special meeting of the court shall be convened if it is not in session at the time. While it is mandatory

[24] Dorsey v. State, 179 Ind. 531, 100 N. E. 369 (1913).

[25] Uzzle v. Commonwealth, 107 Va. 919, 60 S. E. 52 (1908).

[26] Seay v. State, 207 Ala. 453, 93 So. 403 (1922); Fountain v. State, 135 Md. 77, 107 Atl. 554 (1919); Mickle v. State, 85 Tex. Cr. Rep. 560, 213 S. W. 665 (1919).

[27] Ala. Code Ann. (Michie, 1928) §5581.

[28] Patterson v. State, 234 Ala. 342, 175 So. 371 (1937).

[29] Ga. Code Ann. (Michie, 1926) §964.

under this act for the judge to grant a change of venue if the evidence brought forward by the petitioner reasonably shows a probability of lynching or other violence, it is primarily a question of the judge's opinion concerning the existence of such danger. In several instances the alleged criminals have failed to establish that there was any such peril.[30] In one case which arose under this statute the judge of the lower court refused to change the venue because he believed that the court officials could give the Negro defendant ample protection. However, the appellate court reversed the decision. It declared that this might be true and yet there might also exist a distinct possibility of mob violence.[31] It has recently been said that the evidence of danger need not be such as to free the judge's mind of all uncertainty and doubt.[32]

The fact that the militia has been called out to protect the accused from mob violence is not at all fatal to a motion for a continuance or a change of venue. In several instances it apparently has been used as an added circumstance to show that race prejudice really existed.[33] But the mere fact that the military was called, without more, has been held an insufficient ground on which to change the venue.[34]

Undoubtedly some weight will be given by the judge who is deciding on a motion for a change of venue to the preponderance of the affidavits brought before him to substantiate the claims of the state and the accused as to whether the latter would be given a fair trial in the county wherefrom he desired to remove the case.[35] In one Mississippi case, however, other evidence showing that there had been great danger of violence

[30] Wilburn v. State, 140 Ga. 138, 78 S. E. 819 (1913); Shepherd v. State, 141 Ga. 527, 81 S. E. 441 (1914); Nix v. State, 22 Ga. App. 136, 95 S. E. 534 (1918); Broxton v. State, 24 Ga. App. 31, 99 S. E. 635 (1919); Wilson v. State, 28 Ga. App. 574, 112 S. E. 295 (1922); Coggeshall v. State, 33 Ga. App. 613, 126 S. E. 568 (1925); Butler v. State, 56 Ga. App. 126, 192 S. E. 238 (1937); Griffin v. State, 1 S. E. (2d) 41 (Ga. App. 1939).

[31] Bivins v. State, 145 Ga. 416, 89 S. E. 370 (1916).

[32] Johns v. State, 47 Ga. App. 58, 169 S. E. 688 (1933); Geer v. State, 54 Ga. App. 216, 187 S. E. 601 (1936).

[33] Fountain v. State, 135 Md. 77, 107 Atl. 554 (1919); Mickle v. State, 85 Tex. Cr. Rep. 560, 213 S. W. 665 (1919); Uzzle v. Commonwealth, 107 Va. 919, 60 S. E. 52 (1908).

[34] Patterson v. State, 224 Ala. 531, 141 So. 195 (1932).

[35] Jackson v. State, 104 Ala. 1, 16 So. 523 (1894). In this connection see also State v. Wainwright, 119 W. Va. 34, 192 S. E. 121 (1937).

throughout the hearing was held to outweigh the sworn testimony of twenty-three persons who were of the opinion that the accused could be given a fair trial.[36] It has also been remarked that the court should certainly not be concluded by the affidavits or the opinions of witnesses but should look into all of the facts presented and decide for itself.[37]

Whether danger of mob violence really exists, as has been said above in discussing the Georgia statute, is primarily a question for the trial judge.[38] A new trial should never be granted unless it can be shown that the judge abused his discretion in interpreting the evidence or in disregarding the decided weight of the testimony.[39]

It has been suggested in one opinion that the same feeling of antagonism which prevents a Negro from receiving a fair trial in this type of case might also prevent him from obtaining witnesses to testify in his behalf at the hearing of his motion to change the venue, since it is quite possible that a certain type of person might be intimidated by the threat of the possible public reaction against such witnesses.[40]

Evidence of newspaper articles which would tend to arouse racial antagonism has no doubt influenced courts to hold that a refusal to grant a change of venue was erroneous,[41] but not all such articles are considered grave enough in their effects to require a reversal on this ground.[42] It was said in one of the cases which grew out of the Scottsboro incident that allegedly inflammatory newspaper articles, to justify a change of venue, must be of such a character as to mold public opinion in a manner calculated to stir up race prejudice in the particular locality

---

[36] Brown v. State, 83 Miss. 645, 36 So. 73 (1904).

[37] Ware v. State, 146 Ark. 321, 225 S. W. 626 (1920); Browder v. Commonwealth, 136 Ky. 45, 123 S. W. 328 (1909).

[38] Goumas v. State, 44 Ga. App. 210, 160 S. E. 682 (1931).

[39] Seay v. State, 207 Ala. 453, 93 So. 403 (1922). *See also* Goumas v. State, 44 Ga. App. 210, 160 S. E. 682 (1931).

[40] Browder v. Commonwealth, 136 Ky. 45, 123 S. W. 328 (1909).

[41] *See* Jones v. Commonwealth, 111 Va. 862, 69 S. E. 953 (1911).

[42] Collins v. State, 234 Ala. 197, 174 So. 296 (1937); Ware v. State, 146 Ark. 321, 225 S. W. 626 (1920); Holmes v. Commonwealth, 241 Ky. 573, 44 S. W. (2d) 592 (1931). The Ware case grew out of the above-mentioned Elaine riots and was decided by a divided court, the dissenting judges having a good argument for reversal.

where the case is to be tried.[43] In one instance where the appellate court ruled that there were no sufficient grounds for reversal, much emphasis was placed upon the fact that the publicity which had aroused feeling against the Negro defendants was in a newspaper in an adjoining county and not in the one where the crime was committed.[44] But the inference which is thereby drawn, that because of this fact the incendiary articles were less likely to create race feeling, is a very poor one. It can well be supposed that the circulation of this newspaper would include persons in the county where the deed was done, especially when racial antipathies are involved and the crime is the talk of the community.

In one Georgia case there was evidence that race feeling engendered by an alleged crime was very high, amounting to threats of lynching, and that the chief of police had spirited the Negro defendant out of town. The officer had forced the Negro to lie down in the patrol wagon so that the inhabitants would not see him. This was held to be sufficient proof to authorize and require a change of venue.[45] In another case from the same jurisdiction a group of white men administered a beating to a Negro sometime prior to his second trial for the offense with which he was charged. The appellate court ruled that the trial judge had erred in his refusal to change the venue.[46]

In a case from Alabama it was established that a Negro who was accused of rape was a soldier of a certain colored regiment, the members of which had committed so many crimes in the community where it was quartered that a deep-seated prejudice against its personnel had been fixed in the minds of the people. Efforts had been made to mob the accused, and incendiary articles had been published in the newspapers referring to him as "the brutal Negro who assaulted a respectable white woman." The family of the alleged victim resided in the county and she had many relatives and friends therein. In this instance the appellate court declined to rule that the judge's refusal to move the case to another county was erroneous.[47] This decision seems

[43] Powell v. State, 224 Ala. 540, 141 So. 201 (1932).

[44] Benton v. State, 108 Tex. Cr. Rep. 285, 300 S. W. 75 (1927).

[45] Newman v. State, 143 Ga. 270, 84 S. E. 579 (1915).

[46] Mitchell v. State, 55 Ga. App. 842, 191 S. E. 500 (1937).

[47] Thompson v. State, 122 Ala. 12, 26 So. 141 (1899).

a bit off color, as the evidence would appear to establish that the defendant could not be given an unprejudiced trial in that county.

In one case from Kentucky where a Negro was indicted for killing white men the only evidence in support of his application for a change of venue was mere irresponsible talk and the fact that some people believed that he would be at a disadvantage because of the race of his victims. It was held that the judge had not abused his discretion in refusing to grant the defendant's request.[48]

In a Texas case a Negro had been tried three times in the same county for homicide and the race question had been elevated to prominence in the community. It was shown that in one instance, where the mob had failed to catch another whom its members were desirous of lynching, one of the assemblage suggested that it would be a good idea to go to the jail and lynch the Negro who was awaiting his fourth trial. It was ruled that under these circumstances a change of venue should have been granted in spite of the fact that some of the witnesses who testified before the judge were of the opinion that a fair jury could be obtained in the county.[49]

In another instance a Georgia Negro proved that the mob which desired to do violence to him had been appeased only by an illegal promise of immediate conviction and quick execution made by the sheriff, an agreement which that officer did not deny. He alleged that the prejudice against him was so great that he had been prevented from using a good defense which it was possible for him to produce. He also claimed that he would probably be lynched if he were given a sentence of less than death. The appellate court decided that the testimony established beyond the shadow of a doubt that the trial judge had erred in refusing to grant a change of venue.[50]

The above cases show that the appellate courts are usually just in deciding whether a particular judge has been fair or unfair in ruling on these motions. In some of the cases analyzed above the courts may appear to be unfair to the Negro petitioner, but one must not forget that the burden of proving

[48] Stroud v. Commonwealth, 160 Ky. 503, 169 S. W. 1021 (1914).
[49] Smith v. State, 45 Tex. Cr. Rep. 405, 77 S. W. 453 (1903).
[50] Graham v. State, 141 Ga. 812, 82 S. E. 282 (1914).

prejudice in these cases is upon the accused.[51]

A peculiar case came before the Alabama Court during the days of Reconstruction. In a district which was inhabited largely by Negroes a white man was accused of murdering a member of that race. He claimed that false reports had been circulated and that there was widespread feeling among the Negroes that he should perish. The appellate court was of the opinion that the action of the trial judge in refusing to change the venue was not final and ruled that the appellant's motion to that effect should have been granted.[52] The facts of this case are certainly less strong than some of the above instances where the appellate courts in the South have declined to interfere with the adverse decisions of trial judges, the shoe pinching the other foot.

The Maryland Court of Appeals has decided that the discretionary determination of a trial judge in granting or refusing to grant a change of venue is not such a "final action" as will permit a review by that court under the appellate practice of the state.[53] In this instance the trial had not been terminated when the appeal was taken, and the court declared that it was not allowed to take up cases piecemeal.

A portion of the congressional reconstruction legislation authorizes the removal of a case to the federal courts upon a showing of race prejudice.[54] This statute has been construed to apply only to instances where the state involved has enacted prejudicial legislation and not to instances where the administration of the law is unfair to the Negro or where race feeling has been aroused by the action of individuals or is just the natural result of racial antipathy.[55]

In proceedings to extradite an alleged Negro criminal from the jurisdiction to which he has escaped, he may allege that

---

[51] Powell v. State, 224 Ala. 540, 141 So. 201 (1932); Norris v. State, 229 Ala. 226, 156 So. 556 (1934). [52] *Ex parte* Chase, 43 Ala. 303 (1869).

[53] Lee v. State, 161 Md. 430, 157 Atl. 723 (1931).

[54] 28 U. S. C. A. §74 (1926), REV. STAT. §641 (1875).

[55] Texas v. Gaines, 23 Fed. Cas. No. 13,847 (C. C. W. D. Tex. 1874); Folwkes v. Folwkes, 9 Fed. Cas. No. 5005 (C. C. W. D. Va. 1875); Thomas v. State, 58 Ala. 365 (1877); *Ex parte* State, 71 Ala. 363 (1882); Patterson v. State, 234 Ala. 342, 175 So. 371 (1937); Fitzgerald v. Allman, 82 N. C. 492 (1880); State v. Walls, 211 N. C. 487, 191 S. E. 232 (1937); State v. Smalls, 11 S. C. 262 (1878). Whatever is said contrary to this view in State v. Dunlap, 65 N. C. 491 (1871) *and* Gaines v. State, 39 Tex. 606 (1873) can be disregarded.

prejudice against him or his race is so great in the demanding state that he cannot be accorded a fair trial if returned thereto. The mere allegation that such prejudice exists, unsupported by proof, cannot be considered a good foundation for a writ of habeas corpus and hence may not be used as a defense in the extradition proceedings.[56] From principles announced in the jury cases, discussed elsewhere in this treatise,[57] one might be led to believe that the writ would not be granted even if the proof of prejudice was incontrovertible.

Attempts were made by Congress during the period of Reconstruction to protect the newly emancipated Negroes in the exercise of the rights which had been conferred upon them by the postwar constitutional amendments. A considerable portion of this legislation was without doubt framed to protect the colored men from violence and threats of violence on the part of their former masters. In most instances the statutes failed to accomplish this aim. This failure was caused in great part by the fact that the federal courts came to the conclusion that the Fourteenth Amendment authorized only corrective legislation aimed at the action of the states and their officials and not laws which were directed at the acts of individual citizens.[58] The statute known as the Ku Klux Act, which made punishable a conspiracy to go abroad upon the highways in disguise with the intent to deny to certain citizens equal protection of the laws,[59] was declared unconstitutional for this very reason in a case which came up to the Supreme Court from Tennessee.[60] Later the Supreme Court upheld a decision of a lower federal court which had refused to approve an indictment under the the federal statute[61] punishing a conspiracy to deprive a citizen of the enjoyment of any right secured to him by the Federal Constitution or laws. The indictment in this instance charged that a mob had taken a Negro who was accused of murder from the hands of the sheriff and a company of Alabama national

[56] Marbles v. Creecy, 215 U. S. 63, 30 Sup. Ct. 32 (1909); Blevins v. Snyder, 57 App. D. C. 300, 22 F. (2d) 876 (1927).

[57] See chapter on Jury, notes 159-161.

[58] *See* Hodges v. United States, 203 U. S. 1, 27 Sup. Ct. 6 (1906).

[59] REV. STAT. §5519 (1875).

[60] United States v. Harris, 106 U. S. 629, 1 Sup. Ct. 601 (1882). *See also* LeGrand v. United States, 12 Fed. 577 (C. C. Tex. 1882).

[61] 18 U. S. C. A. §51 (1926), REV. STAT. §5508 (1875).

guardsmen which he had summoned to his assistance and lynched him. The court reasoned that the deed was one committed by individuals and not by the state or its officers and that therefore it could not be punished under the said statute, the right here involved not being one which is secured under the Constitution or laws of the United States.[62]

A different result was reached, however, where Negro citizens were accused of larceny in the Indian country, a federal offense. The Negroes were taken from a federal deputy marshal with his connivance and lynched. The Supreme Court came to the conclusion that there was a right of protection from mob violence in this instance which was guaranteed by valid federal laws and that therefore the members of the lynching party were indictable under the above statute.[63] The court declared that the officer had the duty of protection thrust upon him because of his absolute right to hold prisoners who have been taken into custody under federal laws. This duty was said to be one which necessarily implies a corresponding right of the prisoners to be so protected.

In a case arising in Georgia a Negro woman brought a suit in the federal court against the chief of police in the town in which she resided, claiming that she had been whipped by him. She attempted to show that the court had jurisdiction of this offense under certain federal statutes. One of the acts under which she sued provides for the fining or imprisonment of persons who, under color of any law, statute, ordinance, regulation, or custom, subject any inhabitant to the deprivation of any rights, privileges, or immunities secured by the Federal

[62] United States v. Powell, 212 U. S. 564, 29 Sup. Ct. 690 (1908), *aff'g* 151 Fed. 648 (C. C. N. D. Ala. 1907). A demurrer to the indictment was sustained. The court herein refused to adopt the reasoning contained in the circuit court decision in *Ex parte* Riggins, 134 Fed. 404 (C. C. N. D. Ala. 1904), to the effect that the right was one protected by the equal protection and due process clauses of the Fourteenth Amendment and was therefore indictable under the conspiracy statute. The culprit sued out a writ of habeas corpus on the basis that the offense was not indictable under the statute. When the case was taken to the Supreme Court, however, that tribunal refused to consider the validity of the indictment because he had erred in his choice of remedy, habeas corpus never being used to correct errors of this type. The court declared a writ of error to be the proper remedy. Riggins v. United States, 199 U. S. 547, 26 Sup. Ct. 147 (1905). The Riggins and Powell cases grew out of the same set of circumstances.

[63] Logan v. United States, 144 U. S. 263, 12 Sup. Ct. 617 (1892).

Constitution and laws.[64] The other was the civil counterpart thereof, practically the same language being used except that the action authorized is civil instead of criminal.[65] The court, after dismissing the first statute because it authorized criminal actions only, held that the latter act does not empower a person of African descent to sue a white man for an unlawful assault committed under color of executive authority.[66] It was of the opinion that the rights of the individual to life, liberty, and property are primary rights within the proper protective sphere of the state in which the individual resides. Congressional legislation to protect Negro citizens against interference with such rights engineered by state and municipal officials would be a valid exercise of the authority conferred under the Fourteenth Amendment, the acts considered being well within the category of state action. Up to the present time, however, the national legislative body has never seen fit to enact such a law, no doubt believing it best to leave the matter for the states to handle under their ordinary criminal codes.

The comparative scarcity of state legislation dealing with this problem of mob violence against individuals is somewhat disquieting to those who are desirous that this sort of lawlessness shall be stamped out. Only twenty states have statutes which can rightly be termed antilynching laws. These jurisdictions are Alabama,[67] Arkansas,[68] Connecticut,[69] Georgia,[70] Illinois,[71] Indiana,[72] Kansas,[73] Kentucky,[74] Minnesota,[75] Nebraska,[76] New Jersey,[77] New Mexico,[78] North Carolina,[79] Ohio,[80]

---

[64] 18 U. S. C. A. §52 (1926), REV. STAT. §5510 (1875).

[65] 8 U. S. C. A. §43 (1926), REV. STAT. §1979 (1875).

[66] Brawner v. Irvin, 169 Fed. 964 (C. C. N. D. Ga. 1909).

[67] ALA. CONST. §138; ALA. CODE ANN. (Michie, 1928) §4939-40.

[68] ARK. DIG. STAT. (Crawford & Moses, 1921) §§2211-2217.

[69] CONN. GEN. STAT. (1930) §514.

[70] GA. CODE ANN. (Michie, 1926) §§362-365.

[71] ILL. REV. STAT. (Cahill, 1933) c. 38, §§537-549.

[72] IND. STAT. ANN. (Burns, 1933) §§10-3301-05 (Act of 1931), §§10-3306-11 (Act of 1905).

[73] KAN. REV. STAT. (1923) §§12-201-02, 21-1003-09.

[74] KY. STAT. ANN. (Carroll, 1930) §§1151a(1-6).

[75] MINN. STAT. (Mason, 1927) §§10,036-38.

[76] NEB. COMP. STAT. (1929) c. 148, §§1-11.

[77] N. J. COMP. STAT. (Supp. 1924) c. 130, §§1-6.

[78] N. MEX. STAT. ANN. (Courtright, 1929) §§75-125-28.

[79] N. C. CODE ANN. (Michie, 1931) §§1266, 3945, 4376-77, 4570-73, 4600.

[80] OHIO CODE (Throckmorton, 1929) §§6278-89, 12831.

Pennsylvania,[81] South Carolina,[82] Tennessee,[83] Virginia,[84] West Virginia,[85] and Wisconsin.[86] This enumeration does not include statutes which punish the participation in mobs and riots generally, nor does it include those acts authorizing the employment of prison guards or allowing the removal of prisoners from jails which have become unsafe because of threats of lynching, a discussion of which will be entered into later.

Seven of these states, Alabama, Georgia, Indiana, Kansas, Kentucky, North Carolina, and Virginia, make lynching a crime in and of itself. Four others, Illinois, New Jersey, Pennsylvania, and West Virginia, punish an act of the same nature under the head of mob violence, as does also the 1931 Indiana statute. New Mexico inflicts punishment upon those who assault a jail for the purpose of procuring the homicide of any one of the prisoners incarcerated therein, while Ohio punishes anyone who breaks or attempts to break into a jail or attacks or attempts to attack an officer with intent to lynch such a prisoner. Pennsylvania penalizes any attempt to take a prisoner from the custody of an officer, and in Kentucky attempted lynching is made a crime. Under the North Carolina statute a conspiracy to lynch is also punishable. A former Texas statute[87] punished "murder by mob violence" and authorized a change of venue in cases coming within its terms, but this act appears to be no longer in effect.[88]

The constitutionality of this type of antilynching legislation has been upheld in a decision from North Carolina,[89] and there

---

81 PA. STAT. ANN. (Purdon, 1930) tit. 18, §§331-343.

82 S. C. CONST. art. 6, §6; S. C. CODE (1932) §§1128, 3041. See also §§1380-93.

83 TENN. CODE (Will. Shan. & Harsh, 1932) §697. See also §§11602, 11603.

84 VA. CODE ANN. (Michie, 1930) §§4427 (c-h).

85 W. VA. CODE (1931) c. 61, art. 6, §12.

86 WIS. STAT. (1931) §66.07.

87 Tex. Gen. Laws Spec. Sess. 25th Leg. 1897, §§1, 2.

88 The exact date of repeal is elusive. CHADBOURN, LYNCHING AND THE LAW (1933) 27. In a case which arose only a short time after this enactment, Alexander v. State, 40 Tex. Cr. Rep. 395, 50 S. W. 716 (1899), this act was held to apply only to those persons who forcibly take a prisoner from an officer of the law and not to those forming an ordinary conspiracy to kill another because of malice. The language of the act was that they should "be guilty of murder by mob violence," and the court, although it considered the question, did not decide whether the act was to be interpreted as an effort to make a separate and distinct crime of "murder by mob violence" or only as providing for a change of venue in cases involving mob fury.

89 State v. Lewis, 142 N. C. 626, 55 S. E. 600 (1906).

can be no doubt concerning its validity in all the states which have adopted such laws. However, these statutes have never been well enforced, chiefly because of the difficulty of obtaining evidence. In such cases most people, even the best citizens, are disinclined to testify against their neighbors.

In most of the eleven states where lynching or murder by mob violence is a statutory crime the offense may be defined as the killing of a person by a mob. The ultimate accomplishment of the lynching would of course be unnecessary for a successful indictment under the above-mentioned New Mexico and Ohio statutes because of their peculiar wording. An attempt to enter a jail with the intent to lynch a prisoner would be punishable under these two acts. Kentucky defines the crime of lynching as a killing by a mob of a person in the custody of peace officers, while in North Carolina the definition is the entering of a jail for the purpose of killing a prisoner incarcerated therein. Thus both in Kentucky and North Carolina the victim must have been under arrest before the law can be invoked. In both jurisdictions mob action before arrest would not subject the members of the lynching party to punishment under these acts. In Pennsylvania it seems that the lynching must have been in default of the protection of officers of the law or the legally constituted authorities of the county. In Illinois, New Jersey, West Virginia, and under the 1931 Indiana act the violence must be committed upon the pretense of exercising correctional or regulative powers over the proposed victim or else with the intent to inflict injury upon someone charged with the commission of a crime.

While most lynchings which have occurred in the past have had as victims persons who were in the custody of the law or were charged with some heinous crime, it is quite possible that mob violence may occur which would not be covered by these statutes with the above limitations attached. Hence it would probably be better to adopt a statute with a simple and nontechnical definition of the term "lynching" which would not embody such elements and limitations as those noted above. A definition which would describe the offense as the killing of a human being by the act or procurement of a mob, as the Minnesota antilynching statute defines it, is no doubt the best practical solution of the problem.[90] Under such a statutory provision the courts would be free to determine in any given set of circumstances whether or not there has been a lynching, and in doing so would not be hindered by preconceived legislative ideas as to what the elements of the offense should be. Civil liability of members of the mob is specifically provided for by several of these statutes, and such liability would be the rule even in the absence of such a clause. Ordinary principles of the law of torts would no doubt allow a recovery here.

Five of the above states, Alabama, Indiana, Kansas, Kentucky, and Virginia, either specifically provide for accessorial responsibility or else employ language which is subject to the interpretation that such responsibility, before and/or after the fact, is created. The ordinary principles of the criminal law concerning accessories would apply where a statute contained no special clause covering the situation.

In one case which arose under the Virginia act, the person charged with the crime went to the home of the victim with a knowledge of the intent of the mob. When he reached his destination he called the victim out and delivered him to the angry gathering. It was held that by these actions the accused had subjected himself to an indictment under the statute.[91] This case involved a whipping and not a lynching. However, the defendant's conduct is evidently made punishable by a provision in the Virginia act making an assault and battery by persons composing a mob a felony. In Alabama there is a special statute which penalizes any two or more persons who abuse, whip, or beat any human being in order to force a confession of crime or other disclosure or to compel him to leave a locality where his presence is not desired.[92] Kentucky also has a special act punishing persons who band together for the purpose of intimidating, alarming, disturbing, or injuring anyone.[93]

The death of the victim seems to be a prerequisite of responsibility under the laws of these eleven states only with respect to indictments under the statutes of Alabama, Kansas, and Penn-

[90] See Chadbourn, *op. cit. supra* note 88, at 36.

[91] Hagood v. Commonwealth, 157 Va. 918, 166 S. E. 10 (1932). The victim's race is not mentioned.

[92] Ala. Code Ann. (Michie, 1928) §4938.

[93] Ky. Stat. Ann. (Carroll, 1930) §§1241a (1-5).

sylvania, and the Indiana act of 1905.[94] This difficulty has been obviated to a great extent in Alabama by the afore-mentioned assault statute. Death also seems to be a prerequisite to the county liability to the legal representatives of the person lynched which is established by the statutes of Minnesota, North Carolina, Pennsylvania, and South Carolina,[95] and perhaps the same applies to the similar Nebraska act.[96] It would probably be a good thing if this death requirement were removed, as there are cases where an injustice is done because of it. A man who had been beaten and crippled for life could not obtain redress from the county under these laws as they are now worded.

The liability of counties and/or cities for lynching or mob death and/or injury has been established by statute in twelve states. These jurisdictions are Connecticut, Illinois, Kansas, Minnesota, Nebraska, New Jersey, North Carolina, Ohio, Pennsylvania, South Carolina, West Virginia, and Wisconsin. The Indiana statute of 1931 contained such a provision,[97] but this provision of the act was soon repealed.[98] This sudden change in policy was no doubt due to an emergency which was created by the financial embarrassment of certain counties in which mob violence was quite prevalent at the time. An Alabama statute enacted during the days of Reconstruction made counties liable for any murder, assassination, or assault on anyone by outlaws, mobs, or persons in disguise.[99] This statute was evidently aimed at the activities of the Ku Klux Klan. The act was held to be a valid exercise of the state's police power,[100] but no trace of it can be found in the modern compilations.

Recovery cannot be had against a county under the Ohio provision without a showing that the mob had assembled for the purpose and was actuated by the intention of exercising correc-

---

[94] This does not apply to the Indiana act of 1931.

[95] *See* Brazzill v. Lancaster Co., 132 S. C. 347, 128 S. E. 728 (1925).

[96] Section 1 of the Nebraska act seems to include the death of the victim as a prerequisite to recovery, but see §8 where the words used are "killed or seriously injured."

[97] Ind. Acts 1931, c. 85, §§4, 5, 6.

[98] Ind. Acts Spec. Sess. 1932, c. 69.

[99] Ala. Laws 1868, p. 452. *See* Gunter v. Dale County, 44 Ala. 639 (1870); DeKalb County v. Smith, 47 Ala. 407 (1872).

[100] Gunter v. Dale County, 44 Ala. 639 (1870). *Cf.* City of Chicago v. Sturges, 222 U. S. 313, 32 Sup. Ct. 92 (1911).

tional power over a definite victim,[101] and the same has been said to be true in cases arising under the Illinois act[102] and the now defunct Indiana statute.[103] The same may also be said with respect to the Nebraska, New Jersey, and West Virginia acts. In North Carolina it seems that a recovery is permitted only where the county commissioners, after being informed by the sheriff that there is danger of mob violence to a person in the custody of the law, fail to authorize the employment of guards to protect the jail where the victim is incarcerated.

In South Carolina an action against a county for mob injury as distinguished from mob death is authorized, if at all, only where the victim has been interfered with in respect to the exercise of political rights guaranteed by constitution or statute.[104]

In Illinois[105] and South Carolina[106] the victim of the lynching party must have been charged with or suspected of some crime and must have been lynched because of such offense. In the latter state, however, it has been held that a recovery is authorized whether the deceased was a prisoner in the hands of the law or not.[107]

In another case from South Carolina a Negro shot a white man and then in turn was wounded by the latter's cousin. He was seized by a mob from the hands of the sheriff who had arrested him after a temporary escape. The mob carried the wounded man a considerable distance in an automobile and left him lying in the car more dead than alive and without medical attention. That night a Negro lodge burned down and an un-

---

101 Davis v. Bd. of Comm'rs, 8 Ohio App. 30 (1917); Lexa v. Zmunt, 123 Ohio St. 510, 176 N. E. 82 (1931); Hammett v. Cook, 42 Ohio App. 167, 182 N. E. 36 (1932); Reynolds v. Lathrop, 133 Ohio St. 435, 14 N. E. (2d) 599 (1938).

102 Barnes v. City of Chicago, 225 Ill. App. 31 (1922). CHADBOURN in his LYNCHING AND THE LAW (p. 33) says that the court's distaste for this requirement of specific intent is shown by the fact that it finds an ambiguity in another section of the act under which recovery is permitted. The case was reversed on further appeal on a different ground. See note 105 *infra*.

103 Shake v. Bd. of Comm'rs of Sullivan Co., 210 Ind. 61, 1 N. E. (2d) 132 (1936).

104 Brazzill v. Lancaster County, 132 S. C. 347, 128 S. E. 728 (1925), interpreting S. C. CODE (1932) §1384.

105 Barnes v. City of Chicago, 323 Ill. 203, 153 N. E. 821 (1926).

106 Green v. Greenville Co., 176 S. C. 433, 180 S. E. 471 (1935).

107 Brown v. Orangeburg Co., 55 S. C. 45, 32 S. E. 764 (1899); Green v. Greenville Co., 176 S. C. 433, 180 S. E. 471 (1935).

recognizable body with a cable around the neck was found in the ruins. This proved to be the victim of the mob. These facts were said to show that there had been a lynching and a recovery was allowed against the county.[108]

Illinois, Nebraska, and Ohio authorize a recovery by a county which has been mulcted under a statute of this kind against those persons who constitute the mob, and it has been suggested that a provision be added requiring that the sum paid out by the county shall be included in the next tax levy.[109] In Ohio and Nebraska the county where the lynching occurred may recover the amount of the judgment against it from the county from which the mob came.

In the absence of legislative action there is no responsibility on the part of counties or municipalities for lynchings or mob violence which occur within their borders.[110] Therefore a statute is necessary to the creation of any such liability.

It is most unwise to hedge the statutory remedy about with restrictions of the type mentioned above in connection with the North Carolina act. A recovery should be allowed whether the prisoner is in the custody of the law or not and should certainly not depend upon the county commissioners' refusal of the sheriff's request that he be permitted to employ guards to protect the prospective victim. The Minnesota statute, defining lynching as the killing of a person by a mob, is simplicity itself.

It is hard to judge the effectiveness of this type of legislation. There are so many factors which enter into a study of mobs and the spirit of violence. Thus, a county which had six or seven lynchings during the decade preceding the enactment of county-liability legislation may have only one in the next ten-year period. But what does this prove? Only that there have been more lynchings in the first decade than in the second. There may have been fewer occasions for the generation of the mob spirit in the second decade. The police protection may have increased in effectiveness or the sheriff may be a man who is not to be trifled with. Extraneous circumstances may have prevented the mobs from carrying out their purpose until tempers had cooled. These and other unpredictable factors may have

[108] Kirkland v. Allendale County, 128 S. C. 541, 123 S. E. 648 (1924).

[109] Chadbourn, Lynching and the Law (1933) 56.

[110] Wallace v. Town of Norman, 9 Okla. 339, 60 Pac. 108 (1900).

been responsible for the decrease. Hence the fewer lynchings may not have been the result of the legislation at all.

One argument against the desirability of this type of legislation is that it penalizes a community's more respectable citizens, who are usually the largest taxpayers, for the misdeeds of the rougher element who pay very little toward the support of the county or municipal government. A very good answer to this objection is that the more decent element in the community might thereby be made directly conscious of the evils attending upon mob violence. This element might be obliged for financial reasons to take more interest in the affairs of local government and the creation of a more adequate police force to protect the community against the mob spirit engendered by the influence which the excited utterances of firebrands have upon the public mind.

The Kansas statute provides that a municipality which is liable under such an act may show in mitigation of damages the bad reputation or conduct of the victim or the diligence and care which was employed in an attempt to prevent the injury. This statute is worded in such a manner as to cover all damages which occur in consequence of the destructive action of mobs. The word "mob" has received a very liberal construction by the Kansas court, and the statute has been held to be applicable in certain instances where it would appear that there had been little more than an affray.[111]

The West Virginia statute contains a provision which states that the action to enforce the liability of the county may be brought in any state court, and this has been held to change the common law rule that the action should be brought in the county concerned and to allow the suit to be brought in any county court which has jurisdiction of the subject matter.[112] In Pennsylvania the action must be brought in a county other than the one in which the crime occurred. In North Carolina the law provides that the superior court of any county which adjoins the

[111] See the folowing cases: City of Cherryvale v. Hawman, 80 Kan. 170, 101 Pac. 994 (1909); Moon v. City of Wichita, 106 Kan. 636, 189 Pac. 372 (1920); Wilkins v. City of Mineral, 109 Kan. 46, 197 Pac. 863 (1921); Hendren v. Arkansas City, 122 Kan. 361, 252 Pac. 218 (1927); Seigler v. Kansas City, 131 Kan. 504, 292 Pac. 937 (1930). See also Chadbourn, *op. cit. supra* note 109 at c. 4.

[112] Mullens v. Greenbrier County Court, 112 W. Va. 593, 166 S. E. 116 (1932).

county where the crime is committed shall have complete jurisdiction over the offense.

Texas has a special statute allowing a change of venue to an adjoining county in prosecutions for rape.[113] In cases of this kind, as well as in instances of lynching, a change of venue would be permitted in a proper case under the ordinary rules of law governing that subject.

In North Carolina and Virginia an official investigation of the circumstances surrounding a lynching is commanded, and in the former state the costs of this inquiry must be paid by the county where the crime is committed.

The Arkansas statute provides for the calling of a special term of court when any crime is committed which is calculated to arouse the passions of the community to such an extent that mob violence is feared. This act punishes the failure of the sheriff, after receiving a request from seven or more citizens, to apply to the judge for a special term when such circumstances patently exist. The statute has been applied in at least one reported case.[114] Arkansas is the only state which has this type of statute, but this manner of preventing a lynching is probably used a great deal in other jurisdictions under general provisions calling for special terms.[115] The idea behind this device is that no time shall be given for the generation of the mob spirit. However, there is the danger that the speedy trial of the accused will not be fair. Such a trial may result in a mob-dominated verdict.[116] It is easy to frown upon a device because in some instances it has failed to accomplish its purpose, but this method should not be wholly condemned because of this. One can think of instances in which this device would advance the cause of justice no end.

Pennsylvania and West Virginia specifically disqualify as jurors for the trial of such an offense all those persons who have participated in the lynching or have by word or action indicated that they approved of mob violence, and this would no doubt be the rule elsewhere.

[113] TEX. ANN. CODE CRIM. PROC. (Vernon, 1925) art. 207.

[114] Bettis v. State, 164 Ark. 17, 261 S. W. 46 (1924).

[115] See Chadbourn, *op. cit. supra* note 109, at 105. *Cf.* Dingus v. Commonwealth, 153 Va. 846, 149 S. E. 414 (1929). Special terms may be used in the trial of lynchers as well as their victims. State v. Hall, 142 N. C. 710, 55 S. E. 806 (1906).

[116] Downer v. Dunaway, 53 F. (2d) 586 (C. C. A. 5th, 1931).

In North Carolina it is provided that no person may refuse to testify in a lynching case upon the ground that his answers might tend to incriminate him, but, in order to meet constitutional difficulties, a clause is added promising immunity. This state also punishes witnesses for refusing to testify in investigations of lynchings. North Carolina also gives the judge authority to exclude all bystanders at rape trials, a very good precaution against the generation of the mob spirit.[117] This is done in other states also whether express authority is given or not.

There is quite a novel statute in Illinois which prohibits the manufacture, sale, exhibition, or advertisement of any publication or representation by lithograph, motion picture, play, drama, or sketch representing the lynching of a human being.[118]

The Kansas statute and the Indiana act of 1905 making lynching per se an offense against the state provide for prosecution by way of an information filed by the attorney general or prosecuting attorney. In Kansas this must be based upon the affidavit of some reputable person. Indictments are provided for in the Indiana act but no mention is made of this procedure in the Kansas statute. This is no specific provision for an information in the other statutes and the procedure is usually by way of indictment.

The antilynching statutes of Alabama, Georgia, Indiana, Pennsylvania, South Carolina, Tennessee, West Virginia, and Wisconsin make provision for either the criminal or civil liability of sheriffs or, in some instances, other peace officers who are at fault in the performance of their duties with respect to a prisoner in their custody. The Arkansas statute punishes the sheriff if he fails to notify the district judge of the need for a special term after he has received a request from the citizens of the county as provided for in the act. There may also be liability under general statutes punishing officers for a dereliction of duty. In fact, an Arkansas officer was held criminally responsible for a failure on his part to suppress a riot in an instance where a Negro was lynched by a mob.[119] That there is

[117] N. C. Code Ann. (Michie, 1931) §4636.
[118] Ill. Rev. Stat. (Cahill, 1933) c. 38, §458.
[119] Pennewell v. State, 105 Ark. 32, 150 S. W. 114 (1912).

a need for some such statutory requirement is shown by the fact that in one case the Maryland Court held that in the absence of malicious intent neither the sheriff nor his bondsmen were liable in damages for the death of a prisoner at the hands of a mob.[120] The evidence demonstrated that the officer was warned of the gathering of the mob and that the guard had been removed and the keys of the insecure jail given to an old and infirm Negro. The sheriff was also present at the outrage and offered no resistance to the mob. In contrast to this case, however, is an action initiated in the federal courts under a Texas wrongful death statute. In this instance it was held that a United States marshal was liable on his official bond for the lynching of a Negro prisoner by a mob where he delivered the victim into the hands of an incompetent deputy who was shown to have been in league with the mob, the marshal well knowing that the deputy was unfit for the duties which were thrust upon him in the emergency.[121]

Nine states, Alabama, Illinois, Indiana, Kansas, Kentucky, Minnesota, New Jersey, South Carolina, and Tennessee, provide for the removal of sheriffs, or in some instances other like officials such as deputies or jailers, when it can be shown that they were at fault in not sufficiently protecting a prisoner in their charge. In five of these jurisdictions, Illinois, Indiana, Kansas, Kentucky, and New Jersey, the sheriff is automatically suspended at the time the crime is committed and his place taken by the coroner, with provisions for reinstatement by way of petition to the governor in case he can prove to the satisfaction of that official that he has done everything in his power to avert the lynching. In South Carolina the law provides that the officer shall be deposed when the true bill of indictment is found against him. This ouster is, of course, subject to conviction. In Minnesota the same procedure as that provided for the removal of county officers is used. In Tennessee the removal follows conviction, while in Alabama it comes only after successful impeachment proceedings in the State Supreme Court. In the states where there is no automatic ouster at some time before conviction, the burden of proving that the peace officer was negligent or in connivance with the mob is evidently

[120] State, Use of Cocking v. Wade, 87 Md. 529, 40 Atl. 104 (1898).
[121] Asher v. Cabell, 50 Fed. 818 (C. C. A. 5th, 1892).

upon the prosecution.[122] Death of the victim seems to be a prerequisite to an employment of this device except in the three states of Alabama, Kentucky, and South Carolina, and possibly Minnesota.

The cases arising under these statutes which have reached the appellate courts are comparatively few in number. In one instance an Illinois sheriff was ousted for failure to protect a Negro prisoner.[123] In an Alabama case the court held that a removal was called for where a sheriff, notwithstanding the great public feeling against a Negro prisoner, failed to order his henchmen to close the jail's strong doors which had been provided for the protection of prisoners on just such occasions.[124] In this instance the mob had entered the jail through the basement and had seized and lynched its victim after overpowering the guards. The court of the same state came to a like conclusion in another case decided just two years later. In this case[125] the mob accused the sheriff of bad faith in respect to an agreement made with its members to turn a Negro prisoner over to the officer of an adjoining county. The sheriff either would not or could not show that the officer was coming on that day. The mob heard that the sheriff had telegraphed the governor for military aid and broke into the jail and obtained the guns which had been given up as part of the agreement. These guns had been left locked up in the jail but unguarded. Events finally came to a climax with the lynching of the Negro victim. It was held that the sheriff had neglected the "high duties" of his office and he was forthwith removed.

Such legislation is indeed desirable. Sheriffs and other custodians of prisoners will thereby be forced to accept a much greater degree of responsibility for the safety of their captives. It will stimulate these officials to take timely steps to disperse mobs. Sheriffs will perhaps make a greater effort to prevent the formation of angry crowds if they know that their jobs depend upon a strict observance of the duties incumbent upon them. Oftentimes an officer can employ measures which

---

[122] This was also the case in Indiana until the passage of the 1931 act. *See* State *ex rel.* Maxwell v. Dudley, 161 Ind. 431, 68 N. E. 899 (1903).

[123] State *ex rel.* Davis v. Nellis, 249 Ill. 12, 94 N. E. 165 (1911).

[124] State *ex rel.* Garber v. Cazalas, 162 Ala. 210, 50 So. 296 (1909).

[125] State *ex rel.* Att'y Gen. v. Jinwright, 172 Ala. 340, 55 So. 541 (1911).

will prevent mob violence if he is sufficiently alert. It is therefore believed that other states should enact laws of this kind. The best type of statute is probably that which vacates the office immediately and throws the burden upon the sheriff to show that he has not been careless in carrying out the duties which an election to the office entails. Too often there is an attitude among police officers that the upholding of the majesty of the law in a case where a suspected Negro's life is threatened is not worth the risk of one's life. Such an attitude should disqualify a man from holding such an office of trust. The responsibility of the sheriff should not be dependent upon his having custody of the prospective victim, as is now the case in all the states which have this type of legislation. The custody requirement is bad because it tends to make officers none too diligent in making arrests of suspected criminals who are apt to be the victims of lynching parties. It is very easy for a sheriff to sit back and do nothing while a mob is doing its work. Therefore a provision might be added making the officer responsible in this situation. In those states which have the automatic removal, however, the custody requirement should be kept for that purpose only, as the burden of proof of nonfeasance of the type mentioned above should be upon the state. In these states a clause could be added making the distinction between the effects of custody and non-custody in this respect. A statute embodying this change in the rules of evidence, depending upon whether the officer had custody, ought not to be too difficult to frame.

In one case from Tennessee a Negro had been convicted of rape and had appealed to the Federal Supreme Court on the ground that he had been denied due process and equal protection of the laws. While the hearing was pending, the prisoner was lynched and the sheriff and his deputies and the jailer were all shown to have been neglectful of their duties in not doing all that lay within their power to prevent the crime. There was also evidence of complicity with the mob. The Supreme Court held that this conduct constituted contempt of a federal court and that the officers should be punished accordingly.[126] The only reported case which at all resembles this one is a decision

[126] United States v. Ship, 203 U. S. 563, 27 Sup. Ct. 165 (1906), 214 U. S. 386, 29 Sup. Ct. 637 (1909).

by a federal court in Florida that an attorney may be disbarred for participating in a lynching.[127]

Two other methods of combating lynching cannot be overlooked. Kentucky in its mob injury statute provides for rewards to be offered by the governor or county judge for information concerning the identity of offenders which will lead to a conviction.[128] It is doubted if this method will lead to many convictions because of the disinclination of persons who may or may not be in sympathy with the lynchers to inform against them. There is also the fear that members of the mob will wreak vengeance upon anyone who has the audacity to become an informer. However, it is possible that the device might be used in some instances with desirable effect. The other device which it is believed deserves specific mention is the increase in the bail bond. A person who was accused of a bailable offense might well be released on bond only to meet death at the hands of a mob. In one instance the Louisiana Court seems to have approved of this device.[129] It declared that such action on the part of a judge would no doubt be expedient in a proper case, but denied that an increase of the bond from five hundred to five thousand dollars was called for by the circumstances of the instant case. The danger of mob violence to the Negro defendant was not shown to have been so great as to allow such an extraordinary increase.

A mob as mentioned in these antilynching statutes can be defined generally as a collection of persons assembled for the unlawful purpose of injuring any individual by violence and without lawful authority. Of course the definitions of the term vary, and in some of the states it is provided, as seen above, that the act must be committed in the exercise of correctional or regulative power. The statutes differ with respect to the minimum number of persons necessary to constitute a mob. The number varies from one to five, and some of the states have no specific minimum figures. In North Carolina the act is worded in such a manner that one man might be guilty of the crime. In those states which have no minimum figures the statutes usually mention a "collection of persons," although in several acts

[127] *In re* Wall, 13 Fed. 814 (C. C. S. D. Fla. 1882).

[128] KY. STAT. ANN. (Carroll, 1930) §1241a-5.

[129] State v. Richardson, 176 La. 750, 146 So. 737 (1933).

a definition is not even attempted. In South Carolina there are two decisions in which the court has discussed and explained the term. In the first of these cases it was declared that the word "mob" as used in the state constitutional provision concerning the penalties for lynching is synonymous with the term "unlawful assemblage of persons" employed therein.[130] In the other the court approved a judge's charge to a jury in which he defined the term as meaning a group of more than one person assembled together and participating in an act which is in violation of the law.[131] In a case from Ohio where the mob had assembled out of mere curiosity it was held that the motive of the gathering is immaterial where all the elements of a lynching are present, and a charge to the jury which was subject to an opposite interpretation received the disapproval of the court on appeal.[132] The Kansas Court rendered a like decision in a case which involved a "Kangaroo Court" formed by fellow prisoners who were jailed with the victim after an affray in which they had all participated. The court declared that "the circumstances that the persons did not voluntarily come into the jail and did not originally assemble there to whip the plaintiff does not put them outside the definition of a mob. The manner of their coming together or the primary purpose for which they assembled is not material if they, in fact, formed the unlawful purpose and became riotous after they were brought together." [133]

Why should legislators attempt to put limitations of the kind noted above with respect to the meaning of such an indefinite and uncertain term as "mob"? Why not simplify the statute by leaving out these frills? The courts could then decide in each case whether or not there had been a mob without being limited by the type of detailed statute mentioned above. The Minnesota statute again is recommended for its simplicity in this respect.

Under the lynching laws of Georgia, Indiana, and Kansas, the mob injury statute of Kentucky, and the jail assault act in New Mexico, an officer may demand the assistance of ordinary

[130] Cantey v. Clarendon County, 101 S. C. 141, 85 S. E. 228 (1915).

[131] Best v. Barnwell County, 114 S. C. 123, 103 S. E. 479 (1920).

[132] Bd. of Comm'rs of Champaign County v. Church, 62 Ohio St. 318, 57 N. E. 50 (1900).

[133] Blakeman v. City of Wichita, 93 Kan. 444, 144 Pac. 816 (1914).

citizens to aid him in the prevention or suppression of mob violence. A failure on the part of anyone to answer his summons is punishable as a misdemeanor. A special South Carolina statute gives the sheriff authority to call out the *posse comitatus* to his aid with provision for punishment if anyone refuses to obey.[134] The Indiana and Kansas acts also contain provisions which specifically give the sheriff power to call on the governor for military aid if he believes the situation is getting out of hand, and this may be done in other states also. Georgia has a special act authorizing the commanding officer of such a military force guarding a prisoner to prescribe a reasonable area in the neighborhood of the jail where he is confined within which persons may not venture.[135]

There have been many lynchings prevented by a timely request for troops. However, it is sometimes very difficult for the ordinary civil authorities to ascertain just when to call in military aid. Mobs are sometimes very quick and silent about gathering. Officers are usually reluctant about calling for aid of this kind, and they often refuse to believe that the danger is acute until some overt act occurs. Then the officer may hate to call for aid of this kind because of political considerations or because of his belief that his civil guards are sufficient to handle any situation which may develop. Furthermore, the calling in of the militia has sometimes led to dire results. In one interesting case from Alabama members of a military unit which had been sent into a strike zone to keep order lynched a Negro who had had some trouble with one of their number. And the subsequent history of this case shows that a conviction of the culprits for murder was reversed on appeal.[136] However, a device which has shown such good results in so many instances should not be condemned because it has led to dire results in a few isolated cases.

There are also other devices which may be employed to protect prisoners who are in grave danger of being lynched. Twenty states specifically authorize the employment of guards to protect prisoners in the custody of the law.[137] In Kentucky

[134] S. C. CODE (1932) §1952. [135] GA. CODE ANN. (Michie, 1926) §1467 (88).

[136] Lancaster v. State, 214 Ala. 2, 76, 106 So. 609, 617 (1925).

[137] These states are as follows: ALA. CODE ANN. (Michie, 1928) §4817 (applies only where prisoner is being transferred to another county); ARIZ. REV. CODE

a statute directs that the prisoners in a jail which is about to be attacked by a mob may be provided with weapons with which to protect themselves,[138] a device which can be criticized as being too dangerous in most instances but which might be employed in a case where adequate protection could not be afforded in any other manner.

Thirty-one states either expressly or impliedly authorize the removal of prisoners from an insecure or unsafe jail in which they are threatened with mob violence to jails in adjoining counties or in a few instances to other prisons.[139] Some of these statutes merely state that a removal is authorized where there is danger that the jail is insufficient, but this language would surely be interpreted as giving local officers authority to transport prospective victims of would-be lynchers to a place of

ANN. (Struckmeyer, 1928) §5342; ARK. DIG. STAT. (Crawford & Moses, 1921) §6217; CAL. PEN. CODE (Deering, 1931) §1610; COLO. STAT. ANN. (Mills, 1930) §4146; IDAHO CODE ANN. (1932) §20-614; ILL. REV. STAT. (Cahill, 1933) c. 75, §13; KY. STAT. ANN. (Carroll, 1930) §2044; MISS. CODE ANN. (1930) §3336; MO. REV. STAT. (1929) §§8543-44; MONT. REV. CODES (1921) §12,481; N. C. CODE ANN. (Michie, 1931) §3945; OKLA. COMP. STAT. (1921) §6340; R. I. GEN. LAWS (1923) §6451; S. C. CODE (1932) §1952; TENN. CODE (Will. Shan. & Harsh, 1932) §§11,986-88 (§11,892 in removal from jail); TEX. ANN. REV. CIV. STAT. (Vernon, 1925) art. 6871; UTAH REV. STAT. ANN. (1933) §19-19-17; VA. CODE ANN. (Michie, 1930) §4954; W. VA. CODE (1931) c. 7, art. 8, §6.

[138] KY. STAT. ANN. (Carroll, 1930) §1241a-4.

[139] ALA. CODE ANN. (Michie, 1928) §4816; ARIZ. REV. CODE ANN. (Struckmeyer, 1928) §5337; ARK. DIG. STAT. (Crawford & Moses, 1921) §6218; CAL. PEN. CODE (Deering, 1931) §1603; COLO. STAT. ANN. (Mills, 1930) §4143; FLA. COMP. GEN. LAWS (Skillman, 1927) §8541; IDAHO CODE ANN. (1932) §20-607; ILL. REV. STAT. (Cahill, 1933) c. 75, §10; IND. STAT. ANN. (Burns, 1933) §9-1023; IOWA CODE (1931) §13,965; KAN. REV. STAT. (1923) §§19-1916, 21-1008 (latter statute provides for removal to state prison or reformatory); KY. STAT. ANN. (Carroll, 1930) §2238-40, 2240a(1-3) (later statute authorizes removal to penitentiary or reformatory); LA. CODE CRIM. PROC. ANN. (Dart, 1932) art. 1390; ME. REV. STAT. (1930) c. 94, §46; MICH. COMP. LAWS (1929) §17,703; MISS. CODE ANN. (1930) §1256; MO. REV. STAT. (1929) §8545; MONT. REV. CODES (1921) §12,474; NEV. COMP. LAWS (Hillyer, 1929) §11,529; N. H. PUB. LAWS, (1926) c. 397, §§17, 30; N. J. COMP. STAT. (1911) p. 1876, §170; N. M. STAT. ANN. (Courtright, 1929) §75-118; N. Y. CONSOL. LAWS (Cahill, 1930) c. 10b, §504; N. D. COMP. LAWS ANN. (1913) §11,356; OHIO CODE (Throckmorton, 1929) §3170; R. I. GEN. LAWS (1923) §§6447-50; TENN. CODE (Will. Shan & Harsh, 1932) §§11,989-91; TEX. ANN. REV. CIV. STAT. (Vernon, 1925) art. 5118; VT. PUB. LAWS (1933) §§8812, 8826; VA. CODE ANN. (Michie, 1930) §2872; WIS. STAT. (1931) §55.04. There are statutes in other states which might possibly be given a construction which would allow a prisoner to be removed to a place of safety in time of stress, a good example of which is CONN. GEN. STAT. (1930) §2014.

safety, a very common device employed even in jurisdictions where there is no statutory authorization.

A study of the state statutes involving lynching and mob violence would be incomplete without at least some mention of the anti-Ku Klux legislation of 1924 in Louisiana.[140] The most important provisions of this act prohibit people from going about the streets or other places wearing hoods or masks, excepting certain holidays such as Halloween and Mardi gras, and punish certain acts engaged in by those who go about the country disguised in this manner and commit depredations on the community. In one Oklahoma case it is said that courts will take judicial notice of the negrophobe attitude of unfriendly organizations like the Klan.[141]

There has been much agitation in late years for a federal antilynching law which would permit the federal courts to punish lynchers and delinquent officers and penalize any county where a lynching occurred.[142] Southern senators and representatives have always stood ready to filibuster any such legislation by Congress. Senator Borah has been one of the more recent bitter opponents of this type of legislation. His opposition is based upon the ground that the proposed act would be unconstitutional as a usurpation of the powers of the states. This question is as yet a moot one and has been much argued by lawyers and laymen alike.[143]

In the meantime lynching seems fortunately to be steadily declining. According to the records of Tuskegee Institute only three lynchings occurred in 1939. Many factors are responsible for this decline, among them the educational work of the Southern Commission on Interracial Coöperation, the condemnation of lynching by influential editors and other persons in public life in the South, and the growing spirit of liberalism in southern thought.

---

[140] LA. CODE CRIM. PROC. ANN. (Dart, 1932) arts. 871-884.

[141] Johnson v. State, 28 Okla. Cr. Rep. 254, 230 Pac. 525 (1924).

[142] Dyer Bill of 1920 & 1922. See HOUSE REP. 71, 68th Cong., 1st Sess., 16.

[143] See the following: Dyer, *The Constitutionality of a Federal Anti-Lynching Bill* (1928) 13 ST. LOUIS L. REV. 186; MERTINS, HAS THE UNITED STATES THE POWER TO PROSECUTE "LYNCHING" AS A FEDERAL CRIME WITHOUT AN AMENDMENT TO THE CONSTITUTION (1921); *Lynching and Federal Law* (Jan. 1905) 40 CHAUTAUQUAN 408; Note (1938) 38 COL. L. REV. 199.

XII

RACE DISCRIMINATION IN THE SELECTION OF JURIES

Before the Civil War and the adoption of the Fourteenth Amendment there was no provision in the Federal Constitution which would prevent the states from enacting statutes specifically excluding Negroes from service on grand or petit juries.[1] There were no Negro jurors in the South during this period, for state laws or customs prohibited such participation in the judicial process.[2] The amendment guarantees to the Negro equal protection of the laws, the privileges and immunities of citizenship, and the right not to be deprived by the states of life, liberty, or property without due process of law. The equal protection clause is the principal provision which must be considered in analyzing this problem, as most of the cases which discuss the subject are decided on the theory that this guarantee has or has not been violated. However, in a few instances the courts have based their decisions on the application of the due process clause to the particular situation presented. The problem is not confined to the Negro, and therefore cases dealing with discrimination against other races[3] in this manner will be discussed. The same principles apply to these cases that are pertinent to the similar problem with respect to the Negro. Of course the overwhelming majority of the cases concerning this phase of the Negro problem come from the southern and border states, but there have been a few instances of this sort of discrimination in the eastern and northern states as well. The same principles of substantive law govern the grand and petit juries with respect to the Negro,[4] and hence there will be no effort to

---

[1] *See* State v. Taylor, 61 N. C. 508 (1868); Pauska v. Daus, 31 Tex. 67 (1868).

[2] See statement in State v. Brown, 10 Ark. 78 (1849) to the effect that an Arkansas statute provided that every grand juror must be a free white male citizen.

[3] Morris v. State, 62 Okla. Cr. Rep. 337, 71 P. (2d) 514 (1937) (Indians); Juarez v. State, 102 Tex. Cr. Rep. 297, 277 S. W. 1091 (1925) (Mexicans).

[4] Pierre v. Louisiana, 306 U. S. 354, 59 Sup. Ct. 536 (1939).

set off one group of decisions from another because of differences between the two in this respect.

One of the first really important decisions concerning the problem of racial discrimination against Negroes with respect to juries was the *Strauder* case[5] from West Virginia. The Federal Supreme Court held that a state statute[6] expressly restricting jury service to whites clearly violated the equal protection guarantee of the Fourteenth Amendment and was therefore invalid. The court also held that a portion of the Reconstruction legislation[7] which authorized a removal to the federal courts in cases of discrimination was a proper exercise of the authority conferred by the amendment and that it had been properly employed in this instance. In the same year, however, the Supreme Court ruled that the latter statute applied only in those instances where there has been racial discrimination by state statute or constitutional provision and not where the discrimination is practised by state agencies or individuals acting in an official capacity.[8] It was declared that the wording of the act was not subject to a broader interpretation.

This case has been followed in numerous decisions of the state and federal courts.[9] The state statute of Kentucky excluding Negroes from juries had been declared unconstitutional by the state appellate court[10] in accordance with the principles announced in the *Strauder* case. In a case arising in that state the Supreme Court declared that there was no valid law in existence which on its face discriminated against the Negro and therefore

[5] Strauder v. West Virginia, 100 U. S. 303 (1879), *rev'g* 11 W. Va. 745 (1877).

[6] W. Va. Acts 1872-73, p. 102.

[7] 28 U. S. C. A. §74 (1926), Rev. Stat. §641 (1875).

[8] Virginia v. Rives, 100 U. S. 313 (1879), rev'g *Ex parte* Reynolds, 20 Fed. Cas. No. 11,720 (C. C. W. D. Va. 1878).

[9] Gibson v. Mississippi, 162 U. S. 565, 16 Sup. Ct. 904 (1896), *aff'g* 17 So. 892 (Miss. 1895); Smith v. Mississippi, 162 U. S. 592, 16 Sup. Ct. 900 (1896), *aff'g* 18 So. 116 (Miss. 1895); Murray v. Louisiana, 163 U. S. 101, 16 Sup. Ct. 990 (1896), reviewing *Ex parte* Murray, 66 Fed. 297 (C. C. E. D. La. 1895); State v. Chue Fan, 42 Fed. 865 (C. C. N. D. Cal. 1890); Tillman v. State, 121 Ark. 322, 181 S. W. 890 (1915); Cooper v. State, 64 Md. 40, 20 Atl. 986 (1885); Dixon v. State, 74 Miss. 271, 20 So. 839 (1896); Patterson v. Commonwealth, 139 Va. 589, 123 S. E. 657 (1924). The same was held by a federal court in Louisiana before the Rives case was decided. *Ex parte* Wells, 29 Fed. Cas. No. 17,386 (C. C. D. La. 1878). *See also* State v. Walls, 211 N. C. 487, 191 S. E. 232 (1937).

[10] Commonwealth v. Johnson, 78 Ky. 509 (1880).

held that a removal was not authorized, there being no discrimination except that which was the result of administrative unfairness.[11] However, there is a suggestion in the opinion that the court of original jurisdiction should have set aside the indictment because of unlawful racial discrimination in selecting the jury. A like result as to removal was reached in a later federal case from Kentucky where the positive effect of certain jury statutes had never been determined by the state court.[12] In Delaware a statute had limited jury service to those who were qualified electors, and the elective franchise was confined to whites by the terms of a state constitutional provision. A Negro who had been indicted for rape claimed the right of removal to a federal court by virtue of the above act. He claimed that the Delaware laws discriminated against the colored man because members of his race were thereby prohibited from service on juries. The Supreme Court refused to uphold this contention, however, and held that this effect of the state constitutional provision had been automatically annulled by the Fifteenth Amendment and that therefore there was no state law in effect at that time specifically barring Negroes from jury duty.[13] The court declared that if the state had enacted any legislation in conflict with the provisions of the Fourteenth Amendment, repudiated the amendment in her judicial tribunals, or declared that the legislation enacted by Congress to enforce it was inoperative and void, there would have been grounds for removal. As none of these actions had been taken, however, the case was held not to be within the meaning of the statute.

As a portion of the Civil Rights Act of 1875, Congress enacted a criminal statute,[14] a provision which is still in effect,[15] making it a misdemeanor for any officer or other person charged with any duty in the selection or summoning of jurors to exclude or fail to summon any citizen on account of his race, color, or previous condition of servitude. The act has reference to the jury-selecting officials in both state and federal courts and

---

[11] Bush v. Kentucky, 107 U. S. 110, 1 Sup. Ct. 625 (1882), *rev'g* 78 Ky. 268 (1880).

[12] Commonwealth v. Wendling, 182 Fed. 140 (C. C. W. D. Ky. 1910).

[13] Neal v. Delaware, 103 U. S. 370 (1880).

[14] 18 STAT. 336, §4.

[15] 8 U. S. C. A. §44 (1926).

provides for a fine of not more than five thousand dollars. The statute has been held constitutional as being a valid exercise of the power given to Congress by the last section of the Fourteenth Amendment.[16] The court declared that the inhibition of the amendment demands that no state agency or officer or representative through whom the state's authority is exerted shall deny to any person the equal protection of the laws. Such action was considered state action and ministerial in character. These officers, although they derive their authority to carry out the duties imposed by law from the states, are bound in the discharge of these duties to recognize the superior authority of the Federal Constitution and the laws enacted by Congress in pursuance thereof. Since this decision, however, the statute has seen little or no use as a method of enforcing the Negro's right not to be discriminated against in the selection of jurors on account of race or color.

Besides the above-mentioned West Virginia statute, at least one other southern state, Mississippi,[17] enacted legislation which disqualified the Negroes from serving on juries, a type of statute which we have seen was unconstitutional after the ratification of the Fourteenth Amendment. The statutes of Arkansas[18] and Tennessee,[19] enacted during the period of Presidential Reconstruction with the purpose of giving the Negroes certain rights which they had not before possessed, contained provisions which either expressly or impliedly provided that nothing therein contained should be construed to give Negroes the right to sit on juries. But only a short time later Tennessee gave the colored man equal rights in this respect.[20] A Louisiana statute of 1880[21] provided that there should be no distinction in selecting jurors on account of race, color, or previous condition of servitude. A Reconstruction act in South Carolina apportioned the jurors according to the number of Negro and white voters.[22] None of these acts is in effect at present in the form in which it was originally enacted.

---

[16] *Ex parte* Virginia, 100 U. S. 339 (1879), *aff'g* Charge to Grand Jury, Civil Rights Act, 30 Fed. Cas. No. 18,259 (C. C. W. D. Va. 1875).

[17] Miss. Laws 1866-67, p. 233.

[18] Ark. Laws 1866-67, p. 99.

[19] Tenn. Laws 1865-66, pp. 24, 65.

[20] Tenn. Laws 1867-68, p. 32.

[21] La. Acts 1880, no. 54, *cited in* State v. Connor, 142 La. 631, 77 So. 482 (1917).

[22] 14 S. C. Stat. at Large 1868-70, no. 155.

That the discrimination practised against members of the Negro race in respect to jury service is not wholly southern is proved by the fact that six eastern and middle western states, Indiana,[23] Michigan,[24] New Jersey,[25] New York,[26] Ohio,[27] and Rhode Island,[28] have enacted criminal statutes aimed at such conduct on the part of jury-selecting officials. There have also been a few cases involving this type of discrimination in these as well as other sections of the nation. The enabling act which admitted Nebraska to the union in 1867 provided that it should not be effective except upon the condition that there should be no denial of rights on account of race or color, excepting Indians not taxed. The question arose as to whether there was any valid objection to the service of Negroes on juries in that jurisdiction. The state court decided that this provision of the enabling act had become a part of the organic law of Nebraska and therefore binding as such, and that the right to serve on juries was a fundamental right within the meaning of this provision.[29]

In one case there arose the question of the validity of the Mississippi qualifications for jury service. The state constitution of 1890 provided that all persons who were qualified electors were eligible to be jurors. The disfranchising provisions had been placed in the new constitution at the same time. The Negro defendant claimed that these provisions were unconstitutional. Hence it was argued that the qualifications for jury service were also invalid. The case was carried to the Federal Supreme Court and the disfranchising provisions of the state constitution were upheld.[30] The court said that the provisions should not be declared invalid because there was a possibility that the law would

---

[23] IND. STAT. ANN. (Burns, 1933) §10-903.

[24] MICH. COMP. LAWS (1929) §16,811 re-enacted in 1933 Supp. as §17,115-148, *cited in* Ferguson v. Gies, 82 Mich. 358, 46 N. W. 718 (1890).

[25] N. J. COMP. STAT. (1911) p. 1442, §3.

[26] N. Y. CONSOL. LAWS (Cahill, 1930) c. 7, §13.

[27] OHIO CODE (Throckmorton, 1929) §12,868.

[28] R. I. Gen. Laws (1923) §4692.

[29] Brittle v. People, 2 Neb. 198 (1873).

[30] Williams v. Mississippi, 170 U. S. 213, 18 Sup. Ct. 583 (1897). In accord with this decision is Dixon v. State, 74 Miss. 271, 20 So. 839 (1896). In this connection see also Rogers v. Alabama, 192 U. S. 226, 24 Sup. Ct. 257 (1903). In Alabama jurors are not required to be qualified electors.

be improperly administered. The discriminatory administration doctrine of the *Chinese Laundry* case[31] was held not to apply in this instance because there was no sufficient proof of unfairness to the Negro in selecting the jurors.

Following the reasoning here announced, state statutes placing the duty of selecting juries in the hands of administrative bodies, the provisions of which do not as worded discriminate against the Negro in any way, cannot be declared invalid because there is a possibility that they will be administered in such a manner as to deny equal protection of the laws.[32] The requirement of the Mississippi Constitution[33] that no person shall be eligible as a juryman unless he be a qualified elector would not prevent the enactment of a statute providing that persons selected for jury duty must possess intelligence, judgment, and character.[34] The action of the aforesaid administrative bodies in carrying out their duties in a manner which is discriminatory and unfair to the Negro is state action within the terms of the Fourteenth Amendment.[35] The performance of the said duties in a proper and nondiscriminatory manner will be pre-

---

[31] Yick Wo v. Hopkins, 118 U. S. 356, 6 Sup. Ct. 1064 (1885), cited in chapter on Civil Rights, note 241.

[32] Jugiro v. Brush, 140 U. S. 291, 11 Sup. Ct. 770 (1891) (Japanese); Murray v. Louisiana, 163 U. S. 101, 16 Sup. Ct. 990 (1896); Powell v. State, 224 Ala. 540, 141 So. 201 (1932); Washington v. State, 95 Fla. 289, 116 So. 470 (1928), *cert. denied* 278 U. S. 599, 49 Sup. Ct. 8 (1928); State v. Ford, 42 La. Ann. 255, 7 So. 696 (1890); State v. Jackson, 142 La. 636, 77 So. 484 (1917); State v. Ah Chew, 16 Nev. 50 (1881) (Chinese); State v. Franklin, 80 S. C. 332, 60 S. E. 953 (1908), *aff'd* 218 U. S. 161, 30 Sup. Ct. 640 (1910); Thomas v. State, 49 Tex. Cr. Rep. 633, 95 S. W. 1069 (1906), *aff'd* 212 U. S. 278, 29 Sup. Ct. 393 (1909); Roberts v. State, 81 Tex. Cr. Rep. 227, 195 S. W. 189 (1917).

[33] §264.

[34] Gibson v. Mississippi, 162 U. S. 565, 16 Sup. Ct. 904 (1895). That there have been similar laws enacted in other jurisdictions is proved by a glance at the following cases: Haynes v. State, 71 Fla. 585, 72 So. 180 (1916); Thomas v. State, 67 Ga. 460 (1881); Wilson v. State, 69 Ga. 224 (1882); Cooper v. State, 64 Md. 40, 20 Atl. 986 (1885); Lee v. State, 163 Md. 56, 161 Atl. 284 (1932). See also Note (1934) 29 Ill. L. Rev. 498, criticizing selective method.

[35] *Ex parte* Virginia, 100 U. S. 339 (1879); Rogers v. Alabama, 192 U. S. 226, 24 Sup. Ct. 257 (1903); Bonaparte v. State, 65 Fla. 287, 61 So. 633 (1913); State v. Peoples, 131 N. C. 784, 42 S. E. 814 (1902); Carrick v. State, 41 Okla. Cr. Rep. 336, 274 Pac. 896 (1929); Collins v. State, 60 S. W. 42 (Tex. Cr. App. 1900); Juarez v. State, 102 Tex. Cr. Rep. 297, 277 S. W. 1091 (1925) (Mexicans); State v. Cook, 81 W. Va. 686, 95 S. E. 792 (1918); State v. Young, 82 W. Va. 714, 97 S. E. 134 (1918); State v. Frazier, 104 W. Va. 480, 140 S. E. 324 (1927).

sumed,[36] and hence the burden of proving discrimination is upon that party by whom it is alleged.[37]

An allegation of racial discrimination in the selection of jurors without any evidence to support it will be ineffective as a ground for reversal.[38] Such an allegation, even if supported by a verified statement such as an affidavit, cannot be regarded as evidence,[39] and, if controverted by the state, is not enough

---

[36] Tarrance v. Florida, 188 U. S. 519, 23 Sup. Ct. 402 (1902), *aff'g* 43 Fla. 446, 30 So. 685 (1901); Hannah v. State, 183 Ark. 810, 38 S. W. (2d) 1090 (1931); Montgomery v. State, 55 Fla. 97, 45 So. 879 (1908); Haynes v. State, 71 Fla. 585, 72 So. 180 (1916); Washington v. State, 95 Fla. 289, 116 So. 470 (1928); State v. Baptiste, 105 La. 661, 30 So. 147 (1901); State v. Guirlando, 152 La. 570, 93 So. 796 (1922) (Italians); State v. Gill, 186 La. 339, 172 So. 412 (1937).

[37] Haynes v. State, 71 Fla. 585, 72 So. 180 (1916); Royals v. State, 73 Fla. 897, 75 So. 199 (1917); Washington v. State, 95 Fla. 289, 116 So. 470 (1928); People v. Price, 371 Ill. 137, 20 N. E. (2d) 61 (1939); State v. Pierre, 189 La. 764, 180 So. 630 (1938); Lee v. State, 163 Md. 56, 161 Atl. 284 (1932); Hollins v. State, 56 Okla. Cr. Rep. 275, 38 P. (2d) 36 (1934); Whitney v. State, 43 Tex. Cr. Rep. 197, 63 S. W. 879 (1901); Mitchell v. State, 105 Tex. Cr. Rep. 297, 288 S. W. 224 (1926); Wilborn v. State, 111 Tex. Cr. Rep. 299, 12 S. W. (2d) 578 (1929); Lugo v. State, 124 S. W. (2d) 344 (Tex. Cr. App. 1938) (Mexicans).

[38] Franklin v. South Carolina, 218 U. S. 161, 30 Sup. Ct. 640 (1910); Ragland v. State 187 Ala. 5, 65 So. 776 (1914); Hannah v. State, 183 Ark. 810, 38 S. W. (2d) 1090 (1931); State v. Ryan, 141 Kans. 549, 42 P. (2d) 591 (1935); Smith v. Commonwealth, 17 Ky. Law Rep. 1162, 33 S. W. 825 (1896); Montjoy v. Commonwealth, 262 Ky. 426, 90 S. W. (2d) 362 (1936); State v. Jackson, 142 La. 636, 77 So. 484 (1917); State v. Guirlando, 152 La. 570, 93 So. 796 (1922) (Italians); State v. Liston, 318 Mo. 1222, 2 S. W. (2d) 780 (1928); Johnson v. State, 59 N. J. Law 271, 35 Atl. 787 (1896), 59 N. J. Law 535, 37 Atl. 949 (1897); Davis v. State, 53 Okla. Cr. Rep. 411, 12 P. (2d) 555 (1932); Adkins v. State, 65 S. W. 924 (Tex. Cr. App. 1901); Jackson v. State, 71 S. W. 280 (Tex. Cr. App. 1902); Pena v. State, 114 Tex. Cr. Rep. 15, 24 S. W. (2d) 396 (1930) (Mexicans); Rector v. State, 128 Tex. Cr. Rep. 56, 78 S. W. (2d) 976 (1935); Trapper v. State, 129 Tex. Cr. Rep. 53, 84 S. W. (2d) 726 (1935); Brown v. State, 130 Tex. Cr. Rep. 319, 94 S. W. (2d) 449 (1936); Patterson v. Commonwealth, 139 Va. 589, 123 S. E. 657 (1924); Clark v. Commonwealth, 167 Va. 472, 189 S. E. 143 (1937). The same result follows where the record shows nothing that can be taken as proof of discrimination; Merriweather v. Commonwealth, 118 Ky. 870, 82 S. W. 592 (1904); State v. Casey, 44 La. Ann. 969, 11 So. 583 (1892); Hinton v. State, 175 Miss. 308, 166 So. 762 (1936).

[39] Tarrance v. Florida, 188 U. S. 519, 23 Sup. Ct. 402 (1902), *aff'g* 43 Fla. 446, 30 So. 685 (1901); Smith v. Mississippi, 162 U. S. 592, 16 Sup. Ct. 900 (1896), *aff'g* 18 So. 116 (Miss. 1895); Brownfield v. South Carolina, 189 U. S. 426, 23 Sup. Ct. 513 (1903), *aff'g* 60 S. C. 509, 39 S. E. 2 (1901); Franklin v. State, 85 Ark. 534, 109 S. W. 298 (1908); State v. Baptiste, 105 La. 661, 30 So. 147 (1901); State v. Guirlando, 152 La. 570, 93 So. 796 (1922) (Italians); State v. Brown, 119 Mo. 527, 24 S. W. 1027 (1894); Rivers v. State, 117 Tenn.

on which to base a claim of unfairness in this respect.[40] However, an affidavit has been held to be sufficient where the facts stated therein were not denied by the prosecution,[41] and in one Texas case there is an intimation that a motion could be used in evidence if the state consented.[42]

The only right[43] which the Negro possesses in this respect is that his race shall not be discriminated against in the selection of the grand jury which indicts him or the petit jury which tries him, and he is not entitled to juries composed wholly or partially of members of his own race.[44] Therefore the mere absence of Negroes from either type of jury is no reason for a reversal.[45]

235, 96 S. W. 956 (1906) Wilborn v. State, 111 Tex. Cr. Rep. 299, 12 S. W. (2d) 578 (1929).

[40] Cook v. State, 81 W. Va. 686, 95 S. E. 792 (1918).

[41] Neal v. Delaware, 103 U. S. 370 (1880).

[42] McCline v. State, 64 Tex. Cr. Rep. 19, 141 S. W. 977 (1912).

[43] This right is well expressed in a recent Missouri case where it is said that a Negro defendant must not be deprived by design of the chance of having persons of his own race on the jury. State v. Logan, 341 Mo. 1164, 111 S. W. (2d) 110 (1937).

[44] Gibson v. Mississippi, 162 U. S. 365, 16 Sup. Ct. 904 (1896), *aff'g* 17 So. 892 (Miss. 1895); Martin v. Texas, 200 U. S. 316, 26 Sup. Ct. 338 (1905), *aff'g* 44 Tex. Cr. Rep. 538, 72 S. W. 386 (1903); Younge v. United States, 242 Fed. 788 (C. C. A. 4th, 1917); Preleau v. United States, 271 Fed. 361 (App. D. C. 1921); Ware v. State, 146 Ark. 321, 225 S. W. 626 (1920); Montgomery v. State, 53 Fla. 115, 42 So. 894 (1907); Haynes v. State, 71 Fla. 585, 72 So. 180 (1916); Washington v. State, 95 Fla. 289, 116 So. 470 (1928); Haggard v. Commonwealth, 79 Ky. 366 (1881); State v. Ford, 42 La. Ann. 255, 7 So. 696 (1890); State v. Laborde, 120 La. 136, 45 So. 38 (1907) (Creole); State v. Manuel, 133 La. 571, 63 So. 174 (1913) (Creole); State v. Gill, 186 La. 339, 172 So. 412 (1937); Lee v. State, 163 Md. 56, 161 Atl. 284 (1932); Lewis v. State, 91 Miss. 505, 45 So. 360 (1908); State v. Brown, 119 Mo. 527, 24 S. W. 1027 (1894); State v. Sloan, 97 N. C. 499, 2 S. E. 666 (1887); Peters v. State, 22 Okla. Cr. Rep. 245, 211 Pac. 427 (1922); Carrick v. State, 41 Okla. Cr. Rep. 336, 274 Pac. 896 (1929); Powell v. State, 60 Okla. Cr. Rep. 116, 63 P. (2d) 113 (1936); Mayor of Nashville v. Sheperd, 62 Tenn. 373 (1874); Lewis v. State, 42 Tex. Cr. Rep. 278, 59 S. W. 1116 (1900); Thomas v. State, 49 Tex. Cr. Rep. 633, 95 S. W. 1069 (1906); Mitchell v. Commonwealth, 33 Gratt. 845 (Va. 1880); Lawrence v. Commonwealth, 81 Va. 484 (1886); Clark v. Commonwealth, 167 Va. 472, 189 S. E. 143 (1937); State v. Cook, 81 W. Va. 686, 95 S. E. 792 (1918).

[45] Virginia v. Rives, 100 U. S. 313 (1879); Neal v. Delaware, 103 U. S. 370 (1880); Martin v. Texas, 200 U. S. 316, 26 Sup. Ct. 338 (1905), *aff'g* 44 Tex. Cr. Rep. 538, 72 S. W. 386 (1903); Younge v. United States, 242 Fed. 788 (C. C. A. 4th, 1917); Millhouse v. State, 232 Ala. 567, 168 So. 665 (1936); Eastling v. State, 69 Ark. 189, 62 S. W. 584 (1901); Hannah v. State, 183 Ark. 810, 38 S. W. (2d) 1090 (1931); Montgomery v. State, 53 Fla. 115, 42 So. 894 (1907); Washington v. State, 95 Fla. 289, 116 So. 470 (1928); State v. Ryan, 141 Kan. 549, 42 Pac. (2d) 591 (1935); Smith v. Commonwealth, 17 Ky. Law Rep. 1162, 33 S. W.

However, persons of the colored race should be given an opportunity to present the evidence which has been obtained for the purpose of proving discrimination.[46] A failure on the part of the court to allow the presentation of the evidence is a proper ground for reversal whether the opportunity was withheld by the action of the court[47] or was lost due to circumstances which were beyond the control of the Negro defendant's counsel.[48] The same principles apply where a Negro has had no opportunity to object to racial discrimination in the selection of the grand jury because it had been chosen before the commission of the alleged crime.[49] In one Texas case[50] it was intimated that, if the jury was drawn before the crime was committed, any inference of discrimination against a Negro defendant would be negatived. The court declared that the jury-selecting officials would then have no particular defendant in mind and could not therefore be said to have been unfair to any particular criminal be he white or colored. The fallacy in this argument is that the officials could easily discriminate against the Negro without having any particular person of that race in mind.

---

825 (1896); State v. Brown, 119 Mo. 527, 24 S. W. 1027 (1894); Bullock v. State, 65 N. J. Law 557, 47 Atl. 62 (1900); Smith v. State, 4 Okla. Cr. Rep. 328, 111 Pac. 960 (1910); McIntosh v. State, 8 Okla. Cr. Rep. 469, 128 Pac. 735 (1912); Carrick v. State, 41 Okla. Cr. Rep. 336, 274 Pac. 896 (1929); Powell v. State, 60 Okla. Cr. Rep. 166, 63 P. (2d) 113 (1936); Burks v. State, 79 P. (2d) 619 (Okla. Cr. App. 1938); Smith v. State, 93 Atl. 353 (R. I. 1915); State v. Brownfield, 60 S. C. 509, 39 S. E. 2 (1901); Parker v. State, 65 S. W. 1066 (Tex. Cr. App. 1901); Carter v. State, 45 Tex. Cr. Rep. 430, 76 S. W. 437 (1903); Thomas v. State, 49 Tex. Cr. Rep. 633, 95 S. W. 1069 (1906); Roberts v. State, 81 Tex. Cr. Rep. 227, 195 S. W. 189 (1917); Mickle v. State, 85 Tex. Cr. Rep. 560, 213 S. W. 665 (1919); Briscoe v. State, 106 Tex. Cr. Rep. 478, 293 S. W. 573 (1926); Ross v. State, 110 Tex. Cr. Rep. 260, 7 S. W. (2d) 1078 (1928); State v. Cook, 81 W. Va. 686, 95 S. E. 792 (1918).

[46] Fields v. State, 4 Ohio N. P. (N.S.) 401 (1906); Smith v. State, 42 Tex. Cr. Rep. 220, 58 S. W. 97 (1900); Kipper v. State, 42 Tex. Cr. Rep. 613, 62 S. W. 420 (1901).

[47] Carter v. Texas, 177 U. S. 442, 20 Sup. Ct. 687 (1900), *rev'g* 39 Tex. Cr. Rep. 345, 46 S. W. 236 (1898); Castleberry v. State, 69 Ark. 346, 63 S. W. 670 (1901); Ware v. State, 146 Ark. 321, 225 S. W. 626 (1920); State v. Warner, 165 Mo. 399, 65 S. W. 584 (1901); State v. Jones, 115 N. J. Law 257, 179 Atl. 320 (1935); State v. Peoples, 131 N. C. 784, 42 S. E. 814 (1902); Smith v. State, 4 Okla. Cr. Rep. 328, 111 Pac. 960 (1910).

[48] Smith v. State, 45 Tex. Cr. Rep. 405, 77 S. W. 453 (1903).

[49] Carter v. Texas, 177 U. S. 442, 20 Sup. Ct. 687 (1900); Castleberry v. State, 69 Ark. 346, 63 S. W. 670 (1901). *See* Tillman v. State, 121 Ark. 322, 181 S. W. 890 (1915).

[50] Cavitt v. State, 15 Tex. App. 190 (1883).

What type of evidence will be the most efficacious in showing that the Negro has been treated unfairly in the selection of grand and petit jurors, and what is the effect of the different types of testimony on the court's decision as to whether or not there has actually been discrimination? The answer to this query is beclouded by the fact that many types of testimony are introduced in every case, and hence it is rather difficult to determine just how much any one particular bit of evidence influenced the court in its decision in any given case. However, there are certain inferences to be drawn from an analysis of the numerous decisions which have been rendered through the years since the Fourteenth Amendment became a part of the Constitution.

By far the most usual type of evidence brought forward in favor of or in contradiction of such a claim of racial discrimination in the selection of jurors is the testimony of jury commissioners or other jury-selecting officials. Where the examination of these witnesses shows that they have acted unfairly toward the Negro in selecting the grand jurors who had indicted a member of that race or the petit jurors who had tried him, there is a sound basis for the reversal of a conviction.[51] On the other hand, if they testify that there has been no unfairness to the Negro or other race in this respect, the appellate courts will usually decide that there has been no discrimination and will therefore refuse to interfere.[52] However, an opposite con-

[51] Lee v. State, 163 Md. 56, 161 Atl. 284 (1932); Whitney v. State, 42 Tex. Cr. Rep. 283, 59 S. W. 895 (1900); Collins v. State, 60 S. W. 42 (Tex. Cr. App. 1900); Leach v. State, 62 S. W. 422 (Tex. Cr. App. 1901).

[52] Green v. State, 73 Ala. 26 (1882); Eastling v. State, 69 Ark. 189, 62 S. W. 584 (1901); Jordan v. State, 141 Ark. 504, 217 S. W. 788 (1920); Royals v. State, 73 Fla. 897, 75 So. 199 (1917); State v. Joseph, 45 La. Ann. 903, 12 So. 934 (1893); State v. Murray, 47 La. Ann. 1424, 17 So. 832 (1895); State v. Turner, 133 La. 555, 63 So. 169 (1913); State v. Daniels, 134 N. C. 641, 46 S. E. 743 (1904); Peters v. State, 22 Okla. Cr. Rep. 245, 211 Pac. 427 (1922); Bruster v. State, 40 Okla. Cr. Rep. 25, 266 Pac. 486 (1928); Parker v. State, 65 S. W. 1066 (Tex. Cr. App. 1901); Hubbard v. State, 43 Tex. Cr. Rep. 564, 67 S. W. 413 (1902); Martin v. State, 44 Tex. Cr. Rep. 538, 72 S. W. 386 (1903); Thompson v. State, 45 Tex. Cr. Rep. 190, 74 S. W. 914 (1903); Smith v. State, 45 Tex. Cr. Rep. 552, 78 S. W. 694 (1904); Thomas v. State, 49 Tex. Cr. Rep. 633, 95 S. W. 1069 (1906); Washington v. State, 51 Tex. Cr. Rep. 542, 103 S. W. 879 (1907); Macklin v. State, 53 Tex. Cr. Rep. 197, 109 S. W. 145 (1908); McIntosh v. State, 56 Tex. Cr. Rep. 134, 120 S. W. 455 (1909); Pollard v. State, 58 Tex. Cr. Rep. 299, 125 S. W. 390 (1910); Ybarra v. State, 73 Tex. Cr. Rep. 70, 164 S. W. 10 (1914) (Mexicans); Hemphill v. State, 75 Tex. Cr. Rep. 63,

clusion will be reached where there is other evidence which indubitably outweighs such testimony.[53] Evidence of these officials showing that the matter of placing Negroes on the jury had not been discussed or was not even in their minds at the time of selection does not seem to require a reversal.[54]

In one Texas case the Negro defendant offered the testimony of the judge who had presided when the jury commissioners were appointed. The gist of his testimony was that he would not have selected a commissioner who he believed would place Negroes on the county juries. His reason for this was that such action would cause friction between the two races. The lower court rejected his testimony, but this was held to be error on appeal.[55] Evidence that no Negroes had been placed on the jury commission at present or in the past does not seem to be adequate proof of discrimination,[56] and the same is true of testimony by the judge that he did not believe he would ever appoint a Negro commissioner.[57]

Use of the registration books or poll tax lists which in the South do not usually contain the names of many Negroes has been held not to require the courts to interfere.[58] The same is true where the jury was selected with the aid of a city directory, only the names of certain disreputable Negroes not being given consideration.[59] In one Mississippi case it was said that a Negro defendant could not object because there was no registration

---

170 S. W. 154 (1914); Roberts v. State, 81 Tex. Cr. Rep. 227, 195 S. W. 189 (1917); Briscoe v. State, 106 Tex. Cr. Rep. 478, 293 S. W. 573 (1926); Ross v. State, 110 Tex. Cr. Rep. 260, 7 S. W. (2d) 1078 (1928); Freeney v. State, 123 Tex. Cr. Rep. 488, 59 S. W. (2d) 385 (1933); Langrum v. State, 128 Tex. Cr. Rep. 23, 78 S. W. (2d) 973 (1935); State v. Cook, 81 W. Va. 686, 95 S. E. 792 (1918).

[53] Norris v. Alabama, 294 U. S. 587, 55 Sup. Ct. 579 (1935), *rev'g* 229 Ala. 226, 156 So. 556 (1934); Carrick v. State, 41 Okla. Cr. Rep. 336, 274 Pac. 896 (1929).

[54] Eastling v. State, 69 Ark. 189, 62 S. W. 584 (1901); Ross v. State, 110 Tex. Cr. Rep. 260, 7 S. W. (2d) 1078 (1928); Johnson v. State, 121 Tex. Cr. Rep. 548, 50 S. W. (2d) 831 (1932); Langrum v. State, 128 Tex. Cr. Rep. 23, 78 S. W. (2d) 973 (1935).

[55] Smith v. State, 44 Tex. Cr. Rep. 90, 69 S. W. 151 (1902).

[56] Thomas v. State, 49 Tex. Cr. Rep. 633, 95 S. W. 1069 (1906); Hanna v. State, 52 Tex. Cr. Rep. 162, 105 S. W. 793 (1907).

[57] Thompson v. State, 45 Tex. Cr. Rep. 190, 74 S. W. 914 (1903).

[58] State v. Thomas, 35 La. Ann. 24 (1883); State v. Conner, 142 La. 631, 77 So. 482 (1917); Ross v. State, 110 Tex. Cr. Rep. 260, 7 S. W. (2d) 1078 (1928).

[59] State v. Lawrence, 124 La. 378, 50 So. 406 (1909).

book in the county to guide officials in making up the jury list,[60] the state constitution, as above noted, requiring jurors to be qualified voters.

Testimony of men of high standing in the community, including a Negro physician, that there were no Negroes in the county qualified for jury duty has been held to be persuasive of the fact that there was no discrimination.[61] In an Oklahoma case the evidence of certain white witnesses that they had never been selected for jury duty was used to prove a fair selection, the inference being that other men besides Negroes had not been chosen for this service and that some persons did not serve even though they might be Caucasians.[62] This testimony had a tendency to show that individuals, white or colored, may be left off juries for reasons other than race. In the *Royals* case from Florida[63] the simple statement of a jury-selecting official that he had not discriminated against the Negro in choosing jurors seems to have been held to outweigh the testimony of certain other witnesses, some of whom had been connected with the court for quite a while. These witnesses testified that there were many Negroes in the county qualified for jury service and that there had been no person of that race on the local juries for many years. The periods of time during which it was claimed this situation had prevailed varied from five to twenty years according to the experience of the various persons testifying. It would seem that the decided weight of the testimony in this case is with the Negro in his effort to prove unfairness to his race, but one cannot be certain that the court came to an erroneous conclusion. There are other elements, such as the incredibility of witnesses, which might easily have influenced the lower court in its decision.

The fact that there are Negroes who are qualified to serve as jurors has been an important element in reaching a conclusion that there was discrimination against them in the selective process,[64] but evidence of this fact is not always held to require

[60] Dixon v. State, 74 Miss. 271, 20 So. 839 (1896).

[61] Fugett v. State, 45 Tex. Cr. Rep. 313, 77 S. W. 461 (1903).

[62] Bruster v. State, 40 Okla. Cr. Rep. 25, 266 Pac. 486 (1928).

[63] Royals v. State, 73 Fla. 897, 75 So. 199 (1917).

[64] Norris v. Alabama, 294 U. S. 587, 55 Sup. Ct. 579 (1935), *rev'g* 229 Ala. 226, 156 So. 556 (1934); People v. Hines, 81 P. (2d) 1048 (Cal. App. 1938); Montgomery v. State, 55 Fla. 97, 45 So. 879 (1908); Carrick v. State, 41 Okla.

a reversal.[65] In one Louisiana case[66] the testimony showed that there were a number of persons of African descent living in the parish and that all of the three hundred names which had been drawn out of the jury box were those of white persons. This evidence was held not to establish discrimination, as no proof was offered that there were no names of Negroes in the box. Moreover, the fact that there were comparatively few Negroes in the locality who were at all suited for jury service has been influential in making the courts reach the conclusion that no discriminatory tactics had been employed.[67]

Where it is shown that Negroes, no matter how few, have actually served on the jury or had their names on the panel or on the list or in the box from which the panel was drawn, the courts have generally held that there has been no discrimination.[68] The same is true where Negroes have served many times during the last few years.[69] In a recent Texas case the counsel for a Negro defendant attempted to show discrimination by proving that the two Negroes who had been selected by the

---

Cr. Rep. 336, 274 Pac. 896 (1929); Smith v. State, 42 Tex. Cr. Rep. 220, 58 S. W. 97 (1900); Leach v. State, 62 S. W. 422 (Tex. Cr. App. 1901); Johnson v. State, 124 S. W. (2d) 1001 (Tex. Cr. App. 1939); State v. Young, 82 W. Va. 714, 97 S. E. 134 (1918).

[65] Haynes v. State, 71 Fla. 585, 72 So. 180 (1916).

[66] State v. West, 116 La. 626, 40 So. 920 (1906).

[67] State v. Joseph, 45 La. Ann. 903, 12 So. 934 (1893); State v. Pierre, 189 La. 764, 180 So. 630 (1938); McIntosh v. State, 8 Okla. Cr. Rep. 469, 128 Pac. 735 (1912); Lewis v. State, 42 Tex. Cr. Rep. 278, 59 S. W. 1116 (1900); Parker v. State, 65 S. W. 1066 (Tex. Cr. App. 1901); Martin v. State, 44 Tex. Cr. Rep. 538, 72 S. W. 386 (1903), *aff'd* 200 U. S. 316, 26 Sup. Ct. 338 (1905); Thompson v. State, 45 Tex. Cr. Rep. 190, 74 S. W. 914 (1903); Smith v. State, 45 Tex. Cr. Rep. 552, 78 S. W. 694 (1904); Thomas v. State, 49 Tex. Cr. Rep. 633, 95 S. W. 1069 (1906); Pollard v. State, 58 Tex. Cr. Rep. 299, 125 S. W. 390 (1910). *See* Ramirez v. State, 119 Tex. Cr. Rep. 362, 40 S. W. (2d) 138 (1931) (Mexicans).

[68] Beckett v. United States, 84 F. (2d) 731 (C. C. A. 6th, 1936); Collins v. State, 234 Ala. 197, 174 So. 296 (1937); Groce v. Territory, 12 Ariz. 1, 94 Pac. 1108 (1908); Thomas v. State, 67 Ga. 460 (1881); Wilson v. State, 69 Ga. 224 (1882); State v. Murray, 47 La. Ann. 1424, 17 So. 832 (1895); State v. Gill, 186 La. 339, 172 So. 412 (1937); State v. Logan, 126 S. W. (2d) 256 (Mo. 1939); State v. Walls, 211 N. C. 487, 191 S. E. 232 (1937); Scott v. State, 29 Okla. Cr. Rep. 324, 233 Pac. 776 (1925); Whitney v. State, 43 Tex. Cr. Rep. 197, 63 S. W. 879 (1901); Thomas v. State, 49 Tex. Cr. Rep. 633, 95 S. W. 1069 (1906); Macklin v. State, 53 Tex. Cr. Rep. 197, 109 S. W. 145 (1908); McIntosh v. State, 56 Tex. Cr. Rep. 134, 120 S. W. 455 (1909). *See also* State v. Laborde, 120 La. 136, 45 So. 38 (1907) (Creoles).

[69] Vaughn v. State, 235 Ala. 80, 177 So. 553 (1937).

jury commissioners were not chosen for duty. In the absence of a showing as to why the Negroes were not chosen, the court decided that there was no sufficient proof of unfairness in the selective process.[70] The Negro is not entitled to a pro-rata representation on the jury that indicts or tries him,[71] and there seems to have been no instance of a reversal where one or more colored men have actually served. The mere fact that the names of Negroes in the jury box are marked with a different colored ink from those of whites has been held insufficient in itself to require a reversal.[72]

In an early case from Delaware the Federal Supreme Court employed language which can be interpreted as recognizing the doctrine that a long absence of Negroes from all juries in any given locality may be taken as prima-facie evidence of discrimination.[73] For half a century and more this expression of opinion by the high tribunal was disregarded by southern courts. In several instances during this period it was held that a Negro defendant could not predicate error in selecting the jury at his trial upon proof that there had been continued discrimination against his race in that locality which had extended over a period of previous years.[74] It is true that in one Oklahoma case a court's refusal to hear evidence that would substantiate a claim of a continued discrimination of this kind was held to be reversible error.[75] The gist of the offered testimony was that there had been a studied neglect to summon colored jurors during the whole time that the county had been an organized unit. However, this decision seems to be one of the few cases decided during this period which can be said to support the above language of the Supreme Court. In the same fifty-year span testimony to the effect that no Negroes had served in the particular locality involved for lengthy periods such as five,

---

[70] Mitchell v. State, 135 Tex. Cr. Rep. 176, 117 S. W. (2d) 443 (1938).

[71] Beckett v. United States, 84 F. (2d) 731 (C. C. A. 6th, 1936); Thomas v. State, 49 Tex. Cr. Rep. 633, 95 S. W. 1069 (1906); McIntosh v. State, 56 Tex. Cr. Rep. 134, 120 S. W. 455 (1909). *See also* Miera v. Territory, 13 N. Mex. 192, 81 Pac. 586 (1905) (Mexicans).

[72] State v. Walls, 211 N. C. 487, 191 S. E. 232 (1937).

[73] Neal v. Delaware, 103 U. S. 370 (1880).

[74] State v. Thomas, 250 Mo. 189, 157 S. W. 330 (1913); Welch v. State, 30 Okla. Cr. Rep. 330, 236 Pac. 68 (1925); Ransom v. State, 116 Tenn. 355, 96 S. W. 953 (1906).

[75] Smith v. State, 4 Okla. Cr. Rep. 328, 111 Pac. 960 (1910).

ten, or twenty years was held not to be a sufficient showing of discrimination.[76] In one Texas case the court declared that while such evidence might be given weight in a close case, it would be considered of no great consequence in an instance where all the rest of the testimony indicated that there were no discriminatory methods practised.[77]

Then in 1932 the *Euel Lee* case came before the Maryland Court of Appeals. The Negro defendant, charged with murder, presented testimony of the judge who had been responsible for the selection of the petit jury which indicated that his system of drawing jurors began with a collection of the names of eligible white men. This demonstrated that from the very outset there had been unfairness toward the Negro. It was also proved that 10 per cent of the population of the county was colored and that there had been an extended period of time during which no Negro had sat on any jury in that locality. This last circumstance, along with the other evidence introduced, was held to be sufficient proof of discrimination to warrant a reversal[78] of the conviction which had been obtained in the lower court. The tribunal declared that any prolonged absence of colored persons from juries in any particular locality will warrant an inference of a denial of equal protection of the laws. This reasoning has been approved by the Federal Supreme Court in the *Scottsboro*[79] and *Hollins*[80] cases. However, proof that there

---

[76] *See* Haynes v. State, 71 Fla. 585, 72 So. 180 (1916); Royals v. State, 73 Fla. 897, 75 So. 199 (1917); Thompson v. State, 45 Tex. Cr. Rep. 397, 77 S. W. 449 (1903).

[77] Pollard v. State, 58 Tex. Cr. Rep. 299, 125 S. W. 390 (1910).

[78] Lee v. State, 163 Md. 56, 161 Atl. 284 (1932).

[79] Norris v. Alabama, 294 U. S. 587, 55 Sup. Ct. 579 (1935), *rev'g* 229 Ala. 226, 156 So. 556 (1934). The case in its various stages has been the subject of much editorial comment, as is attested by the following: (1934) 29 ILL. L. REV. 498, (1935) 35 COL. L. REV. 776, (1936) 24 ILL. B. J. 233, (1935) 33 MICH. L. REV. 1252, (1935) 8 MISS. L. REV. 196, (1935) 3 GEO. WASH. L. REV. 388, (1935) 10 WIS. L. REV. 395, (1933) 36 L. NOTES 104. In the Patterson case, which grew out of the same set of circumstances, the Negro defendant failed to file a bill of exceptions within ninety days after the judgment was rendered in accordance with the Alabama law. His attorney was responsible for the neglect through a misapprehension of the law. The state court held that this was fatal to the defendant's case. Patterson v. State, 229 Ala. 270, 156 So. 567 (1934). This case was considered by the Supreme Court along with the Norris case, and that tribunal declared that it was not convinced that the state court would have upheld the conviction on this legal technicality had that court held that there was a denial of equal protection as concluded by the Supreme Court. The

has been none of the defendant's race on juries in the county for a short time like two years or less has been said not to show unfairness.[81] The same is true of testimony to the effect that there have been no Negro jurors "for some time," such evidence being entirely too indefinite.[82] This systematic exclusion of Negroes from juries for any lengthy period must be proved, for a court may not take judicial notice of this fact.[83] In order to sustain such a claim, the Texas Court has declared that the Negro defendant must prove that during the period of exclusion there have been Negroes who possessed the statutory qualifications for jury service.[84]

It has been said in an Alabama case that a court cannot refuse to permit a Negro defendant's attorney to question a jury commissioner as to whether colored persons had been systematically excluded from the grand jury, whether additional names had been placed in the jury box prior to the drawing of such jury, and whether the names of certain Negroes were placed therein as a colorable compliance with the law as announced in the *Scottsboro* case.[85] It has also been held reversible error for the court to refuse to allow a Negro defendant's counsel to interrogate a deputy sheriff as to whether or not he had ever selected a colored man to serve on any jury in the

---

tribunal was of the opinion that the state court should be given an opportunity to re-examine its decision in the light of the situation which had arisen in connection with the Norris case. This was not an attempt to review the finding of a state court on a nonfederal question, but only an effort to give that court an opportunity to deal properly with the peculiar situation presented. Patterson v. Alabama, 294 U. S. 600, 55 Sup. Ct. 575 (1935). In connection with the problem presented in the Patterson case see also Hale v. Commonwealth, 269 Ky. 743, 108 S. W. (2d) 716 (1937), *rev'g* Hale v. Kentucky, 303 U. S. 613, 58 Sup. Ct. 753 (1938).

80 Hollins v. Oklahoma, 295 U. S. 394, 55 Sup. Ct. 784 (1935), *rev'g* 56 Okla. Cr. Rep. 275, 38 P. (2d) 36 (1934). *See also* Holland v. State, 61 Okla. Cr. Rep. 215, 67 P. (2d) 58 (1937).

81 Binyon v. United States, 4 Ind. Ter. 642, 76 S. W. 265 (1903); Hanna v. State, 52 Tex. Cr. Rep. 162, 105 S. W. 793 (1907); Carrasco v. State, 130 Tex. Cr. Rep. 659, 95 S. W. (2d) 433 (1936) (Mexicans).

82 Brown v. State, 130 Tex. Cr. Rep. 276, 94 S. W. (2d) 169 (1936).

83 Montjoy v. Commonwealth, 262 Ky. 426, 90 S. W. (2d) 362 (1936). *See also* Hinton v. State, 175 Miss. 308, 166 So. 762 (1936). Neither may a court take judicial notice of the percentage of persons of African descent in a county. Bruster v. State, 40 Okla. Cr. Rep. 25, 266 Pac. 486 (1928).

84 Mitchell v. State, 132 Tex. Cr. Rep. 491, 105 S. W. (2d) 246 (1937). *See also* Brown v. State, 130 Tex. Cr. Rep. 323, 94 S. W. (2d) 455 (1936).

85 Millhouse v. State, 232 Ala. 567, 168 So. 665 (1936).

county.[86] Such a question is proper because discrimination during a certain period of time will tend to prove that there had been unfairness in the instant case.

After a presentation of all the evidence, a trial judge's decision that there was no discrimination should not be disturbed unless it can be shown that he did not give the matter proper consideration.[87] In the *Thomas* case,[88] moreover, the Federal Supreme Court declared that the judge's decision is not reviewable unless there has been such an abuse of the discretion given him in such cases as to deprive the Negro defendant of due process of law. This discretion of the trial judge should be carefully exercised with a view to obtaining the best jurors possible.[89] In a Texas case[90] involving unfairness to Mexicans it was said that a judge has the authority to set aside the jury commissioners' returns in an instance where he believes discrimination against the defendant's race has been shown, may decline to accept the lists of prospective jurors, and is allowed to reconvene the commission for instructions concerning the law in this respect or appoint a new set of commissioners.

What degree of respect is due to a state appellate court's decision that there has been no racial discrimination in the selection of jurors? The Federal Supreme Court has only recently remarked that, although the state court's opinion is entitled to great respect, the highest tribunal can re-examine the evidence in order to ascertain whether the decision is supported by the facts.[91]

There seems to be a difference of opinion as to whether a judge may direct that Negro jurors be called in cases where the rights of persons of that race are involved. In one instance the Virginia Court held that an order of this kind was not improper.[92] The court declared that a Negro might very well be called on account of his qualifications for jury duty and not on

[86] Bonaparte v. State, 65 Fla. 287, 61 So. 633 (1913).

[87] Royals v. State, 73 Fla. 897, 75 So. 199 (1917).

[88] Thomas v. Texas, 212 U. S. 278, 29 Sup. Ct. 393 (1909), *aff'g* 49 Tex. Cr. Rep. 633, 95 S. W. 1069 (1906). In accord with this decision are State v. Cooper, 205 N. C. 657, 172 S. E. 199 (1934); State v. Walls, 211 N. C. 487, 191 S. E. 232 (1937); State v. Henderson, 216 N. C. 99, 3 S. E. (2d) 357 (1939).

[89] Montgomery v. State, 55 Fla. 97, 45 So. 879 (1908).

[90] Pena v. State, 114 Tex. Cr. Rep. 15, 24 S. W. (2d) 396 (1930).

[91] Pierre v. Louisiana, 306 U. S. 354, 59 Sup. Ct. 536 (1939).

[92] Coleman v. Commonwealth, 84 Va. 1, 3 S. E. 878 (1887).

account of his race or color. The North Carolina[93] and Tennessee[94] courts, however, have come to the conclusion that such a command is improper. The fact that in the Virginia case both the prosecutrix and the defendant were Negroes, while the other two cases involved civil actions between Negroes and whites, may well have influenced the courts in coming to what seem to be opposite conclusions. However this may be, it was stated in a Maryland case that the intentional placing of Negroes on juries is just as much a violation of the law as discrimination against them.[95] It has also been held that a white man cannot object because there were no Negroes on the grand jury which indicted him,[96] and he cannot take exception to the fact that Negroes have served.[97]

In one Mississippi case the action of jury-selecting officials in intentionally leaving the names of Negroes off the lists from which juries are selected was said to violate not only the Fourteenth Amendment but also the due process clause of the Fifth Amendment, the impartial jury provision of the Sixth, and the guarantee of a republican form of government contained in the Constitution.[98] However, this ruling disregards the fact that the Supreme Court has held that the first eight amendments apply only to the federal government and not to the states,[99] and the argument that such action violates the guarantee of a republican form of government is rather farfetched.

A plea in abatement or a motion to quash an indictment on account of discrimination against the Negro in the selection of jurors must state that members of that race were excluded because of race or color.[100] It was said in one Louisiana case that

---

[93] Capehart v. Stewart, 80 N. C. 101 (1879). The decision was affirmed, however, because the objecting party had not exhausted his full quota of peremptory challenges.

[94] Mayor of Nashville v. Sheperd, 62 Tenn. 373 (1874).

[95] Cooper v. State, 64 Md. 40, 20 Atl. 986 (1885).

[96] Griffin v. State, 183 Ga. 775, 190 S. E. 2 (1937); Commonwealth v. Wright, 79 Ky. 22 (1880); State v. Dierlamm, 189 La. 544, 180 So. 135 (1938); State v. Sims, 213 N. C. 590, 197 S. E. 176 (1938) (dictum).

[97] Lee v. State, 45 Miss. 114 (1871); Brittle v. People, 2 Neb. 198 (1873).

[98] Farrow v. State, 91 Miss. 509, 45 So. 619 (1908). The case is discussed in (1908) 66 Cent. L. J. 481.

[99] Barron v. Mayor of Baltimore, 7 Pet. 243 (U. S. 1833).

[100] Younge v. United States, 242 Fed. 788 (C. C. A. 4th, 1917); Patterson v. Commonwealth, 139 Va. 589, 123 S. E. 657 (1924). That the allegation must be *solely* because of race or color: *See* Hale v. Commonwealth, 269 Ky. 743, 108

an allegation that the list of three hundred names from which a jury was drawn did not contain the name of a single Negro and that one-fourth of the population of the parish were of that race, while pregnant with the affirmation of discrimination, does not sufficiently allege it, as there might be a legitimate omission of this kind however improbable it may appear to be.[101] If the state demurs, the facts alleged are to be taken as true for the purpose of ruling upon the pleading,[102] but in one Florida case it was declared that the state should be permitted to take issue on the pleadings in case its demurrer is overruled.[103]

A party may waive his right to object to the discrimination practised against his race in this respect.[104] When a Negro defendant has had a reasonable opportunity to challenge the formation of the grand jury which found the bill of indictment against him and fails to do so, he will not generally be allowed to raise the objection later, so as to invalidate the proceedings as a whole.[105] If there has been no such opportunity to challenge the grand jury, the defendant must allege and prove the circumstances which excuse his failure to so object.[106] In one Texas case it was declared that the objection could nevertheless be brought forward by a later motion to quash the particular indictment when the case came before the court.[107] In another case from the same jurisdiction it is said that the objection does not come too late even after the return.[108] In some states, like North Carolina, the procedure is such that the defendant is really afforded no opportunity to make such an objection before trial, and in such jurisdictions it would probably be proper to

S. W. (2d) 716 (1937); Clark v. Commonwealth, 167 Va. 472, 189 S. E. 143 (1937).

[101] State v. Baptiste, 105 La. 661, 30 So. 147 (1901).

[102] *See* Montgomery v. State, 53 Fla. 115, 42 So. 894 (1907); Washington v. State, 95 Fla. 289, 116 So. 470 (1928); State v. Young, 82 W. Va., 714, 97 S. E. 134 (1918); State v. Frazier, 104 W. Va. 480, 140 S. E. 324 (1927). The Frazier case is commented upon in (1928) 26 MICH. L. REV. 815.

[103] Montgomery v. State, 53 Fla. 115, 42 So. 894 (1907).

[104] Washington v. State, 95 Fla. 289, 116 So. 470 (1928); Haggard v. Commonwealth, 79 Ky. 366 (1881); Keith v. State, 53 Ohio App. 58, 4 N. E. (2d) 220 (1936); White v. State, 128 S. W. (2d) 51 (Tex. Cr. App. 1939).

[105] Tillman v. State, 121 Ark. 322, 181 S. W. 890 (1915); State v. King, 342 Mo. 975, 119 S. W. (2d) 277 (1938); Jackson v. State, 71 S. W. 280 (Tex. Cr. App. 1902); McCline v. State, 64 Tex. Cr. Rep. 19, 141 S. W. 977 (1912).

[106] State v. King, 342 Mo. 975, 119 S. W. (2d) 277 (1938).

[107] Thomas v. State, 49 Tex. Cr. Rep. 633, 95 S. W. 1069 (1906).

[108] Roberts v. State, 81 Tex. Cr. Rep. 227, 195 S. W. 189 (1917).

object to the formation at that time. An objection to the panel of petit jurors alleging racial discrimination in the selective process has been declared by the Arkansas Court[109] not to be in the nature of a plea in abatement and therefore not one of those motions that must be brought at the very beginning of proceedings. The court also said that this objection differs from a motion to quash an indictment because of such unfairness in choosing the grand jury, such motion being similar to a plea in abatement and hence required to be brought before the plea in bar. In an Oklahoma case of recent date, however, it was said that a challenge to the panel of trial jurors must come before a plea of not guilty and must be taken in writing before the jury is sworn.[110] In one Maryland case it is said that while the court in its discretion may permit a plea in bar to be withdrawn and a plea in abatement filed, its refusal to do this is not subject to review.[111] An objection to tales jurors because no Negroes were chosen must be made when they are first brought into court.[112]

It has been held that the refusal of the trial judge to delay a hearing a reasonable time in order to enable a Negro defendant to procure the attendance of witnesses by whom he hoped to prove unfairness to his race in this respect was an abuse of discretion.[113] However, a different result was reached where no explanation was forthcoming for the delay in obtaining the desired evidence.[114]

The question of racial discrimination in selecting jurors must be raised in apt time. It is too late to object for the first time after conviction,[115] or on appeal,[116] or on a motion for a new trial.[117] Moreover, in a recent Georgia decision it was said that

[109] Ware v. State, 146 Ark. 321, 225 S. W. 626 (1920).

[110] Powell v. State, 60 Okla. Cr. Rep. 166, 63 P. (2d) 113 (1936).

[111] Cooper v. State, 64 Md. 40, 20 Atl. 986 (1885).

[112] Carter v. State, 45 Tex. Cr. Rep. 430, 76 S. W. 437 (1903).

[113] Whitney v. State, 42 Tex. Cr. Rep. 283, 59 S. W. 895 (1900).

[114] Franklin v. State, 85 Ark. 534, 109 S. W. 298 (1908).

[115] Carruthers v. Reed, 102 F. (2d) 933 (C. C. A. 8th, 1939); Watts v. State, 75 Tex. Cr. Rep. 330, 171 S. W. 202 (1914).

[116] Clayton v. State, 191 Ark. 1070, 89 S. W. (2d) 732 (1935); Merriweather v. Commonwealth, 118 Ky. 870, 82 S. W. 592 (1904). *See also* Lee v. State, 45 Miss. 114 (1871).

[117] Powell v. State, 224 Ala. 540, 141 So. 201 (1932); Hicks v. State, 143 Ark. 158, 220 S. W. 308 (1920); Garnett v. State, 60 S. W. 765 (Tex. Cr. App. 1900); White v. State, 128 S. W. (2d) 51 (Tex. Cr. App. 1939).

rulings against a Negro defendant in this respect which he claimed were erroneous could not be asserted as a proper basis for a motion for new trial, the proper procedure being to except to these rulings *pendente lite* or to assign them as error in the bill of exceptions.[118] In Florida an attempt was made to employ the writ *coram nobis*, a writ of error directed to another branch of the same court, as a means of challenging the legality of the verdict of a trial jury to which the culprit had not objected. At the original hearing no mention had been made of discrimination against the convicted Negro's race in the selection of the jury. The court declared that this writ was not available where the defendant had had an opportunity to object at the trial and had not done so, especially where there is no suggestion of an unfair trial, duress, or use of undue influence.[119]

The issue as to whether there is discrimination against Negroes in this respect in any given case has been brought to the attention of the various courts in several ways. There is the plea in abatement, the motion to quash, and the challenge to the array or panel. All three of these methods are not in use in every jurisdiction. The local practice controls the mode of procedure adopted. In some states one or more of these methods of raising the question may be employed while the others may not, but a state may make use of all three as is shown by an examination of certain Maryland decisions.[120] In West Virginia the proper way to raise the question is by a plea in abatement,[121] but a plea of this type which has all the necessary allegations will not be thrown out simply because the defendant's counsel misnamed it a motion to quash.[122] The Indiana Court has decided that racial discrimination in the selection of grand jurors must be raised by a plea in abatement and not by a motion to quash the indictment.[123] In Florida it was held in one instance that the proper way to raise the issue of discrimination against

[118] Herndon v. State, 178 Ga. 832, 174 S. E. 597 (1934).

[119] Washington v. State, 95 Fla. 289, 116 So. 470 (1928). *But see* Swain v. State, 18 N. E. (2d) 921 (Ind. 1939).

[120] Cooper v. State, 64 Md. 40, 20 Atl. 986 (1885); Lee v. State, 163 Md. 56, 161 Atl. 284 (1932).

[121] State v. Cook, 81 W. Va. 686, 95 S. E. 792 (1918); State v. Young, 82 W. Va. 714, 97 S. E. 134 (1918).

[122] *Ibid.*

[123] Johnson v. State, 213 Ind. 659, 14 N. E. (2d) 96 (1938).

Negroes in selecting jurors is the plea in abatement and not the motion to quash,[124] but in all the later cases from this jurisdiction the challenge to the array has been used.[125] In Oklahoma both the challenge to the array or panel[126] and the motion to quash[127] have been employed, while in New Jersey the former has been the only method used.[128] The usual manner of raising the issue in Arkansas,[129] Louisiana,[130] and Missouri[131] is evidently a motion to quash, but in all three jurisdictions the challenge to the array has been used.[132] A motion to discharge the jury seems to be another way of raising the issue in Arkansas,[133] a method which was also followed in the only case to come before the Kansas Court.[134]

A motion to set aside the indictment or a challenge to the panel seems to have been the method approved by the earlier

---

[124] Tarrance v. State, 43 Fla. 446, 30 So. 685 (1901).

[125] Montgomery v. State, 53 Fla. 115, 42 So. 894 (1907); Bonaparte v. State, 65 Fla. 287, 61 So. 633 (1913); Haynes v. State, 71 Fla. 585, 72 So. 180 (1916); Royals v. State, 73 Fla. 897, 75 So. 199 (1917).

[126] Smith v. State, 4 Okla. Cr. Rep. 328, 111 Pac. 960 (1910); Peters v. State, 22 Okla. Cr. Rep. 245, 211 Pac. 427 (1922); Welch v. State, 30 Okla. Cr. Rep. 330, 236 Pac. 68 (1925); Hollins v. State, 56 Okla. Cr. Rep. 275, 38 P. (2d) 36 (1934); Powell v. State, 60 Okla. Cr. Rep. 166, 63 P. (2d) 113 (1936).

[127] McIntosh v. State, 8 Okla. Cr. Rep. 469, 128 Pac. 735 (1912); Scott v. State, 29 Okla. Cr. Rep. 324, 233 Pac. 776 (1925); Bruster v. State, 40 Okla. Cr. Rep. 25, 266 Pac. 486 (1928); Carrick v. State, 41 Okla. Cr. Rep. 336, 274 Pac. 896 (1929); Davis v. State, 53 Okla. Cr. Rep. 411, 12 P. (2d) 555 (1932); Holland v. State, 61 Okla. Cr. Rep. 215, 67 P. (2d) 58 (1937).

[128] Johnson v. State, 59 N. J. Law 271, 35 Atl. 787 (1896); Bullock v. State, 65 N. J. Law 557, 47 Atl. 62 (1900); State v. Jones, 115 N. J. Law 257, 179 Atl. 320 (1935).

[129] Eastling v. State, 69 Ark. 189, 62 S. W. 584 (1901); Castleberry v. State, 69 Ark. 346, 63 S. W. 670 (1901); Ware v. State, 146 Ark. 321, 225 S. W. 626 (1920); Hannah v. State, 183 Ark. 810, 38 S. W. (2d) 1090 (1931).

[130] State v. Joseph, 45 La. Ann. 903, 12 So. 934 (1893); State v. Baptiste, 105 La. 661, 30 So. 147 (1901); State v. West, 116 La. 626, 40 So. 920 (1906); State v. Lawrence, 124 La. 378, 50 So. 406 (1909); State v. Turner, 133 La. 555, 63 So. 169 (1913); State v. Connor, 142 La. 631, 77 So. 482 (1917); State v. Gill, 186 La. 339, 172 So. 412 (1937); State v. Pierre, 189 La. 764, 180 So. 630 (1938).

[131] State v. Brown, 119 Mo. 527, 24 S. W. 1027 (1894); State v. Warner, 165 Mo. 399, 65 S. W. 584 (1901); State v. Liston, 318 Mo. 1222, 2 S. W. (2d) 780 (1928); State v. Logan, 341 Mo. 1164, 111 S. W. (2d) 110 (1937); State v. King, 342 Mo. 975, 119 S. W. (2d) 277 (1938).

[132] *See* Franklin v. State, 85 Ark. 534, 109 S. W. 298 (1908); State v. Murray, 47 La. Ann. 1424, 17 So. 832 (1895); State v. Thomas, 250 Mo. 189, 157 S. W. 330 (1913).

[133] Jordan v. State, 141 Ark. 504, 217 S. W. 788 (1920).

[134] State v. Ryan, 141 Kans. 549, 42 P. (2d) 591 (1935).

Kentucky decisions,[135] but in the more recent cases the plea in abatement and the motion to quash have been employed.[136] In California both the motion to quash and the challenge to the panel seem to be proper procedure.[137] In one recent case from North Carolina the plea in abatement was used,[138] but in most of the cases from that jurisdiction the motion to quash has been employed.[139] In Alabama it was said in an early decision that the statutes which were in effect at that time did not permit a plea in abatement for error or irregularity in drawing or summoning grand jurymen because of racial discrimination in their selection.[140] However, this decision would probably not be followed today in view of what has been said to the contrary in a later case.[141] The procedure used in more recent Alabama cases is the motion to quash,[142] and this method seems to have been the only one employed in Delaware,[143] Mississippi,[144] South Carolina,[145] Tennessee,[146] and Virginia.[147] In Georgia all three of the usual ways of bringing the issue before the courts have been attempted,[148] and there is nothing in the language of the

---

[135] *See* Haggard v. Commonwealth, 79 Ky. 366 (1881); Smith v. Commonwealth, 17 Ky. Law. Rep. 1162, 33 S. W. 825 (1896).

[136] Miller v. Commonwealth, 127 Ky. 387, 105 S. W. 899 (1907); Owens v. Commonwealth, 188 Ky. 498, 222 S. W. 524 (1920); Montjoy v. Commonwealth, 262 Ky. 426, 90 S. W. (2d) 362 (1936); Hale v. Commonwealth, 269 Ky. 743, 108 S. W. (2d) 716 (1937).

[137] People v. Hines, 81 P. (2d) 1048 (Cal. App. 1938).

[138] State v. Henderson, 216 N. C. 99, 3 S. E. (2d) 357 (1939).

[139] State v. Peoples, 131 N. C. 784, 42 S. E. 814 (1902); State v. Daniels, 134 N. C. 641, 46 S. E. 743 (1904); State v. Cooper, 205 N. C. 657, 172 S. E. 199 (1934); State v. Walls, 211 N. C. 487, 191 S. E. 232 (1937). See N. C. CODE ANN. (Michie, 1931) §2335.

[140] Boulo v. State, 51 Ala. 18 (1874). [141] Green v. State, 73 Ala. 26 (1882).

[142] Ragland v. State, 187 Ala. 5, 65 So. 776 (1914); Norris v. State, 229 Ala. 226, 156 So. 556 (1934); Collins v. State, 234 Ala. 197, 174 So. 296 (1937); Vaughn v. State, 235 Ala. 80, 177 So. 553 (1937).

[143] Neal v. Delaware, 103 U. S. 370 (1880).

[144] Smith v. State, 18 So. 116 (Miss. 1895); Dixon v. State, 74 Miss. 271, 20 So. 839 (1896); Lewis v. State, 91 Miss. 505, 45 So. 360 (1907); Farrow v. State, 91 Miss. 509, 45 So. 619 (1908).

[145] State v. Brownfield, 60 S. C. 509, 39 S. E. 2 (1901); State v. Franklin, 80 S. C. 332, 60 S. E. 953 (1908).

[146] Ransom v. State, 116 Tenn. 355, 96 S. W. 953 (1906); Rivers v. State, 117 Tenn. 235, 96 S. W. 956 (1906).

[147] Patterson v. Commonwealth, 139 Va. 589, 123 S. E. 657 (1924); Clark v. Commonwealth, 167 Va. 472, 189 S. E. 143 (1937).

[148] *See* Wilson v. State, 69 Ga. 224 (1882); Herndon v. State, 178 Ga. 832, 174 S. E. 597 (1934).

tribunal which could be said to disapprove any of them. In Texas a statute provides for only two reasons for challenging the array of grand jurymen.[149] As the right to challenge for racial discrimination did not come within the purview of either of these provisions, it was held in several early cases that there could be no such objection to the jury.[150] This position was soon abandoned, however, and it is now held that a defendant may assert his constitutional right in this respect by means of either a plea in abatement or a motion to quash.[151] In considering a similar Missouri statute, the court of that state remarked that "whenever a constitutional right comes in contact with a statute, the former tolls the latter; and whenever a constitutional right, such as is now under discussion, has no statute specifically adapted to enforce it, by its own inherent potency, and leaning not on its adventitious aids of statutory regulations, it supplies the lack of statutory provisions, and enforces itself." [152]

Subject to certain restrictions, it is provided by statute that the local rules and regulations governing the summoning and selection of jurors and the methods of objecting to any irregularity which may be noted in the manner of choosing such jurors shall also apply to the federal courts in the various states.[153] There is also a statute providing that no citizen possessing all other qualifications shall be disqualified for service as a grand or petit juror in any federal court on account of race, color, or previous condition of servitude.[154] Hence it is necessary to follow the procedure of the state where the case is tried in raising the issue of discrimination against the Negro in the formation of juries.[155]

The Kentucky legislature enacted a statute which provided that there should be no exception to rulings upon challenges to

---

[149] TEX. CRIM. CODE ANN. (Vernon, 1925) §§358, 361.

[150] Williams v. State, 44 Tex. 34 (1875); Cavitt v. State, 15 Tex. App. 190 (1883); Carter v. State, 39 Tex. Cr. Rep. 345, 46 S. W. 236 (1898).

[151] *See* Carter v. State, 48 S. W. 508 (Tex. Cr. App. 1898), approved on this point by Carter v. Texas, 177 U. S. 442, 20 Sup. Ct. 687 (1900); Garnett v. State, 60 S. W. 765 (Tex. Cr. App. 1900); Thomas v. State, 49 Tex. Cr. Rep. 633, 95 S. W. 1069 (1906); Juarez v. State, 102 Tex. Cr. Rep. 297, 277 S. W. 1091 (1925).

[152] State v. Warner, 165 Mo. 399, 65 S. W. 584 (1901).

[153] 28 U. S. C. A. §§411, 729 (1926). *See* United States v. Eagan, 30 Fed. 608 (C. C. E. D. Mo. 1887).

[154] 28 U. S. C. A. §415 (1926).

[155] Beckett v. United States, 84 Fed. (2d) 731 (C. C. A. 6th, 1936). *See also* Younge v. United States, 242 Fed. 788 (C. C. A. 4th, 1917).

the panel, motions for new trial, and motions to set aside indictments.[156] There could be no appeal from adverse rulings of the lower courts on motions of this kind. In cases involving claims by Negroes that their race had been discriminated against in the selection of jurors, this statute was held not to deny equal protection of the laws. The State Court of Appeals came to the conclusion that the right of appeal from adverse rulings of the trial judge is purely statutory and not in the nature of an inherent right to which everyone is entitled.[157] The court declared that there was nothing in this statute which could be interpreted as giving any group of citizens any privilege withheld from others. The issue was never taken to the Federal Supreme Court, and there is now no reason to do so. A recent change in the statute makes it possible for rulings of this kind to be appealed from.[158]

The Supreme Court has decided that a writ of habeas corpus brought in a lower federal court is not a proper method of obtaining a review of state court decisions concerning racial discrimination in the selection of jurors.[159] The correct procedure was said to be a writ of error to the court of final appeal in the state where the particular controversy arises, a mode of appeal which has now been superseded by certiorari.[160] The same principles apply where an accused Negro who has escaped from the state where he has been indicted by a grand jury, in the selection of which he alleges unfairness toward his race, petitions for a writ of habeas corpus in an attempt to avoid extradition from the jurisdiction to which he has fled. It has been decided that the question of discrimination must be determined in the first instance by the courts of the demanding state and no other.[161]

---

[156] Ky. Codes Ann. (Carroll, 1932) Crim. Prac. §281.

[157] Miller v. Commonwealth, 127 Ky. 387, 105 S. W. 899 (1907); Owens v. Commonwealth, 188 Ky. 498, 222 S. W. 524 (1920).

[158] Ky. Codes Ann. (Carroll, 1938) Crim. Prac. §281.

[159] Wood v. Brush, 140 U. S. 278, 11 Sup. Ct. 738 (1891); Jugiro v. Brush, 140 U. S. 291, 11 Sup. Ct. 770 (1891) (Japanese); Andrews v. Swartz, 156 U. S. 272, 15 Sup. Ct. 389 (1895). See also in this connection Virginia v. Rives, 100 U. S. 313 (1879); *Ex parte* Caesar, 27 F. Supp. 690 (N. D. Tex. 1939).

[160] Note (1934) 29 Ill. L. Rev. 498. *See also* Hale v. Crawford, 65 Fed. (2d) 739 (C. C. A. 1st, 1933).

[161] Blevins v. Snyder, 57 App. D. C. 300, 22 Fed. (2d) 876 (1927); Hale v. Crawford, 65 Fed. (2d) 739 (C. C. A. 1st, 1933).

Only one other case merits consideration at this point. In Utah a Negro sued a white man for damages because the latter had written a letter to the authorities in which he had objected to serving on a jury with colored persons. The plaintiff claimed that he was humiliated and had been deprived of the jury fees which he would have received if the defendant's objection had not been heeded. The court held that the facts pleaded failed to establish a case against the defendant, declaring that the action was frivolous, unwarranted, and unworthy.[162] The officials who acceded to the defendant's wishes by refusing to allow the Negro to serve were not in any way bound to listen to the objection of a prejudiced white man or any other ordinary citizen.

It is too early to judge the ultimate results of the *Scottsboro* decision. The white man in the South is certainly not going to care for the service of Negroes on juries to any great extent. The probable result of this attitude is almost certain to be an extensive use of subterfuges of one kind or another, such as placing Negroes on jury lists and then excusing them for some reason, or placing names of colored men in the jury box as a colorable compliance with the law, which was actually claimed in one recent Alabama case.[163] In states like Mississippi where the local law provides that jurymen must also be electors, Negroes may be kept off the panel by the use of such devices as the understanding clause and other disfranchising provisions in the state constitutions.[164] Those Negroes who do actually qualify may oftentimes be barred by challenges, either peremptory or for cause.[165] It is very probable, however, that the *Scottsboro* decision will greatly increase the numbers of Negro jurors in those courts where there have been few if any men of that race on either the grand or petit juries for a long time. The South will certainly have to pay at least some attention to the decision or else face the reversal of every case in which a person of color has been convicted. Of course the cost of an appeal to the Supreme Court is very high and hence the number of requests for review would be comparatively few.[166] Never-

[162] McPherson v. McCarrick, 22 Utah 232, 61 Pac. 1004 (1900).

[163] Millhouse v. State, 232 Ala. 567, 168 So. 665 (1936).

[164] See Note (1935) 8 Miss. L. Rev. 196.

[165] See Note (1936) 24 Ill. B. J. 233.

[166] See Note (1934) 29 Ill. L. Rev. 498.

theless, a sufficient number of these jury cases would probably be taken to that tribunal to make the recalcitrant state feel the result of its failure to obey the law, whether the cost be financial or a blow to its judicial prestige. Furthermore, the Supreme Court can almost surely be said to have abandoned its former conservative attitude that the decision of the trial judge is not reviewable unless the Negro is able to prove an abuse of discretion in ruling upon the issue,[167] and it is very probable that the court will make a much more thorough inquiry into the facts of future cases than it has done in the past.[168]

It must be perceived, however, that familiarity with local race problems is essential to a complete and thorough understanding of the difficulties involved, for "to view such a situation through the inflamed eyes of race prejudice, or the no less inflamed eyes of anti-race prejudice, only increases the confusion and sets the ends of justice beyond reach."[169] Furthermore, there are other difficulties which present themselves. Petit jurors serving at important trials must oftentimes be herded together for hours or even days in the same room and may even be required not to separate during the time that no actual consideration is being given the case in hand. Such circumstances present difficulties for those who desire better interracial relations. However, there can be no doubt that at least some Negroes have actually served on juries since the turn of the century.[170] The great majority of these are presumably from the urban centers where the members of the colored race have acquired a greater degree of economic independence and the educational facilities are better. In the small towns and rural communities there are few Negro jurors. There is no consistency about this, however, as there are many cities and large towns where Negro jurymen are unheard of.

There has been a great deal of comment during the last few years concerning this phase of the race problem. It has probably received more editorial attention in the newspapers, magazines, and periodicals than any other aspect of the problem

[167] *See* Thomas v. Texas, 212 U. S. 278, 29 Sup. Ct. 393 (1909), cited *supra* note 88.

[168] See Note (1936) 24 Ill. B. J. 233.

[169] Note (1933) 36 L. Notes 104.

[170] See replies to questionnaire on actual service in a number of states. Stephenson, Race Distinctions in American Law (1910) 253-272.

with the possible exception of the primary election. The ostensible reason for this is of course the great amount of publicity which has been given to the *Scottsboro* case. The public interest will no doubt continue until this famous case ceases to be news. Whether the interest in the jury issue will then endure or die out altogether is a question which only time can answer.

XIII

RACE PREJUDICE OF JURORS

A good many problems have arisen in connection with questions put to jurors and answers made by them when they are asked on their preliminary examination, technically known as the examination on the *voir dire*, whether they have any race prejudice which will unduly interfere with a fair consideration and thorough sifting of the evidence in the case before them. These problems usually arise in criminal prosecutions against Negroes, but they also occur in civil cases where Negroes and whites are contesting. There are also instances of such questions being asked where the prejudice was against some other minority racial group.

A failure on the part of a trial judge to permit such questions to be asked of prospective jurors is beyond a doubt unjustified.[1] In the case which attracted the most attention to this phase of the race problem, the *Aldridge* case from the District of Columbia, the trial judge overruled the request of a Negro defendant charged with the murder of a white man that each and every juror be interrogated concerning racial prejudice. In this instance the Federal Supreme Court held that the refusal of this request was erroneous, thus reversing[2] the District of Columbia Court of Appeals. In coming to its fallacious conclusion the latter court had followed one of its former decisions[3] in expressing the novel but erroneous view that even if such a question were a proper one in the Lower South, it was not proper in the District of Columbia because racial prejudice there is certainly not so pronounced. The Court of Appeals had also declared that the prejudice in the District of Columbia is not of such a character as to prevent fair treat-

---

[1] Pinder v. State, 27 Fla. 370, 8 So. 837 (1891); Hill v. State, 112 Miss. 260, 72 So. 1003 (1916); State v. Pyle, 123 S. W. (2d) 167 (Mo. 1938); State v. McAfee, 64 N. C. 339 (1870). *See* People v. Reyes, 5 Cal. 347 (1855) (persons of Spanish extraction); People v. Car Soy, 57 Cal. 102 (1880) (Chinese).

[2] Aldridge v. United States, 283 U. S. 308, 51 Sup. Ct. 470 (1931), *rev'g* 60 App. D. C. 45, 47 F. (2d) 407 (1931), (1931) 10 N. C. L. Rev. 86.

[3] Crawford v. United States, 59 App. D. C. 356, 41 F. (2d) 979 (1930).

ment of any Negro charged with crime, nor is it influenced so much by the density of the Negro population as it is in the states farther to the south; but these arguments can well be answered by calling attention to the fact that the city of Washington is the nation's capital and the center of political activity, and one would therefore suppose that all controversial subjects, including the race issue, would be in the foreground of political and social discussion in that jurisdiction. This has been proved by the publicity which was given the incident of the refusal to serve the guests of Representative Oscar DePriest in the congressional restaurant. The race problem is not merely a sectional one. It applies to the North and West as well as to the South, and this particular phase of it cannot be said to have any peculiar angles which make special treatment necessary. Futhermore, Washington is below the Mason and Dixon Line.

Where the court has allowed a Negro defendant to ask the panel of jurors whether they are prejudiced against him because of his race, a refusal to permit each separate juror to be so examined was ruled not to amount to a denial of due process or equal protection.[4]

In one case from Missouri a juror was permitted to serve where he admitted some prejudice against Negroes but not to such a degree as would prevent him from giving a Negro charged with the murder of a white man an impartial trial. The appellate court evidently did not believe that the juror was thereby rendered incompetent to serve.[5] However, as the case was remanded on another ground, the court said that it probably would be better to select for the second trial of the accused, jurors who had no unkindly feeling toward the Negro race. In South Carolina a Negro's attorney was not allowed to ask a juror if he would be influenced by the fact that the defendant was colored. The appellate court refused to interfere, basing its decision on the ground that the statutory questions concerning the presence of any prejudice or bias against the accused had already been asked and that there was therefore no sufficient reason for further questioning along this line.[6]

---

[4] Herndon v. State, 178 Ga. 832, 174 S. E. 597 (1934).

[5] State v. Brown, 188 Mo. 451, 87 S. W. 519 (1905).

[6] State v. Bethune, 93 S. C. 195, 75 S. E. 281 (1912).

However, it is believed that these two decisions are not in line with the more recent cases and may be said to be unsound. Race prejudice in the South is of such a quality as to require special latitude of inquiry in cases of this type, and this is borne out by the later cases in respect to this problem. The Missouri Court certainly seems to admit that the selection of unprejudiced jurors would be desirable. How is it possible to obtain jurors who are not prejudiced against Negroes without permitting a direct inquiry as to whether one is so prejudiced? In a previous appeal of the South Carolina case the court had called attention to the fact that the trial judge, when faced with the necessity of deciding whether such a specific question should be put to one of the jurors, had replied: "You can't go into that sea. It might swamp us all."[7]

On the other hand, courts have decided that, where it appears that a juror stated that he had no race prejudice against the accused and that he could give him the same treatment meted out to a white man, he is certainly competent to serve.[8] Furthermore, if he answers the question put to him concerning his ability to give the Negro a fair trial by saying "I believe so" or "I think so," he is not thereby disqualified, as many persons express their honest convictions in this somewhat indefinite and uncertain manner.[9]

In one recent Mississippi case a juror was asked by the court whether he could render a "white man's verdict." The appellate court disapproved of the question but refused to reverse the case in view of the fact that all the jurors, including the one particularly objected to, had testified that they would give a Negro the same impartial trial that they would give anyone else.[10] The trial judge had also stated that he had used the above expression only to emphasize the duty of jurors to render a fair verdict to people of all races, and this undoubtedly had a great deal to do with the decision.

Three southern courts have held that it is not proper to question jurors as to the comparative credence they would give

---

[7] State v. Bethune, 86 S. C. 143, 67 S. E. 466 (1910).

[8] State v. Buford, 158 Iowa 173, 139 N. W. 464 (1913); Hubbard v. State, 43 Tex. Cr. Rep. 564, 67 S. W. 413 (1902).

[9] Strong v. State, 85 Ark. 536, 109 S. W. 536 (1908).

[10] Owen v. State, 177 Miss. 488, 171 So. 345 (1936).

to the testimony of white and Negro witnesses,[11] but the California Court has held that it was reversible error for a judge to refuse to permit a Chinese defendant to ask a juror whether he could give the defendant's testimony the same credence as if vouched for by a white man.[12] The Texas Court has decided that jurors are not objectionable because on being questioned they stated that they would give more weight to a white person's tesimony than to a Negro's, but had no prejudice against the Negro defendant and were of the opinion that they could give him a fair trial.[13] In this instance all the witnesses except an unimportant one were Negroes, and this fact may have had something to do with the outcome. In comparatively recent times, however, the South Carolina Court held that a juror was disqualified because he made a statement that he intended to disregard incriminating testimony for the sole reason that the witness testifying was a Negro.[14]

The fact that the Negro defendant is being tried for the homicide of a member of his own race may have an influence in deciding whether or not a particular juror is competent. Even if he declares that he cannot give a Negro as fair a trial as he would a white man, the fact that an affirmative answer was given to the further question as to whether he could render an impartial verdict where one Negro had killed another renders him fit for service.[15] In the trial of a white man for the murder of a Negro, it was said to be proper to ask a juror if he would return the same verdict against a white defendant for killing a Negro as for killing another white man where the evidence was the same in both instances.[16] In a case where a Negro killed a white man for insulting his wife it was said to be proper to ask whether a juror would render the same verdict

---

[11] Jenkins v. State, 31 Fla. 196, 12 So. 677 (1893); State v. Dyer, 154 La. 379, 97 So. 563 (1923); Lee v. State, 164 Md. 550, 165 Atl. 614 (1933). The Dyer case is most certainly influenced by the fact that in Louisiana a defendant is not permitted to inquire as to the juror's opinion concerning the credibility of any witness.

[12] People v. Car Soy, 57 Cal. 102 (1880).

[13] Moore v. State, 52 Tex. Cr. Rep. 336, 107 S. W. 540 (1908).

[14] State v. Rector, 166 S. C. 335, 164 S. E. 865 (1931).

[15] Hamlin v. State, 101 Ark. 257, 142 S. W. 151 (1911); Williams v. State, 60 Tex. Cr. Rep. 453, 132 S. W. 345 (1910). *See also* State v. Mayfield, 104 La. 173, 28 So. 997 (1900).

[16] Lester v. State, 2 Tex. App. 432 (1877).

in this instance as he would if a Negro had insulted a white man's wife and had been killed by him.[17]

The fact that a white juror does not regard the Negro as his social equal fails to render him incompetent,[18] and he is not disqualified because he believes that the white race is superior.[19] A juror is incompetent when he states that he cannot give fair consideration to a case in which trouble had followed intermarriage between the races,[20] and the same is true when he testifies that he has an antipathy to a Negro lawyer pleading before a white jury.[21]

The Maryland Court has decided that a juror cannot be asked whether he knows of the various forms of Negro segregation practiced in the Eastern Shore counties,[22] while in Kentucky it was declared that only those jurors who would wholly disregard their own private opinions on the question as to whether Negroes should be permitted to travel in the same bus as white persons should be retained in event the court should instruct the jury that the Negroes had such a right.[23]

A juror is not disqualified because he has become embroiled in a personal difficulty with a Negro other than the defendant because he refused to drink at the same public bar with the said Negro.[24] In one Louisiana case the court refused to approve questions as to the opinion of certain jurors with respect to the race problem, the superiority of the white race, and the trial of Negroes by members of the white race exclusively. The appellate court declared that the answers to these questions could not affect the qualifications of these jurors.[25] There are expressions in this case, however, which might lead one to be-

[17] Fendrick v. State, 39 Tex. Cr. Rep. 147, 45 S. W. 589 (1898).

[18] Lee v. State, 164 Md. 550, 165 Atl. 614 (1933); Cavitt v. State, 15 Tex. App. 190 (1883); Bass v. State, 59 Tex. Cr. Rep. 186, 127 S. W. 1020 (1910). The question whether the friendship the juror felt for a Negro defendant was the friendship of a white man for another white man or for a Negro was asked in State v. Brady, 124 La. 951, 50 So. 806 (1909), a case where the defendant claimed that he was white and that he had intermarried and associated with whites, but the court found that a decision on the point was unnecessary.

[19] Johnson v. State, 88 Neb. 565, 130 N. W. 282 (1911).

[20] People v. Decker, 157 N. Y. 186, 51 N. E. 1018 (1898).

[21] State v. Sanders, 103 S. C. 216, 88 S. E. 10 (1916).

[22] Lee v. State, 164 Md. 550, 165 Atl. 614 (1933).

[23] Brumfield v. Consolidated Coach Corp., 240 Ky. 1, 40 S. W. (2d) 356 (1931).

[24] State v. Green, 229 Mo. 642, 129 S. W. 700 (1910).

[25] State v. Casey, 44 La. Ann. 969, 11 So. 583 (1892).

lieve that the test adopted in Louisiana at that time was the juror's prejudice against the particular Negro defendant who was being tried, and this makes the case of uncertain value as a precedent.

In Oklahoma[26] and Texas[27] it has been held that prospective jurors may be asked whether they are members of a negrophobe organization or secret society such as the Ku Klux Klan, but in Missouri[28] an opposite conclusion has been reached.

In a case from Texas a juror had declared he did not have race prejudice against a Negro defendant which would prevent him from giving the case fair consideration. The court ruled that he was not rendered incompetent to serve simply because of a further statement that he would not employ a Negro because his neighbors objected.[29]

In another Texas case an alleged criminal libel contained a harangue against Jews. The defendant was said to be entitled to bring out the fact that several of the proposed jurors were Jews, and his challenges on this ground were sustained.[30] The court stated, however, that prejudice should never be confused with opinion in this respect and that, if the juror had an opinion which he could lay aside, he should not be declared incompetent to serve.

In an action for damages brought by a Negro woman for the wrongful death of her husband, questions propounded to jurors as to whether they would be influenced by her color were said to be nonprejudicial. The court said that there was no danger that the jurors would be so influenced, since there should be no difference in the amount which may be recovered by white and Negro women suffering the same pecuniary damages.[31]

In one Maryland case a conviction of a Negro for murder

[26] Johnson v. State, 28 Okla. Cr. Rep. 254, 230 Pac. 525 (1924).

[27] Reich v. State, 94 Tex. Cr. Rep. 449, 251 S. W. 1072 (1923); Benson v. State, 95 Tex. Cr. Rep. 311, 254 S. W. 793 (1923).

[28] State v. Griffith, 311 Mo. 630, 279 S. W. 135 (1925); State v. Logan, 126 S. W. (2d) 256 (Mo. 1939). In the Logan case the question concerned the prospective jurors' past membership in the Ku Klux organization.

[29] Hubbard v. State, 43 Tex. Cr. Rep. 564, 67 S. W. 413 (1902).

[30] Potter v. State, 86 Tex. Cr. Rep. 380, 216 S. W. 886 (1919). Another case involving inquiries into jurors' prejudice against Jews is People v. Simon, 80 Cal. App. 675, 252 Pac. 758 (1927).

[31] Hawkins v. Missouri P. Ry., 182 Mo. App. 323, 170 S. W. 459 (1914).

had been reversed because of discrimination against his race in the selection of the trial jury. At a second hearing, the defendant argued that certain prospective jurors were disqualified because they had been on the jury list at the former trial, but the court refused to uphold this contention.[32]

There is some support in certain cases for the proposition that a case will not be reversed on the ground of race prejudice of jurors where the challenger of said jurors has not exhausted all the peremptory challenges allowed him by law,[33] and this is in accordance with the principles of law which govern objections to jurors generally.[34]

The more recent cases appear to be headed in the right direction, tending toward a recognition of an undeniable right to challenge a juror for race prejudice, except that he may not be asked concerning his desire to live socially apart from the Negro, a desire which the law cannot hope to control. There is a very thin line between social and legal prejudice, but this is probably the only criterion available under the circumstances, especially in the South where a more rigid rule would certainly disqualify most of the white candidates for jury duty.

[32] Lee v. State, 164 Md. 550, 165 Atl. 614 (1933).

[33] Hamlin v. State, 101 Ark. 257, 142 S. W. 151 (1911); State v. Bethune, 86 S. C. 143, 67 S. E. 466 (1910).

[34] Capehart v. Stewart, 80 N. C. 101 (1879); Carter v. State, 45 Tex. Cr. Rep. 430, 76 S. W. 437 (1903) (motion for rehearing).

XIV

THE RIGHT TO EFFICIENT COUNSEL

A man accused of crime must be given the fairest trial which can be obtained under the circumstances of his particular case. If this is not done, he is accorded less than he is entitled to under our system of jurisprudence. The average person knows very little about the rules of substantive law and less concerning the technicalities of procedure and evidence. Therefore it may be said that he is in no position to conduct a case in court. If he should attempt to do so, he would be at a very great disadvantage in his effort to obtain justice. The province of an attorney at law is to supply this need. The attorney offers his services for hire and may be employed to conduct a trial for a client. The arrangement for the attorney's fee is usually a matter of private concern between the parties. However, it may be that a person is too poor to hire an attorney to defend him against a charge that he has been involved in some crime. To supply this need for attorneys to defend paupers charged with offenses against the common weal, laws have been enacted which authorize the judges to appoint counsel to represent such persons who are financially unable to provide themselves with proper legal aid.

There are many Negroes in our southern states as well as elsewhere who are too poor to hire counsel to represent them in the courts. In the South the colored persons who are in this predicament probably outnumber the white. The court frequently will appoint some young lawyer without much experience. Sometimes a prominent attorney will be asked to serve where the case is of special significance. Generally speaking, it is probably true that these charity lawyers are not as efficient as privately employed attorneys, but in many instances such is not the case. Some of these young attorneys are far better trained and equipped than lawyers who have been at the bar for years. However, the young attorney is often handicapped by the lack of the thorough knowledge of the rules of procedure and evidence which is only obtained through continuous practice in the courts. Experience also counts heavily with respect to the questioning and cross-questioning of witnesses. An experienced attorney knows how to talk to a jury and in many instances is possessed of a great knowledge of human nature. Therefore he is usually better able to cope with the legal formulae than a young attorney who is just out of law school or some other lawyer's office. Hence a Negro pauper who is assigned one of these young attorneys may not always be adequately represented. His lawyer may be one of those persons who antagonize a jury with every statement he makes and has yet to find out that he does so. He may be a person who has made a great record in law school and yet not be a good trial attorney.

A situation of this kind was presented in the greatly publicized Mississippi torture case. In this instance confessions had been wrung from three ignorant Negroes who were suspected of murdering a white man. At the trial the court appointed counsel to defend the Negroes. The attorney made what he thought to be a sufficient objection to the use of the confessions in evidence. He failed to move for the exclusion of the confessions after it was shown that they were obtained by torture. The state appellate court ruled that this was fatal to the Negroes' cause and sustained the conviction which had been obtained largely through the use of the confessions.[1] The case was taken to the Federal Supreme Court, and that tribunal ruled that the use of the confessions under the circumstances amounted to a denial of due process of law.[2] The tribunal recognized the right of the state to regulate the practice in its own courts, but said that such rules must not offend against fundamental principles of justice. The court evidently felt that it would be a miscarriage of justice to allow these Negroes to suffer because of the attorney's ignorance of the practice in the state courts.

Back in 1884 an important case from California came before the Federal Supreme Court. In this instance the tribunal ruled that an indictment by grand jury was not an essential element of the due process of law which is guaranteed by the Fourteenth Amendment, and that another procedural device

[1] Brown v. State, 173 Miss. 542, 158 So. 339, 161 So. 465 (1935).

[2] Brown v. Mississippi, 297 U. S. 278, 56 Sup. Ct. 461 (1936).

could be employed if it served the same purpose in a manner which was fair and just to the accused.[3] In arguing the case, however, the court made some unfortunate remarks to the effect that the due process clause of the Fourteenth Amendment was coextensive with the similar provision relating to the Federal Government which is contained in the Fifth Amendment, a portion of the Federal Bill of Rights, and that therefore the rights guaranteed by other portions of the Bill of Rights could not be considered as coming within the terms of the post-civil-war amendment. In 1932 the *Scottsboro* cases came before the Supreme Court for the first time. One of the appellants' contentions was that they had not been provided with adequate and sufficient counsel. The right of an accused person to have the assistance of counsel for his defense is guaranteed in the federal courts by the Sixth Amendment and not the Fifth. It was argued by those who were attempting to sustain the conviction which had been obtained in the state court that the tribunal should follow the dictum of its predecessors and hold that the rights guaranteed by the Fourteenth Amendment did not include adequate counsel for the defense of accused persons. The court, however, could not see its way clear to the adoption of a doctrine which would so limit the scope of the due process clause. It held that such a failure to provide adequate counsel in a capital case would constitute a denial of the due process guarantee as interpreted in a manner which is at once reasonable and progressive.[4] Thus the court took a forward step in broadening the scope of the due process clause. It reaffirmed its right to examine a specific fact situation in order to determine whether a person has been accorded a trial which is up to its own standard of fairness.

A somewhat similar case had arisen in Oklahoma only a few months earlier. Fearful of an assembled mob, an ignorant Negro had pleaded guilty to a charge of rape. Afterwards he applied

---

[3] Hurtado v. California, 110 U. S. 516, 4 Sup. Ct. 111 (1884).

[4] Powell v. Alabama, 287 U. S. 45, 53 Sup. Ct. 55 (1932). The case is discussed in the following Notes: (1933) 13 B. U. L. REV. 92, (1933) 21 CALIF. L. REV. 484, (1932) 32 COL. L. REV. 1430, (1932) 1 GEO. WASH. L. REV. 116, (1933) 18 IOWA L. REV. 383, (1932) 31 MICH. L. REV. 245, (1933) 17 MINN. L. REV. 415, (1933) 10 N. Y. U. L. Q. REV. 389, (1933) 12 ORE. L. REV. 227, (1932) 7 ST. JOHN'S L. REV. 126, (1933) 18 ST. LOUIS L. REV. 161, (1933) 7 SO. CALIF. L. REV. 90, (1933) 11 TEX. L. REV. 546, (1933) 8 WIS. L. REV. 370.

for a writ of habeas corpus, and one of the grounds of his petition was that he had not had the benefit of counsel. At the hearing the trial judge stated that he had not appointed counsel under the pauper laws because he supposed it to be useless after the Negro's confession of guilt. The appellate court held that this denial of a conference with an attorney constituted a denial of the due process of law guaranteed by a state constitutional provision and directed that the writ of habeas corpus should be granted.[5]

In one case from Georgia certain evidence brought before a federal court in a habeas corpus proceeding seemed to suggest that the attorneys appointed to defend a Negro prisoner had construed their appointment to cover only the incidents of the actual trial, such as impaneling the jury, examining and cross-examining witnesses, and arguing the case before the court, and not as extending to the making of motions for change of venue, continuance, or new trial. In coming to the conclusion that the desired relief should be granted under these circumstances, the court declared that such an interpretation of an appointment to defend an accused person was much too narrow and that the Negro would thereupon be deprived of proper representation in court in violation of his constitutional rights.[6]

In a South Carolina case it was shown that counsel appointed by the court to defend a Negro was hurried in his preparations for trial by threats of mob violence which convinced him that his client would be lynched if he asked for sufficient time in which to make arrangements for the best possible defense. The defendant was convicted but the appellate court granted a new trial because of the above circumstance.[7]

An attorney who has been appointed to defend a pauper must be allowed sufficient time in which to make preparations for the trial. If the circumstances indicate that insufficient time has been given, the accused is entitled to a continuance.[8] In one Kentucky case it was shown that an attorney appointed by the court to defend a Negro was called away and therefore

[5] *Ex parte* Hollins, 54 Okla. Cr. Rep. 70, 14 P. (2d) 243 (1932).

[6] Downer v. Dunaway, 53 Fed. (2d) 586 (C. C. A. 5th, 1931). Habeas corpus granted in 1 Fed. Supp. 1001 (M. D. Ga. 1932).

[7] State v. Weldon, 91 S. C. 29, 74 S. E. 43 (1912).

[8] Jackson v. Commonwealth, 215 Ky. 800, 287 S. W. 17 (1926); State v. Collins, 104 La. 629, 29 So. 180 (1900).

had had no opportunity to confer with his client until the day of the trial. The appellate court declared that a continuance should be granted under such circumstances.[9] The same would be true in any case where an untoward event occurs which prevents the attorney assigned to the defendant from giving him proper attention.

There is a lack of uniformity in the statutes which authorize the appointment of charity counsel to defend accused persons who are financially unable to employ attorneys of their own choice. They differ widely with respect to the type of cases to which they apply. Some of these statutes, like those of Oklahoma[10] and Tennessee,[11] would seem to apply to all types of crimes. The Maryland statute[12] leaves the matter of appointing counsel to the discretion of the trial judge. In some states, like Arkansas[13] and Missouri,[14] the duty to appoint seems to be limited to cases of felony. In others, like Alabama,[15] Mississippi,[16] South Carolina,[17] and Texas,[18] it is limited to capital cases. In Delaware[19] the courts of oyer and terminer, which have jurisdiction of all cases involving capital crimes and homicides, are authorized to assign counsel to indigent persons. Louisiana[20] provides charity counsel in all cases of felony, whether capital or not, but a clause is added which states that the appointee in a capital case must have had at least five years' experience at the bar. This provision prevents the appointment of inexperienced attorneys in instances where a man's life is at stake, and might well be copied in other jurisdictions. The federal statute[21] authorizes the assignment of counsel in trials for treason and other capital crimes.

---

[9] Stroud v. Commonwealth, 160 Ky. 503, 169 S. W. 1021 (1914).

[10] OKLA. COMP. STAT. (1921) §2590.

[11] TENN. CODE (Will. Shan. & Harsh, 1932) §11,734.

[12] MD. ANN. CODE (Bagby, 1924) art. 26, §7.

[13] ARK. DIG. STAT. (Crawford & Moses, 1921) §3051.

[14] MO. REV. STAT. (1929) §3614.

[15] ALA. CODE ANN. (Michie, 1928) §5567. *See* Bethune v. State, 26 Ala. App. 72, 153 So. 892 (1934).

[16] MISS. CODE ANN. (1930) §1262. *See* Reed v. State, 143 Miss. 686, 109 So. 715 (1926).

[17] S. C. CODE (1932) §980.

[18] TEX. ANN. CODE CRIM. PROC. (Vernon, 1925) arts. 491, 494. *See* Brown v. State, 118 Tex. Cr. Rep. 582, 40 S. W. (2d) 118 (1931).

[19] DEL. REV. CODE (1915) §3794.

[20] LA. CODE CRIM. PROC. ANN. (Dart, 1932) art. 143.

[21] 18 U. S. C. A. §563 (1926).

The New York Court of Appeals has declared that the courts of that state have inherent power, apart from statute, to assign counsel for the defense of indigent persons who are charged with crime.[22] The rule would probably be the same in other states. In spite of the fact that the trial courts in Alabama are under no statutory duty to appoint counsel for the accused except in capital cases, the appellate court of that state has declared that a judge may assign counsel in any felony case if he sees fit to do so.[23]

Not only must it appear that the accused is financially unable to employ counsel, but it also must be shown that he desires legal advice.[24] In one Kentucky case it is said that in the absence of a request for counsel and a showing of inability to pay for the services of an attorney, it is not the duty of the court to assign counsel to the accused unless the latter is mentally incapable of conducting his own defense.[25] In an Arkansas case evidence was presented concerning the mental capacity of a defendant who had been allowed to defend himself without the benefit of counsel. As a mental defective should not be permitted to waive his right to have an attorney appointed to defend him, the appellate court ruled that it could examine the evidence adduced at the trial in order to determine whether the lower court had erred in refusing to grant a new trial.[26] There is no reason why a normal person should not be allowed to waive the right to counsel which is guaranteed to him by a state constitutional provision.[27] It has also been held that a pauper may waive his statutory right to be represented by charity counsel,[28] but in every instance of this kind the surrounding circumstances should be well scrutinized for the least bit of unfairness or coercion.

The language used by the Supreme Court in the *Scottsboro* case expressly limits the decision to capital cases. The court deemed it unnecessary to discuss issues not presented in the case, such as the extension of the doctrine to cases involving crimes

---

[22] People v. Price, 262 N. Y. 410, 187 N. E. 298 (1933).
[23] Bethune v. State, 26 Ala. App. 72, 153 So. 892 (1934).
[24] Dorris v. Crowder, 26 Cal. App. (2d) 49, 78 P. (2d) 1039 (1938).
[25] Holland v. Commonwealth, 241 Ky. 813, 45 S. W. (2d) 476 (1932).
[26] Williams v. State, 163 Ark. 623, 260 S. W. 721 (1924).
[27] Gatlin v. State, 17 Ga. App. 406, 87 S. E. 151 (1915).
[28] McKee v. State, 118 Tex. Cr. Rep. 479, 42 S. W. (2d) 77 (1931).

for which the death penalty is not inflicted. Some commentators have favored the further extension of the principles announced in this case to instances involving crimes of a less serious nature.[29] The problem presents itself as to just where we are going to draw the line. Are we going to expand the doctrine to include all crimes, whether felonies or misdemeanors, or will we limit its operation to cases involving capital crimes or perhaps felonies? These are questions which will have to be answered by the Supreme Court in future controversies.

Other cases will arise concerning the clarification of the doctrine announced in the *Scottsboro* case. For example, a federal court recently held that the principles announced in that decision would cover an instance where the charity counsel did not have sufficient time to prepare his client's case for trial.[30]

Only one other case merits attention here. In Arkansas a convicted Negro applied to a federal court for a writ of habeas corpus. He claimed that he had been denied a fair trial in the state court because his attorney had failed to object that there had been racial discrimination in the selection of the jury. The attorney testified that, after due consideration, he had refrained from making the objection because he believed that the action would lead to an increase of race prejudice in the community. He argued that this would not be favorable to the defendant's cause. The Circuit Court of Appeals ruled that the due process and equal protection guarantees had not been violated and therefore declined to issue the writ.[31] While the decision may be technically correct in this particular case, it is believed that other cases might arise where a wall of race prejudice would surround the court and make it impossible to raise objections of this kind. If a case of this sort should arise, relief would no doubt be forthcoming from the federal courts.

[29] See Notes: (1932) 31 MICH. L. REV. 245, (1933) 17 MINN. L. REV. 415.

[30] Jones v. Commonwealth of Kentucky, 97 F. (2d) 335 (C. C. A. 6th, 1938).

[31] Carruthers v. Reed, 102 F. (2d) 933 (C. C. A. 8th, 1939).

XV

THE NEGRO AS A WITNESS

Before the Civil War and the abolition of slavery the codes of all of the southern states and a good many others prohibited Negroes from testifying in the courts to a varying extent.[1] One writer on this subject has said that "the Negro slave had been either deemed incompetent as a witness, or, if deemed competent, his testimony was admitted only in certain actions."[2] While not generally permitted to testify in cases where a white man was a party, Negroes, both slave and free, were in the period preceding the war being given increased rights to give evidence in cases which involved them alone.

After the abolition of slavery became an accomplished fact in 1865, Congress immediately took steps toward giving the freedmen the rights of citizenship. The Civil Rights Act of 1866[3] was then formulated, which, among other things, guaranteed the right to give evidence in the courts. A controversy immediately arose over the constitutionality of this statute. Some of the cases which came before the courts involved the competency of Negro witnesses, since some of the prewar statutes disqualifying them had not as yet been repealed by the state legislatures. While most of the courts considering the question from this standpoint held that the act was valid,[4] there were at least some dissenting voices.[5] The most usual argument for the validity of the statute seems to have been that this legislation was authorized by the Thirteenth Amendment to the Federal Constitution, the antislavery amendment. The question never reached the Supreme Court. As there appeared to be some

[1] See Century Digest (American Digest System), Witnesses, ¶¶88-92, for cases dealing with the competency of Negro witnesses during ante-bellum days.

[2] Stephenson, Race Distinctions in American Law (1910) 242.

[3] 14 Stat. 27 (1866).

[4] United States v. Rhodes, 27 Fed. Cas. No. 16,151 (C. C. D. Ky. 1866); Kelley v. State, 25 Ark. 392 (1869); Handy v. Clark, 4 Houst. 16 (Del. 1869); *Ex parte* Warren, 31 Tex. 143 (1868). *See also* People v. Washington, 36 Cal. 658 (1869).

[5] State v. Rash, Houst. Cr. Cas. 271 (Del. 1867); Bowlin v. Commonwealth, 2 Bush 5 (Ky. 1867).

doubt as to the validity of the act, the congressional leaders forced the passage of the Fourteenth Amendment. This amendment was soon ratified and embodied most of the more important features of the Civil Rights Act and clothed Congress with power to protect the rights guaranteed thereby. In 1870 the civil rights legislation was practically re-enacted,[6] and the portion of this statute which grants all persons an equal right to give evidence is still on the statute books.[7] This statute is clearly authorized by the equal protection clause of the Fourteenth Amendment.

An attempt was made in a Georgia federal court to make this statute the basis of an indictment under another federal act[8] punishing a conspiracy to deprive a citizen of any right secured to him by the Federal Constitution or laws. The case involved the acts of certain individuals who had killed a witness who had testified in a criminal prosecution under the internal revenue laws. The court held that the indictment could not be so justified.[9] In arguing the case, the court made the statement that the indictment did not allege that the act of violence had been committed because of the race or color of the victim. This might possibly lead one to the erroneous conclusion that the decision would have been different had the indictment contained an allegation that the witness had been attacked because of racial antagonism. The statute evidently applies to all persons of whatever race within the jurisdiction of the United States, and therefore it cannot be said that such an allegation would be necessary in any action based upon its provisions. Nevertheless, there was a factor in this case which was fatal to the claimed jurisdiction of the federal court over the alleged crime here involved. The killing of the victim of the conspiracy was the act of individuals who had no connection with state, county, or municipal authorities.

The Fourteenth Amendment, as has been said in the *Civil Rights Cases*,[10] authorizes only corrective legislation aimed at

---

[6] 16 STAT. 144 (1870).

[7] 8 U. S. C. A. §41 (1926), REV. STAT. §1977 (1875).

[8] 18 U. S. C. A. §51 (1926), REV. STAT. §5508 (1875).

[9] United States v. Sanges, 48 Fed. 78 (C. C. N. D. Ga. 1891). The case was dismissed on a writ of error to the Supreme Court because of procedural difficulties. 144 U. S. 310, 12 Sup. Ct. 609 (1892).

[10] Civil Rights Cases, 109 U. S. 3, 3 Sup. Ct. 18 (1883).

the state or local governments or their officials, and not direct legislation dealing with the acts of private citizens. It is probable that the only authorization for a statute of this kind is to be found in the Fourteenth Amendment, and hence it can be valid only if interpreted not to protect witnesses from the wrongful act of individuals. It would be unreasonable to contend that a statute could form the basis of a right which it was not possible to protect in a direct manner. Hence the right was not one of those which is secured under this law of the United States, nor is it one which could be protected under any past or present federal statute which could have been validly enacted.

In 1882 an attempt was made in Texas to found an indictment for interfering with a Negro witness upon another Reconstruction statute[11] which was worded in such a way as to punish individuals for conspiring and going out in disguise for the purpose of depriving any person of the equal protection of the laws. This act was evidently aimed at the activities of the Ku Klux Klan. As the Fourteenth Amendment authorizes no such direct legislation, the statute was held to be unconstitutional and void.[12]

In the period which immediately followed the collapse of armed resistance in the South, laws were passed by the legislatures of the subjugated states with a view to taking care of the problems created by emancipation. Some of these laws were very harsh, but we must not forget that the Negroes were terribly ignorant and easily influenced. As an example of the laws which were enacted at this time as compromise measures, we note that a North Carolina act of 1866[13] provided that persons of color were competent witnesses in cases where one of their race was accused of a crime or had an interest in the controversy. The radicals soon obtained control of the machinery of government and immediately these laws were replaced by laws which reflected the attitude of those in power. New constitutions were adopted as a prerequisite to readmission to the union. These constitutions and the statutes enacted by the radical legislatures removed many of the racial distinctions which remained in the laws of the states after the war and emancipation. In Georgia it

---

[11] REV. STAT. §5519 (1875).

[12] LeGrand v. United States, 12 Fed. 577 (Cir. Ct. Tex. 1882).

[13] N. C. Pub. Laws 1866, c. 40, §9. *See* State v. Henderson, 61 N. C. 229 (1867).

was held that a state statute of 1866[14] had wiped out all distinctions on account of color as far as the competency of witnesses was concerned.[15] In 1869 the North Carolina Court held that racial distinctions in respect to the competency of witnesses was contrary to the spirit of the new constitution of that state.[16] Today all such distinctions which were aimed at the Negro have been erased from the statute books. At present Texas seems to be the only one of these states which notices the matter in the modern compilations. In that state a statute provides that "no person shall be incompetent to testify on account of race or color." [17]

In an early case the California Court held that a statute which denied the privilege of testifying to Chinese was not violative of the provisions of the Fourteenth Amendment.[18] Judging from what is said by the Federal Supreme Court in the important *Chinese Laundry* case,[19] however, the amendment's equal protection clause applies to all persons who are rightfully within the borders of the United States. Such a statute, whether the discriminatory provisions are aimed at Negroes, Chinese, or any other race, would certainly be violative of the principles of constitutional law which have grown up around the Fourteenth Amendment. There have been many decisions where statutory racial distinctions similar to this one have been held to be violative of the equal protection clause. Hence we may say that any statute which on its face discriminates against resident[20] Chinese or Negroes is unconstitutional. Therefore it may be concluded that the decision in the above California case was erroneous.

There is not a court in the nation where a Negro who is competent in other respects is not given the privilege of testifying in the same manner and under the same restrictions as are white witnesses. In fact it was held in a Virginia case that acts done and statements made by an ex-slave while in a state

---

[14] Ga. Pamp. Acts 1866, p. 239.

[15] Clarke v. State, 35 Ga. 75 (1866).

[16] State v. Underwood, 63 N. C. 98 (1869).

[17] Tex. Ann. Rev. Civ. Stat. (Vernon, 1925) art. 3714.

[18] People v. Brady, 40 Cal. 198 (1870).

[19] Yick Wo v. Hopkins, 118 U. S. 356, 6 Sup. Ct. 1064 (1885).

[20] In regard to non-residents see Fong Yue Ting v. United States, 149 U. S. 698, 13 Sup. Ct. 1016 (1893).

of slavery are admissible in evidence if the testimony is otherwise competent.[21]

It is only natural that a race which has held a servile position in a community should be considered by some persons as careless of the truth.[22] It is not believed that any race or people can be termed liars per se. Personal veracity is a matter of individual honesty and character. There are many Negroes who can be trusted to tell the truth. While there are a goodly number of colored persons who would not hesitate to tell a lie on the witness stand, there are also many members of the white and other races who would not be averse to testifying to an untruth if it was to their advantage to do so. The ingrained prejudice of some white jurors is largely responsible for the feeling that Negroes on the whole are not as credible as white witnesses. These white jurors will have to be shown that Negro witnesses are as reliable as the whites, and the colored man is challenged to prove it to their satisfaction. One might perhaps think that Negro jurors would be more apt to believe witnesses of their own race than would white jurors, but, generally speaking, it is doubted if such would be the case. The better class of colored persons in the South are frequently far less sympathetic than the whites toward the criminal element in their midst. Therefore, with the possible exception of instances where a Negro is accused of the rape or murder of a white person, it is believed that Negro jurors would be just as doubtful of the veracity of colored witnesses as would jurors of the white race.

It has been held not to be improper for a judge in his charge to the jury to remark that no lack of credibility can be attached to witnesses because of their race or color.[23] While every allusion made in the courtroom to the race or color of a witness is not taboo, any such reference which is unnecessary or irrelevant is improper.[24] Furthermore, remarks by prosecuting

---

[21] Richmond Cedar Works v. Foreman Blades Co., 267 Fed. 363 (C. C. A. 4th, 1920).

[22] See Note (1926) 30 L. NOTES 45. There is a statement to much this same effect about the Chinese laboring classes in United States v. Lee Huen, 118 Fed. 442 (N. D. N. Y. 1902).

[23] Dolan v. State, 81 Ala. 11, 1 So. 707 (1887); McDaniel v. Monroe, 63 S. C. 307, 41 S. E. 456 (1902).

[24] Fonville v. State, 91 Ala. 39, 8 So. 688 (1891); Sills v. State, 2 Ala. App. 73, 57 So. 89 (1911).

officials which were derogatory to the credibility of Negro witnesses as compared with those of the white race have been held to constitute reversible error.[25]

The presumption in favor of the good character of a witness should be the same, no matter to what race he or she may belong. Hence a Texas court has declared that the proponent of a Negro witness will not be permitted to introduce evidence of the witness' good character unless his adversary attacks it, following the familiar rule to that effect.[26]

There are many cases in which white men are held to be accountable or unaccountable for their deeds on the basis of the testimony of Negro witnesses. Sometimes their word is taken in preference to that of white witnesses. Furthermore, judges will oftentimes prevent colored witnesses from being browbeaten on cross-examination by opposing attorneys. On the whole it can hardly be said that there is much discrimination against Negro witnesses in the courts of the South or in any other section of the nation.

---

[25] Tannehill v. State, 159 Ala. 51, 48 So. 662 (1909); Hardaway v. State, 99 Miss. 223, 54 So. 833 (1911); Hamilton v. State, 38 Okla. Cr. Rep. 62, 259 Pac. 168 (1927).

[26] Houston Electric Co. v. Jones, 61 Tex. Civ. App. Rep. 281, 129 S. W. 863 (1910).

XVI

PREJUDICIAL REMARKS

Many cases have arisen in which the language of some court official or attorney has been made the grounds for an appeal because it was believed that the race prejudice of white jurors had been aroused thereby. While all references to the race of an accused person are not taboo, such language should never be permitted where it tends to provoke race hatred or to increase prejudice which is already present, as it surely is in the southern states. Such prejudicial argument oftentimes occurs in cases where a Negro is being tried for the murder or rape of a white person, but it is also found in other criminal prosecutions and in a few civil cases.

Language which is calculated to arouse such prejudice at murder trials has been held to constitute reversible error in many instances.[1] The courts have also reversed homicide cases where the prosecutor called attention to the fact that a Negro had either called or felt a white man to be a "son of a bitch."[2] However, there are cases where the language was not deemed of sufficient gravity to justify a reversal. In one case of this kind from Texas a suggestion was made to the jury that it should not let it be said that a jury of that county could only hang a white man. The defendant's attorney had objected and the prosecutor had replied that the remark was made because of questions asked by the attorney concerning the race prejudice of jurors. The appellate court declined to reverse the adverse decision on the objection.[3] In a California case the court held that a mere reference to the race of a Negro defendant was nonprejudicial where he was in court for all to see.[4]

---

[1] *See* Cooper v. State, 186 So. 230 (Fla. 1939); State v. Lee, 130 La. 477, 58 So. 155 (1912); State v. Brown, 148 La. 357, 86 So. 912 (1921); People v. Hill, 258 Mich. 79, 241 N. W. 873 (1932); Hamilton v. State, 38 Okla. Cr. Rep. 62, 259 Pac. 168 (1927); Blocker v. State, 112 Tex. Cr. Rep. 275, 16 S. W. (2d) 253 (1929).

[2] Roby v. State, 147 Miss. 575, 113 So. 185 (1927); Taylor v. State, 50 Tex. Cr. Rep. 560, 100 S. W. 393 (1907).

[3] Gibson v. State, 53 Tex. Cr. Rep. 349, 110 S. W. 41 (1908).

[4] People v. DeVaughn, 2 Cal. App. (2d) 447, 38 P. (2d) 192 (1934). *See also*

It has been held improper to argue that a female bootlegger be sent out of the county for the protection of the white boys who purchased liquor from her,[5] or to make the somewhat ambiguous statement in a liquor case that the jury "must deal with a Negro in the light of the fact that he is a Negro and applying your reason and common sense." [6] In one Louisiana arson case it was held to be improper to remind the jury of a former race war in which the whites had narrowly escaped massacre.[7] Convictions for carrying concealed weapons have been reversed because the prosecutor had remarked that the fact that white jurors backed up Negroes in carrying a pistol caused white mobs,[8] or had said that a Negro defendant had frightened a white woman and child by drawing a pistol and threatening to kill the man of the family.[9]

On the trial of Negro defendants for rape or other crimes, it has usually been held that any unnecessary reference by a prosecuting official to the general subject of sexual intercourse between a Negro man and a white woman is reversible error.[10] Such language is viewed as an attempt to inflame the feelings of white jurors on this subject, the sentiment against which may sometimes amount to what may be called a phobia. In some instances, however, courts have held that arguments of this kind were justified because the prosecutor stayed well within the bounds of the fact situations.[11]

It has been held that it is reversible error to use language

National Life & Accident Ins. Co. v. Harris, 118 S. W. (2d) 838 (Tex. Civ. App. 1938).

[5] Walton v. State, 147 Miss. 17, 112 So. 601 (1927).

[6] Simmons v. State, 14 Ala. App. 103, 71 So. 979 (1916).

[7] State v. Jones, 127 La. 694, 53 So. 959 (1911).

[8] State v. Cook, 132 Mo. App. 167, 112 S. W. 710 (1908).

[9] Cofield v. State, 14 Ga. App. 813, 82 S. E. 355 (1914).

[10] Williams v. State, 25 Ala. App. 342, 146 So. 422 (1933); Thompson v. State, 27 Ga. App. 637, 109 So. 516 (1921); Hoskins v. Commonwealth, 152 Ky. 805, 154 S. W. 919 (1913); State v. Perry, 124 La. 931, 50 So. 799 (1909); Sykes v. State, 89 Miss. 766, 42 So. 875 (1907); Garner v. State, 120 Miss. 744, 83 So. 83 (1919); Story v. State, 133 Miss. 476, 97 So. 806 (1923); State v. Jackson, 336 Mo. 1069, 83 S. W. (2d) 87 (1935); Vickers v. United States, 1 Okla. Cr. Rep. 452, 98 Pac. 467 (1908); Derrick v. State, 100 Tex. Cr. Rep. 223, 272 S. W. 458 (1925). *But see* Weems v. State, 236 Ala. 261, 182 So. 3 (1938), where such argument was held not reversible error because provoked by inflammatory remarks by defendant's counsel.

[11] Norman v. Commonwealth, 31 Ky. Law Rep. 1283, 104 S. W. 1024 (1907); Johnson v. State, 121 Tex. Cr. Rep. 392, 50 S. W. (2d) 831 (1932).

calling attention to the probability of mob violence if the jury fails to convict a Negro for slaying a white man,[12] and the same is true of a remark praising the citizens of a town for permitting a Negro to have a fair trial rather than resorting to violence.[13] Courts have also disapproved of language which indicated that the defendant's life should be forfeited because the citizens had restrained themselves from lynching him,[14] and a remark to the effect that a Negro defendant was fortunate in that the citizens had allowed a fair trial was also ruled improper.[15] In one Louisiana case a Negro's attorney harangued the jury on the subject of lynching for assaulting white women and argued that his client was innocent because he had not been lynched. The district attorney replied that Negro domination had forced the whites to adopt this method of defending themselves and that every man was entitled to a fair trial, the necessity for lynching having passed away. The appellate court declared that the whole discussion was improper, but refused to consider it reversible error as an appeal to race prejudice.[16]

In one Texas case the prosecution used language urging the jury to punish a Negro defendant severely because he had murdered a Negro woman for being unfaithful to him and calling attention to the generally accepted notion that in such instances the white man kills the other man while the Negro kills the woman. This language was held to require a reversal.[17]

Cases have been reversed because of the use of opprobrious epithets, such as "a brute of his race,"[18] "enough African blood in him to make him as mean as Hades itself,"[19] "coal-black murderer,"[20] or "black rascal."[21] It was considered harmless, however, for a witness to refer to a Negro as a "darkey."[22]

---

[12] Harris v. State, 96 Miss. 379, 50 So. 626 (1909).

[13] Williams v. State, 122 Miss. 151, 433, 84 So. 8 (1920).

[14] Thompson v. State, 33 Tex. Cr. Rep. 472, 26 S. W. 987 (1894); Anderson v. State, 85 Tex. Cr. Rep. 422, 214 S. W. 353 (1919).

[15] Cleveland v. State, 130 Tex. Cr. Rep. 357, 94 S. W. (2d) 746 (1936).

[16] State v. Petit, 119 La. 1013, 44 So. 848 (1907).

[17] Neal v. State, 50 Tex. Cr. Rep. 583, 99 S. W. 1012 (1907).

[18] Garner v. State, 120 Miss. 744, 83 So. 83 (1919).

[19] Funches v. State, 125 Miss. 140, 87 So. 487 (1921).

[20] Morehead v. State, 12 Okla. Cr. Rep. 62, 151 Pac. 1183 (1915).

[21] Bailum v. State, 17 Ala. App. 679, 88 So. 200 (1921).

[22] Herndon v. State, 178 Ga. 832, 174 S. E. 597 (1934).

It has also been held prejudicial for a prosecuting official to state that "if the Negro was taken out of court there would not be much left," [23] or to declare that he had lost the Negro vote because of his activity in prosecuting members of that race.[24]

The question of the prejudicial effect of remarks in court may also arise in civil cases, although it is not nearly so apt to occur. An attorney will not be permitted to refer too pointedly and unnecessarily to the difference in the race of the parties.[25] However, an argument that a Negro is entitled to the same rights as a white man has been said to be merely an attempt to obtain justice and therefore unobjectionable.[26] The courts will refuse to permit a Negro's counsel in a personal injury suit against a railway corporation to prejudice the jury unduly by indicating without supporting evidence that the Negro plaintiff had been hurt because he had been carried beyond the station platform in order to allow the white passengers to alight more comfortably.[27] In another case against a corporate defendant it was held to be improper for the Negro plaintiff's counsel to state that he knew the veracity of Negroes, thereby implying that he had seldom known one to lie, and to declare that the jury would probably lean toward the Negro.[28] An inference made in a civil suit that a Negro cannot enforce his rights because of his race has also been declared to be an improper attempt to influence the jury in his favor, but the effect of this argument was not deemed of sufficient importance to require a reversal.[29]

At the trial it is permissible for the judge to instruct the jury that a Negro is entitled to the equal protection of the law regardless of his color.[30] It is also deemed legitimate at the trial

[23] James v. State, 170 Ala. 72, 54 So. 494 (1911).

[24] People v. Brigham, 226 App. Div. 104, 234 N. Y. Supp. 567 (3d Dep't 1929).

[25] Thomas v. Posey, 15 Ala. App. 419, 73 So. 747 (1916).

[26] Texas & N. O. Ry. v. McCoy, 54 Tex. Civ. App. Rep. 278, 117 S. W. 446 (1909).

[27] St. Louis, I. M. & S. Ry. v. Briggs, 87 Ark. 581, 113 S. W. 644 (1908).

[28] Cooke-Teague Motor Co. v. Johnson, 50 S. W. (2d) 399 (Tex. Civ. App. 1932).

[29] St. Louis, B. & M. Ry. v. Green, 196 S. W. 555 (Tex. Civ. App. 1917).

[30] McLaurin v. Williams, 175 N. C. 291, 95 S. E. 559 (1918); Wilson v. Singer Sewing Machine Co., 184 N. C. 40, 113 S. E. 508 (1922); Ganaway v. Salt Lake Dramatic Ass'n, 17 Utah 37, 53 Pac. 830 (1898). *See also* McDaniel v. Monroe, 63 S. C. 307, 41 S. E. 456 (1902).

of a white man for the murder of a Negro for the judge to instruct the jury that it was as much its duty to convict under these circumstances as it would be in an instance where a Negro had killed a white man.[31] Furthermore, it has been held that there were no grounds for a reversal where a judge remarked that obscene and suggestive language used by a Negro in accosting a white girl on the street would naturally cause great apprehension on her part and then continued by expatiating on the "white man's burden." [32] In a rape case from Missouri a judge was held to be justified in refusing to instruct the jury that the defendant was "part Negro" and the prosecutrix "white" and that in arriving at its verdict the defendant should be accorded the same fair consideration as a white man would be entitled to under the same circumstances.[33] In an Alabama case it was said that a reversal cannot be had where the judge permits an eyewitness to testify that the defendant was "the Negro" who had committed the murder.[34]

In one Texas case, however, it was said to be improper for a judge to remark to a defendant bus company's attorney that the latter only made a certain statement to prejudice the jury against the Negro plaintiff.[35] This remark offended the rule that the judge should refrain from making unnecessary comments which may prejudice either of the litigants, for such comments may greatly affect the minds of the jurors.

Sometimes it seems as though a court's adverse ruling on an objection to language of this kind has been influenced by the fact that the victim of the crime was also a Negro.[36] In one Mississippi case, however, it was said to be improper for a prosecutor to make the remarks that "this bad nigger killed a good nigger" and "the dead nigger was a white man's nigger and these bad niggers like to kill that kind." [37]

In a case involving manslaughter while driving an automo-

---

[31] Dolan v. State, 81 Ala. 11, 1 So. 707 (1886).

[32] State v. Williams, 186 N. C. 627, 120 S. E. 224 (1923).

[33] State v. Pyle, 343 Mo. 876, 123 S. W. (2d) 166 (1938).

[34] Peterson v. State, 227 Ala. 361, 150 So. 156 (1933).

[35] Southland Greyhound Lines v. Matthews, 74 S. W. (2d) 713 (Tex. Civ. App. 1934).

[36] State v. Webb, 149 La. 93, 88 So. 156 (1921); Pitts v. State, 53 Okla. Cr. Rep. 165, 8 P. (2d) 78 (1932).

[37] Collins v. State, 100 Miss. 435, 56 So. 527 (1911).

bile, it was said to be improper for the prosecuting official to remark that the mulatto driver "was trying to save his own yellow head and that of his black mammy and pickaninny." [38] It was also deemed injurious for a special prosecutor to say that he was hired by members of both races in an effort to show that public opinion, white and colored, was crying for a conviction.[39]

Remarks derogatory to the credibility of Negro witnesses as compared with those of the white race have been frequently disapproved,[40] and the Alabama Court has refused to give its sanction to a state attorney's inquiry concerning the race of absent material witnesses.[41] Casting aspersions at white witnesses who testify in favor of a Negro has also been declared to be beyond the pale.[42] There is some sentiment for allowing such remarks to be made if properly controlled,[43] and some of the cases which have arisen seem to go this far if not farther. Thus it has been held nonprejudicial to refer unnecessarily to the fact that the defense had asked the jury to believe a couple of Negroes rather than the white girls whom they were accused of assaulting,[44] to argue that witnesses will be influenced by the fact that they belong to the defendant's race,[45] to refer to a Negro witness who had laid himself open to criticism as a "black rascal" and request the jury not to consider his testimony,[46] or to point to a Negro defendant and ask the jury whether it was going to believe that Negro sitting over there with "a face on him like that" rather than the testimony of a deputy officer.[47]

---

[38] Jones v. State, 21 Ala. App. 234, 109 So. 189 (1926).

[39] Collins v. State, 100 Miss. 435, 56 So. 527 (1911).

[40] Battle v. United States, 209 U. S. 36, 28 Sup. Ct. 422 (1908); Tannehill v. State, 159 Ala. 51, 48 So. 662 (1909); Jones v. State, 21 Ala. App. 234, 109 So. 189 (1926); Harris v. State, 22 Ala. App. 119, 113 So. 318 (1927); State v. Brice, 163 La. 392, 111 So. 798 (1927); Hardaway v. State, 99 Miss. 223, 54 So. 833 (1911); Moseley v. State, 112 Miss. 854, 73 So. 791 (1916); Hamilton v. State, 38 Okla. Cr. Rep. 62, 259 Pac. 168 (1927); Arnold v. State, 96 Tex. Cr. Rep. 214, 256 S. W. 919 (1923).

[41] Fonville v. State, 91 Ala. 39, 8 So. 688 (1890). *See also* Sills v. State, 2 Ala. App. 73, 57 So. 89 (1911).

[42] Roland v. State, 137 Tenn. 663, 194 S. W. 1097 (1917).

[43] Note (1926) 30 L. NOTES 45 replying to a former Note (1926) 29 L. NOTES 185.

[44] Allen v. State, 22 Ala. App. 74, 112 So. 117 (1927).

[45] State v. Howard, 120 La. 311, 45 So. 260 (1907).

[46] State v. Miles, 199 Mo. 530, 98 S. W. 25 (1906).

[47] James v. State, 18 Ala. App. 618, 92 So. 909 (1922).

Oftentimes the effect of prejudicial remarks will be declared to have been eradicated by the action of the trial judge in sustaining the Negro's objections or warning the jury to pay no attention to them.[48] In some instances, however, it has been said that the pernicious effect of the language used cannot be erased by this means and new trials have been ordered.[49] The reprimand must be positive and unmistakable and must also come promptly.[50] In one instance it was said that there could be no basis for a reversal where no objection was offered and the prosecutor, immediately after making the improper remark, stated that he did not wish to appeal to race prejudice.[51] In a Louisiana case it was decided that the prejudicial language of a prosecuting official could not be justified because the attorney for the Negro defendant argued that there would have been a prompt acquittal if he had been white.[52] Language to the effect that mulattoes should be spurned by both Negroes and whites and that no respectable Negro had dared to testify in their behalf has been held highly improper,[53] and there seems to be no doubt that the same is true of remarks which are derogatory to other racial groups, such as Creoles,[54] Italians,[55] Japanese,[56] Indians,[57] and Jews.[58]

---

[48] Davis v. State, 209 Ala. 409, 96 So. 187 (1923); Owens v. State, 215 Ala. 42, 109 So. 109 (1926); Davis v. State, 233 Ala. 202, 172 So. 344 (1936), *rev'g case in* 27 Ala. App. 342, 172 So. 343 (1936); Warren v. State 103 Ark. 165, 146 S. W. 477 (1912); Smith v. State, 165 Ind. 180, 74 N. E. 983 (1905); Hoskins v. Commonwealth, 152 Ky. 805, 154 S. W. 919 (1913); State v. Baker, 209 Mo. 444, 108 S. W. 6 (1908); Watkins v. State, 84 Tex. Cr. Rep. 412, 207 S. W. 926 (1919); Dial v. State, 133 Tex. Cr. Rep. 610, 113 S. W. (2d) 905 (1938).

[49] Moulton v. State, 199 Ala. 411, 74 So. 454 (1917); Jones v. State, 21 Ala. App. 234, 109 So. 189 (1926).

[50] Harris v. State, 22 Ala. App. 119, 113 So. 318 (1927).

[51] People v. Jeans, 79 Cal. App. 464, 249 Pac. 1089 (1926).

[52] State v. Brice, 163 La. 392, 111 So. 798 (1927).

[53] Hampton v. State, 88 Miss. 257, 40 So. 545 (1906).

[54] State v. Bessa, 115 La. 259, 38 So. 985 (1905).

[55] Fontanello v. United States, 19 F. (2d) 921 (C. C. A. 8th, 1927); State v. Shuler, 300 S. W. 318 (Mo. App. 1927).

[56] International Lumber Export Co. v. M. Furuya Co., 121 Wash. 350, 209 Pac. 858 (1922).

[57] People v. Frost, 37 Cal. App. 120, 174 Pac. 106 (1918). Improper but not reversible.

[58] Rosenthal v. United States, 45 F. (2d) 1000 (C. C. A. 8th, 1930); People v. Simon, 80 Cal. App. 675, 252 Pac. 758 (1927); Freeman v. Dempsey, 41 Ill. App. 554 (1891); Hyman v. Kirt, 153 Mich. 113, 116 N. W. 536 (1908); Hiller v. State, 164 Tenn. 388, 50 S. W. (2d) 225 (1932); Garritty v. Rankin, 55 S. W.

On the whole the appellate courts, and those in the southern states are no exception, have displayed an increasing willingness to rule out any improper argument derogatory to the Negro as a race. Although some of the decided cases seem somewhat unfair, there is reason to believe that the day is not far distant when a prosecuting attorney will face a rebuke every time he uses language of this sort which is at all unjustifiable, and a judge will be confronted with a reversal every time he overrules an objection to vicious argument or so far forgets the proprieties as to employ such unwarranted language himself.

---

367 (Tex. Civ. App. 1900). *See also* Gross v. Blecker, 105 S. W. (2d) 282 (Tex. Civ. App. 1937).

XVII

PUNISHMENTS AND SENTENCES

Before the Civil War and the adoption of the postwar amendments to the Federal Constitution, the southern states had statutes which provided harsher penalties for certain crimes when committed by Negroes than they did when the same crime was committed by a white person. There were also laws which made certain acts crimes only if they were perpetrated by Negroes. Such statutes were very common and there seems to have been no provision in the state constitutions of that period which could have been said to invalidate them.

During this period, therefore, there was nothing in the existing law to prevent the Alabama legislature from enacting a statute which punished the crime of rape upon a white woman more severely when the act was perpetuated by a slave, free Negro, or mulatto than when the same illegal act was committed by a white man.[1] In fact a somewhat similar Arkansas statute was held to be a valid exercise of legislative authority in spite of a state constitutional provision which stated that any slave convicted of a capital offense should suffer the same degree of punishment as a white man who had been convicted of a like crime.[2] The court construed the constitutional provision as preventing discrimination in the mode of inflicting the punishment meted out by the courts rather than interpreting it to mean that the state legislature might not inflict a graver penalty upon slaves than upon white men for the same offense.

The North Carolina Court upheld a statute which made it unlawful for free Negroes to carry arms.[3] To uphold such legislation, the court employed reasoning somewhat resembling the reasonable classification argument which was later used to support legislation under the equal protection clause of the Fourteenth Amendment. A North Carolina statute which di-

[1] Thurman v. State, 18 Ala. 276 (1850).

[2] Charles v. State, 11 Ark. 389 (1850); Pleasant v. State, 13 Ark. 360 (1852).

[3] State v. Newsom, 27 N. C. 250 (1844).

rected the hiring out of free Negroes who were convicted of any criminal offense was also held to be a valid act.[4] The court refused to declare that this statute was in conflict with that clause in the state's constitution which forbade the deprivation of the liberty of a free person "but by the law of the land."

Then came the War Between the States and the passage of the antislavery amendment to the Federal Constitution. The Civil Rights Act of 1866 was enacted into law. One provision of this statute stated that all persons within the jurisdiction of the United States shall be subject to like punishments, pains, and penalties, and this portion of the enactment is still on the statute books.[5] In one case from Alabamá it was held that the infliction of the punishment of banishment upon a freedman was in conflict with this act.[6] All doubt as to the validity of federal legislation of this type was removed by the passage of the Fourteenth Amendment with its guarantees of the privileges and immunities of citizenship, due process of law, and the equal protection of the laws. Before the passage of the amendment, certain state legislatures were asked to enact statutes similar to the above federal act. Thus we have the Delaware[7] and Mississippi[8] acts guaranteeing that the punishment of whites and Negroes shall be the same for like offenses.

The question soon arose as to whether the Fourteenth Amendment invalidated the miscegenation laws which were in force in a number of states. These laws outlawed interracial marriages between whites and Negroes and affixed greater penalties to an act of illicit sexual intercourse when indulged in by persons of different races than when indulged in by persons of the same race.[9] It was claimed that these statutes violated the equal protection guarantee of the amendment. The controversy finally reached the Federal Supreme Court in the *Pace* case from Alabama. The court held that the Alabama miscegenation act was a legitimate exercise of the state's police power.[10] It declared that the penalties are aimed at the

[4] State v. Manuel, 20 N. C. 144 (1838).

[5] 8 U. S. C. A. §41 (1926), REV. STAT. §1977 (1875).

[6] United States v. Horton, 26 Fed. Cas. No. 15, 392 (D. Ala. 1867).

[7] Del. Laws 1867, c. 168.

[8] Miss. Laws 1867, p. 233.

[9] See chapter on Intermarriage, notes 6 and 117.

[10] Pace v. Alabama, 106 U. S. 583, 1 Sup. Ct. 637 (1882), *aff'g* 69 Ala. 231 (1881). In Ellis v. State, 42 Ala. 525 (1868), it was held that this statute did

illicit act itself and not at the individuals, white or colored, who have committed the offense. A former Texas statute which penalized only the white person concerned received the approval of both state[11] and federal[12] courts. The federal court declared that the whites were mainly to blame for such unnatural unions. It was argued that this might well "furnish some excuse, if not a justification, for punishing them alone, as a means of prevention." The Texas statute was enacted before emancipation and remained in force until after the Reconstruction government was overthrown, but was repealed soon afterwards and replaced by a statute which penalized both parties to the crime equally. While the above reason for sustaining the statute was probably a sufficient one during and immediately after Reconstruction, it is believed that a present-day miscegenation statute which punished the whites alone would be held unconstitutional. The Negroes have undoubtedly become far more morally responsible than they were when this Texas statute was in effect. At present West Virginia seems to be the only state which has such a statute.[13]

The type of miscegenation statute in effect today punishes both white and Negro participants in the illegal act. Under this kind of statute both parties are equally guilty. In one Alabama case a Negro male offender was convicted while his white female paramour was given her freedom. The appellate court refused to sustain the conviction, however, since the illicit sexual relationship is such that one person cannot commit the criminal offense.[14] Some statutes require a guilty knowledge, and in this case one of the participants may be held responsible and the other exonerated.[15]

In one Texas case it was held that an enactment which penalized betting on any game except card playing in private

---

not contravene the 1866 Civil Rights Act. For additional authority with respect to these matters see chapter on Intermarriage, notes 9 and 11.

[11] Frasher v. State, 3 Tex. App. 263, 30 Am. Rep. 131 (1877); Francois v. State, 9 Tex. App. 144 (1880).

[12] *Ex parte* Francois, 9 Fed. Cas. No. 5,047 (C. C. W. D. Tex. 1879).

[13] W. VA. CODE (1931) c. 48, art. 1, §19. For further discussion see chapter on Intermarriage, note 20.

[14] Reed v. State, 20 Ala. App. 496, 103 So. 97 (1925).

[15] Bell v. State, 33 Tex. Cr. Rep. 163, 25 S. W. 769 (1894).

residences was not invalid because it permits wagering on the white man's game of cards and prohibits gambling on the Negro's game of craps.[16] An ante-bellum Tennessee statute made it a misdemeanor for a white man to play cards with a slave or a free Negro. Some years after the Civil War an attempt was made to apply this act in a criminal proceeding. The court declared that the statute was obsolete, as the evil which it had been intended to eradicate had passed away when the slaves were emancipated.[17] This may be said to be at least theoretically true.

Criminal statutes which are expressly directed against persons of any one race or color with no sufficient reason why they should be so aimed have been held to violate the equal protection guarantee. Thus a Massachusetts statute which made it unlawful for women under twenty-one years of age to enter a hotel or restaurant which was conducted by Chinese proprietors was declared invalid.[18] There was nothing in this act to keep young women out of establishments of this kind if they were conducted by members of other races, no matter how they were managed. A hotel or restaurant conducted by Chinese might be the best place of its kind in the state and yet the statute would apply. A hotel or restaurant conducted by other persons might be a low dive and yet the statute would have no application. Hence this was said to be an unwarranted and discriminatory exercise of the police power. A statute of this type which was aimed at Negroes instead of Chinese would likewise be unconstitutional.

Suppose a statute or ordinance which is fair and nondiscriminatory on its face is administered by state, county, or municipal authorities in a manner which is unfair to a particular racial group. In the celebrated *Chinese Laundry* case[19] it was held that such unjustifiable treatment clearly violated the equal protection guarantee of the Fourteenth Amendment. In order to invoke this principle, however, the proponent must allege and prove that

[16] Sparks v. State, 64 Tex. Cr. Rep. 610, 142 S. W. 1183 (1912).

[17] Wells v. State, 71 Tenn. 70 (1879).

[18] Opinion of the Justices, 207 Mass. 601, 94 N. E. 558 (1911).

[19] Yick Wo v. Hopkins, 118 U. S. 356, 6 Sup. Ct. 1064 (1885). See also case concerning Chinese Queue Ordinance. Ho Ah Kow v. Nunan, 12 Fed. Cas. No. 6,546 (C. C. D. Cal. 1879).

the administration was discriminatory or that the conditions at which the enactment was aimed did not exclusively exist among the members of his race and that there were other racial groups against whom the law was not enforced.[20]

In the matter of the comparative sentences imposed upon members of the two races, white and colored, there seems to be a startling lack of reliable statistical information. In fact the available information is so fragmentary that it cannot be employed as a basis for a scientific study of the problem. Hence one is obliged to confine oneself to a brief discussion of the matter from a standpoint of general knowledge. It is believed that there is very little discrimination on the basis of race alone in respect to the sentences imposed by the courts of the nation, even in the South. Most of the instances which have been unearthed in an effort to prove that such unfairness really exists are so complicated by the presence of other social phenomena as to be practically useless in an attempt to show that the injustice was due to the racial distinction alone. Many other things of a social and economic nature, such as wealth, political power and influence, social prestige, and community feeling, may influence a judge in sentencing a convicted criminal. In many instances he is unaware that he is being influenced by forces other than those which will be best for the community as a whole. While there is undoubtedly some racial discrimination of this kind in the courts of the country, particularly in the South, it could hardly be said that such unfairness is prevalent or at all common. Oftentimes a judge will be lenient just because the culprit is a Negro. Most judges are fair-minded and upright men who would never consciously stoop to unfairness. There have been cases, however, in which jurists seemed a bit callous to a Negro culprit's plea for leniency. Furthermore, discrimination of this kind might be more evident if better statistical information concerning the race of the victim were available. It should occasion no great surprise if more complete data of this kind would show, especially in interracial homicide and sex crimes, a decided tendency toward a longer or more severe sentence where the victim was white and a lighter

[20] Ah Sin v. Wittman, 198 U. S. 500, 25 Sup. Ct. 756 (1905); Chicago Park District v. Lattipee, 364 Ill. 182, 4 N. E. (2d) 86 (1936).

Death Sentences and Executions During Specific Period

State	Period Covered	Number Sentenced to Death		Number Executed		Ratio of Executions to Sentences	
		White	Negro	White	Negro	White	Negro
Florida	8/1928-12/1938	27	42	15	31	55.5	73.5
Kentucky	1928-1938	44	36	26	23	59.	64.
Missouri	1938 (only)	4	6	3	5	75.	83.3
North Carolina	1/1909-7/1928	51	149	13	81	25.5 } 39	54.4 } 52
	7/1927-7/1938	56	174	29	85	51.4 }	48.8 }
Oklahoma	1915-1937	102	57	35	22	34.3	38.6
South Carolina	4/3/1912-11/20/1938	39	174	16	126	41.	72.3
Tennessee	1/1928-12/1938	26	48	9	32	34.6	66.6
Texas	2/8/1924-12/1/1938	63	119	50	99	79.4	83.2
Virginia	1/1928-12/1938	12	43	5	26	41.6	60.5

punishment where the victim was colored. It is also interesting to note that a greater percentage of condemned colored felons are actually executed than whites, as is shown in the preceding tabulation of data obtained for several of the southern states.[21] This subject has received little or no attention from social scientists and statisticians. It presents a great opportunity for further investigation and research.

---

[21] Data in this table were obtained from state prison departments and state departments of public welfare.

XVIII

THE VOTING FRANCHISE

In considering this topic the material naturally falls into four periods. The first of these periods will be a study of the status of the Negro in this respect before the Civil War and the adoption of the Thirteenth, Fourteenth, and Fifteenth amendments to the Federal Constitution. The second period will be a discussion of the construction given these amendments in the courts, the efforts to enforce the statutes enacted by Congress in pursuance of the power given by the amendments, and the limitations engrafted on the power of Congress in this respect by a strict judicial construction thereof. The third period will be a legal analysis of the constitutional and statutory provisions adopted by the southern states in the nineties and early nineteen-hundreds with a view toward Negro disfranchisement and the administrational and procedural subterfuges made possible thereby. Lastly a discussion will be entered into concerning the efforts made to deny the vote to Negroes by those who believe, sincerely or not, that they are not as yet ready to be entrusted with the franchise. The white primary has been one of the most effective of the instruments employed to accomplish this purpose, and the legal aspects of this device are not as yet completely settled by our courts.

The Status of Negro Suffrage Before the Civil War

In 1860 even free Negroes were disfranchised throughout the South, and the same applied as well to almost all of the North and West. However, all New England, with the exception of Connecticut, permitted the Negro to vote. New York granted Negroes the suffrage if they owned a specified amount of property, a qualification which the state laws did not require of whites. Wisconsin extended the suffrage to them in1849. On the other hand, several northern and border states, in which Negroes had not previously been explicitly barred, disfranchised them from time to time, Delaware in 1792, Kentucky in 1799, Maryland in 1809, Connecticut in 1818, New Jersey in

1820, and Pennsylvania in 1838.[1] The question arose in the constitutional conventions of Tennessee and North Carolina in the years 1834 and 1835 respectively, and it was decided, not without opposition, that the franchise should be limited to the white race. There is a statement by one authority that no Negroes voted in North Carolina before this date.[2] However, a judge in that jurisdiction declared in one opinion that, although Negroes did not vote during colonial times, it was a notorious fact that free Negroes had exercised the privilege of suffrage under the provisions of the state constitution of 1776 until explicitly barred by the 1835 amendment to that document.[3] Virginia disfranchised the free Negro by constitutional provision in 1830 without opposition. In the remaining states of the West and South Negroes were not permitted to vote.

The cases during this early period which discuss the Negro's right to vote are few and scattered. The Maine Court held that Negroes, being citizens of that state, could vote therein.[4] The Illinois Court decided that anyone could vote who came within the statutory qualifications of being a white male twenty-one years of age.[5] In South Carolina the court stated that neither Indians, Negroes, nor mulattoes came within the term "free white men" used in the state constitutional provision determining voters.[6]

There are two decisions which show that even in the North the opponents of Negro suffrage were attempting to take advantage of legal technicalities in order to keep the Negro from the polls. In the first of these cases it was ruled that although the word "white" before the word "freeman" in the suffrage provision of the Pennsylvania Constitution of that period had been left out by the constitutional convention, this was not to be construed as giving free Negroes the right to vote, since the account of the convention stated that the purpose of the omission was to prevent dark-complexioned white men from being embarrassed at the polls.[7] The other instance involved a pro-

---

[1] See in this connection Porter, History of Suffrage in the United States (1918); Stephenson, Race Distinctions in American Law (1910) c. 11.

[2] Porter, *op. cit. supra* note 1, at 82. [3] State v. Manuel, 20 N. C. 144 (1838).

[4] Opinions of the Justices, 44 Me. 505 (1857).

[5] Spragins v. Houghton, 3 Ill. 377 (1840).

[6] State v. Managers of Elections, 1 Bailey 215 (S. C. 1829).

[7] Hobbs v. Fogg, 6 Watts 553 (Pa. 1837).

vision in the Wisconsin Constitution to the effect that the legislature could extend the suffrage to any group by submitting the question to a referendum. This was done in 1849 with respect to Negroes. At the ensuing election the proposal received a majority of the votes cast on that particular issue, but the opponents of the measure claimed that the proponents had not carried the election because the proposal had not received a majority of the votes cast on all subjects submitted for the people's approval at the election. The court, however, refused to give this contention its approbation and hence decided in favor of Negro suffrage.[8]

Some of the western states had a rule of law at this time that one in whom the white blood preponderated was within the constitutional restriction limiting the privilege of voting to whites. This doctrine was upheld by the Ohio Court in several instances,[9] and it was said in a Michigan case that persons who were predominantly white and had less than one-fourth African blood would have the right to vote in that state.[10]

The Period of Reconstruction and its Eventual Overthrow (1865-1890)

The Civil War was fought and won, and Lincoln's Emancipation Proclamation and the Thirteenth Amendment had abolished slavery. The southern legislators, in their efforts to deal with the serious situation which confronted them, enacted the so-called Black Codes and thereby precipitated the overthrow of Presidential Reconstruction and the adoption by Congress of the ultraradical policies of such men as Stevens and Sumner. The Fourteenth Amendment, guaranteeing to the Negro citizenship and the privileges and immunities thereof together with the equal protection of the laws and the right not to be deprived of life, liberty, or property by any state without due process of law, was passed by Congress and its ratification made a prerequisite to readmission to the Union. There seemed to be some doubt as to whether the Fourteenth Amendment guaran-

[8] Gillespie v. Palmer, 20 Wis. 544 (1866).

[9] Thacker v. Hawk, 11 Ohio Rep. 376 (1842); Anderson v. Millikin, 9 Ohio St. 568 (1859); Monroe v. Collins, 17 Ohio St. 665 (1867). There is a strong dissenting opinion in the Thacker case based on the suggestion that the word "white" meant wholly white.

[10] People v. Dean, 14 Mich. 406 (1866).

teed the Negro the right to vote, and so the Fifteenth Amendment was also passed and ratified. The context of this amendment is that neither the United States nor any state shall abridge the right to vote on account of race, color, or previous condition of servitude. Each of these amendments contains a provision giving Congress the power to carry out its mandates by appropriate legislation. Thus the ignorant freedmen, controlled by "carpetbaggers" and "scalawags," were given the voting privilege while the ex-Confederates were disfranchised. This led to the unsettled political conditions in the South during Reconstruction.

The Fourteenth Amendment changed the law as declared in the famous *Dred Scott* case,[11] for the court in that case had decided against Negro national citizenship. However, in a Michigan case where two Negro slaves had migrated from slave territory to Canada before 1860 and their issue came back to this country and settled in Detroit, a peculiar situation was presented. The court held that the progeny of this union was not a citizen of the United States because he was born in Canada and hence did not come under the first section of the amendment which provides that all persons born or naturalized in the United States are citizens thereof and also citizens of the state in which they reside. His parents might come back and become citizens, but their child could not claim the same privilege because of their previous condition as slaves and because they had moved out of the country while the law was in accordance with the *Dred Scott* decision.[12] The fact that this case was contested is an indication that there still existed a sentiment even as far north as Michigan against the Negro's exercise of the voting franchise.

The Fifteenth Amendment of course automatically put an end to all the state constitutional and statutory provisions limiting the elective franchise to persons of the white race.[13] However, it is interesting to note that even as late as 1884 the Kentucky Court mentioned the fact that the constitutional provision governing the right to vote in that state limited such

[11] Dred Scott v. Sandford, 19 How. 393 (U. S. 1856).

[12] People *ex rel.* Hedgman v. Bd. of Registration, 26 Mich. 51 (1872).

[13] Neal v. Delaware, 103 U. S. 370 (1880); Wood v. Fitzgerald, 3 Ore. 568 (1870).

right to white men only.[14] In New York the state constitution adopted before the Civil War provided that in reorganizing the state senate districts persons of color not taxed should be excluded from the enumeration of the inhabitants for that purpose. This provision was evidently overlooked when the state repealed a similar clause regarding the lower branch of the assembly and the above-mentioned property qualification for Negro suffrage. The Court of Appeals declared that the provision was repealed by implication,[15] thereby reversing the lower court which had held that the provision was still the law, although manifestly an inadvertence, and that it did not conflict with the Fifteenth Amendment or the privileges and immunities clause of the Fourteenth.[16]

In a famous case from Missouri[17] a woman claimed the right to vote under the Fourteenth Amendment, contending that the state constitutional provision limiting the suffrage to males was in conflict therewith and therefore invalid. The Supreme Court held that the states have the right to limit the suffrage within their borders and that the Fourteenth Amendment did not change the law in this respect, the right to vote not being one of the privileges or immunities of United States citizenship guaranteed thereby. The same result had been reached in two earlier cases.[18] In several decisions courts have said that the right of the states to control the elective franchise was only limited by the Fifteenth Amendment.[19] However, the final de-

[14] Buckner v. Gordon, 81 Ky. 665 (1884).

[15] People *ex rel.* Carter v. Rice, 135 N. Y. 473, 31 N. E. 921 (1892).

[16] People *ex rel.* Pond v. Bd. of Supervisors, 19 N. Y. Supp. 978 (Supt. Ct. 1892).

[17] Minor v. Happersett, 21 Wall. 162 (U. S. 1874).

[18] United States v. Anthony, 24 Fed. Cas. No. 14,459 (C. C. N. D. N. Y. 1873); Van Valkenberg v. Brown, 43 Cal. 43 (1872). *See* Gougar v. Timberlake, 148 Ind. 38, 46 N. E. 339 (1897). The right of the states to control the franchise had been decided in several cases in the state courts before the amendment was ratified. Spragins v. Houghton, 3 Ill. 377 (1840); Anderson v. Baker, 23 Md. 531 (1865); Huber v. Reily, 53 Pa. St. 112 (1866). In the Pennsylvania case, however, it was ruled that Congress may deprive one of his citizenship where there has been an evasion of the draft act and may thus affect his right to vote.

[19] Pope v. Williams, 193 U. S. 621, 24 Sup. Ct. 573 (1904); McKay v. Campbell, 16 Fed. Cas. No. 8839 (D. Ore. 1870); United States v. Anthony, 24 Fed. Cas. No. 14,459 (N. D. N. Y. 1873); Gardina v. Bd. of Registrars, 160 Ala. 155, 48 So. 788 (1909); Van Valkenburg v. Brown, 43 Cal. 43 (1872); State v. Dillon, 32 Fla. 545, 14 So. 383 (1893); Gougar v. Timberlake, 148 Ind. 38, 46 N. E. 339 (1897); Kinneen v. Wells, 144 Mass. 497, 11 N. E. 916 (1887); Sproule v.

cision that the elective franchise was not one of the privileges or immunities guaranteed by the amendment was not reached without opposition on the part of some of the judges on the Federal Bench. It was actually held that the right to vote was one of the privileges assured to every citizen thereby,[20] and it was said in one instance that the prosecution need not bring its case under federal statutes against officials at state elections within the terms of the Fifteenth Amendment.[21] This was an erroneous view of the law which will receive attention later.

An analogous situation arose when the courts began to consider the question as to whether or not all the rights guaranteed by the first eight amendments to the Federal Constitution were privileges or immunities within the meaning of the Fourteenth Amendment. One court took the position that these rights and privileges were guaranteed by the amendment,[22] but such a holding was later positively repudiated by the Supreme Court.[23] However, some of the guarantees of the said Federal Bill of Rights have been held to be within the meaning and protection of the due process clause of the Fourteenth Amendment, as witness what is decided in the *Scottsboro* case.[24] The Supreme Court, in considering a statute adopted in Michigan which changed the method of electing presidential electors, has also held that none of the postwar amendments affect the constitutionality of the act under Article II, Section 1, of the Federal Constitution, leaving the manner of choosing electors to the states. The amendments do not change the methods thus prescribed. They do not make immutable the method which was used at the time they were adopted, nor do they give every citizen who reaches his majority the right to vote for presidential electors.[25]

And now it becomes necessary to consider the respective

Fredericks, 69 Miss. 898, 11 So. 472 (1892). *See also* Davis v. Teague, 220 Ala. 309, 125 So. 51 (1929).

[20] United States v. Canter, 25 Fed. Cas. No. 14, 719 (C. C. S. D. Ohio 1870); Opinion of Bond, J., in United States v. Petersburg Judges of Election, 27 Fed. Cas. No. 16,036 (C. C. E. D. Va. 1875).

[21] *Ibid.*

[22] United States v. Hall, 26 Fed. Cas. No. 15,282 (C. C. S. D. Ala. 1871).

[23] Maxwell v. Dow, 176 U. S. 581, 20 Sup. Ct. 448 (1899).

[24] Powell v. Alabama, 287 U. S. 45, 53 Sup. Ct. 55 (1932).

[25] McPherson v. Blacker, 146 U. S. 1, 13 Sup. Ct. 3 (1892), *aff'g* 92 Mich. 377, 52 N. W. 469 (1892).

powers of Congress and the states in regard to both national and state elections. Under the Federal Constitution Congress is given power to make regulations or to alter all rules prescribed by the state legislatures as to the time, place, and manner of choosing United States senators and representatives, except the place of choosing senators.[26] The power granted by the postwar amendments is merely additional to the authority over congressional elections contained in this portion of the fundamental document. Hence some of the legislation passed by Congress with a view to forcing the South to accept the Negro voters at the polls was upheld as a proper exercise of the power granted by this section. Thus two counts of an indictment under the Enforcement Act were declared to state causes of action by a South Carolina federal court.[27] The tribunal stated that the power to regulate congressional elections was derived from this clause of the Constitution.

Congress enacted much legislation of this nature about this time, and all of these statutes which could be construed to apply to congressional elections alone were held constitutional.[28] For jurisdictional purposes an indictment under statutes which have been enacted in pursuance of this power over national

---

[26] U. S. CONST. Art. I, §4.

[27] United States v. Crosby, 25 Fed. Cas. No. 14,893 (C. C. D. S. C. 1871).

[28] These statutes were placed, along with others which were declared invalid and some dealing with the elective franchise, in the Federal Revised Statutes of 1875. See §§2002-31, 5506-32. Sections 2021-22 were declared valid in *In re* Engle, 8 Fed. Cas. No. 4488 (C. C. D. Md. 1877). The validity of §§5511-12, 5514-15, 5522 had also been recognized in a number of cases: *Ex parte* Siebold, 100 U. S. 371 (1879); *Ex parte* Clark, 100 U. S. 399 (1879); United States v. Gale, 109 U. S. 65, 3 Sup. Ct. 1 (1883); *In re* Coy, 127 U. S. 731, 8 Sup. Ct. 1263 (1888), *aff'g* 31 Fed. 794 (C. C. D. Ind. 1887); U. S. v. Nicholson, 27 Fed. Cas. No. 15,877 (C. C. D. La. 1878); United States v. Fisher, 8 Fed. 414 (C. C. S. D. Ohio 1881); United States v. Bader, 16 Fed. 116 (C. C. E. D. La. 1883); United States v. Jackson, 25 Fed. 548 (C. C. W. D. Tenn. 1885); United States v. Kelsey, 42 Fed. 882 (W. D. Tex. 1890). See also in this connection §§1979-81 of REV. STAT. (1875). The application of §5511 to congressional elections alone is pointed out in United States v. Souders, 27 Fed. Cas. No. 16,358 (D. N. J. 1871), in which the court held that interference with Negroes when they offered to vote was punishable under this section, in spite of the fact that the Negroes finally succeeded in voting. Section 5511 did not apply to purely state elections. *Ex parte* Perkins, 29 Fed. 900 (C. C. D. Ind. 1887). A good many of these statutes have been repealed. See note 71 *infra*. The general federal jurisdiction over congressional elections is illustrated by two later cases. Wiley v. Sinkler, 179 U. S. 58, 21 Sup. Ct. 17 (1900); Swofford v. Templeton, 185 U. S. 487, 22 Sup. Ct. 783 (1902).

elections must allege that the act complained of was committed at an election where a membership in Congress was being determined by the voters.[29] However, an indictment under some of these acts charging the alteration of tally sheets of the vote for local officials in pursuance of a conspiracy was held insufficient despite the fact that a congressman was up for election at the same time.[30] Congress is not authorized to legislate for state elections in this manner except with respect to federal officials. In a habeas corpus proceeding instituted by one who had been convicted of bribery at a Virginia election, the United States Supreme Court declared that presidential electors were state officers and hence the state courts would have jurisdiction of any action pertaining thereto in spite of the fact that a congressman was voted upon at the same election.[31] In this instance the Supreme Court reversed the lower federal court which had granted the writ on the ground that the state court had no jurisdiction. Even in congressional elections, a voter must comply with valid state regulations.[32]

The portion of the Reconstruction laws which punished any conspiracy to prevent any citizen who was lawfully entitled to vote from giving his support to a lawful and qualified candidate for a seat in Congress, the means employed being force, intimidation, or threats,[33] was given the approval of the courts.[34] The statute was said to be a proper exercise of the authority over federal elections granted by the above provision of the Constitution.

There can be no doubt that most of the provisions of the

---

[29] United States v. Cahill, 9 Fed. 80 (C. C. E. D. Mo. 1881); United States v. Wright, 16 Fed. 112 (C. C. E. D. La. 1883); United States v. Seaman, 23 Fed. 882 (C. C. S. D. N. Y. 1885); United States v. Morrissey, 32 Fed. 147 (C. C. E. D. Mo. 1887). *See also* United States v. McKenna, 127 Fed. 88 (C. C. A. 6th, 1904). In so far as the decision in United States v. McBosley, 29 Fed. 897 (D. Ind. 1886) is contrary to this rule of pleading, it is probably erroneous.

[30] *Ex parte* Perkins, 29 Fed. 900 (C. C. D. Ind. 1886).

[31] *In re* Green, 134 U. S. 377, 10 Sup. Ct. 586 (1890).

[32] Wiley v. Sinkler, 179 U. S. 58, 21 Sup. Ct. 17 (1900); Pope v. Williams, 193 U. S. 621, 24 Sup. Ct. 573 (1904).

[33] Rev. Stat. §5520 (1875).

[34] *Ex parte* Yarbrough, 110 U. S. 651, 4 Sup. Ct. 152 (1884); United States v. Goldman, 25 Fed. Cas. No. 15,225 (C. C. D. La., 1878). This statute also mentions presidential electors, and a glance at the recent Supreme Court decision in United States v. Burroughs, 290 U. S. 534, 54 Sup. Ct. 287 (1934), gives one an inkling as to what would have been the court's ruling had the problem in the Green case, *supra* note 31, arisen with respect to this statute.

Enforcement Act of 1870[35] were enacted for the ostensible purpose of enforcing the guarantees of the Fifteenth Amendment. Congress evidently had no idea that the amendment did not give it the authority to enact direct legislation punishing interference with the voting of the newly made citizens. The first section of this statute, one of the few portions of it which is still in effect,[36] gave all citizens without distinction of race or color who are otherwise qualified to vote at any state, territorial, district, county, city, parish, township, school district, municipal, or other similar sub-divisional election the right not to be discriminated against at the polls, any law of any state or territory notwithstanding. With respect to the other pertinent sections of the act, practically all of which were placed in the Revisal of the Federal Statutes in 1875,[37] there seems to have been a controversy as to their validity almost from the day of their enactment. It was decided in the *Reese*[38] and *Cruikshank*[39] cases that the Fifteenth Amendment did not actually confer the right to vote on the Negro population, but only invested citizens with the right not to be discriminated against in the exercise of the voting privilege on account of race, color, or previous condition of servitude. Hence in bringing an indictment pertaining to state elections under the various portions of the Enforcement Act it was held that it was necessary to allege that the crime charged was committed because of the race, of the victims.[40]

[35] 16 STAT. 140-146, c. 94.

[36] 8 U. S. C. A. §31 (1925), REV. STAT. §2004 (1875). This section has been said to be merely declaratory of the amendment and hence not to support an action against state officials for interference with the Negroes in the exercise of the suffrage. Karem v. United States, 121 Fed. 250 (C. C. A. 6th, 1903).

[37] *See* REV. STAT. §§2002-31, 5506-23 (1875). All of these provisions are not pertinent to the problem raised here but most of them are.

[38] United States v. Reese, 92 U. S. 214 (1875).

[39] United States v. Cruikshank, 92 U. S. 542 (1875), *aff'g* 25 Fed. Cas. No. 14,987 (C. C. D. La. 1874).

[40] United States v. Cruikshank, 92 U. S. 542 (1875); McKay v. Campbell, 16 Fed. Cas. No. 8839 (D. Ore. 1870); Opinion of Hughes, J., in United States v. Petersburg Judges of Elections, 27 Fed. Cas. No. 16,036 (C. C. E. D. Va. 1875) (Opinion of Bond, J., contra). The same was held in United States v. Mason, 26 Fed. Cas. No. 15,734 (D. Md.) and United States v. Schumenant, 27 Fed. Cas. No. 16,236 (D. Md.), cases in which the opinions are now lost but which are mentioned in Cully v. Baltimore, 6 Fed. Cas. No. 3,466 (D. Md. 1876). The same was true of an action under the statute which allowed a contest of an election in which persons have been deterred from voting by reason of race or

In the above-mentioned *Reese* case[41] the Supreme Court was given its first opportunity to construe the legislation enacted by Congress for the purpose of carrying out the mandate of the Fifteenth Amendment. The case arose out of an attempt to punish certain local election officials in Kentucky under Section 4 of the Enforcement Act which provided for the punishment of those who interfered with persons in their attempt to vote. The statute was held to cover more offenses than are punishable under legitimate legislation under the terms of the amendment, for it was not confined to the action of state officials in interfering with the suffrage on account of race or color. The court remarked that although the statute manifestly included the offense committed in this instance, an offense which no doubt could be made a crime under proper legislation, it would include within the natural interpretation given its terms other offenses which are clearly beyond the powers given to Congress with respect to elections. The court also stated that it would not step within the act and declare that certain offenses made punishable thereby were indictable, when it was clearly in excess of the power of Congress to legislate with respect to other offenses equally within the natural meaning of the words of the statute. The act was therefore held unconstitutional. Before this ruling was made, however, the statute had been placed in the codification of 1875.[42]

An attempt was made to resurrect the act and in several cases it is said that Congress had reënacted it and made it apply only to federal elections, thereby making it a valid exercise of the authority invested in that body by Article I, Section 4, of the Constitution.[43] However, the change made in this statute

---

color, REV. STAT. §2010 (1875), a portion of the act which was undoubtedly valid because its language brought it within the authority given by the amendment. *See* Kellog v. Warmouth, 14 Fed. Cas. No. 7,667 (C. C. D. La. 1872); Harrison v. Hadley, 11 Fed. Cas. No. 6,137 (C. C. E. D. Kans. 1873). In a case arising under §4 of the act, Seeley v. Koox, 21 Fed. Cas. No. 12,630 (C. C. S. D. Ga. 1874), it was declared that the declaration must allege that the unlawful means by which the plaintiff was prevented from voting was wilful or malicious, and hence a declaration in which it was alleged that the conduct of the official at the polls was due to a mistaken view of the law was held to be demurrable. This appears to be a civil action under a criminal statute.

41 United States v. Reese, 92 U. S. 214 (1875).

42 REV. STAT. §5506 (1875).

43 United States v. Munford, 16 Fed. 223 (C. C. E. D. Va. 1883); United States

is not of such a nature as would allow such a conclusion, for the original act was not limited to acts committed on account of race or color. At least such is the case if one does not construe this section with relation to other portions of the Enforcement Act which do come within the authority conferred by the amendment and read words into it that are not there. Where the acts are so limited, as they are in Section 2 of the statute, this argument could be advanced with better reason,[44] but in the case of Section 4 it is extremely doubtful that this decision would have received the sanction of the federal appellate tribunals.

There is also another objection to the statute. It is not limited to state action, but applies to the acts of individuals as well. This last ground was the basis of the decisions in the federal courts that Section 5 of the Enforcement Act,[45] which also punished interference with the voting franchise, was unconstitutional.[46] The courts also declared that the latter act was invalid because of the reasons which had been advanced in the *Reese* case in respect to Section 4. The Supreme Court accepted this reasoning when the question was finally brought before it in 1903.[47] State action includes the acts of state officials,[48] but the authority given by the amendment cannot be extended to protect the Negro from the depredations of individuals who are

v. Belvin, 46 Fed. 381 (C. C. E. D. Va. 1891). The same was held with respect to §§2005-06 of the Rev. Stat., punishing interference with any prerequisite of the right to vote. Brown v. Munford, 16 Fed. 175 (C. C. E. D. Va. 1883).

[44] See *ibid.*

[45] Afterwards Rev. Stat. §5507 (1875).

[46] United States v. Amsden, 6 Fed. 819 (D. Ind. 1881); Lackey v. United States, 107 Fed. 114 (C. C. A. 6th, 1901), *rev'g* 99 Fed. 952 (D. Ky. 1900), in which the court had held that an averment that the offences were committed by reason of the victim's race or color would make an indictment under this section valid. The Supreme Court affirmed the Lackey case without opinion in 181 U. S. 621, 21 Sup. Ct. 925 (1901). In the case of United States v. Miller, 107 Fed. 913 (D. Ind. 1901), the judge unearthed an obscure dictum in the opinion of the lower court in the Cruikshank case, *supra* note 39, to the effect that the Fifteenth Amendment authorizes legislation in respect to individuals. The Fourteenth Amendment is worded like the Fifteenth in this respect, and hence it is very strange that this judge should have paid any attention at all to this dictum in view of the fact that Rev. Stat. §5519 (1875), the authority for which was supposed to arise under the Fourteenth Amendment, had been held to be invalid on this ground in United States v. Harris, 106 U. S. 629, 1 Sup. Ct. 601 (1882). In fact there are indications in the Supreme Court opinion in the Cruikshank case itself that the amendments apply only to state action.

[47] James v. Bowman, 190 U. S. 127, 23 Sup. Ct. 678 (1903).

[48] Virginia v. Rives, 100 U. S. 313 (1879).

not connected with the national, state, or municipal governments.

Section 2 of the act, from which other sections of the codification of 1875 were taken but placed therein in a more or less mutilated form,[49] was worded in such a manner that the above objections to its constitutionality did not apply.[50] This section penalized any officer of elections who refused to allow a citizen to perform any prerequisite to the right to vote at an election on account of race, color, or previous condition of servitude. An indictment under this portion of the act was required to allege that the crime charged was committed because of race or color, and hence indictments which did not state that such was the reason for the illegal act were not sufficient.[51] This applies also to an indictment under the twenty-third section of the Enforcement Act[52] which provided for a contest of any election at which persons entitled to vote were prevented from doing so because of their race or color.[53] It was also held in cases arising under this section that the federal courts had no jurisdiction except in instances involving discriminations on account of race and that they had this only when the complaining candidate for office was defeated in the election.[54]

In considering Section 6 of the Enforcement Act,[55] one of the few portions of the statute which is still in effect,[56] one must pay marked attention to its peculiar wording. The statute in its present form begins with a clause punishing a conspiracy to threaten, injure, oppress, or intimidate any citizen in the free

[49] REV. STAT. §§2005-07 (1875).

[50] *See* United States v. Given, 25 Fed. Cas. Nos. 15, 210-11 (C. C. D. Del. 1873).

[51] McKay v. Campbell, 16 Fed. Cas. No. 8839 (D. Ore. 1870).

[52] Afterwards REV. STAT. §2010 (1875).

[53] Kellog v. Warmouth, 14 Fed. Cas. No. 7667 (C. C. D. La. 1872); Harrison v. Hadley, 11 Fed. Cas. No. 6,137 (C. C. E. D. Ark. 1873). In the Louisiana case the governor made application to the Federal Supreme Court for a writ of prohibition forbidding the circuit court to proceed with the case. However, that tribunal declined to issue the writ because it was of the opinion that it has no jurisdiction until an appeal was taken at the final disposition of the case in the lower court. *Ex parte* Warmouth, 17 Wall. 64 (U. S. 1872).

[54] Dubuclet v. Louisiana, 103 U. S. 550 (1880); Johnson v. Jumel, 13 Fed. Cas. No. 7392 (C. C. D. La. 1877). In the Johnson case it is said that the federal courts have no jurisdiction of an action brought to enable a party to retain physically an office to which he has been duly elected and into which he has been inducted but from which he has been subsequently ejected, it being the province of the executive department of the government to enforce such rights.

[55] Afterwards REV. STAT. §5508 (1875).

[56] 18 U. S. C. A. §51 (1926).

exercise or enjoyment of any right or privilege secured to him by the Constitution or laws of the United States or because of his having exercised the same. The statute also contains a clause, originally placed first but now relegated to a less conspicuous position in the latter portion of the act,[57] providing punishment for those who go in disguise on the highway or onto the premises of another with intent to prevent or hinder the free exercise of any right or privilege so secured. This portion of the statute, evidently intended to curb the activities of the Ku Klux Klan, has been held not to render the whole act invalid.[58]

The right to vote at a congressional election has been held to be a right secured by Article I, Section 4, of the Constitution and hence within the meaning of the statute, and therefore indictments under this act which charged the culprits with a conspiracy to interfere with certain Negro voters at such an election were upheld in the *Yarbrough*[59] and *Mosley*[60] cases. That this was no new view of the law is seen when one examines an earlier case from South Carolina.[61]

The application of this statute to state elections in its relation to Negro suffrage seems to have never been fully clarified by the decisions, and hence there has been some confusion in the cases as to just what the law really is. In the early *Cruikshank* case[62] an indictment under this act charged the defendants with conspiracy to prevent certain Negroes from exercising their right to vote at an election, claiming that this was a right guaranteed by the Constitution and hence protected by the

[57] Compare original statute with REV. STAT. §5508 (1875).

[58] *Ex parte* Yarbrough, 110 U. S. 651, 4 Sup. Ct. 152 (1884); United States v. Mosley, 238 U. S. 383, 35 Sup. Ct. 904 (1915).

[59] *Ex parte* Yarbrough, 110 U. S. 651, 4 Sup. Ct. 152 (1884).

[60] United States v. Mosley, 238 U. S. 383, 35 Sup. Ct. 904 (1915).

[61] United States v. Butler, 25 Fed. Cas. No. 14,700 (C. C. D. S. C. 1877). In an earlier opinion in this same case it is said that the proper method of procedure under this statute is an indictment and not an information. United States v. Butler, 25 Fed. Cas. No. 14,701 (C. C. D. S. C. 1876). It has also been held that an indictment under this section and REV. STAT. §5509 (1875) (the latter punishing an infraction of §5508) must aver that the persons conspired against are citizens, it being insufficient to allege that the victims are officers conspired against in the attempt to perform their official duties. United States v. Patrick, 53 Fed. 356 (C. C. M. D. Tenn. 1892).

[62] United States v. Cruikshank, 92 U. S. 542 (1875), *aff'g* 25 Fed. Cas. No. 14,897 (C. C. D. La. 1874).

statute. In deciding the case the Supreme Court declared that the Constitution did not guarantee citizens the right to vote but only the right not to be discriminated against by the states on account of race, color, or previous condition of servitude. It was not alleged that the victims had been prevented from exercising the voting franchise for any one of the above reasons, and therefore the court held that the indictment did not state a cause of action within the meaning of the statute. The only rights protected by the statute are those secured by the Constitution. This is the basic theory on which the decision was placed, and the fact that there was also another ground that might have been used to defeat the indictment is therefore of no particular significance. There is nowhere in the opinion any indication that the culprits were state officials, the amendment being directed at state action alone, and hence the case could without a doubt have been thrown out on this reasoning also. The necessity for alleging that the prospective voters had been interfered with because of their race or color seems also to be supported by the charge to the jury in the above-mentioned South Carolina case,[63] but the alleged interference in that instance appears to have been with Negroes who were desirous of voting for a certain candidate for a seat in Congress and hence the force of the language used is weakened.

The most natural interpretation to be put upon the language used in the *Cruikshank* case is that the indictment would have been approved if there had been an allegation that the culprits had acted because of the race or color of their victims. Therefore the only possible conclusion to be drawn is that the right not to be discriminated against by a state on account of race or color is a right which is guaranteed by the Constitution and therefore is within the meaning of this statute. Hence an indictment charging a conspiracy on the part of state or county officials to interfere with this right certainly ought to be good.

However, in the face of this seeming assertion by the Supreme Court, the Circuit Court of Appeals in the *Karem* case from Kentucky decided that this statute was not appropriate legislation under which to enforce the right secured by the Fifteenth Amendment and therefore refused to approve an indictment

[63] United States v. Butler, 25 Fed. Cas. No. 14,700 (C. C. D. S. C. 1877).

under this act which alleged that certain election officials had conspired to deprive Negro citizens of a right guaranteed by the Constitution, further describing it as the "right and privilege to vote at the election hereafter named, without distinction of race, color, or previous condition of servitude."[64] An excerpt from this case will further clarify the grounds of the decision:

"This section has for its object the punishment of all persons who conspire to prevent the free enjoyment of any right or privilege secured by the Constitution or laws of Congress, without regard to whether the persons so conspiring are private individuals or officials exercising the power of the United States or of a State. Neither does it draw any distinction between a conspiracy directed against the exercise of the right of suffrage based upon race or color, and a conspiracy not so grounded. It is therefore not legislation appropriate to the enforcement of the fifteenth amendment; and, if the only warrant for its enactment was that article, we should be obliged to hold that Congress had exceeded its jurisdiction, because broad enough to cover wrongful acts without as well as within its jurisdiction. That it is not within the province of the courts to so limit an act by judicial construction as to make it operate only on that which Congress may rightfully prohibit and punish is now a well-settled principle of constitutional interpretation."

The court also said that the warrant for this section is found in other portions of the Constitution and that other parts of the Enforcement Act were intended to secure the right granted by the Fifteenth Amendment. The court for these reasons refused to hold that the indictment was a proper one.

How this result was reached passes understanding. The Fifteenth Amendment is just as much a part of the Constitution as any other portion thereof and hence the right secured thereby should be included within the terms of the statute which by any reasonable interpretation would include all rights guaranteed by the fundamental document. To come to any other conclusion would be to discriminate between the several sections thereof. Such a decision as the one in the *Karem* case gives an

[64] Karem v. United States, 121 Fed. 250 (C. C. A. 6th, 1903).

efficacy to one portion of the Constitution which it withholds from another. In the *Mosley* case[65] it is said this statute deals with all federal rights and protects them "in the lump," and this would seem to include the right secured by the Fifteenth Amendment. The allegations are sufficient to bring the right claimed within the terms of the amendment, and hence it is believed that the *Karem* decision is erroneous.

There is other legislation of this period still in effect which it is pertinent to mention here. There are two statutes, one criminal[66] and the other authorizing a civil action,[67] which are worded in much the same manner as the above-mentioned conspiracy act. These statutes respectively provide that any person who, under color of any statute, ordinance, regulation, or custom, subjects, or causes to be subjected, any inhabitant of the country within the jurisdiction of the United States to the deprivation of any rights, privileges, or immunities secured by the Constitution or laws shall be subject to the action provided by the particular statute. This type of statute is constitutional, as it is limited to action on the part of state, county, or municipal officials and also protects only those rights which are secured under federal law. There seems to be no doubt that these statutes could be used to punish state or municipal election officers for unfairness to Negroes at the polls or during the process of registration. Certain attempts to use these statutes in this manner have met with varying success and will be discussed later.

A clause in another statute of this same period, which is still on the books,[68] provides civil liability in case of a conspiracy to prevent any qualified citizen, by force or intimidation, from giving his support or advocacy in favor of the election of a member of Congress or a presidential elector. This clause would probably be valid if it stood alone, but it is doubted if the whole statute could be sustained in view of the fact that some portions of it seem to be directed at individual rather than at state action. These portions seem to be authorized by no such special provision of the Constitution as that which authorizes legislation

---

[65] United States v. Mosley, 238 U. S. 383, 35 Sup. Ct. 904 (1915). See *supra* note 60.

[66] 18 U. S. C. A. §52 (1926), Rev. Stat. §5510 (1875).

[67] 8 U. S. C. A. §43 (1926), Rev. Stat. §1979 (1875).

[68] 8 U. S. C. A. §47 (1926), Rev. Stat. §1980 (1875).

with respect to national elections. Other parts may be authorized by congressional jurisdiction over the federal courts and the right to protect federal officials from being molested in the exercise of their duties, but the provision which penalizes conspiring or going abroad on the highway with the intent to deprive any class of persons of the equal protection of the laws is certainly just as subject to claims of invalidity as the Ku Klux Act which was declared unconstitutional in the *Harris* case from Tennessee.[69]

The next section of the code[70] provides that any person who knows that any of the wrongs mentioned in the preceding section are about to be committed and who refuses or neglects to aid in the prevention of the same is civilly liable to the victims. This is connected with the above statute and is dependent upon it, and if the one were declared invalid the other would fall with it.

All of the above-mentioned congressional legislation which is pertinent to the Negro suffrage question except those statutes declared to be still in effect has been either declared unconstitutional or repealed. Most of the repealing was done by an act of 1894.[71] Two of the statutes which could have been used to protect the Negro's right to vote were declared invalid in the *Bowman*[72] and *Harris*[73] cases. Congress evidently decided to let the states handle the problem for themselves, at least as far as the constitutional guarantees would permit.

State legislation seeking to guarantee Negro suffrage was not very plentiful during this period. New York enacted a statute forbidding election officials to require any oath or ask any questions of Negroes that was not demanded of whites or to reject the registration of a Negro except for some reason applicable to both races alike.[74] It is assumed that this law died a natural death, since no mention is found of it in the index of

---

[69] United States v. Harris, 106 U. S. 629, 1 Sup. Ct. 601 (1882).

[70] 8 U. S. C. A. §48 (1926), Rev. Stat. §1981 (1875).

[71] 28 Stat. 36, 37 (1893). The statutes repealed by this act were Rev. Stat. §§2002, 2005-31, 5506, 5511-15, 5520-23 (1875). The repeal of Rev. Stat. §5509 (1875) came at a later date.

[72] James v. Bowman, 190 U. S. 127, 23 Sup. Ct. 678 (1903), invalidating Rev. Stat. §§5507 (1875).

[73] United States v. Harris, 106 U. S. 629, 1 Sup. Ct. 601 (1882), invalidating Rev. Stat. §5519 (1875).

[74] N. Y. Laws 1870, c. 388.

the latest New York code and there is really no reason for such a statute at the present time, as the necessity for it has disappeared in that state.

It will be seen from an examination of the above authorities that the southern states were considerably helped in their fight against Negro domination at the polls by the strict construction given the postwar amendments by the Supreme Court and the lower federal courts as well. But even after the whites had regained control in the late seventies, they considered it necessary to prevent a recurrence of the frightful conditions through which they had just passed. At first the threat of force and various forms of duress were used. Out and out fraud and bribery were practiced wholesale. Various fraudulent devices were employed in order to keep the Negro vote as small as possible. Among these devices were the use of tissue ballots, the stuffing of ballot boxes, the employment of more ballot boxes than were necessary, and the surreptitious removal of the polls at the last moment. But the trouble with all this was that it led to serious results. A state cannot long exist under such grave conditions. Besides, no matter how much circumstances may seem to justify a system such as this, and we believe that the best of the southern whites were sincere, no voting system which is built upon fraud and duress can possibly live long in any land where the people are so intelligent and liberty-loving. Furthermore, there was always present the fact that this system encouraged crooked politicians and put a premium upon dishonesty. And the fraud was not always confined to the Negro. Hence, after fifteen or twenty years of this fraudulent system of elections, the reformers in the South began to cast about in an attempt to discover legal means of excluding the Negro from the suffrage.

Of course the rise of the Populist party in the South and its union with Republicanism in some states had its effect on the Democratic party, which had again become the dominant force in southern politics as soon as the Reconstruction governments were overthrown. This coalition obtained control of the state governments in some of the states and even succeeded in electing representatives and senators to Congress. The Negroes again became restive in some localities and, in the opinion of the whites, insolent to their former masters, as shown in the circumstances which led up to the race riots in Wilmington, North Carolina. Hence the Democrats were desirous of finding some legitimate method of cutting down the Negro vote, for the members of that race were mostly Republican at the time.

DISFRANCHISEMENT (1890-1920)

The first method devised to keep the Negroes away from the polls which met with the approval of the lawmakers was the requirement of a poll tax and the presentation of tax receipts as a prerequisite to voting. It was believed that many Negroes would not pay the tax and hence would be disqualified. The Negroes were notoriously careless about keeping receipts of any kind. Tennessee adopted a poll tax qualification in her constitution of 1870. Alabama, Arkansas, Georgia, Louisiana, Mississippi, North Carolina, South Carolina, Texas, and Virginia followed suit. In Georgia the constitution of 1877 provided that all taxes must be paid. In Florida the constitution of 1885 permitted the legislature to require payment of a poll tax as a prerequisite to the right to vote, and such a qualification was put into effect. That this policy was not confined to the states which had seceded from the Union is shown by the fact that Delaware adopted a similar policy.

In North Carolina the poll tax qualification was deleted from the constitution in 1920.[75] In recent years there has been quite a movement to follow the lead of that state in this respect, which has had the support of quite a few southern liberals. Their efforts have been successful in Florida[76] and Louisiana,[77] but have met with defeat in Arkansas and Tennessee.

The poll tax qualification has been held not to violate the Fourteenth Amendment,[78] although in many instances an un-

[75] By inadvertence the statute which was enacted as a compliment to the voting provisions of the North Carolina Constitution was left untouched when the document was amended. See N. C. CODE ANN. (Michie, 1931) §5941. This statute is probably rendered inoperative, since a proper interpretation of N. C. CONST. Art. VI, §1, seems to establish the proposition that the legislature cannot add to the voting qualifications which are set out in the fundamental document.

[76] Fla. Laws 1937, p. 755.

[77] La. Acts 1934, No. 230 (constitutional amendment adopted Nov. 6th, 1934).

[78] *See* Williams v. Mississippi, 170 U. S. 213, 18 Sup. Ct. 583 (1898); Breedlove v. Suttles, 302 U. S. 277, 58 Sup. Ct. 205 (1937).

fair administration of the law tended to disfranchise the Negro. It is certain that more Negroes than whites were so disqualified. There is nothing in the text of the provisions that could possibly be said to expressly discriminate because of race or color, for the fact that Negroes were generally delinquent in the payment of taxes was not the fault of the statute and therefore not properly to be urged against it.[79] The practice of paying a Negro's poll tax in exchange for his vote grew up among unscrupulous politicians. In Texas the conduct of certain politicians became so flagrant as to call forth an effort to put a stop to it. Thus the Terrell Election Law[80] was enacted making such conduct a misdemeanor. The validity of this statute was upheld by a Texas court.[81] Unjust discrimination against Negroes in the administration of the poll tax requirement is strikingly illustrated in another case from Texas. In this instance it was held that the failure of certain voters to present poll tax receipts when such presentation was not demanded by election officials did not justify the throwing out of the ballots.[82] The voters in this instance were not Negroes, and the inference is that the poll holders did not even request presentation except in the case of men of African descent.

In 1890 a constitutional convention met in Mississippi with the avowed purpose of getting rid of the Negro vote by truly legal means. The constitution adopted by this body provided that after 1892 a voter must be able to read the constitution, understand it when read to him, or else give a reasonable interpretation of certain passages. A voter must also take an oath that he will answer truthfully all questions concerning his right to vote, and may be disfranchised for the commission of various specified crimes, many of which are peculiarly adaptable to the Negro's known propensities. The presentation of a two-dollar poll tax receipt was also required. Many of the delegates were not satisfied with the wording of the constitution as enacted, these representatives preferring an educational test honestly administered. However, this group was in the minority and hence was outvoted. The majority wished to disfranchise as

[79] Freiszleben v. Shallcross, 9 Houst. 1, 19 Atl. 576 (Del. 1890).
[80] Tex. Acts 1st Called Sess. 1905, c. 11, §170.
[81] Watts v. State, 61 Tex. Cr. Rep. 364, 135 S. W. 585 (1911).
[82] Ramsay v. Wilhelm, 52 S. W. (2d) 757 (Tex. Civ. App. 1932).

many Negroes as possible without depriving a single white man of the voting privilege. Of course this was unfair, but, in the opinion of the whites, the end justified the means. The only weakness in the document finally adopted was thought by its proponents to be its failure to fully protect the illiterate white man.

In South Carolina a convention met in 1895 to revise the constitution of that state. It was able to improve upon the disfranchising methods used in Mississippi at least to a certain extent. The constitution adopted provided for payment of all taxes as a prerequisite for voting and set up an educational test with a provision for permanent registration before 1898. Various crimes of a kind apt to be committed by Negroes were made to entail the loss of the elective franchise. This was the method which South Carolina employed to disfranchise over half of her population. The permanent registration clause was for the obvious purpose of protecting the illiterate whites.

Other states of the Deep and Middle South soon followed the lead of these two states to a greater or lesser extent: Louisiana, in 1898; North Carolina, in 1901; Alabama, in 1901; Virginia, in 1902; and Georgia, in 1908. North Carolina, and later Oklahoma, adopted the famous grandfather clause, the ostensible purpose of which was to disfranchise the Negroes while leaving illiterate whites free to vote. Some of the other states mentioned also adopted either this provision or a similar one. These clauses provided that anyone who could vote at a certain period, the date being set at a time when the Negro could not legally vote, or a descendant of such person, would be able to qualify as a permanent voter at any time previous to a given date without submitting to educational or other tests prescribed by the constitutions. Some of the states had alternative property qualifications. Alabama and Virginia allowed war veterans and their descendants to become permanent voters, and to this Alabama added all persons of good character who understood the duties and obligations of citizenship under a Republican form of government. The Georgia and Louisiana provisions contain some but not all of the above clauses. All of these provisions are still effective,[83] although the grandfather

[83] ALA. CONST. §§180-182; GA. CONST. Art. II, §1, par. 4; LA. CONST. Art. VIII, §1; MISS. CONST. §§243-244; N. C. CONST. Art VI, §4; S. C. CONST. Art II,

clauses have either become obsolete or have been declared unconstitutional. Maryland made two abortive attempts to amend its constitution but failed each time.[84] However, the state legislature did enact a special local statute applying to the city of Annapolis alone with a provision sounding very much like a grandfather clause attached.[85] The rest of the former slave states found it unnecessary to adopt measures of this type.

Even before this time efforts had been made to find some legal means of disfranchisement. Thus use was made of the provision in the older constitution of Alabama disqualifying voters for certain crimes, including larceny. This clause was held to be constitutional in a case where a voter attempted to exercise the privilege in spite of this provision. It was said that the state had the right to limit the voting franchise in any way it saw fit except as limited by the Fifteenth Amendment. The provision was held not to limit the right to vote on account of race or color in spite of the fact that it would probably disfranchise more Negroes than whites.[86]

The city of Wilmington, North Carolina, amended its charter in a manner which was disadvantageous to the Negroes living within its boundaries, since the method of redistricting the city prescribed thereby was unfair to them. A bill in equity praying for an injunction was brought in a federal court for the purpose of preventing an election which was to be held under the provisions of the amended charter. In accordance with a familiar principle of equity jurisprudence the court held that there was a sufficient and adequate remedy at law in that if the election were illegal the plaintiff had the remedy by quo warranto, and if legal a remedy could be had by an action under the appropriate provisions of the Enforcement Act of 1870.[87] However, these or previous similar redistricting pro-

§§4, 6; Va. Const. §§19-22. The Oklahoma provision is still on the books, OKLA. CONST. Art. III, §4a, although it was declared invalid in the Guinn case, *infra* note 105. [84] STEPHENSON, RACE DISTINCTIONS IN AMERICAN LAW (1910) 295.

[85] Md. Laws 1908, c. 525.

[86] Washington v. State, 75 Ala. 582 (1884). It made no difference in an indictment for illegal voting in spite of this provision that the defendant had forgotten that he had been convicted of larceny and was therefore acting in good faith. Gandy v. State, 82 Ala. 61, 2 So. 465 (1886), 86 Ala. 20, 5 So. 520 (1888). The provision covered petit as well as grand larceny. Anderson v. State, 72 Ala. 187 (1882).

[87] Holmes v. Oldham, 12 Fed. Cas. No. 6,643 (C. C. E. D. N. C. 1877).

visions in the city charter had been declared unconstitutional by the state court.[88]

Residence and registration requirements had also been used to defeat actions by voters for being unwarrantably deprived of the voting privilege. Thus an action by a Kansas Negro failed because the plaintiff did not allege that he had established a residence of thirty days in the township as required by the state election law.[89] An action started in South Carolina failed because the plaintiff did not allege that he was registered.[90]

Maryland in the early years of the century enacted the Wilson Ballot Law which made it possible for officials in certain districts where there was a large Negro population to increase the difficulty of voting the Republican ticket. Criminal proceedings against election officials were started under various valid statutes of Reconstruction times.[91] The indictments alleged that officials in a certain congressional election had prepared the ballots in such a way that it would be much easier for ignorant persons to vote the Democratic ticket than the Republican. The defendants claimed that the indictments failed to state a cause of action, but the court would not listen to this contention and convicted the culprits.[92] The court answered the argument that the statute was valid on its face by citing the famous *Chinese Laundry* case[93] in which the Supreme Court had held in effect that discriminatory administration amounted to the same thing as discriminatory legislation, both being in the category of state action.

The natural result of all these provisions and the other means employed to accomplish the purpose of the white man was the general disfranchisement of the southern Negro. With white politicians in charge of the polls and the election machinery, a fair administration of these laws was practically impossible. The average election official was of the opinion that

---

[88] People *ex rel.* Van Bokkelen v. Canady, 73 N. C. 198, 21 Am. Rep. 465 (1875).

[89] Anthony v. Halderman, 7 Kans. 50 (1871).

[90] Wiley v. Sinkler, 179 U. S. 58, 21 Sup. Ct. 17 (1900).

[91] 18 U. S. C. A. §51 (1926), Rev. Stat. §5508 (1875); 18 U. S. C. A. §89 (1926), Rev. Stat. §5440 (1875). The latter punishes a conspiracy to commit the offense indictable under 18 U. S. C. A. §52 (1926), Rev. Stat. §5510 (1875).

[92] United States v. Stone, 188 Fed. 836 (D. Md. 1911).

[93] Yick Wo v. Hopkins, 118 U. S. 356, 6 Sup. Ct. 1064 (1885).

he had been given a mandate by the people to exclude the Negro from the polls entirely and acted accordingly with no regard for the intelligence of the particular Negro who came before him to qualify. The more conscientious whites deplored these conditions but thought that even this was better than a return to the former state. The Negroes themselves suffered from apathy or else fear of what might happen to them if they demanded a fairer deal. Such fear had been engendered by race riots, notably those which occurred at the time when the disfranchising amendments were adopted, and was the result of the threatening gestures of the whites to adopt again the methods of the Ku Klux Klan.

The feeling aroused by the Civil War had about died away in the North, and more and more the attitude of the people of that section became that of hands off. There was much talk of decreasing the representation of the southern states in Congress in accordance with the provision of the Fourteenth Amendment calling for such procedure, but nothing ever came of the propaganda. The North had finally lost interest in the cause of the Negro, and the fight was carried on only by the more rabid of the supporters of the black man and by those who in every age believe in an abstract justice and are willing to fight for it. Furthermore, there had arisen among the Negro leaders themselves a group who believed that the Negro's cause in society as a whole would be better served by not antagonizing the southern whites and by going along with them in peace and harmony. This school of thought did not desire to assert civil rights and thereby cause friction between the races; it would wait until the number of educated and independent Negroes increased to an extent sufficient to make themselves civilly and economically felt in the body politic. Of course this method was hard on certain individuals who were perfectly capable of an unprejudiced and thoughtful exercise of the right of suffrage as well as other civil rights, but these leaders believed that this would be offset in the long run by the improved relations between the races. Such belief has been to some extent justified by the improved Negro schools and sanitary conditions which the South has today. To assert that there was some injustice in this action on the part of the southern white man is to declare an obvious fact, but what is being attempted here is an effort to demonstrate his attitude toward the problem and the reasoning and circumstances which led up to the policy of disfranchisement. The same reasoning was used as an argument for keeping the Negro disfranchised. Any argument for abstract justice was always met by recalling the horrible political conditions of the past thirty-five years. This sentiment continued to be the prevailing one in spite of the fact that goodly numbers of Negroes had become capable of exercising intelligently the obligations which a grant of the voting privilege entails. The conditions during these thirty-five years were always used as a talking point by those who opposed Negro suffrage.

The disfranchising provisions of the Mississippi Constitution were held to be valid restrictions by the highest court of that state soon after their adoption in spite of the fact that more Negroes than whites were kept from the polls thereby,[94] and the Supreme Court took the same view of the matter when the question reached that tribunal.[95] The court added that this was true even though there was a distinct possibility of unjust discrimination against Negroes in the administration of the scheme. It stated that it would not interfere unless unfair administration was proved, and declared that the possibility of evil under these provisions was not enough to defeat their validity. This reasoning was closely followed in a case from Oklahoma in which the state court declared that if election officials administered the understanding clause in the constitution of that state in such a manner as to discriminate against the Negro, either by delaying other electors from entering the polling place or by giving him an unusual amount of interpretation to do, the election might be questioned.[96] However, it has been said in another Oklahoma decision that the burden of proving an unfair administration of the educational qualification is upon the voter himself, as a just administration is presumed.[97]

[94] Dixon v. State, 74 Miss. 271, 20 So. 839 (1896). For a decision upholding the validity of these provisions, *see* Sproule v. Fredericks, 69 Miss. 898, 11 So. 472 (1892). [95] Williams v. Mississippi, 170 U. S. 213, 18 Sup. Ct. 583 (1898).

[96] Snyder v. Blake, 35 Okla. 294, 129 Pac. 34 (1912).

[97] Storm v. Parman, 43 Okla. 495, 143 Pac. 38 (1914).

The Louisiana provision requiring a registrant to be able to read or give a reasonable interpretation of the constitution was held not to conflict with either the Fourteenth or Fifteenth Amendment, and the court declared that state election officials do not have arbitrary power under this clause.[98] In this state, moreover, a voter must not only satisfy the prescribed educational test, but must also fill out the blanks on the application correctly and without any aid.[99]

In another case in which the Mississippi poll tax was being discussed, the state court made the statement that in its opinion the poll tax requirement "was primarily intended by the framers of the Constitution as a clog upon the franchise." [100] This is interesting as an example of the frankness with which the South acted in its effort to rid itself of the Negro vote. The legislators were evidently in a mood to employ any means, fair or unfair, to accomplish their purpose. They were certainly not deterred by any possible reaction in other sections of the country.

Educational qualifications are not confined to the South, as states in other sections have adopted such provisions either by constitution or statute. Thus one finds such a statute in Massachusetts which was held by the court of that state not to be in conflict with either the Fourteenth or the Fifteenth Amendment.[101] An examination of the manner in which these provisions have been interpreted will be helpful in the extreme. The Washington Court has held that its educational provision is satisfied if the voter can read to some extent; he does not have to read well.[102] Two cases arose out of a statute allowing women to vote at school elections in Kentucky. The court was of the opinion that the ability to write means that the voter

---

[98] Trudeau v. Barnes, 65 Fed. (2d) 563 (C. C. A. 5th, 1933), *aff'g* 1 Fed. Supp. 453 (E. D. La. 1932). The lower court stated that the petition must allege that the prospective voter is able to make a reasonable interpretation or that he understands the duties of citizenship.

[99] Bishop v. Sherburne, 122 La. 429, 47 So. 759 (1908); Lorio v. Sherburne, 122 La. 434, 47 So. 760 (1908).

[100] Ratliff v. Beale, 74 Miss. 247, 20 So. 865 (1896).

[101] Stone v. Smith, 159 Mass. 413, 34 N. E. 521 (1893). A similar qualification is mentioned in a much later case in which it is said that voters are thus able to understand the physical arrangement of the ballot. O'Brien v. Bd. of Election Comm'rs, 257 Mass. 332, 153 N. E. 553 (1926).

[102] Hill v. Howell, 70 Wash. 603, 127 Pac. 211 (1912).

must be able to express herself by the use of alphabetical symbols in a fairly legible manner in words of common use and average difficulty, and the ability to read signifies that the voter must be able to read and interpret in a reasonably intelligent manner sentences composed of words of average difficulty.[103] The court also said that the words need not be accurately spelled.

The Oklahoma Court several times ruled that the grandfather clause in the constitution of that state was not in conflict with either the Fifteenth Amendment or a like provision in the Enabling Act which admitted Oklahoma to the Union.[104] And then the Supreme Court, realizing that this clause was an indirect violation of the amendment, declared it unconstitutional in the famous *Guinn* case.[105] The court based its opinion upon the fact that, although the grandfather clause purported to give those who had the franchise before a certain date and their descendants the right to register permanently before a certain time had elapsed without complying with the educational qualifications required of all other voters, the date chosen had been selected with an ulterior motive. The court declared that the date was fixed at a time when Negroes were not permitted to vote. The device was clearly designed to allow all the illiterate whites to exercise the privilege of suffrage while disfranchising all of the ignorant blacks. The provision therefore was an indirect attempt to circumvent the Fifteenth Amendment and hence could not be declared valid without leaving the door open for future attempts of the same kind which would completely disfranchise the Negro.

As this clause was an essential portion of the system of suffrage adopted by Oklahoma, the whole provision, educational qualifications and all, was declared invalid. Therefore an indictment under the Reconstruction conspiracy statute protect-

[103] Justice v. Meade, 162 Ky. 421, 172 S. W. 678 (1915); Williams v. Hays, 175 Ky. 170, 193 S. W. 1046 (1917).

[104] Atwater v. Hassett, 27 Okla. 292, 111 Pac. 802 (1910); *Ex parte* Show, 4 Okla. Cr. Rep. 416, 113 Pac. 1062 (1910); Snyder v. Blake, 35 Okla. 294, 129 Pac. 34 (1912); Cofield v. Farrell, 38 Okla. 608, 134 Pac. 407 (1913).

[105] Guinn v. United States, 238 U. S. 347, 35 Sup. Ct. 926 (1915). A good analysis of the problem and the supposed conflict of the provision with the equal protection clause of the Fourteenth Amendment as well as the Fifteenth is presented by Monnet, *The Latest Phase of Negro Disfranchisement* (1912) 26 HARV. L. REV. 42.

ing constitutional rights,[106] in which it was alleged that certain Negroes had been deprived of a constitutional right by the action of election officials in not permitting them to vote because of the state constitutional provision, was held to state a good cause of action. The case was sent back to the lower court where the evidence was held to be sufficient to support a conviction. This court also declared that it was not error to exclude an opinion of the state tribunal sustaining the validity of the grandfather clause when offered in evidence to establish the necessary element of bad faith, as it was not shown that the defendants had read or knew about such opinion.[107]

The afore-mentioned similar clause in the Maryland local act applying only to the city of Annapolis was also questioned in a case brought under the federal statute which provided for a civil action in case any state official or other person acting under color of law interfered with anyone in the exercise of rights secured by the Federal Constitution or laws.[108] Certain election officials, acting under the authority of this state law, had excluded Negroes from the polls. The circuit court used the above reasoning in declaring this statute invalid, and also stated that the Fifteenth Amendment could be properly applied to municipal elections.[109] The case was appealed to the Supreme Court, but it took five years to get the decision reviewed. The court finally rendered its decision and declared the statute unconstitutional in accordance with the principles announced in the *Guinn* case.[110]

These decisions outlawing the grandfather clause were handed down in 1915. A year later the Oklahoma legislature enacted a statute[111] which required registrars to enroll all those persons who had voted in 1914 and provided that other persons were to be registered only if the officials "shall be satisfied" of their qualifications. In 1914 few, if any, Negroes voted, since the constitutional provisions which were invalidated in the *Guinn* case were still in effect at that time. This statute went

[106] 18 U. S. C. A. §51 (1926), Rev. Stat. §5508 (1875).
[107] Guinn v. United States, 228 Fed. 103 (C. C. A. 8th, 1915).
[108] 8 U. S. C. A. §43 (1926), Rev. Stat. §1979 (1875).
[109] Anderson v. Myers, 182 Fed. 223 (C. C. D. Md. 1910).
[110] Myers v. Anderson, 238 U. S. 368, 35 Sup. Ct. 932 (1915).
[111] Okla. Comp. Stat. (1921) §§6252, 6255.

unchallenged for a long while. In the recent *Lane* case, however, the Tenth Circuit Court of Appeals refused to hold that the statute was invalid.[112] The court declared that there was nothing on the face of the statute which discriminated between white and Negro voters. The case was taken to the Federal Supreme Court, and that tribunal, after disposing of certain procedural difficulties, ruled that the statute was only an indirect method of perpetuating the discriminations against the Negro race and held the act unconstitutional.[113] One commentator has remarked that "the establishment of participation in the election of 1914 as the standard is but an indirect continuation of the restrictions which were declared invalid by the 1915 decision." [114]

In 1918 another rather peculiar situation arose in Oklahoma which came about as a result of the decision in the *Guinn* case. Certain local election officials, after taking into consideration the voting setup in a precinct in which the whites were considerably in the minority and relying upon the disqualification of the Negroes which was the natural result of the above provisions, had placed the polling place at the edge of a certain precinct at some distance from Negro towns. A writ of mandamus was brought to correct this, and, it having been shown that 90 per cent of the population of the precinct resided in these towns, the court ordered that the precinct be broken up.[115] Thus the court gave a practical solution of the difficulty.

From what has been said concerning the *Guinn* case it might possibly be thought that it decided the above-mentioned query in respect to the *Karem* case in accordance with the principles contended for, but it is so closely tied in with a congressional election as not to be wholly applicable to the problem presented by that decision.

It was thought for a time that the decision of the Supreme Court outlawing the grandfather clauses might mark a turning point in the court's attitude toward Negro suffrage. However, one must remember that the device was merely a temporary

[112] Lane v. Wilson, 98 F. (2d) 980 (C. C. A. 10th, 1938).

[113] Lane v. Wilson, 59 Sup. Ct. 872 (U. S. 1939). Justices Butler and McReynolds dissented. See Notes: (1939) 6 U. of Chi. L. Rev. 269, (1939) 87 U. of Pa. L. Rev. 348.

[114] Note (1939) 87 U. of Pa. L. Rev. 348.

[115] Becknell v. State, 68 Okla. 264, 172 Pac. 1094 (1918).

measure and that the time limit for registration under its terms has passed in every state in which it was adopted. The decision in the *Lane* case is but a reaffirmance of these principles, although there are certain procedural ramifications which will be discussed later in a more appropriate place. Hence there may not be such an about-face as has been supposed. While the first two Texas primary cases[116] seemed to indicate a more liberal sentiment in respect to Negro suffrage, more recent developments[117] in the white primary controversy have been less favorable.

There have been other instances, however, where Negroes have successfully asserted their right not to be discriminated against at the polls. A case of this kind occurred in Oklahoma, where certain Negroes asked for a writ of mandamus to compel county and precinct registrars to enroll them for an election at which presidential electors and a congressman were to be selected. The mandamus was granted in the lower federal court. That tribunal was of the opinion that the allegations of the petition were sufficient to raise a federal question, and the Circuit Court of Appeals refused to review the case because the appellant had not followed the correct appellate procedure.[118]

Before 1915 the hands-off attitude of the northern people was reflected in the decisions of the Supreme Court. The Republican party remained in power until 1913 with the exception of Cleveland's two administrations, and hence the personnel of the court was predominantly Republican. But practically every case that came before the court during this time to test the constitutionality of the suffrage clauses in southern state constitutions went against the Negro for various reasons, some of which are technical in the extreme. Furthermore, in certain localities, the activities of various white organizations like the Red Shirts, groups which were of the same ilk as the old Ku Klux Klan, had made the Negro afraid to insist on his just rights. Then too the colored man developed an apathy which has been one of the chief obstacles in the way of those who have

---

[116] Nixon v. Herndon, 273 U. S. 536, 47 Sup. Ct. 446 (1927); Nixon v. Condon, 286 U. S. 73, 52 Sup. Ct. 484 (1932). See notes 195 and 212 *infra.*

[117] Grovey v. Townsend, 295 U. S. 45, 55 Sup. Ct. 622 (1935). See note 225 *infra.*

[118] Berry v. Davis, 15 F. (2d) 488 (C. C. A. 8th, 1926).

enlisted in his cause.[119] The above-mentioned technical decisions will now be discussed.

The first of these came about as a result of a proceeding in equity in the federal court to restrain South Carolina election officials from carrying out the terms of a state statute providing for an entirely new registration and the closing of the books with the exception of once a month thereafter. This was to be the procedure after the general election in each year until the first of July preceding the next election. Voters who became of age could register after the closing of the books in any given year. Persons not producing their registration certificates were not to be permitted to vote. When a person moved from one county to another, onerous conditions were placed upon the transfer and renewal of the certificates. These provisions were no doubt meant to cut down the Negro vote, although there was nothing in the wording which was discriminatory. The lower court held that these were unreasonable restrictions which had manifestly been enacted for the purpose of legalizing discriminatory tactics against the Negro and were therefore unconstitutional.[120] The Circuit Court of Appeals, however, reversed the decision on jurisdictional grounds. It held that there was a remedy at law under the above-mentioned Reconstruction statutes and that an equity court had no jurisdiction over this type of case, equity not being permitted to enjoin political acts or to interfere in respect to political controversies.[121] The case was taken to the Supreme Court and was dismissed on the ground that the question was moot, for the election at which the plaintiff had claimed a right to vote was a thing of the past and those chosen thereat were seated.[122]

[119] In respect to the apathy which developed over most of the nation see Monnet, *The Latest Phase of Negro Disfranchisement* (1912) 26 HARV. L. REV. 42.

[120] Mills v. Green, 67 Fed. 818 (C. C. D. S. C. 1895).

[121] Green v. Mills, 69 Fed. 852 (C. C. A. 4th, 1895). In Gowdy v. Green, 69 Fed. 865 (C. C. D. S. C. 1895), the same circuit judge who had decided the Mills case bowed in deference to the Circuit Court of Appeals, but declared that his opinion of the issues involved, which were the same as those considered in that case, had remained unchanged.

[122] Mills v. Green, 159 U. S. 651, 16 Sup. Ct. 132 (1895). A similar decision was handed down in a case where the plaintiff demanded a writ of prohibition, declaring that the Virginia constitutional provisions had not been properly submitted to the people of the state. Jones v. Montague, 194 U. S. 147, 24 Sup. Ct. 611 (1904).

And then came the much discussed *Harris* case from Alabama. This case was brought in a federal equity court under the above civil statute[123] protecting individuals against a deprivation of constitutional rights by any person under color of law. The action was brought to compel the State Board of Registrars to enroll the names of certain Negroes on the voting lists. The plaintiff's contention was that the disfranchising provisions in the new Alabama Constitution were in conflict with the Fourteenth and Fifteenth amendments. The Supreme Court, with several justices dissenting, came to the conclusion that a court of equity could not enforce registration under provisions which the plaintiff himself is contending are invalid, giving as an additional reason for its decision the broad generalization that a court of equity will not enforce political rights.[124] Justice Holmes, who delivered the opinion of the court, remarked upon the argument that the statute was not applicable because it failed to mention state constitutional provisions in its enumeration of types of legislation under color of which the defendant would have to act in order for the statute to apply, but the point was left undecided because there were other grounds upon which the action was unsustainable.[125]

In the *Teasley* case from Alabama two actions were commenced in the state courts, one a civil action to recover damages for the failure of election officials to register the Negro plaintiff,[126] the other an application for a writ of mandamus to enforce the plaintiff's alleged right to register.[127] Both actions failed. The state court declared that if the afore-mentioned constitutional provisions were void, then the board of registrars which had refused to let the plaintiff get on the voting list was without authority to register him, there being no law under which a proper registration could be had. Therefore the refusal on the part of election officials to allow this prerequisite of the right to vote could not be said to render the members of the board liable in an action for damages or subject to mandamus proceedings. The court also declared that if the

[123] 8 U. S. C. A. §43 (1926), Rev. Stat. §1979 (1875). See note 67 *supra*.

[124] Giles v. Harris, 189 U. S. 475, 23 Sup. Ct. 639 (1903).

[125] See Monnet, *The Latest Phase of Negro Disfranchisement* (1912) 26 Harv. L. Rev. 42.

[126] Giles v. Teasley, 136 Ala. 164, 33 So. 819 (1902).

[127] Giles v. Teasley, 136 Ala. 228, 33 So. 820 (1902).

said provisions were valid, then by their very terms judicial discretion was conferred upon the board for the exercise of which authority its members would be liable in neither of the aforesaid actions. The case was taken to the Supreme Court, but that tribunal dismissed the proceeding and refused to consider the constitutional question because the state court had decided the cases on the above independent procedural grounds. Therefore, the high tribunal held that it had no jurisdiction, there being no federal question involved.[128] The court did not even discuss the validity of the disfranchising provisions.

After a consideration of principles announced in these two Alabama cases, the query presented itself as to just how the validity of these state constitutional and statutory provisions could be brought to a test in the Supreme Court. When the argument of no effective registration under a statute which the plaintiff himself claims is void was set up by the defendant in the *Maryland Grandfather Clause* case,[129] the court decided that this did not leave the plaintiff without a remedy. The justices avoided the difficulty by holding that a former registration act was revived by the declaration of the invalidity of the statute. Therefore there was an authorized action against the officials who had wrongfully refused to register the plaintiff in conformity with the provisions of the older act. It was declared that this statute had never ceased to be the law according to the plaintiff's theory of the case.

It was inevitable that the argument which had been employed to defeat the Negro plaintiffs' actions in the *Harris* and *Teasley* cases would be set up in some future controversy involving Negro suffrage. An opportunity presented itself in the recent *Lane* case in which an Oklahoma Negro claimed that a state statute was invalid because it discriminated against persons of his race. The action was brought under the same federal statute[130] which had been employed in the *Harris* case. The only difference in the two cases appeared to be that in the *Harris* case the action was in equity while in the *Lane* case the action was at law. In the *Harris* case Justice Holmes in the majority opinion remarked that the court was "not prepared

[128] Giles v. Teasley, 193 U. S. 146, 24 Sup. Ct. 359 (1903).

[129] Myers v. Anderson, 238 U. S. 368, 35 Sup. Ct. 932 (1915).

[130] 8 U. S. C. A. §43 (1926), Rev. Stat. §1979 (1875). See note 123 *supra*.

to say that an action at law could not be maintained on the facts alleged in the bill." Through this loophole the court plunged[131] and thereby distinguished the two cases. The sophistry of this distinction can be better understood when it is noted that the statute authorizes a suit in equity as well as an action at law. Hence it is believed that the present liberal court made a wide departure from its former stand in regard to this procedural point. As we have noted above, the court in the *Harris* case declared that a court of equity cannot undertake to enforce political rights. In answer to this argument as applied to present-day cases it may be said that equity courts have of late been taking a distinct interest in some controversies in which political rights were involved, thus making the rule less rigid. It is believed that in the *Lane* case the present liberal justices disdained to follow the legalistic quibble with which their predecessors had dismissed the earlier cases.

Two federal courts have declared that a plaintiff in this type of case must first exhaust his remedies in the state courts before resorting to the federal tribunals.[132] In the *Lane* case,[133] however, the Supreme Court negatived this objection to the original jurisdiction of the federal courts.

To what elections is the Fifteenth Amendment applicable? This query is not easily answered in view of the confused state of the authorities. The application of the amendment to municipal elections has been settled affirmatively by the decision of the Supreme Court in the case from Maryland involving the grandfather clause.[134] The court cited Section 1 of the Enforcement Act.[135] This statute is still in effect[136] and specifically mentions such elections. In Georgia an act incorporating a town which limited the right to vote at municipal elections to whites was held to be in direct conflict with the amendment and therefore void.[137]

[131] Lane v. Wilson, 59 Sup. Ct. 872 (U. S. 1939).

[132] Trudeau v. Barnes, 65 F. (2d) 563 (C. C. A. 5th, 1933); Lane v. Wilson, 98 F. (2d) 980 (C. C. A. 10th, 1938).

[133] Lane v. Wilson, *supra* note 131.

[134] Myers v. Anderson, 238 U. S. 368, 35 Sup. Ct. 932 (1915).

[135] 16 STAT. 144 (1870).

[136] 8 U. S. C. A. §31 (1926), REV. STAT. §2004 (1875).

[137] Howell v. Pate, 119 Ga. 537, 46 S. E. 667 (1904). However, certain state constitutional provisions in Florida were held not to apply to municipal elections, these being controlled by statute. State v. Dillon, 32 Fla. 545, 14 So. 383 (1893).

A school-district election has been said to be within the purview of the Fifteenth Amendment, the court citing the above declaratory federal statute which also expressly mentions this type of election.[138] In an early Illinois case, moreover, a Negro was held to be entitled to recover damages against officials who had denied him the right to vote at a school election.[139]

However, local option elections to decide questions of special interest to a particular locality like prohibition, which are not mentioned in the above statute, have been held not to be within the scope of the amendment.[140] But such elections have been held to be within the meaning of state constitutional provisions affecting the elective franchise in other ways, such as disfranchisement for crime[141] and a clause providing that elections shall be by ballot.[142]

The White Primary

Almost universally in this country the primary has superseded the convention as the method employed by political parties to select candidates for office. These parties are somewhat in the nature of voluntary associations,[143] but may be subject to reasonable regulation by the state.[144] In some states,

[138] Porter v. Kingfisher County Comm'rs, 6 Okla. 550, 51 Pac. 741 (1898). For a discussion of statutes providing for a vote by each race alone concerning problems of its own schools, see chapter on Education, pp. 120-126. *See also* Wright v. Lyddan, 191 Ky. 58, 229 S. W. 74 (1921); Bd. of Education of Meade County v. Bunger, 240 Ky. 155, 41 S. W. (2d) 908 (1931); Ratliff v. State *ex rel.* Woods, 79 Okla. 152, 191 Pac. 1038 (1920).

[139] Bernier v. Russell, 89 Ill. 60 (1878).

[140] McClure v. Topf & Wright, 112 Ark. 342, 166 S. W. 174 (1914); Hickey v. State, 114 Ark. 526, 170 S. W. 562 (1914); Havis v. Philpot, 115 Ark. 250, 170 S. W. 1005 (1914); Willis v. Kalmbach, 109 Va. 475, 64 S. E. 342 (1909).

[141] Anderson v. State, 72 Ala. 187 (1882); Washington v. State, 75 Ala. 582 (1884); Gandy v. State, 82 Ala. 61, 2 So. 465 (1886).

[142] State *ex rel.* Birchmore v. State Bd. of Canvassers, 78 S. C. 461, 59 S. E. 145 (1907).

[143] Walls v. Brundidge, 109 Ark. 250, 160 S. W. 230 (1913); Waples v. Marrast, 108 Tex. 5, 184 S. W. 180 (1916). The Arkansas Court declared that the state had "nothing to do with the holding of primary elections. The statute fixes the date for holding primary elections, but the state appoints no officers to hold a Democratic primary. It does not pay the costs thereof. The machinery for holding a Democratic primary election in Arkansas is entirely an instrumentality created by the party with which the state, as a state, has nothing to do, whereas in a general election the entire machinery for holding such election is the creation of the state."

[144] People *ex rel.* Breckōn v. Bd. of Election Comm'rs, 221 Ill. 9, 77 N. E. 321

like Oklahoma and Virginia, this regulation has been of such a quality that the primary has become an integral part of the state election machinery.[145] In fact primaries are mentioned in the Virginia Constitution. However, political parties are allowed to regulate their own particular affairs whenever the legislature has not seen fit to interfere,[146] and it has been held that an equity court cannot interfere with the management of political parties.[147]

Is a primary an "election" within the meaning of that term as used at common law or in various constitutional and statutory provisions? In the *Newberry* case the primary was held by the Supreme Court not to be an election within that portion of the Federal Constitution[148] which gives Congress authority to control national elections.[149] There is a contrariety of opinion in the state courts regarding this problem. Thus some states consistently hold that the primary is an election, while a number of others hold just as consistently that the opposite interpretation is the proper one. There is also a third group which has been inconsistent in its interpretation of such provisions. Of course the decisions in a number of instances have been influenced to a great extent by the peculiar wording of the pro-

(1906); State v. Michel, 121 La. 374, 46 So. 340 (1908); Ladd v. Holmes, 40 Ore. 167, 66 Pac. 714 (1901).

145 *Ex parte* Wilson, 7 Okla. Cr. Rep. 610, 125 Pac. 739 (1912); Commonwealth v. Willcox, 111 Va. 849, 69 S. E. 1027 (1911).

146 Ferguson v. Montgomery, 148 Ark. 83, 229 S. W. 30 (1921).

147 Wilkinson v. Henry, 221 Ala. 254, 128 So. 362 (1930); Winnet v. Adams, 71 Nebr. 817, 99 N. W. 681 (1904). *See also* Ferguson v. Montgomery, 148 Ark. 83, 229 S. W. 30 (1921); Brown v. Costen, 176 N. C. 63, 96 S. E. 659 (1918). In the Wilkinson case one of the party regulations was that only white persons could vote, but there is no indication that the complainant was a Negro.

148 Art. I, §4.

149 Newberry v. United States, 256 U. S. 232, 41 Sup. Ct. 469 (1921). The five to four decision in this case deserves mention because one commentator (see Note (1932) 17 St. Louis L. Rev. 155) claims that the case was not decided by a majority of the court on the point that is here important, remarking that the opinion of Justice McKenna was reserved on constitutional grounds. However, an examination of the case shows that his opinion was reserved because of the possible application of the Seventeenth Amendment to the particular problem involved in the determination of that controversy; namely, whether Congress could legislate for senatorial primaries, a point which is not germane to the present problem. The case is fully analyzed by Evans, *Primary Elections and the Constitution* (1934) 32 Mich. L. Rev. 451; Note (1921) 19 Mich. L. Rev. 860. *See also* United States v. Gradwell, 243 U. S. 476, 37 Sup. Ct. 407 (1917).

vision which is being interpreted, and no doubt this accounts for some of the confusion which has developed with respect to this problem.

Those jurisdictions which have consistently held that a primary is an election are Nebraska,[150] North Carolina,[151] Oklahoma,[152] and Oregon,[153] while Virginia could almost certainly be placed in the same category because, as stated above,[154] the constitution of that state mentions primaries. Illinois has been one of the most consistent proponents of this view.[155] However, it has been said in a recent case from that state that a primary election law is within the scope of the provisions of the state constitution only so far as it affects or has to do with rights which are guaranteed by that document. The court said that the primary is not an election in the sense that all voters having the constitutional qualifications may vote thereat, and that therefore the primary act of 1927 giving equal voice to all qualified members of the party to select candidates is not unconstitutional as being in conflict with the cumulative voting provisions of the said constitution.[156] The Florida Court has held that a primary is an "election" within the state constitutional provision authorizing the enactment of legislation to keep down the exertion of undue influence by the use of improper practices.[157] However, it was held in an earlier Florida case that members of a political party's county executive committee are not "officers" within the meaning of the state constitutional provision[158] relating to the continuance in office of state,

[150] State *ex rel.* Adair v. Drexel, 74 Nebr. 776, 105 N. W. 174 (1905); State *ex rel.* Ragan v. Junkin, 85 Nebr. 1, 122 N. W. 473 (1909). In the Drexel case, however, primaries were said not to be elections within a statute mentioning "official ballots."

[151] State v. Cole, 156 N. C. 618, 72 S. E. 221 (1911).

[152] Dove v. Oglesby, 114 Okla. 144, 244 Pac. 798 (1926). See also *Ex parte* Wilson, 7 Okla. Cr. Rep. 610, 125 Pac. 739 (1912).

[153] Ladd v. Holmes, 40 Ore. 167, 66 Pac. 714 (1901).

[154] See note 145 *supra*.

[155] People *ex rel.* Breckon v. Bd. of Election Comm'rs, 221 Ill. 9, 77 N. E. 321 (1906); Rouse v. Thompson, 228 Ill. 522, 81 N. E. 1109 (1907); People *ex rel.* Phillips v. Strassheim, 240 Ill. 279, 88 N. E. 821 (1909); People *ex rel.* Espey v. Deneen, 247 Ill. 289, 93 N. E. 437 (1910); People v. Fox, 294 Ill. 263, 128 N. E. 505 (1920); McAlpine v. Dimick, 326 Ill. 240, 157 N. E. 235 (1927).

[156] People *ex rel.* Lindstrand v. Emmerson, 333 Ill. 606, 165 N. E. 217 (1929). Whatever is said contrary to this view in the Breckon case, cited *supra* note 155, is overruled.

[157] *Ex parte* Hawthorne, 116 Fla. 608, 156 So. 619 (1934); State *ex rel.* Gandy v. Page, 125 Fla. 348, 169 So. 854 (1936).

[158] FLA. CONST. Art. XVI, §14.

county, and municipal officers until their successors are duly qualified.[159]

Those states which have consistently held the opposing view that a primary is not an election are Arkansas,[160] Georgia,[161] Iowa,[162] Kentucky,[163] Louisiana,[164] Michigan,[165] Minnesota,[166] Mississippi,[167] Nevada,[168] New Jersey,[169] New York,[170] North Dakota,[171] Ohio,[172] Tennessee,[173] and West Virginia.[174] Missouri could almost be said to be within the same category,[175]

---

[159] Moore v. Bd. of County Comm'rs, 96 Fla. 519, 118 So. 476 (1928).

[160] Hester v. Bourland, 80 Ark. 145, 95 S. W. 992 (1906); State v. Simmons, 117 Ark. 159, 174 S. W. 238 (1915); McClain v. Fish, 159 Ark. 199, 251 S. W. 686 (1923).

[161] George v. State, 18 Ga. App. 753, 90 S. E. 493 (1916); Mark v. State, 18 Ga. App. 754, 90 S. E. 493 (1916).

[162] Jones v. Fisher, 156 Iowa 582, 137 N. W. 940 (1912); State *ex rel.* Hatfield v. Carrington, 194 Iowa 785, 190 N. W. 390 (1922).

[163] Commonwealth v. Helm, 9 Ky. Law Rep. 532 (1887); Montgomery v. Chelf, 118 Ky. 766, 82 S. W. 388 (1904); Hodge v. Bryan, 149 Ky. 110, 148 S. W. 21 (1912); Runyon v. Trent, 270 Ky. 134, 109 S. W. (2d) 396 (1937).

[164] State *ex rel.* Rees v. Foster, 111 La. 1087, 36 So. 200 (1904); Reid v. Brunot, 153 La. 490, 96 So. 43 (1923).

[165] Line v. Bd. of Election Canvassers, 154 Mich. 329, 117 N. W. 730 (1908).

[166] State *ex rel.* Gulden v. Johnson, 87 Minn. 221, 91 N. W. 604, 840 (1902); State *ex rel.* Nordin v. Erickson, 119 Minn. 152, 137 N. W. 385 (1912).

[167] Ramey v. Woodward, 90 Miss. 777, 44 So. 769 (1907).

[168] Riter v. Douglass, 32 Nev. 400, 109 Pac. 444 (1910).

[169] State v. Woodruff, 68 N. J. Law 89, 52 Atl. 294 (1902); State v. Bienstock, 78 N. J. Law 256, 73 Atl. 530 (1909).

[170] People v. Foster, 60 Misc. 3, 112 N. Y. Supp. 706 (Ct. Gen. Sess. N. Y. Co. 1908).

[171] State *ex rel.* McCue v. Blaisdell, 18 N. D. 55, 118 N. W. 141 (1908); State *ex rel.* Miller v. Flaherty, 23 N. D. 313, 136 N. W. 76 (1912); Leu v. Montgomery, 31 N. D. 1, 5, 148 N. W. 662 (1914); Walton v. Olsen, 40 N. D. 571, 170 N. W. 107 (1918). The later opinion in Johnson v. Grand Forks County, 22 N. D. 613, 135 N. W. 179 (1912) certainly throws doubt upon the apparently contrary holding in that same case, 16 N. D. 363, 113 N. W. 1071 (1907).

[172] State *ex rel.* Webber v. Felton, 77 Ohio St. 554, 84 N. E. 85 (1908).

[173] Lillard v. Mitchell, 37 S. W. 702 (Tenn. Ch. App. 1896); Ledgerwood v. Pitts, 122 Tenn. 570, 125 S. W. 1036 (1909); Mathes v. State, 121 S. W. (2d) 548 (Tenn. 1938). *But see* State v. Matthews, 173 Tenn. 302, 117 S. W. (2d) 2 (1938).

[174] Baer v. Gore, 79 W. Va. 50, 90 S. E. 530 (1916); Fansler v. Rightmire, 115 W. Va. 492, 177 S. E. 288 (1934).

[175] Dooley v. Jackson, 104 Mo. App. 21, 78 S. W. 330 (1904); Haas v. City of Neosho, 139 Mo. App. 293, 123 S. W. 473 (1909); State *ex rel.* Von Stade v. Taylor, 220 Mo. 618, 119 S. W. 373 (1909); State *ex rel.* Dunn v. Coburn, 260 Mo. 177, 168 S. W. 956 (1914); State *ex rel.* McDonald v. Lollis, 326 Mo. 644, 33 S. W. (2d) 98 (1930). *See also* State *ex rel.* Neu v. Waechter, 332 Mo. 574, 58 S. W. (2d) 971 (1933).

although language has been employed in a recent decision from that state which seems to indicate that a primary is an "election" within the state constitutional provision requiring elections to be free and open.[176] Furthermore, one might also place Rhode Island in this same general class, as the court of that state has held that a party caucus is not to be considered as an election.[177]

There are several jurisdictions where there has been no consistency in the decisions as to whether a primary is or is not to be considered an election within such provisions. In this classification would be California,[178] Indiana,[179] Maryland,[180] Pennsylvania,[181] Texas,[182] and Washington.[183]

Thus it seems that a clear majority of the jurisdictions which have had occasion to pass upon this proposition in the past have been in favor of considering the primary as separate and apart from the general election when such constitutional and statutory provisions are being considered.[184] Furthermore, in some states

[176] *Ibid.* See also in this connection State *ex rel.* Hollman v. McElhinney, 315 Mo. 731, 286 S. W. 951 (1926) and State *ex rel.* Dengel v. Hartman, 339 Mo. 200, 96 S. W. (2d) 329 (1936).

[177] *In re* Jamestown Caucus Law, 43 R. I. 421, 112 Atl. 900 (1921).

[178] Those cases holding that the primary is an election are: Marsh v. Hanly, 111 Cal. 368, 43 Pac. 975 (1896); Spier v. Baker, 120 Cal. 370, 52 Pac. 659 (1898); Britton v. Bd. of Election Comm'rs, 129 Cal. 337, 61 Pac. 1115 (1900). Those holding that it is not are: People v. Cavanaugh, 112 Cal. 674, 44 Pac. 1057 (1896); McDonald v. Neuner, 5 Cal. App. (2d) 751, 43 P. (2d) 813 (1935). *See also* Bigelow v. Bd. of Supervisors, 18 Cal. App. 715, 124 Pac. 554 (1912).

[179] That the primary is an election: State v. Hirsch, 125 Ind. 207, 24 N. E. 1062 (1890). That it is not: Gray v. Seitz, 162 Ind. 1, 69 N. E. 456 (1904); Kelso v. Cook, 184 Ind. 173, 110 N. E. 987 (1916).

[180] That the primary is an election: Strasburger v. Burk, 13 Am. L. Reg. (N.S.) 607 (City Ct. of Baltimore, 1874). That it is not: Foxwell v. Beck, 117 Md. 1, 82 Atl. 657 (1911).

[181] That the primary is an election: Leonard v. Commonwealth, 112 Pa. St. 607, 4 Atl. 220 (1886). That it is not: Commonwealth v. Wells, 110 Pa. St. 463, 1 Atl. 310 (1885).

[182] That the primary is an election: Anderson v. Ashe, 62 Tex. Civ. App. Rep. 262, 130 S. W. 1044 (1910); Ashford v. Goodwin, 103 Tex. 491, 131 S. W. 535 (1910). That it is not: Koy v. Schneider, 110 Tex. 369, 218 S. W. 479, 221 S. W. 880 (1920); Hamilton v. Davis, 217 S. W. 431 (Tex. Civ. App. 1920); Walker v. Hopping, 226 S. W. 146 (Tex. Civ. App. 1920); Iles v. Walker, 120 S. W. (2d) 418 (Tex. 1938).

[183] That the primary is an election: State v. Robinson, 69 Wash. 172, 124 Pac. 379 (1912). That it is not: State *ex rel.* Zent v. Nichols, 50 Wash. 508, 97 Pac. 728 (1908).

[184] A statement to the contrary in a Note (1930) 15 CORN. L. Q. 262 may therefore be disregarded.

like Arkansas[185] and Texas,[186] political parties have been held not to be governmental instrumentalities, in spite of the fact that they are subject to a certain amount of control by the state.

As the Negro became better and better educated, the southern whites, who had never forgotten or forgiven Reconstruction, realized that the disfranchising constitutional provisions could no longer be depended upon to effect the purpose for which they had been enacted and that, if the Negro vote was to be kept down, some other method would have to be found to accomplish this purpose. The white primary was hit upon as the best possible way of doing this. The Democratic primary is far more important in the South than the general election because of the overwhelming preponderance of people of that political faith in this section of the nation. Hence there is usually far more interest and political activity engendered by the former than by the latter. According to Mr. Lewinson,[187] in all of the states which comprised the Confederacy the Democratic party had attempted to bar the Negro from its primaries to a certain extent by 1932. In Alabama, Arkansas, Georgia, Louisiana, Mississippi, and Virginia a party rule prevented Negroes from participating in the primary. There is a similar rule now in force in Texas, but it is disregarded in some counties. In Florida they were disqualified by county rule. In order to be allowed to vote in the South Carolina primaries a Negro was compelled to procure affidavits of ten white men to the effect that he voted for Wade Hampton in 1876 and had since voted the Democratic ticket. In North Carolina Negroes vote in the primaries in a number of urban districts, while in Tennessee they are only permitted to vote in the urban centers of Memphis and Nashville and to a varying extent in other towns and cities over the state.[188] In the border states there are no general primary regulations to this effect. The "lily-white" movement made its appearance in the Republican party in the South, leaving the Negro without any effective means of organization for the purpose of bettering his political lot.

---

[185] Walls v. Brundidge, 109 Ark. 250, 160 S. W. 230 (1913).

[186] Waples v. Marrast, 108 Tex. 5, 184 S. W. 180 (1916); Cunningham v. McDermatt, 277 S. W. 218 (Tex. Civ. App. 1925).

[187] Race, Class, and Party (1932) App. III.

[188] *Id.* at 153.

Hence the Negro turned to the courts in an effort to avoid this stalemate. The first case came before the Louisiana Court in 1912 and involved a state Democratic committee resolution to the effect that only members of the white race were to be permitted to vote in the primary. A number of mulattoes voted in the primary as white persons, and the defeated candidate brought an action to contest the election because they were permitted to cast their ballot notwithstanding the resolution. However, in this instance the complainant was thrown out of court on the ground that there were not enough of these contested votes to affect the result of the election,[189] and hence the constitutional problems involved were not even considered. The next case did not arise until 1922 and involved a petition filed by a Negro asking that he be permitted to vote in a certain Texas Democratic primary, the party executive committee in that state having adopted a resolution restricting participation therein to whites. As the election in which the Negro desired to vote had passed before a review of the case could be obtained in the appellate court, it was held that no relief could be given, the question being a moot one.[190] Another point of this nature was used to defeat a later attempt to invalidate a similar county rule in Florida. In this instance the court said that the objection that Negroes were not allowed to vote could not be set up by white persons who had challenged the validity of the primary law of that state.[191]

The Democrats of Texas, disgusted with the situation which had developed in several cities, particularly San Antonio, where rival political factions in the party had been making efforts to control the ignorant Negro vote by means of bribery and other unfair methods, decided that they would do something really drastic in order to prevent the recurrence of such conditions. In 1923 the legislature enacted a statute which specifically excluded Negroes from all Democratic primaries in the state.[192] It has been remarked that this presents "the strange picture of one race disfranchising another to save it-

[189] Marrero v. Middleton, 131 La. 432, 59 So. 863 (1912).

[190] Love v. Griffith, 236 S. W. 239 (Tex. Civ. App. 1922), *aff'd* 266 U. S. 32, 45 Sup. Ct. 12 (1924).

[191] State *ex rel.* Landis v. Dyer, 109 Fla. 33, 148 So. 201 (1933).

[192] TEX. ANN. REV. CIV. STAT. (Vernon, 1925) art. 3107.

self from the consequences of its own vices."[193] The supporters of Negro suffrage were not long in bringing a test case in the federal court to enjoin the enforcement of this statute. In this instance relief was denied on the ground that a primary cannot be put into the same category as a general election in this respect, as it is merely a method of selecting the candidates of a political party, and that the right to vote therein would not be protected by the Fourteenth and Fifteenth amendments.[194] The court said that the pertinent provisions of the amendments apply only to state action and not to the acts of voluntary associations like political parties. When the question reached the Supreme Court in the *Herndon* case, however, a different view of the matter was taken. In that case a Negro brought an action for damages in the federal court for the refusal of poll officials to allow him to vote in a primary. The Supreme Court ruled that the statute was a direct and patent violation of the equal protection guarantee of the Fourteenth Amendment, as the enactment of such legislation by the representatives of the people was undoubtedly state action of a most definite nature.[195] In the course of his opinion Justice Holmes remarked that it was unnecessary to decide whether or not the Fifteenth Amendment would apply to such a situation because one could not well imagine a more flagrant violation of the Fourteenth.

Texas' answer to the Supreme Court's decision in the *Herndon* case was the immediate passage of a statute giving the party executive committee authority to fix the qualifications for membership in the party.[196] Under the provisions of this act the Democratic Executive Committee adopted a resolution to the effect that no Negroes would be permitted to vote in the coming primary. The idea back of this scheme was that the action of the committee in this respect would be considered by

---

[193] Note (1932) 41 YALE L. J. 1212.

[194] Chandler v. Neff, 298 Fed. 515 (W. D. Tex. 1924).

[195] Nixon v. Herndon, 273 U. S. 536, 47 Sup. Ct. 446 (1927). There was a good deal of comment devoted to this decision in the law journals. See Notes: (1927) 5 TEX. L. REV. 393, (1927) 12 ST. LOUIS L. REV. 199, (1932) 17 ST. LOUIS L. REV. 155, (1930) 15 CORN. L .Q. 262, (1930) 28 MICH. L. REV. 613, (1930) 43 HARV. L. REV. 467, (1932) 21 CALIF. L. REV. 62, (1932) 41 YALE L. J. 1212. One commentator went so far as to reproach the Texas legislature for enacting a statute so patently unconstitutional. Note (1927) 11 MARQ. L. REV. 259.

[196] Tex. Gen. & Sp. Laws 1927, c. 67.

the courts as that of a purely voluntary political association and not that of a state agency, for the guarantees of the above constitutional provisions only protected the rights secured thereby as against state action. Thus Texas sought to circumvent the Supreme Court's decision.

The statute's only material opposition in the legislature came from those politicians who feared an extension of its application beyond the purposes it was meant to serve. Their apprehension was aroused by the probability that this power given to the executive committee would be used to punish party bolters.[197] It seems that the party leaders were bent upon keeping the Negroes away from the polls. Immediately the Negroes, with the financial aid of organizations like the National Association for the Advancement of Colored People, began legal proceedings with the purpose of contesting the validity of the resolution.

The *Grigsby* case was the first reported controversy to arise under this statute. A Negro applied to the federal district court for an injunction to prevent a county executive committee from putting the resolution into effect. It was held that such a resolution in pursuance of the authority invested in the committee by the statute was not state action and hence not within the prohibitions of the above-mentioned constitutional amendments.[198] The court also mentioned the fact that in Texas, as has been said above, political parties are merely political instrumentalities and not governmental instrumentalities. The same reasoning was followed by the state court in the *Lubbock* case.[199] The proceeding in this instance was a mandamus

[197] For further discussion of this subject see Note (1932) 41 YALE L. J. 1212.

[198] Grigsby v. Harris, 27 Fed. (2d) 942 (S. D. Tex. 1928). Procedural difficulties prevented an appeal to the Supreme Court. 27 Fed. (2d) 945 (S. D. Tex. 1928). The case is commented upon in sundry legal periodicals. Notes: (1929) 13 MINN. L. REV. 375, (1928) 4 NOTRE DAME LAWYER 209, (1929) 3 TEMP. L. Q. 217, (1929) 33 L. NOTES 101.

[199] White v. Lubbock, 30 S. W. (2d) 722 (Tex. Civ. App. 1930). This case has also been noticed in various law journals. Notes: (1930) 8 N. Y. U. L. Q. REV. 309, (1930) 79 U. OF PA. L. REV. 220, (1931) 34 L. NOTES 212, (1931) 9 TEX. L. REV. 439, (1931) 25 ILL. L. REV. 699. In the comment in the TEXAS LAW REVIEW the writer remarks that there was little need for the resolution, a statement which would seem to be open to serious doubt in view of the large amount of litigation concerning the white primary which has recently been coming before the courts, both state and federal, in the state of Texas. In fact it was said by

brought against party officials by a Negro to enforce his alleged right to vote in the party primaries. The court placed its decision upon the additional ground that there was no provision in the state law for a mandamus to compel party officials to do their duty, but it was not long before the party chieftains, faced with the problems created by the bolting Hooverites, shoved through an act which provided for such a remedy.[200]

While all this was happening in Texas, the Democratic party in other southern states was also having difficulties in trying to restrict its membership to whites. A statute had been enacted in Virginia which provided that persons who are not disqualified by reason of other requirements in the law of the party to which they belong may vote at the party primaries.[201] In pursuance of the authority recognized by this act the State Democratic Convention adopted a regulation excluding all Negroes from the party primaries. A Negro brought an action in the federal court for damages under one of the abovementioned Reconstruction statutes authorizing a civil action for deprivation of constitutional rights.[202] He alleged that the statute was unconstitutional in authorizing the disqualification of voters in primary elections by discriminatory rules based on color. The court came to the conclusion that party primaries in Virginia had become such an integral part of the state election machinery that any action in respect to them was now regarded as state action and that the statute was invalid because it authorized the making of discriminatory regulations by those in charge of the party affairs.[203] The court stressed the fact that the expenses of the Virginia primaries are paid for by the state. Since the statute is not discriminatory on its face, this decision can be approved only on the theory that the statute constituted an effort by the legislature to make a delegation of authority which was altogether too broad, as a blanket authority such as is attempted here is unauthorized and fraught with the danger of being used in a discriminatory manner.

---

the commentator in the ILLINOIS LAW REVIEW, *supra,* that the necessity for some sort of legislation was deemed so great at the time the statute was passed that the constitutional requirement of reading a bill three times was suspended.

[200] See Note (1932) 41 YALE L. J. 1212, 1216-17.

[201] VA. CODE ANN. (Michie, 1930) §228.

[202] 8 U. S. C. A. §43 (1926), REV. STAT. §1979 (1875).

[203] West v. Bliley, 33 Fed. (2d) 177 (E. D. Va. 1929).

The court might possibly have avoided the issue of the validity of the statute by employing the doctrine of discriminatory administration by a state agency as approved in the often-cited *Chinese Laundry* case.[204] It might very well be argued that a political party in Virginia was made a state agency by this statute which gave it power to control its membership. The court seems to recognize that this statute and others which regulate political parties have changed the character of these voluntary associations and made them state agencies. However, the court evidently preferred to rest its decision on the above reasoning. The Circuit Court of Appeals affirmed this case,[205] and in doing so declared its approval of the language of the lower tribunal. The court stressed the argument that, were all the political parties to bar the Negroes from the primaries, they would then be deprived of any participation in the selection of candidates to be nominated for office, a privilege which is of great importance to them because of the one-party system which has developed in the South.

In the *Robinson* case from Arkansas a Negro brought an action in the state court to establish his alleged right to vote in the Democratic primaries, a privilege which was denied members of his race because of a party rule barring them from participating therein. It was held that the action of the State Democratic Central Committee in so limiting the party's membership to whites was to be considered as a proper exercise of the party's inherent power to control its own membership and that it was not state action proscribed by the Fourteenth and Fifteenth amendments.[206] The Supreme Court refused to interfere, declaring that it had no jurisdiction.[207] It is evident, there-

[204] Yick Wo v. Hopkins, 118 U. S. 356, 6 Sup. Ct. 1064 (1885). See chapter on Civil Rights, note 241.

[205] Bliley v. West, 42 Fed. (2d) 101 (C. C. A. 4th, 1930). The case has been discussed in various legal periodicals. See Notes: (1929) 33 L. Notes 101, (1931) 34 L. Notes 212, (1930) 8 N. Y. U. L. Q. Rev. 309, (1930) 15 Corn. L. Q. 262, (1930) 43 Harv. L. Rev. 467, (1931) 5 Tulane L. Rev. 309, (1931) 9 N. C. L. Rev. 207, (1929) 14 Minn. L. Rev. 83, (1929) 16 Va. L. Rev. 193, (1932) 17 St. Louis L. Rev. 155, (1932) 41 Yale L. J. 1212. The commentator in the St. Louis Law Review makes the statement that the privilege of participating in the party primary is a constitutional right, but, as will be seen later, this is not absolutely true as here expressed, although the West case is certainly persuasive of the recognition of such a proposition in Virginia as an isolated instance.

[206] Robinson v. Holman, 181 Ark. 428, 26 S. W. (2d) 66 (1930).

[207] Robinson v. Holman, 282 U. S. 804, 51 Sup. Ct. 88 (1930).

fore, that the reasoning of the state court was at least not disapproved by that tribunal.

Going back to Texas, it is to be noted that the militant leaders among the Negroes were certainly not satisfied with the result obtained in the *Grigsby* and *Lubbock* cases. Hence it was decided that another test case should be pushed through to the Supreme Court. The same Dr. Nixon who had been the plaintiff in the *Herndon* case brought an action for damages under the same federal statute which was employed in the Virginia case. He claimed that the resolution of the Democratic Executive Committee restricting the party membership to whites deprived Negroes of their constitutional rights. For convenience' sake this will be alluded to as the *Condon* case. The District Court[208] held that action of the Executive Committee was not state action within the meaning of the Fourteenth and Fifteenth amendments and that the statute authorizing the resolution was a valid exercise of legislative authority. The opinion stated that the first proposition was especially true in Texas because the candidates themselves bore the expenses of the primaries. A previous attempt by the legislature to place this burden on the state had been declared invalid in the *Waples* case[209] because the expenditure was not considered as being for a public purpose as required by the state constitution. The case was distinguished from the above Virginia decision on this latter ground, as it is permissible in that jurisdiction for the state treasury to bear such expense. The court went on to declare that the resolution was not state action because the primary in Texas had not become so much a part of the state election machinery as to be termed an exclusively state function, and this was said to be true in spite of the fact that political parties have been regulated to a certain extent by the state legislature. An additional reason given for the decision was that the primary is not to be considered as an election within the meaning of the Fifteenth Amendment.

The Circuit Court of Appeals approved the decision of the lower court,[210] but the last-mentioned point is not listed as one of the reasons for the affirmance. The case was then taken on a

[208] Nixon v. Condon, 34 Fed. (2d) 464 (W. D. Tex. 1929).
[209] Waples v. Marrast, 108 Tex. 5, 184 S. W. 180 (1916).
[210] Nixon v. Condon, 49 Fed. (2d) 1012 (C. C. A. 5th, 1931).

writ of certiorari to the Supreme Court, and that tribunal, in a five to four decision,[211] reversed the case on the ground that the statute had set up the party committee and made it a state agency with certain powers and duties.[212] The court said the acts of the committee were state action within the terms of the Fourteenth Amendment. Hence the committee regulation that white persons only might vote was held to be in conflict with the equal protection clause of the said amendment. An excerpt from Justice Cardozo's opinion will serve to clarify the decision:

"The pith of the matter is simply this, that when these agencies are invested with an authority independent of the will of the association in whose name they undertake to speak, they become to that extent the organs of the State itself, the repositories of official power. They are then the governmental instruments whereby parties are organized and regulated to the end that government itself may be established or continued. What they do in that relation, they must do in submission to the mandates of equality and liberty that bind officials everywhere. They are not acting in matters of merely private concern like the directors or agents of business corporations. They are acting in matters of highly public interest, matters intimately connected with the capacity of government to exercise its functions unbrokenly and smoothly. Whether in given circumstances parties or their committees are agencies of government within the Fourteenth or Fifteenth Amendment is a question which this court will determine for itself. It is not concluded upon such an inquiry by decisions rendered elsewhere. The test is not whether the members of the Executive Committee are the representatives of the State in the strict sense in which an agent is the representative of his principal. The test is whether they are to be classified as representatives of the

---

[211] Butler, McReynolds, Sutherland, and Van Davanter dissenting.

[212] Nixon v. Condon, 286 U. S. 73, 52 Sup. Ct. 484 (1932). The case in its various stages received copious comment from the legal periodicals. Notes: (1932) 6 FLA. STATE B. A. L. J. 141, (1931) 5 So. CALIF. L. REV. 162, (1932) 32 COL. L. REV. 88, 135, 1069, (1930) 15 CORN L. Q. 262, (1930) 39 YALE L. J. 423, (1932) 41 YALE L. J. 1212, (1932) 10 N. Y. U. L. Q. REV. 77, (1930) 43 HARV. L. REV. 467, (1932) 17 ST. LOUIS L. REV. 155, (1932) 1 GEO. WASH. L. REV. 131, (1932-33) 21 CALIF. L. REV. 62, 240, (1932) 12 B. U. L. REV. 689, (1932) 7 ST. JOHN'S L. REV. 128, (1933) 27 ILL. L. REV. 686. The decisions in the lower courts and both the majority and minority opinions of the justices of the Supreme Court are discussed in these comments.

State to such an extent and in such a sense that the great restraints of the Constitution set limits to their action."

Justice McReynolds' dissenting opinion is based upon the theory that the statute did not set up a state agency apart from the party and that the act only recognized the inherent right of the party to limit its own membership as it sees fit. He says that in Texas political parties have been held not to be governmental instrumentalities and therefore should be permitted to control their activities and membership except where they are regulated by statute.[213]

The Texas view that money paid out of state funds to defray the expenses of a primary election cannot be considered as an expenditure for a public purpose and is therefore an illegal diversion of public funds is out of line with authorities in other states, for most jurisdictions have held that such an outlay is perfectly legitimate.[214] Hence the decision in the abovementioned *Waples* case does not have the significance as a precedent which it might have were it the general rule and not just a local ruling.

The decision in the *Condon* case, however, was based upon the theory that the statute vested in the Executive Committee an authority independent of the will of the party as a whole and that therefore its discriminatory acts amounted to state action within the terms of the Fourteenth Amendment. Thus the way was left open for other forms of discriminatory action against the Negroes by political parties.[215] The Democrats of Texas were not slow in taking advantage of the opportunity which was open to them. Three weeks after the decision by the Supreme Court in the *Condon* case the State Democratic Convention adopted a resolution to the effect that in the future only white persons might vote in the party primaries. The State

---

[213] In this connection see Note (1932) 41 YALE L. J. 1212 and also the following Texas cases: Waples v. Marrast, 108 Tex. 5, 184 S. W. 180 (1916); Cunningham v. McDermatt, 277 S. W. 218 (Tex. Civ. App. 1925); Briscoe v. Boyle, 286 S. W. 275 (Tex. Civ. App. 1926); Love v. Wilcox, 119 Tex. 256, 28 S. W. (2d) 515 (1930); Love v. Buckner, 121 Tex. 369, 49 S. W. (2d) 425 (1932).

[214] Kenneweg v. County Comm'rs of Allegany County, 102 Md. 119, 62 Atl. 249 (1905); State *ex rel.* Labauve v. Michel, 121 La. 374, 46 So. 430 (1908); State *ex rel.* Webber v. Felton, 77 Ohio St. 554, 84 N. E. 85 (1908); Commonwealth v. Willcox 111 Va. 849, 69 S. E. 1027 (1911).

[215] See Note (1931) 5 So. CALIF. L. REV. 453.

Executive Committee put this resolution into effect at once.

Almost immediately proceedings were started in both state and federal courts to test the validity of this resolution. The first case to arise was a mandamus proceeding initiated by a Negro to compel party officials to allow the complainant to vote in the forthcoming primary, they having refused to permit him to do so. The federal court[216] was of the opinion that the convention resolution and its approval by the Executive Committee amounted to state action in view of the statutory control over primaries and political parties which is exercised in Texas.[217] The court declared that the authority to determine the personnel of the party was derived from the state by virtue of these statutes and not from an inherent right of the party to govern its own affairs, but denied the relief asked for because it had no power to issue a writ of mandamus in such a case.

A year later this same court refused injunctive relief to a Negro who was seeking to prevent party officials from enforcing a similar resolution adopted by the Executive Committee for Houston.[218] It distinguished the case from its former decision by saying that in the latter instance the action of the local committee was the exercise of the inherent power of the party to regulate its own affairs, while in the former the action of the convention which was approved and put into effect by the State Executive Committee was the action of the state because the committee had been given authority by the above statute to prescribe rules for party membership and had exercised that authority in its approval of the convention resolution. This was a very strained interpretation of the previous language of the court in view of the fact that the reasoning in the first case seems to be based on the theory that the action of the convention in excluding the Negroes was state action because the power of the convention to do this was derived from the state

[216] White v. Harris County Executive Committee, 60 Fed. (2d) 973 (S. D. Tex. 1932). The case is commented upon in the law journals. Notes: (1933) 46 Harv. L. Rev. 812, (1933) 6 So. Calif. L. Rev. 172, (1933) 27 Ill. L. Rev. 686, (1933) 11 Tex. L. Rev. 382, (1933) 1 U. of Chi. L. Rev. 142.

[217] Tex. Ann. Rev. Civ. Stat. (Vernon, 1925) arts. 3100-3173.

[218] Drake v. Houston Democratic Executive Committee, 2 Fed. Supp. 486 (S. D. Tex. 1933). This case has also received attention in the periodicals. Notes: (1933) 46 Harv. L. Rev. 812, (1933) 81 U. of Pa. L. Rev. 769.

statutes regulating primaries and not from the party's inherent right to regulate its own membership. The distinction here sought to be sustained does not seem to be a very reasonable one, and it is doubted that this proposition would receive the approval of a higher court.[219] However, later developments in Texas have rendered any further argument on this point unnecessary in view of the present situation in that state.

In 1932 an injunction was sought in the state courts to restrain a county committee from enforcing the convention resolution. This injunction was refused on the ground that a political party in convention assembled has an inherent power to determine its own membership and that the resolution was a valid exercise of this power, the action of the convention not being state action and hence not within the Reconstruction amendments.[220] Two years later mandamus proceedings, provided for by a recent statute[221] evidently enacted with the afore-mentioned *Lubbock* case in mind, failed to bring the Negro plaintiffs relief because the courts came to a like conclusion.[222] The State Supreme Court declared in the *Bell* case[223] that an interpretation of the above statute which would permit the State Executive Committee to make rules and regulations determining party membership independent of the will of the party as a whole would violate certain personal rights guaranteed by the Bill of Rights of the state constitution.[224] Therefore the statute would not be so interpreted. Hence the resolution of the party convention was effective to prevent Negroes from voting in the primaries, as this is not considered as state action in Texas.

The controversy finally reached the Federal Supreme Court

---

[219] See Evans, *Primary Elections and the Constitution* (1934) 32 MICH. L. REV. 451, 461.

[220] Bexar County Committee v. Booker, 53 S. W. (2d) 123 (Tex. Civ. App. 1932). The state supreme court refused to review the case because the associate primary judge was not made a party to the action. 122 Tex. 89, 52 S. W. (2d) 908 (1932). This case has received attention in the periodicals. Notes: (1933) 46 HARV. L. REV. 812, (1933) 6 SO. CALIF. L. REV. 172, (1933) 1 GEO. WASH. L. REV. 273.

[221] Tex. Gen. Laws 4th Called Sess. 1930, c. 4.

[222] Bell v. Hill, 123 Tex. 531, 74 S. W. (2d) 113 (1934); Mason v. Dallas County Executive Committee, 74 S. W. 326 (Tex. Civ. App. 1934).

[223] Bell v. Hill, 123 Tex. 531, 74 S. W. (2d) 113 (1934).

[224] TEX. CONST. Art. I, §§2, 27, 29.

in the *Grovey* case.[225] In this instance a Negro sued for ten dollars in damages in a Texas justice's court. He claimed that the action of party officials in carrying out the above-mentioned convention mandate and in not permitting him to vote in a primary was discriminatory and violated the rights guaranteed to him by the Fourteenth and Fifteenth amendments. The justice's court was the highest state tribunal to which such a controversy might go, and therefore the record was ordered to be brought directly to the Supreme Court by a writ of certiorari. A unanimous court came to the conclusion that the convention resolution was not state action within the meaning of the said amendments but was the action of the political party in exercising its inherent right to determine its own policies and membership. Justice Roberts, who wrote the opinion, cited the *Bell* case as establishing the proposition that political parties have such powers in Texas by virtue of the state constitution and that this is true in spite of what had been said in previous cases. The above-mentioned state constitutional provisions were said not to violate the postwar amendments by reason of their failure to forbid political organizations to make membership qualifications based on race or color.

In answer to the argument that the State Democratic Convention had become an agency or instrumentality of the state because of the statutory regulation of political parties in respect to certain aspects of the primary and other party activities, the opinion points out the fact that the expenses of primaries in Texas are borne by the candidates; that the ballots are furnished by the party and not by the state; that the votes are counted by party officials; and that the state recognizes the convention as the organ of the party for the declaration of principles and the formulation of policies. Therefore it may be said that the action of the Democratic Convention is not state action because in Texas political parties have been held not to be governmental instrumentalities but merely political instrumentalities and that this is not so inaccurate as to require the Supreme Court to hold otherwise. It might also

[225] Grovey v. Townsend, 295 U. S. 45, 55 Sup. Ct. 622 (1935). This case has received much attention in the legal periodicals. Notes: (1935) 35 Col. L. Rev. 607, (1935) 33 Mich. L. Rev. 955, (1935) 48 Harv. L. Rev. 1436, (1935) 2 U. of Chi. L. Rev. 640, (1935) 83 U. of Pa. L. Rev. 1027, (1935) 22 Va. L. Rev. 91.

be said that the court, by approving this theory of the nature of a political party in Texas, has adopted the view that the party has not been so regulated and is not of such a nature that it has become an integral part of the state governmental machinery.

This decision, however, could not be used as a precedent in any other jurisdiction other than those where the political parties have been treated in practically the same way that they have been in Texas. Such a state is Arkansas, where the decision in the *Grovey* case was foreshadowed by the conclusion reached in the *Robinson* case[226] and the failure of the Supreme Court to render an opinion on the question raised in that case because of the want of jurisdiction. In a state like Virginia where the primary has been held to be an integrated part of the state election machinery a different result might well be reached. The problem boils down to a query as to whether in any given jurisdiction political parties are treated as governmental or political instrumentalities in respect to the particular problem here involved, the exclusion of Negroes from the primaries because of race or color. Each state would undoubtedly present a different problem, and therefore there is no reasonable limit to the amount of litigation which may be expected in the future with respect to this phase of the problem. Should the political party be held to have become a governmental instrumentality and its action in regard to the primary to have become state action in dealing with the situation in any given state, it has been predicted that the jurisdiction concerned would repeal all laws relating to primaries and leave them uncontrolled by anything except party supervision and regulation.[227] However, it is hardly conceivable that any such dire result would follow.

There are undoubtedly a great number of educated and intelligent colored men and women in the South who are better qualified to vote in any form of election than many of the whites who exercise this great privilege of self-government. However, a slow and thoughtful approach is probably much better in the long run. Some Negroes have always voted even in this section

---

[226] Robinson v. Holman, 181 Ark. 428, 26 S. W. (2d) 66 (1930). See *supra* note 206.

[227] Notes: (1932) 41 YALE L. J. 1212, (1932) 6 FLA. STATE B. A. L. J. 141.

of the country. In fact Arkansas has enacted a statute requiring alternate voting by members of the two races at the polls in precincts where more than a hundred votes were cast at the preceding election.[228] The urban Negroes have been permitted to exercise the franchise in certain cities in the South, notably those in some of the largest cities in North Carolina and Tennessee,[229] but this cannot be said to be the general rule. A Negro precinct committeeman was recently elected at a political meeting in Raleigh, North Carolina.[230]

There is the danger that party machines, which control election machinery and are therefore far more able than the opposition to decide when and where the Negro will be permitted to vote, will make use of the ignorant Negro vote to accomplish their sometimes nefarious schemes. In answer to the argument that the Negro should not be allowed to vote for this and similar reasons, it is urged that the Negro will not be given a square deal in regard to appropriations, treatment in the courts, and preferment in other fields of human endeavor until he can make his weight felt at the polls.[231]

In the rural communities it is very unusual to have anything like a considerable Negro vote, and about the only general rule worth notice in respect to the size of this vote is that it varies with the population of the city in which the voting is being done. The urban districts are usually more favorable to Negro participation, but this is not always the case.[232]

It seems that one of the best ways for the Negro to obtain a better measure of political equality is by being a good citizen and by making an effort to obtain a definite place in the economic life which goes on about him. The acquisition of property and wealth will certainly not hinder a demand for the recognition of political rights, for the power of wealth in this country is still a thing with which it is rather difficult to cope. In many places where he has acquired wealth the Negro has been accorded political recognition, as witness the situation which has developed in Durham, North Carolina.

The one-party system which prevails in the South today is

---

[228] ARK. DIG. STAT. (Crawford & Moses, 1921) §3808.

[229] See LEWINSON, RACE, CLASS AND PARTY (1932) 138-142.

[230] Greensboro Daily News, June 11, 1934, p. 1.

[231] See Lewinson, *op. cit. supra* note 229, at 196-197.

[232] *Id.* at 145-146.

one of the chief factors in the continued disfranchisement of the Negro. If the South had two evenly balanced political parties, there would be continual rivalry between them as to which one should control the majority of the Negro vote, as is the case in some of the eastern and middle western states at the present time. Such a balance might induce the removal of at least some of the prejudice against the exercise of the voting franchise by the Negro. From the standpoint of the whites, however, the desirability of such a change in the political setup is the crux of the matter. At present the great majority of the southern whites are in favor of keeping the Negro out of politics as much as possible. An all-too-vivid picture of the horrors of Reconstruction remains in the minds of the southern people, especially the old aristocracy which has not lost all of its influence in southern politics. The South is still afraid of the Negro vote as manipulated by unscrupulous politicians.

It is not believed that legislation, either state or federal, is the remedy for this situation. Every such attempt that has been made has resulted in utter failure, and any further effort would be met by the same wall of subterfuge and prejudice that rang the knell of its predecessors. But this does not mean that nothing can be done. The remedy seems to lie in a twofold program of education. The Negro must be educated along the lines of civic consciousness and responsibility. The Negro high schools should be urged to adopt courses which would lead to a better understanding of things political. The white man must be persuaded to permit intelligent and well-educated Negroes to vote. They have just as much right to exercise that privilege as the white man who, down in his innermost soul, must certainly recognize the justice of the Negro's claims in this respect which are in accordance with the true principles of democratic government. A plan must be devised which will educate the white man in the South to a point where he will give heed to the righteousness of the Negro's cause.

SELECTED BIBLIOGRAPHY

American Digest (Century edition). 50 vols. Minneapolis

Asbury, Herbert. The French Quarter. New York, London, 1936

Baker, Jay N. The Segregation of White and Colored Passengers on Interstate Trains. (1910) 19 Yale L. J.

Baldwin, Simeon E. The Schooling Rights Under Our Treaty with Japan. (1907) 7 Col. L. Rev.

Baldwin's Ohio Code Service

Benson, T. B. Segregation Ordinances. (1915) 1 Va. L. Reg. (N.S.)

Bond, Horace Mann. The Education of the Negro in the American Social Order. New York, 1934

Bruce, A. A. Racial Zoning by Private Contract in the Light of the Constitution and the Rule Against Restraints on Alienation. (1927) 21 Ill. L. Rev.

———. Racial Zoning by Private Contract. (1928) 13 Va. Law Reg. (N.S.)

Chadbourn, James H. Lynching and the Law. Chapel Hill, 1933

Daggett, Harriet S. The Legal Aspect of Amalgamation in Louisiana. (1933) 11 Tex. L. Rev.

Dyer, L. C. and Dyer, C. C. The Constitutionality of a Federal Anti-Lynching Bill. (1928) 13 St. Louis L. Rev.

Evans, L. H. Primary Elections and the Constitution. (1934) 32 Mich. L. Rev.

Holmes, Dwight O. W. The Evolution of the Negro College. New York, 1934

Hunting, Warren B. The Constitutionality of Race Distinctions and the Baltimore Negro Segregation Ordinance. (1911) 11 Col. L. Rev.

Johnson, Franklin. Development of State Legislation Concerning the Free Negro. New York, 1919

Leavell, Ullin W. Philanthropy in Negro Education. Nashville, 1930

Lewinson, Paul. Race, Class, and Party. London and New York, 1932

Lynching and Federal Law. (Jan., 1905) 40 Chatauquan

Mahon, J. The Japanese Question. (1914) 48 Am. L. Rev.

Martin, A. T. Segregation of Negroes. (1934) 32 Mich. L. Rev.

Maryland State Manual of Standards
Mertins, Leon Evans. "Has the United States Government the Power to Prosecute 'Lynching' as a Federal Crime Without an Amendment to the Constitution?" New York, 1921
Minor, James F. Constitutionality of Segregation Ordinances. (1912) 18 Va. L. Reg.
Monnet, Julien C. The Latest Phase of Negro Disfranchisement. (1912) 26 Harv. L. Rev.
Negro Education. Bul. 38, 1916. Bureau of Education, Department of the Interior Negro Year Book (ed., Work)
Peck, Melville. Necessity for Prior Valid Marriage in Prosecution for Bigamy. (1910) 15 Va. L. Reg.
Porter, Kirk H. A History of Suffrage in the United States. Chicago, 1918
Quindry, F. E. Airline Passenger Discriminations. (1932) 3 J. Air L.
Report of North Carolina Charitable, Penal, and Correctional Institutions. Raleigh, 1934
Saxon, Lyle. Fabulous New Orleans. New York, London, 1928
Schofield, Henry. Federal Courts and Mob Domination of State Courts: Leo Frank's Case. (1916) 10 Ill. L. Rev.
Schrieke, Bertram J. O. Alien Americans. New York, 1936
Shannon, R. W. Racial Integrity of the American Negro. (1933) 144 Contemp. Rev.
Statutory Changes in North Carolina. (1939) 17 N. C. L. Rev.
Stephenson, Gilbert Thomas. Race Distinctions in American Law. London and New York, 1910
Survey of Statutory Changes in North Carolina in 1929, A. (1929) 7 N. C. L. Rev.
Sydnor, Charles S. Slavery in Mississippi. New York, London, 1933

INDEX

www.ingramcontent.com/pod-product-compliance
Lightning Source LLC
Chambersburg PA
CBHW031544260326
41914CB00002B/265

* 9 7 8 1 5 8 4 7 7 0 8 1 7 *